PRE-GROUPING

# ATLAS

AND RCH JUNCTION DIAGRAMS

First published 2014

ISBN 978 0 7110 3460 03810 3

Published by Ian Allan Publishing Ltd, Hersham, Surrey, KT12 4RG

Printed in Bulgaria

Visit the Ian Allan Publishing website at www.ianallanpublishing.com

# Contents

Introduction 3

Index to map numbers 5

Maps and RCH diagrams 6

Gazetteer 140

1 List of abbreviations 141

2 Index to Tunnels 143

3 Index to Water troughs 145

4 Index to Summits 146

5 Index to Bridges and Viaducts 146

6 Index of Locations 147

7 Index to Junction Diagrams 190

## Introduction to the First Edition of *Pre-Grouping Atlas and Gazetteer*

Just 35 years ago many of the separate railway companies operating in Britain as self-contained units were grouped into four major systems by the provisions of the Railways Act 1921, and on the 1st January 1923 these individual units lost their titles in the initials LMSR, LNER and SR, only the GWR keeping its identity although extending its territory by the accretion of the many small railways in Wales. Many of these lines were in fact controlled by the GW somewhat earlier than the date above mentioned. Similarly, the L&YR was amalgamated with the L&NWR in 1921. It can be noted here that in the sheets that follow, all these railways are shown as independent concerns as a matter of interest, but the general picture presented is of the railway system of Britain as it existed in the years prior to 1923.

Taking into account all the minor narrow-gauge lines, the various joint undertakings, committees, etc, there were something like 150 titles extant in the period depicted on these maps and many of these names still live. Through the 25 years of the grouped systems and even now, in Nationalisation days, many of the old names not only are used by members of the railway staffs in day to day working, but such names are currently quoted in official documents, working timetables, etc.

An examination of this Atlas will show that numbers of station names of the 1920s have disappeared, either due to re-naming or to the abandonment of the station through lack of passenger usage. Many branch lines were closed after the amalgamations either to passenger working (a goods and parcel service being maintained) or in their entirety. Since Nationalisation much more has been done in this respect. However, some lines and stations which had in fact been closed by 1922 have been shown in this atlas for the sake of interest and as a record of their existence.

In addition to the inclusion of every railway company at work in the years before 1923, much other matter has been shown. A great many junctions, many still in use as timing points in working timetables, are indicated together with physical features such as the more important viaducts, tunnels, etc, locomotive shed locations and railway workshops. Track water troughs also receive attention and in areas of tourist interest scenic features in the railway vicinity are indicated. It is hoped that such data will add to the interest and usefulness of this volume.

Many towns with complicated railway layouts have been shown as enlarged insets, and in addition areas such as London, South Wales, The West Riding, etc, with ramified railway routes and connecting lines points receive attention in separate sheets. Interpretation of the initials of the various companies will be found in the list of abbreviations shown on pp 141-142.

Both the checking of the sheets which follow and the compilation of the gazetteer have been undertaken by Mr U. A. Vincent and the writer is greatly indebted to him for his valued guidance and interest in unearthing obscure matters of cartographic importance and in generally keeping him 'on the right lines' in the draughting of these maps.

W. Philip Conolly

(1958)

## Introduction to the *Pre-Grouping Atlas and RCH Junction Diagrams*

The *British Railways Pre-Grouping Atlas and Gazetteer* was first published in 1958. Since that time there have been five separate editions together with numerous reprints. Indeed, it would be fair to say that most railway enthusiasts will either have their own or at least have used a copy – participants of railtours may still often be seen studying the pages!

Changing customer demands has meant that our more recently published atlases have been to a larger page format, appreciated we know by those whose eyesight may perhaps not be quite what it once was! When the decision was made to reprint the 'Pre-Group' atlas, the decision was also made to increase to the new page size while at the same time taking the opportunity to update the index and redraw the maps. The result is a completely new book complete with a much enlarged and expanded index, the latter alone now having in the order 8,500 entries.

Even allowing for the new page size, the complexity of the railway network, especially in areas where original companies had conjoined, meant that maps of a number of locations would still perhaps not provide the detail required. Here a remedy was at hand in the form of the *Railway Clearing House Junction Diagrams*. These latter drawings distinguished railway companies in similar fashion to the atlas while also affording enhanced detail that was just not possible to incorporate otherwise.

While several editions of RCH drawings were produced in the early years of the 20th century, bound copies are rare – and expensive. Odd pages do appear from time to time, but a complete book has only ever been reprinted once and also some years ago.

The opportunity was thus taken to combine the two. Wherever possible we have placed adjacent location maps/plans next to each other, but from both a design and rail complexity purpose there are of necessity a few exceptions.

This new book will provide the enthusiast and student of railway history a more detailed glimpse of the past than has been available before – and at a size that it may still be carried on trips or studied at leisure at home.

## Acknowledgements
The publisher would like to thank the following for their assistance in the production of this title: Lawrie Bowles, Alan Butcher, Angela Connolly, Colin McCarthy (Map Creation), Sue Frost, Nick Lerwill, Alistair Plumb, Kevin Robertson, Colin Woodman.

# Index to map numbers

1 Cornwall; Devon W. 6
2 Devon 7
3 Somerset; Dorset; Wilts. W. 10
4 Wilts. E.; Hants.; Berks. S.; Sussex W. 11
5 Sussex; Surrey; Kent W.; Greater London; Essex S. 16
6 Sussex E.; Kent E.; Essex E. 17
7 Devon N., South Wales W.; Pembroke 22
8 South Wales E.; Monmouth; Somerset; Gloucester W. 23
9 Hereford; Gloucester; Wilts. N. 36
10 Warwicks.; Northants.; Bucks.; Beds. W.; Oxford; Berks. N. 37
11 Beds. E.; Hunts.; Cambs.; Essex N. 40
12 Norfolk S.; Suffolk; Essex E. 41
13 Pembroke N.; Cardigan; Carmarthen; Birmingham 46
14 Montgomery; Brecknock; Radnor; Hereford W.; Salop W. 47
15 Cheshire; Salop.; Staffs.; Warwicks. N.; Derby W. 54
16 Derby; Notts.; Leics.; Rutland; Lincs. W. 55
17 Lincs. S.; Norfolk W.; Cambs. N. 64
18 Norfolk 65
19 North Wales 70
20 Denbigh; Flint; Cheshire; Lancs.; Salop. N.; Staffs. N. 71
21 Yorks. W. & S. 78
22 Yorks. E.; Lincs. N. 79
23 Isle of Man 88
24 Lancs.; Yorks. N. & W. 89
25 Wigtown; Ayr S.; Kirkcudbright 94
26 Kirkcudbright E.; Dumfries S.; Cumberland 95
27 Northumberland W.; Durham W.; Westmorland 100
28 Northumberland E.; Durham E.; North Yorkshire 101
29 Stirling W.; Dumbarton; Ayr; Glasgow; Clyde Coast 106
30 Stirling E.; Dunfermline; Lanarks. E.; The Lothians; Edinburgh 107
31 Berwick; Northumberland N.; Roxburgh 112
32 Oban, Mallaig & West Highlands 113
33 Kinross, Perth & Central Highlands 116
34 Aberdeen S.; Kincardine; Angus; Dundee; Fife 117
35 Ross & Cromarty 120
36 Inverness; Nairn; Moray; Banff W. 121
37 Banff E.; Aberdeenshire 122
38 Caithness 123

## Enlargements

39 London – West Side 126
40 London – East Side 127
41 Nottingham-Sheffield Area 132
42 Leeds-Sheffield-West Riding Area 133
43 South Wales 136
44 Glasgow Area 137
45 Liverpool-Manchester Area 138

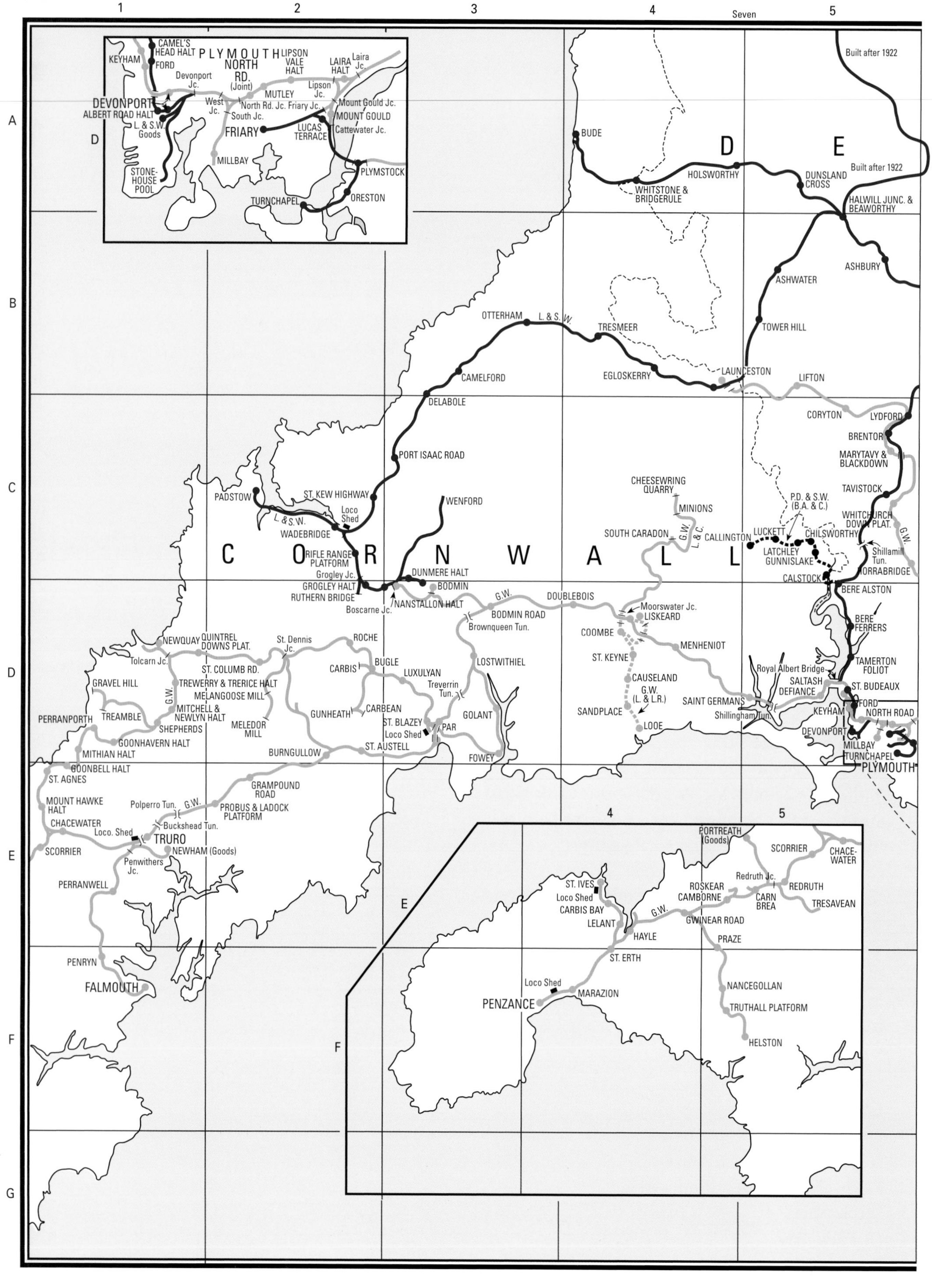

1 2 3 4 Seven 5

A B C D E F G

KEYHAM
CAMEL'S HEAD HALT
FORD
PLYMOUTH NORTH RD. (Joint)
LIPSON VALE HALT
LAIRA HALT
Laira Jc.
Devonport Jc.
Lipson Jc.
MUTLEY
DEVONPORT
ALBERT ROAD HALT
L. & S.W. Goods
West Jc.
North Rd. Jc.
Friary Jc.
South Jc.
Mount Gould Jc.
MOUNT GOULD
FRIARY
LUCAS TERRACE
Cattewater Jc.
D
MILLBAY
STONEHOUSE POOL
PLYMSTOCK
TURNCHAPEL
ORESTON

Built after 1922
BUDE
D
E
Built after 1922
HOLSWORTHY
WHITSTONE & BRIDGERULE
DUNSLAND CROSS
HALWILL JUNC. & BEAWORTHY
ASHBURY
ASHWATER
TOWER HILL
OTTERHAM
L. & S. W.
TRESMEER
EGLOSKERRY
LAUNCESTON
LIFTON
CAMELFORD
DELABOLE
CORYTON
LYDFORD
BRENTOR
MARYTAVY & BLACKDOWN
PORT ISAAC ROAD
TAVISTOCK
CHEESEWRING QUARRY
MINIONS
P.D. & S.W. (B.A. & C.)
WHITCHURCH DOWN PLAT.
G.W.
PADSTOW
ST. KEW HIGHWAY
WENFORD
Loco Shed
L. & S.W.
WADEBRIDGE
SOUTH CARADON
G.W.
L. & C.
CALLINGTON
LUCKETT
CHILSWORTHY
LATCHLEY
GUNNISLAKE
Shillamill Tun.
HORRABRIDGE
C O R N W A L L
RIFLE RANGE PLATFORM
Grogley Jc.
DUNMERE HALT
GROGLEY HALT
RUTHERN BRIDGE
BODMIN
CALSTOCK
BERE ALSTON
Boscarne Jc.
NANSTALLON HALT
G.W.
DOUBLEBOIS
BODMIN ROAD
Brownqueen Tun.
Moorswater Jc.
LISKEARD
BERE FERRERS
COOMBE
MENHENIOT
NEWQUAY
QUINTREL DOWNS PLAT.
St. Dennis Jc.
ROCHE
Tolcarn Jc.
ST. COLUMB RD.
CARBIS
BUGLE
LOSTWITHIEL
ST. KEYNE
TAMERTON FOLIOT
Royal Albert Bridge
GRAVEL HILL
TREWERRY & TRERICE HALT
LUXULYAN
Treverrin Tun.
CAUSELAND
SALTASH
DEFIANCE
ST. BUDEAUX
G.W.
MELANGOOSE MILL
G.W. (L. & L.R.)
SAINT GERMANS
MITCHELL & NEWLYN HALT
GUNHEATH
CARBEAN
SANDPLACE
KEYHAM
FORD
PERRANPORTH
TREAMBLE
SHEPHERDS
MELEDOR MILL
ST. BLAZEY
GOLANT
Shillingham Tun.
NORTH ROAD
Loco Shed
PAR
LOOE
DEVONPORT
GOONHAVERN HALT
BURNGULLOW
ST. AUSTELL
MILLBAY
MITHIAN HALT
FOWEY
TURNCHAPEL
PLYMOUTH
GOONBELL HALT
ST. AGNES
GRAMPOUND ROAD
MOUNT HAWKE HALT
Polperro Tun.
G.W.
PROBUS & LADOCK PLATFORM
CHACEWATER
Buckshead Tun.
Loco. Shed
TRURO
SCORRIER
NEWHAM (Goods)
Penwithers Jc.
PERRANWELL
PENRYN
FALMOUTH

4 5
PORTREATH (Goods)
SCORRIER
CHACEWATER
ST. IVES
Redruth Jc.
Loco Shed
ROSKEAR
REDRUTH
CAMBORNE
CARN BREA
TRESAVEAN
E
CARBIS BAY
G.W.
LELANT
GWINEAR ROAD
HAYLE
PRAZE
ST. ERTH
Loco Shed
NANCEGOLLAN
MARAZION
PENZANCE
TRUTHALL PLATFORM
HELSTON
F

5
Seven
4
3
2
Eight
1
A
B
C
D
E
F
G
Three
V O N S H I R E
L. & S.W.
EGGESFORD
LAPFORD
MORCHARD ROAD
COPPLESTONE
TIVERTON
BURLESCOMBE
CULMSTOCK
HEMYOCK
UFFCULME
TIVERTON JUNC.
CADELEIGH
CULLOMPTON
G.W.
UP EXE
THORVERTON
SILVERTON
HELE & BRADNINCH
CHARD (Joint)
L. & S.W. Goods
Summit
Honiton Tun.
HONITON
SAMPFORD COURTENAY
NORTH TAWTON
BOW
Coleford Jc.
YEOFORD JUNC.
CREDITON
NEWTON ST. CYRES
LION'S HOLT HALT
QUEEN STREET
BRAMPFORD SPEKE
STOKE CANON
WHIMPLE
SIDMOUTH JUNC.
AXMINSTER
SEATON JUNC.
EXETER
Cowley Bridge Jc.
ST. DAVIDS
Loco Shed
Loco Shed
PINHOE
BROAD CLYST
OTTERY ST MARY
COLYTON
COLYFORD
COMBPYNE
SEATON
OKEHAMPTON
Meldon Jc.
Summit
Exmouth Jc.
ST. THOMAS
City Basin Jc.
MOUNT PLEASANT ROAD HALT
POLSLOE BRIDGE HALT
CLYST ST MARY & DIGBY HALT
TIPTON ST JOHN'S
NEWTON POPPLEFORD
SIDMOUTH
LONGDOWN
IDE
TOPSHAM
Yes Tor
BRIDESTOWE
MORETONHAMPSTEAD
CHRISTOW
EXMINSTER
Watertroughs
WOODBURY ROAD
LYMPSTONE
EAST BUDLEIGH
LITTLEHAM
EXMOUTH
BUDLEIGH SALTERTON
ASHTON
LUSTLEIGH
TRUSHAM
STARCROSS
BOVEY FOR ILSINGTON
CHUDLEIGH
DAWLISH WARREN
DAWLISH
HEATHFIELD
TEIGNGRACE
TEIGNMOUTH
PRINCETOWN
NEWTON ABBOT
Works
Loco. Shed
ASHBURTON
Aller Jc.
DOUSLAND
KINGSKERSWELL
YELVERTON
Summit
Dainton Tun.
TORRE
BUCKFASTLEIGH
TORQUAY
SHAUGH BRIDGE PLATFORM
STAVERTON
PRESTON PLAT.
BICKLEIGH
BRENT
Marley Tun.
TOTNES
Ashburton Jc.
PAIGNTON
PLYM BRI. PLAT.
CORNWOOD
MARSH MILLS
WRANGATON
Summit
AVONWICK
BRIXHAM
PLYMPTON
IVYBRIDGE
BITTAFORD PLATFORM
CHURSTON
Tavistock Jc.
PLYMSTOCK
GARA BRIDGE
BILLACOMBE
KINGSWEAR
ELBURTON CROSS
YEALMPTON
BRIXTON RD.
DARTMOUTH (Ferry service from Kingswear)
STEER POINT
LODDISWELL
KINGSBRIDGE
Plymouth to Brest G.W.R.

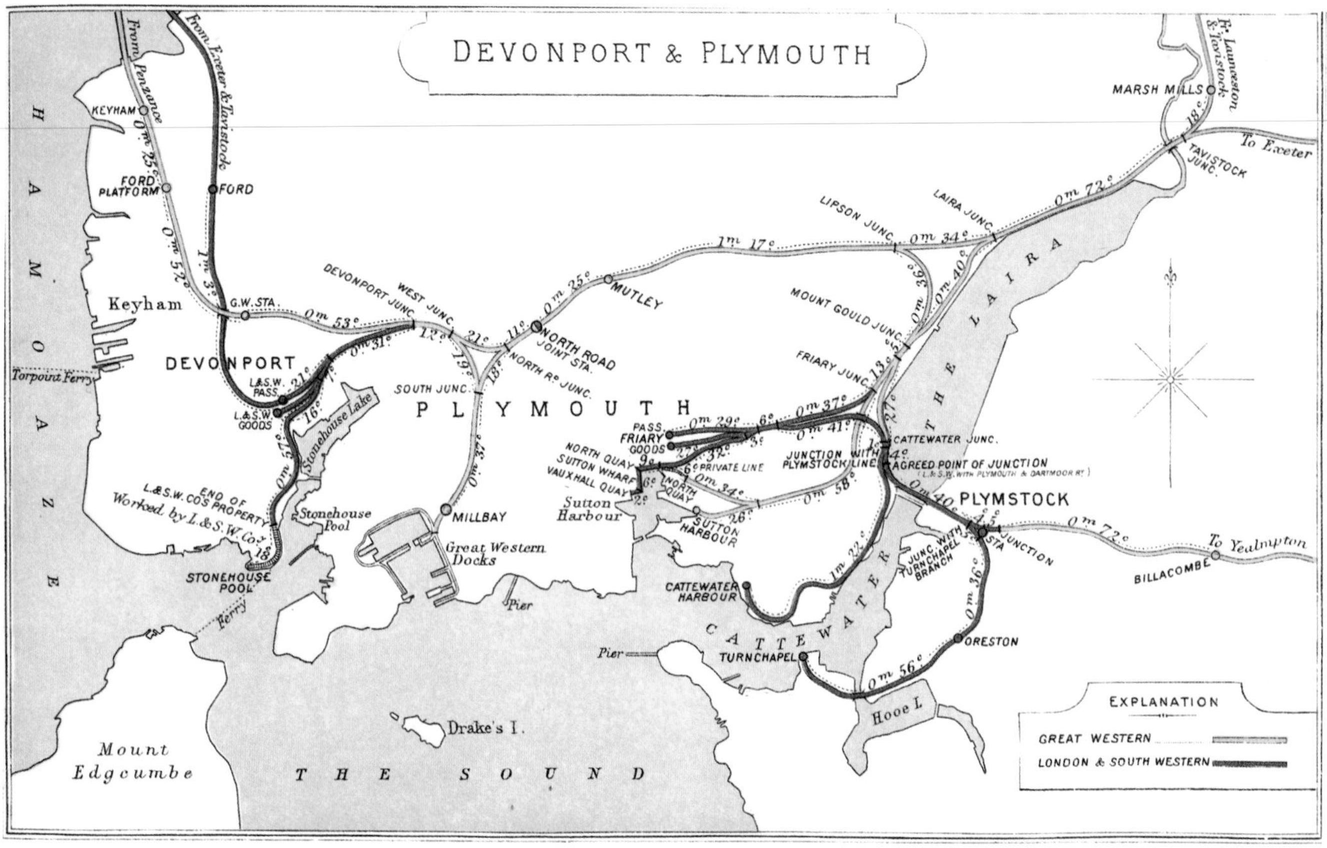

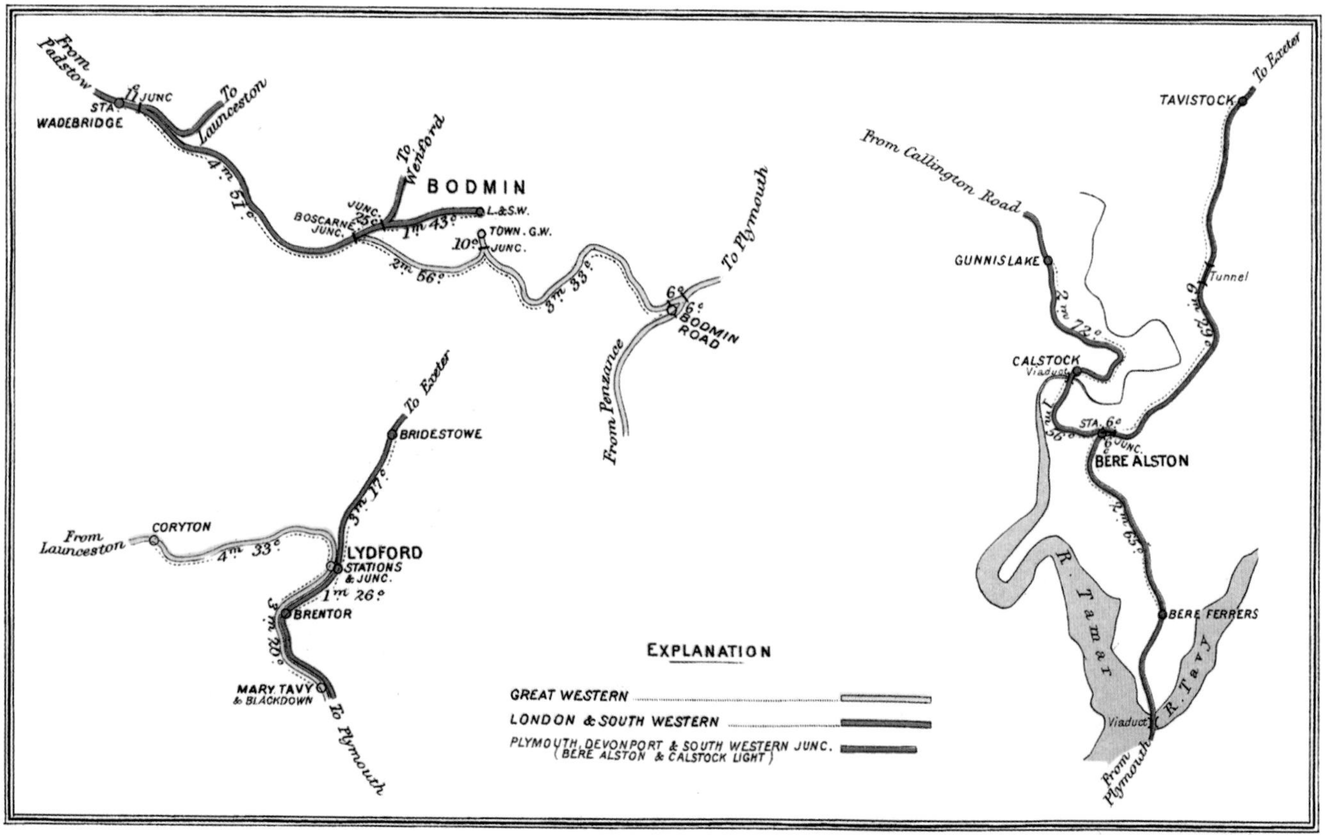

## DEVONPORT & PLYMOUTH





**Bere Alston–Bodmin–Lydford**

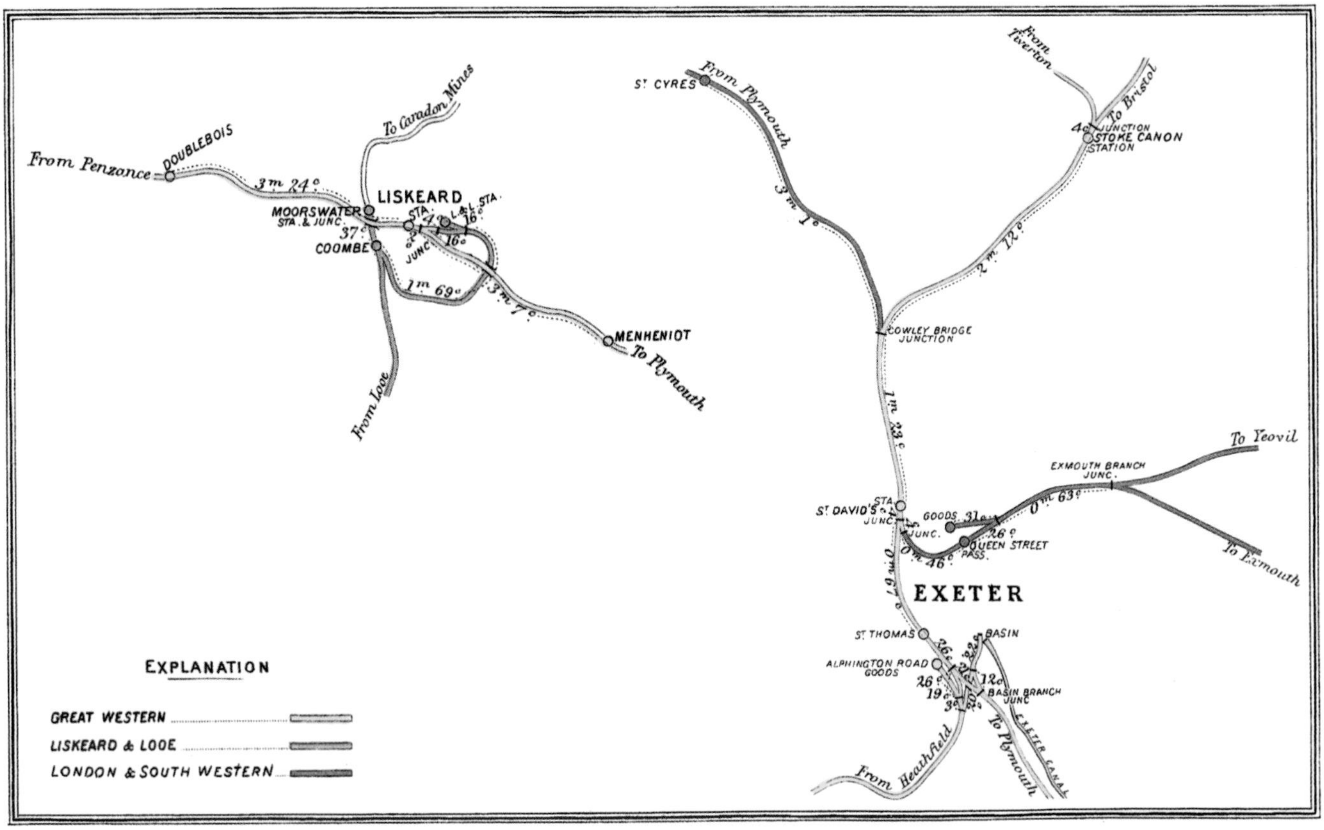

**Exeter–Liskeard**

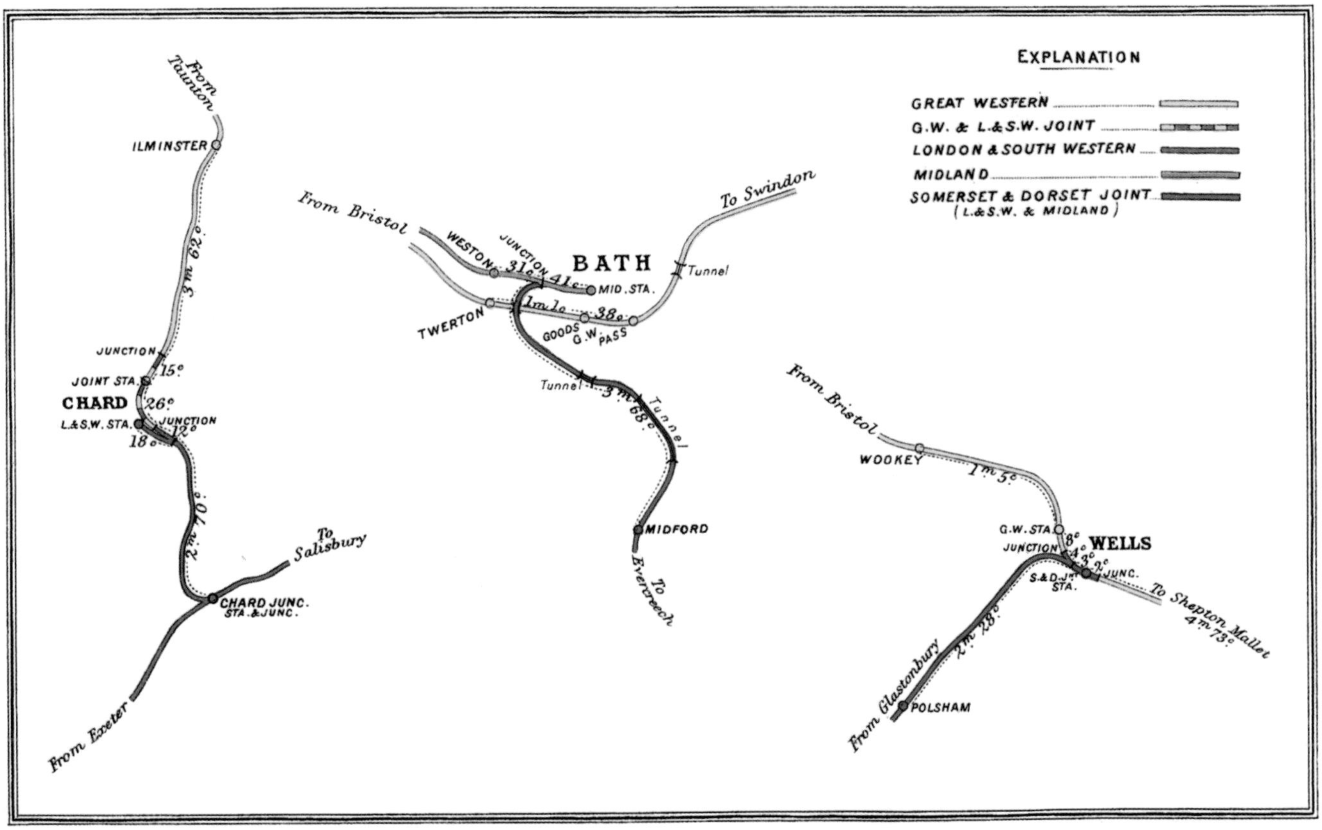

**Bath–Chard–Wells**

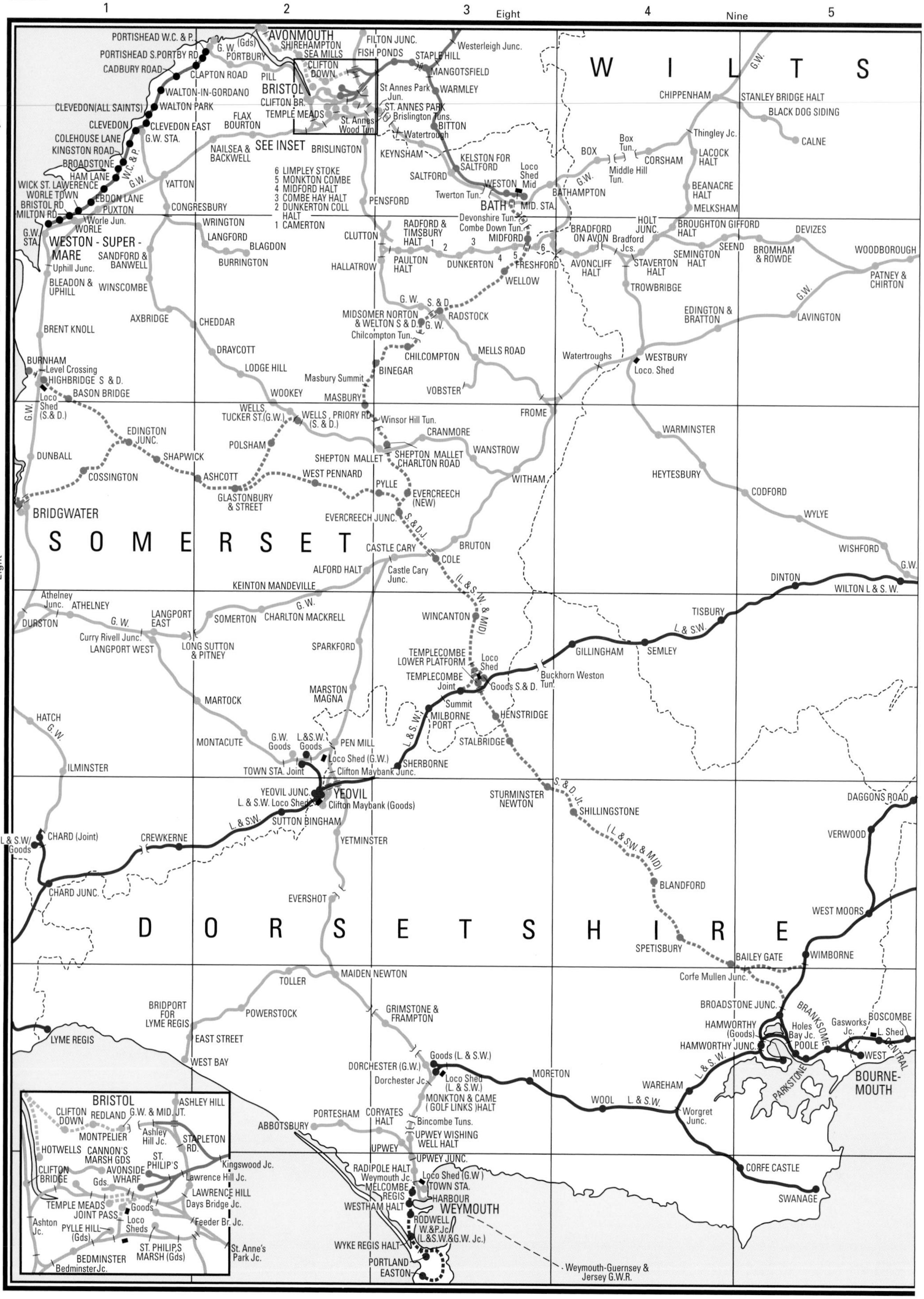

## THREE

1 2 3 Eight 4 Nine 5

A B C D E F G

W I L T S

S O M E R S E T

D O R S E T S H I R E

PORTISHEAD W.C. & P.
PORTISHEAD S.PORTBY RD.
CADBURY ROAD
G. W. (Gds)
PORTBURY
AVONMOUTH
SHIREHAMPTON
SEA MILLS
CLIFTON DOWN
PILL
CLAPTON ROAD
WALTON-IN-GORDANO
WALTON PARK
CLEVEDON(ALL SAINTS)
CLEVEDON
CLEVEDON EAST
G.W. STA.
COLEHOUSE LANE
KINGSTON ROAD
BROADSTONE
W.C. & P.
HAM LANE
WICK ST. LAWRENCE
WORLE TOWN
BRISTOL RD
MILTON RD
EBDON LANE
PUXTON
G.W.
Worle Jun.
WORLE
G.W. STA.
WESTON - SUPER - MARE
Uphill Junc.
BLEADON & UPHILL
SANDFORD & BANWELL
WINSCOMBE
BRENT KNOLL
AXBRIDGE
CHEDDAR
YATTON
CONGRESBURY
NAILSEA & BACKWELL
FLAX BOURTON
SEE INSET
BRISTOL
CLIFTON BR.
TEMPLE MEADS
St. Annes Wood Tun.
BRISLINGTON
FILTON JUNC.
FISH PONDS
STAPLE HILL
Westerleigh Junc.
MANGOTSFIELD
St Annes Park Jun.
WARMLEY
ST. ANNES PARK
Brislington Tuns.
BITTON
Watertrough
KEYNSHAM
KELSTON FOR SALTFORD
SALTFORD
Loco Shed Mid
WESTON
Twerton Tun.
BATH
MID. STA.
BATHAMPTON
G.W.
BOX
Box Tun.
Middle Hill Tun.
CORSHAM
CHIPPENHAM
STANLEY BRIDGE HALT
BLACK DOG SIDING
CALNE
Thingley Jc.
LACOCK HALT
BEANACRE HALT
MELKSHAM
6 LIMPLEY STOKE
5 MONKTON COMBE
4 MIDFORD HALT
3 COMBE HAY HALT
2 DUNKERTON COLL HALT
1 CAMERTON
PENSFORD
WRINGTON
LANGFORD
BLAGDON
BURRINGTON
CLUTTON
HALLATROW
RADFORD & TIMSBURY HALT
PAULTON HALT
DUNKERTON
Devonshire Tun.
Combe Down Tun.
MIDFORD
FRESHFORD
WELLOW
BRADFORD ON AVON
Bradford Jcs.
AVONCLIFF HALT
HOLT JUNC.
BROUGHTON GIFFORD HALT
STAVERTON HALT
SEMINGTON HALT
SEEND
BROMHAM & ROWDE
DEVIZES
WOODBOROUGH
PATNEY & CHIRTON
TROWBRIBGE
G.W.
LAVINGTON
EDINGTON & BRATTON
G. W. S. & D.
MIDSOMER NORTON & WELTON S & D.
G. W.
RADSTOCK
Chilcompton Tun.
CHILCOMPTON
BINEGAR
MELLS ROAD
Watertroughs
WESTBURY
Loco. Shed
VOBSTER
Masbury Summit
MASBURY
FROME
BURNHAM
Level Crossing
HIGHBRIDGE S & D.
BASON BRIDGE
Loco Shed (S.& D.)
G.W.
DRAYCOTT
LODGE HILL
WOOKEY
WELLS, TUCKER ST.(G.W.)
WELLS, PRIORY RD (S. & D.)
Winsor Hill Tun.
CRANMORE
WANSTROW
WARMINSTER
EDINGTON JUNC.
POLSHAM
SHAPWICK
DUNBALL
COSSINGTON
ASHCOTT
SHEPTON MALLET
SHEPTON MALLET CHARLTON ROAD
WEST PENNARD
WITHAM
HEYTESBURY
CODFORD
GLASTONBURY & STREET
PYLLE
EVERCREECH (NEW)
EVERCREECH JUNC.
S. & D.J.
WYLYE
BRIDGWATER
CASTLE CARY
BRUTON
COLE
WISHFORD
G.W.
ALFORD HALT
Castle Cary Junc.
(L & S.W. & MID)
KEINTON MANDEVILLE
DINTON
WILTON L & S. W.
Athelney Junc.
ATHELNEY
DURSTON
G. W.
LANGPORT EAST
SOMERTON
CHARLTON MACKRELL
G.W.
Curry Rivell Junc.
LANGPORT WEST
LONG SUTTON & PITNEY
WINCANTON
TISBURY
L & S.W.
SEMLEY
GILLINGHAM
SPARKFORD
TEMPLECOMBE LOWER PLATFORM
Loco Shed
TEMPLECOMBE Joint
Goods S.& D.
Buckhorn Weston Tun.
MARSTON MAGNA
MARTOCK
Summit
MILBORNE PORT
HENSTRIDGE
HATCH
G.W.
L.& S.W.
STALBRIDGE
MONTACUTE
G.W. Goods
L.&S.W. Goods
PEN MILL
Loco Shed (G.W.)
SHERBORNE
ILMINSTER
TOWN STA. Joint
Clifton Maybank Junc.
YEOVIL JUNC.
YEOVIL
L. & S.W. Loco Shed
Clifton Maybank (Goods)
STURMINSTER NEWTON
S. & D. Jt.
SHILLINGSTONE
DAGGONS ROAD
L. & S.W.
SUTTON BINGHAM
(L & S.W. & MID)
VERWOOD
L & S.W. Goods
CHARD (Joint)
CREWKERNE
YETMINSTER
CHARD JUNC.
EVERSHOT
BLANDFORD
WEST MOORS
SPETISBURY
BAILEY GATE
WIMBORNE
Corfe Mullen Junc.
MAIDEN NEWTON
TOLLER
BROADSTONE JUNC.
BRANKSOME
BRIDPORT FOR LYME REGIS
POWERSTOCK
GRIMSTONE & FRAMPTON
HAMWORTHY (Goods)
Holes Bay Jc.
Gasworks Jc.
BOSCOMBE
L. Shed
CENTRAL
LYME REGIS
EAST STREET
HAMWORTHY JUNC.
POOLE
WEST
WEST BAY
Goods (L. & S.W.)
L. & S. W.
PARKSTONE
BOURNE-MOUTH
DORCHESTER (G.W.)
MORETON
Dorchester Jc.
Loco Shed (L. & S.W.)
WAREHAM
MONKTON & CAME (GOLF LINKS) HALT
WOOL
L & S.W.
Worgret Junc.
PORTESHAM
CORYATES HALT
Bincombe Tuns.
ABBOTSBURY
UPWEY WISHING WELL HALT
UPWEY
UPWEY JUNC.
CORFE CASTLE
RADIPOLE HALT
Weymouth Jc.
Loco Shed (G.W.)
MELCOMBE REGIS
TOWN STA.
HARBOUR
WESTHAM HALT
WEYMOUTH
SWANAGE
RODWELL
W.&P.Jc.
(L.&S.W.&G.W. Jc.)
WYKE REGIS HALT
PORTLAND
EASTON
Weymouth-Guernsey & Jersey G.W.R.

BRISTOL
ASHLEY HILL
CLIFTON DOWN
REDLAND
G.W. & MID. JT.
MONTPELIER
Ashley Hill Jc.
STAPLETON RD.
HOTWELLS
CANNON'S MARSH GDS
ST. PHILIP'S
Kingswood Jc.
CLIFTON BRIDGE
AVONSIDE WHARF
Gds.
Lawrence Hill Jc.
LAWRENCE HILL
TEMPLE MEADS
Goods
Days Bridge Jc.
JOINT PASS.
Ashton Jc.
Loco Sheds
Feeder Br. Jc.
PYLLE HILL (Gds)
ST. PHILIPS MARSH (Gds)
St. Anne's Park Jc.
BEDMINSTER
Bedminster Jc.

Eight

Two

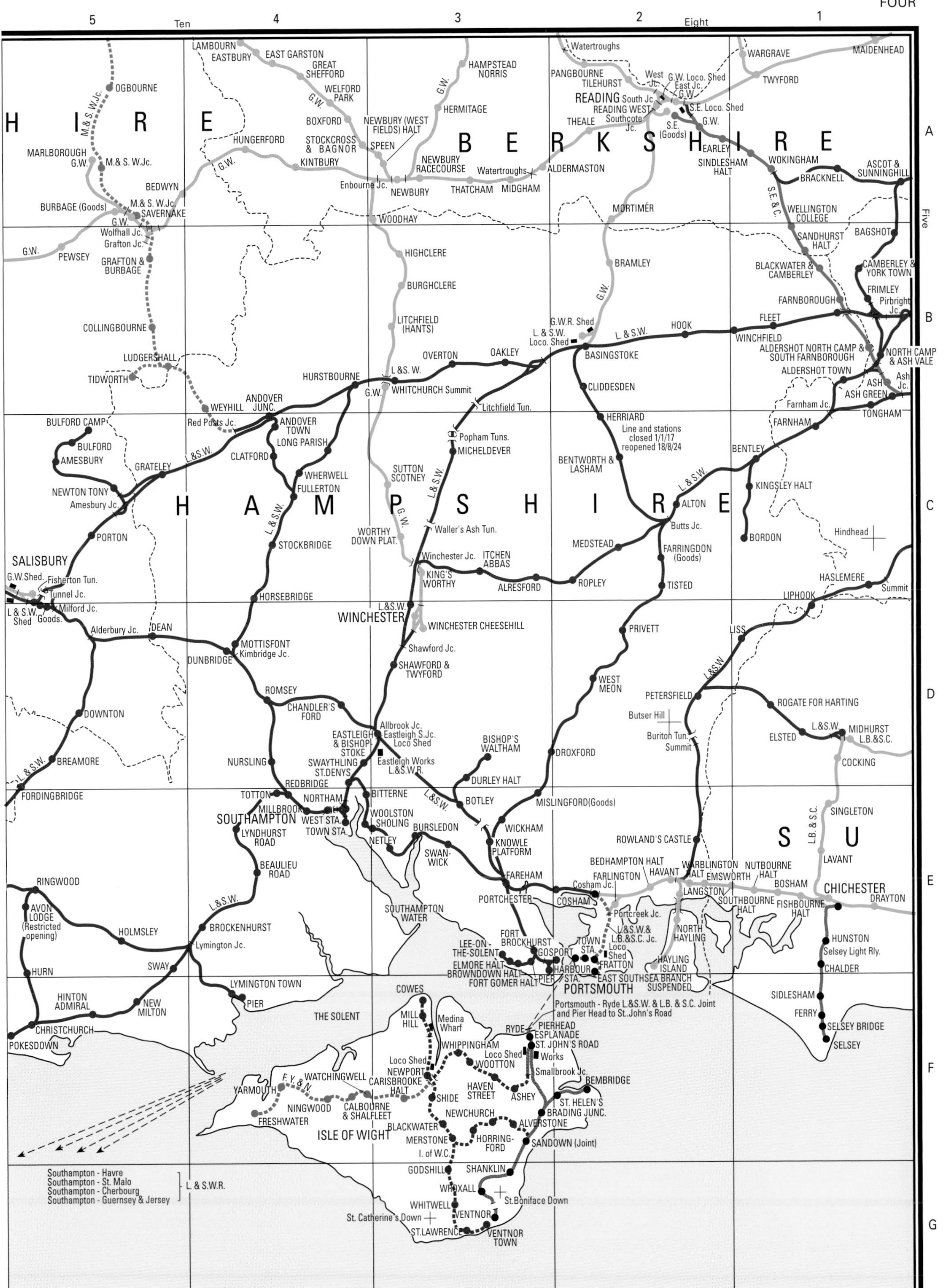
5
Ten
4
3
2
Eight
1
A
B
C
D
E
F
G
Five
H I R E
B E R K S H I R E
H A M P S H I R E
S U
LAMBOURN
EASTBURY
EAST GARSTON
GREAT SHEFFORD
WELFORD PARK
BOXFORD
HAMPSTEAD NORRIS
HERMITAGE
NEWBURY (WEST FIELDS) HALT
STOCKCROSS & BAGNOR
SPEEN
HUNGERFORD
KINTBURY
NEWBURY RACECOURSE
Enbourne Jc.
NEWBURY
THATCHAM
MIDGHAM
Watertroughs
ALDERMASTON
Watertroughs
PANGBOURNE
TILEHURST
READING
West Jc.
G.W. Loco. Shed
East Jc.
South Jc.
READING WEST
Southcote Jc.
THEALE
S.E. (Goods)
S.E. Loco. Shed
EARLEY
SINDLESHAM HALT
WARGRAVE
TWYFORD
MAIDENHEAD
WOKINGHAM
BRACKNELL
ASCOT & SUNNINGHILL
WELLINGTON COLLEGE
SANDHURST HALT
BAGSHOT
CAMBERLEY & YORK TOWN
FRIMLEY
Pirbright Jc.
BLACKWATER & CAMBERLEY
FARNBOROUGH
OGBOURNE
M.& S. W.Jc.
MARLBOROUGH G.W.
M.& S. W.Jc.
BEDWYN
BURBAGE (Goods)
M.& S. W.Jc.
SAVERNAKE
Wolfhall Jc.
Grafton Jc.
G.W.
PEWSEY
GRAFTON & BURBAGE
COLLINGBOURNE
LUDGERSHALL
TIDWORTH
WEYHILL
Red Posts Jc.
ANDOVER JUNC.
ANDOVER TOWN
LONG PARISH
HURSTBOURNE
WOODHAY
HIGHCLERE
BURGHCLERE
LITCHFIELD (HANTS)
MORTIMER
BRAMLEY
G.W.R. Shed
L. & S.W. Loco. Shed
BASINGSTOKE
HOOK
FLEET
WINCHFIELD
ALDERSHOT NORTH CAMP & SOUTH FARNBOROUGH
NORTH CAMP & ASH VALE
ALDERSHOT TOWN
ASH
Ash Jc.
ASH GREEN
Farnham Jc.
FARNHAM
TONGHAM
OVERTON
OAKLEY
WHITCHURCH Summit
Litchfield Tun.
Popham Tuns.
MICHELDEVER
CLIDDESDEN
HERRIARD
Line and stations closed 1/1/17 reopened 18/8/24
BENTWORTH & LASHAM
BENTLEY
KINGSLEY HALT
BORDON
Hindhead
ALTON
Butts Jc.
BULFORD CAMP
BULFORD
AMESBURY
GRATELEY
CLATFORD
WHERWELL
FULLERTON
NEWTON TONY
Amesbury Jc.
PORTON
SUTTON SCOTNEY
Waller's Ash Tun.
WORTHY DOWN PLAT.
STOCKBRIDGE
MEDSTEAD
FARRINGDON (Goods)
SALISBURY
G.W.Shed
Fisherton Tun.
Tunnel Jc.
Milford Jc.
L & S.W. Shed
Goods.
Winchester Jc.
KING'S WORTHY
ITCHEN ABBAS
ALRESFORD
ROPLEY
TISTED
HASLEMERE
Summit
LIPHOOK
HORSEBRIDGE
WINCHESTER
WINCHESTER CHEESEHILL
Alderbury Jc.
DEAN
MOTTISFONT
Kimbridge Jc.
DUNBRIDGE
Shawford Jc.
SHAWFORD & TWYFORD
PRIVETT
LISS
DOWNTON
ROMSEY
CHANDLER'S FORD
WEST MEON
PETERSFIELD
ROGATE FOR HARTING
Allbrook Jc.
Eastleigh S.Jc.
Loco Shed
EASTLEIGH & BISHOPSTOKE
Eastleigh Works L.&S.W.R.
BISHOP'S WALTHAM
Butser Hill
Buriton Tun.
Summit
ELSTED
MIDHURST
L.B.& S.C.
BREAMORE
NURSLING
SWAYTHLING
ST.DENYS
REDBRIDGE
DURLEY HALT
DROXFORD
COCKING
FORDINGBRIDGE
TOTTON
NORTHAM
BITTERNE
BOTLEY
MISLINGFORD(Goods)
SINGLETON
MILLBROOK
SOUTHAMPTON
WEST STA.
TOWN STA.
WOOLSTON
SHOLING
NETLEY
BURSLEDON
WICKHAM
KNOWLE PLATFORM
ROWLAND'S CASTLE
LYNDHURST ROAD
BEAULIEU ROAD
SWANWICK
LAVANT
RINGWOOD
AVON LODGE (Restricted opening)
BEDHAMPTON HALT
FARLINGTON
HAVANT
WARBLINGTON HALT
EMSWORTH
NUTBOURNE HALT
BOSHAM
CHICHESTER
DRAYTON
FAREHAM
PORTCHESTER
Cosham Jc.
COSHAM
LANGSTON
SOUTHBOURNE HALT
FISHBOURNE HALT
SOUTHAMPTON WATER
Portcreek Jc.
L.&S.W.& L.B.&S.C. Jc.
NORTH HAYLING
HUNSTON
Selsey Light Rly.
HOLMSLEY
BROCKENHURST
Lymington Jc.
FORT BROCKHURST
LEE-ON-THE-SOLENT
ELMORE HALT
BROWNDOWN HALT
FORT GOMER HALT
GOSPORT
TOWN STA.
Loco Shed
FRATTON
HARBOUR STA.
PIER
HAYLING ISLAND
CHALDER
HURN
SWAY
LYMINGTON TOWN
PIER
EAST SOUTHSEA BRANCH SUSPENDED
PORTSMOUTH
Portsmouth - Ryde L.&S.W. & L.B. & S.C. Joint and Pier Head to St.John's Road
SIDLESHAM
FERRY
SELSEY BRIDGE
SELSEY
HINTON ADMIRAL
NEW MILTON
CHRISTCHURCH
POKESDOWN
THE SOLENT
COWES
MILL HILL
Medina Wharf
RYDE
PIERHEAD
ESPLANADE
ST. JOHN'S ROAD
Works
Loco Shed
WHIPPINGHAM
WOOTTON
Smallbrook Jc.
Loco Shed
NEWPORT
WATCHINGWELL
CARISBROOKE HALT
F.Y.& N.
YARMOUTH
HAVEN STREET
ASHEY
SHIDE
BEMBRIDGE
ST. HELEN'S
BRADING JUNC.
NINGWOOD
CALBOURNE & SHALFLEET
FRESHWATER
NEWCHURCH
ALVERSTONE
BLACKWATER
ISLE OF WIGHT
MERSTONE
HORRINGFORD
SANDOWN (Joint)
I. of W.C.
GODSHILL
SHANKLIN
WROXALL
St.Boniface Down
WHITWELL
VENTNOR
St. Catherine's Down
ST.LAWRENCE
VENTNOR TOWN
Southampton - Havre
Southampton - St. Malo
Southampton - Cherbourg
Southampton - Guernsey & Jersey
L. & S.W.R.
G.W.
L.& S.W.
L.&S.W.
L.&S.W.
S.E.& C.
L.B.& S.C.

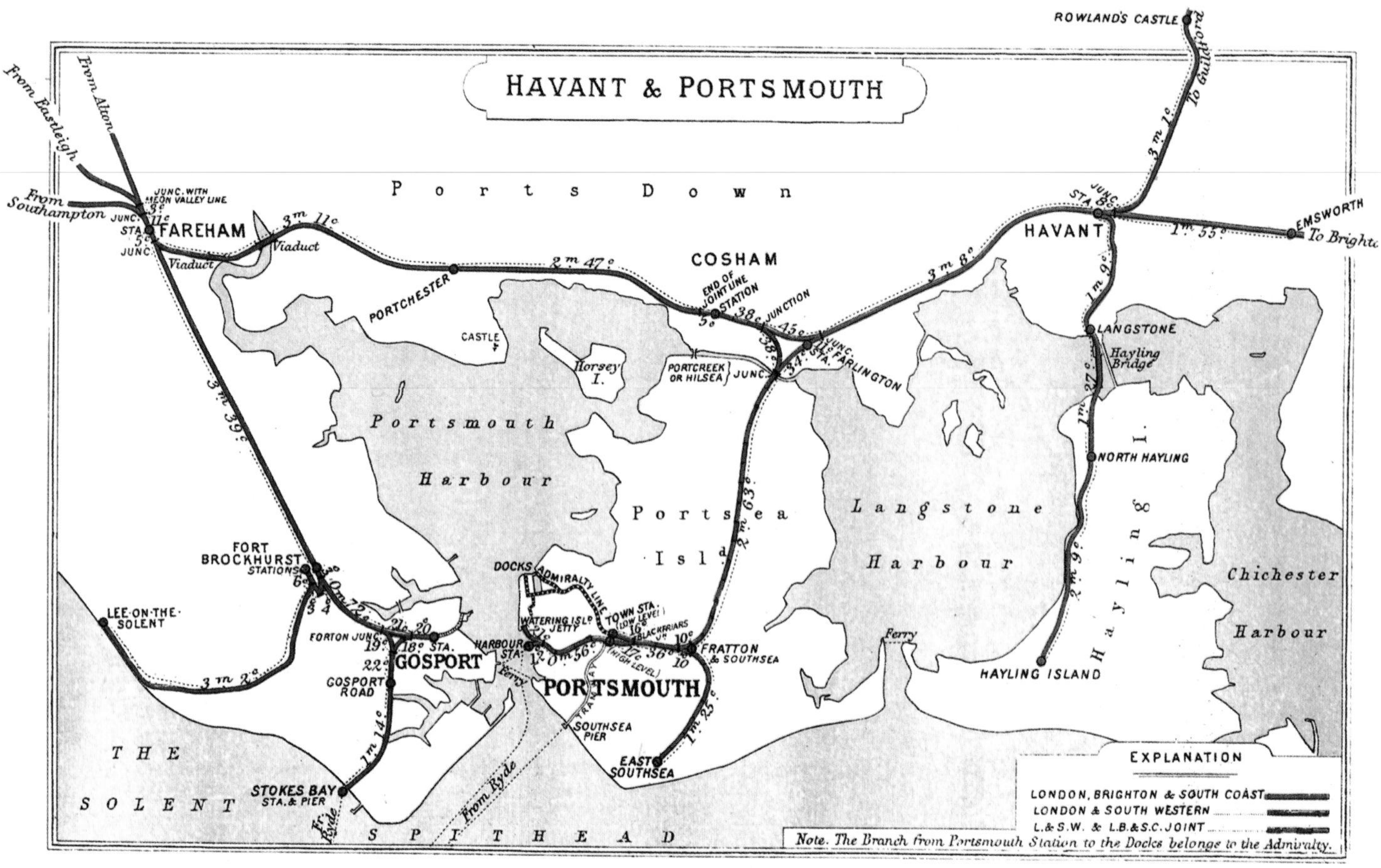

# HAVANT & PORTSMOUTH

Rowland's Castle
To Guildford
From Eastleigh
From Alton
From Southampton
Junc. with Meon Valley Line
Fareham
Viaduct
Ports Down
Portchester
Cosham
End of Joint Line Station
Junction
Havant
Emsworth
To Brighton
Langstone
Hayling Bridge
Junc. Farlington Sta.
Portcreek or Hilsea Junc.
Castle
Horsey I.
Portsmouth Harbour
Portsea Isld.
Langstone Harbour
North Hayling
Hayling I.
Chichester Harbour
Fort Brockhurst Stations
Lee-on-the-Solent
Forton Junc.
Gosport
Gosport Road
Docks
Admiralty Line
Watering Isl. Jetty
Town Sta. (Low Level)
(High Level)
Blackfriars Jn.
Harbour Sta.
Fratton & Southsea
Portsmouth
Ferry
Southsea Pier
East Southsea
Hayling Island
The Solent
Stokes Bay Sta. & Pier
From Ryde
To Ryde
Spithead

EXPLANATION

London, Brighton & South Coast
London & South Western
L.& S.W. & L.B.& S.C. Joint

Note. The Branch from Portsmouth Station to the Docks belongs to the Admiralty.

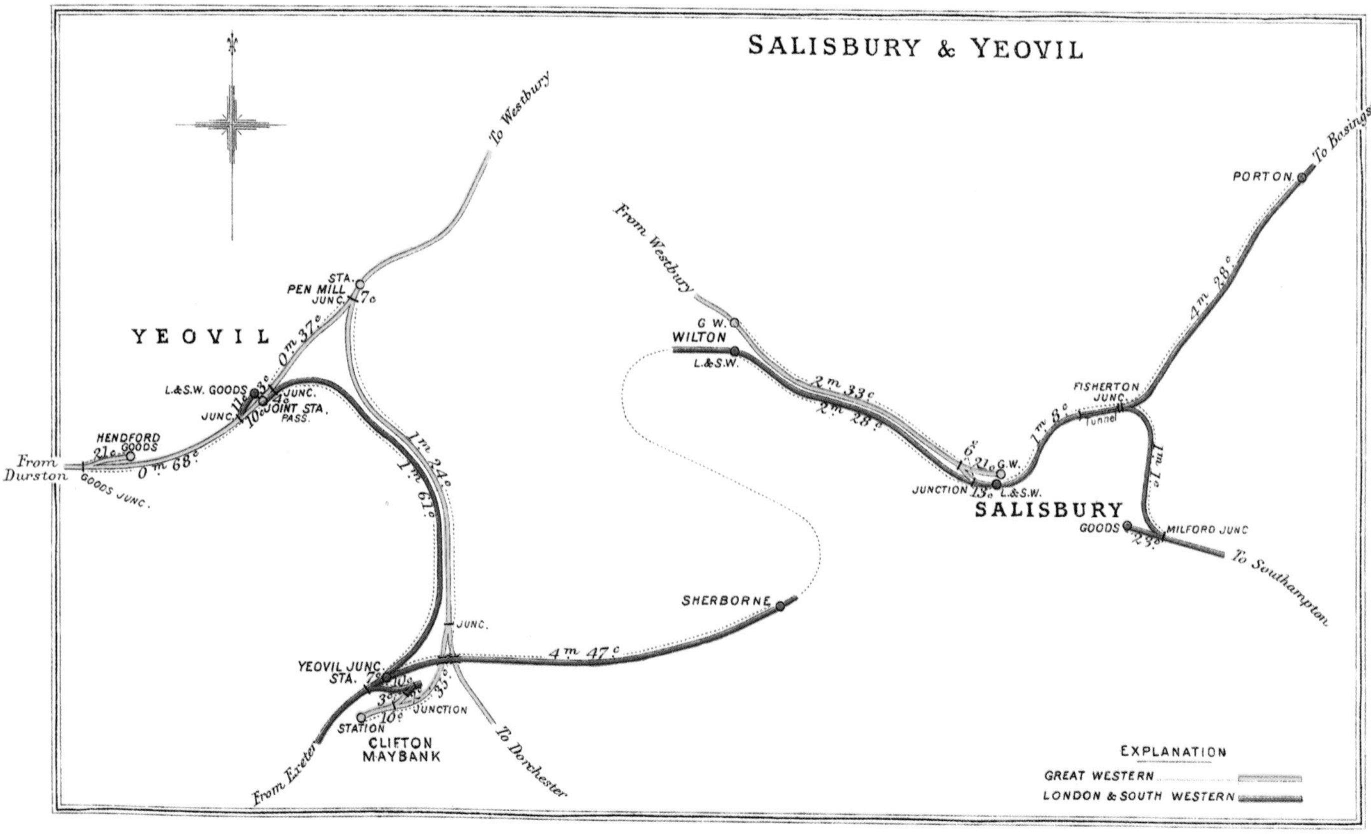

# SALISBURY & YEOVIL

To Westbury
Pen Mill Sta. Junc.
Yeovil
L.& S.W. Goods
Junc.
Junc. Joint Sta. Pass.
Hendford Goods
From Durston
Goods Junc.
Junc.
Yeovil Junc. Sta.
Junction
Station
Clifton Maybank
From Exeter
To Dorchester
Sherborne
From Westbury
G.W. Wilton L.& S.W.
Porton
To Basingstoke
Fisherton Junc.
Tunnel
Junction
G.W.
L.& S.W.
Salisbury
Goods
Milford Junc.
To Southampton

EXPLANATION

Great Western
London & South Western

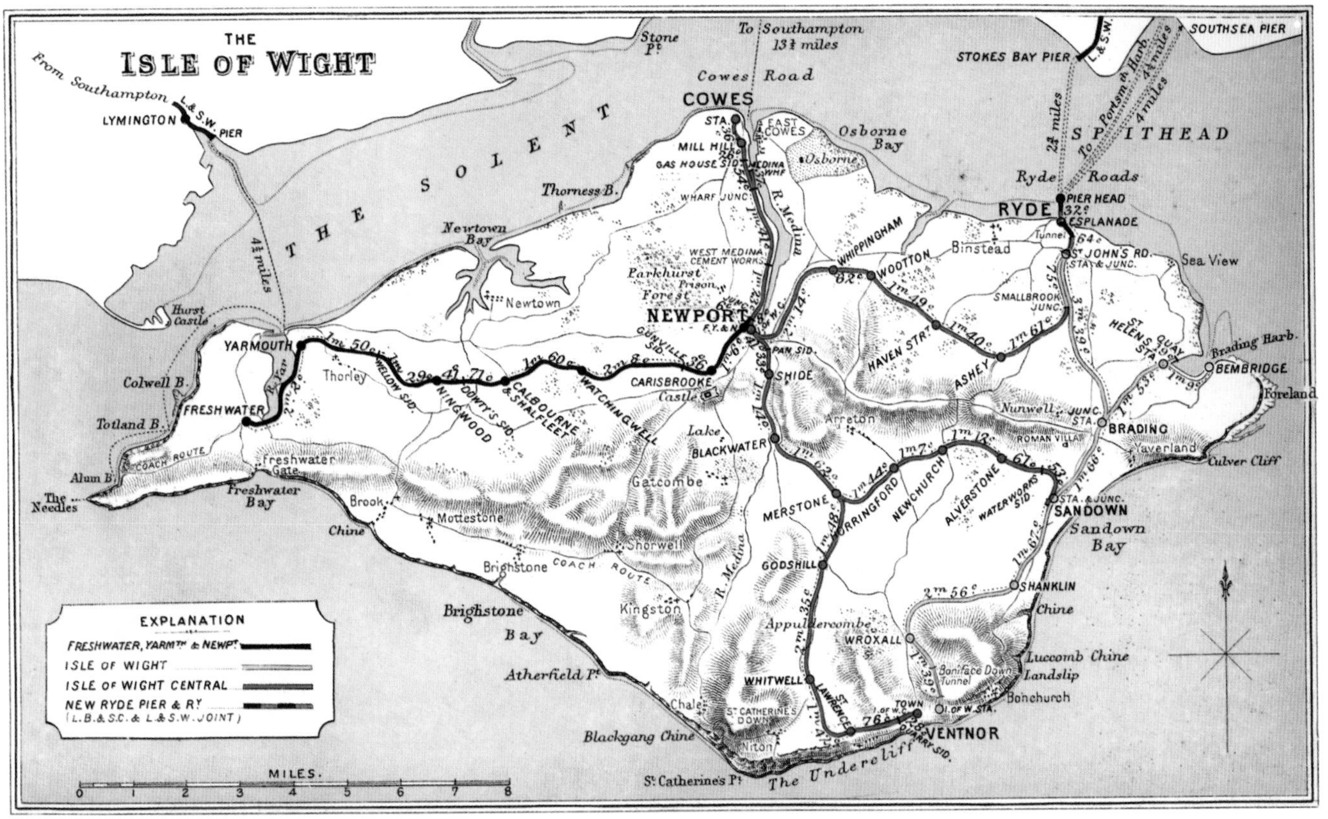

THE

# ISLE OF WIGHT

EXPLANATION

FRESHWATER, YARM.TH & NEWP.T

ISLE OF WIGHT

ISLE OF WIGHT CENTRAL

NEW RYDE PIER & R.Y (L.B.&S.C. & L.&S.W. JOINT)

MILES.

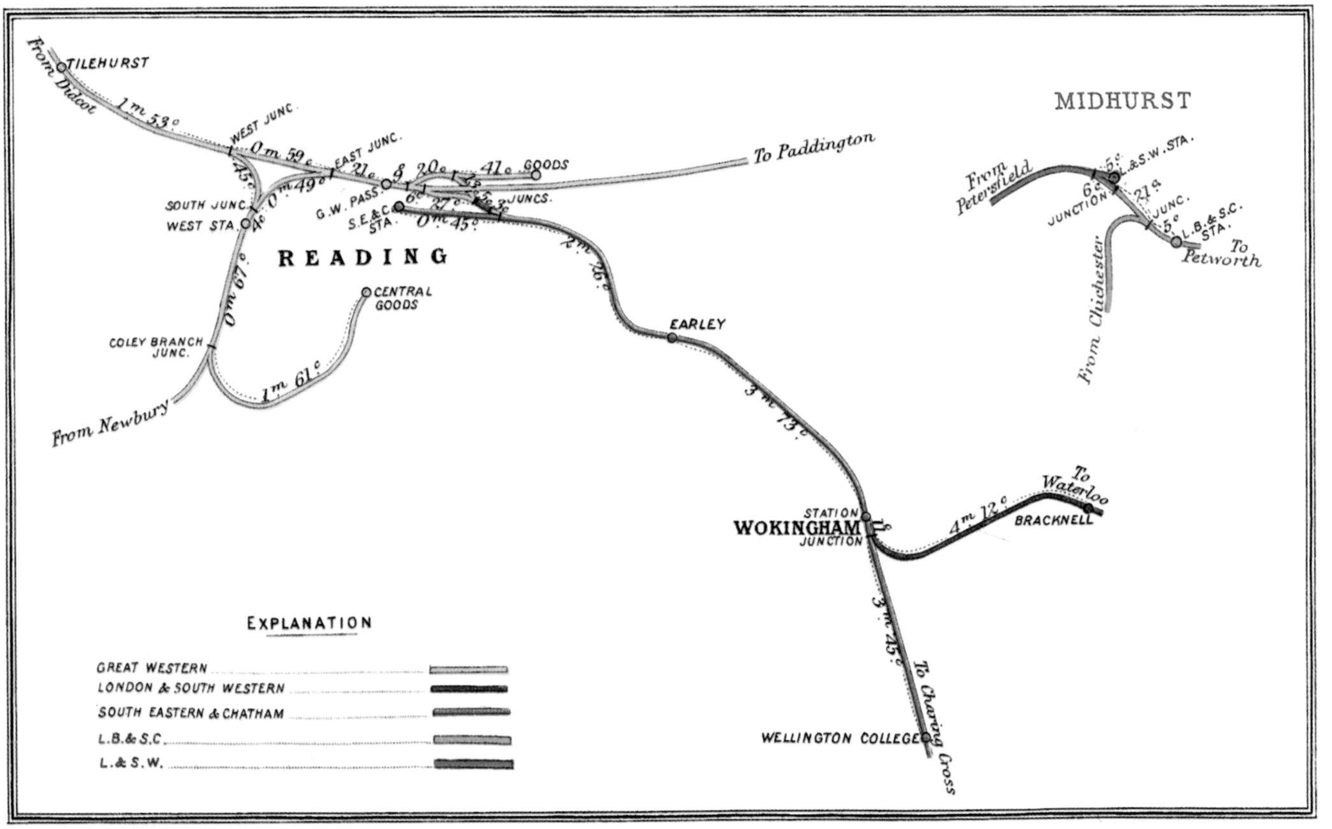

0 1 2 3 4 5 6 7 8

# READING

# MIDHURST

EXPLANATION

GREAT WESTERN

LONDON & SOUTH WESTERN

SOUTH EASTERN & CHATHAM

L.B.& S.C.

L.& S.W.

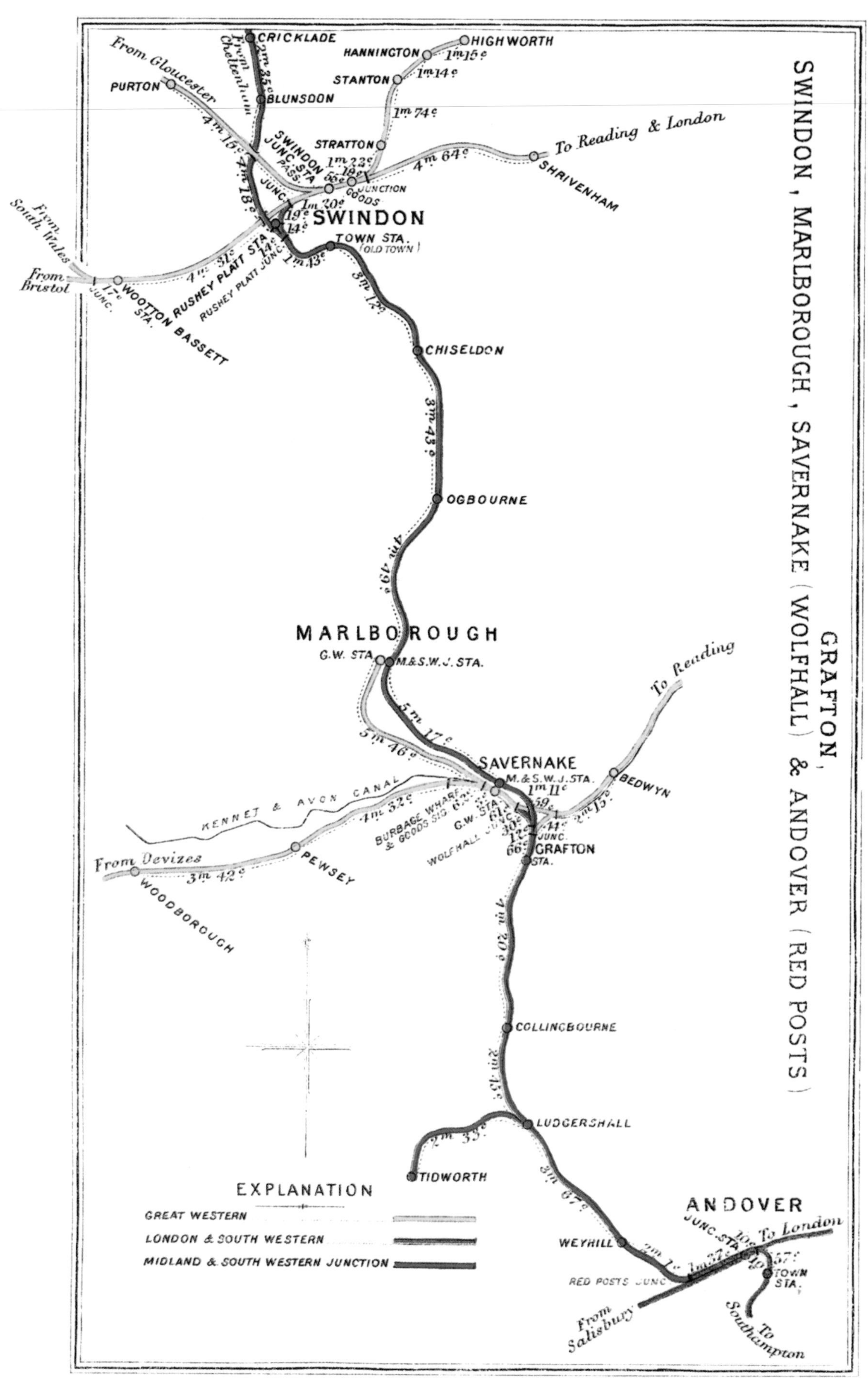
SWINDON, MARLBOROUGH, SAVERNAKE (WOLFHALL) & ANDOVER (RED POSTS)
GRAFTON,
CRICKLADE
From Cheltenham
HIGHWORTH
HANNINGTON
STANTON
PURTON
From Gloucester
BLUNSDON
STRATTON
To Reading & London
SHRIVENHAM
SWINDON JUNC. STA.
JUNCTION
GOODS
SWINDON
TOWN STA. (OLD TOWN)
From South Wales
From Bristol
RUSHEY PLATT STA.
RUSHEY PLATT JUNC.
WOOTTON BASSETT
CHISELDON
OGBOURNE
MARLBOROUGH
G.W. STA.
M.&S.W.J. STA.
To Reading
SAVERNAKE
M.&S.W.J. STA.
G.W. STA.
BEDWYN
KENNET & AVON CANAL
BURBAGE WHARF & GOODS SIG
WOLFHALL JUNC.
GRAFTON STA.
From Devizes
PEWSEY
WOODBOROUGH
COLLINGBOURNE
LUDGERSHALL
TIDWORTH
EXPLANATION
GREAT WESTERN
LONDON & SOUTH WESTERN
MIDLAND & SOUTH WESTERN JUNCTION
ANDOVER
JUNC. STA.
To London
WEYHILL
RED POSTS JUNC.
TOWN STA.
From Salisbury
To Southampton

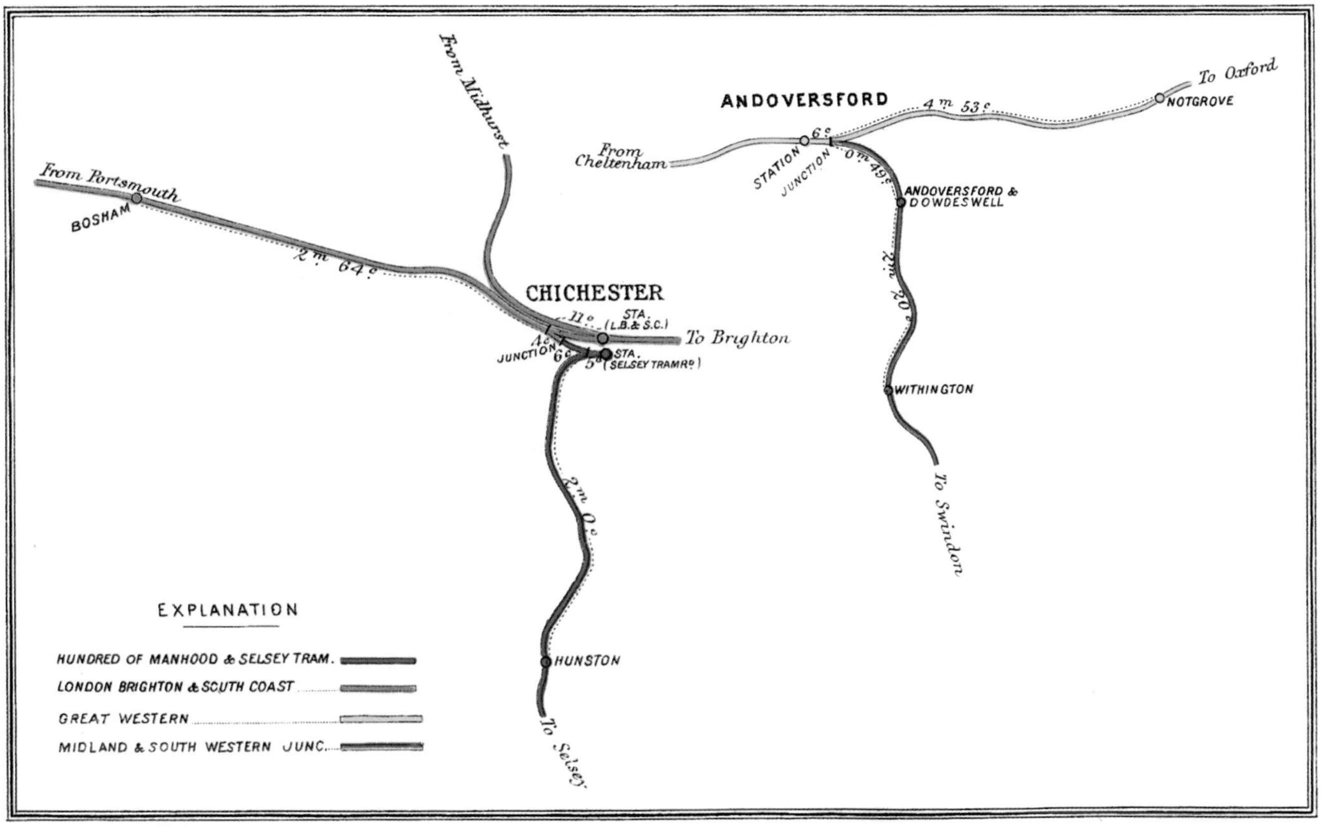

EXPLANATION

HUNDRED OF MANHOOD & SELSEY TRAM.

LONDON BRIGHTON & SOUTH COAST

GREAT WESTERN

MIDLAND & SOUTH WESTERN JUNC.

**Andoversford–Chichester**

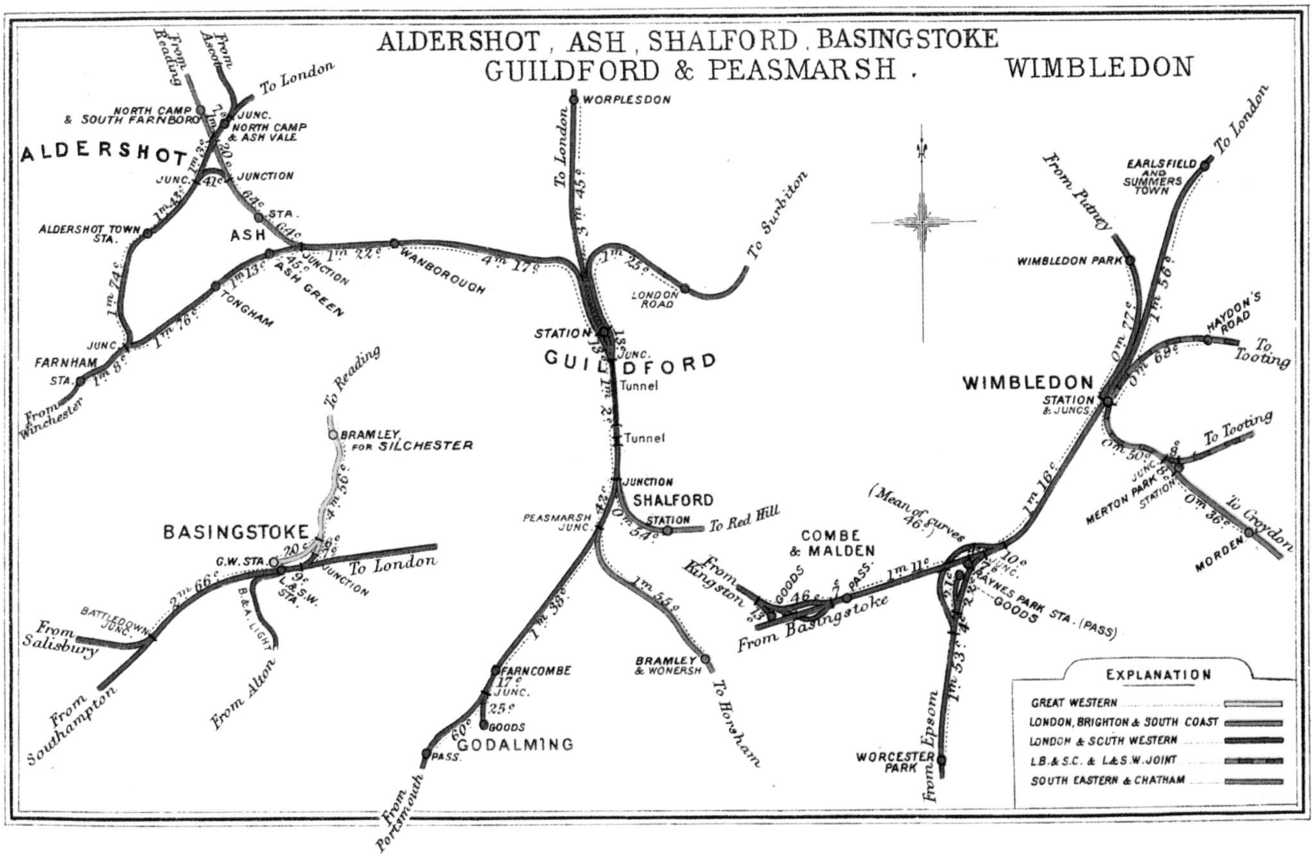

ALDERSHOT, ASH, SHALFORD, BASINGSTOKE
GUILDFORD & PEASMARSH. WIMBLEDON

EXPLANATION

GREAT WESTERN

LONDON, BRIGHTON & SOUTH COAST

LONDON & SOUTH WESTERN

L.B.& S.C. & L.& S.W. JOINT

SOUTH EASTERN & CHATHAM

## FIVE

1 2 3 4 5
Eleven
A B C D E F G
Four

CHORLEY WOOD & CHENIES
CROXLEY GREEN
WATFORD JUNC.
HIGH ST.
RICKSMANWORTH
BUSHEY & OXHEY
ELSTREE
HIGH BARNET
NEW BARNET
ENFIELD
ENFIELD TOWN
BRIMSDOWN
CHURCHBURY
PONDER'S END
CHIGWELL LANE
LOUGHTON
OAKLEIGH PARK
TOTTERIDGE
MILL HILL
RUSH HILL PARK
CHINGFORD
(SEE SHEETS THIRTY NINE & FORTY)
SHENFIELD & HUTTON
Summit
BILLERICAY
Whitehouse Farm Tun.
BEACONSFIELD
SEER GREEN HALT
SANDY LODGE
HATCH END
EDGWARE
PALMERS GREEN
WOODSIDE PK
LOWER EDMONTON
HIGHAMS PARK
CHIGWELL
STANMORE
MILL HILL
ANGEL ROAD
PALACE GATES
WOODFORD
FAIRLOP
BRENTWOOD & WARLEY
LOUDWATER
NORTHWOOD
PINNER
HARROW & WEALD-STONE
FINCHLEY
MUSWELL HILL
WOODGREEN
GEORGE LANE
SNARESBROOK
GIDEA PARK
HAROLD WOOD
GERRARDS CROSS
WOOBURN GREEN
DENHAM
NORTH HARROW
HARROW-ON-THE-HILL
EAST FINCHLEY
HIGHGATE
SEVEN SISTERS
ROMFORD
SEVEN KINGS
EMERSON PARK HALT
LAINDON
BOURNE END
DENHAM GOLF CLUB PLAT
RUISLIP
HENDON
WEMBLEY PK
LEYTONSTONE
UPMINSTER
COOKHAM
S. HARROW
NEASDEN
CRICKLEWOOD
FINSBURY PARK
HACKNEY DOWNS
ILFORD
G.E.
HORNCHURCH
EAST HORNDON
UXBRIDGE HIGH ST
NORTHHOLT JUNC.
WEMBLEY
KENTISH TOWN
BARKING
MID
DAGENHAM
BURNHAM BEECHES
UXBRIDGE VINE STREET
COWLEY
GREENFORD
EALING BR'WAY
WILLESDEN JC.
ST PANCRAS
EUSTON
KINGS CROSS
BROAD ST.
LIVERPOOL ST.
L.T. & S.
DAGENHAM DOCK
TAPLOW
HAYES & HARLINGTON
HANWELL
MARYLEBONE
PADDINGTON
HOLBORN VIA
FENCHURCH
BLACKWALL
BECKTON
RAINHAM
OCKENDON
STANFORD-LE-HOPE
G.W.
LANGLEY
CHARING X
CANNON ST.
LONDON BRIDGE
N. WOOLWICH
PURFLEET RIFLE RANGE
Thames Haven Jc.
MAIDENHEAD
SLOUGH
ACTON
KENSINGTON
PURFLEET
WEST DRAYTON
SOUTHALL
BRENTFORD
OSTERLEY
ABBEY WOOD
BELVEDERE
W.Thurrock Jc.
GRAYS
LOW STREET
DATCHET
COLNBROOK
HOUNSLOW TOWN
VICTORIA
WATERLOO
CHARLTON
WOOLWICH DOCKYARD
ERITH
WINDSOR & ETON
HOUNSLOW BARRACKS
RICHMOND
CHELSEA
BATTERSEA
BARNES
BRIXTON
GREENWICH
SLADES GREEN
TILBURY DOCKS
HOUNSLOW
MORTLAKE
BLACKHEATH
BARNEHURST
WRAYSBURY
RUNEMEDE (Goods)
RUNEMEDE RANGE
TWICKENHAM
PUTNEY
CLAPHAM JUNC.
HERNE HILL
WELL HALL
WELLING
GREENHITHE
TILBURY
HIGH ST.
L.& S.W.
FULWELL
STRAWBERRY HILL
BALHAM
LEE
BEXLEY-HEATH
NORTHFLEET
WEST ST.
GRAVESEND
EGHAM
FELTHAM
TEDDINGTON
EARLSFIELD
STREATHAM
TULSE HILL
ELTHAM
NEW ELTHAM
CRAYFORD
STONE CROSSING HALT
ROSHERVILLE
STAINES JUNC.
ASHFORD
WIMBLEDON
GROVE PARK
SIDCUP
BEXLEY
DARTFORD
ASCOT & SUNNINGHILL
SUNBURY
HAMPTON
NORBITON
CRYSTAL PALACE
CHISLEHURST
FARINGHAM RD & SUTTON-AT-HONE
SOUTHFLEET
VIRGINIA WATER
HAMPTON COURT
KINGSTON
MALDEN
RAYNES PARK
SHORTLANDS
BROMLEY NORTH
LONGFIELD HALT FOR RINDON & WESTWOOD
S.E.& C.
SHEPPERTON
THORNTON HEATH
SELHURST
ELMERS END
ST.MARY CRAY
SWANLEY
SUNNINGDALE
THAMES DITTON
MITCHAM
NORWOOD JUNC.
EDEN PARK
BROMLEY SOUTH
FAWKHAM FOR HARTLEY & LONGFIELD
MEOPHAM
CHERTSEY
ESHER
SURBITON
MITCHAM JUNC
WOODSIDE
W.WICKHAM
ORPINGTON
SOLE STREET
Hampton Court Jc.
WORCESTER PARK
WEST CROYDON
COOMBE LANE
HAYES
BAGSHOT
ADDLESTONE
WALTON FOR HERSHAM
SUTTON
CARSHALTON
EAST CROYDON
CHELSFIELD
EYNSFORD
CLAYGATE
CHEAM
PURLEY OAKS
SELSDON RD
KNOCKHOLT
Summit
WEYBRIDGE
EWELL
BELMONT
PURLEY
SANDERSTEAD
Polhill Tun.
BYFLEET
OXSHOTT
EPSOM
KENLEY
WHYTELEAFE
SHOREHAM (KENT)
L.& S.W.
COBHAM FOR STOKE D'ABERNON
EPSOM DOWNS
BANSTEAD
SMITHAM
UPPER WARLINGHAM
FRIMLEY
Bisley Camp
BROOKWOOD
WOKING
ASHTEAD
TATTENHAM CORNER
COULSDON
WARLINGHAM
OTFORD
KEMSING
MALLING
CHIPSTEAD
COULSDON & CANE HILL
WOLDINGHAM
LEATHERHEAD
KINGSWOOD
TADWORTH & WALTON ON THE HILL
DUNTON GREEN
Pirbright Jc.
Brookwood Cemetery
WORPLESDON
EFFINGHAM JUNC.
CHEVENING HALT
BRASTED
SEVENOAKS BAT & BALL
WROTHAM & BOROUGH GREEN
BOOKHAM
CATERHAM
HORSLEY
Mickleham Tun.
Merstham Tuns.
WESTERHAM
SEVENOAKS TUBS HILL
Summit
Sevenoaks Tun.
ALDERSHOT NORTH CAMP & SOUTH FARNBOROUGH
BOX HILL & BURFORD BRI.
MERSTHAM
OXTED FOR LIMPSFIELD
ASH
Ash Jc.
GUILDFORD
CLANDON
Box Hill
DORKING
REIGATE
Hurst Green Jc.
ASH GREEN
WANBORO
DORKING
REDHILL
HURST GREEN HALT
MONKS LANE HALT
YALDING
TONGHAM
LONDON ROAD
BETCHWORTH
Redhill Tun.
Shalford Jc.
CHILWORTH & ALBURY
BOX HILL
NUTFIELD
Crowhurst Jc.
HILDENBOROUGH
Peasmarsh Jc.
Betchworth Tun.
EARLSWOOD
Bletchingley Tun.
GODSTONE
EDENBRIDGE
S.E.& C.
TONBRIDGE
PADDOCK WOOD
SHALFORD
GOMSHALL & SHERE
SALFORDS (Goods)
PENSHURST
LYGHE HALT
Loco Shed
FRANCOMBE
BRAMLEY & WONERSH
EDENBRIDGE TOWN
Somerhill Tun.
S U R R E Y
GODALMING
Goods
L.B.& S.C.
HEVER
HOLMWOOD
HORLEY
LINGFIELD
L.B.& S.C.
Viaduct
Leith Hill
SOUTHBOROUGH
MILFORD
GATWICK (RACECOURSE)
DORMANS
COWDEN
CRANLEIGH
OCKLEY FOR CAPEL
Wells Tun.
Grove Tun.
TUNBRIDGE WELLS
GROOMBRIDGE
Loco Shed
Strawberry Hill Tun.
THREE BRIDGES
St. Margarets Jc.
ASHURST
WITLEY & CHIDDINGFOLD
EAST GRINSTEAD
HL
LL
HIGH ROCKS HALT
TUNBRIDGE WELLS WEST
BAYNARDS
CRAWLEY
GRANGE RD.
FOREST ROW
HARTFIELD
WITHYHAM
FRANT
HASLEMERE
Loco Shed
ROWFANT
KINGSCOTE
WARNHAM
IFIELD HALT
FAY GATE
ERIDGE
RUDGWICK
ROFFEY RD. HALT
Balcombe Tun.
WEST HOATHLY
WADHURST
LITTLEHAVEN HALT
Wadhurst Tun.
SLINFOLD
Loco Shed
HORSHAM
BALCOMBE
Ouse Via.
CROWBOROUGH & JARVIS BROOK
ROTHERFIELD & MARK CROSS
Itchingfield Jc.
Stammerham Jc.
CHRISTS HOSPITAL (WEST HORSHAM)
HORSTED KEYNES
ARDINGLY
MAYFIELD
TICEHURST ROAD
L.B.& S.C.
SOUTHWATER
Copyhold Jc.
SHEFFIELD PARK
Haywards Heath Tun.
HAYWARDS HEATH
S U S S E X
BILLINGSHURST
BUXTED
NEWICK & CHAILEY
WEST GRINSTEAD
HEATHFIELD
MIDHURST
SELHAM
UCKFIELD
WIVELSFIELD
Keymer Jc.
PULBOROUGH
PARTRIDGE GREEN
PETWORTH
BURGESS HILL
FITTLEWORTH
Hardham Jc.
ISFIELD
WALDRON & HOREHAM ROAD
BARCOMBE
BARCOMBE MILLS
HENFIELD
HASSOCKS
PLUMPTON
Clayton Tun.
COOKSBRIDGE
EAST SUSSEX MEMORIAL HOSPITAL
AMBERLEY
North Stoke Tun.
HELLINGLY
STEYNING
THE DYKE
Southerham Jc.
FALMER
GOLF CLUB PLATFORM
GLYNDE
BRAMBER
LEWES
HAILSHAM
Patcham Tun.
DRAYTON
ARUNDEL
PRESTON PARK
LONDON ROAD
NORMANS BAY HALT
PORT-LADE
BERWICK
L.B.& S.C.
BARNHAM JUNC.
FORD JUNC.
Arundel Jc.
SHOREHAM-BY-SEA
LEWES ROAD
SOUTHEASE & RODMELL HALT
STONE CROSS HALT
Stone Cross Jct
PEVENSEY BAY HALT
Works
WEST WORTHING
LANCING
KEMP TOWN
Littlehampton Jc.
GORING-BY-SEA
KINGSTON (Goods)
HOVE
Goods
CENTRAL
POLEGATE
PEVENSEY & WESTHAM
Willingdon Jc.
WORTHING
SOUTHWICK
BRIGHTON
Loco Shed
NEWHAVEN TOWN
ANGMERING
HAMPDEN PARK
LITTLEHAMPTON
HARBOUR STA.
BISHOPSTONE
1 HOLLAND ROAD HALT
2 DYKE JUNC. HALT
3 FISHERGATE HALT
4 BUNGALOW TOWN HALT
5 HAM BRIDGE HALT
Loco Shed
BOGNOR
SEAFORD
EASTBOURNE
Newhaven-Dieppe L.B.& S.C.

## SIX

5 4 3 Twelve 2 1

A B C D E F G

BURNHAM ON CROUCH
G.E.
BATTLESBRIDGE
FAMBRIDGE
ALTHORNE
WICKFORD
WOODHAM FERRERS
G.E.
HOCKLEY
RAYLEIGH
ROCHFORD
MID. L.T. & S.
PITSEA
BENFLEET
SOUTHEND - ON - SEA FOR WESTCLIFF & THORPE BAY
PRITTLEWELL
L. Shed
LEIGH - ON SEA
THORPE BAY
Independent Light Railway
WESTCLIFF-ON-SEA
SOUTHEND-ON- SEA
SHOEBURYNESS
CORRINGHAM
CORYTON
Canvey Island
THAMESHAVEN

URALITE HALT
HIGH HALSTOW HALT
GRAIN CROSSING HALT
CLIFFE
MIDDLE STOKE HALT
PORT VICTORIA
DOCKYARD
SHEERNESS- ON-SEA
SHEERNESS EAST
SHARNAL ST.
HIGHAM
BELUNCLE HALT
QUEENBOROUGH
EAST MINSTER-ON-SEA
Hoo Jc.
Rochester Br. Jc.
ROCHESTER BRI.
MINSTER-ON-SEA
EASTCHURCH
STROOD
Fort Pitt Tun.
L. Shed
GILLINGHAM
BRAMBLEDOWN HALT
HARTY RD. HALT
LEYSDOWN
CUXTON
Gillingham Tun.
Chatham Tun.
RAINHAM
King's Ferry Bri.
ROCHESTER
CHATHAM
NEWINGTON
WHITSTABLE HARB.
WHITSTABLE TOWN & TANKERTON
TANKERTON HALT
HERNE BAY
S.E. & C.
WESTGATE-ON-SEA
SANDS
MARGATE
EAST
WEST
BIRCHINGTON-ON-SEA
BROADSTAIRS
RAMSGATE TOWN
HARB.
Minster East Jc.
Minster West Jc.

HALLING
West Jc.
SITTINGBOURNE
East Jc.
TEYNHAM
GRAVENEY (Goods)
SOUTH STR.HALT
MINSTER
Minster 'B'.Jc.
SNODLAND
FAVERSHAM
Loco. Shed
Faversham Jc.
BLEAN & TYLER HILL HALT
STURRY
GROVE FERRY
CHISLET COLLIERY HALT
ASH TOWN
SANDWICH ROAD
SANDWICH
EAST MALLING HALT
AYLESFORD
Preston Hall Tuns.
SELLING
Selling Tun.
WEST
CANTERBURY
EAST
STAPLE
BEKESBOURNE
WINGHAM
ROMAN ROAD
WOODNESBOROUGH
BARMING
EAST
BEARSTED & THURNHAM
SOUTH
CHARTHAM
EASTRY
TESTON CROSSING HALT
BARRACKS
WEST
HOLLINGBOURNE
CHILHAM
BRIDGE
ADISHAM
EASTRY SOUTH OPENED 1927
TOVIL
MAIDSTONE
HARRIETSHAM
EAST FARLEIGH
LENHAM
KNOWLTON
DEAL
BISHOPSBOURNE
ELVINGTON
WATERINGBURY
EYTHORNE
WALMER
CHARING
BARHAM
East Kent Light R.
SHEPHERDS WELL

HOTHFIELD
WYE
Lydden Tun.
MARTIN HILL
MARDEN
STAPLEHURST
KEARSNEY
Guston Tun.
ELHAM
Buckland Jc.
Charlton Tun.
Priory Tun.
S.E. & C.
HEADCORN
PLUCKLEY
Loco Shed
PRIORY
HORSMONDEN
LYMINGE
Abbotscliff Tun.
HARBOUR
Harb.Tun.
CHERITON HALT
Archcliffe Jc.
Martello Tun.
DOVER
ASHFORD
Ashford Works
FRITTENDEN ROAD
Saltwood Tun.
Loco Shed
MARINE
Dover to Calais. S.E. & C.
TOWN
SMEETH
CENT.
Shakespeare Tun.
GOUDHURST
BIDDENDEN
Sandling Tun.
SANDLING JUNC.
JUNC. STA.
FOLKESTONE
WESTENHANGER
HARB.
HIGH HALDEN ROAD
SANDGATE
SHORNCLIFFE CAMP
CRANBROOK
HYTHE
TENTERDEN ST. MICHEALS
Folkestone to Boulogne. S.E.&
HAM STREET & ORLESTONE
TENTERDEN TOWN
HAWKHURST
ROLVENDEN

Kent & East Sussex Light Railway
APPLEDORE
WITTERSHAM ROAD
ETCHINGHAM
NORTHIAM
SALEHURST HALT
BODIAM
BROOKLAND
JUNCTION ROAD
ROBERTSBRIDGE
S.E.& C.
NEW ROMNEY & LITTLESTONE-ON- SEA.
RYE
Mountfield Tun.
Tramway
LYDD
CAMBER
WINCHELSEA
HARBOUR
DUNGENESS

BATTLE
CROWHURST
Bopeep Tunnel
Ore Tun.
WEST ST. LEONARDS
ORE
Loco Shed
Mount Pleasant Tun.
SIDLEY
WEST MARINA
HASTINGS
BEXHILL
Hastings Tun.
WARRIOR SQUARE
Bopeep Jc.

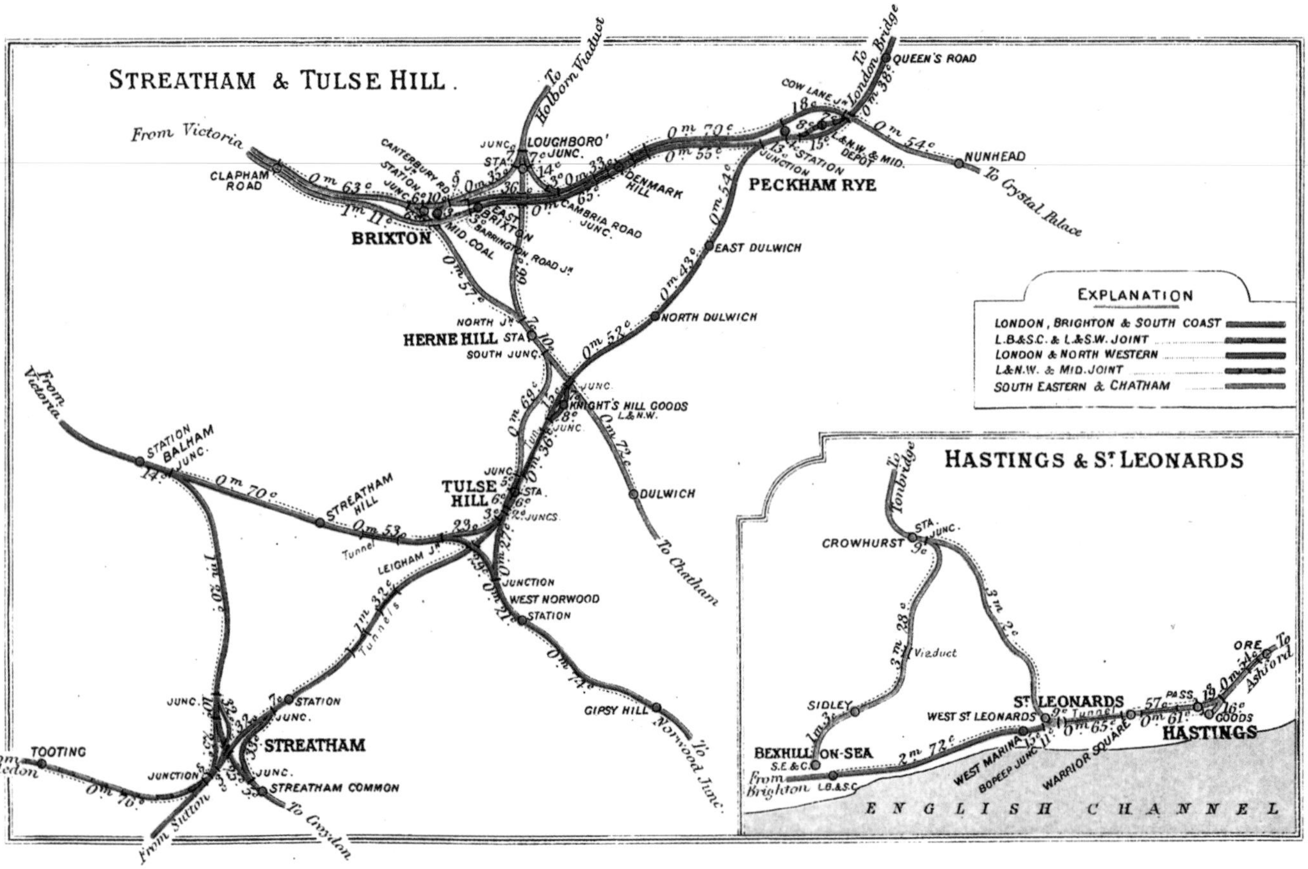

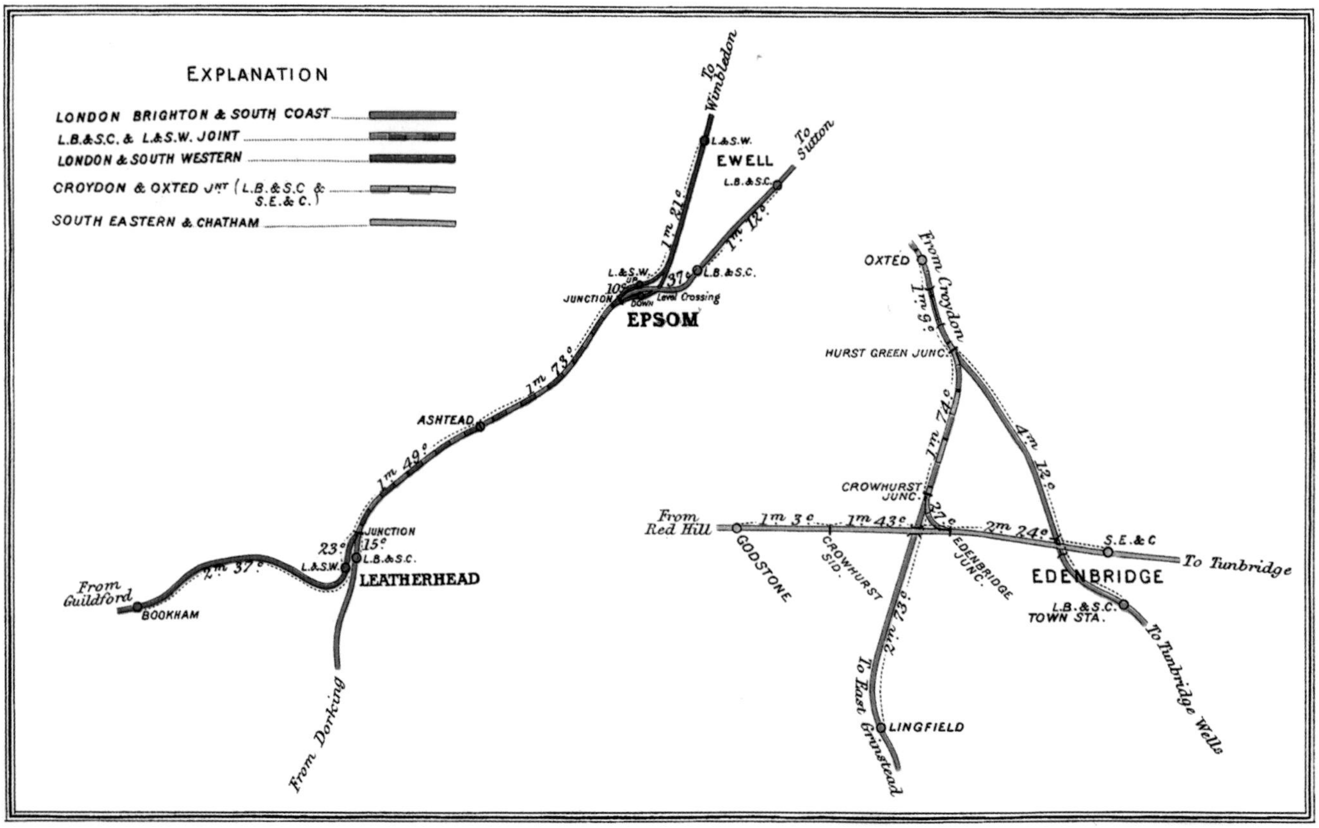

## STREATHAM & TULSE HILL.

EXPLANATION

- LONDON, BRIGHTON & SOUTH COAST
- L.B.&S.C. & L.&S.W. JOINT
- LONDON & NORTH WESTERN
- L.&N.W. & MID. JOINT
- SOUTH EASTERN & CHATHAM

## HASTINGS & S^T LEONARDS

ENGLISH CHANNEL

EXPLANATION

- LONDON BRIGHTON & SOUTH COAST
- L.B.&S.C. & L.&S.W. JOINT
- LONDON & SOUTH WESTERN
- CROYDON & OXTED J^NT (L.B.&S.C & S.E.&C.)
- SOUTH EASTERN & CHATHAM

Leatherhead–Epsom–Edenbridge

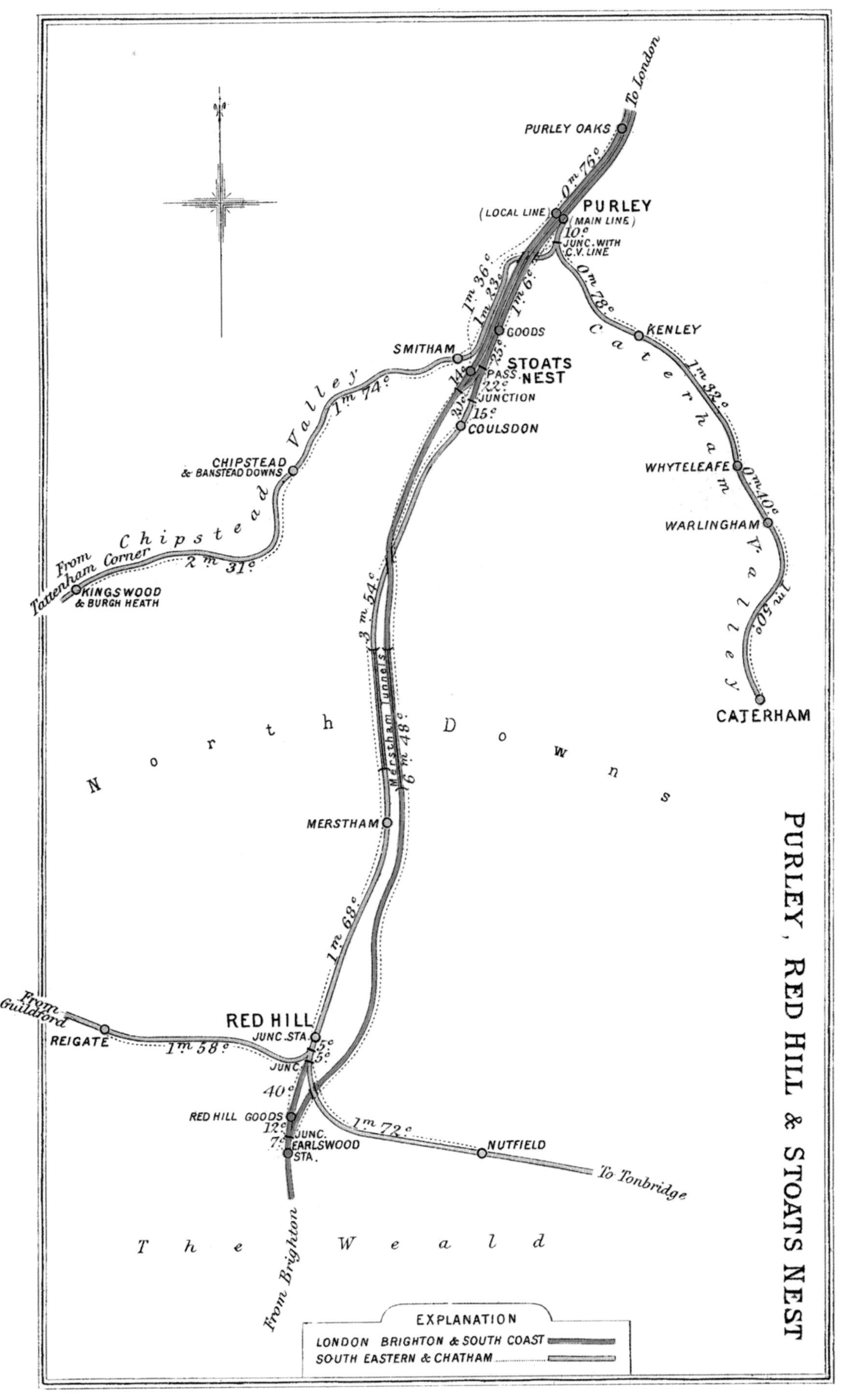
PURLEY, RED HILL & STOATS NEST
To London
PURLEY OAKS
PURLEY
(LOCAL LINE)
(MAIN LINE)
JUNC. WITH C.V. LINE
GOODS
SMITHAM
STOATS NEST
PASS.
JUNCTION
COULSDON
KENLEY
Caterham Valley
WHYTELEAFE
WARLINGHAM
CATERHAM
Chipstead Valley
CHIPSTEAD & BANSTEAD DOWNS
From Tattenham Corner
KINGSWOOD & BURGH HEATH
North Downs
Merstham Tunnels
MERSTHAM
From Guildford
REIGATE
RED HILL
JUNC. STA.
JUNC.
RED HILL GOODS
JUNC.
EARLSWOOD STA.
NUTFIELD
To Tonbridge
From Brighton
The Weald
EXPLANATION
LONDON BRIGHTON & SOUTH COAST
SOUTH EASTERN & CHATHAM

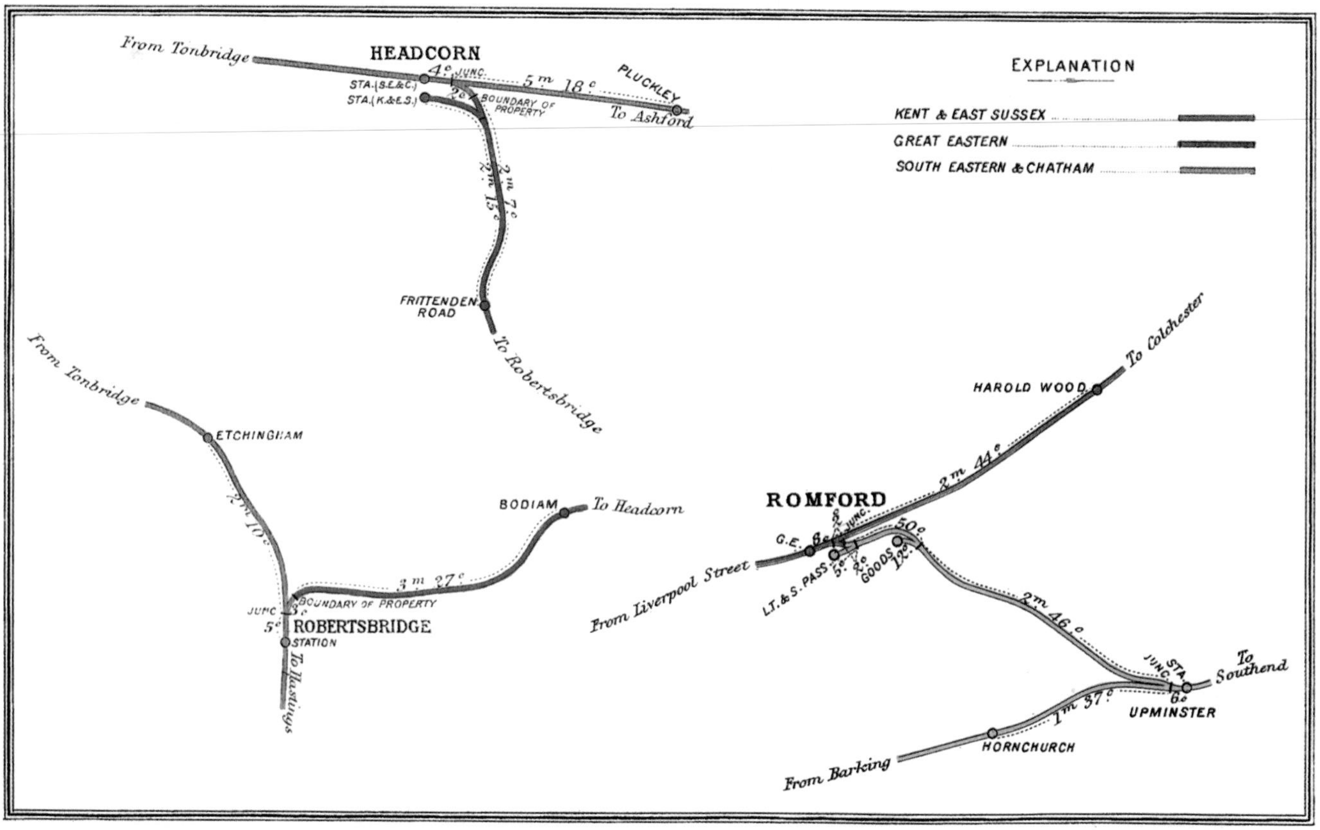

Headcorn–Robertsbridge–Romford

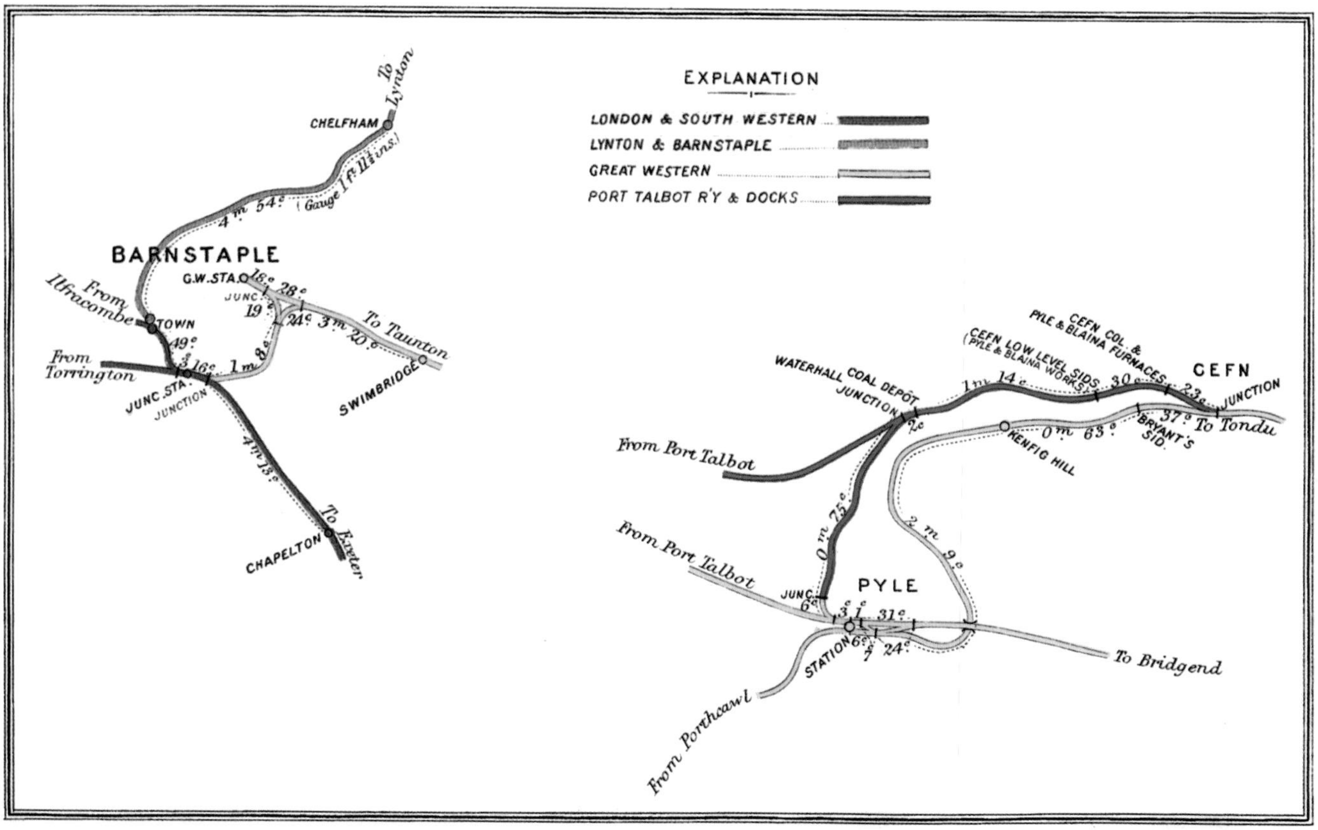

Barnstaple–Pyle

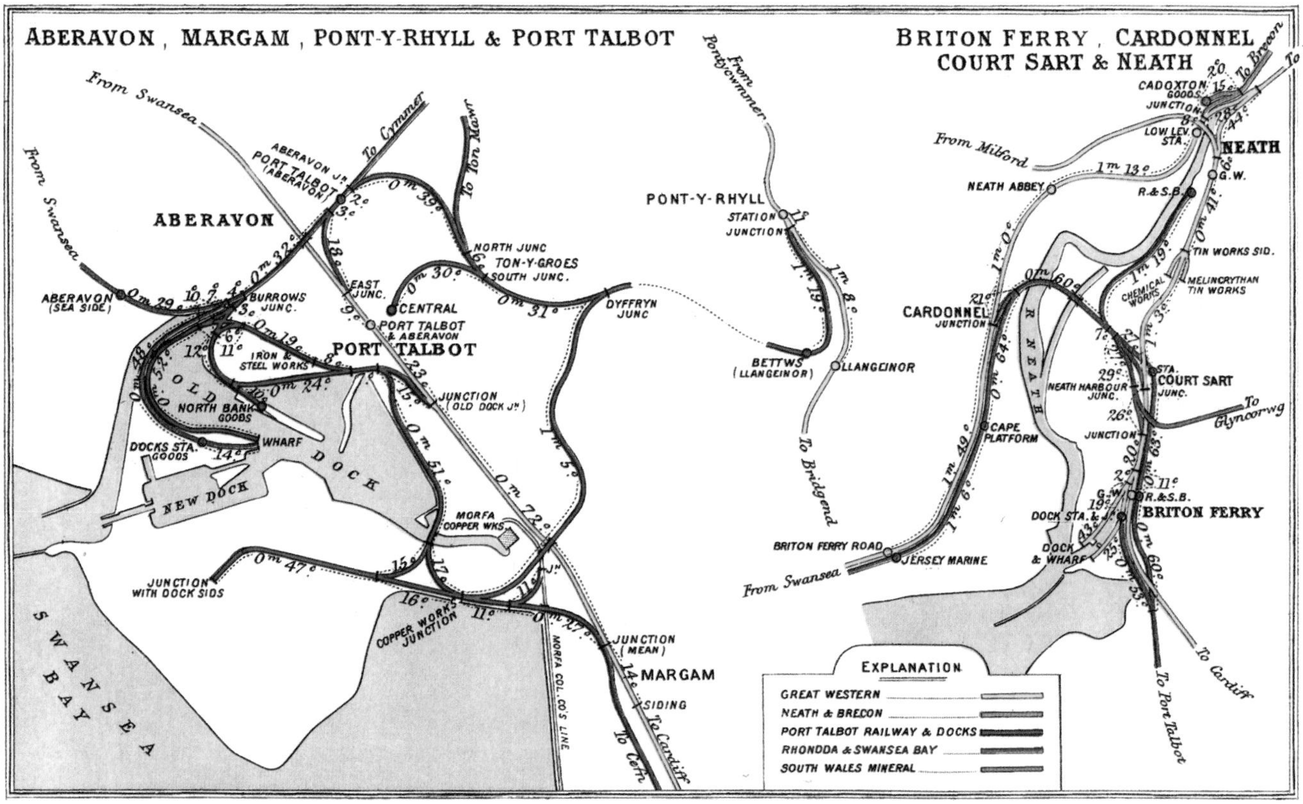
ABERAVON, MARGAM, PONT-Y-RHYLL & PORT TALBOT
BRITON FERRY, CARDONNEL COURT SART & NEATH
From Swansea
To Cymmer
To Ton Mawr
ABERAVON
ABERAVON (SEA SIDE)
BURROWS JUNC.
NORTH JUNC
TON-Y-GROES SOUTH JUNC.
EAST JUNC.
CENTRAL
PORT TALBOT & ABERAVON
PORT TALBOT
IRON & STEEL WORKS
DYFFRYN JUNC
OLD DOCK
NORTH BANK GOODS
DOCKS STA. GOODS
WHARF
NEW DOCK
JUNCTION (OLD DOCK Jn.)
MORFA COPPER WKS.
JUNCTION WITH DOCK SIDS
COPPER WORKS JUNCTION
NORFA COL. CO'S LINE
JUNCTION (MEAN)
MARGAM
SIDING
To Cardiff
To Cefn
SWANSEA BAY
From Pontycymmer
PONT-Y-RHYLL
STATION JUNCTION
BETTWS (LLANGEINOR)
LLANGEINOR
To Bridgend
From Milford
CADOXTON GOODS
JUNCTION
LOW LEV. STA.
NEATH
G.W.
R.&S.B.
To Brecon
To Merthyr
NEATH ABBEY
TIN WORKS SID.
CHEMICAL WORKS
MELINCRYTHAN TIN WORKS
CARDONNEL JUNCTION
RIVER NEATH
COURT SART
COURT SART JUNC.
NEATH HARBOUR JUNC.
To Glyncorwg
JUNCTION
CAPE PLATFORM
G.W.
R.&S.B.
BRITON FERRY
DOCK STA.
DOCK & WHARF
BRITON FERRY ROAD
JERSEY MARINE
From Swansea
To Port Talbot
To Cardiff
EXPLANATION
GREAT WESTERN
NEATH & BRECON
PORT TALBOT RAILWAY & DOCKS
RHONDDA & SWANSEA BAY
SOUTH WALES MINERAL

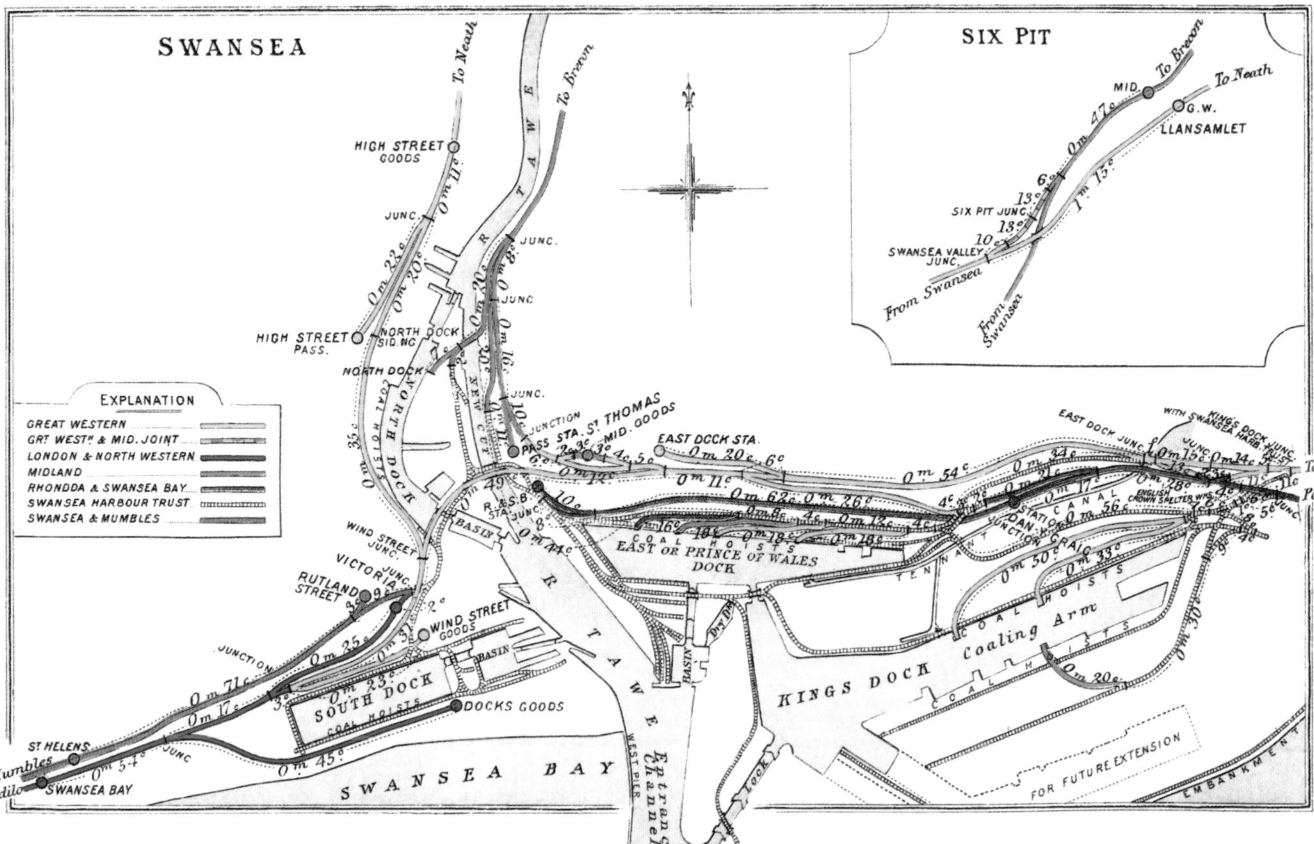
SWANSEA
SIX PIT
To Neath
To Brecon
HIGH STREET GOODS
JUNC.
HIGH STREET PASS.
NORTH DOCK SIDING
NORTH DOCK
NORTH DOCK
NEW CUT
JUNCTION
PASS STA. ST THOMAS
MID. GOODS
EAST DOCK STA.
R.&S.B. STA.
BASIN
WIND STREET JUNC.
VICTORIA
RUTLAND STREET
WIND STREET GOODS
SOUTH DOCK
COAL HOISTS
DOCKS GOODS
JUNCTION
ST HELENS
Fr. Mumbles
Llandilo
SWANSEA BAY
SWANSEA BAY
RIVER TAWE
EAST OR PRINCE OF WALES DOCK
COAL HOISTS
EAST DOCK JUNC.
KINGS DOCK JUNC.
WITH SWANSEA HARB. TRUST
PORT TENNANT
DAN-Y-GRAIG
ENGLISH CROWN SPELTER WKS.
KINGS DOCK
Coaling Arm
COAL HOISTS
FOR FUTURE EXTENSION
EMBANKMENT
Entrance Channel
WEST PIER
To Port Talbot
EXPLANATION
GREAT WESTERN
GRT. WESTn. & MID. JOINT
LONDON & NORTH WESTERN
MIDLAND
RHONDDA & SWANSEA BAY
SWANSEA HARBOUR TRUST
SWANSEA & MUMBLES
To Brecon
To Neath
MID.
G.W.
LLANSAMLET
SIX PIT JUNC.
SWANSEA VALLEY JUNC.
From Swansea
From Swansea

SEVEN
1
2
Thirteen
3
4
Fourteen
5
A
B
C
D
E
F
G
Inset
Cardigan Jc.
WHITLAND
G.W.
ST CLEARS
SARNAU
CARMARTHEN
DRYSLLWYN
DERWYDD ROAD
LLANDEBIE
Y Fan Gihirach
CRAIGYNOS (PEHWYLLT)
SEE SHEET NO.
CROSS HANDS
CWM MAWR
TUMBLE
CWM BLAWD
Watertroughs
MYNYDD-Y-GARREG
PONTYBEREM
B.P. & G.V.
FERRYSIDE
GLYN ABBEY
PONTHENRY
KIDWELLY
G.V.
PONT YATES
TRIMSARAN ROAD
CYNHEIDRE
HOREB
Tycoch Junc.
PINGED
TRIMSARAN (GDS.)
LLANELLY QUEEN VICTORIA ROAD
L. & M.M.
PEMBREY
FELIN FOEL
LLAN-GENNECH
PEMBREY & BURRY PORT
BURRY PORT
LLANELLY
Dock Goods
L.C. BYNEA
PENCLAWDD
LLANMORLAIS
TIRYDAIL
GARNANT
BRYNAMMAN
GLANAMMAN
CWMLLYNFELL
MID
VARTEG
GWYS
ABERCRAVE
STRAD-GYNLAIS
COLBREN JUNC
ONLLWTH
AMMANFORD
PANTYFFYNNON
GURNOS (Gds)
YSTALYFERA
SEVEN SISTERS
Ynys-Y-Geinon Jc.
GLYN NEATH
G.W.
CRYNANT
G L A M.
PONTARDULAIS (Joint)
PONTARDAWE
N. & B.
RESOLVEN
PONT LLIW
CLYDACH-ON-TAWE
GROVES END
LLAN GYFELACH
CILFREW
L.&N.W.
GLAIS
GORSEINON
ABERDYLAIS
S.W.M.
BLAENRHONDDA
BLAEN-GWYNFY
LOUGHOR
MORRISTON
FELIN FRAN
SKEWEN
NEATH
PLAS MARL
LANDORE
Summit
NEATH ABBEY
COURT SART
TREHERBERT
ABERGWYNFI
GOWERTON
COCKETT
UP. BANK
CWM AVON
CAERAU
CYMMER
BLAEN GARW
NANTYMOEL
DUNVANT
RUTLAND ST
HIGH ST.
NANTY FFYLLON
KILLAY
S.&M.
SWAN-SEA BAY
DAN-Y-GRAIG
JERSEY MARINE
BRITON FERRY
BRYN
CWMDU
PONTY CYMMER
MUMBLES ROAD
SWANSEA
ABERAVON (SEASIDE)
MAESTEG
PONTY RHYLL
OGMORE VALE
MUMBLES PIER
PORT TALBOT DOCK
TROEDYRHIEW GARTH
LLANGONOYD
Margam Junc.
LLETTY BRONGU
LLANGEINOR
BETTWS (LLANGEINDRO)
BRYNMENYN
BLACK HILL
Cefn Junc.
TONDU
KENFIG HILL
Bryncethin Junc.
PYLE
G.W.
Coity Junc.
BRIDGEND
PORTHCAWL
SOUTHERNDOWN ROAD
BARRY
HAVERFORDWEST
G.W.
NARBERTH
JOHNSTON
TEMPLETON
MILFORD HAVEN
NEYLAND
KILGETTY
SAUNDERSFOOT
DOCK STA.
GOLDEN HILL PLAT.
PEMBROKE
G.W.
TENBY
LAMPHEY
MANORBIER
LYDSTEP
PENALLY
B R I S T O L
LYNTON
ILFRACOMBE
Summit
MORTEHOE
WOODY BAY
PARRACOMBE (Closed 1917 - 1924)
BLACKMOOR
L.&S.W.
BRATTON FLEMING
BRAUNTON
SNAPPER
CHELFHAM
L.&B.
WRAFTON
TOWN STA.
BARNSTAPLE
FREMING-TON
JUNC STA.
Loco Shed
APPLEDORE
NORTHAM
INSTOW
SWIMBRIDGE
FILLEIGH
WESTWARD HO!
B.W.H.& A.
ABBOTSHAM ROAD
BIDEFORD
CHAPELTON
G.W.
BISHOP'S NYMPTON & MOLLAND
SOUTH MOLTON
DULVERTON
EAST ANSTEY
UMBERLEIGH
TORRINGTON
PORTSMOUTH ARMS
BAMPTON (DEVON)
Built after 1922
SOUTH MOLTON ROAD
D E V O N S H I R E
L.&S.W.
TIVERTON
WATERGATE
EGGESFORD
One
Two

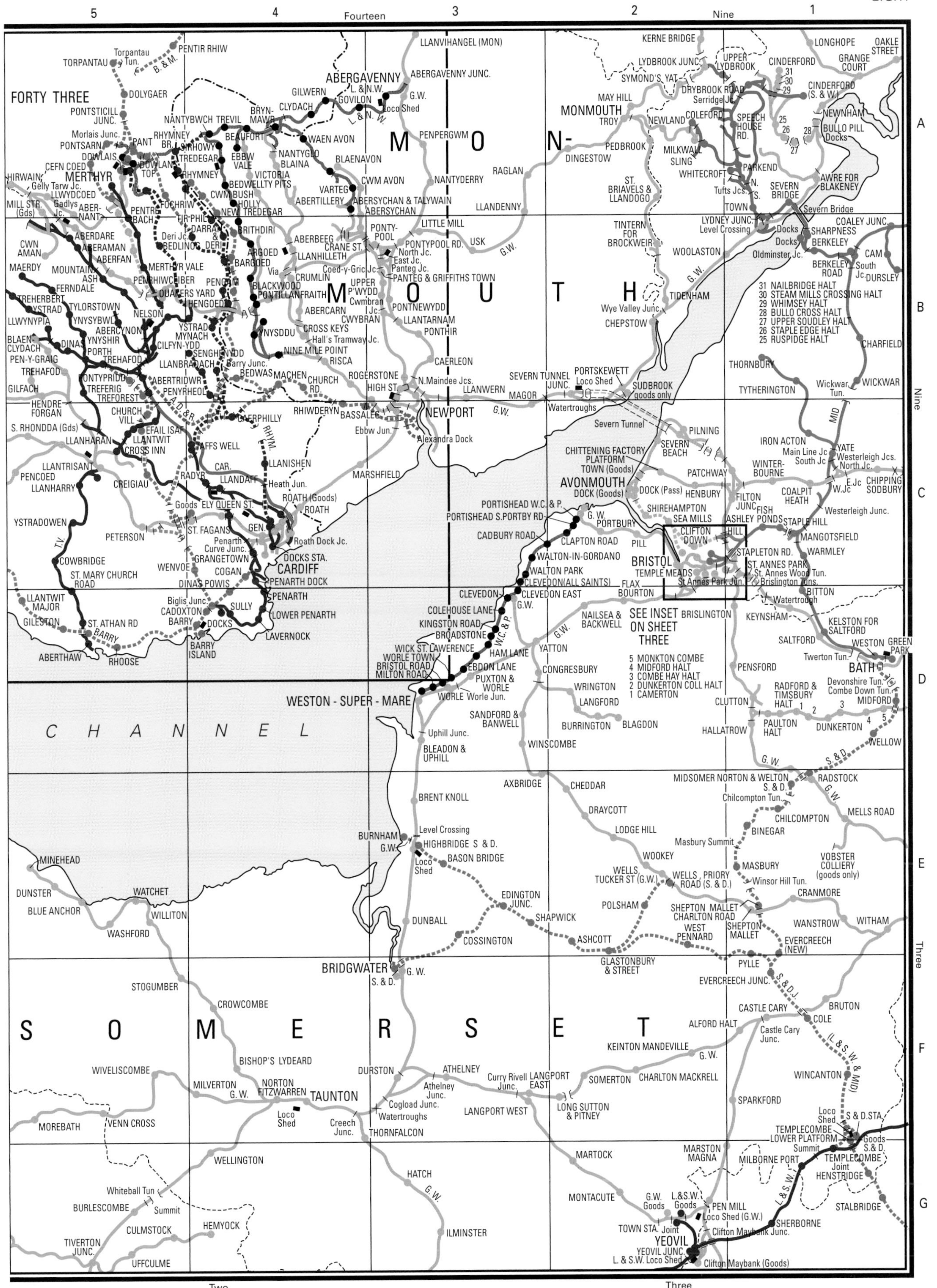

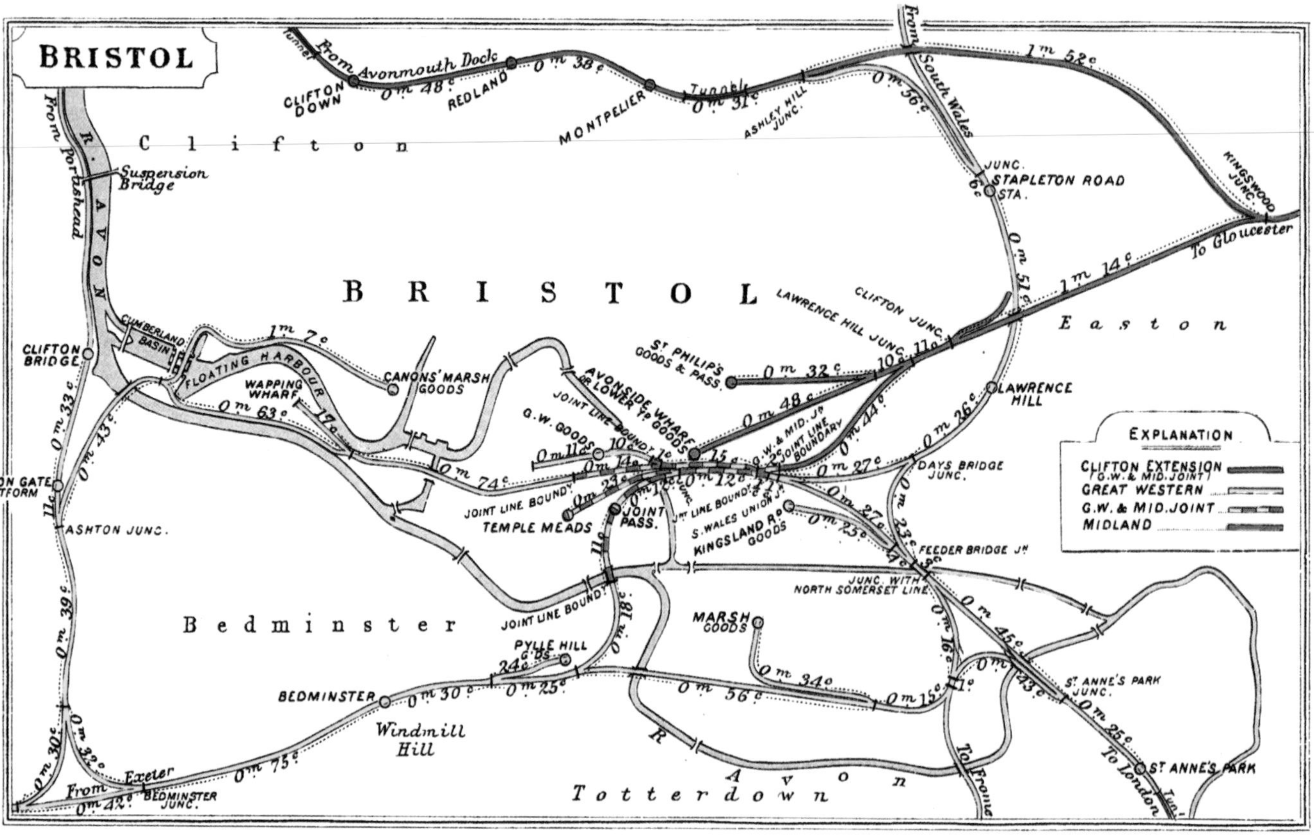

## EIGHT

BRISTOL

From Avonmouth Dock
CLIFTON DOWN
REDLAND
MONTPELIER
Tunnel
ASHLEY HILL JUNC.
From South Wales
KINGSWOOD JUNC.
JUNC. STAPLETON ROAD STA.
To Gloucester
From Portishead
R. AVON
Clifton
Suspension Bridge
BRISTOL
LAWRENCE HILL JUNC.
CLIFTON JUNC.
Easton
CLIFTON BRIDGE
CUMBERLAND BASIN
FLOATING HARBOUR
WAPPING WHARF
CANONS' MARSH GOODS
AVONSIDE WHARF OR LOWER Yd GOODS
ST PHILIP'S GOODS & PASS.
LAWRENCE HILL
G.W. GOODS
JOINT LINE BOUNDY
G.W. & MID. Jn JOINT LINE BOUNDARY
DAYS BRIDGE JUNC.
ASHTON GATE PLATFORM
ASHTON JUNC.
TEMPLE MEADS
JOINT PASS.
S. WALES UNION Jn
KINGSLAND Rd GOODS
FEEDER BRIDGE Jn
JUNC. WITH NORTH SOMERSET LINE
Bedminster
MARSH GOODS
PYLLE HILL G. Ds
BEDMINSTER
Windmill Hill
ST ANNE'S PARK JUNC.
ST ANNE'S PARK
To London
To Frome
From Exeter
BEDMINSTER JUNC.
R. Avon
Totterdown

EXPLANATION
CLIFTON EXTENSION (G.W. & MID. JOINT)
GREAT WESTERN
G.W. & MID. JOINT
MIDLAND

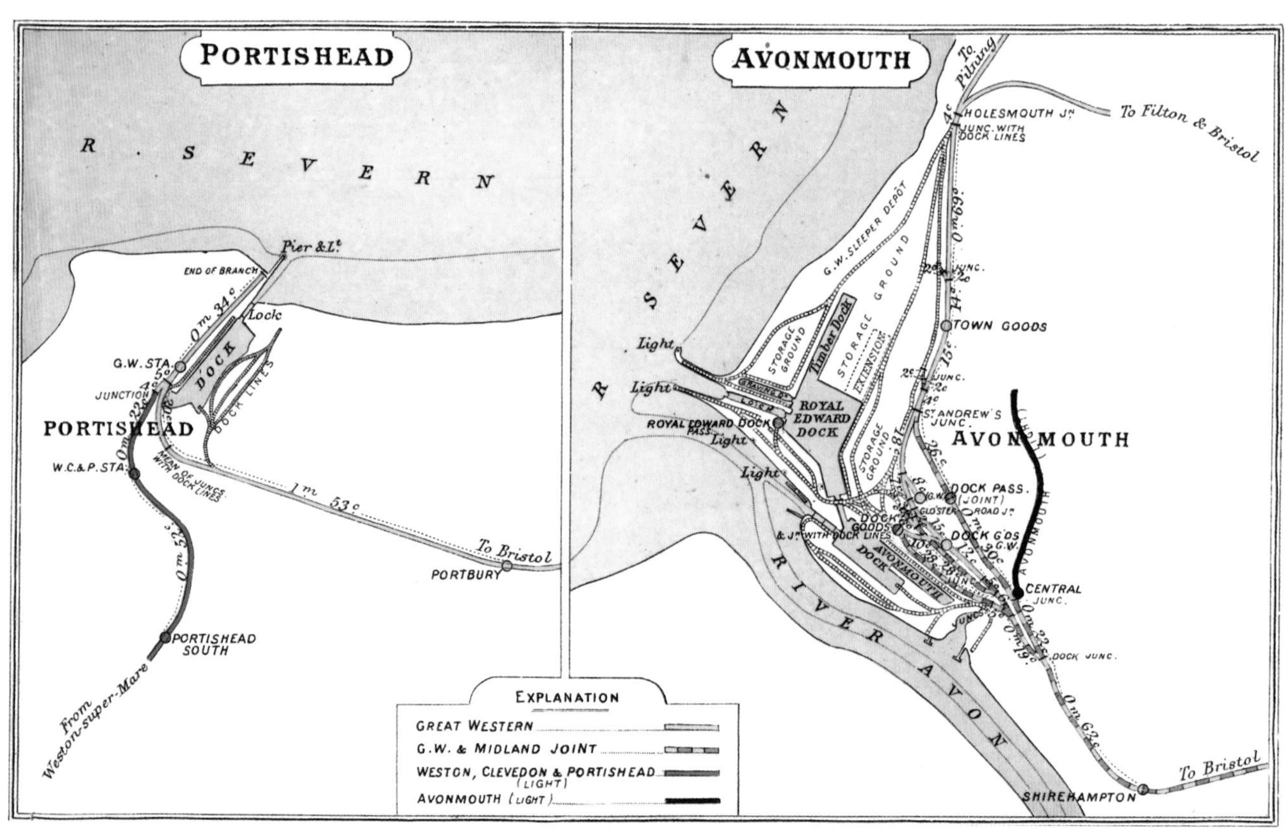

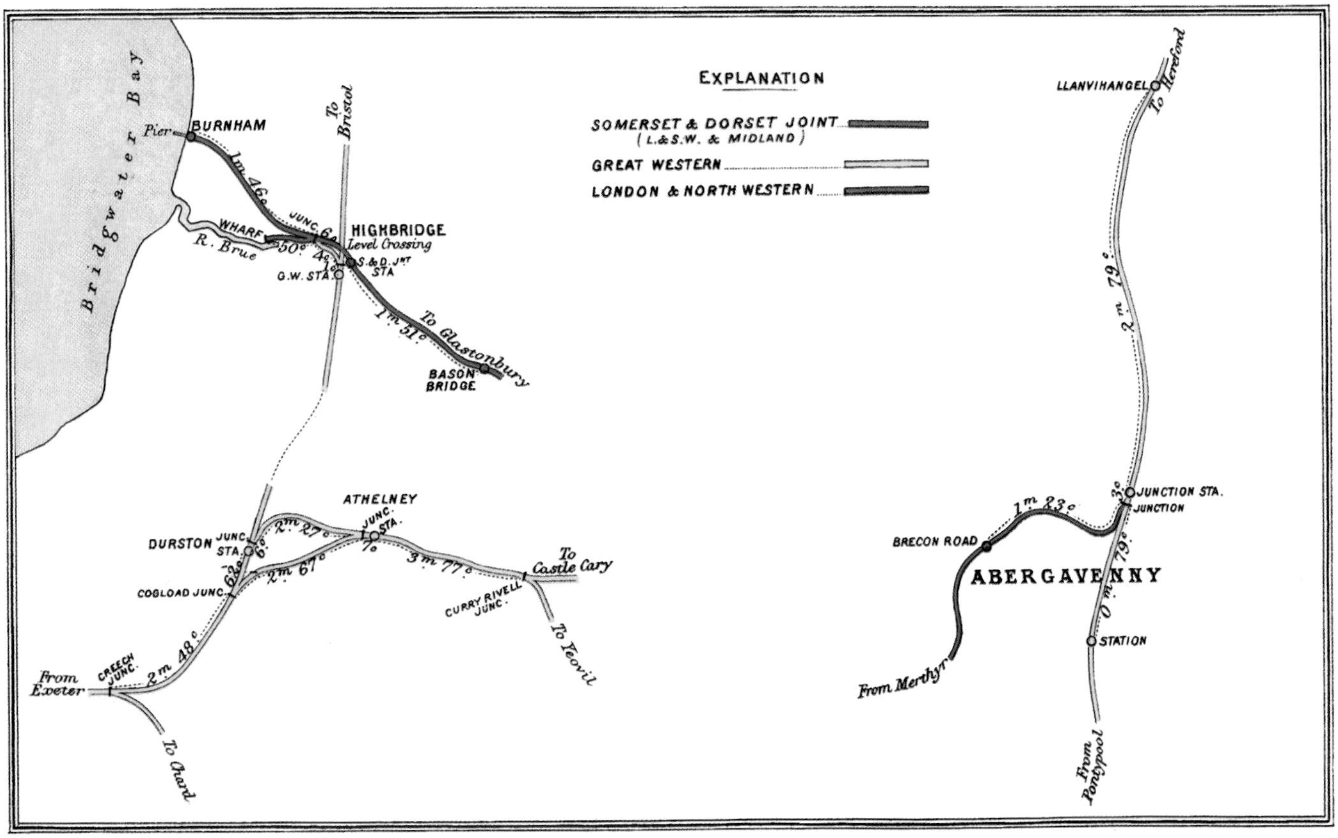

Burnham–Highbridge–Abergavenny

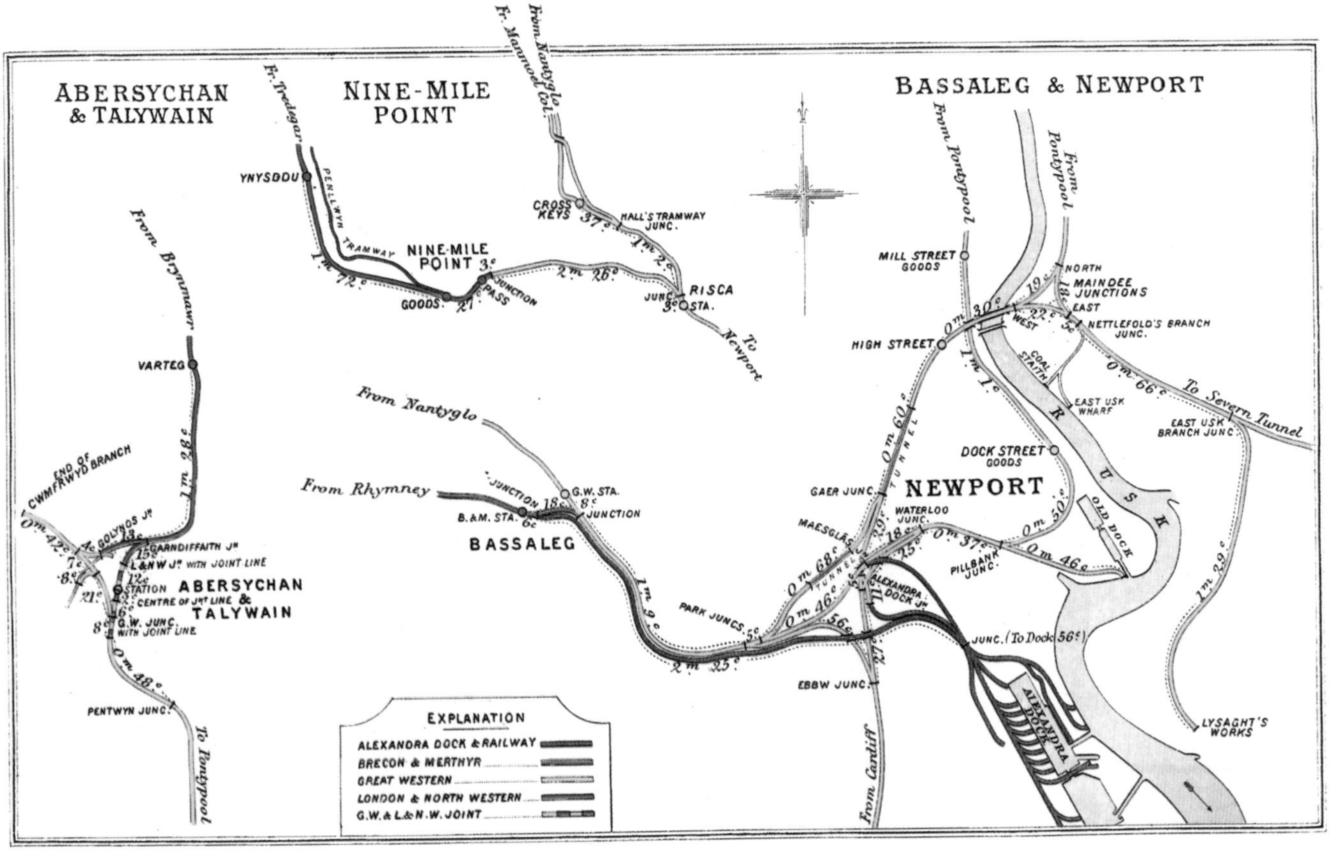

ABERDARE
(Continued below)
LLANCAIACH, MOUNTAIN ASH & QUAKER'S YARD
CWMBACH JUNC.
MIDDLE DUFFRYN COL.
BEDLINOG
From Dowlais
From Merthyr
ABERFAN FOR MERTHYR VALE
MERTHYR VALE
HIRWAIN
From Swansea
GELLY TARW JUNC.
MOUNTAIN ASH
LLWYDCOED
Viaduct
PENRHIWCEIBER
G.W. MILL STREET
CYNON TIN PLATE WORKS
ABERNANT
GADLY'S JUNC.
WERFA COL.
WERFA SID.
To Merthyr
DARE VALLEY JUNC.
ABERDARE
BWLLFA DARE COLLIERY
DARE JUNC.
Tunnel
JOINT LINE JUNC.
HIGH LEVEL
BRANCH JUNC.
TREHARRIS
LOW LEVEL
QUAKER'S YARD
LLANCAIACH
JOINT LINE JUNC.
TAFF BARGOED JUNC.
STATION
To Pontypool
NELSON
PONTCYNON JUNC.
WERFA COL. SID.
ABERAMAN
EXPLANATION
GREAT WESTERN
QUAKER'S YARD & MERTHYR JOINT (GREAT WESTERN & RHYMNEY)
TAFF BARGOED JOINT (G.W. & RHYMNEY)
TAFF VALE
PRIVATE LINES
CWMBACH JUNC.
MIDDLE DUFFRYN COL.
From Cwm Aman
(Continued above)
ABERCYNON
ABERDARE BRANCH Jn.
TRAVELLERS' REST
YNYS-Y-DWR JUNC.
STORMSTOWN JUNC. & SID.
To Cardiff
To Pontypridd

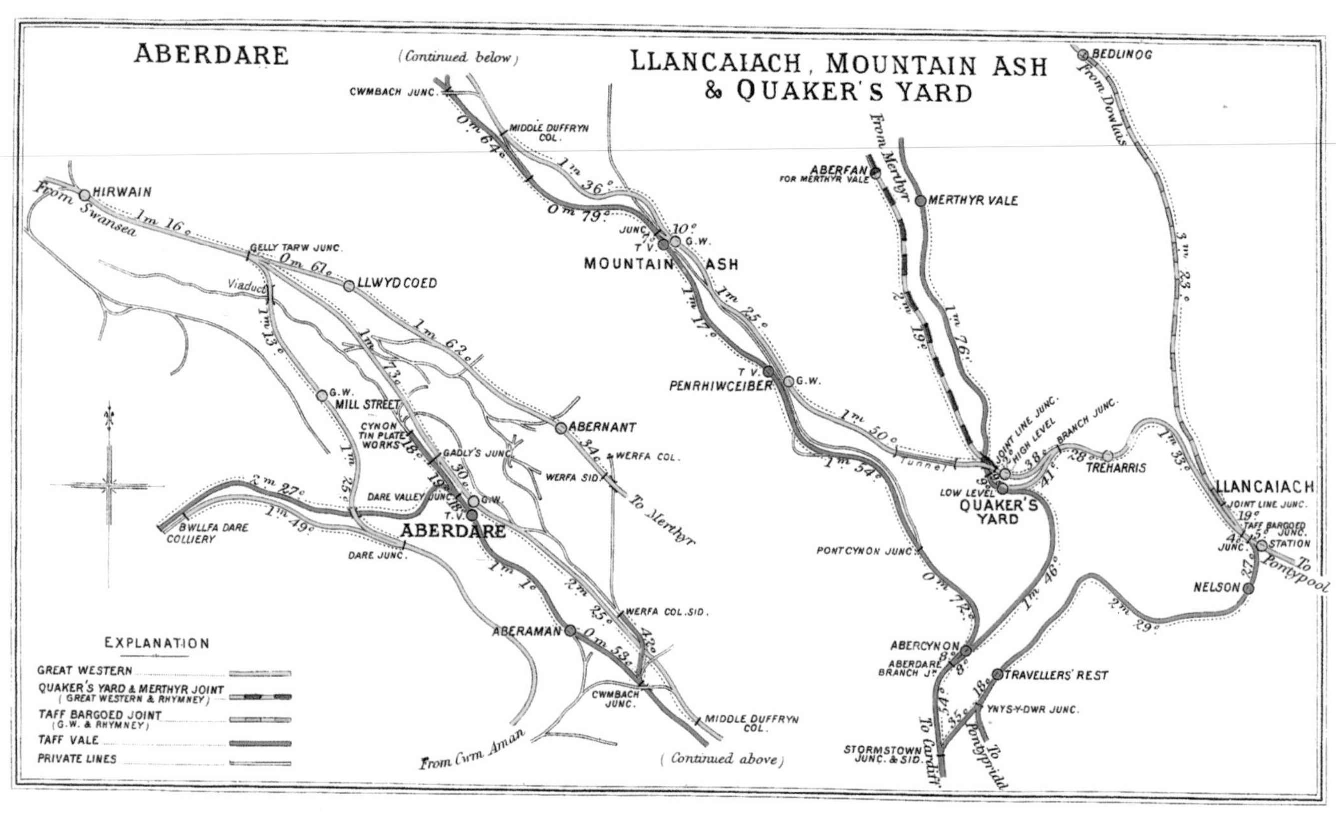

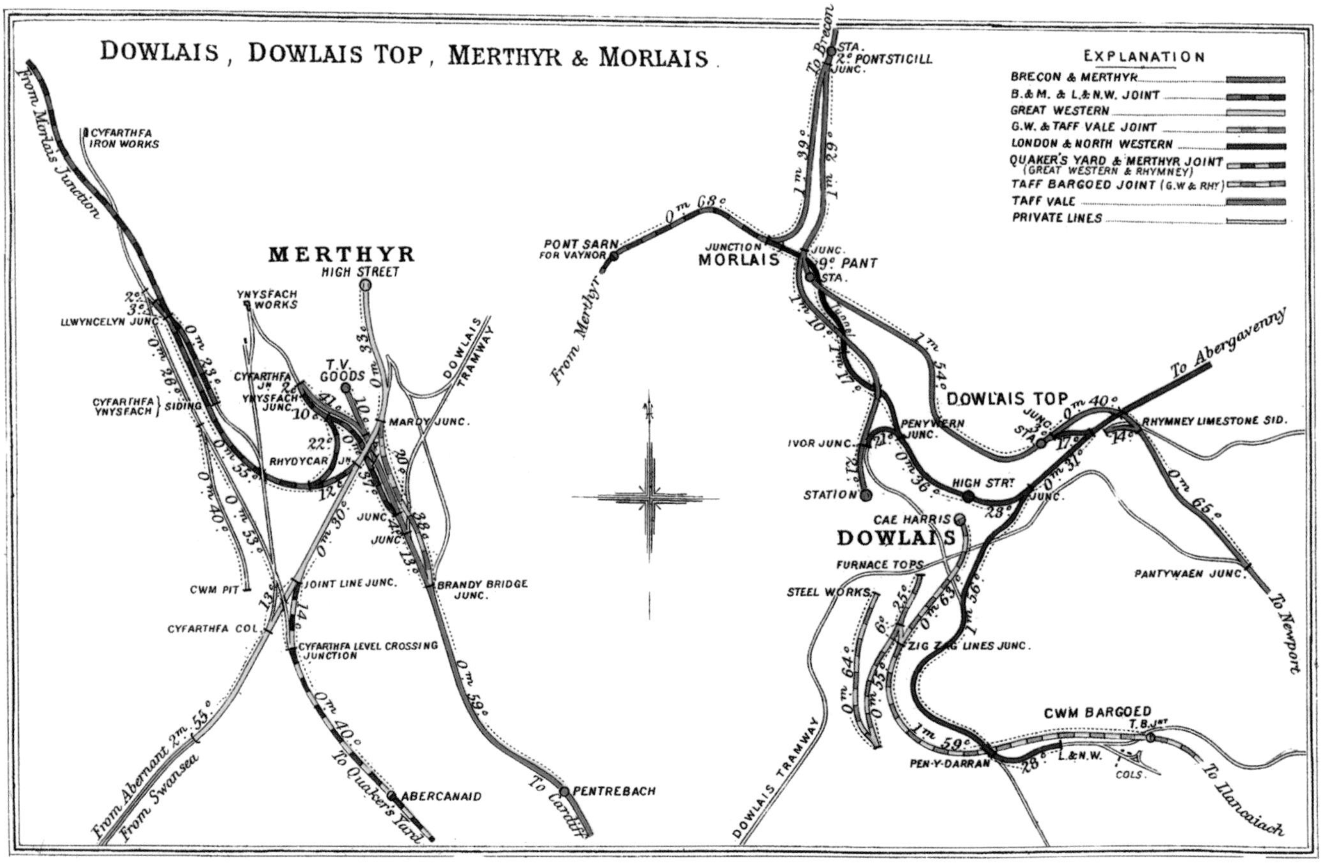

DOWLAIS, DOWLAIS TOP, MERTHYR & MORLAIS.
To Brecon
STA.
PONTSTICILL JUNC.
EXPLANATION
BRECON & MERTHYR
B.&M. & L.&N.W. JOINT
GREAT WESTERN
G.W. & TAFF VALE JOINT
LONDON & NORTH WESTERN
QUAKER'S YARD & MERTHYR JOINT (GREAT WESTERN & RHYMNEY)
TAFF BARGOED JOINT (G.W. & RHY.)
TAFF VALE
PRIVATE LINES
From Morlais Junction
CYFARTHFA IRON WORKS
PONT SARN FOR VAYNOR
JUNCTION
MORLAIS
JUNC.
PANT
STA.
MERTHYR
HIGH STREET
YNYSFACH WORKS
DOWLAIS TRAMWAY
LLWYNCELYN JUNC.
From Merthyr
To Abergavenny
T.V. GOODS
CYFARTHFA Jn.
YNYSFACH JUNC.
CYFARTHFA YNYSFACH SIDING
MARDY JUNC.
DOWLAIS TOP
JUNC.
STA.
RHYMNEY LIMESTONE SID.
RHYDYCAR Jn.
PENYWERN JUNC.
IVOR JUNC.
HIGH STR.
JUNC.
STATION
JUNC.
JUNC.
CAE HARRIS
DOWLAIS
FURNACE TOPS
PANTYWAEN JUNC.
CWM PIT
JOINT LINE JUNC.
BRANDY BRIDGE JUNC.
STEEL WORKS
To Newport
CYFARTHFA COL.
CYFARTHFA LEVEL CROSSING JUNCTION
ZIG ZAG LINES JUNC.
CWM BARGOED
T.B. Jnct.
PEN-Y-DARRAN
L.&N.W.
COLS.
From Abernant
From Swansea
To Quaker's Yard
ABERCANAID
To Cardiff
PENTREBACH
DOWLAIS TRAMWAY
To Llancaiach

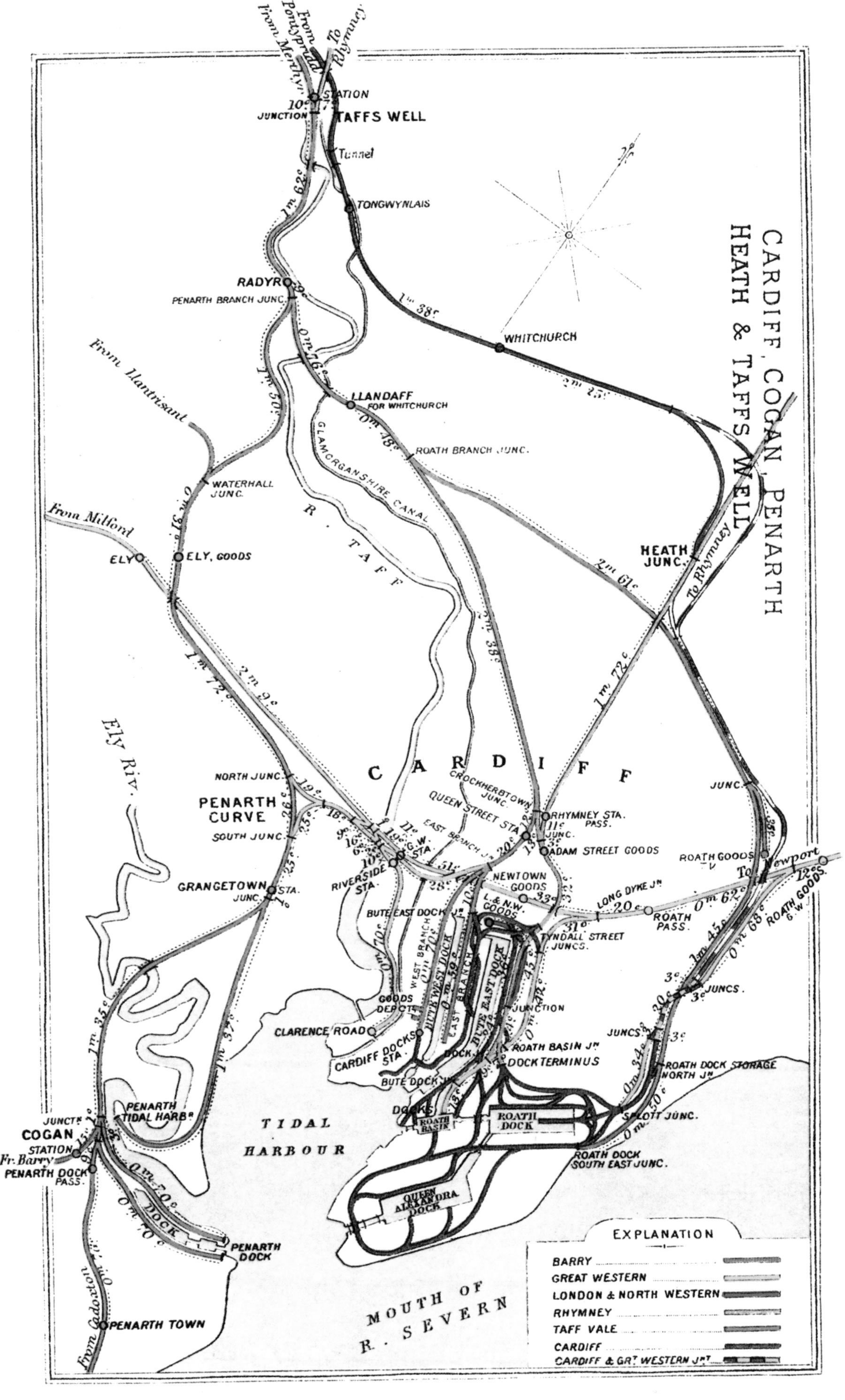
CARDIFF, COGAN, PENARTH
HEATH & TAFFS WELL
TAFFS WELL
STATION
JUNCTION
Tunnel
TONGWYNLAIS
RADYR
PENARTH BRANCH JUNC.
WHITCHURCH
LLANDAFF
FOR WHITCHURCH
ROATH BRANCH JUNC.
GLAMORGANSHIRE CANAL
R. TAFF
From Llantrisant
WATERHALL JUNC.
From Milford
ELY
ELY, GOODS
HEATH JUNC.
To Rhymney
From Pontypridd
From Merthyr
To Rhymney
Ely Riv.
CARDIFF
NORTH JUNC.
PENARTH CURVE
SOUTH JUNC.
GRANGETOWN
JUNC.
STA.
CROCKHERBTOWN JUNC.
QUEEN STREET STA.
EAST BRANCH JN
RHYMNEY STA. PASS.
JUNC.
ADAM STREET GOODS
G.W. STA.
RIVERSIDE STA.
NEWTOWN GOODS
L.& N.W. GOODS
BUTE EAST DOCK JN
LONG DYKE JN
ROATH PASS.
ROATH GOODS
To Newport
ROATH GOODS G.W.
TYNDALL STREET JUNCS.
WEST BRANCH
BUTE WEST DOCK
EAST BRANCH
BUTE EAST DOCK
JUNCTION
GOODS DEPOT
CLARENCE ROAD
CARDIFF DOCKS STA.
BUTE DOCK
DOCKS
ROATH BASIN
ROATH BASIN JN
DOCK TERMINUS
ROATH DOCK
ROATH DOCK STORAGE NORTH JN
SPLOTT JUNC.
ROATH DOCK SOUTH EAST JUNC.
JUNCS.
QUEEN ALEXANDRA DOCK
TIDAL HARBOUR
PENARTH TIDAL HARBR
JUNCTN
COGAN
STATION
Fr. Barry
PENARTH DOCK PASS.
DOCK
PENARTH DOCK
From Cadoxton
PENARTH TOWN
MOUTH OF R. SEVERN
EXPLANATION
BARRY
GREAT WESTERN
LONDON & NORTH WESTERN
RHYMNEY
TAFF VALE
CARDIFF
CARDIFF & GRT WESTERN JNT

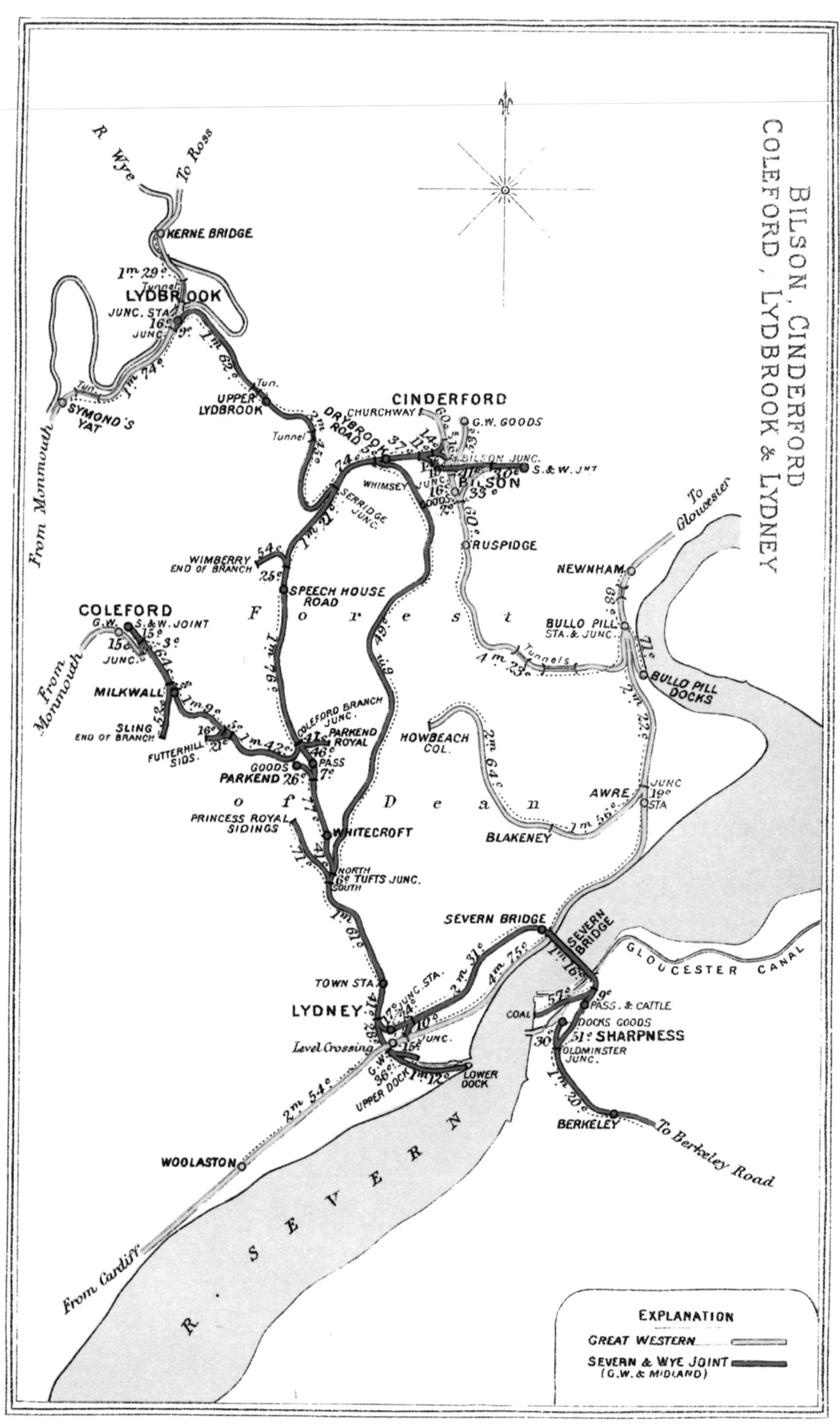
BILSON, CINDERFORD
COLEFORD, LYDBROOK & LYDNEY
R Wye
To Ross
KERNE BRIDGE
LYDBROOK
JUNC. STA.
UPPER LYDBROOK
SYMOND'S YAT
From Monmouth
CINDERFORD
CHURCHWAY
G.W. GOODS
DRYBROOK ROAD
BILSON JUNC.
S.& W. JNT
BILSON
WHIMSEY
SERRIDGE JUNC.
RUSPIDGE
To Gloucester
NEWNHAM
WIMBERRY END OF BRANCH
SPEECH HOUSE ROAD
COLEFORD
G.W. S.&W. JOINT
BULLO PILL STA. & JUNC.
Tunnels
BULLO PILL DOCKS
From Monmouth
MILKWALL
SLING END OF BRANCH
FUTTERHILL SIDS.
COLEFORD BRANCH JUNC.
PARKEND ROYAL
HOWBEACH COL.
PARKEND
PASS
Forest of Dean
AWRE
JUNC STA
PRINCESS ROYAL SIDINGS
WHITECROFT
BLAKENEY
NORTH TUFTS JUNC. SOUTH
SEVERN BRIDGE
SEVERN BRIDGE
GLOUCESTER CANAL
TOWN STA.
LYDNEY
JUNC. STA.
PASS. & CATTLE
COAL
DOCKS GOODS
SHARPNESS
Level Crossing
OLDMINSTER JUNC.
LOWER DOCK
UPPER DOCK
BERKELEY
To Berkeley Road
WOOLASTON
R. SEVERN
From Cardiff
EXPLANATION
GREAT WESTERN
SEVERN & WYE JOINT (G.W. & MIDLAND)

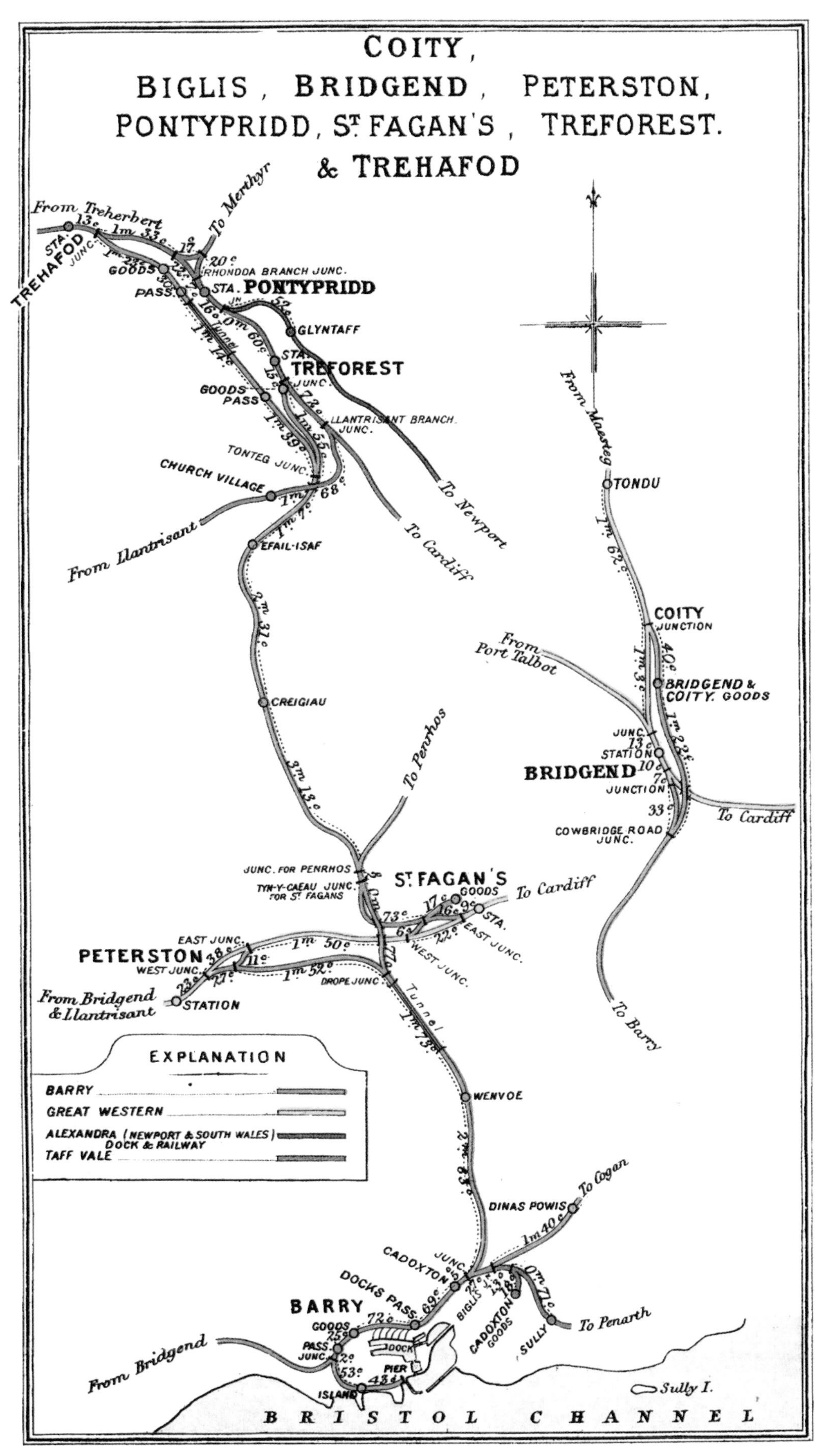
COITY,
BIGLIS, BRIDGEND, PETERSTON,
PONTYPRIDD, ST FAGAN'S, TREFOREST.
& TREHAFOD
From Treherbert
To Merthyr
TREHAFOD
RHONDDA BRANCH JUNC.
PONTYPRIDD
GLYNTAFF
TREFOREST
LLANTRISANT BRANCH JUNC.
TONTEG JUNC.
CHURCH VILLAGE
From Llantrisant
To Newport
To Cardiff
EFAIL-ISAF
CREIGIAU
To Penrhos
From Maesteg
TONDU
COITY JUNCTION
From Port Talbot
BRIDGEND & COITY GOODS
BRIDGEND
To Cardiff
COWBRIDGE ROAD JUNC.
JUNC. FOR PENRHOS
TYN-Y-CAEAU JUNC. FOR ST FAGANS
ST FAGAN'S
To Cardiff
PETERSTON
From Bridgend & Llantrisant
DROPE JUNC.
To Barry
EXPLANATION
BARRY
GREAT WESTERN
ALEXANDRA (NEWPORT & SOUTH WALES) DOCK & RAILWAY
TAFF VALE
WENVOE
DINAS POWIS
To Cogan
CADOXTON
DOCKS PASS.
BIGLIS
CADOXTON GOODS
SULLY
To Penarth
BARRY
From Bridgend
PIER
ISLAND
Sully I.
BRISTOL CHANNEL

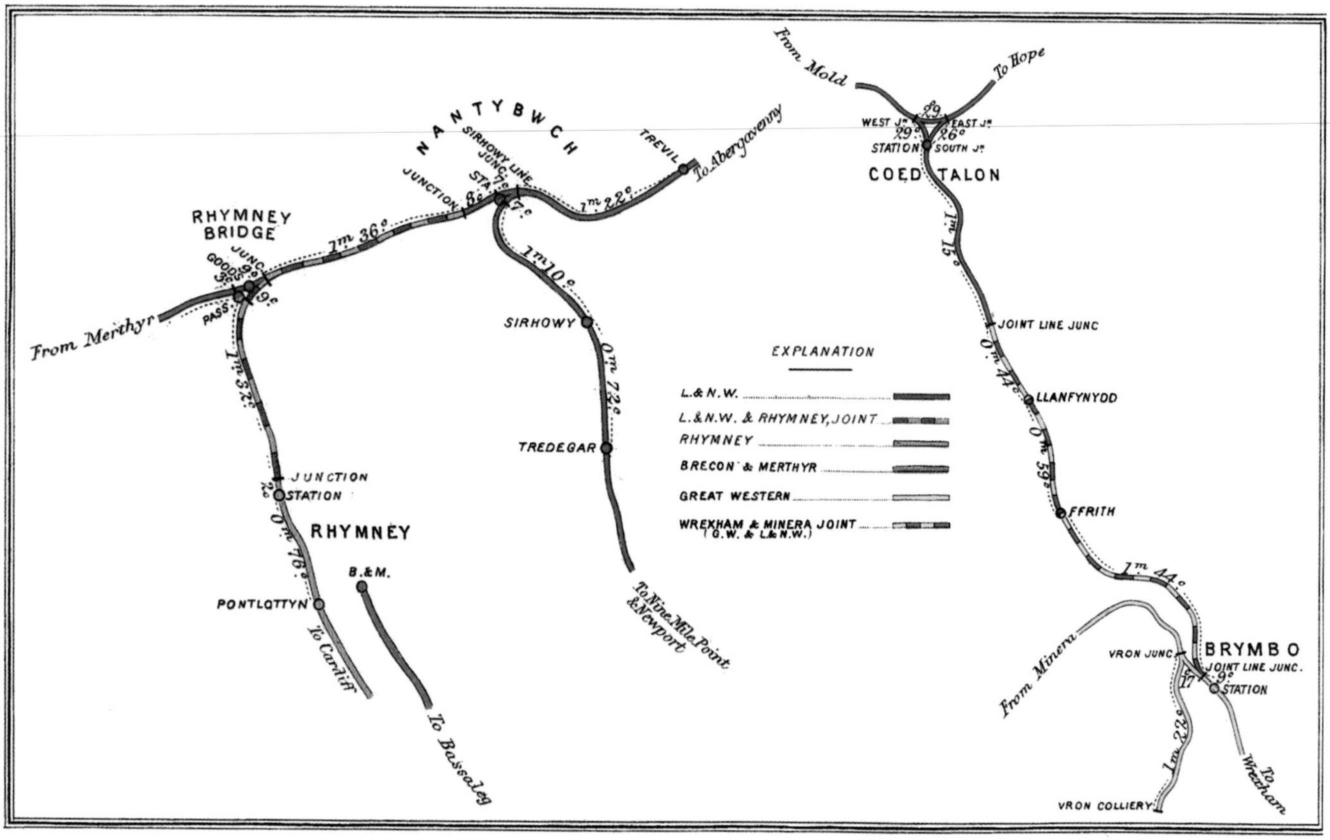

EXPLANATION

- L.& N.W.
- L.& N.W. & RHYMNEY, JOINT
- RHYMNEY
- BRECON & MERTHYR
- GREAT WESTERN
- WREXHAM & MINERA JOINT (G.W. & L.& N.W.)

Rhymney–Rhymney Bridge–Nantybwch–Coedtalon–Brymbo

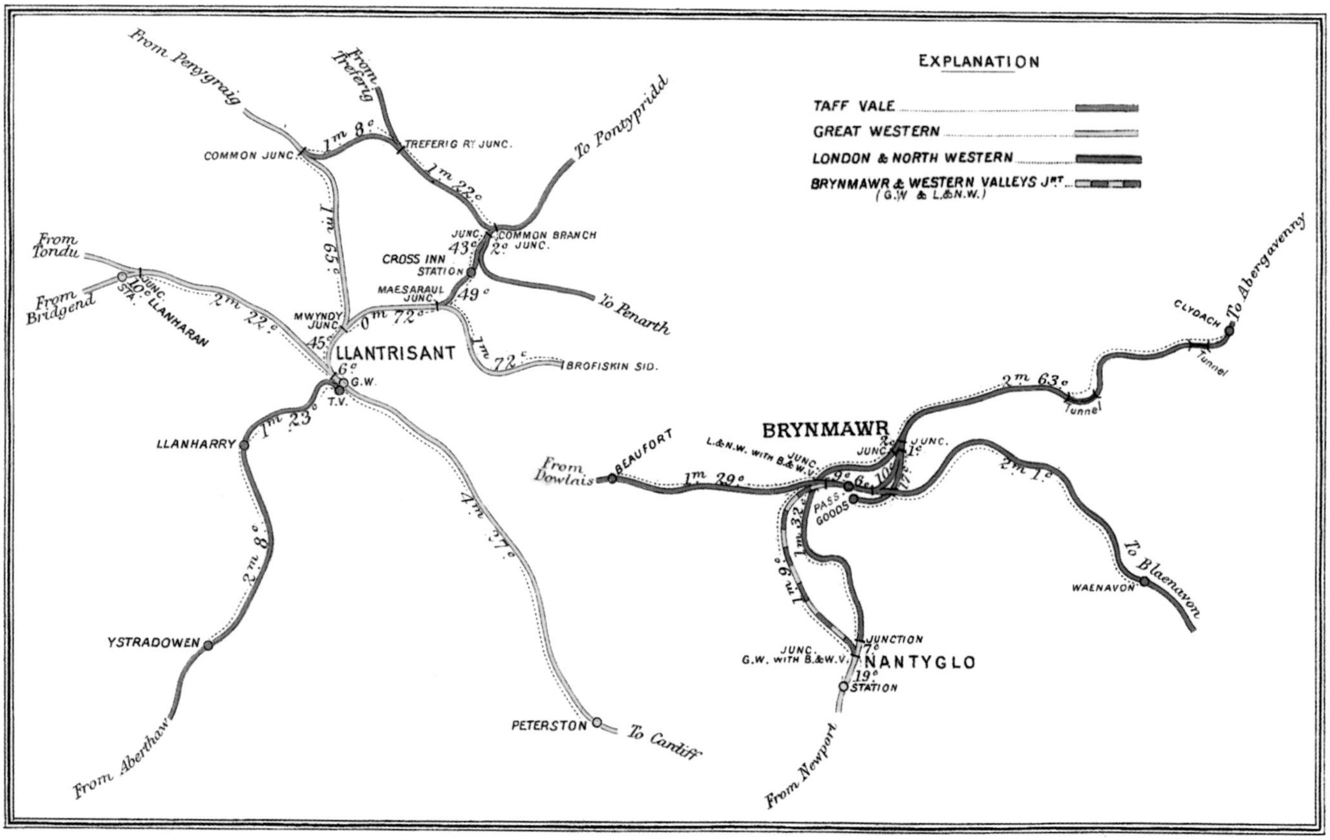

EXPLANATION

- TAFF VALE
- GREAT WESTERN
- LONDON & NORTH WESTERN
- BRYNMAWR & WESTERN VALLEYS J^NT (G.W & L.& N.W.)

Llantrisant–Nantyglo–Brynmawr

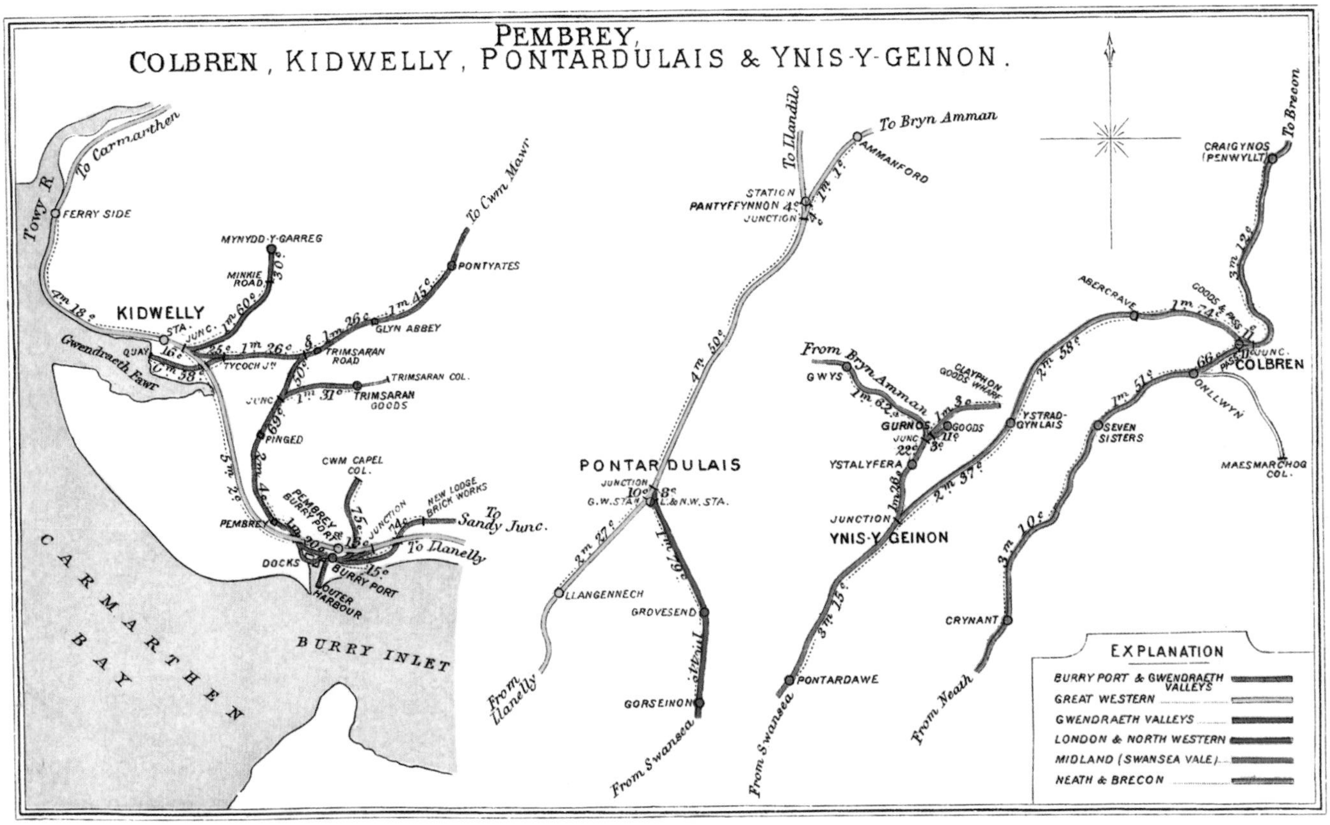

# PEMBREY, COLBREN, KIDWELLY, PONTARDULAIS & YNIS-Y-GEINON.

To Carmarthen
Towy R.
FERRY SIDE
KIDWELLY
STA.
JUNC.
QUAY
Gwendraeth Fawr
TYCOCH JN.
MYNYDD-Y-GARREG
MINKIE ROAD
To Cwm Mawr
PONTYATES
GLYN ABBEY
TRIMSARAN ROAD
TRIMSARAN COL.
TRIMSARAN GOODS
PINGED
CWM CAPEL COL.
NEW LODGE BRICK WORKS
To Sandy Junc.
To Llanelly
PEMBREY
PEMBREY & BURRY PORT
DOCKS
BURRY PORT
OUTER HARBOUR
CARMARTHEN BAY
BURRY INLET
To Llandilo
To Bryn Amman
AMMANFORD
PANTYFFYNNON STATION JUNCTION
PONTARDULAIS
G.W. STA.
L.&N.W. STA.
LLANGENNECH
GROVESEND
GORSEINON
From Llanelly
From Swansea
From Bryn Amman
GWYS
GURNOS
GOODS
CLAYPHON GOODS WHARF
YSTALYFERA
JUNCTION
YNIS-Y-GEINON
PONTARDAWE
From Swansea
YSTRAD-GYNLAIS
ABERCRAVE
GOODS & PASS.
CRAIGYNOS (PENWYLLT)
To Brecon
COLBREN
ONLLWYN
SEVEN SISTERS
MAESMARCHOG COL.
CRYNANT
From Neath

**EXPLANATION**

- BURRY PORT & GWENDRAETH VALLEYS
- GREAT WESTERN
- GWENDRAETH VALLEYS
- LONDON & NORTH WESTERN
- MIDLAND (SWANSEA VALE)
- NEATH & BRECON

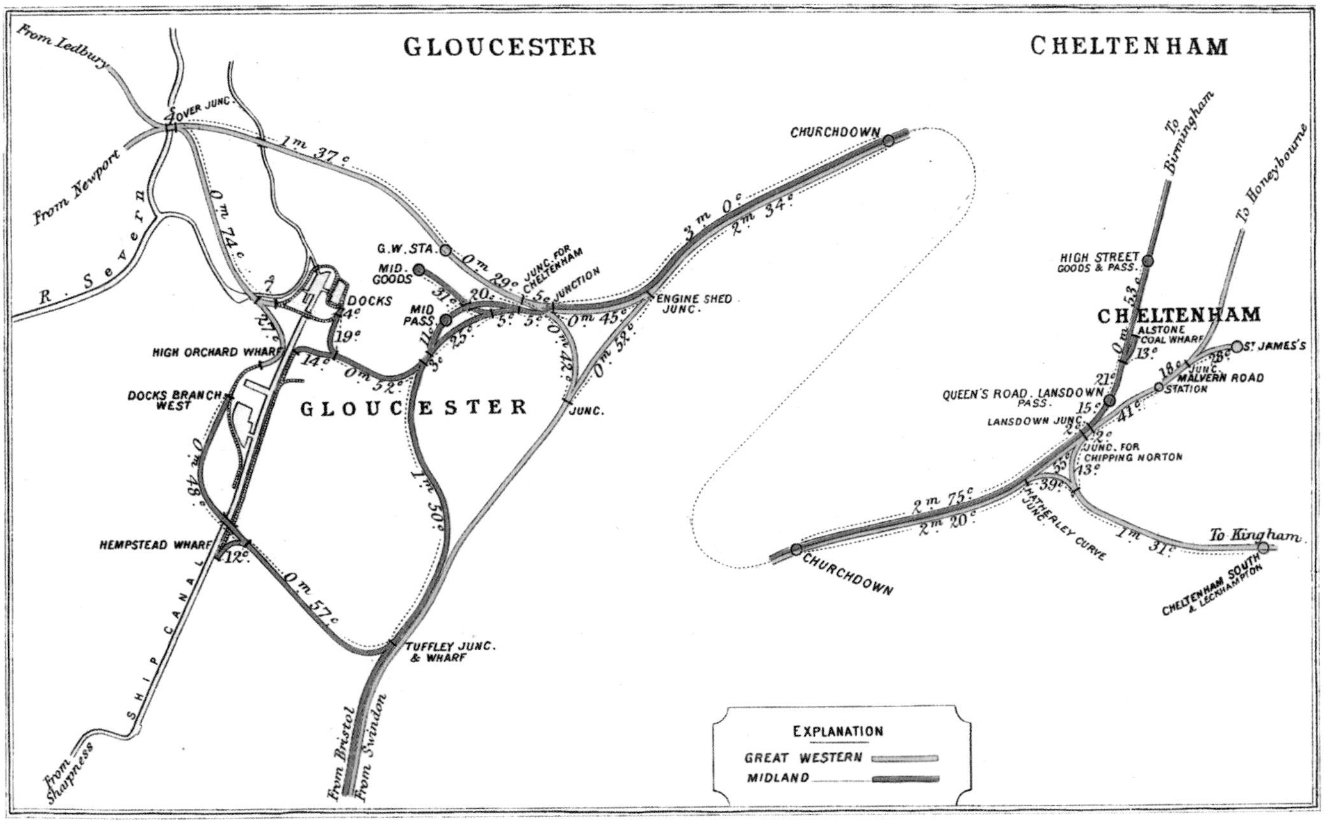

# GLOUCESTER

From Ledbury
OVER JUNC.
From Newport
R. Severn
G.W. STA.
MID. GOODS
MID. PASS.
JUNC. FOR CHELTENHAM
JUNCTION
DOCKS
ENGINE SHED JUNC.
CHURCHDOWN
HIGH ORCHARD WHARF
DOCKS BRANCH WEST
GLOUCESTER
JUNC.
HEMPSTEAD WHARF
SHIP CANAL
TUFFLEY JUNC. & WHARF
From Sharpness
From Bristol
From Swindon

# CHELTENHAM

To Birmingham
To Honeybourne
HIGH STREET GOODS & PASS.
CHELTENHAM
ALSTONE COAL WHARF
ST. JAMES'S
MALVERN ROAD STATION
QUEEN'S ROAD, LANSDOWN PASS.
LANSDOWN JUNC.
JUNC. FOR CHIPPING NORTON
HATHERLEY JUNC.
HATHERLEY CURVE
CHURCHDOWN
To Kingham
CHELTENHAM SOUTH & LECKHAMPTON

**EXPLANATION**

- GREAT WESTERN
- MIDLAND

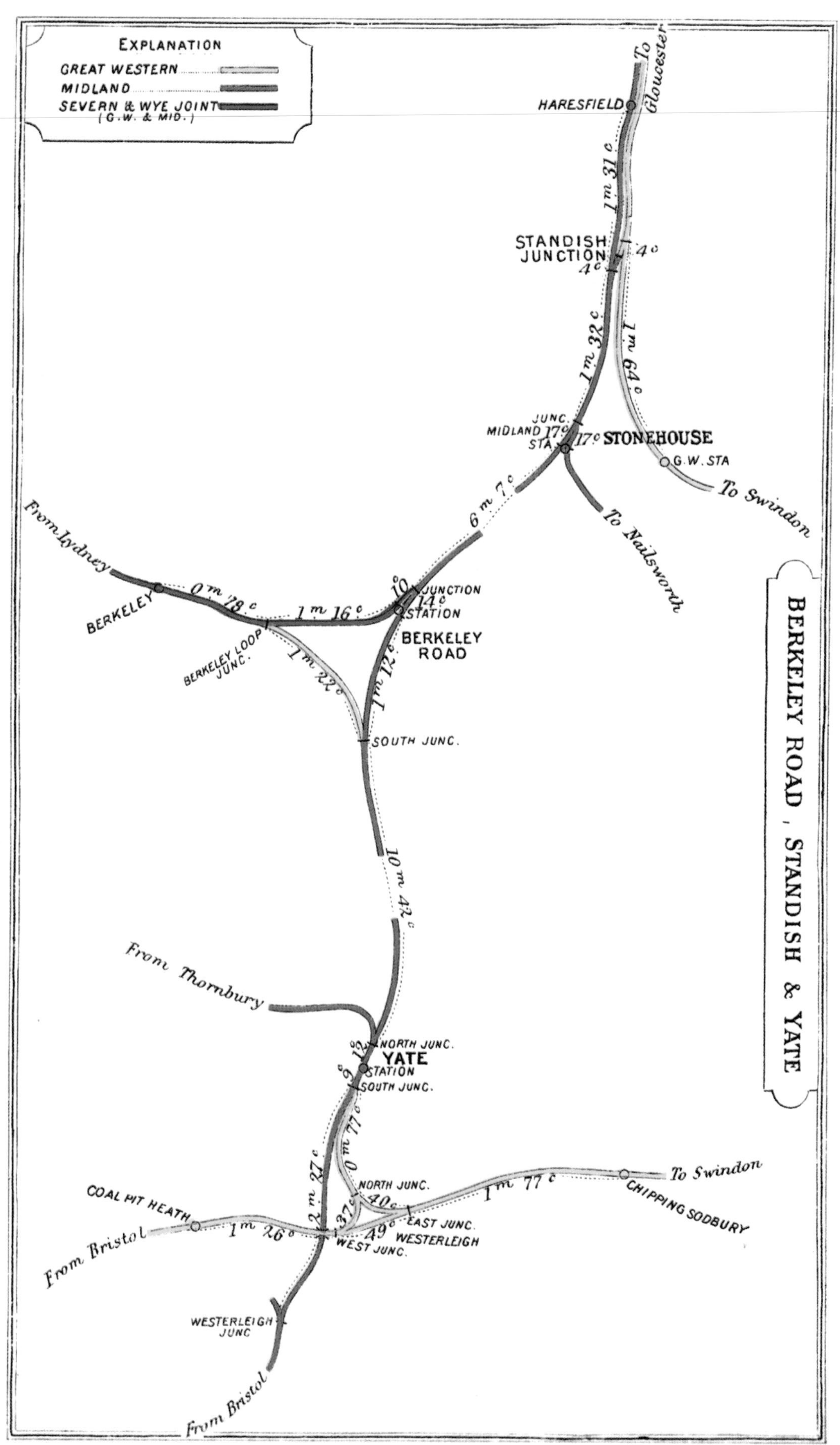
BERKELEY ROAD, STANDISH & YATE
EXPLANATION
GREAT WESTERN
MIDLAND
SEVERN & WYE JOINT
(G.W. & MID.)
To Gloucester
HARESFIELD
STANDISH JUNCTION
STONEHOUSE
G.W. STA
To Swindon
To Nailsworth
From Lydney
BERKELEY
BERKELEY LOOP JUNC.
JUNCTION
STATION
BERKELEY ROAD
SOUTH JUNC.
From Thornbury
NORTH JUNC.
YATE
STATION
SOUTH JUNC.
COAL PIT HEATH
From Bristol
WEST JUNC.
NORTH JUNC.
EAST JUNC.
WESTERLEIGH
CHIPPING SODBURY
To Swindon
WESTERLEIGH JUNC
From Bristol

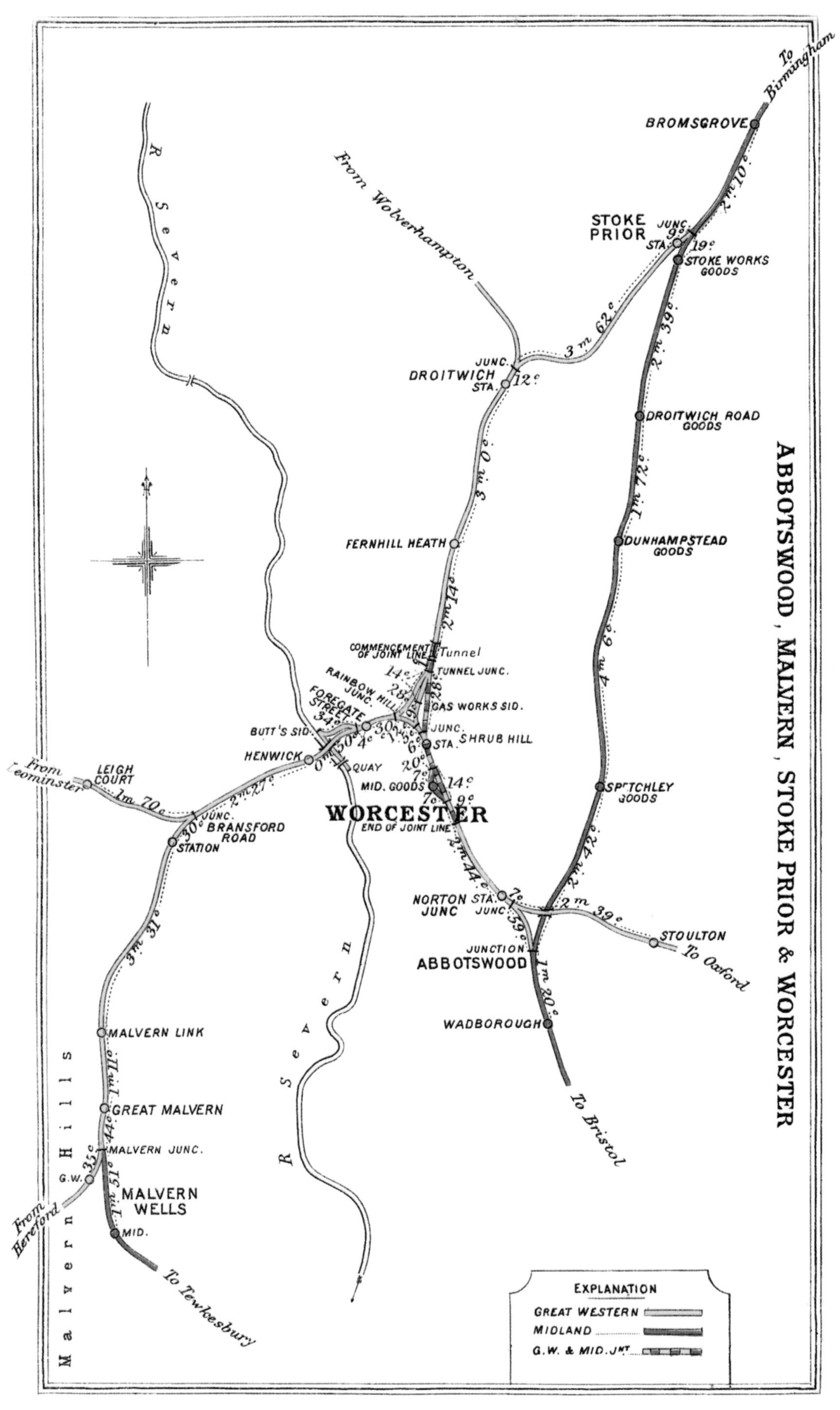
ABBOTSWOOD, MALVERN, STOKE PRIOR & WORCESTER
To Birmingham
BROMSGROVE
STOKE PRIOR
JUNC.
STA.
STOKE WORKS GOODS
From Wolverhampton
R. Severn
JUNC.
DROITWICH
STA.
DROITWICH ROAD GOODS
FERNHILL HEATH
DUNHAMPSTEAD GOODS
COMMENCEMENT OF JOINT LINE
Tunnel
TUNNEL JUNC.
RAINBOW HILL JUNC.
FOREGATE STREET
GAS WORKS SID.
BUTT'S SID.
JUNC.
STA. SHRUB HILL
HENWICK
QUAY
From Leominster
LEIGH COURT
MID. GOODS
SPETCHLEY GOODS
WORCESTER
END OF JOINT LINE
JUNC.
BRANSFORD ROAD
STATION
NORTON JUNC.
STA.
JUNC.
STOULTON
To Oxford
JUNCTION
ABBOTSWOOD
WADBOROUGH
MALVERN LINK
To Bristol
GREAT MALVERN
MALVERN JUNC.
G.W.
MALVERN WELLS
MID.
From Hereford
To Tewkesbury
Malvern Hills
EXPLANATION
GREAT WESTERN
MIDLAND
G.W. & MID. JNT

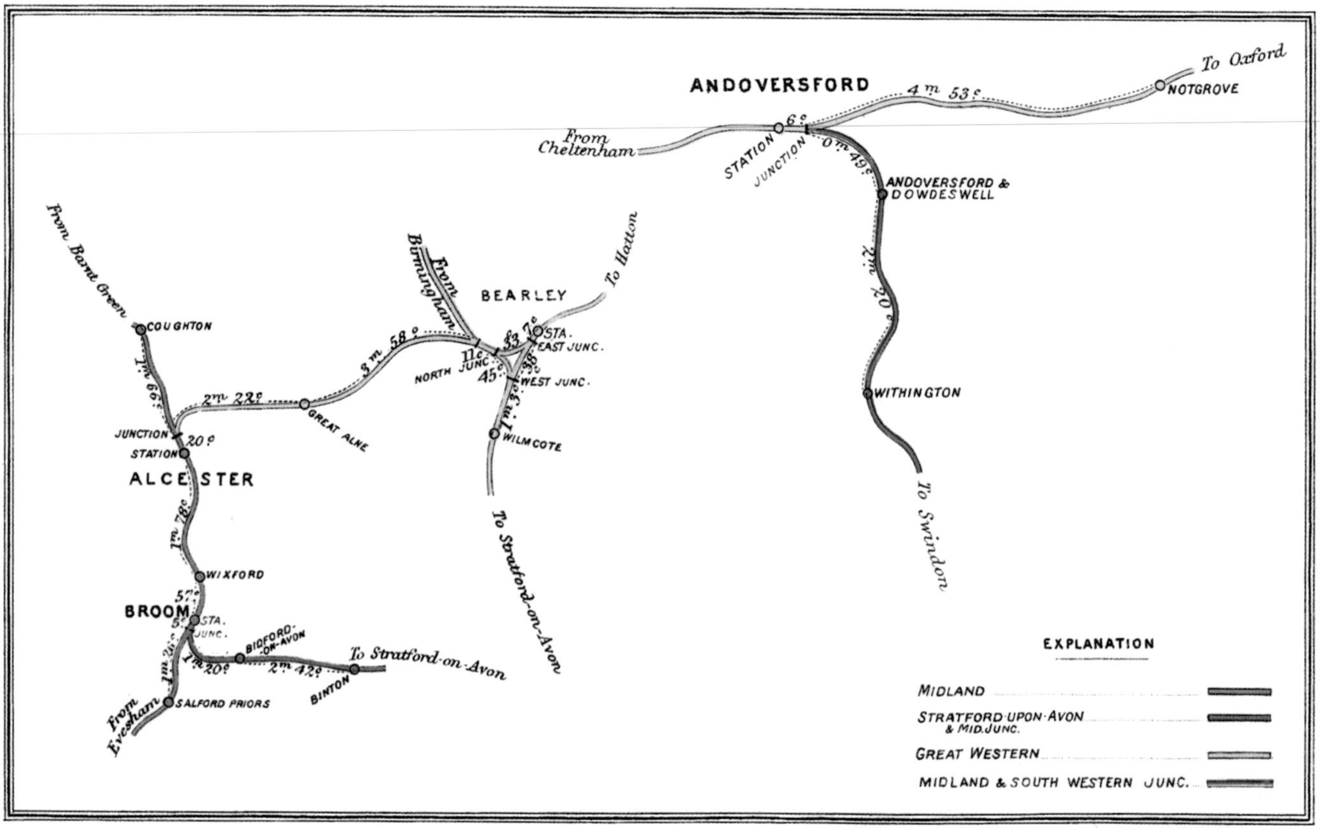

Broom–Alcester–Bearley–Andoversford

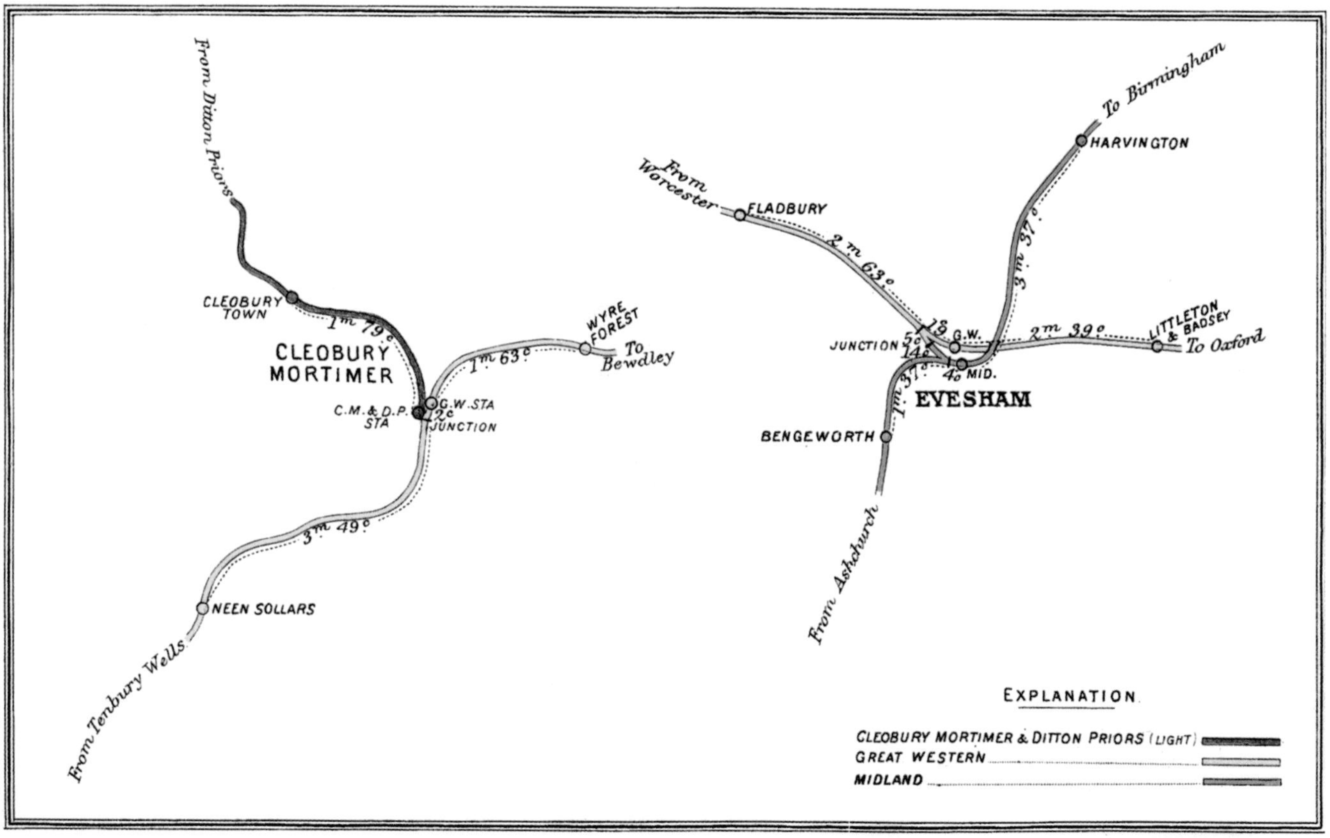

Cleobury Mortimer–Evesham

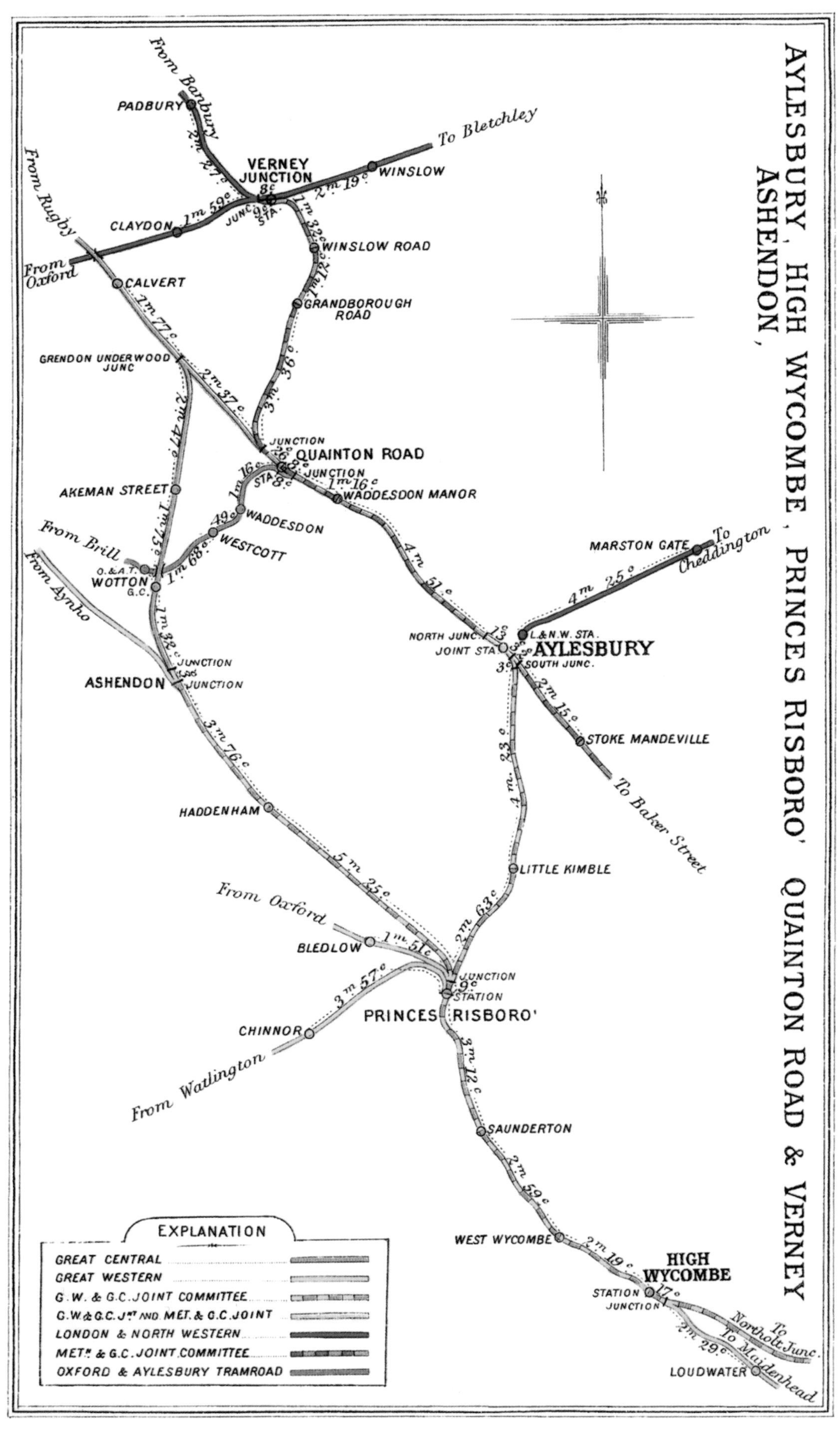
AYLESBURY, HIGH WYCOMBE, PRINCES RISBORO' QUAINTON ROAD & VERNEY
ASHENDON,
From Banbury
PADBURY
To Bletchley
VERNEY JUNCTION
WINSLOW
From Rugby
CLAYDON
WINSLOW ROAD
From Oxford
CALVERT
GRANDBOROUGH ROAD
GRENDON UNDERWOOD JUNC
JUNCTION
QUAINTON ROAD
JUNCTION
STA
WADDESDON MANOR
AKEMAN STREET
WADDESDON
From Brill
WESTCOTT
O.&A.T.
WOTTON
G.C.
From Aynho
MARSTON GATE
To Cheddington
NORTH JUNC
L.&N.W. STA.
JOINT STA
AYLESBURY
SOUTH JUNC.
JUNCTION
ASHENDON
JUNCTION
STOKE MANDEVILLE
To Baker Street
HADDENHAM
LITTLE KIMBLE
From Oxford
BLEDLOW
JUNCTION
STATION
PRINCES RISBORO'
CHINNOR
From Watlington
SAUNDERTON
WEST WYCOMBE
HIGH WYCOMBE
STATION
JUNCTION
To Northolt Junc.
To Maidenhead
LOUDWATER
EXPLANATION
GREAT CENTRAL
GREAT WESTERN
G.W. & G.C. JOINT COMMITTEE
G.W.& G.C. J^T AND MET. & G.C. JOINT
LONDON & NORTH WESTERN
MET^N & G.C. JOINT COMMITTEE
OXFORD & AYLESBURY TRAMROAD

## NINE

1 2 3 4 5

Fifteen

A B C D E F G

Fourteen

Eight

WORCESTER

HEREFORD

GLOUCESTER

WAR

WILTSHIRE

ONIBURY
BROMFIELD
Titterstone Clee
Watertroughs
BITTERLEY
MIDDLETON
CLEE HILL
LUDLOW
WOOFERTON
TENBURY WELLS
EASTON COURT
BERRINGTON & EYE
G.W.
W. Jt.
LEOMINSTER
S. & H. G.W. & L.N.
FORD BRIDGE
Dinmore Tun.
DINMORE
FENCOTE
STEENS BRIDGE
ROWDEN MILL
BROMYARD
KNIGHTWICK
SUCKLEY
STOTTESDON
HIGHLEY
C.M. & D.P.
PRESCOTT SIDING
DETTON ROAD SIDING
ARLEY
CLEOBURY TOWN STA
CLEOBURY MORTIMER
WYRE FOREST
BEWDLEY
NEEN SOLLARS
NEWNHAM BRIDGE
STOURBRIDGE TOWN
LYE
STOURBRIDGE JC.
HAGLEY
CHURCHILL & BLAKEDOWN
KIDDERMINSTER
RIFLE RANGE HALT
FOLEY PARK HALT
STOURPORT
HARTLEBURY
DROITWICH
FERNHILL HEATH
Tunnel Jc.
Loco Shed
Rainbow Hill Jc.
WORCESTER
LEIGH COURT
HENWICK
Leominster Jc.
Works
FOREGATE ST.
SHRUB HILL
G.W. & M. Joint
MID Goods
NORTON JC.
BRANSFORD RD.
Abbotswood Jc.
SOMERSET RD
HALESOWEN
HARBORNE
MOSELEY
KING'S HEATH
ACOCKS GREEN
OLTON
MID.
HAMPTON-IN-ARDEN
L & N.W.
HUNNINGTON
SELLY OAK
KING'S NORTON
HAZELWELL
LIFFORD
HALL GREEN
YARDLEY WOOD PLATFORM
SOLIHULL
BERKSWELL
NORTHFIELD
Northfield Jc.
RUBERY
SHIRLEY
WIDNEY MANOR
GRIMES HILL & WYTHALL HALT
Summit
EARLSWOOD LAKES
KNOWLE & DORRIDGE
BARNT GREEN
BLACKWELL
WOOD END PLATFORM
DANZEY FOR TANWORTH
LAPWORTH
ALVECHURCH
Lickey Incline
BROMSGROVE
Loco Shed
REDDITCH
Watertroughs
E.Jc.
N. Jc.
HATTON
S.Jc.
Pass
Stoke Works Jc.
STOKE WORKS (Goods)
HENLEY-IN-ARDEN
Goods
CLAVERDON
STUDLEY & ASTWOOD BANK
WOOTTON WAWEN PLAT
DROITWICH ROAD (Goods)
COUGHTON
N.Jc.
BEARLEY
E.Jc.
W.Jc.
DUNHAMPSTEAD (Goods)
ALCESTER
GREAT ALNE
WILMCOTE
WIXFORD
Goods
STRATFORD-ON-AVON
BROOM JUNCTION
BINTON
Loco Shed
SPETCHLEY (Goods)
BIDFORD -ON-AVON
SALFORD PRIORS
MILCOTE
STOULTON
PERSHORE
HARVINGTON
WADBOROUGH
FLADBURY
EVESHAM
LITTLETON & BADSEY
LONG MARSTON
HONEYBOURNE
MALVERN LINK
GREAT MALVERN
Malvern Jc.
MALVERN WELLS
MID
DEFFORD
ECKINGTON
BENGEWORTH
WESTON-SUB-EDGE
HINTON
Campden Tun.
SHIPSTON-ON-STOUR
LONG ROAD
CAMPDEN
WILLERSLEY HALT
BRECON Curve Jc.
Barrs Ct Jc. N.
Shelwick Jc.
CREDENHILL
MOORFIELDS (Gds)
BARTON (Gds)
Loco Shed
BARRS COURT
Barrs Ct Jc. S
HEREFORD
Rotherwas Jc.
Red Hill Jc.
L & N.W.
WITHINGTON
STOKE EDITH
ASHPERTON
COLWALL
LEDBURY
UPTON-ON-SEVERN
RIPPLE
BREDON
ASHTON-UNDER-HILL
BROADWAY
STRETTON-ON-FOSSE
BLOCKLEY
LAVERTON HALT
BECKFORD
HOLME LACY
MORETON-ON-LUGG
TRAM INN
BALLINGHAM
FAWLEY
DYMOCK
TEWKESBURY
Level Crossing
ASHCHURCH
GRETTON HALT
Greet Tun.
TODDINGTON
MORETON-IN-MARSH
Summit
GOTHERINGTON
WINCHCOMBE
CLEEVE
BISHOP'S CLEEVE
ADLESTROP
CHELTENHAM RACECOURSE
Hunting Butts Tun.
ST. JAMES'S
NEWENT
STOW-ON-THE-WOLD
LANSDOWN
Honeybourne Line Jc.
Banbury Line Jc.
MALVERN ROAD
CHELTENHAM
ROSS-ON-WYE
MITCHELDEAN ROAD
BARBER'S BRIDGE
CHURCHDOWN
CHELTENHAM S. & LECKHAMPTON
ANDOVERSFORD
NOTGROVE
KINGHAM
BOURTON-ON-THE-WATER
Hatherley Curve Jc.
KERNE BRIDGE
LONGHOPE
OAKLE STREET
Over Jc.
G.W.
Engine Shed Jc.
CHARLTON KINGS
ANDOVERSFORD & DOWDESWELL
WITHINGTON
LYDBROOK JUNC.
UPPER LYDBROOK
SYMOND'S YAT
CINDERFORD
GRANGE COURT
Docks
MID.
Level Crossing
GLOUCESTER
DRYBROOK ROAD
Serridge Jc.
CINDERFORD (S. & W.)
Tuffley Jc.
MAY HILL
MONMOUTH
TROY
COLEFORD FOR STAUNTON
NEWLAND
SPEECH HOUSE RD.
NEWNHAM
BULLO PILL
Docks
CHEDWORTH
HARESFIELD
FOSS CROSS
PEDBROOK
DINGESTOW
MILKWALL FOR CLEARWELL
PARKEND
Standish Jc.
ST. BRIAVELS & LLANDOGO
WHITECROFT
Tufts Jcs.
N.
S.
SEVERN BRIDGE
AWRE FOR BLAKENEY
TOWN
Level Crossing
LYDNEY JUN.
Docks
Severn Bridge
STONEHOUSE
Viaduct
FROCESTER
COALEY JUNC.
MID'S SW.
KELMSCOTT & LANGFORD
TINTERN FOR BROCKWEIR
WOOLASTON
SHARPNESS
Docks
BERKELEY
Oldminster Jc.
CAM
WOODCHESTER
Sapperton Tun.
Summit
CIRENCESTER
FAIRFORD
LECHLADE
BERKELEY ROAD
South Jc.
DURSLEY
NAILSWORTH
CERNEY & ASHTON KEYNES
TIDENHAM
Wye Valley Junc.
RODMARTON PLAT.
KEMBLE JUNC.
CULKERTON
CHEPSTOW
CHARFIELD
TETBURY
CRICKLADE
THORNBURY
HANNINGTON
HIGHWORTH
SEVERN TUNNEL JC.
Loco Shed
PORTSKEWETT
SUDBROOK
WICKWAR
Wickwar Tun.
TYTHERINGTON
MINETY & ASHTON KEYNES
BLUNSDON
STANTON
STRATTON
PURTON
MALMESBURY
SHRIVENHAM
Severn Tunnel
PILNING
CHITTENING FACTORY PLATFORM
SEVERN BEACH
IRON ACTON
Main Line Jc.
South Jc.
YATE
Westerleigh Jcs.
North Jc.
LITTLE SOMERFORD
BRINKWORTH
Works
Highworth Jc.
Junc.
SWINDON
TOWN STA.
TOWN (Goods)
WINTER-BOURNE
Sodbury Tun.
BADMINTON
Alderton Tun.
HULLAVINGTON
GREAT SOMERFORD
Rushey Platt Jc.
RUSHEY PLATT (Goods)
AVONMOUTH
DOCK (Pass)
DOCK (Goods)
PATCHWAY
E.Jc
W.Jc
CHIPPING SODBURY
WOOTTON BASSETT
CHISELDON
PORTISHEAD
HENBURY
FILTON JUNC.
COAL PIT HEATH
DAUNTSEY
SHIREHAMPTON
SEA MILLS
G.W.
PORTBURY
ASHLEY HILL
FISH PONDS
STAPLE HILL
Westerleigh Junc.
CLIFTON DOWN
PILL
CLAPTON RD
MANGOTSFIELD
G.W.

1 STONEHOUSE
2 EBLEY CROSSING HALT
3 DOWNFIELD CROSSING HALT
4 STROUD (G. W.)
5 RYEFORD
6 DUDBRIDGE
7 BOWBRIDGE CROSSING HALT
8 HAM MILL CROSSING HALT
9 BRIMSCOMBE BRIDGE HALT
10 BRIMSCOMBE
11 ST. MARY'S CROSSING HALT
12 CHALFORD
13 STROUD (MID.)

31 NAILBRIDGE HALT
30 STEAM MILLS CROSSING HALT
29 WHIMSEY HALT
28 BULLO CROSS HALT
27 UPPER SOUDLEY HALT
26 STAPLE EDGE HALT
25 RUSPIDGE HALT

Eight

Three

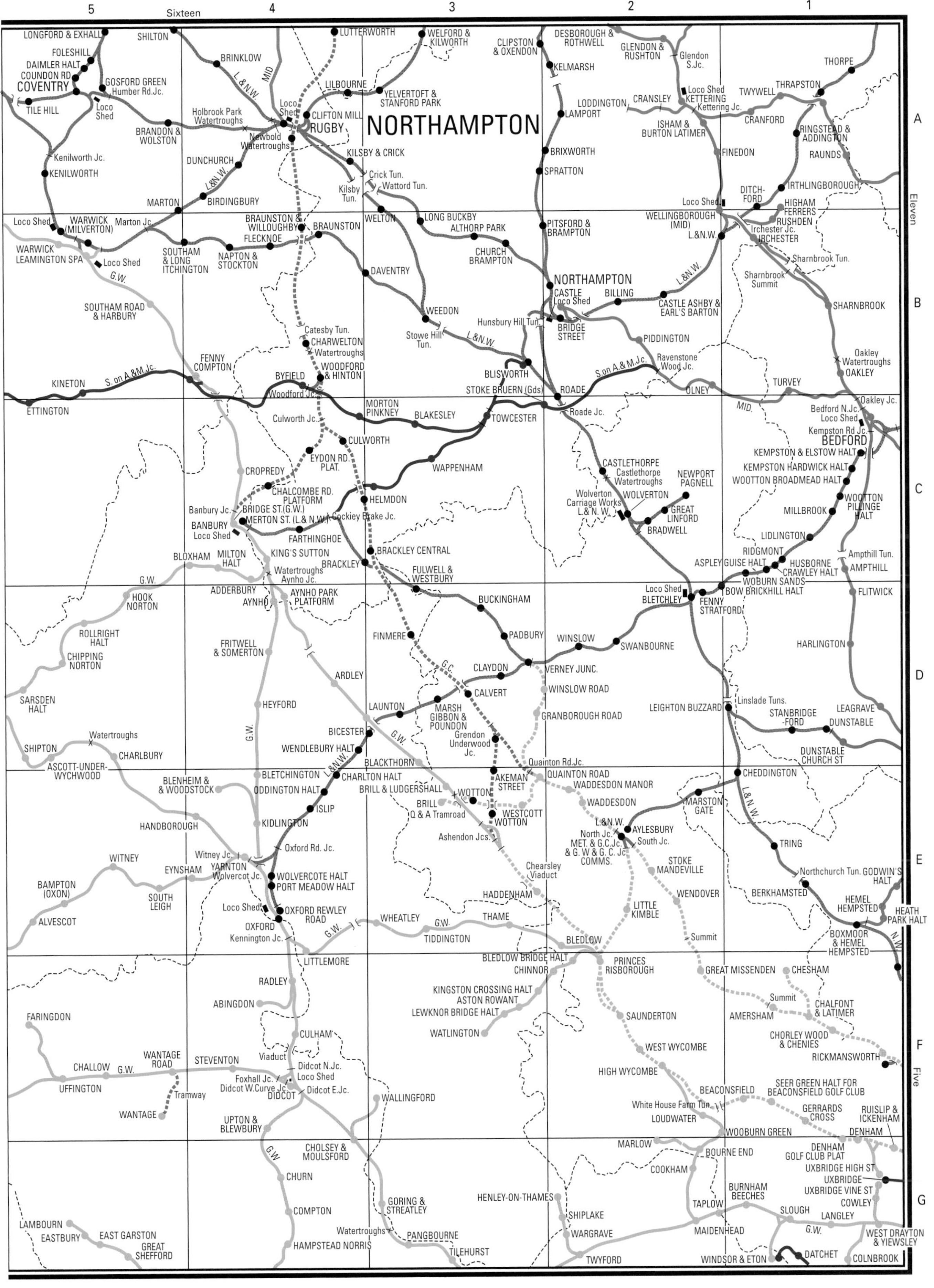
5
Sixteen
4
3
2
1
A
B
C
D
E
F
G
Eleven
Five
NORTHAMPTON
LONGFORD & EXHALL
FOLESHILL
DAIMLER HALT
COUNDON RD
COVENTRY
GOSFORD GREEN
Humber Rd.Jc.
TILE HILL
Loco Shed
SHILTON
BRINKLOW
L.&N.W.
MID
LUTTERWORTH
WELFORD & KILWORTH
CLIPSTON & OXENDON
DESBOROUGH & ROTHWELL
GLENDON & RUSHTON
Glendon S.Jc.
THORPE
LILBOURNE
YELVERTOFT & STANFORD PARK
CLIFTON MILL
RUGBY
Holbrook Park Watertroughs
BRANDON & WOLSTON
Newbold Watertroughs
KELMARSH
LODDINGTON
CRANSLEY
LAMPORT
KETTERING
Kettering Jc.
TWYWELL
THRAPSTON
CRANFORD
ISHAM & BURTON LATIMER
RINGSTEAD & ADDINGTON
RAUNDS
FINEDON
Kenilworth Jc.
KENILWORTH
DUNCHURCH
KILSBY & CRICK
BRIXWORTH
SPRATTON
Crick Tun.
Kilsby Tun.
Wattord Tun.
DITCH-FORD
IRTHLINGBOROUGH
HIGHAM FERRERS
RUSHDEN
MARTON
BIRDINGBURY
WARWICK (MILVERTON)
Marton Jc.
WARWICK
LEAMINGTON SPA
SOUTHAM & LONG ITCHINGTON
NAPTON & STOCKTON
FLECKNOE
BRAUNSTON & WILLOUGHBY
BRAUNSTON
WELTON
LONG BUCKBY
ALTHORP PARK
CHURCH BRAMPTON
PITSFORD & BRAMPTON
WELLINGBOROUGH (MID)
L.&N.W.
Irchester Jc.
IRCHESTER
Sharnbrook Tun.
Sharnbrook Summit
G.W.
DAVENTRY
NORTHAMPTON
CASTLE
BILLING
CASTLE ASHBY & EARL'S BARTON
SOUTHAM ROAD & HARBURY
WEEDON
Catesby Tun.
CHARWELTON
Watertroughs
Stowe Hill Tun.
Hunsbury Hill Tun.
BRIDGE STREET
PIDDINGTON
SHARNBROOK
FENNY COMPTON
KINETON
S. on A.&M.Jc.
BYFIELD
WOODFORD & HINTON
Woodford Jc.
BLISWORTH
STOKE BRUERN (Gds)
ROADE
Ravenstone Wood Jc.
Oakley Watertroughs
OAKLEY
TURVEY
OLNEY
ETTINGTON
MORTON PINKNEY
BLAKESLEY
TOWCESTER
Roade Jc.
Culworth Jc.
CULWORTH
MID.
Oakley Jc.
Bedford N.Jc.
Kempston Rd Jc.
BEDFORD
KEMPSTON & ELSTOW HALT
KEMPSTON HARDWICK HALT
WOOTTON BROADMEAD HALT
EYDON RD. PLAT.
WAPPENHAM
CASTLETHORPE
Castlethorpe Watertroughs
NEWPORT PAGNELL
CROPREDY
CHALCOMBE RD. PLATFORM
HELMDON
WOLVERTON
Wolverton Carriage Works
L.& N. W.
GREAT LINFORD
BRADWELL
WOOTTON PILLINGE HALT
MILLBROOK
Banbury Jc.
BRIDGE ST.(G.W.)
MERTON ST. (L.& N.W.)
Cockley Brake Jc.
BANBURY
FARTHINGHOE
LIDLINGTON
RIDGMONT
Ampthill Tun.
AMPTHILL
BLOXHAM
MILTON HALT
KING'S SUTTON
BRACKLEY CENTRAL
BRACKLEY
FULWELL & WESTBURY
ASPLEY GUISE HALT
HUSBORNE CRAWLEY HALT
WOBURN SANDS
BOW BRICKHILL HALT
Aynho Jc.
ADDERBURY
AYNHO
AYNHO PARK PLATFORM
BUCKINGHAM
BLETCHLEY
FENNY STRATFORD
FLITWICK
HOOK NORTON
ROLLRIGHT HALT
CHIPPING NORTON
FRITWELL & SOMERTON
FINMERE
PADBURY
WINSLOW
SWANBOURNE
HARLINGTON
ARDLEY
G.C.
CLAYDON
VERNEY JUNC.
SARSDEN HALT
HEYFORD
CALVERT
WINSLOW ROAD
LAUNTON
MARSH GIBBON & POUNDON
GRANBOROUGH ROAD
LEIGHTON BUZZARD
Linslade Tuns.
STANBRIDGE -FORD
LEAGRAVE
DUNSTABLE
SHIPTON
Watertroughs
CHARLBURY
ASCOTT-UNDER-WYCHWOOD
BICESTER
WENDLEBURY HALT
Grendon Underwood Jc.
BLACKTHORN
Quainton Rd.Jc.
DUNSTABLE CHURCH ST
CHEDDINGTON
BLENHEIM & WOODSTOCK
BLETCHINGTON
CHARLTON HALT
ODDINGTON HALT
BRILL & LUDGERSHALL
AKEMAN STREET
QUAINTON ROAD
WADDESDON MANOR
WADDESDON
MARSTON GATE
ISLIP
BRILL
Q & A Tramroad
WOTTON
WESTCOTT
HANDBOROUGH
KIDLINGTON
Ashendon Jcs.
North Jc.
MET. & G.C.Jc.
& G. W & G. C. Jc.
COMMS.
AYLESBURY
South Jc.
TRING
Witney Jc.
Oxford Rd. Jc.
WITNEY
EYNSHAM
YARNTON
Wolvercot Jc.
WOLVERCOTE HALT
PORT MEADOW HALT
STOKE MANDEVILLE
Chearsley Viaduct
Northchurch Tun.
GODWIN'S HALT
BAMPTON (OXON)
SOUTH LEIGH
OXFORD REWLEY ROAD
OXFORD
Kennington Jc.
HADDENHAM
LITTLE KIMBLE
WENDOVER
BERKHAMSTED
HEMEL HEMPSTED
HEATH PARK HALT
ALVESCOT
WHEATLEY
THAME
TIDDINGTON
BLEDLOW
Summit
BOXMOOR & HEMEL HEMPSTED
LITTLEMORE
BLEDLOW BRIDGE HALT
CHINNOR
PRINCES RISBOROUGH
GREAT MISSENDEN
CHESHAM
RADLEY
FARINGDON
ABINGDON
KINGSTON CROSSING HALT
ASTON ROWANT
LEWKNOR BRIDGE HALT
SAUNDERTON
AMERSHAM
CHALFONT & LATIMER
CULHAM
WATLINGTON
CHORLEY WOOD & CHENIES
WEST WYCOMBE
RICKMANSWORTH
CHALLOW
WANTAGE ROAD
STEVENTON
Viaduct
Didcot N.Jc.
Loco Shed
Foxhall Jc.
Didcot W.Curve Jc.
DIDCOT
Didcot E.Jc.
UFFINGTON
Tramway
WANTAGE
WALLINGFORD
HIGH WYCOMBE
BEACONSFIELD
SEER GREEN HALT FOR BEACONSFIELD GOLF CLUB
White House Farm Tun.
GERRARDS CROSS
RUISLIP & ICKENHAM
LOUDWATER
UPTON & BLEWBURY
WOOBURN GREEN
DENHAM
MARLOW
BOURNE END
DENHAM GOLF CLUB PLAT
CHOLSEY & MOULSFORD
COOKHAM
UXBRIDGE HIGH ST
UXBRIDGE
UXBRIDGE VINE ST
CHURN
GORING & STREATLEY
HENLEY-ON-THAMES
BURNHAM BEECHES
TAPLOW
SLOUGH
COWLEY
LANGLEY
COMPTON
SHIPLAKE
LAMBOURN
EASTBURY
EAST GARSTON
GREAT SHEFFORD
HAMPSTEAD NORRIS
Watertroughs
PANGBOURNE
TILEHURST
WARGRAVE
MAIDENHEAD
WEST DRAYTON & YIEWSLEY
TWYFORD
WINDSOR & ETON
DATCHET
COLNBROOK

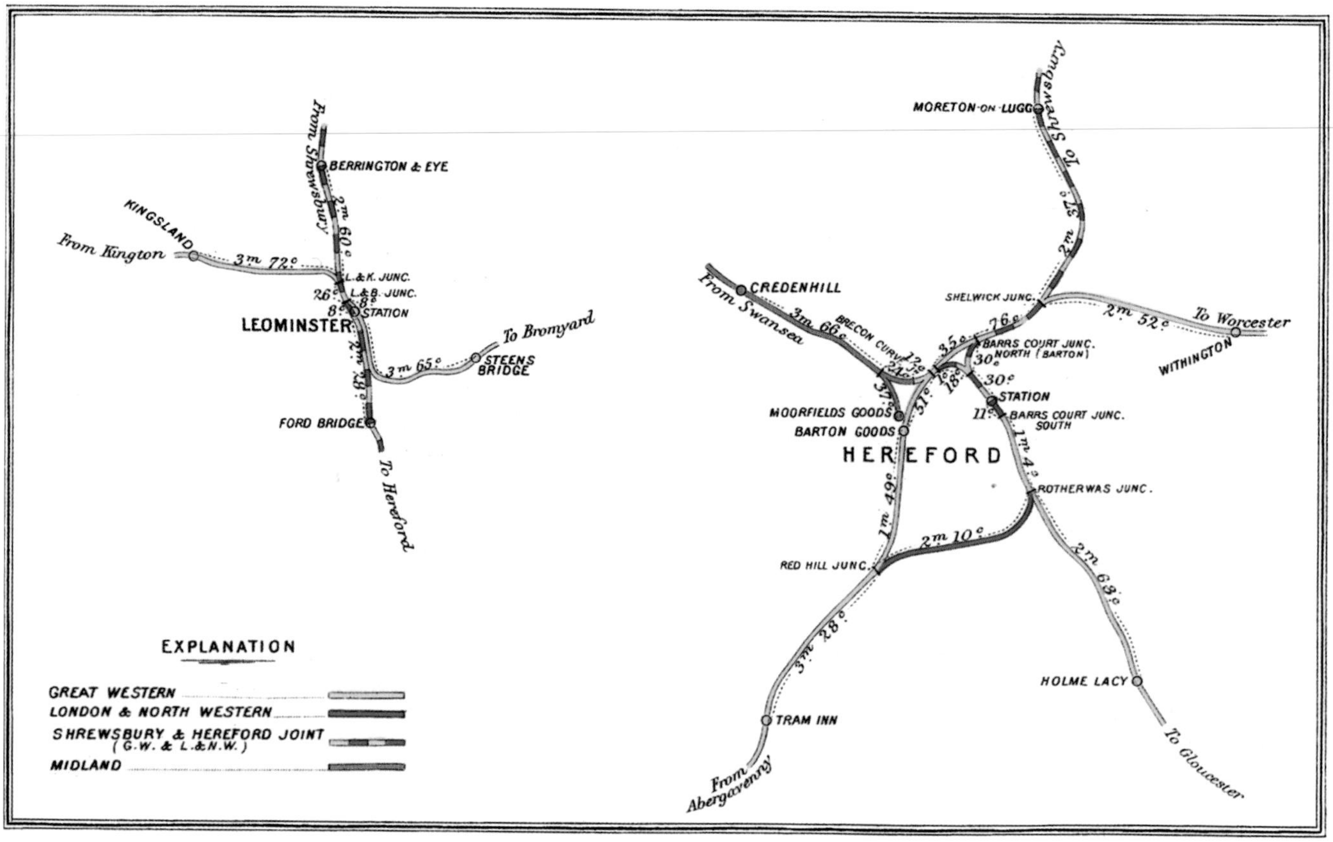
EXPLANATION
GREAT WESTERN
LONDON & NORTH WESTERN
SHREWSBURY & HEREFORD JOINT (G.W. & L.&N.W.)
MIDLAND
LEOMINSTER
HEREFORD
BERRINGTON & EYE
KINGSLAND
From Kington
From Shrewsbury
STEENS BRIDGE
To Bromyard
FORD BRIDGE
To Hereford
MORETON-ON-LUGG
To Shrewsbury
CREDENHILL
From Swansea
SHELWICK JUNC.
To Worcester
WITHINGTON
BARRS COURT JUNC. NORTH (BARTON)
STATION
BARRS COURT JUNC. SOUTH
MOORFIELDS GOODS
BARTON GOODS
ROTHERWAS JUNC.
RED HILL JUNC.
HOLME LACY
TRAM INN
From Abergavenny
To Gloucester

**Leominster–Hereford**

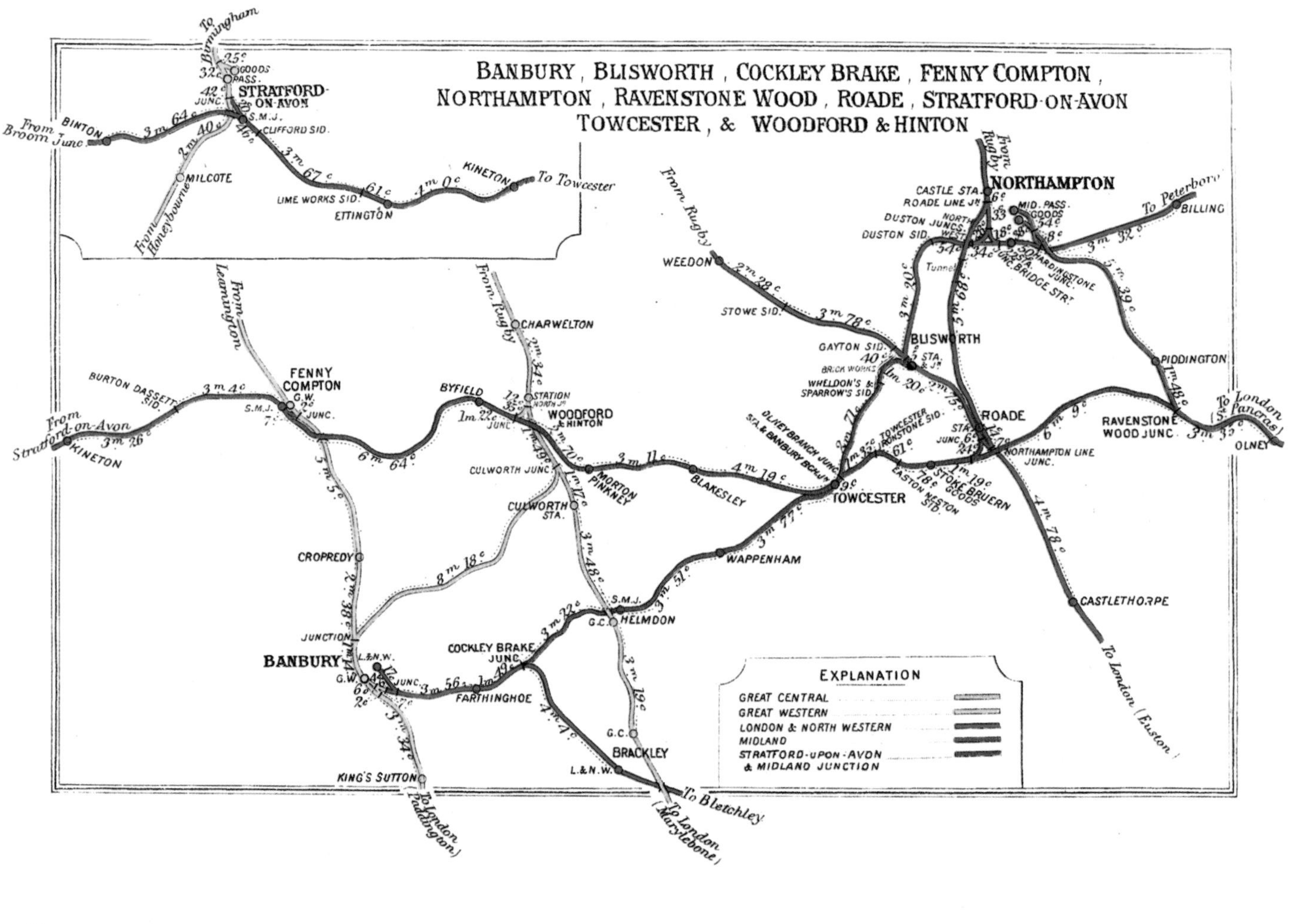
BANBURY, BLISWORTH, COCKLEY BRAKE, FENNY COMPTON, NORTHAMPTON, RAVENSTONE WOOD, ROADE, STRATFORD-ON-AVON TOWCESTER, & WOODFORD & HINTON
EXPLANATION
GREAT CENTRAL
GREAT WESTERN
LONDON & NORTH WESTERN
MIDLAND
STRATFORD-UPON-AVON & MIDLAND JUNCTION
STRATFORD-ON-AVON
To Birmingham
From Broom Junc
BINTON
MILCOTE
From Honeybourne
CLIFFORD SID.
LIME WORKS SID.
ETTINGTON
KINETON
To Towcester
From Leamington
FENNY COMPTON
BURTON DASSETT SID.
From Stratford-on-Avon
KINETON
CROPREDY
BANBURY
KING'S SUTTON
To London (Paddington)
From Rugby
CHARWELTON
BYFIELD
WOODFORD & HINTON
CULWORTH JUNC.
CULWORTH STA.
MORTON PINKNEY
BLAKESLEY
HELMDON
COCKLEY BRAKE JUNC.
FARTHINGHOE
BRACKLEY
To Bletchley
To London (Marylebone)
WEEDON
STOWE SID.
BLISWORTH
GAYTON SID.
TOWCESTER
WAPPENHAM
NORTHAMPTON
CASTLE STA.
To Peterboro'
BILLING
PIDDINGTON
RAVENSTONE WOOD JUNC.
To London (St. Pancras)
OLNEY
ROADE
STOKE BRUERN
CASTLETHORPE
To London (Euston)

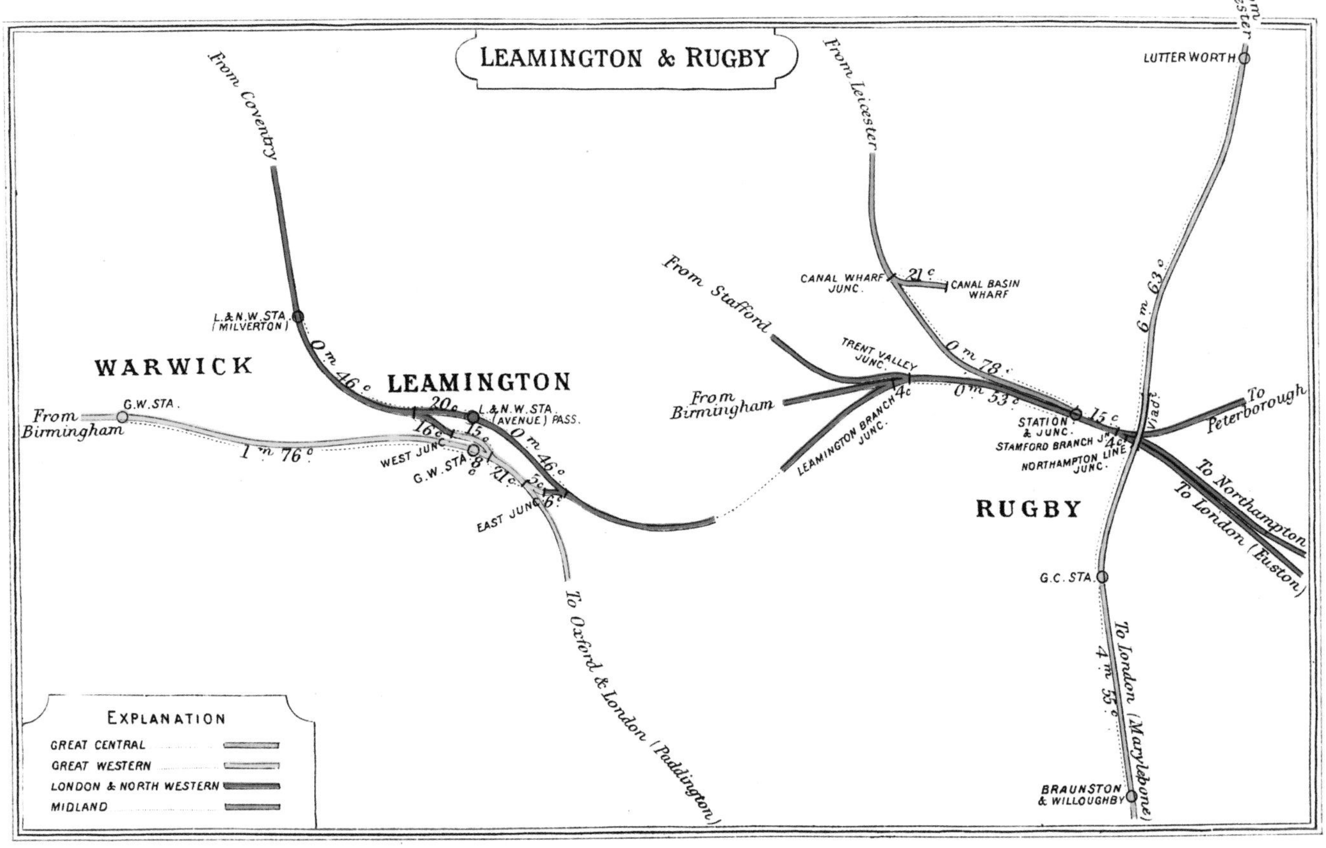

## LEAMINGTON & RUGBY

From Coventry
L.&N.W. STA. (MILVERTON)
WARWICK
LEAMINGTON
From Birmingham
G.W. STA.
1 m 76 c
0 m 46 c
20 c
L.&N.W. STA. (AVENUE) PASS.
16 c
15 c
WEST JUNC.
G.W. STA.
8 c
0 m 46 c
EAST JUNC.
To Oxford & London (Paddington)
From Leicester
CANAL WHARF JUNC.
21 c
CANAL BASIN WHARF
From Stafford
TRENT VALLEY JUNC.
From Birmingham
LEAMINGTON BRANCH JUNC.
4 c
0 m 78 c
0 m 53 c
STATION & JUNC.
15 c
STAMFORD BRANCH JN.
NORTHAMPTON LINE JUNC.
To Peterborough
To Northampton
To London (Euston)
RUGBY
From Leicester
LUTTERWORTH
6 m 63 c
G.C. STA.
4 m 55 c
To London (Marylebone)
BRAUNSTON & WILLOUGHBY

### EXPLANATION

GREAT CENTRAL
GREAT WESTERN
LONDON & NORTH WESTERN
MIDLAND

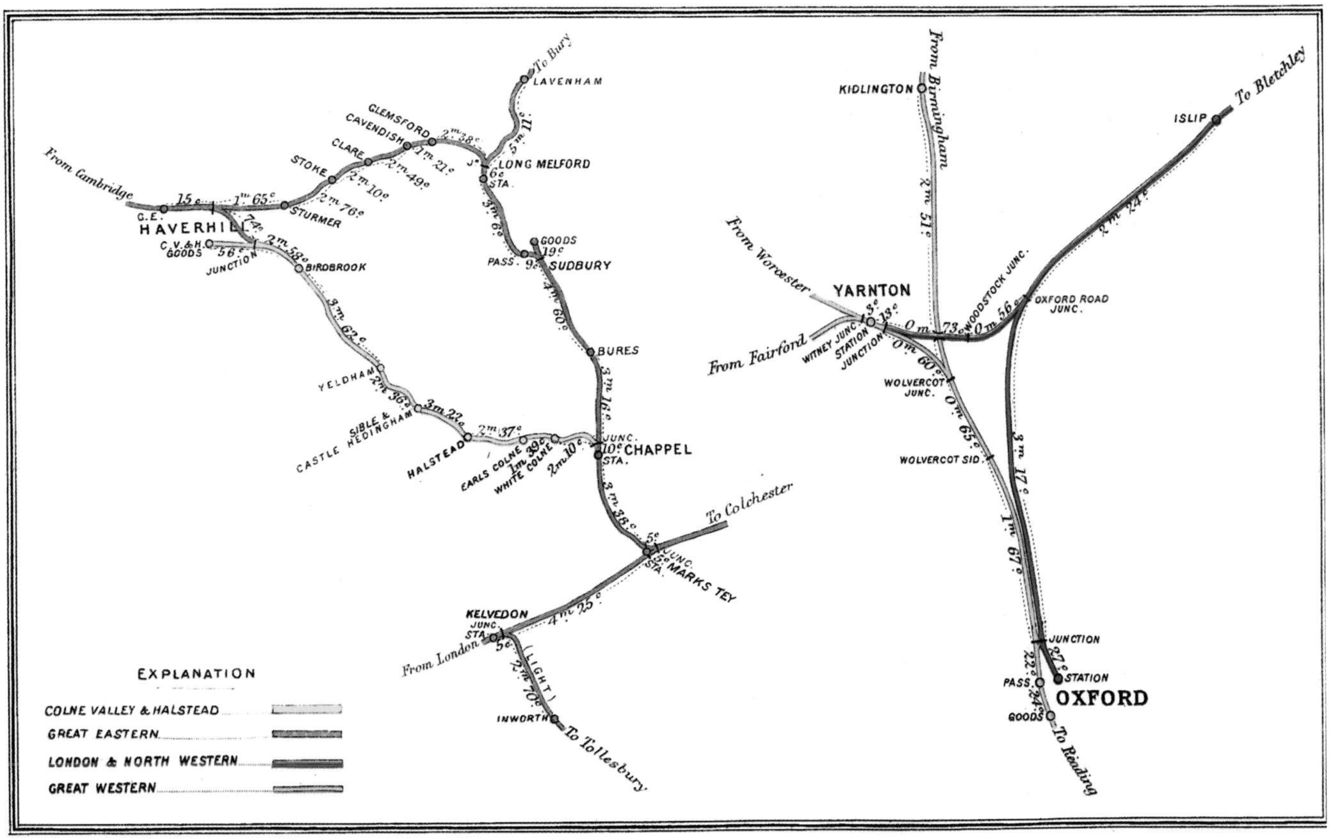

---

To Bury
LAVENHAM
From Cambridge
C.E.
HAVERHILL
15 c
1 m 65 c
STURMER
2 m 76 c
STOKE
2 m 10 c
CLARE
2 m 49 c
CAVENDISH
1 m 21 c
GLEMSFORD
2 m 38 c
5 m 11 c
LONG MELFORD
6 c STA.
3 m 6 c
GOODS
19 c
PASS. 9 c
SUDBURY
4 m 60 c
BURES
3 m 14 c
JUNC.
10 c CHAPPEL
STA.
C.V.&H. GOODS
56 c
JUNCTION
2 m 58 c
BIRDBROOK
3 m 62 c
YELDHAM
2 m 36 c
SIBLE & CASTLE HEDINGHAM
3 m 22 c
HALSTEAD
2 m 37 c
EARLS COLNE
1 m 39 c
WHITE COLNE
2 m 10 c
3 m 38 c
5 c
JUNC. STA.
MARKS TEY
To Colchester
KELVEDON JUNC. STA.
5 c
4 m 25 c
From London
(LIGHT)
2 m 70 c
INWORTH
To Tollesbury

From Birmingham
KIDLINGTON
2 m 51 c
ISLIP
To Bletchley
2 m 24 c
From Worcester
YARNTON
3 c
13 c
From Fairford
WITNEY JUNC.
STATION
JUNCTION
0 m 73 c
WOODSTOCK JUNC.
0 m 56 c
OXFORD ROAD JUNC.
0 m 60 c
WOLVERCOT JUNC.
0 m 65 c
WOLVERCOT SID.
3 m 17 c
1 m 67 c
JUNCTION
27 c
22 c
STATION
PASS.
OXFORD
24 c
GOODS
To Reading

### EXPLANATION

COLNE VALLEY & HALSTEAD
GREAT EASTERN
LONDON & NORTH WESTERN
GREAT WESTERN

**Haverhill–Chappel–Yarnton–Oxford**

## ELEVEN

1 2 3 4 Seventeen 5

A B C D E F G

KINGSCLIFFE
WANSFORD ROAD
CASTOR
NASSINGTON
WANSFORD
Yarwell Jc.
ELTON
L. & N. W.
OUNDLE
BARNWELL
Loco Shed
New England Sidings
G.N.
Loco Shed
L & N.W. & G.E.
PETERBOROUGH
G.E.
ORTON WATERVILLE
Longville Jc.
FLETTON (Goods)
YAXLEY & FARCET
WHITTLESEA
Grassmoor Jc.
WHITEMOOR(Goods)
Loco Shed
West Jc.
North Jc.
MARCH
March S.Jc.
South Jc.
QUAKERS DROVE
WEST FEN DROVE
BURNT HOUSE
JONES' DROVE
WHITE FEN
BENWICK (Goods)
STONEA
MANEA
WIMBLINGTON
CHATTERIS
DENVER
RYSTON
ABBEY FOR WEST DEREHAM
STOKE FERRY
HILGAY
LITTLEPORT
G.E.
BLACK BANK
BRANDON
LAKENHEATH
HOLME
ST MARY'S
RAMSEY
RAMSEY HIGH STREET
WARBOYS
G.N.& G.E. Jc.
G.N.
ABBOTS RIPTON
THORPE
THRAPSTON
CHETTISHAM
G.E.
SHIPPEA HILL
ELY
Dock Jc.
Sutton Branch Jc.
H U N T I N G T O N
SOMERSHAM
G.E.
SUTTON
HADDENHAM
WILBURTON
STRETHAM
EARITH BRIDGE
RAUNDS
KIMBOLTON
LONG STOW (Goods)
Mid.
HUNTINGDON
GODMANCHESTER
Mid.
Needingworth Jc.
BLUNTISHAM
ST.IVES
SWAVESEY
SOHAM
ISLEHAM
MILDENHALL
WORLINGTON GOLF LINKS HALT
FORDHAM
GRAFHAM
BUCKDEN
OFFORD & BUCKDEN
LONG STANTON
OAKINGTON
HISTON
WATERBEACH
BURWELL
Snailwell Jc.
Chippenham Jc.
NEWMARKET WARREN HILL
Warren Hill Jc.
NEWMARKET
KENNETT
HIGHAM
SAXHAM & RISBY
SWAFFHAMPRIOR
QUY
BOTTISHAM & LODE
SHARNBROOK
ST. NEOTS
G.N.
C A M B R I D G E
Coldham Lane Jc.
BARNWELL
MID. Goods
Loco Shed
G.N.Goods
L.N.W. Goods
G.E.Goods.
CAMBRIDGE
FULBOURNE
G.E.
DULLINGHAM
SIX MILE BOTTOM
MID.
Oakley Watertroughs
OAKLEY
TEMPSFORD
TOFT & KINGSTON (Goods)
L. & N.W.
OLD NORTH ROAD
LORDS BRIDGE
Shepreth Branch Jc.
Oakley Jc.
Bedford N.Jc.
Loco Shed
BEDFORD
GDS
Kempston Rd Jc.
ST JOHNS
Level Crossing
BLUNHAM
WILLINGTON
GAMLINGAY
SANDY
POTTON
SHELFORD
HARSTON
FOXTON
SHEPRETH
PAMPISFORD
WHITTLESFORD
LINTON
CARDINGTON
KEMPSTON & ELSTOW HALT
KEMPSTON HARDWICK HALT
WOOTTON BROADMEAD HALT
WOOTTON PILLINGE HALT
MILLBROOK
BIGGLESWADE
SOUTHILL
MELDRETH & MELBOURN
G.E.
HAVERHILL
CAVENDISH
BARTLOW
STURMER
C.V.
CLARE
STOKE
BIRDBROOK
B E D F O R D
SHEFFORD
ROYSTON
ASHWELL & MORDEN
G.N.
GREAT CHESTERFORD
ASHDON HALT
Ampthill Tun.
AMPTHILL
ARLESEY & SHEFFORD ROAD
SAFFRON WALDEN
YELDHAM
FLITWICK
HENLOW
THREE COUNTIES
BALDOCK
AUDLEY END
SIBLE & CASTLE HEDINGHAM
LETCHWORTH
NEWPORT
HARLINGTON
MID.Goods
Loco Shed.
HITCHIN
G.N.
HENHAM HALT
THAXTED
MILL ROAD HALT
CUTLERS GREEN HALT
HALSTEAD
BUNTINGFORD
WESTMILL
ELSENHAM
Summit
SIBLEYS FOR CHICKNEY & BROXTED
STEVENAGE
LEAGRAVE
DUNSTABLE
G.N.Goods.
Langley Watertroughs
Langley Jc.
BRAUGHING
STANDON
STANSTED
HOCKERILL HALT
EASTON LODGE
DUNMOW
BANNISTER GREEN HALT
RAYNE
BRAINTREE & BOCKING
LUTON
DUNSTABLE CHURCH STREET
KNEBWORTH
BISHOP'S STORTFORD
FELSTEAD
G.E.
STANE STREET HALT
TAKELEY
LUTON HOO
CHILTERN GREEN
H E R T F O R D
HADHAM
CRESSING
WHITE NOTLEY
HARPENDEN
Harpenden Jc.
WHEAT-HAMSTEAD
AYOT
Welwyn N.Tun.
Welwyn S.Tun.
WELWYN
Welwyn Viaduct
WIDFORD
SAWBRIDGEWORTH
REDBOURN
WELWYN GDN. CITY HALT
HERTFORD COWBRIDGE
MARDOCK
HERTFORD
G.E.
WARE
HARLOW
HATFIELD PEVEREL
GODWIN'S HALT
BEAUMONT'S HALT
Loco Shed
HERTINGFORDBURY
ST. MARGARETS
BURNT MILL
COLE GREEN
HATFIELD
ROYDON
RYE HOUSE
HEMEL HEMPSTED
HEATH PARK HALT
ST.ALBANS LONDON ROAD
ST. ALBANS
Loco Shed
NAST HYDE HALT
SMALLFORD
Pansbourne Tun.
Broxbourne Jc.
BROXBOURNE & HODDESDON
HILL END
G.N.
CHELMSFORD
BOXMOOR & HEMEL HEMPSTED
L.N.W.
PARK STREET & FROGMORE
NAPSBURY
G.N.
CUFFLEY & GOFFS OAK
NORTH WEALD
BLAKE HALL
ONGAR
MARGARETTING HALT
G.E.
KING'S LANGLEY & ABBOTS LANGLEY
BRICKET WOOD
RADLETT
POTTERS BAR
Potters Bar Tun.
CREWS HILL
CHESHUNT
Loco Shed
EPPING
E S S E X
THEOBALD'S GROVE
WALTHAM CROSS & ABBEY
Watford Tun.
Loco Shed
CALLOWLAND
Hadley H.Tun.
Hadley S. Tun.
HADLEY WOOD
GORDON HILL
FOURTY HILL
ENFIELD LOCK
THEYDON BOIS
INGATESTONE
WOODHAM FERRERS
CHORLEY WOOD & CHENIES
WATFORD JUNC
HIGH STR
NEW BARNET
GORDON HILL
ENFIELD TOWN
BRIMSDOWN
CHIGWELL LANE
CROXLEY GREEN
ELSTREE
HIGH BARNET
OAKLEIGH PARK
CHURCHBURY
PONDER'S END
LOUGHTON
BATTLESBRIDGE
RICKSMANWORTH
BUSHEY & OXHEY
Elstree Tun.
MID.
TOTTERIDGE
ENFIELD
RUSH HILL PARK
CHINGFORD
LOWER EDMONTON
SHENFIELD & HUTTON
Summit
BILLERICAY

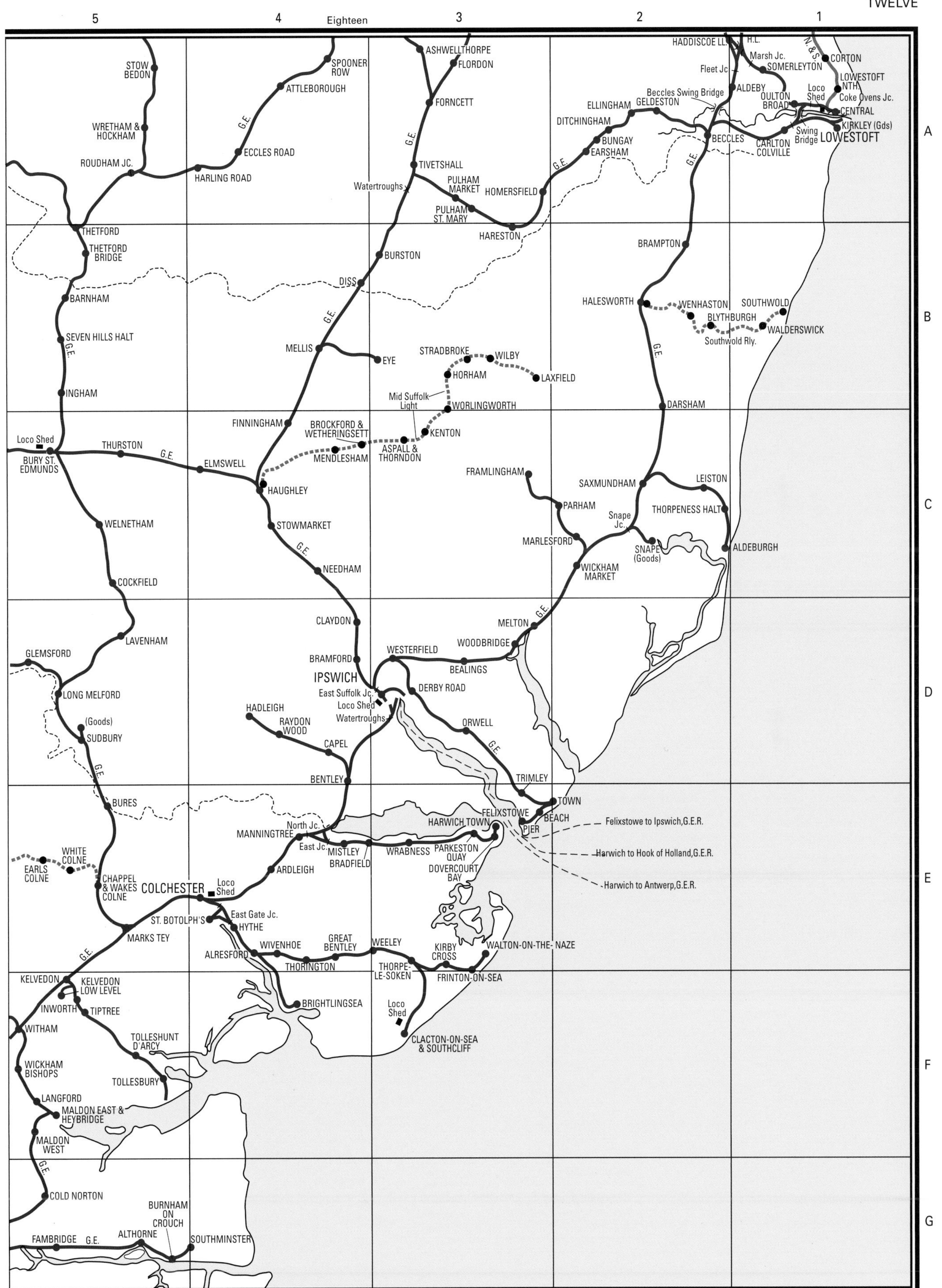
5
4
Eighteen
3
2
1
A
B
C
D
E
F
G
STOW BEDON
SPOONER ROW
ATTLEBOROUGH
ASHWELLTHORPE
FLORDON
FORNCETT
HADDISCOE LL.
H.L.
N & S
Marsh Jc.
SOMERLEYTON
CORTON
Fleet Jc.
ALDEBY
LOWESTOFT NTH.
Loco Shed
Coke Ovens Jc.
Beccles Swing Bridge
OULTON BROAD
CENTRAL
ELLINGHAM
GELDESTON
KIRKLEY (Gds)
DITCHINGHAM
Swing Bridge
LOWESTOFT
BECCLES
CARLTON COLVILLE
BUNGAY
EARSHAM
WRETHAM & HOCKHAM
G.E.
ECCLES ROAD
ROUDHAM JC.
HARLING ROAD
TIVETSHALL
Watertroughs
PULHAM MARKET
HOMERSFIELD
PULHAM ST. MARY
HARESTON
THETFORD
THETFORD BRIDGE
BURSTON
BRAMPTON
DISS
BARNHAM
HALESWORTH
WENHASTON
SOUTHWOLD
BLYTHBURGH
WALDERSWICK
Southwold Rly.
SEVEN HILLS HALT
MELLIS
EYE
STRADBROKE
WILBY
HORHAM
LAXFIELD
INGHAM
Mid Suffolk Light
WORLINGWORTH
DARSHAM
FINNINGHAM
BROCKFORD & WETHERINGSETT
KENTON
Loco Shed
THURSTON
MENDLESHAM
ASPALL & THORNDON
BURY ST. EDMUNDS
ELMSWELL
FRAMLINGHAM
LEISTON
SAXMUNDHAM
HAUGHLEY
PARHAM
THORPENESS HALT
WELNETHAM
Snape Jc.
STOWMARKET
MARLESFORD
SNAPE (Goods)
ALDEBURGH
WICKHAM MARKET
NEEDHAM
COCKFIELD
CLAYDON
MELTON
LAVENHAM
WOODBRIDGE
GLEMSFORD
BRAMFORD
WESTERFIELD
BEALINGS
IPSWICH
East Suffolk Jc.
DERBY ROAD
LONG MELFORD
Loco Shed
Watertroughs
HADLEIGH
RAYDON WOOD
ORWELL
(Goods)
SUDBURY
CAPEL
BENTLEY
TRIMLEY
BURES
TOWN
FELIXSTOWE
BEACH
HARWICH TOWN
PIER
Felixstowe to Ipswich, G.E.R.
North Jc.
MANNINGTREE
East Jc.
MISTLEY
BRADFIELD
WRABNESS
PARKESTON QUAY
Harwich to Hook of Holland, G.E.R.
WHITE COLNE
EARLS COLNE
ARDLEIGH
DOVERCOURT BAY
CHAPPEL & WAKES COLNE
COLCHESTER
Loco Shed
Harwich to Antwerp, G.E.R.
ST. BOTOLPH'S
East Gate Jc.
HYTHE
MARKS TEY
ALRESFORD
WIVENHOE
GREAT BENTLEY
WEELEY
KIRBY CROSS
WALTON-ON-THE-NAZE
THORINGTON
THORPE-LE-SOKEN
FRINTON-ON-SEA
KELVEDON
KELVEDON LOW LEVEL
INWORTH
TIPTREE
BRIGHTLINGSEA
Loco Shed
WITHAM
CLACTON-ON-SEA & SOUTHCLIFF
TOLLESHUNT D'ARCY
WICKHAM BISHOPS
TOLLESBURY
LANGFORD
MALDON EAST & HEYBRIDGE
MALDON WEST
COLD NORTON
BURNHAM ON CROUCH
FAMBRIDGE
ALTHORNE
SOUTHMINSTER

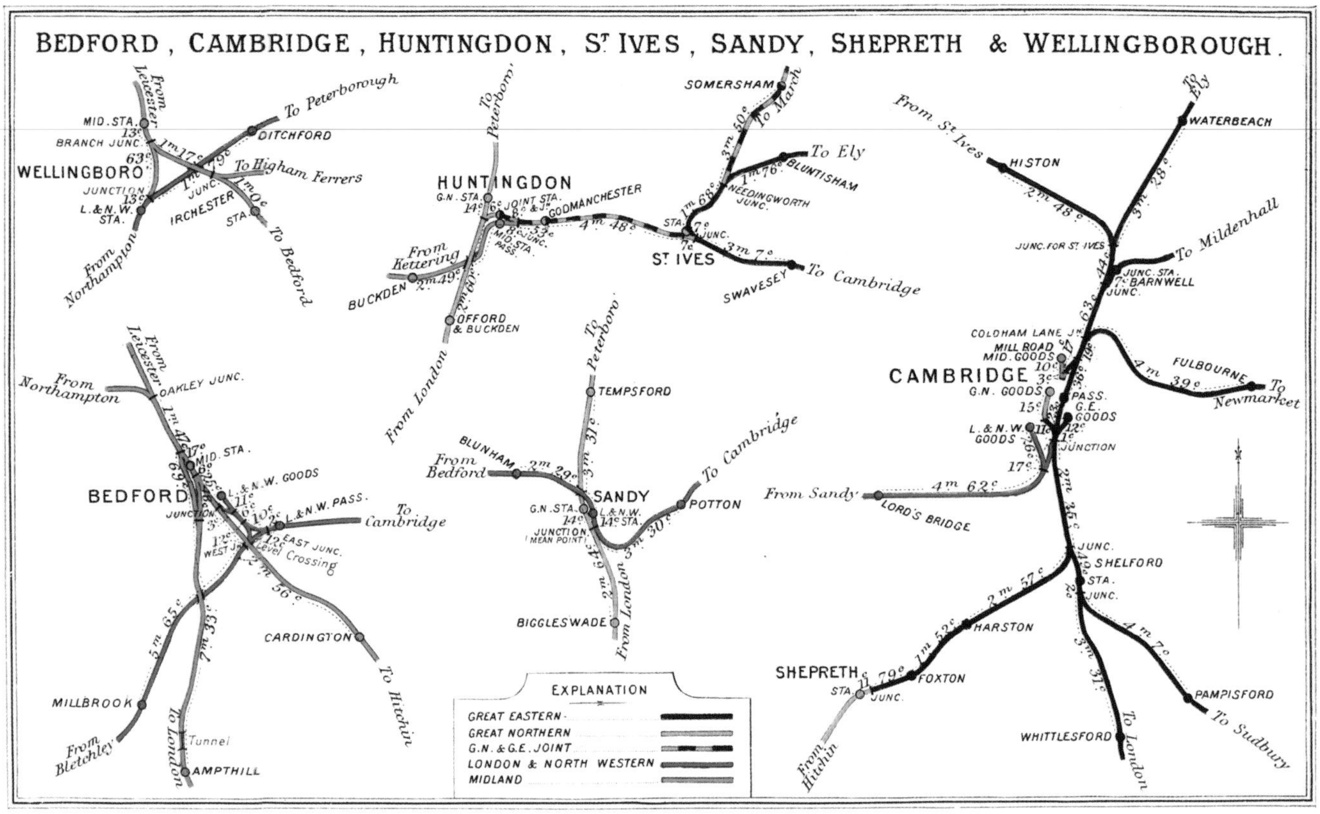
BEDFORD, CAMBRIDGE, HUNTINGDON, ST IVES, SANDY, SHEPRETH & WELLINGBOROUGH.
From Leicester
To Peterborough
MID. STA.
BRANCH JUNC.
DITCHFORD
WELLINGBORO'
To Higham Ferrers
JUNCTION
L.&N.W. STA.
IRCHESTER
JUNC.
STA.
From Northampton
To Bedford
To Peterboro'
HUNTINGDON
G.N. STA.
JOINT STA.
GODMANCHESTER
MID. STA.
PASS.
From Kettering
BUCKDEN
OFFORD & BUCKDEN
From London
SOMERSHAM
To March
To Ely
BLUNTISHAM
NEEDINGWORTH JUNC.
STA.
JUNC.
ST IVES
SWAVESEY
To Cambridge
From St Ives
HISTON
To Ely
WATERBEACH
JUNC. FOR ST IVES
To Mildenhall
JUNC. STA.
BARNWELL JUNC.
COLDHAM LANE JN.
MILL ROAD
MID. GOODS
CAMBRIDGE
G.N. GOODS
PASS.
G.E. GOODS
L.&N.W. GOODS
JUNCTION
FULBOURNE
To Newmarket
From Sandy
LORD'S BRIDGE
From Leicester
From Northampton
OAKLEY JUNC.
MID. STA.
L.&N.W. GOODS
BEDFORD
L.&N.W. PASS.
To Cambridge
JUNCTION
EAST JUNC.
WEST JN.
Level Crossing
CARDINGTON
MILLBROOK
From Bletchley
Tunnel
To London
AMPTHILL
To Hitchin
To Peterboro'
TEMPSFORD
BLUNHAM
From Bedford
SANDY
G.N. STA.
L.&N.W. STA.
JUNCTION (MEAN POINT)
To Cambridge
POTTON
BIGGLESWADE
From London
JUNC.
SHELFORD
STA.
JUNC.
HARSTON
SHEPRETH
STA.
JUNC.
FOXTON
From Hitchin
WHITTLESFORD
To London
PAMPISFORD
To Sudbury
EXPLANATION
GREAT EASTERN
GREAT NORTHERN
G.N. & G.E. JOINT
LONDON & NORTH WESTERN
MIDLAND

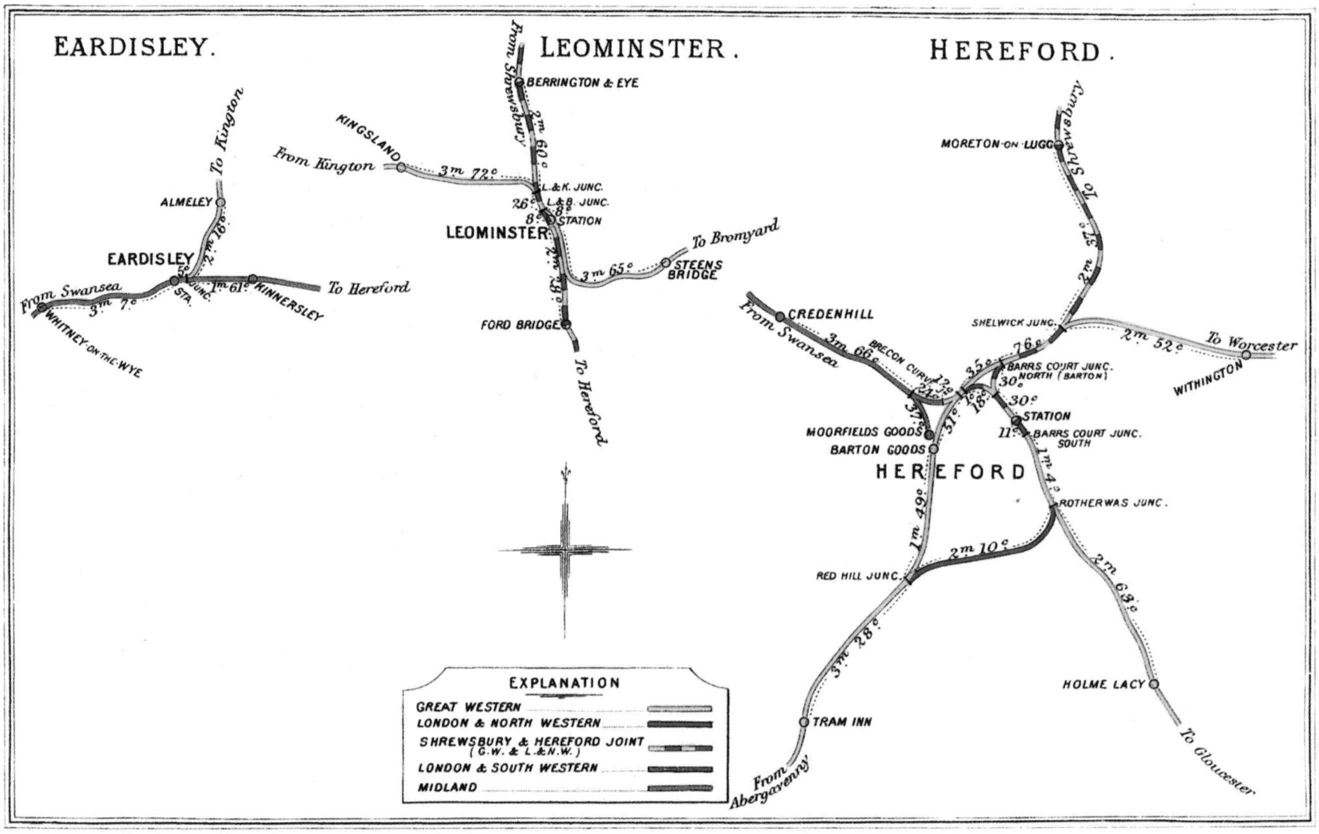
EARDISLEY.
LEOMINSTER.
HEREFORD.
To Kington
ALMELEY
EARDISLEY
From Swansea
STA.
JUNC.
KINNERSLEY
To Hereford
WHITNEY ON THE WYE
From Shrewsbury
BERRINGTON & EYE
KINGSLAND
From Kington
L.&K. JUNC.
L.&B. JUNC.
STATION
LEOMINSTER
To Bromyard
STEENS BRIDGE
FORD BRIDGE
To Hereford
To Shrewsbury
MORETON-ON-LUGG
CREDENHILL
From Swansea
BRECON CURVE
SHELWICK JUNC.
To Worcester
WITHINGTON
BARRS COURT JUNC. NORTH (BARTON)
STATION
BARRS COURT JUNC. SOUTH
MOORFIELDS GOODS
BARTON GOODS
HEREFORD
ROTHERWAS JUNC.
RED HILL JUNC.
HOLME LACY
TRAM INN
From Abergavenny
To Gloucester
EXPLANATION
GREAT WESTERN
LONDON & NORTH WESTERN
SHREWSBURY & HEREFORD JOINT (G.W. & L.&N.W.)
LONDON & SOUTH WESTERN
MIDLAND

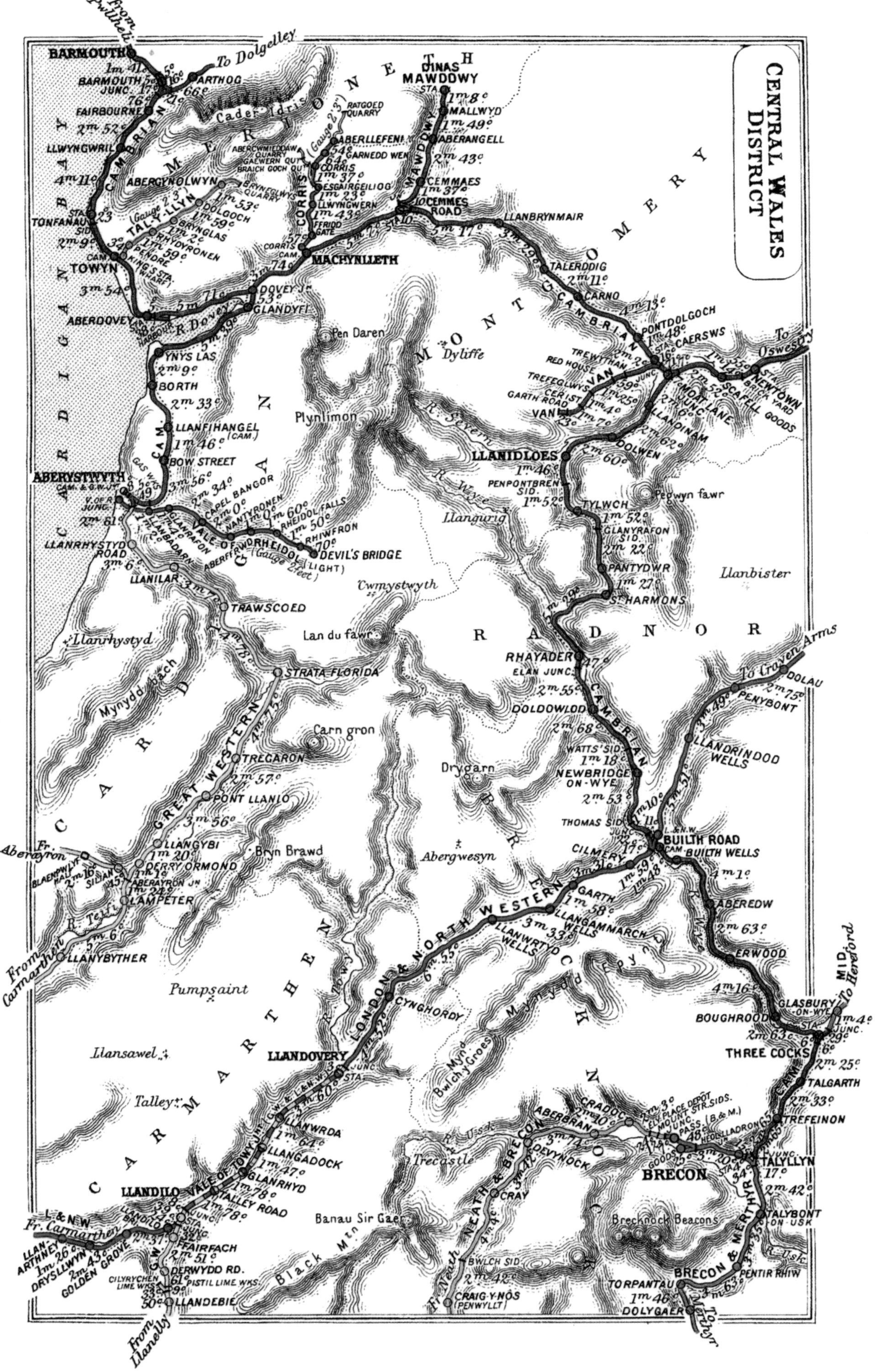
CENTRAL WALES DISTRICT
From Pwllheli
To Dolgelley
BARMOUTH
BARMOUTH JUNC.
ARTHOG
FAIRBOURNE
LLWYNGWRIL
Cader Idris
RATGOED QUARRY
ABERLLEFENI
GARNEDD WEN
CORRIS
ESGAIRGEILIOG
LLWYNGWERN
FFRIDD GATE
CORRIS
MACHYNLLETH
ABERCYNOLWYN
TALY-LLYN
DOLGOCH
BRYNGLAS
RHYDYRONEN
PENDRE
KING'S STA. (WHARF)
TONFANAU
TOWYN
ABERDOVEY
DOVEY JN
GLANDYFI
R. Dovey
DINAS MAWDDWY
MALLWYD
ABERANGELL
CEMMAES
CEMMES ROAD
LLANBRYNMAIR
TALERDDIG
CARNO
PONTDOLGOCH
CAERSWS
To Oswestry
NEWTOWN
SCAFELL GOODS
MOAT LANE JUNC.
LLANDINAM
DOLWEN
LLANIDLOES
TREWYTHAN
RED HOUSE
TREFEGLWYS
CERIST
GARTH ROAD
VAN
M E R I O N E T H
M O N T G O M E R Y
C A R D I G A N
R A D N O R
B R E C K N O C K
C A R M A R T H E N
CARDIGAN BAY
Pen Daren
Dyliffe
Plynlimon
R. Severn
R. Wye
Llangurig
Pegwyn fawr
PENPONTBREN SID.
TYLWCH
GLANYRAFON SID.
PANTYDWR
ST HARMONS
Llanbister
YNYS LAS
BORTH
LLANFIHANGEL (CAM.)
BOW STREET
ABERYSTWYTH
CAPEL BANGOR
NANTYRONEN
RHEIDOL FALLS
RHIWFRON
DEVIL'S BRIDGE
VALE OF RHEIDOL (LIGHT)
LLANBADARN
GLANRAFON
ABERFFRWD
LLANRHYSTYD ROAD
LLANILAR
TRAWSCOED
Cwmystwyth
Llanrhystyd
Lan du fawr
STRATA FLORIDA
Mynydd bach
RHAYADER
ELAN JUNC.
DOLDOWLOD
To Craven Arms
DOLAU
PENYBONT
LLANDRINDOD WELLS
Carn gron
TREGARON
GREAT WESTERN
PONT LLANIO
Drygarn
WATTS' SID.
NEWBRIDGE ON-WYE
THOMAS SID.
BUILTH ROAD
BUILTH WELLS
CILMERY
Abergwesyn
Bryn Brawd
Fr. Aberayron
LLANGYBI
DERRY ORMOND
ABERAYRON JN
LAMPETER
R. Teifi
From Carmarthen
LLANYBYTHER
GARTH
LLANGAMMARCH WELLS
LLANWRTYD WELLS
LONDON & NORTH WESTERN
ABEREDW
ERWOOD
To Hereford
MID
GLASBURY ON-WYE
BOUGHROOD
THREE COCKS
TALGARTH
TREFEINON
Pumpsaint
CYNGHORDY
Mynydd Eppynt
Mynd Bwlch y Groes
LLANDOVERY
Llansawel
Talley
LLANWRDA
LLANGADOCK
GLANRHYD
TALLEY ROAD
LLANDILO
VALE OF TOWY
CRADOC
ABERBRAN
DEVYNOCK
Trecastle
NEATH & BRECON
CRAY
BRECON
TALYLLYN
TALYBONT ON-USK
Brecknock Beacons
BRECON & MERTHYR
PENTIR RHIW
TORPANTAU
DOLYGAER
To Merthyr
Banau Sir Gaer
Black Mtn
BWLCH SID.
CRAIG-Y-NOS (PENWYLLT)
L. & N.W.
Fr. Carmarthen
LLANARTHNEY
DRYSLLWYN
GOLDEN GROVE
FFAIRFACH
DERWYDD RD.
CILYRYCHEN LIME WKS.
PISTIL LIME WKS.
LLANDEBIE
From Llanelly

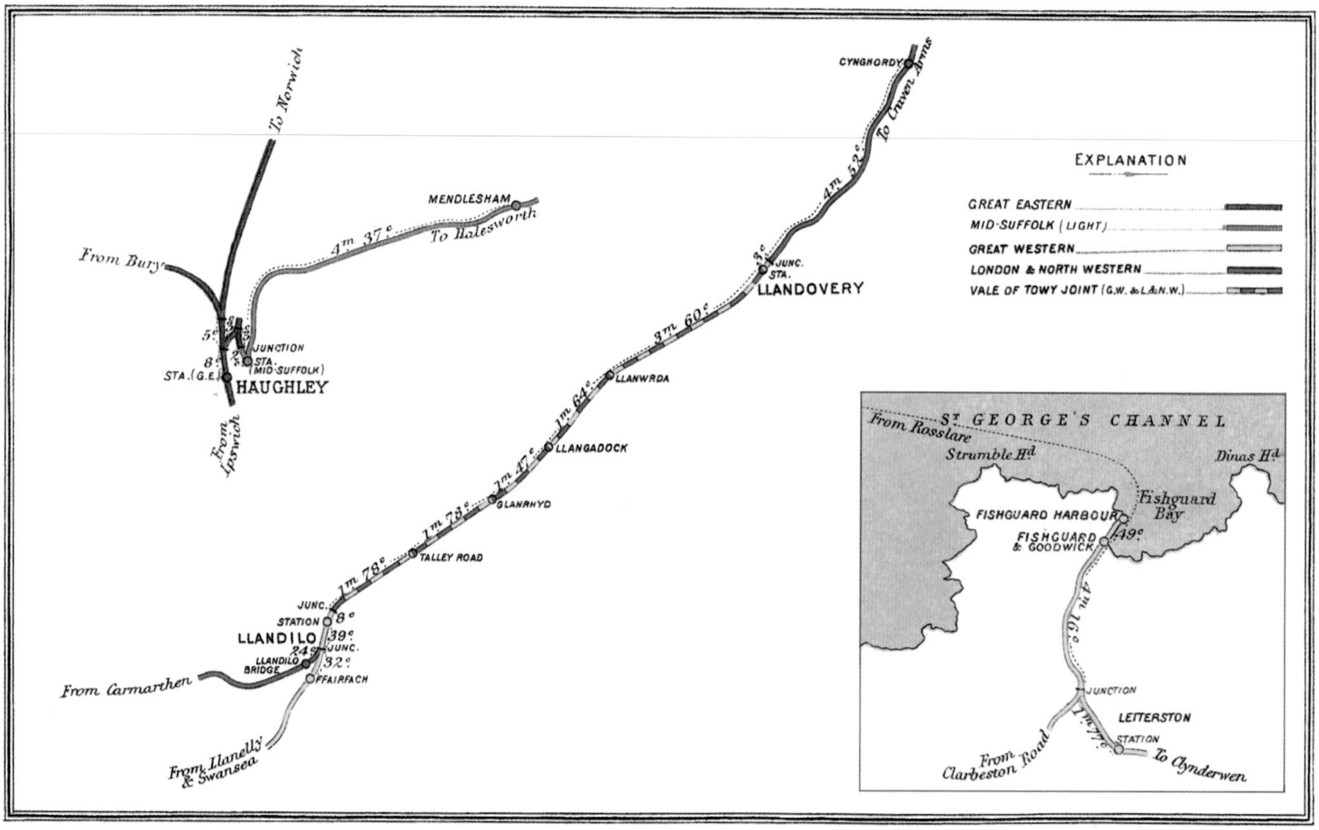

EXPLANATION

GREAT EASTERN
MID-SUFFOLK (LIGHT)
GREAT WESTERN
LONDON & NORTH WESTERN
VALE OF TOWY JOINT (G.W. & L.& N.W.)

Haughley–Llandilo–Llandovery–Fishguard

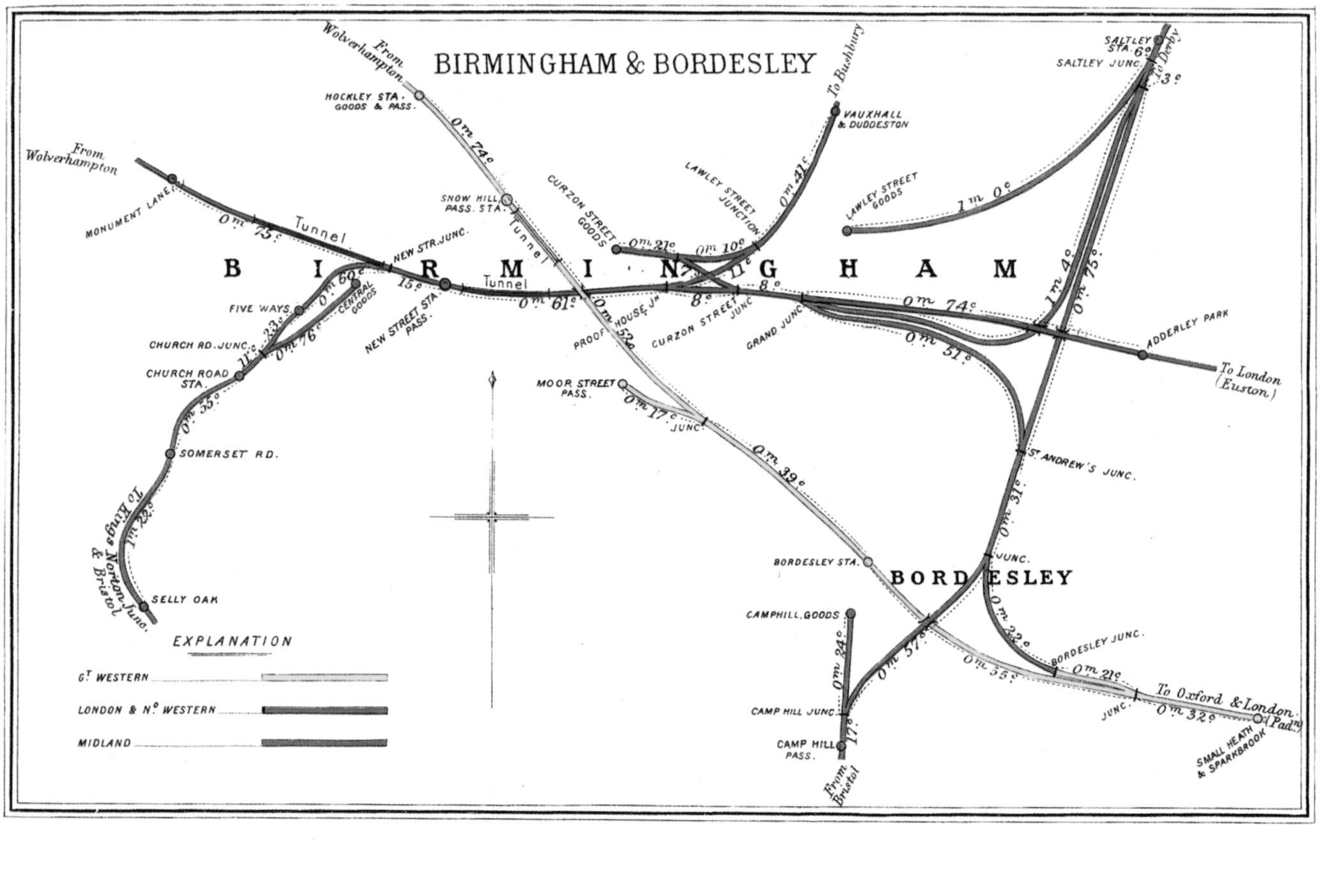

BIRMINGHAM & BORDESLEY

EXPLANATION

G.T WESTERN
LONDON & N.O WESTERN
MIDLAND

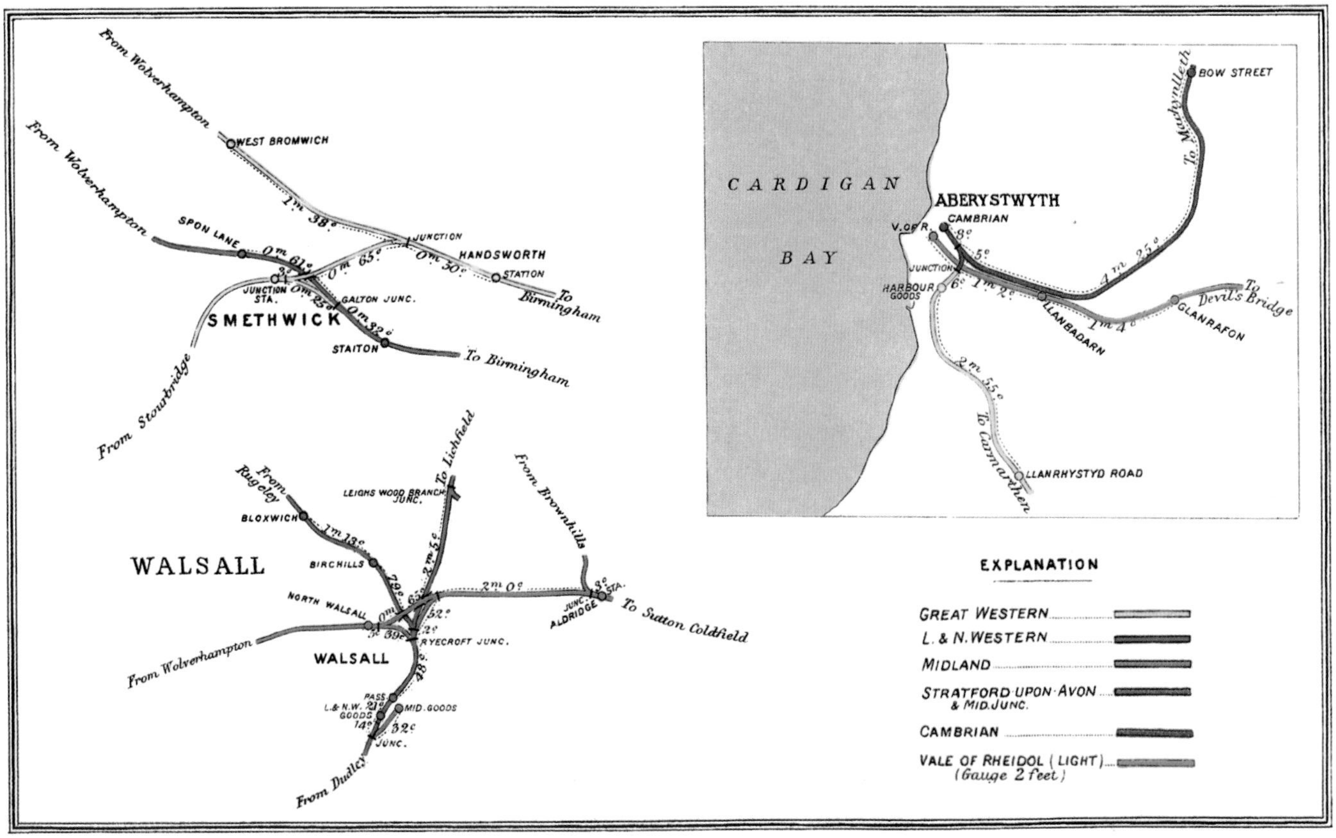

EXPLANATION

GREAT WESTERN

L. & N. WESTERN

MIDLAND

STRATFORD UPON AVON & MID. JUNC.

CAMBRIAN

VALE OF RHEIDOL (LIGHT) (Gauge 2 feet)

**Walsall–Smethwick–Aberystwyth**

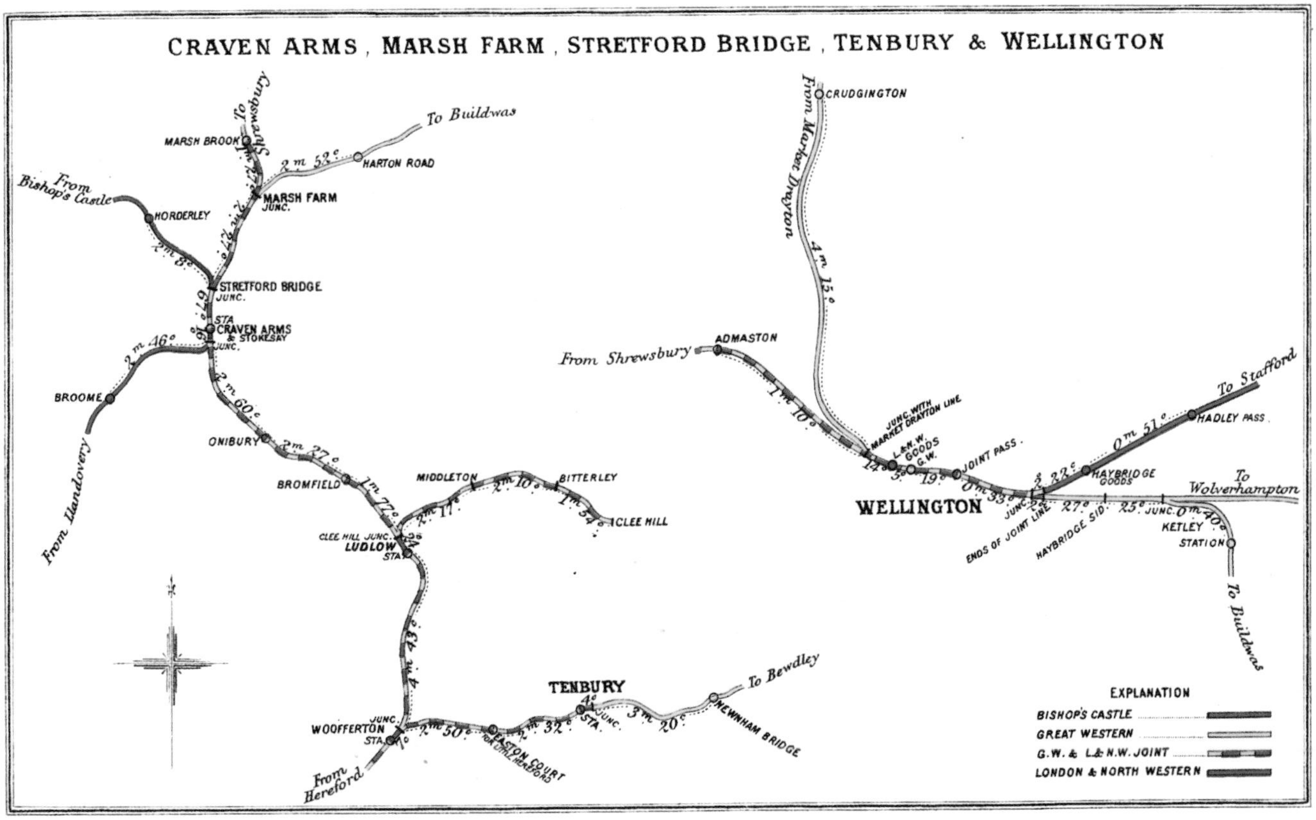

## CRAVEN ARMS, MARSH FARM, STRETFORD BRIDGE, TENBURY & WELLINGTON

EXPLANATION

BISHOP'S CASTLE

GREAT WESTERN

G.W. & L.& N.W. JOINT

LONDON & NORTH WESTERN

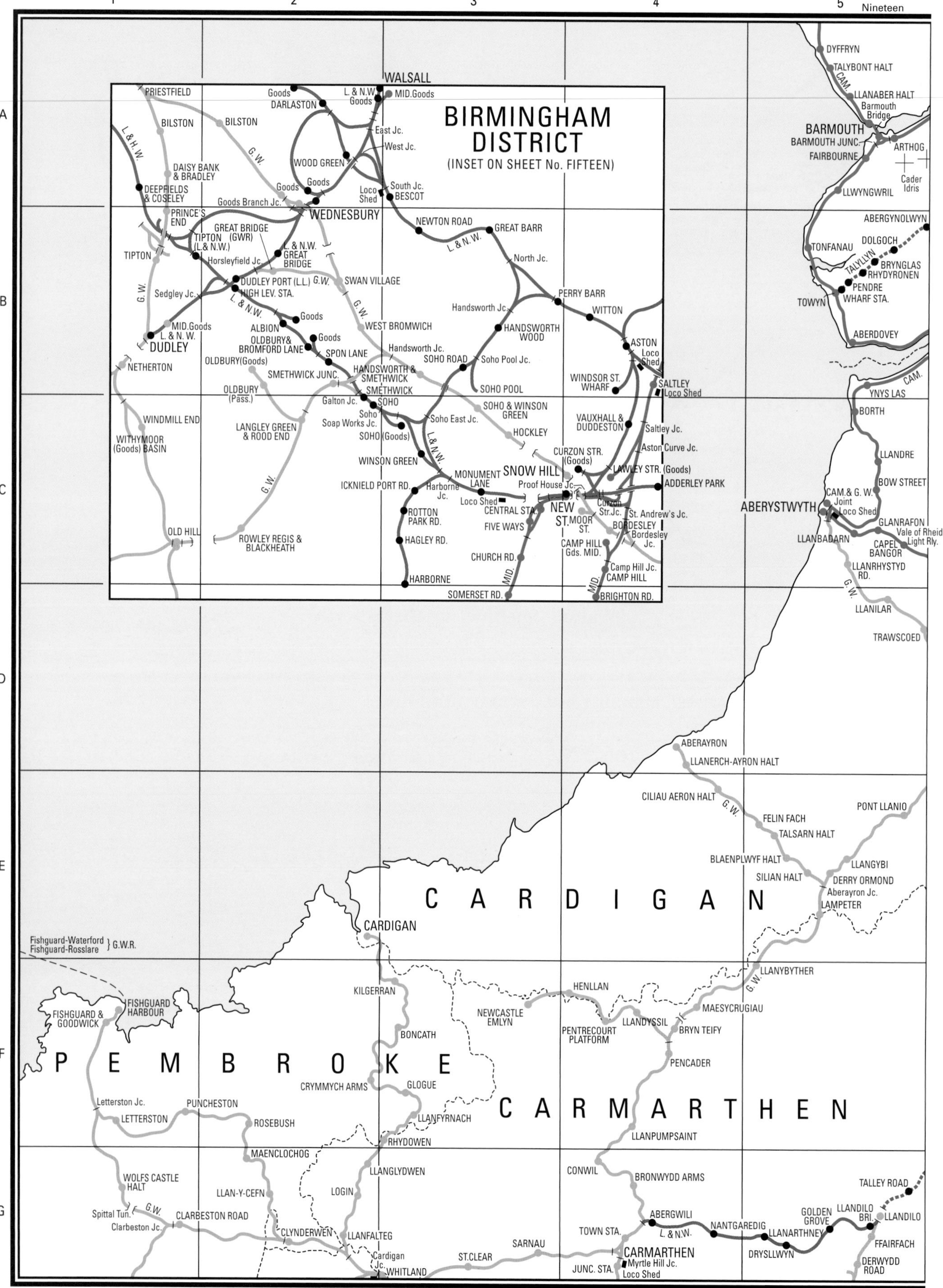
1
2
3
4
5
Nineteen
A
B
C
D
E
F
G
BIRMINGHAM
DISTRICT
(INSET ON SHEET No. FIFTEEN)
WALSALL
PRIESTFIELD
Goods
DARLASTON
L. & N.W. Goods
MID.Goods
BILSTON
BILSTON
L. & H.W.
G.W.
East Jc.
West Jc.
WOOD GREEN
DAISY BANK & BRADLEY
DEEPFIELDS & COSELEY
Goods
Goods
Loco Shed
South Jc.
BESCOT
Goods Branch Jc.
WEDNESBURY
PRINCE'S END
GREAT BRIDGE (GWR)
TIPTON (L.& N.W.)
L. & N.W. GREAT BRIDGE
NEWTON ROAD
GREAT BARR
L. & N.W.
TIPTON
Horsleyfield Jc.
North Jc.
G.W.
Sedgley Jc.
DUDLEY PORT (L.L.)
HIGH LEV. STA.
G.W.
SWAN VILLAGE
PERRY BARR
WITTON
L. & N.W.
Handsworth Jc.
G.W.
Goods
MID.Goods
L. & N. W.
DUDLEY
ALBION
WEST BROMWICH
HANDSWORTH WOOD
OLDBURY& BROMFORD LANE
Goods
ASTON
SPON LANE
Handsworth Jc.
Loco Shed
NETHERTON
OLDBURY(Goods)
SOHO ROAD
Soho Pool Jc.
SMETHWICK JUNC.
HANDSWORTH & SMETHWICK
WINDSOR ST. WHARF
SMETHWICK
SOHO POOL
SALTLEY
Loco Shed
OLDBURY (Pass.)
Galton Jc.
SOHO
SOHO & WINSON GREEN
WINDMILL END
Soho Soap Works Jc.
Soho East Jc.
VAUXHALL & DUDDESTON
LANGLEY GREEN & ROOD END
HOCKLEY
Saltley Jc.
SOHO (Goods)
WITHYMOOR (Goods) BASIN
L&N.W.
Aston Curve Jc.
CURZON STR. (Goods)
WINSON GREEN
LAWLEY STR. (Goods)
SNOW HILL
MONUMENT LANE
ICKNIELD PORT RD.
Harborne Jc.
Proof House Jc.
ADDERLEY PARK
G.W.
Loco Shed
CENTRAL STA.
NEW ST.
Curzon Str.Jc.
St. Andrew's Jc.
ROTTON PARK RD.
FIVE WAYS
MOOR ST.
BORDESLEY
OLD HILL
Bordesley Jc.
ROWLEY REGIS & BLACKHEATH
HAGLEY RD.
CAMP HILL Gds. MID.
CHURCH RD.
Camp Hill Jc.
CAMP HILL
HARBORNE
MID.
MID.
SOMERSET RD.
BRIGHTON RD.
DYFFRYN
TALYBONT HALT
CAM.
LLANABER HALT
Barmouth Bridge
BARMOUTH
BARMOUTH JUNC.
ARTHOG
FAIRBOURNE
Cader Idris
LLWYNGWRIL
ABERGYNOLWYN
DOLGOCH
TONFANAU
TALYLLYN
BRYNGLAS
RHYDYRONEN
PENDRE
TOWYN
WHARF STA.
ABERDOVEY
CAM.
YNYS LAS
BORTH
LLANDRE
BOW STREET
CAM.& G. W. Joint
Loco Shed
ABERYSTWYTH
GLANRAFON
Vale of Rheidol Light Rly.
LLANBADARN
CAPEL BANGOR
LLANRHYSTYD RD.
G.W.
LLANILAR
TRAWSCOED
ABERAYRON
LLANERCH-AYRON HALT
CILIAU AERON HALT
G.W.
PONT LLANIO
FELIN FACH
TALSARN HALT
BLAENPLWYF HALT
LLANGYBI
SILIAN HALT
DERRY ORMOND
Aberayron Jc.
LAMPETER
C A R D I G A N
CARDIGAN
Fishguard-Waterford
Fishguard-Rosslare
G.W.R.
LLANYBYTHER
G.W.
KILGERRAN
HENLLAN
MAESYCRUGIAU
FISHGUARD HARBOUR
FISHGUARD & GOODWICK
NEWCASTLE EMLYN
PENTRECOURT PLATFORM
LLANDYSSIL
BRYN TEIFY
BONCATH
P E M B R O K E
PENCADER
CRYMMYCH ARMS
GLOGUE
Letterston Jc.
PUNCHESTON
LETTERSTON
ROSEBUSH
LLANFYRNACH
C A R M A R T H E N
LLANPUMPSAINT
RHYDOWEN
MAENCLOCHOG
LLANGLYDWEN
CONWIL
BRONWYDD ARMS
WOLFS CASTLE HALT
TALLEY ROAD
LLAN-Y-CEFN
LOGIN
Spittal Tun.
G.W.
CLARBESTON ROAD
Clarbeston Jc.
ABERGWILI
GOLDEN GROVE
LLANDILO BRI.
LLANDILO
NANTGAREDIG
TOWN STA.
L. & N.W.
LLANARTHNEY
CLYNDERWEN
LLANFALTEG
SARNAU
DRYSLLWYN
FFAIRFACH
Cardigan Jc.
ST.CLEAR
CARMARTHEN
Myrtle Hill Jc.
Loco Shed
JUNC. STA.
DERWYDD ROAD
WHITLAND
Seven

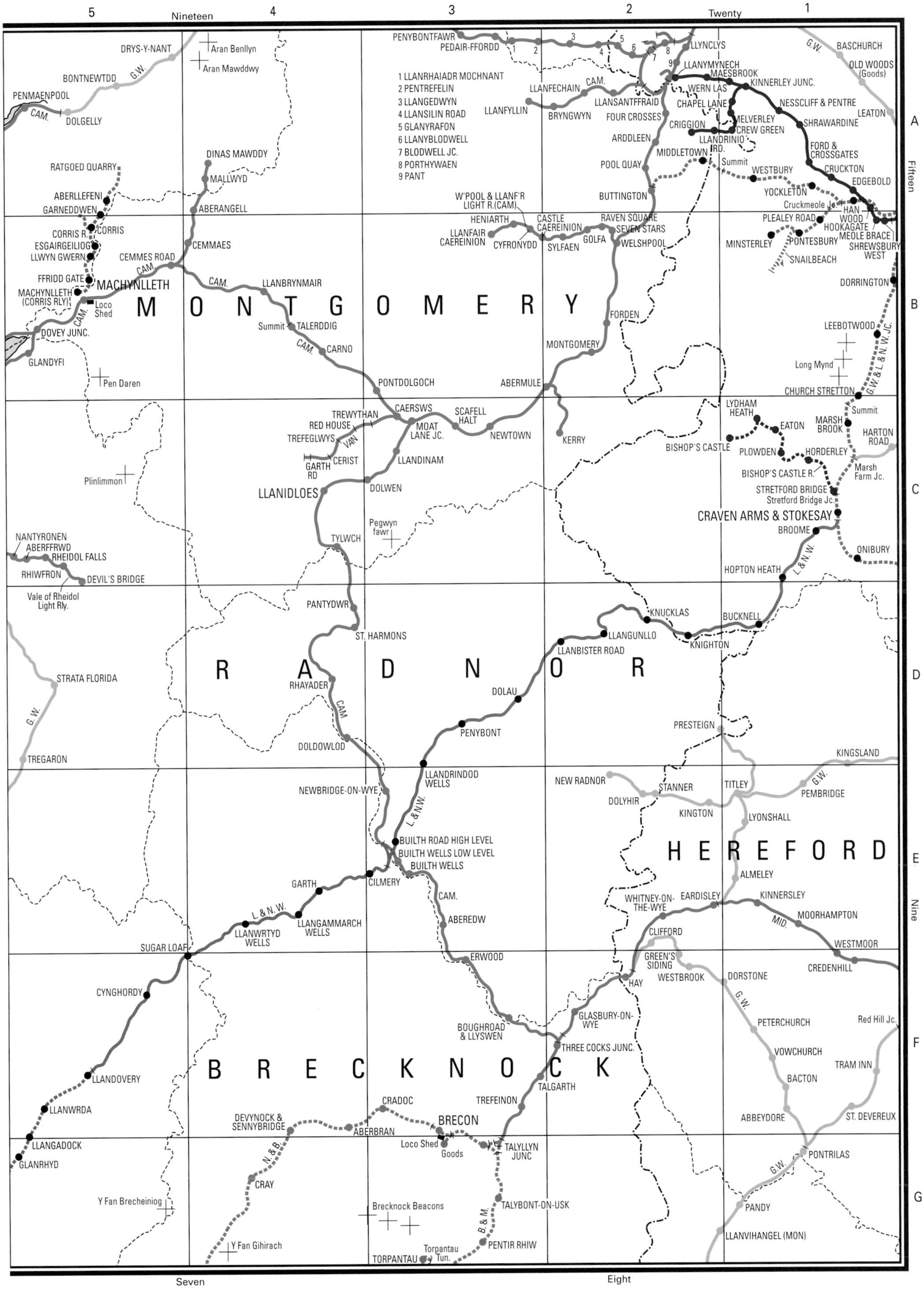

## FOURTEEN

5 Nineteen 4 3 2 Twenty 1

A B C D E F G

Fifteen Nine

Seven Eight

1 LLANRHAIADR MOCHNANT
2 PENTREFELIN
3 LLANGEDWYN
4 LLANSILIN ROAD
5 GLANYRAFON
6 LLANYBLODWELL
7 BLODWELL JC.
8 PORTHYWAEN
9 PANT

**MONTGOMERY**

**RADNOR**

**BRECKNOCK**

**HEREFORD**

DRYS-Y-NANT
G.W.
Aran Benllyn
Aran Mawddwy
BONTNEWTDD
PENMAENPOOL
CAM.
DOLGELLY
DINAS MAWDDY
MALLWYD
ABERANGELL
RATGOED QUARRY
ABERLLEFENI
GARNEDDWEN
CORRIS R.
CORRIS
ESGAIRGEILIOG
LLWYN GWERN
CEMMES ROAD
CEMMAES
FFRIDD GATE
MACHYNLLETH
MACHYNLLETH (CORRIS RLY)
Loco Shed
DOVEY JUNC.
GLANDYFI
Pen Daren
LLANBRYNMAIR
Summit
TALERDDIG
CARNO
PONTDOLGOCH
CAERSWS
TREWYTHAN
RED HOUSE
TREFEGLWYS
VAN
GARTH RD
CERIST
MOAT LANE JC.
SCAFELL HALT
NEWTOWN
LLANDINAM
DOLWEN
LLANIDLOES
Plinlimmon
Pegwyn fawr
TYLWCH
NANTYRONEN
ABERFFRWD
RHEIDOL FALLS
RHIWFRON
DEVIL'S BRIDGE
Vale of Rheidol Light Rly.
PANTYDWR
ST. HARMONS
STRATA FLORIDA
TREGARON
RHAYADER
DOLDOWLOD
NEWBRIDGE-ON-WYE
PENYBONTFAWR
PEDAIR-FFORDD
LLANFECHAIN
LLANFYLLIN
BRYNGWYN
LLANSANTFFRAID
FOUR CROSSES
ARDDLEEN
POOL QUAY
BUTTINGTON
W'POOL & LLANF'R LIGHT R.(CAM)
HENIARTH
LLANFAIR CAEREINION
CYFRONYDD
CASTLE CAEREINION
SYLFAEN
GOLFA
RAVEN SQUARE
SEVEN STARS
WELSHPOOL
FORDEN
MONTGOMERY
ABERMULE
KERRY
LLYNCLYS
LLANYMYNECH
MAESBROOK
WERN LAS
CHAPEL LANE
CRIGGION
MELVERLEY
CREW GREEN
LLANDRINIO RD.
MIDDLETOWN
Summit
WESTBURY
YOCKLETON
Cruckmeole Jc.
KINNERLEY JUNC.
NESSCLIFF & PENTRE
SHRAWARDINE
FORD & CROSSGATES
CRUCKTON
EDGEBOLD
HANWOOD
HOOKAGATE
MEOLE BRACE
SHREWSBURY WEST
BASCHURCH
OLD WOODS (Goods)
LEATON
PLEALEY ROAD
MINSTERLEY
PONTESBURY
SNAILBEACH
DORRINGTON
LEEBOTWOOD
G.W. & L.& N.W. JC.
Long Mynd
CHURCH STRETTON
Summit
LYDHAM HEATH
EATON
MARSH BROOK
HARTON ROAD
BISHOP'S CASTLE
PLOWDEN
HORDERLEY
BISHOP'S CASTLE R.
Marsh Farm Jc.
STRETFORD BRIDGE
Stretford Bridge Jc.
CRAVEN ARMS & STOKESAY
BROOME
ONIBURY
HOPTON HEATH
L.& N.W.
KNUCKLAS
BUCKNELL
LLANGUNLLO
KNIGHTON
LLANBISTER ROAD
DOLAU
PENYBONT
LLANDRINDOD WELLS
PRESTEIGN
KINGSLAND
NEW RADNOR
STANNER
TITLEY
PEMBRIDGE
DOLYHIR
KINGTON
LYONSHALL
BUILTH ROAD HIGH LEVEL
BUILTH WELLS LOW LEVEL
BUILTH WELLS
GARTH
CILMERY
ABEREDW
LLANGAMMARCH WELLS
LLANWRTYD WELLS
SUGAR LOAF
ERWOOD
ALMELEY
WHITNEY-ON-THE-WYE
EARDISLEY
KINNERSLEY
MID.
MOORHAMPTON
WESTMOOR
CREDENHILL
CLIFFORD
GREEN'S SIDING
WESTBROOK
DORSTONE
HAY
GLASBURY-ON-WYE
BOUGHROAD & LLYSWEN
THREE COCKS JUNC.
PETERCHURCH
Red Hill Jc.
VOWCHURCH
TRAM INN
BACTON
ABBEYDORE
ST. DEVEREUX
PONTRILAS
PANDY
LLANVIHANGEL (MON)
CYNGHORDY
LLANDOVERY
LLANWRDA
LLANGADOCK
GLANRHYD
TALGARTH
TREFEINON
CRADOC
DEVYNOCK & SENNYBRIDGE
ABERBRAN
BRECON
Loco Shed
Goods
TALYLLYN JUNC
N.& B.
CRAY
Y Fan Brecheiniog
Brecknock Beacons
TALYBONT-ON-USK
B.& M.
PENTIR RHIW
Y Fan Gihirach
TORPANTAU
Torpantau Tun.

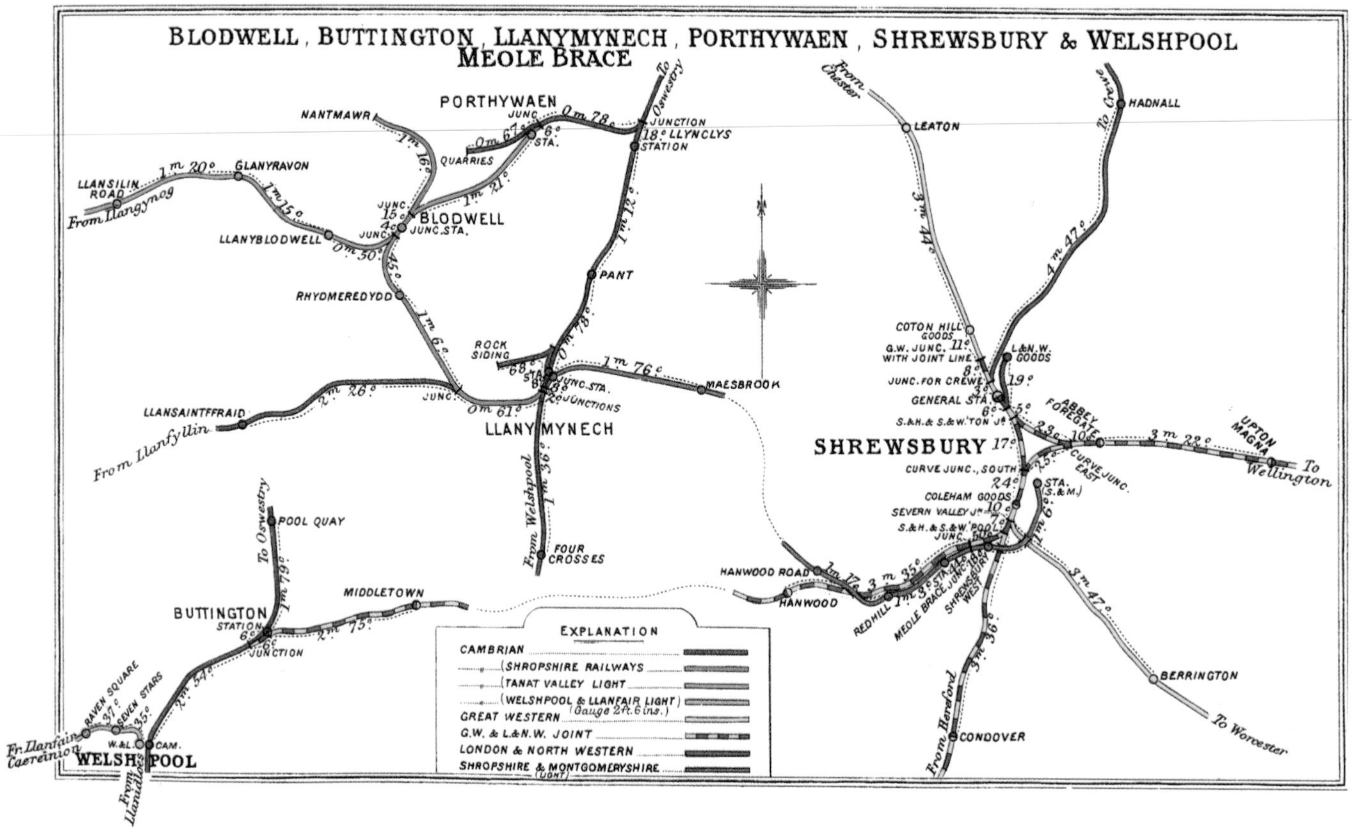

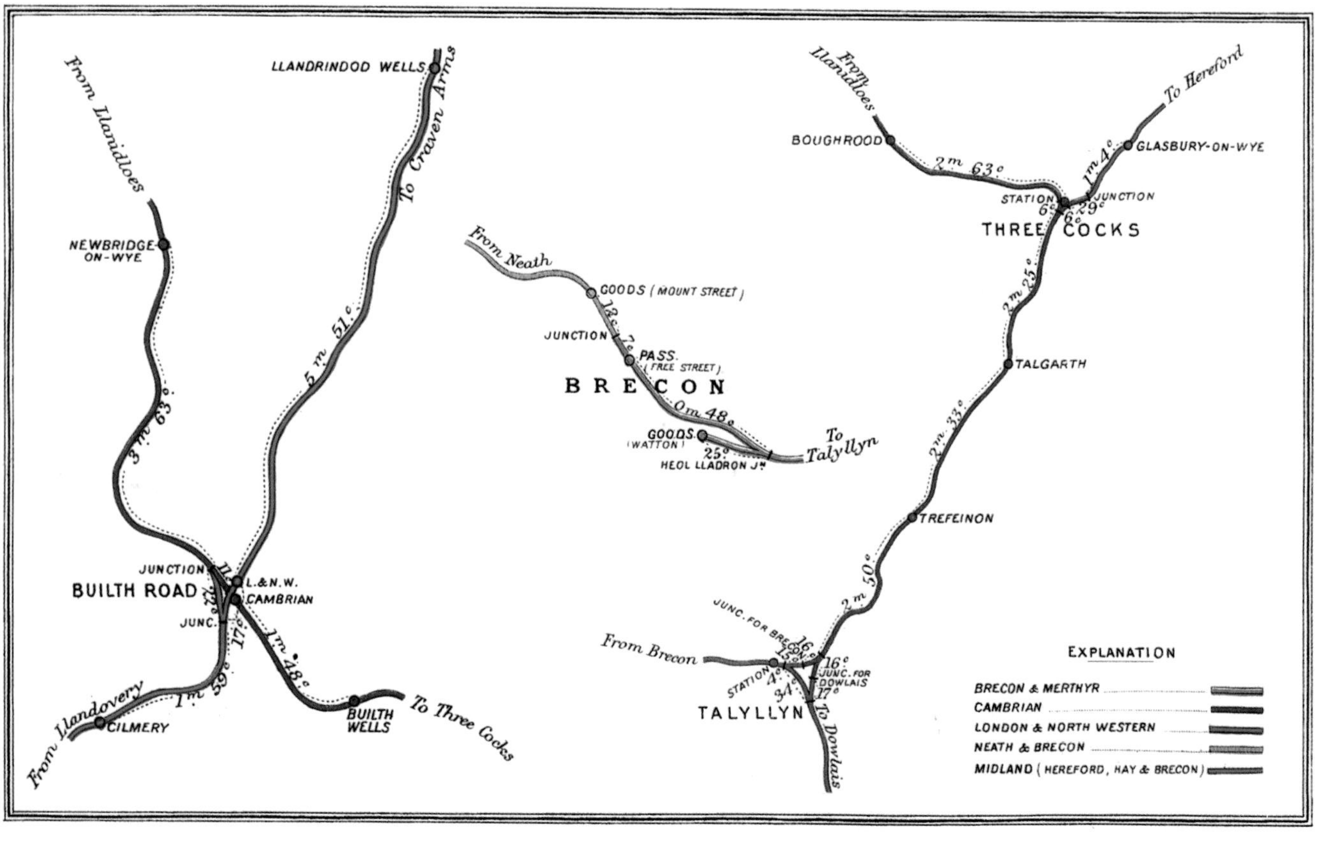

BLODWELL, BUTTINGTON, LLANYMYNECH, PORTHYWAEN, SHREWSBURY & WELSHPOOL
MEOLE BRACE

Builth Road–Brecon–Talyllyn–Three Cocks

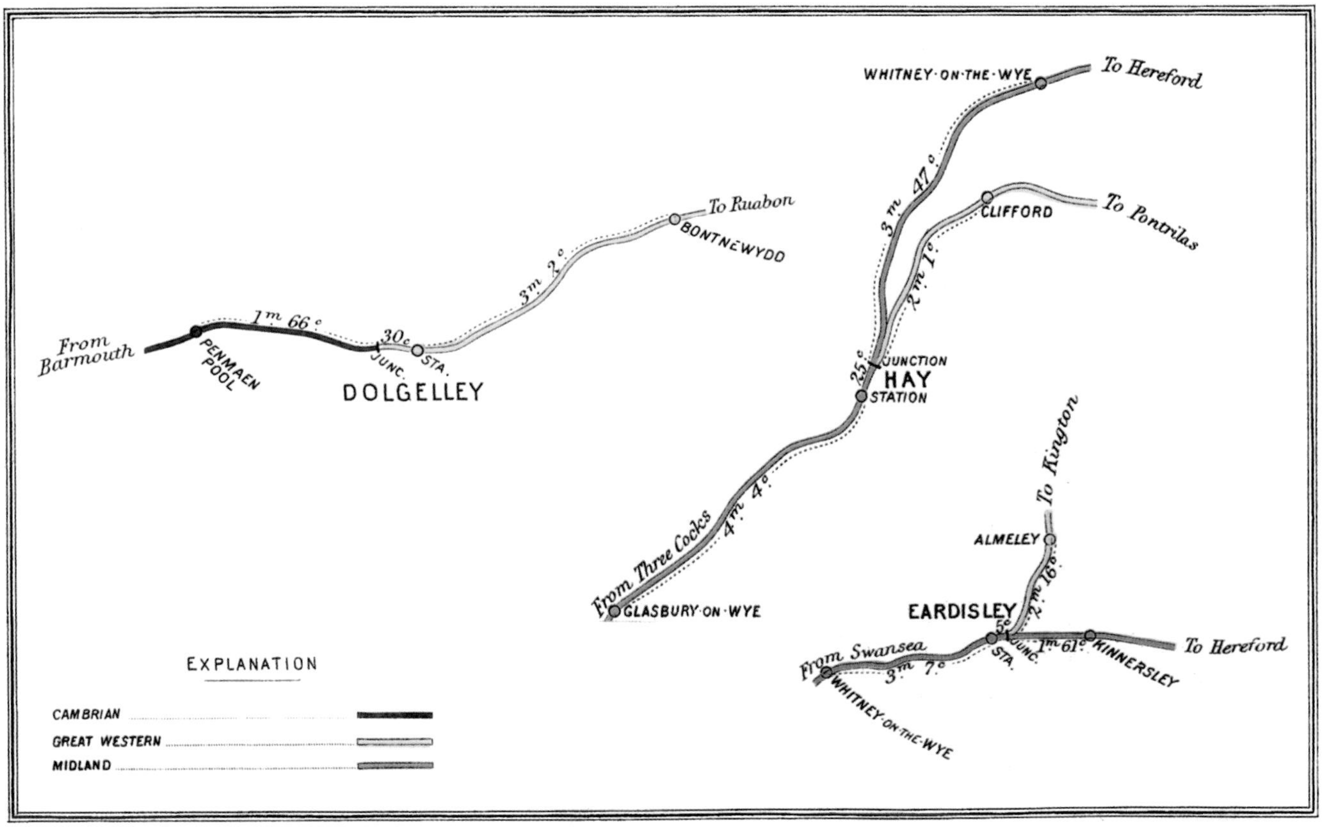

**Dolgelley–Hay–Eardisley**

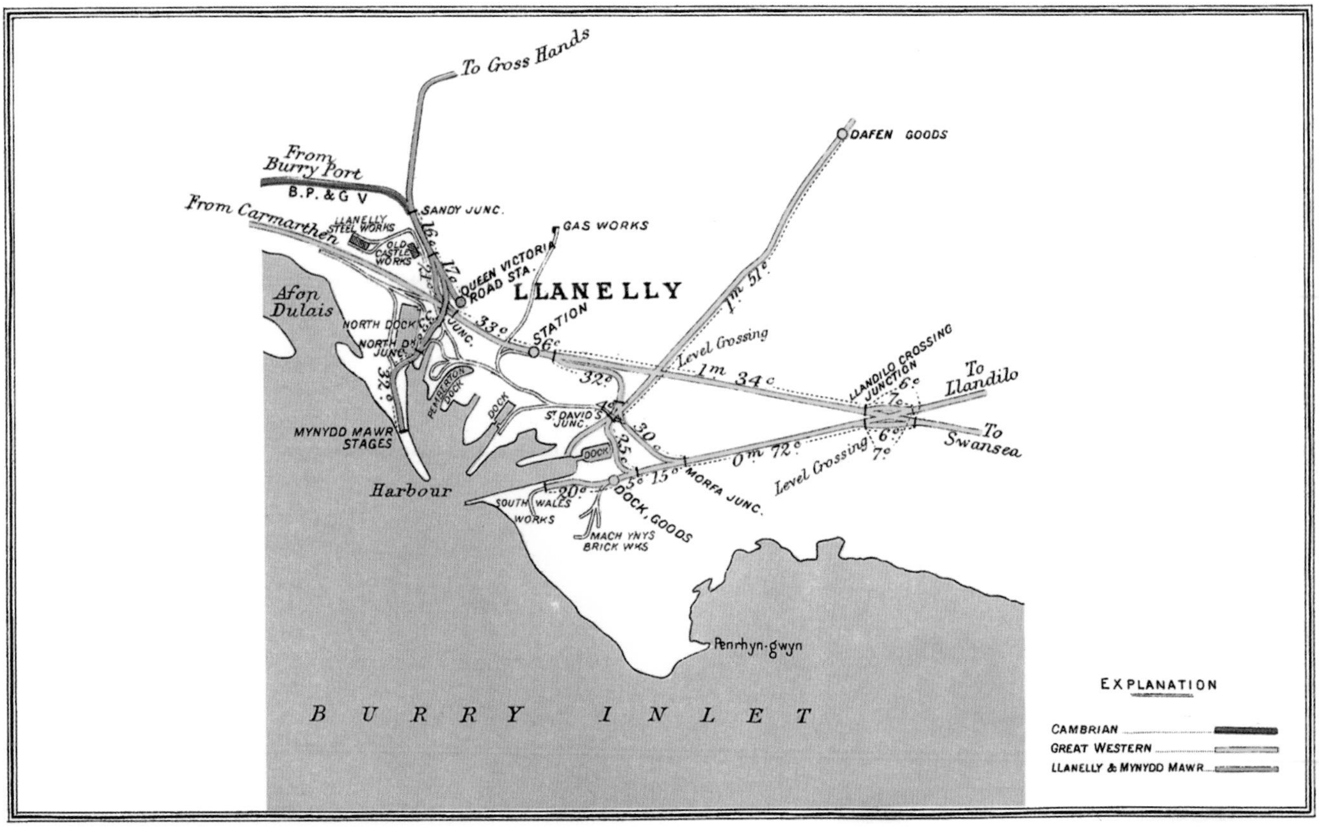

**Llanelly**

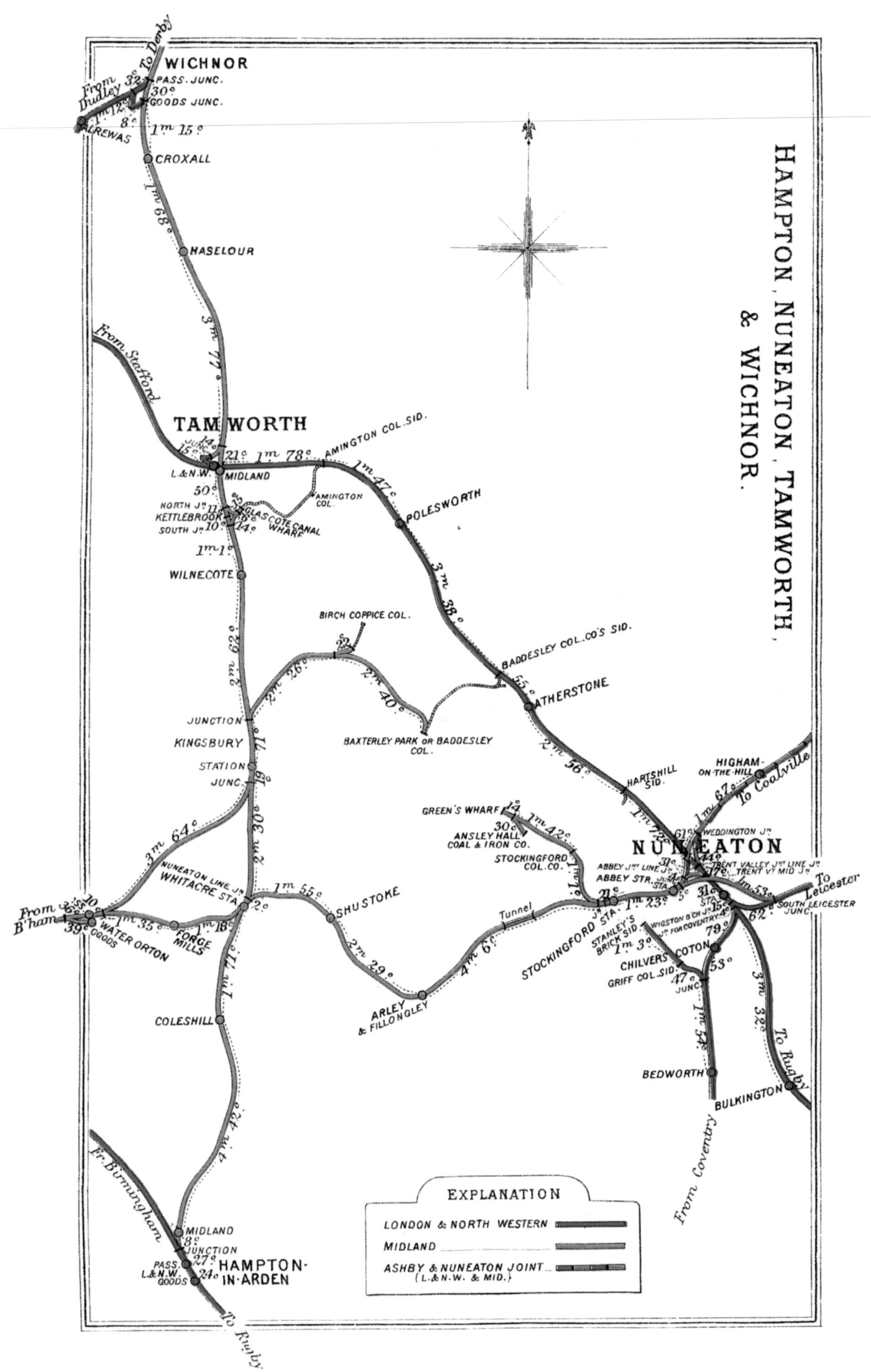
HAMPTON, NUNEATON, TAMWORTH, & WICHNOR.
WICHNOR
PASS. JUNC.
GOODS JUNC.
CROXALL
HASELOUR
From Stafford
TAMWORTH
L.&N.W.
MIDLAND
AMINGTON COL. SID.
AMINGTON COL.
POLESWORTH
NORTH JN.
KETTLEBROOK
SOUTH JN.
GLASCOTE CANAL WHARF
WILNECOTE
BIRCH COPPICE COL.
BADDESLEY COL. CO'S SID.
ATHERSTONE
BAXTERLEY PARK OR BADDESLEY COL.
JUNCTION
KINGSBURY
STATION
JUNC.
HARTSHILL SID.
HIGHAM-ON-THE-HILL
To Coalville
WEDDINGTON JN.
GREEN'S WHARF
ANSLEY HALL COAL & IRON CO.
STOCKINGFORD COL. CO.
NUNEATON
ABBEY JN. LINE JN.
ABBEY STR. STA.
TRENT VALLEY JN. LINE JN.
TRENT VY. MID JN.
To Leicester
SOUTH LEICESTER JUNC.
NUNEATON LINE JN.
WHITACRE STA.
From B'ham
WATER ORTON
GOODS
FORGE MILLS
SHUSTOKE
Tunnel
STOCKINGFORD STA.
STANLEY'S BRICK SID.
WIGSTON B'CH JN.
JN. FOR COVENTRY
COTON
CHILVERS
GRIFF COL. SID.
JUNC.
ARLEY & FILLONGLEY
COLESHILL
BEDWORTH
BULKINGTON
To Rugby
From Coventry
Fr. Birmingham
MIDLAND
JUNCTION
PASS.
L.&N.W.
GOODS
HAMPTON-IN-ARDEN
To Rugby
EXPLANATION
LONDON & NORTH WESTERN
MIDLAND
ASHBY & NUNEATON JOINT (L.&N.W. & MID.)

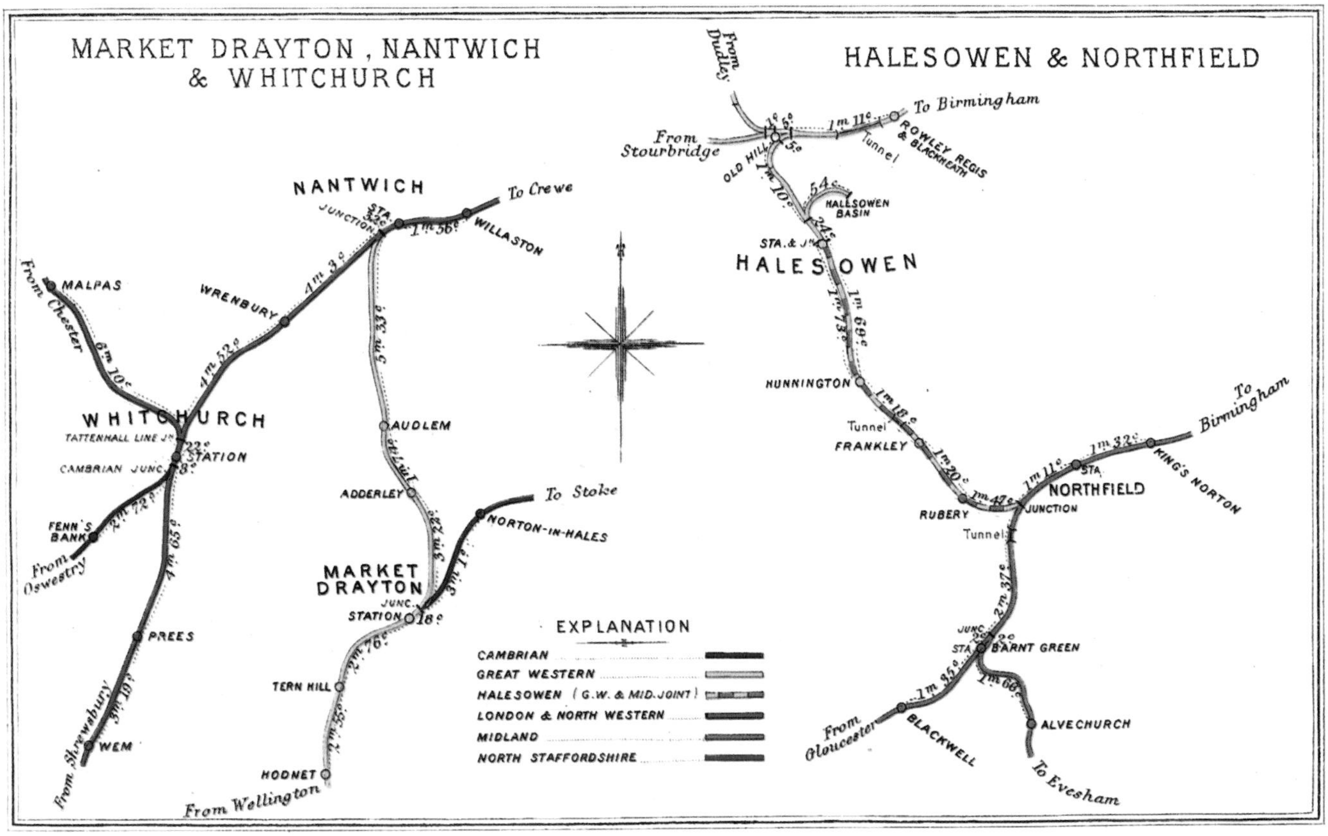
MARKET DRAYTON, NANTWICH & WHITCHURCH
NANTWICH
To Crewe
WILLASTON
WRENBURY
From Chester
MALPAS
WHITCHURCH
TATTENHALL LINE Jn.
STATION
CAMBRIAN JUNC.
FENN'S BANK
From Oswestry
PREES
WEM
From Shrewsbury
AUDLEM
ADDERLEY
To Stoke
NORTON-IN-HALES
MARKET DRAYTON
JUNC.
STATION
TERN HILL
HODNET
From Wellington
EXPLANATION
CAMBRIAN
GREAT WESTERN
HALESOWEN (G.W. & MID. JOINT)
LONDON & NORTH WESTERN
MIDLAND
NORTH STAFFORDSHIRE
HALESOWEN & NORTHFIELD
From Dudley
To Birmingham
From Stourbridge
OLD HILL
ROWLEY REGIS & BLACKHEATH
Tunnel
HALESOWEN BASIN
STA. & Jn.
HALESOWEN
HUNNINGTON
Tunnel
FRANKLEY
RUBERY
To Birmingham
KING'S NORTON
STA.
NORTHFIELD
JUNCTION
Tunnel
JUNC.
STA.
BARNT GREEN
From Gloucester
BLACKWELL
ALVECHURCH
To Evesham

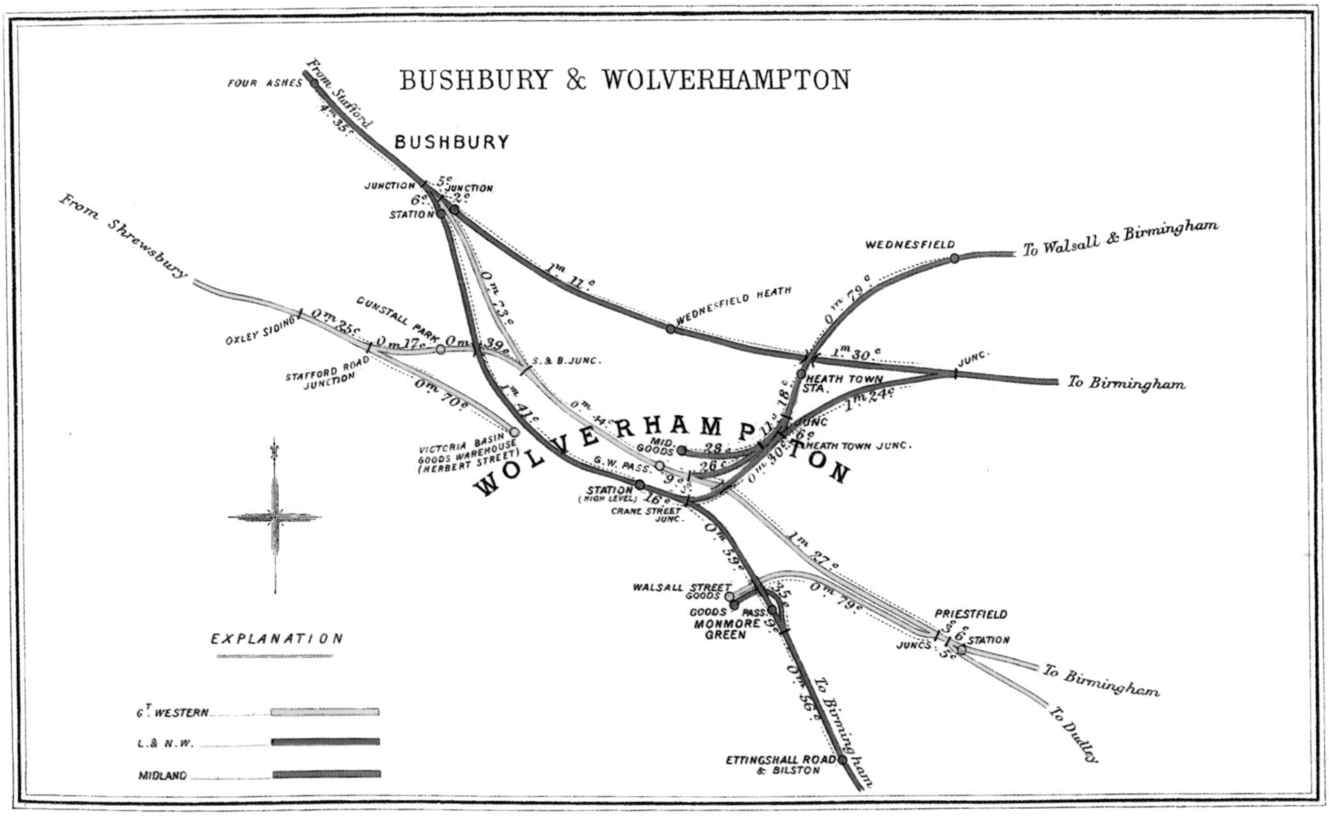
BUSHBURY & WOLVERHAMPTON
FOUR ASHES
From Stafford
BUSHBURY
JUNCTION
JUNCTION
STATION
From Shrewsbury
OXLEY SIDING
DUNSTALL PARK
S. & B. JUNC.
STAFFORD ROAD JUNCTION
WEDNESFIELD HEATH
WEDNESFIELD
To Walsall & Birmingham
JUNC.
To Birmingham
HEATH TOWN STA.
JUNC.
HEATH TOWN JUNC.
VICTORIA BASIN GOODS WAREHOUSE (HERBERT STREET)
WOLVERHAMPTON
MID. GOODS
G.W. PASS.
STATION (HIGH LEVEL)
CRANE STREET JUNC.
WALSALL STREET GOODS
GOODS
PASS.
MONMORE GREEN
PRIESTFIELD
STATION
JUNCS.
To Birmingham
To Dudley
To Birmingham
ETTINGSHALL ROAD & BILSTON
EXPLANATION
Gt. WESTERN
L. & N. W.
MIDLAND

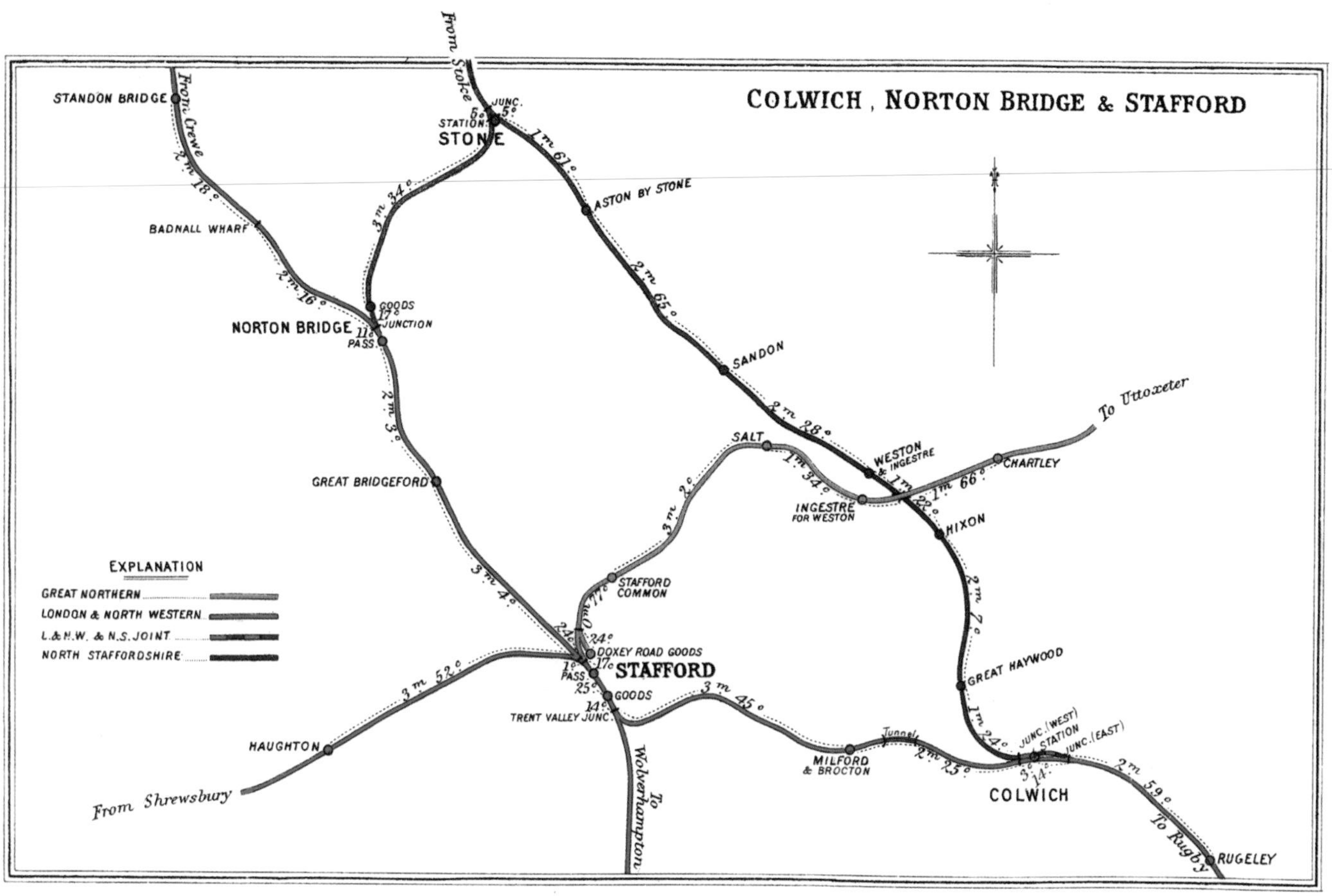

## COLWICH, NORTON BRIDGE & STAFFORD

EXPLANATION

GREAT NORTHERN

LONDON & NORTH WESTERN

L.&N.W. & N.S. JOINT

NORTH STAFFORDSHIRE

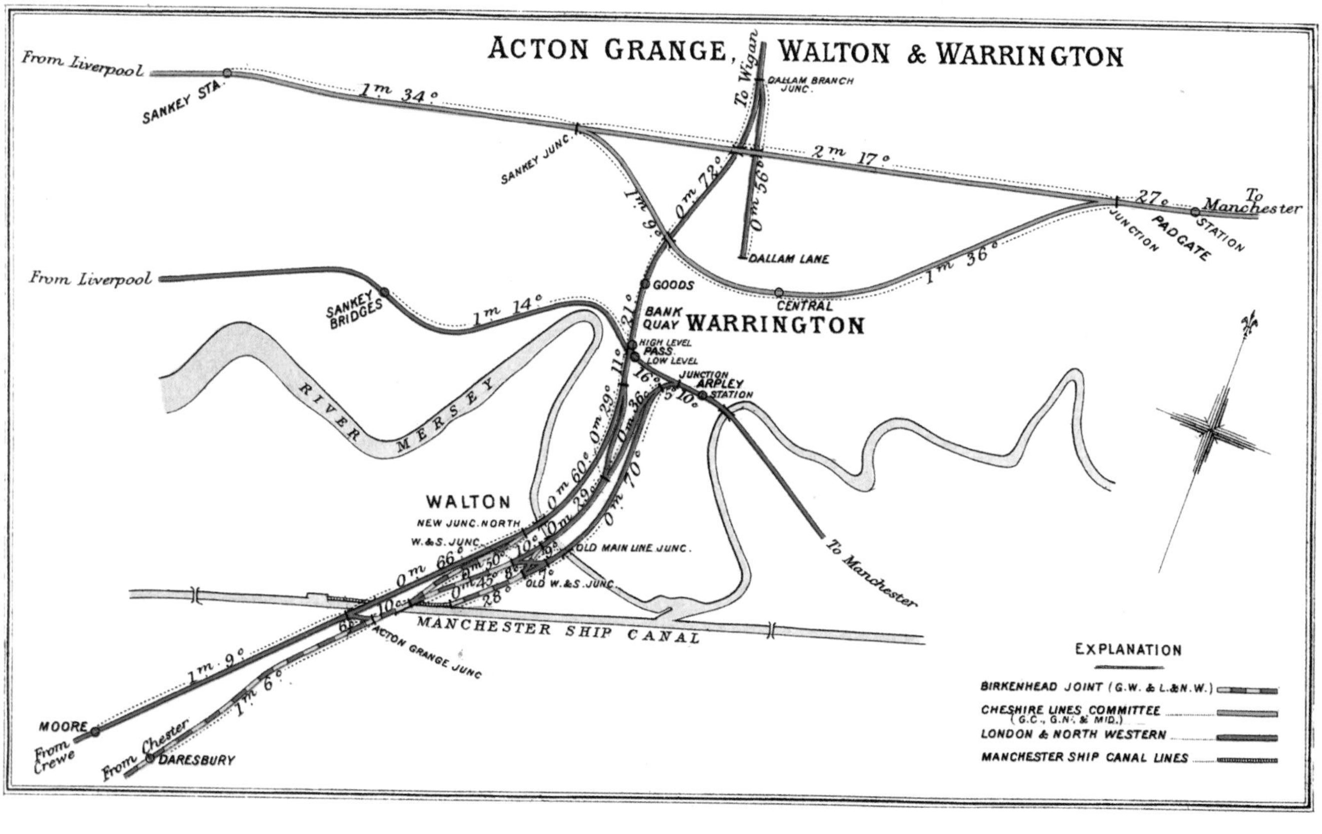

## ACTON GRANGE, WALTON & WARRINGTON

EXPLANATION

BIRKENHEAD JOINT (G.W. & L.&N.W.)

CHESHIRE LINES COMMITTEE (G.C., G.N. & MID.)

LONDON & NORTH WESTERN

MANCHESTER SHIP CANAL LINES

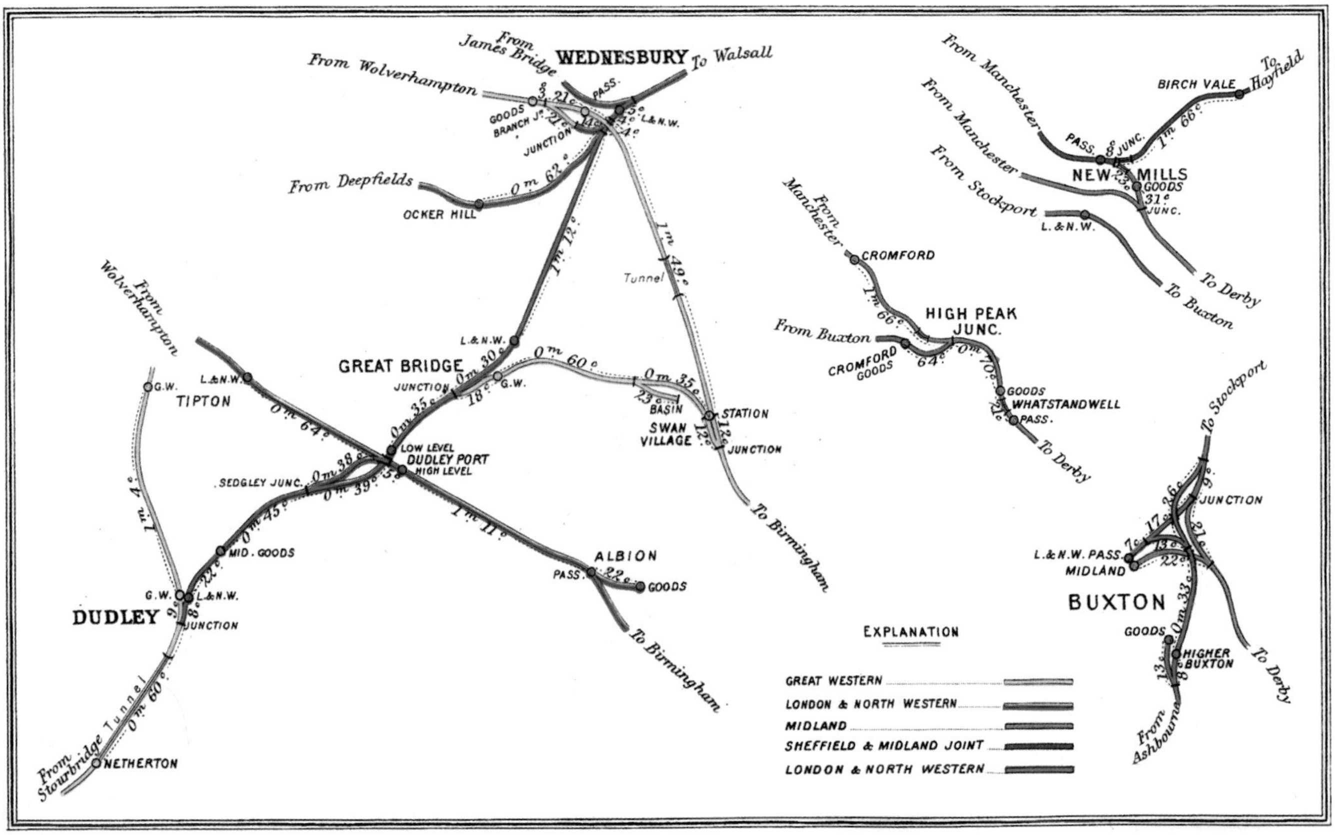

Dudley–Great Bridge–Wednesbury–High Peak Junc–New Mills–Buxton

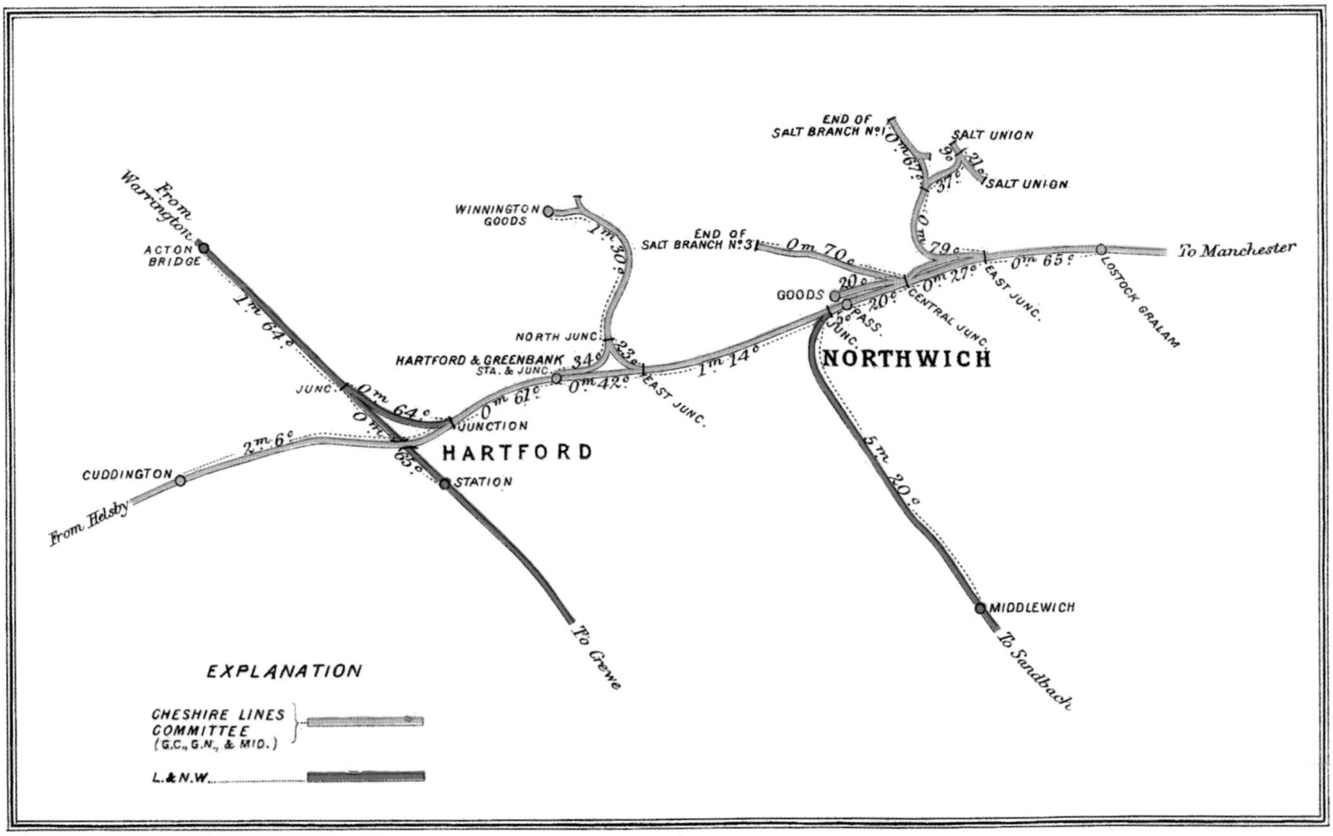

Hartford–Northwich

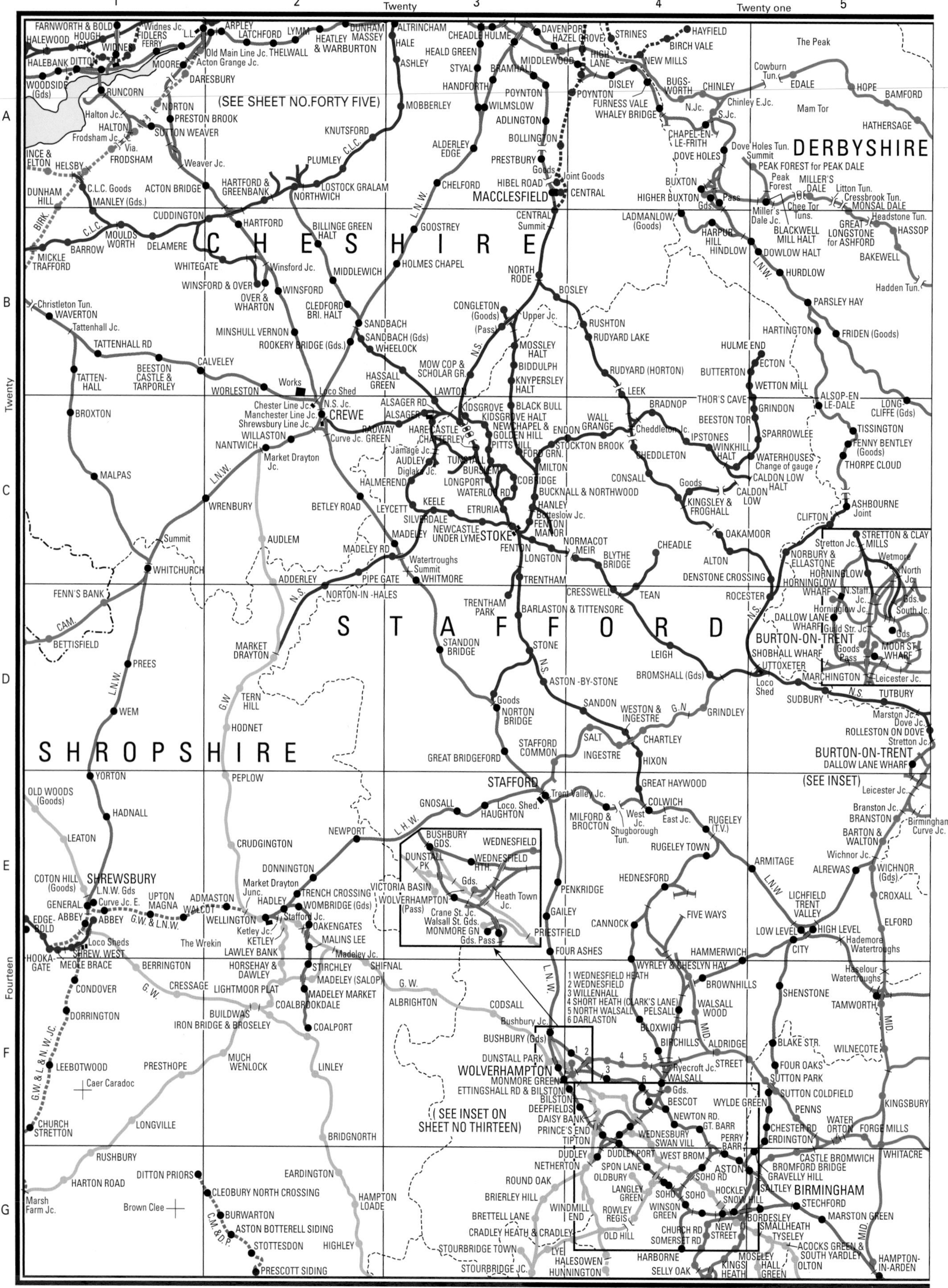
1
2
3
4
5
Twenty
Twenty one
Nine
Fourteen
A
B
C
D
E
F
G
FARNWORTH & BOLD
HALEWOOD
HALEBANK
DITTON
WIDNES
Widnes Jc.
FIDLERS FERRY
ARPLEY
LATCHFORD
LYMM
HEATLEY & WARBURTON
DUNHAM MASSEY
Old Main Line Jc. THELWALL
Acton Grange Jc.
MOORE
DARESBURY
WOODSIDE (Gds)
RUNCORN
NORTON
PRESTON BROOK
SUTTON WEAVER
(SEE SHEET NO.FORTY FIVE)
Halton Jc.
HALTON
Frodsham Jc.
FRODSHAM
INCE & ELTON
HELSBY
Weaver Jc.
DUNHAM HILL
C.L.C. Goods
MANLEY (Gds.)
ACTON BRIDGE
HARTFORD & GREENBANK
LOSTOCK GRALAM
NORTHWICH
PLUMLEY
KNUTSFORD
CUDDINGTON
HARTFORD
MOULDSWORTH
DELAMERE
BARROW
MICKLE TRAFFORD
C H E S H I R E
WHITEGATE
Winsford Jc.
WINSFORD & OVER
OVER & WHARTON
WINSFORD
BILLINGE GREEN HALT
MIDDLEWICH
CLEDFORD BRI. HALT
Christleton Tun.
WAVERTON
Tattenhall Jc.
TATTENHALL RD
MINSHULL VERNON
ROOKERY BRIDGE (Gds.)
SANDBACH
SANDBACH (Gds)
WHEELOCK
BEESTON CASTLE & TARPORLEY
CALVELEY
TATTEN-HALL
WORLESTON
Works
Loco Shed
BROXTON
Chester Line Jc.
Manchester Line Jc.
Shrewsbury Line Jc.
N.S. Jc.
CREWE
Curve Jc.
WILLASTON
NANTWICH
Market Drayton Jc.
MALPAS
WRENBURY
Summit
WHITCHURCH
AUDLEM
FENN'S BANK
BETTISFIELD
ADDERLEY
PREES
WEM
MARKET DRAYTON
TERN HILL
HODNET
S H R O P S H I R E
YORTON
OLD WOODS (Goods)
HADNALL
LEATON
PEPLOW
CRUDGINGTON
COTON HILL (Goods)
SHREWSBURY
L.N.W. Gds
GENERAL
Curve Jc. E.
ABBEY
EDGE-BOLD
Loco Sheds
SHREW. WEST
HOOKAGATE
MEOLE BRACE
UPTON MAGNA
WALCOT
ADMASTON
WELLINGTON
The Wrekin
BERRINGTON
CONDOVER
DORRINGTON
LEEBOTWOOD
Caer Caradoc
CHURCH STRETTON
LONGVILLE
RUSHBURY
HARTON ROAD
Marsh Farm Jc.
Brown Clee
DITTON PRIORS
CLEOBURY NORTH CROSSING
BURWARTON
ASTON BOTTERELL SIDING
STOTTESDON
PRESCOTT SIDING
HIGHLEY
HAMPTON LOADE
EARDINGTON
BRIDGNORTH
LINLEY
MUCH WENLOCK
PRESTHOPE
BUILDWAS
IRON BRIDGE & BROSELEY
CRESSAGE
LIGHTMOOR PLAT
COALBROOKDALE
COALPORT
MADELEY MARKET
MADELEY (SALOP)
STIRCHLEY
SHIFNAL
HORSEHAY & DAWLEY
LAWLEY BANK
KETLEY
Ketley Jc.
MALINS LEE
OAKENGATES
HADLEY
TRENCH CROSSING
WOMBRIDGE (Gds)
DONNINGTON
NEWPORT
ALBRIGHTON
CODSALL
ALTRINCHAM
HALE
ASHLEY
MOBBERLEY
CHEADLE HULME
HEALD GREEN
STYAL
BRAMHALL
HANDFORTH
WILMSLOW
ALDERLEY EDGE
CHELFORD
GOOSTREY
HOLMES CHAPEL
POYNTON
ADLINGTON
BOLLINGTON
PRESTBURY
HIBEL ROAD
MACCLESFIELD
CENTRAL
Joint Goods
CENTRAL Summit
NORTH RODE
BOSLEY
DAVENPORT
HAZEL GROVE
MIDDLEWOOD
HIGH LANE
STRINES
NEW MILLS
DISLEY
FURNESS VALE
WHALEY BRIDGE
HAYFIELD
BIRCH VALE
BUGSWORTH
CHINLEY
Chinley E.Jc.
CHAPEL-EN-LE-FRITH
DOVE HOLES
Dove Holes Tun.
BUXTON
HIGHER BUXTON
LADMANLOW (Goods)
HARPUR HILL
HINDLOW
The Peak
Cowburn Tun.
EDALE
HOPE
BAMFORD
Mam Tor
HATHERSAGE
DERBYSHIRE
PEAK FOREST for PEAK DALE
MILLER'S DALE
Litton Tun.
Cressbrook Tun.
MONSAL DALE
Headstone Tun.
HASSOP
GREAT LONGSTONE for ASHFORD
BAKEWELL
BLACKWELL MILL HALT
DOWLOW HALT
HURDLOW
Hadden Tun.
PARSLEY HAY
HARTINGTON
FRIDEN (Goods)
HULME END
ECTON
BUTTERTON
WETTON MILL
THOR'S CAVE
GRINDON
BEESTON TOR
SPARROWLEE
WATERHOUSES
Change of gauge
CALDON LOW HALT
ALSOP-EN-LE-DALE
LONG CLIFFE (Gds)
TISSINGTON
FENNY BENTLEY (Goods)
THORPE CLOUD
ASHBOURNE
CLIFTON
CONGLETON (Goods)
Upper Jc.
RUSHTON
RUDYARD LAKE
RUDYARD (HORTON)
LEEK
BRADNOP
Cheddleton Jc.
IPSTONES
WINKHILL HALT
CHEDDLETON
CONSALL
KINGSLEY & FROGHALL
OAKAMOOR
ALTON
DENSTONE CROSSING
ROCESTER
CHEADLE
MOSSLEY HALT
BIDDULPH
KNYPERSLEY HALT
MOW COP & SCHOLAR GR.
HASSALL GREEN
ALSAGER RD.
ALSAGER
LAWTON
KIDSGROVE
BLACK BULL
KIDSGROVE HALT
NEWCHAPEL & GOLDEN HILL
PITTS HILL
FORD GRN.
ENDON
STOCKTON BROOK
WALL GRANGE
HARECASTLE
CHATTERLEY
RADWAY GREEN
Jamage Jc.
AUDLEY
Diglake Jc.
TUNSTALL
BURSLEM
LONGPORT
WATERLOO RD
COBRIDGE
MILTON
BUCKNALL & NORTHWOOD
HANLEY
ETRURIA
KEELE
HALMEREND
LEYCETT
BETLEY ROAD
SILVERDALE
NEWCASTLE UNDER LYME
STOKE
FENTON
FENTON MANOR
Botteslow Jc.
NORMACOT
MEIR
BLYTHE BRIDGE
LONGTON
MADELEY
MADELEY RD
Whitmore Summit
Watertroughs
WHITMORE
PIPE GATE
NORTON-IN-HALES
TRENTHAM
TRENTHAM PARK
CRESSWELL
TEAN
BARLASTON & TITTENSORE
S T A F F O R D
STANDON BRIDGE
STONE
ASTON-BY-STONE
LEIGH
BROMSHALL (Gds)
UTTOXETER
MARCHINGTON
SUDBURY
Loco Shed
NORBURY & ELLASTONE
HORNINGLOW
BURTON-ON-TRENT
DALLOW LANE WHARF
SHOBHALL WHARF
Stretton Jc.
STRETTON & CLAY MILLS
TUTBURY
Marston Jc.
Dove Jc.
ROLLESTON ON DOVE
Stretton Jc.
BURTON-ON-TRENT
DALLOW LANE WHARF
(SEE INSET)
Leicester Jc.
Branston Jc.
BRANSTON
BARTON & WALTON
Birmingham Curve Jc.
Wichnor Jc.
WICHNOR (Gds)
ALREWAS
CROXALL
ELFORD
Goods
NORTON BRIDGE
SANDON
WESTON & INGESTRE
GRINDLEY
SALT
CHARTLEY
INGESTRE
HIXON
STAFFORD COMMON
GREAT BRIDGEFORD
STAFFORD
Trent Valley Jc.
GREAT HAYWOOD
COLWICH
MILFORD & BROCTON
West Jc.
East Jc.
Shugborough Tun.
RUGELEY (T.V.)
RUGELEY TOWN
GNOSALL
Loco. Shed.
HAUGHTON
BUSHBURY GDS.
WEDNESFIELD
DUNSTALL PK
WEDNESFIELD HTH.
VICTORIA BASIN
WOLVERHAMPTON (Pass)
Heath Town Jc.
Crane St. Jc.
Walsall St. Gds.
MONMORE GN
Gds. Pass
PENKRIDGE
GAILEY
PRIESTFIELD
FOUR ASHES
CANNOCK
HEDNESFORD
FIVE WAYS
HAMMERWICH
ARMITAGE
LICHFIELD TRENT VALLEY
LOW LEVEL
HIGH LEVEL
CITY
Hademore Watertroughs
WYRLEY & CHESLYN HAY
BROWNHILLS
1 WEDNESFIELD HEATH
2 WEDNESFIELD
3 WILLENHALL
4 SHORT HEATH (CLARK'S LANE)
5 NORTH WALSALL
6 DARLASTON
PELSALL
WALSALL WOOD
BLOXWICH
BIRCHILLS
ALDRIDGE
Bushbury Jc.
BUSHBURY (Gds)
DUNSTALL PARK
WOLVERHAMPTON
MONMORE GREEN
ETTINGSHALL RD & BILSTON
Ryecroft Jc.
STREET
WALSALL
SHENSTONE
Haselour Watertroughs
TAMWORTH
BLAKE STR.
WILNECOTE
FOUR OAKS
SUTTON PARK
SUTTON COLDFIELD
KINGSBURY
PENNS
WATER ORTON
FORGE MILLS
CHESTER RD
ERDINGTON
WHITACRE
WYLDE GREEN
BESCOT
NEWTON RD.
GT. BARR
PERRY BARR
BILSTON
DEEPFIELDS
DAISY BANK
PRINCE'S END
TIPTON
WEDNESBURY
SWAN VILL
DUDLEY PORT
WEST BROM
DUDLEY
NETHERTON
SPON LANE
OLDBURY
ASTON
SOHO RD
CASTLE BROMWICH
BROMFORD BRIDGE
GRAVELLY HILL
SALTLEY
BIRMINGHAM
STECHFORD
MARSTON GREEN
ROUND OAK
BRIERLEY HILL
LANGLEY GREEN
SOHO
SOHO
HOCKLEY
SNOW HILL
WINDMILL END
ROWLEY REGIS
WINSON GREEN
BORDESLEY
SMALLHEATH
TYSELEY
BRETTELL LANE
CRADLEY HEATH & CRADLEY
OLD HILL
CHURCH RD
SOMERSET RD
NEW STREET
ACOCKS GREEN & SOUTH YARDLEY
OLTON
HAMPTON-IN-ARDEN
STOURBRIDGE TOWN
STOURBRIDGE JC.
LYE
HALESOWEN
HUNNINGTON
HARBORNE
SELLY OAK
KINGS HEATH
MOSELEY
HALL GREEN
(SEE INSET ON SHEET NO THIRTEEN)
L.N.W.
N.S.
G.W.
C.L.C.
MID.
G.N.
CAM.
BIRK.
S.&M.J.
C.M.& D.P.
G.W.& L.& N.W. JC.
G.W.& L.N.W.
L.& N.W.

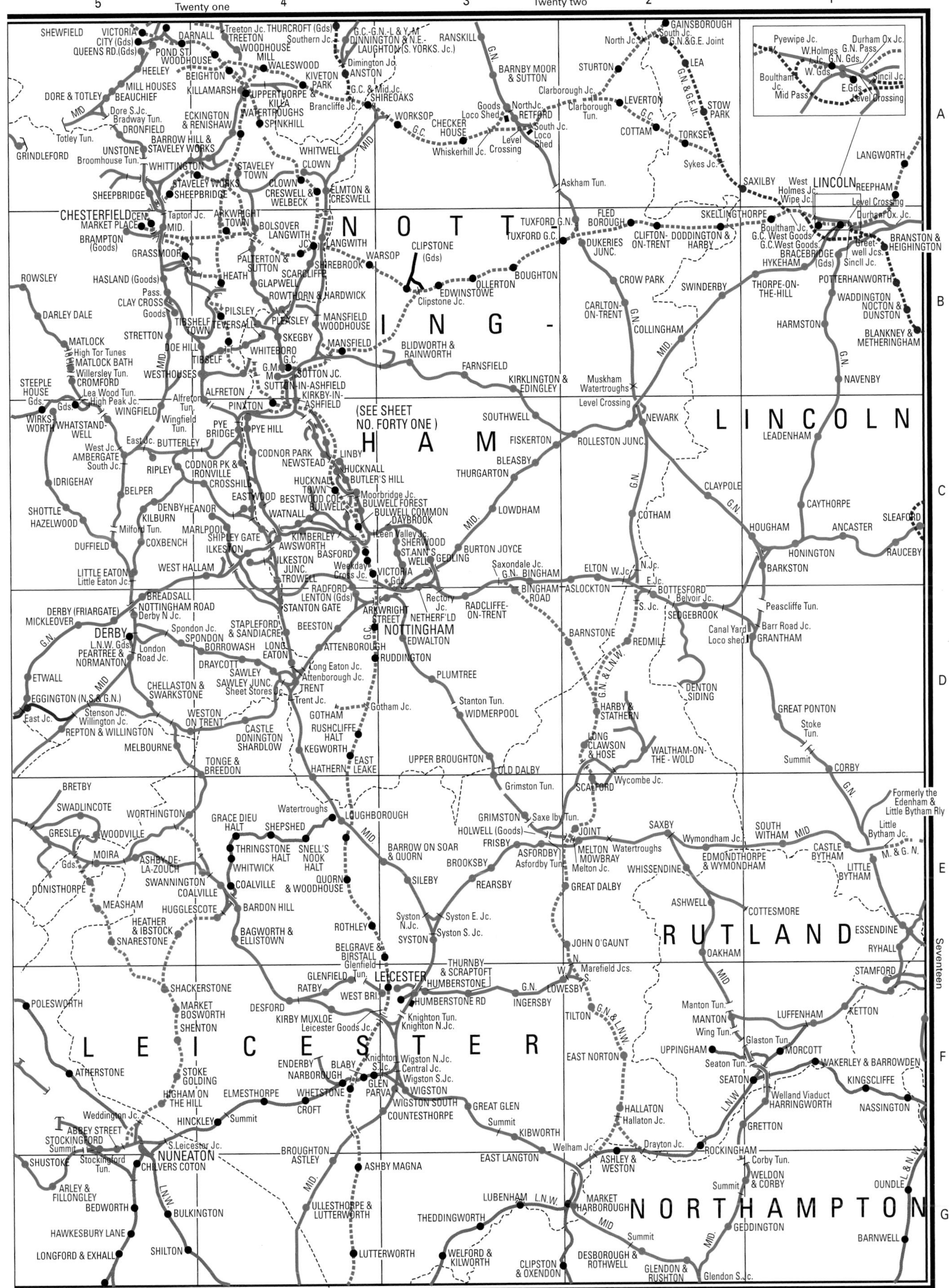
5
Twenty one
4
3
Twenty two
2
1
A
B
C
D
E
F
G
Seventeen
SHEWFIELD
VICTORIA
CITY (Gds)
QUEENS RD.(Gds)
DARNALL
Treeton Jc.
TREETON
THURCROFT (Gds)
Southern Jc.
G.C.-G.N.-L & Y.-M.
DINNINGTON & N.E.-
LAUGHTON (S. YORKS. Jc.)
RANSKILL
GAINSBOROUGH
South Jc.
G.N.&G.E. Joint
North Jc.
LEA
STURTON
POND ST.
WOODHOUSE
WOODHOUSE
MILL
WALESWOOD
Dinnington Jc.
ANSTON
BARNBY MOOR
& SUTTON
HEELEY
BEIGHTON
KIVETON
PARK
Clarborough Jc.
LEVERTON
STOW
PARK
MILL HOUSES
BEAUCHIEF
KILLAMARSH
UPPERTHORPE &
KILLA
WATERTROUGHS
SPINKHILL
G.C. & Mid.Jc.
SHIREOAKS
Brancliffe Jc.
WORKSOP
CHECKER
HOUSE
Goods
Loco Shed
North Jc.
RETFORD
Clarborough
Tun.
COTTAM
TORKSEY
DORE & TOTLEY
MID
Dore S.Jc.
Bradway Tun.
DRONFIELD
ECKINGTON
& RENISHAW
Totley Tun.
GRINDLEFORD
UNSTONE
BARROW HILL &
STAVELEY WORKS
Broomhouse Tun.
WHITTINGTON
WHITWELL
CLOWN
Whiskerhill Jc.
Level
Crossing
South Jc.
Loco
Shed
Sykes Jc.
Pyewipe Jc.
W.Holmes
Durham Ox Jc.
G.N. Pass
G.N. Gds.
W. Gds
Boultham
Jc.
Mid Pass
E.Gds
Sincil Jc.
Level Crossing
LANGWORTH
STAVELEY
TOWN
STAVELEY WORKS
SHEEPBRIDGE
SHEEPBRIDGE
CLOWN
CRESWELL &
WELBECK
ELMTON &
CRESWELL
Askham Tun.
SAXILBY
West
Holmes Jc.
Wipe Jc.
LINCOLN
REEPHAM
Level Crossing
CHESTERFIELD
CEN.
MID.
MARKET PLACE
Tapton Jc.
ARKWRIGHT
TOWN
BOLSOVER
LANGWITH
JC.
LANGWITH
N O T T
TUXFORD G.N.
TUXFORD G.C.
FLED
BOROUGH
CLIFTON-
ON-TRENT
DODDINGTON &
HARBY
SKELLINGTHORPE
Boultham Jc.
G.C. West Goods
G.C.West Goods
Durham Ox. Jc.
BRANSTON &
HEIGHINGTON
BRAMPTON
(Goods)
GRASSMOOR
PALTERTON &
SUTTON
SCARCLIFFE
SHIREBROOK
WARSOP
CLIPSTONE
(Gds)
DUKERIES
JUNC.
BRACEBRIDGE
(Gds)
Greet-
well Jcs.
Sincil Jc.
HYKEHAM
ROWSLEY
HASLAND (Goods)
HEATH
GLAPWELL
ROWTHORN & HARDWICK
EDWINSTOWE
Clipstone Jc.
OLLERTON
BOUGHTON
CROW PARK
SWINDERBY
THORPE-ON-
THE-HILL
POTTERHANWORTH
WADDINGTON
NOCTON &
DUNSTON
Pass.
CLAY CROSS
Goods
DARLEY DALE
PILSLEY
TEVERSALL
PLEASLEY
MANSFIELD
WOODHOUSE
I N G -
CARLTON-
ON-TRENT
G.N.
COLLINGHAM
HARMSTON
BLANKNEY &
METHERINGHAM
MATLOCK
High Tor Tunes
MATLOCK BATH
Willersley Tun.
CROMFORD
STRETTON
TIBSHELF
TOWN
DOE HILL
SKEGBY
MANSFIELD
BLIDWORTH &
RAINWORTH
MID.
TIBSELF
WHITEBORO
WESTHOUSES
G.M.
G.C.
SUTTON JC.
SUTTON-IN-ASHFIELD
KIRKBY-IN-
ASHFIELD
FARNSFIELD
KIRKLINGTON &
EDINGLEY
Muskham
Watertroughs
Level Crossing
NAVENBY
STEEPLE
HOUSE
Gds
Lea Wood Tun.
High Peak Jc.
Alfreton
Tun.
ALFRETON
PINXTON
WINGFIELD
WIRKS-
WORTH
WHATSTAND-
WELL
Wingfield
Tun.
PYE
BRIDGE
PYE HILL
(SEE SHEET
NO. FORTY ONE )
SOUTHWELL
NEWARK
L I N C O L N
LEADENHAM
West Jc.
AMBERGATE
South Jc.
East Jc.
BUTTERLEY
CODNOR PARK
NEWSTEAD
LINBY
H A M
FISKERTON
ROLLESTON JUNC.
RIPLEY
CODNOR PK &
IRONVILLE
CROSSHILL
HUCKNALL
HUCKNALL
TOWN
BUTLER'S HILL
BLEASBY
THURGARTON
IDRIGEHAY
BELPER
EASTWOOD
BESTWOOD COL.
Moorbridge Jc.
BULWELL FOREST
BULWELL
BULWELL COMMON
DAYBROOK
LOWDHAM
CLAYPOLE
COTHAM
CAYTHORPE
SHOTTLE
HAZELWOOD
DENBY
KILBURN
HEANOR
Milford Tun.
WATNALL
MARLPOOL
SHIPLEY GATE
ILKESTON
COXBENCH
KIMBERLEY
AWSWORTH
BASFORD
Leen Valley Jc.
SHERWOOD
ST.ANN'S
WELL
GEDLING
BURTON JOYCE
HOUGHAM
ANCASTER
SLEAFORD
HONINGTON
RAUCEBY
BARKSTON
DUFFIELD
LITTLE EATON
Little Eaton Jc.
WEST HALLAM
ILKESTON
JUNC.
TROWELL
Weekday
Cross Jc.
VICTORIA
Gds
Saxondale Jc.
G.N.
BINGHAM
ELTON
W.Jc.
N.Jc.
E.Jc.
BOTTESFORD
Belvoir Jc.
BREADSALL
NOTTINGHAM ROAD
Derby N Jc.
RADFORD
LENTON (Gds)
STANTON GATE
ARKWRIGHT
STREET
Rectory
Jc.
NETHERF'LD
RADCLIFFE-
ON-TRENT
BINGHAM
ROAD
ASLOCKTON
S. Jc.
SEDGEBROOK
Peascliffe Tun.
DERBY (FRIARGATE)
MICKLEOVER
DERBY
Spondon Jc.
SPONDON
STAPLEFORD
& SANDIACRE
BEESTON
NOTTINGHAM
EDWALTON
BARNSTONE
REDMILE
Canal Yard
Loco shed
Barr Road Jc.
GRANTHAM
G.N.
L.N.W. Gds
PEARTREE &
NORMANTON
London
Road Jc.
BORROWASH
LONG
EATON
ATTENBOROUGH
RUDDINGTON
DRAYCOTT
SAWLEY
SAWLEY JUNC.
Sheet Stores Jc.
Long Eaton Jc.
Attenborough Jc.
TRENT
Trent Jc.
PLUMTREE
G.N. & L.N.W.
DENTON
SIDING
ETWALL
MID
EGGINGTON (N.S.& G.N.)
East Jc.
CHELLASTON &
SWARKSTONE
Stenson Jc.
Willington Jc.
REPTON & WILLINGTON
WESTON
ON TRENT
CASTLE
DONINGTON
SHARDLOW
Gotham Jc.
GOTHAM
RUSHCLIFFE
HALT
Stanton Tun.
WIDMERPOOL
HARBY &
STATHERN
GREAT PONTON
Stoke
Tun.
MELBOURNE
KEGWORTH
LONG
CLAWSON
& HOSE
WALTHAM-ON-
THE - WOLD
Summit
CORBY
TONGE &
BREEDON
HATHERN
EAST
LEAKE
UPPER BROUGHTON
OLD DALBY
Grimston Tun.
SCALFORD
Wycombe Jc.
BRETBY
SWADLINCOTE
WORTHINGTON
GRACE DIEU
HALT
Watertroughs
LOUGHBOROUGH
GRIMSTON
Saxe Iby Tun.
Formerly the
Edenham &
Little Bytham Rly
GRESLEY
WOODVILLE
SHEPSHED
HOLWELL (Goods)
JOINT
SAXBY
Wymondham Jc.
SOUTH
WITHAM
MID
Little
Bytham Jc.
M. & G. N.
MOIRA
Gds.
ASHBY DE-
LA-ZOUCH
THRINGSTONE
HALT
SNELL'S
NOOK
HALT
WHITWICK
MID.
BARROW ON SOAR
& QUORN
FRISBY
ASFORDBY
Asfordby Tun.
MELTON
MOWBRAY
Melton Jc.
Watertroughs
WHISSENDINE
EDMONDTHORPE
& WYMONDHAM
CASTLE
BYTHAM
LITTLE
BYTHAM
DONISTHORPE
SWANNINGTON
COALVILLE
COALVILLE
QUORN
& WOODHOUSE
BROOKSBY
SILEBY
REARSBY
GREAT DALBY
ASHWELL
COTTESMORE
MEASHAM
HUGGLESCOTE
BARDON HILL
HEATHER
& IBSTOCK
SNARESTONE
Syston
N.Jc.
SYSTON
Syston E. Jc.
Syston S. Jc.
ROTHLEY
BAGWORTH &
ELLISTOWN
R U T L A N D
ESSENDINE
JOHN O'GAUNT
BELGRAVE &
BIRSTALL
Glenfield
OAKHAM
RYHALL
THURNBY
& SCRAPTOFT
GLENFIELD
Tun.
LEICESTER
HUMBERSTONE
Marefield Jcs.
W.
N.
S.
STAMFORD
SHACKERSTONE
RATBY
WEST BRI.
G.N.
LOWESBY
HUMBERSTONE RD
INGERSBY
POLESWORTH
MARKET
BOSWORTH
DESFORD
KIRBY MUXLOE
Leicester Goods Jc.
Knighton Tun.
Knighton N.Jc.
TILTON
G.N. & L.N.W.
Manton Tun.
MANTON
Wing Tun.
LUFFENHAM
KETTON
SHENTON
L E I C E S T E R
Glaston Tun.
MORCOTT
UPPINGHAM
EAST NORTON
ATHERSTONE
ENDERBY
BLABY
NARBOROUGH
Knighton
S.Jc.
Wigston N.Jc.
Central Jc.
Wigston S.Jc.
WIGSTON
Seaton Tun.
SEATON
WAKERLEY & BARROWDEN
KINGSCLIFFE
STOKE
GOLDING
HIGHAM ON
THE HILL
ELMESTHORPE
WHETSTONE
GLEN
PARVA
WIGSTON SOUTH
COUNTESTHORPE
GREAT GLEN
HALLATON
Hallaton Jc.
Welland Viaduct
HARRINGWORTH
NASSINGTON
Weddington Jc.
ABBEY STREET
STOCKINGFORD
Summit
HINCKLEY
Summit
CROFT
Summit
KIBWORTH
L.N.W.
GRETTON
S.Leicester Jc.
NUNEATON
Drayton Jc.
ROCKINGHAM
SHUSTOKE
Stockingford
Tun.
CHILVERS COTON
BROUGHTON
ASTLEY
ASHBY MAGNA
EAST LANGTON
Welham Jc.
ASHLEY &
WESTON
Corby Tun.
WELDON
& CORBY
Summit
ARLEY &
FILLONGLEY
BEDWORTH
L.N.W.
BULKINGTON
MID.
ULLESTHORPE &
LUTTERWORTH
LUBENHAM
L.N.W.
MARKET
HARBOROUGH
N O R T H A M P T O N
OUNDLE
L.&N.W.
HAWKESBURY LANE
THEDDINGWORTH
MID
Summit
MID.
GEDDINGTON
LONGFORD & EXHALL
SHILTON
LUTTERWORTH
WELFORD &
KILWORTH
CLIPSTON
& OXENDON
DESBOROUGH &
ROTHWELL
GLENDON &
RUSHTON
Glendon S.Jc.
BARNWELL

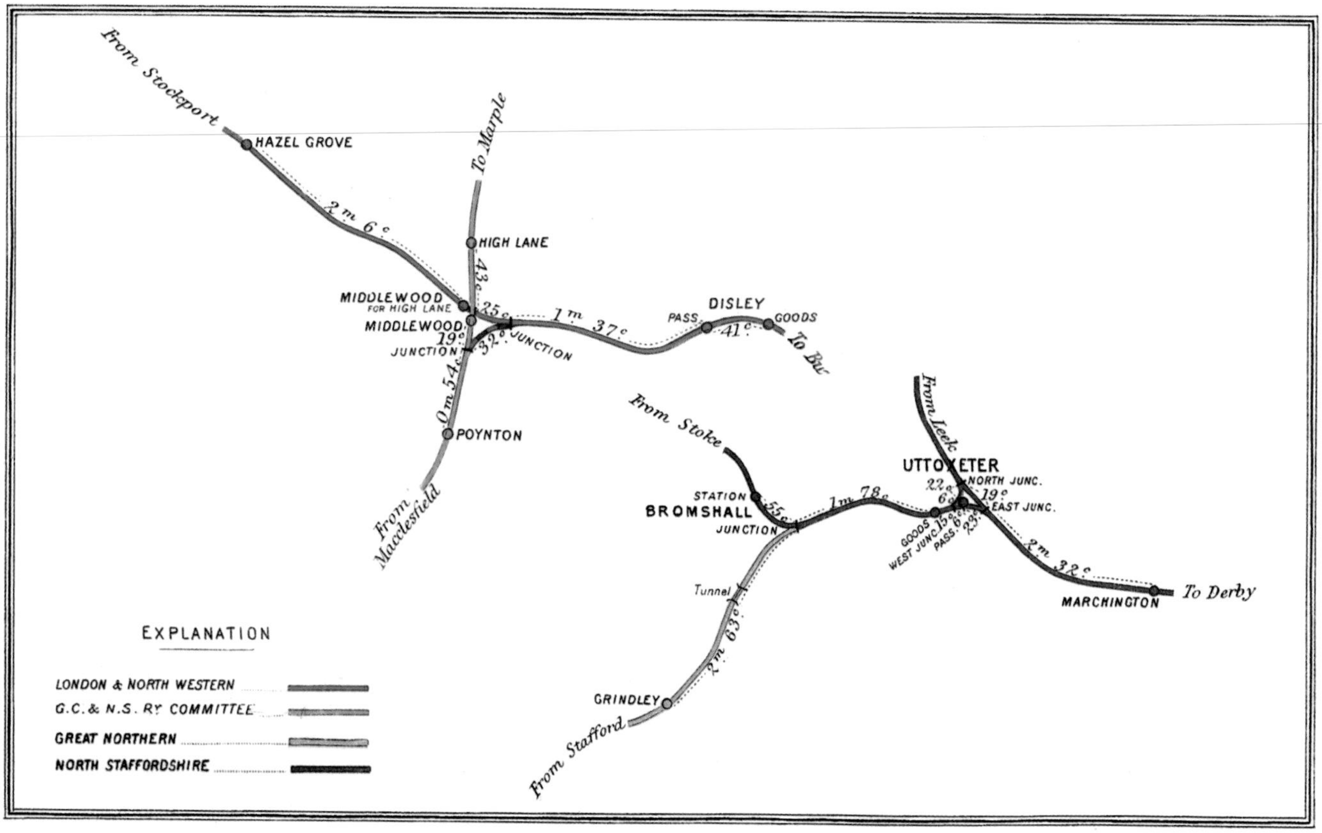

From Stockport
HAZEL GROVE
2m 6c
To Marple
HIGH LANE
43c
MIDDLEWOOD FOR HIGH LANE
MIDDLEWOOD
JUNCTION
25c
19c
32c
JUNCTION
1m 37c
PASS.
DISLEY
GOODS
41c
To Bu
0m 54c
POYNTON
From Macclesfield
From Stoke
STATION
BROMSHALL
JUNCTION
55c
1m 78c
From Leek
UTTOXETER
NORTH JUNC.
EAST JUNC.
22c
6c
19c
GOODS
WEST JUNC.
PASS
2m 32c
MARCHINGTON
To Derby
Tunnel
2m 63c
GRINDLEY
From Stafford

EXPLANATION
LONDON & NORTH WESTERN
G.C. & N.S. RY COMMITTEE
GREAT NORTHERN
NORTH STAFFORDSHIRE

**Middlewood–Bromshall–Uttoxeter**

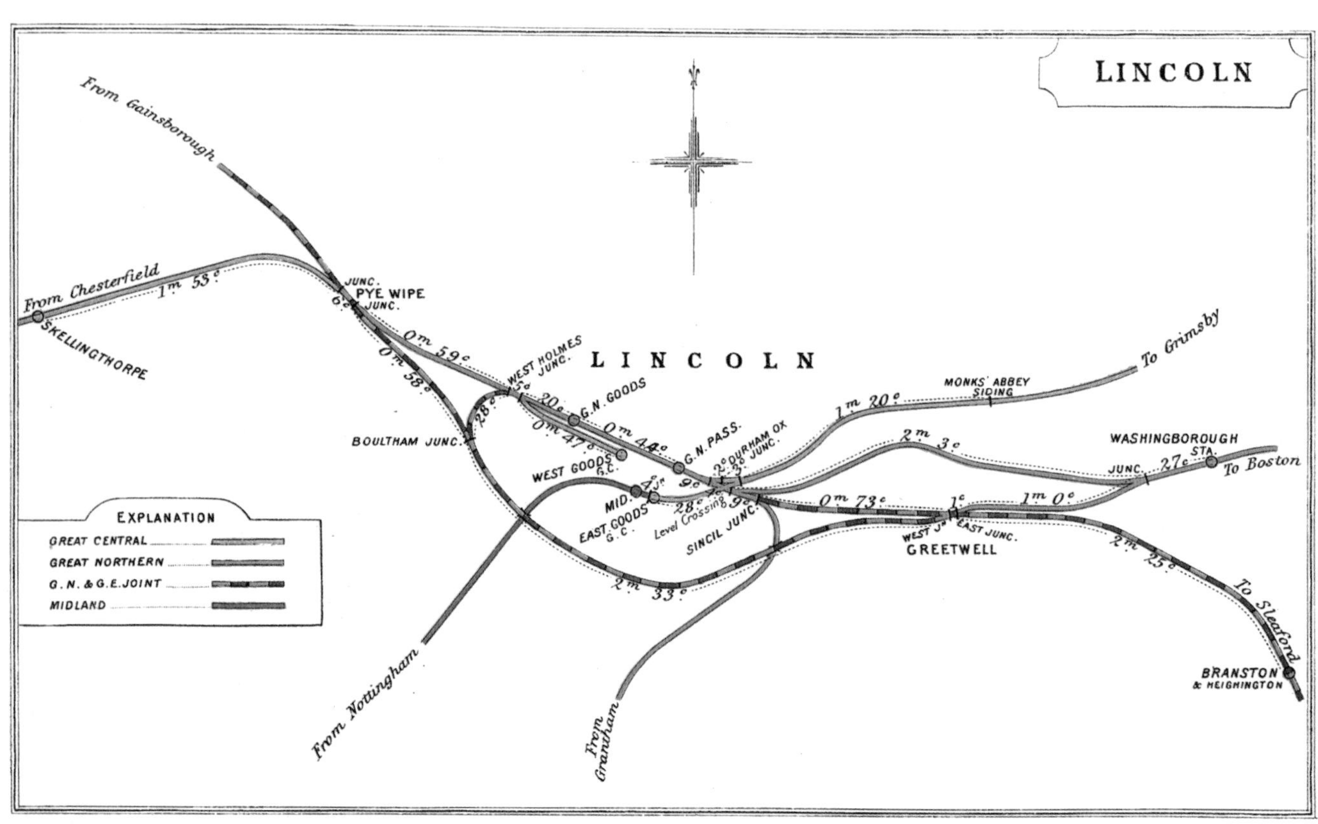

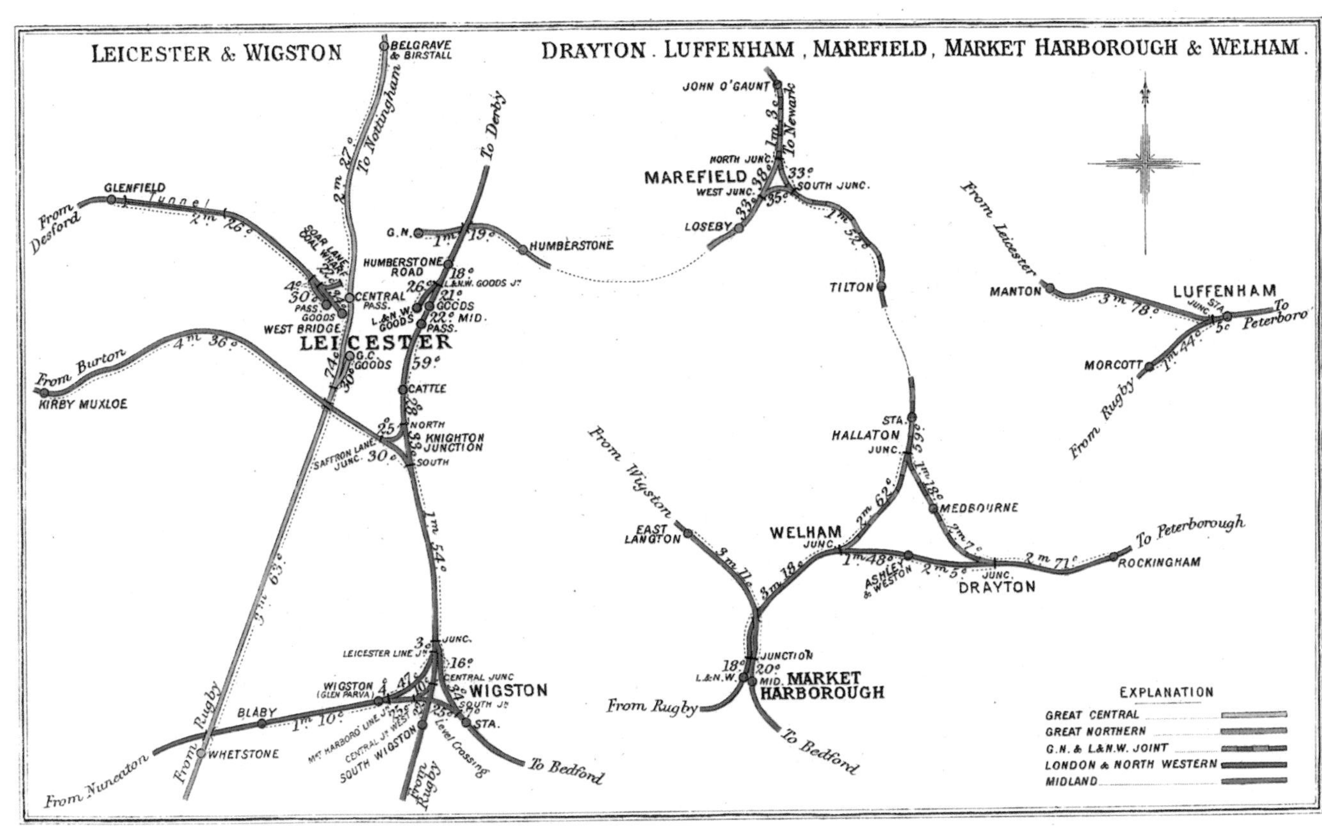


From Lincoln
RUSKINGTON
2m 18c
EXPLANATION
GREAT NORTHERN
GRT NORTHERN & GRT EASTERN JNT
NORTH JUNC.
SLEAFORD
2m 8c
1m 35c
4m 77c
RAUCEBY
1m 68c
WEST JUNC.
STA. & JUNC.
EAST JUNC.
SOUTH JUNC.
From Grantham
HECKINGTON
To Boston
3m 71c
3m 48c
HELPRINGHAM
To Spalding
ASWARBY
To Bourne

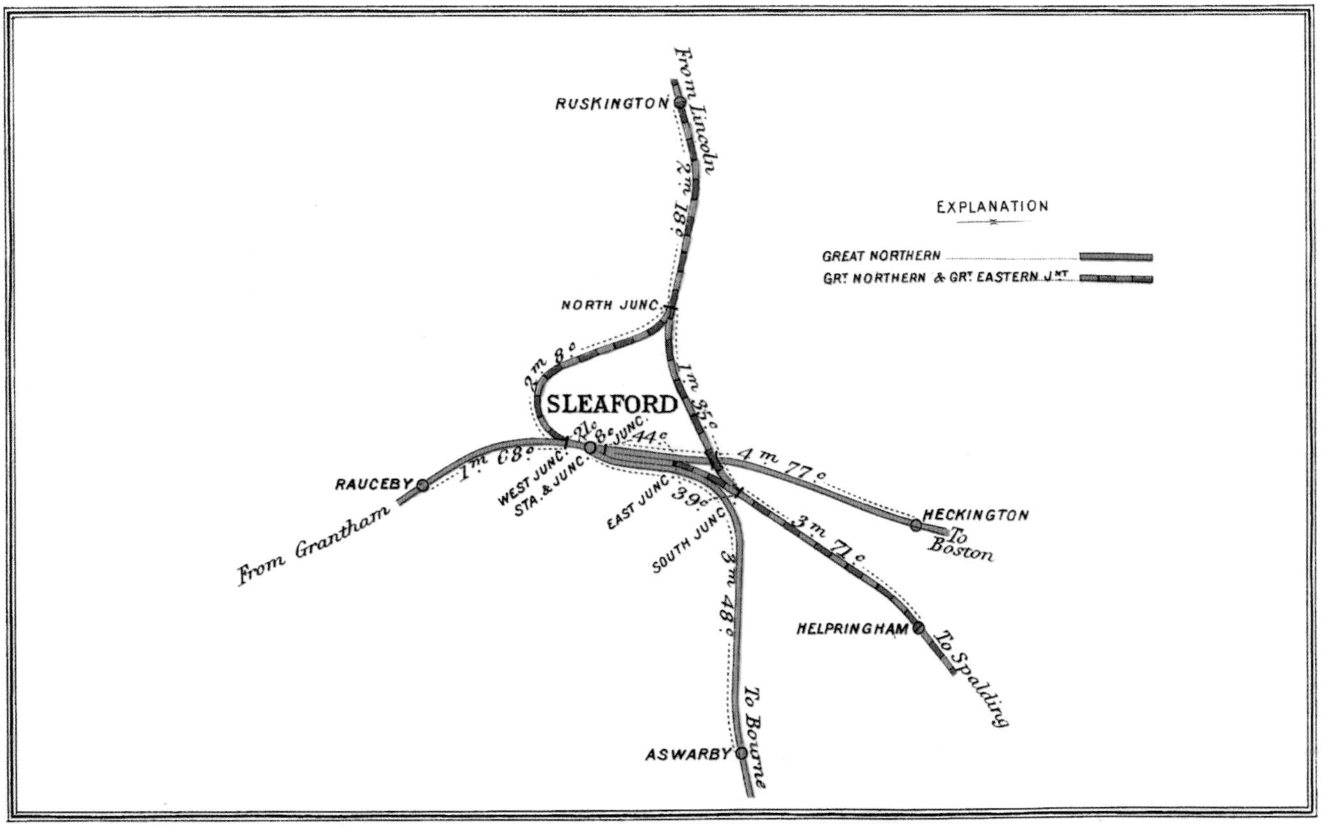

**Sleaford**

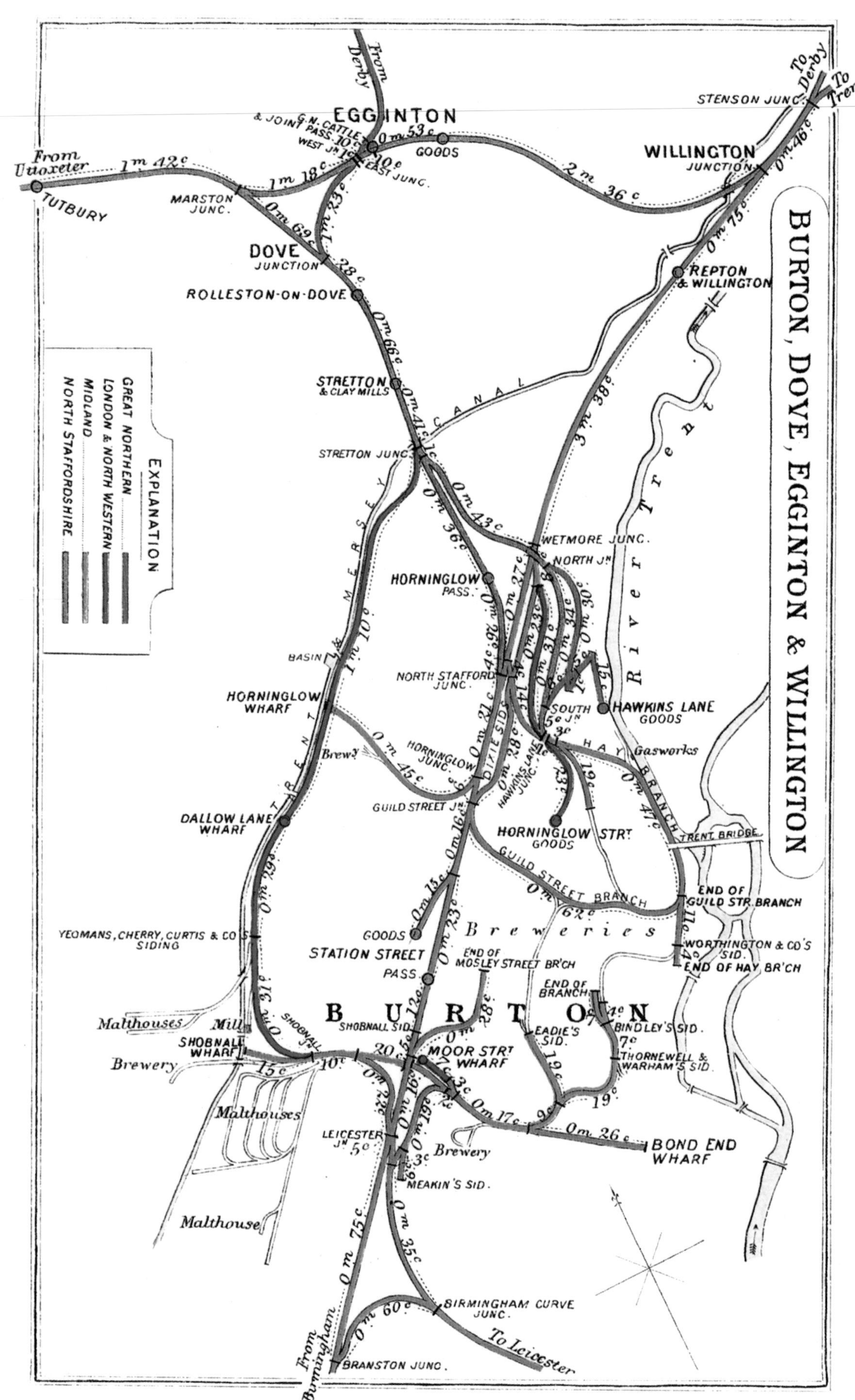
BURTON, DOVE, EGGINTON & WILLINGTON
EXPLANATION
GREAT NORTHERN
LONDON & NORTH WESTERN
MIDLAND
NORTH STAFFORDSHIRE
EGGINTON
WILLINGTON JUNCTION
STENSON JUNC.
TUTBURY
MARSTON JUNC.
DOVE JUNCTION
ROLLESTON-ON-DOVE
STRETTON & CLAY MILLS
STRETTON JUNC.
REPTON & WILLINGTON
WETMORE JUNC.
HORNINGLOW PASS.
NORTH STAFFORD JUNC.
HORNINGLOW WHARF
HAWKINS LANE GOODS
DALLOW LANE WHARF
HORNINGLOW STRT GOODS
GUILD STREET BRANCH
TRENT BRIDGE
END OF GUILD STR. BRANCH
YEOMANS, CHERRY, CURTIS & CO'S SIDING
STATION STREET PASS.
WORTHINGTON & CO'S SID.
END OF HAY BR'CH
END OF MOSLEY STREET BR'CH
BURTON
SHOBNALL WHARF
MOOR STRT WHARF
BINDLEY'S SID.
THORNEWELL & WARHAM'S SID.
EADIE'S SID.
LEICESTER JN
MEAKIN'S SID.
BOND END WHARF
BIRMINGHAM CURVE JUNC.
BRANSTON JUNC.
From Birmingham
To Leicester
From Uttoxeter
From Derby
To Derby
To Trent
River Trent
Breweries
Malthouses
Malthouse
Brewery
Gasworks

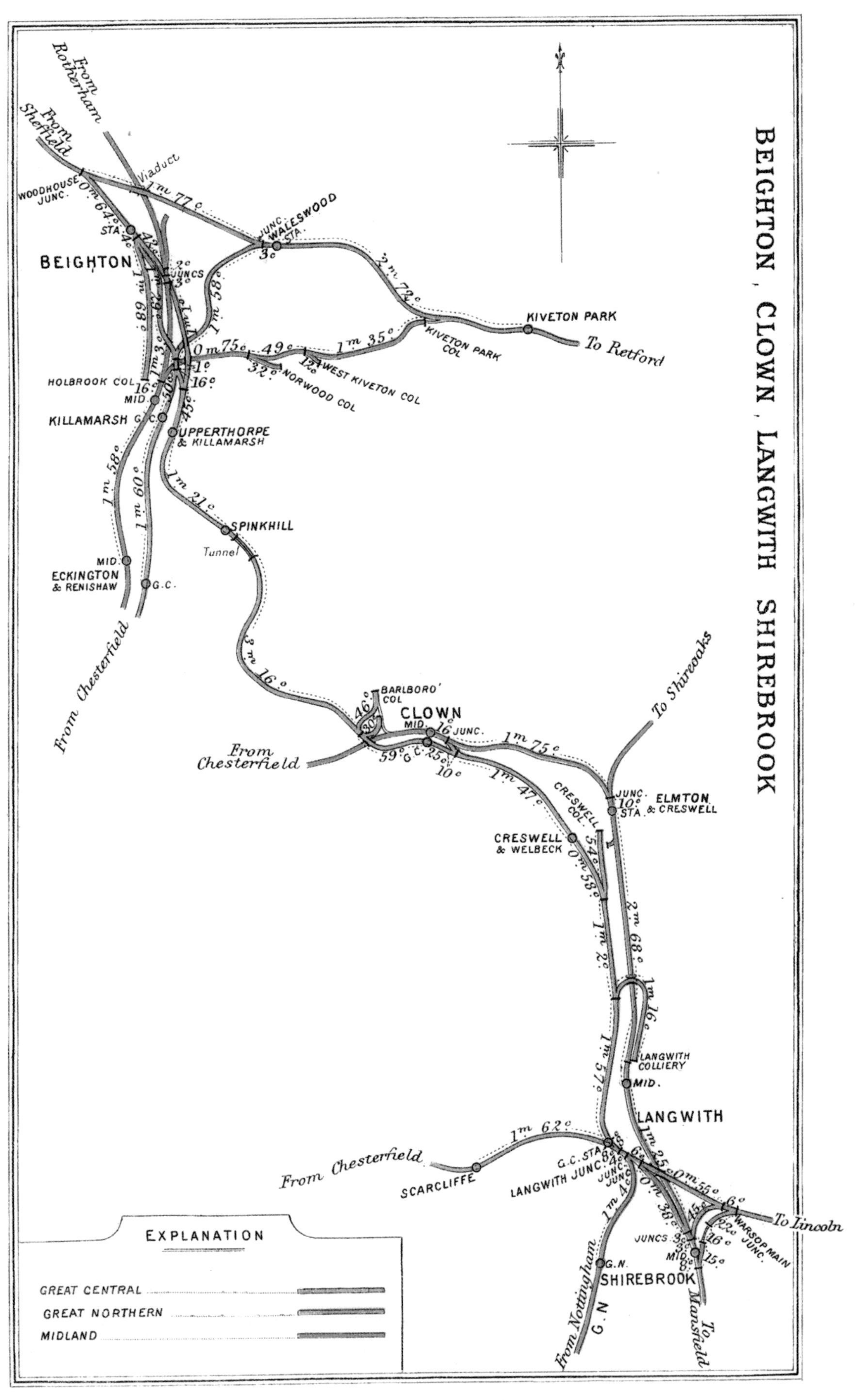
BEIGHTON, CLOWN, LANGWITH SHIREBROOK
From Rotherham
From Sheffield
Viaduct
WOODHOUSE JUNC.
BEIGHTON
JUNCS
JUNC. WALESWOOD STA.
KIVETON PARK
To Retford
KIVETON PARK COL
WEST KIVETON COL
NORWOOD COL
HOLBROOK COL
KILLAMARSH
UPPERTHORPE & KILLAMARSH
SPINKHILL
Tunnel
ECKINGTON & RENISHAW
From Chesterfield
BARLBORO' COL
CLOWN
From Chesterfield
To Shireoaks
ELMTON & CRESWELL
CRESWELL COL
CRESWELL & WELBECK
LANGWITH COLLIERY
LANGWITH
From Chesterfield
SCARCLIFFE
LANGWITH JUNC
To Lincoln
WARSOP MAIN JUNC.
SHIREBROOK
From Nottingham
To Mansfield
EXPLANATION
GREAT CENTRAL
GREAT NORTHERN
MIDLAND

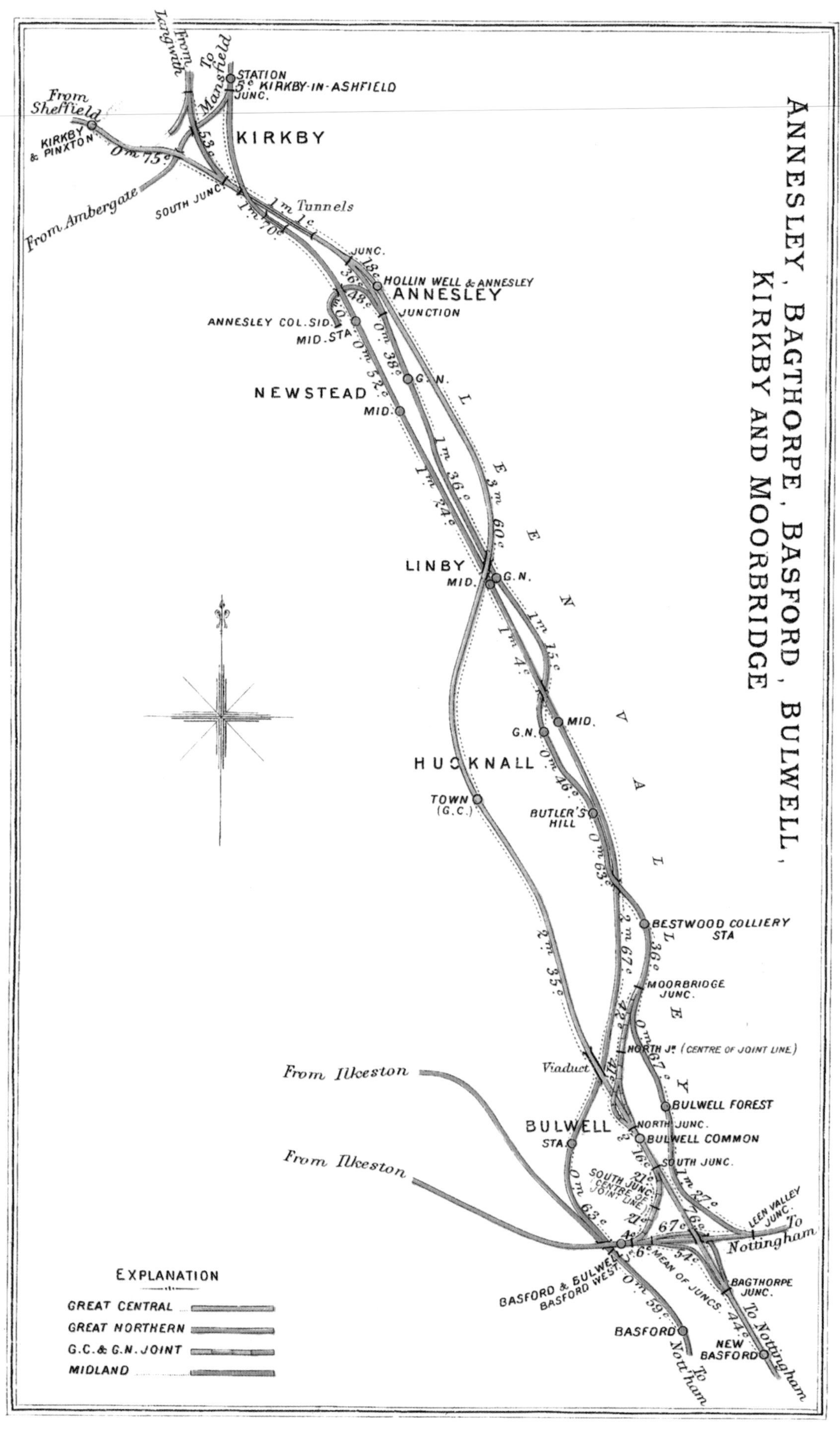
ANNESLEY, BAGTHORPE, BASFORD, BULWELL, KIRKBY AND MOORBRIDGE
From Langwith
To Mansfield
STATION
KIRKBY-IN-ASHFIELD JUNC.
From Sheffield
KIRKBY & PINXTON
KIRKBY
From Ambergate
SOUTH JUNC.
Tunnels
JUNC.
HOLLIN WELL & ANNESLEY
ANNESLEY
JUNCTION
ANNESLEY COL. SID.
MID. STA.
G.N.
NEWSTEAD
MID.
LEEN VALLEY
LINBY
MID.
G.N.
MID.
G.N.
HUCKNALL
TOWN (G.C.)
BUTLER'S HILL
BESTWOOD COLLIERY STA
MOORBRIDGE JUNC.
NORTH Jn. (CENTRE OF JOINT LINE)
Viaduct
From Ilkeston
BULWELL FOREST
BULWELL
STA.
NORTH JUNC.
BULWELL COMMON
From Ilkeston
SOUTH JUNC.
SOUTH JUNC. (CENTRE OF JOINT LINE)
LEEN VALLEY JUNC.
To Nottingham
BASFORD & BULWELL
BASFORD WEST
MEAN OF JUNCS.
BAGTHORPE JUNC.
BASFORD
NEW BASFORD
To Northam
To Nottingham
EXPLANATION
GREAT CENTRAL
GREAT NORTHERN
G.C. & G.N. JOINT
MIDLAND

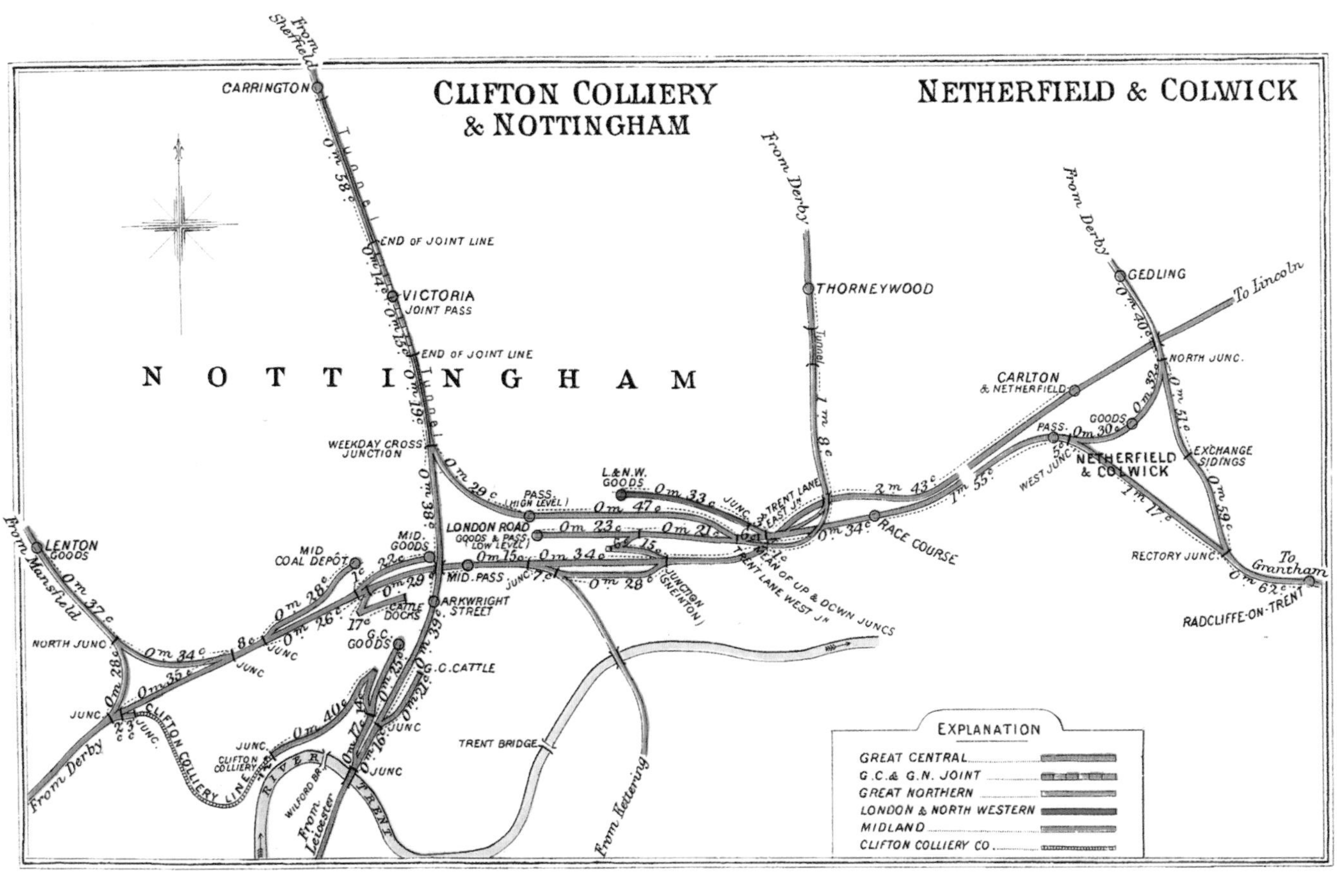

## CLIFTON COLLIERY & NOTTINGHAM

## NETHERFIELD & COLWICK

NOTTINGHAM

From Sheffield
CARRINGTON
Tunnel
0m 58c
END OF JOINT LINE
0m 14c
VICTORIA
JOINT PASS
0m 13c
END OF JOINT LINE
0m 19c
WEEKDAY CROSS JUNCTION
0m 29c
PASS. (HIGH LEVEL)
L.&N.W. GOODS
0m 33c
0m 47c
LONDON ROAD GOODS & PASS. (LOW LEVEL)
0m 23c
0m 21c
MID. GOODS
0m 38c
MID. PASS
0m 15c
0m 34c
JUNCTION (SNEINTON)
0m 28c
ARKWRIGHT STREET
CATTLE DOCKS
G.C. GOODS
G.C. CATTLE
MID COAL DEPÔT
LENTON GOODS
From Mansfield
0m 37c
0m 28c
0m 26c
NORTH JUNC.
0m 34c
0m 35c
JUNC.
From Derby
CLIFTON COLLIERY LINE
CLIFTON COLLIERY JUNC.
0m 40c
RIVER TRENT
WILFORD BR.
From Leicester
JUNC.
TRENT BRIDGE
From Kettering
From Derby
THORNEYWOOD
Tunnel
1m 8c
TRENT LANE EAST JN.
TRENT LANE WEST JN.
REAR OF UP & DOWN JUNCS
0m 34c
RACE COURSE
2m 43c
1m 55c
From Derby
GEDLING
0m 40c
To Lincoln
NORTH JUNC.
CARLTON & NETHERFIELD
GOODS
0m 32c
0m 51c
PASS.
0m 30c
WEST JUNC.
NETHERFIELD & COLWICK
EXCHANGE SIDINGS
1m 17c
0m 59c
RECTORY JUNC.
To Grantham
0m 62c
RADCLIFFE-ON-TRENT

EXPLANATION

GREAT CENTRAL
G.C. & G.N. JOINT
GREAT NORTHERN
LONDON & NORTH WESTERN
MIDLAND
CLIFTON COLLIERY CO.

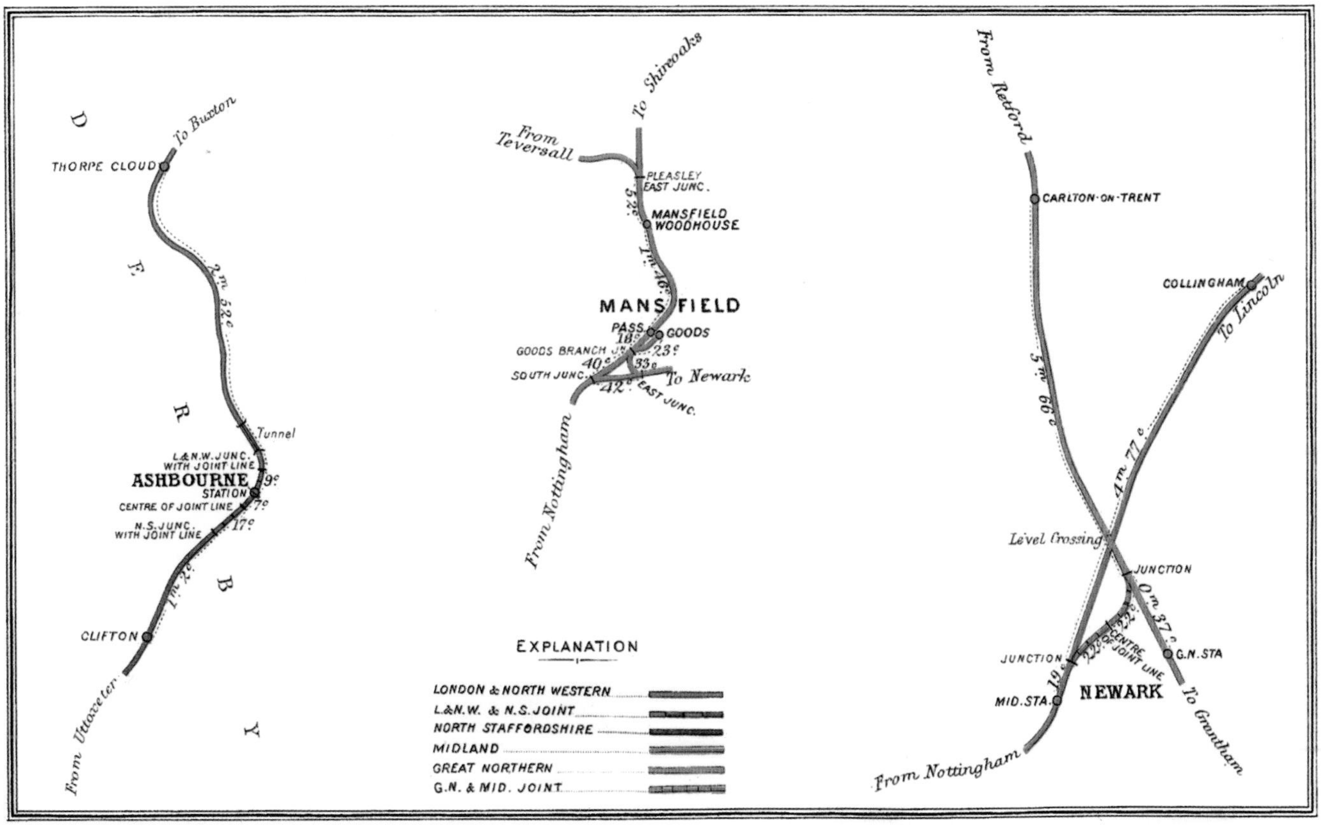

DERBY

To Buxton
THORPE CLOUD
3m 52c
Tunnel
L.&N.W. JUNC. WITH JOINT LINE
ASHBOURNE STATION
9c
CENTRE OF JOINT LINE
7c
N.S. JUNC. WITH JOINT LINE
17c
1m 2c
CLIFTON
From Uttoxeter

To Shireoaks
From Teversall
PLEASLEY EAST JUNC.
52c
MANSFIELD WOODHOUSE
1m 46c
MANSFIELD
PASS.
GOODS
18c
GOODS BRANCH JN.
23c
40c
SOUTH JUNC.
33c
42c
To Newark
EAST JUNC.
From Nottingham

EXPLANATION

LONDON & NORTH WESTERN
L&N.W. & N.S. JOINT
NORTH STAFFORDSHIRE
MIDLAND
GREAT NORTHERN
G.N. & MID. JOINT

From Retford
CARLTON-ON-TRENT
5m 66c
COLLINGHAM
To Lincoln
4m 77c
Level Crossing
JUNCTION
0m 37c
JUNCTION
CENTRE OF JOINT LINE
G.N. STA.
19c
MID. STA.
NEWARK
To Grantham
From Nottingham

**Ashbourne–Mansfield–Newark**

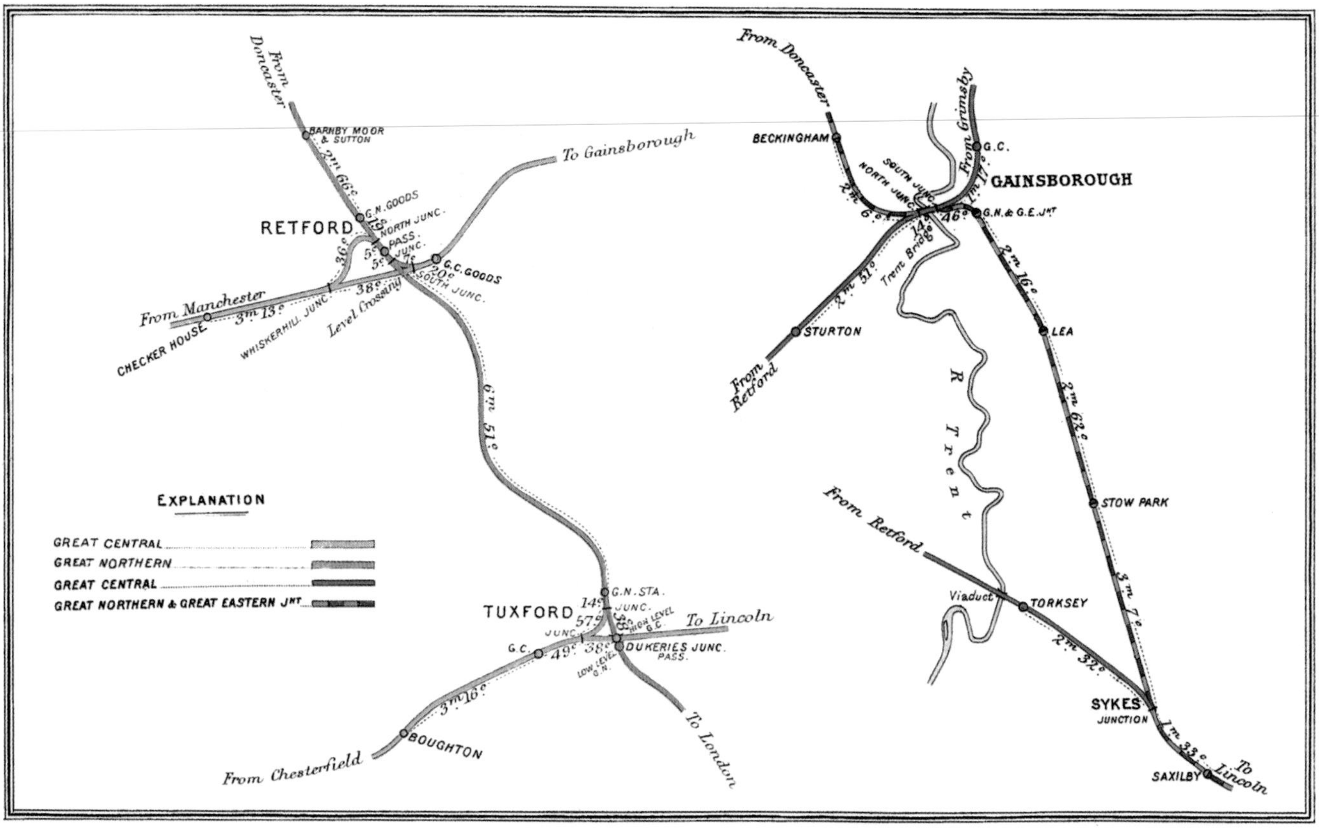

Retford–Tuxford–Gainsborough

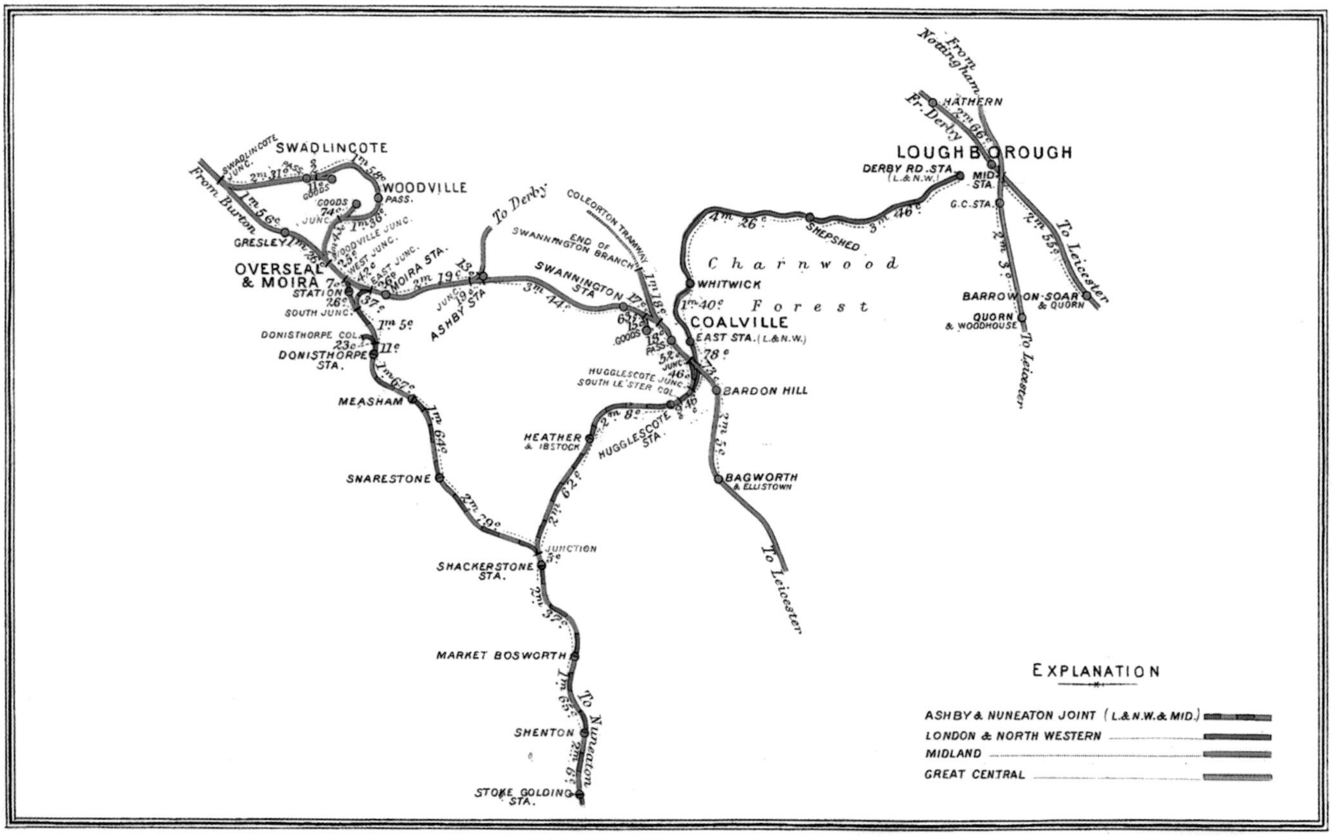

Overseal & Moira–Coalville–Loughborough

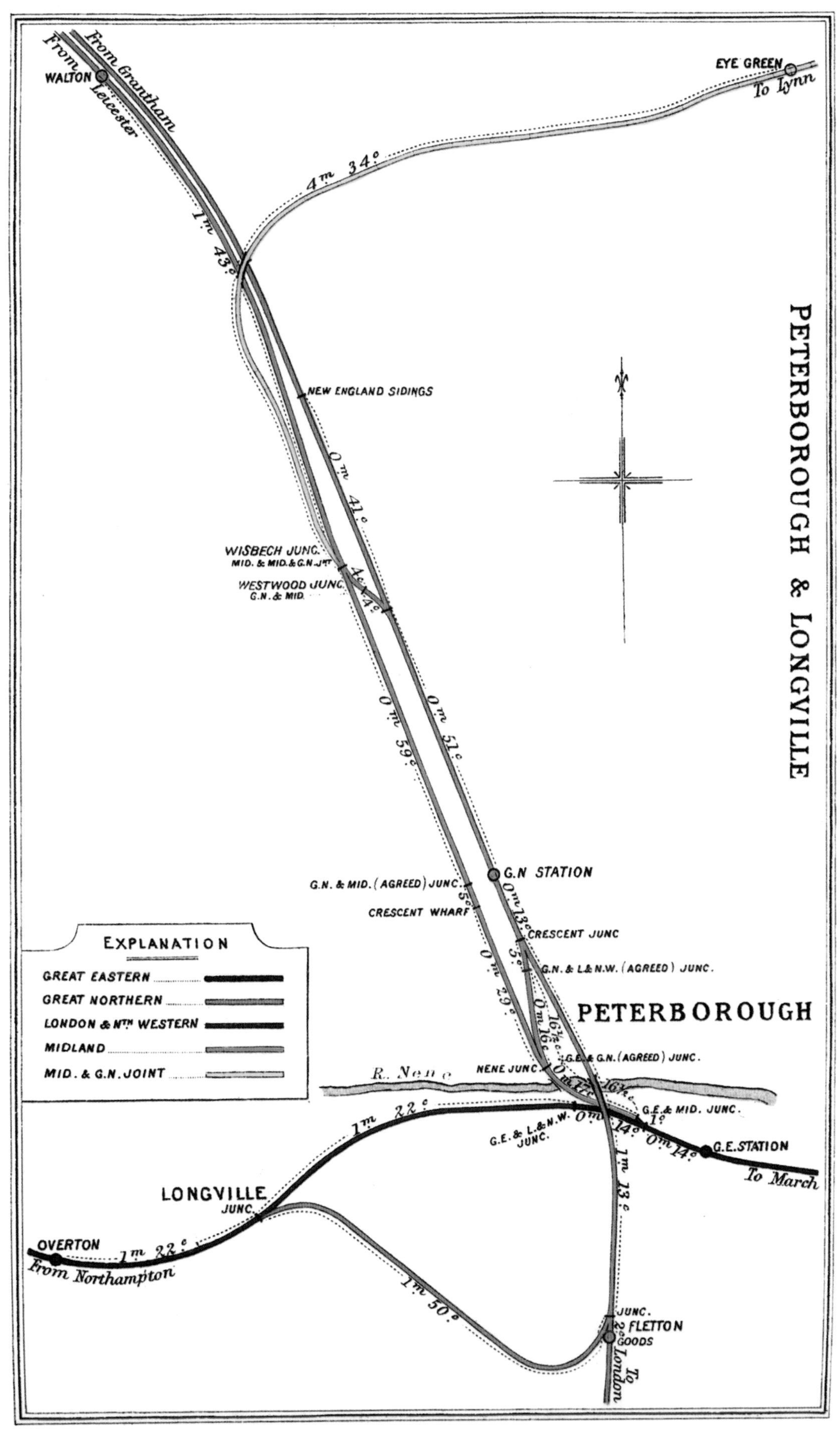
PETERBOROUGH & LONGVILLE
From Grantham
From Leicester
WALTON
EYE GREEN
To Lynn
4m 34c
1m 43c
NEW ENGLAND SIDINGS
0m 41c
WISBECH JUNC.
MID. & MID. & G.N. JNT
WESTWOOD JUNC.
G.N. & MID.
0m 51c
0m 59c
G.N STATION
G.N. & MID. (AGREED) JUNC.
CRESCENT WHARF
0m 13c
CRESCENT JUNC
G.N. & L.& N.W. (AGREED) JUNC.
0m 29c
PETERBOROUGH
EXPLANATION
GREAT EASTERN
GREAT NORTHERN
LONDON & NTH WESTERN
MIDLAND
MID. & G.N. JOINT
R. Nene
NENE JUNC.
G.E. & G.N. (AGREED) JUNC.
G.E. & MID. JUNC.
1m 22c
G.E. & L.& N.W. JUNC.
G.E. STATION
To March
1m 13c
LONGVILLE JUNC.
OVERTON
1m 22c
From Northampton
1m 50c
JUNC.
FLETTON GOODS
To London

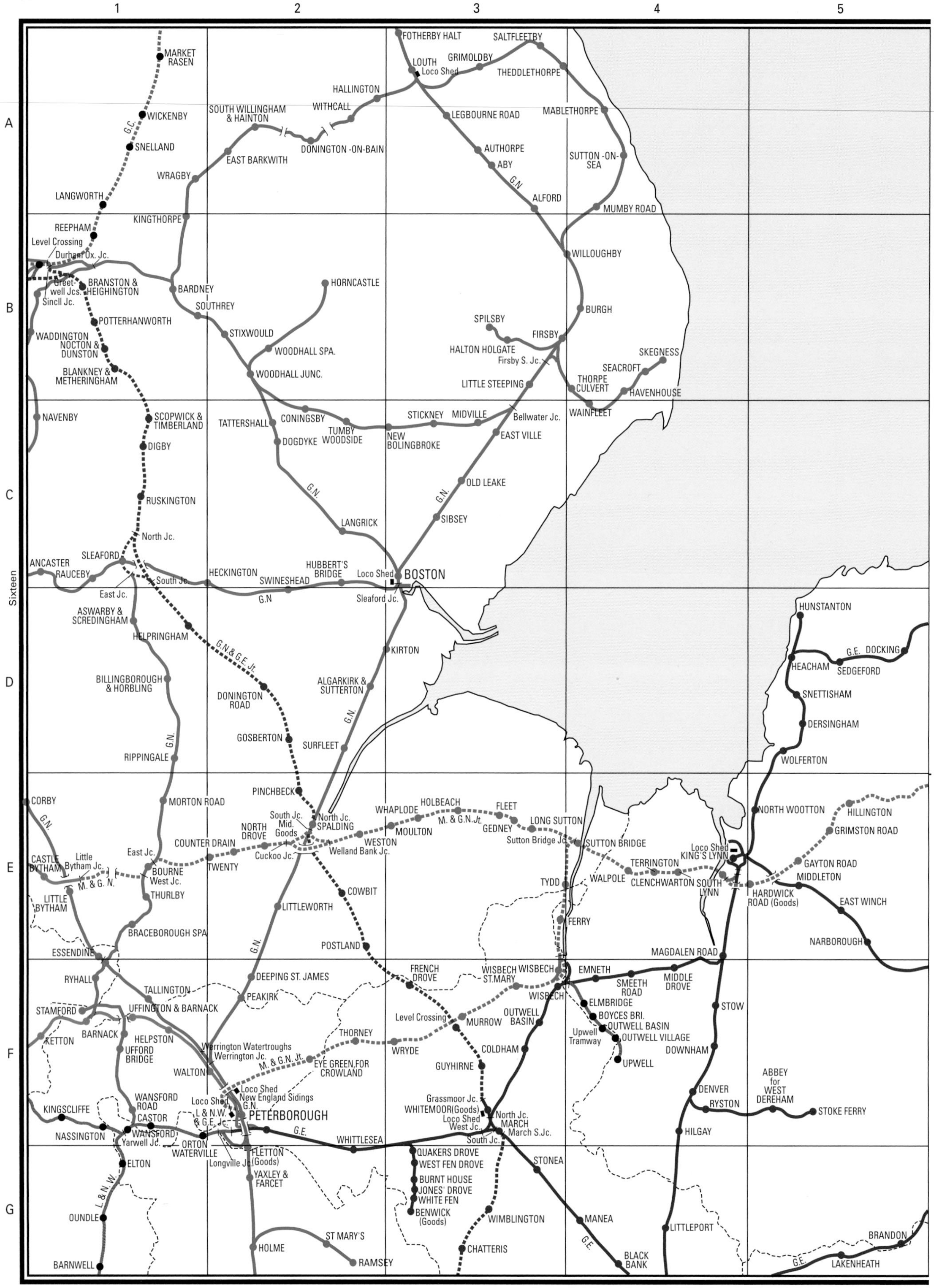

## SEVENTEEN

1 2 3 4 5

A B C D E F G

Sixteen

MARKET RASEN
WICKENBY
G.C.
SNELLAND
LANGWORTH
REEPHAM
Level Crossing
Durham Ox. Jc.
Greetwell Jcs.
Sincil Jc.
BRANSTON & HEIGHINGTON
POTTERHANWORTH
WADDINGTON
NOCTON & DUNSTON
BLANKNEY & METHERINGHAM
NAVENBY
SCOPWICK & TIMBERLAND
DIGBY
RUSKINGTON
North Jc.
SLEAFORD
ANCASTER
RAUCEBY
East Jc.
South Jc.
ASWARBY & SCREDINGHAM
HELPRINGHAM
BILLINGBOROUGH & HORBLING
RIPPINGALE
G.N.
MORTON ROAD
CORBY
G.N.
CASTLE BYTHAM
Little Bytham Jc.
M. & G. N.
LITTLE BYTHAM
East Jc.
BOURNE
West Jc.
THURLBY
BRACEBOROUGH SPA
ESSENDINE
RYHALL
TALLINGTON
STAMFORD
UFFINGTON & BARNACK
KETTON
BARNACK
HELPSTON
UFFORD BRIDGE
WALTON
KINGSCLIFFE
NASSINGTON
WANSFORD ROAD
CASTOR
WANSFORD
Yarwell Jc.
ORTON WATERVILLE
ELTON
L. & N. W.
OUNDLE
BARNWELL

SOUTH WILLINGHAM & HAINTON
WITHCALL
HALLINGTON
DONINGTON -ON-BAIN
EAST BARKWITH
WRAGBY
KINGTHORPE
BARDNEY
SOUTHREY
HORNCASTLE
STIXWOULD
WOODHALL SPA.
WOODHALL JUNC.
TATTERSHALL
CONINGSBY
TUMBY WOODSIDE
DOGDYKE
G.N.
LANGRICK
HECKINGTON
SWINESHEAD
HUBBERT'S BRIDGE
G.N
Loco Shed
BOSTON
Sleaford Jc.
KIRTON
G.N.& G.E. Jt.
DONINGTON ROAD
GOSBERTON
ALGARKIRK & SUTTERTON
SURFLEET
G.N.
PINCHBECK
South Jc.
Mid. Goods
North Jc.
SPALDING
NORTH DROVE
COUNTER DRAIN
TWENTY
Cuckoo Jc.
WESTON
Welland Bank Jc.
COWBIT
LITTLEWORTH
G.N.
POSTLAND
DEEPING ST. JAMES
PEAKIRK
Werrington Watertroughs
Werrington Jc.
M. & G.N. Jt.
EYE GREEN FOR CROWLAND
Loco Shed
New England Sidings
Loco Shed
G.N.
L & N.W. & G.E. Jc.
PETERBOROUGH
G.E.
WHITTLESEA
FLETTON (Goods)
Longville Jc.
YAXLEY & FARCET
HOLME
ST MARY'S
RAMSEY

FOTHERBY HALT
SALTFLEETBY
LOUTH
Loco Shed
GRIMOLDBY
THEDDLETHORPE
LEGBOURNE ROAD
MABLETHORPE
AUTHORPE
ABY
G.N.
SUTTON -ON-SEA
ALFORD
MUMBY ROAD
WILLOUGHBY
BURGH
SPILSBY
FIRSBY
HALTON HOLGATE
Firsby S. Jc.
SKEGNESS
SEACROFT
THORPE CULVERT
HAVENHOUSE
LITTLE STEEPING
WAINFLEET
STICKNEY
MIDVILLE
Bellwater Jc.
NEW BOLINGBROKE
EAST VILLE
OLD LEAKE
G.N.
SIBSEY
WHAPLODE
HOLBEACH
FLEET
M. & G.N. Jt.
MOULTON
GEDNEY
LONG SUTTON
Sutton Bridge Jc.
SUTTON BRIDGE
FRENCH DROVE
WISBECH ST.MARY
WISBECH
Level Crossing
MURROW
THORNEY
WRYDE
GUYHIRNE
Grassmoor Jc.
WHITEMOOR(Goods)
Loco Shed
West Jc.
North Jc.
MARCH
March S.Jc.
South Jc.
QUAKERS DROVE
WEST FEN DROVE
BURNT HOUSE
JONES' DROVE
WHITE FEN
BENWICK (Goods)
WIMBLINGTON
CHATTERIS
STONEA
MANEA
G.E.
BLACK BANK

TYDD
WALPOLE
FERRY
TERRINGTON
CLENCHWARTON
SOUTH LYNN
Loco Shed
KING'S LYNN
WISBECH
EMNETH
SMEETH ROAD
MIDDLE DROVE
MAGDALEN ROAD
ELMBRIDGE
BOYCES BRI.
OUTWELL BASIN
OUTWELL BASIN
OUTWELL VILLAGE
Upwell Tramway
UPWELL
COLDHAM
STOW
DOWNHAM
DENVER
RYSTON
HILGAY
LITTLEPORT

HUNSTANTON
G.E.
DOCKING
HEACHAM
SEDGEFORD
SNETTISHAM
DERSINGHAM
WOLFERTON
NORTH WOOTTON
HILLINGTON
GRIMSTON ROAD
GAYTON ROAD
MIDDLETON
HARDWICK ROAD (Goods)
EAST WINCH
NARBOROUGH
ABBEY for WEST DEREHAM
STOKE FERRY
BRANDON
G.E.
LAKENHEATH

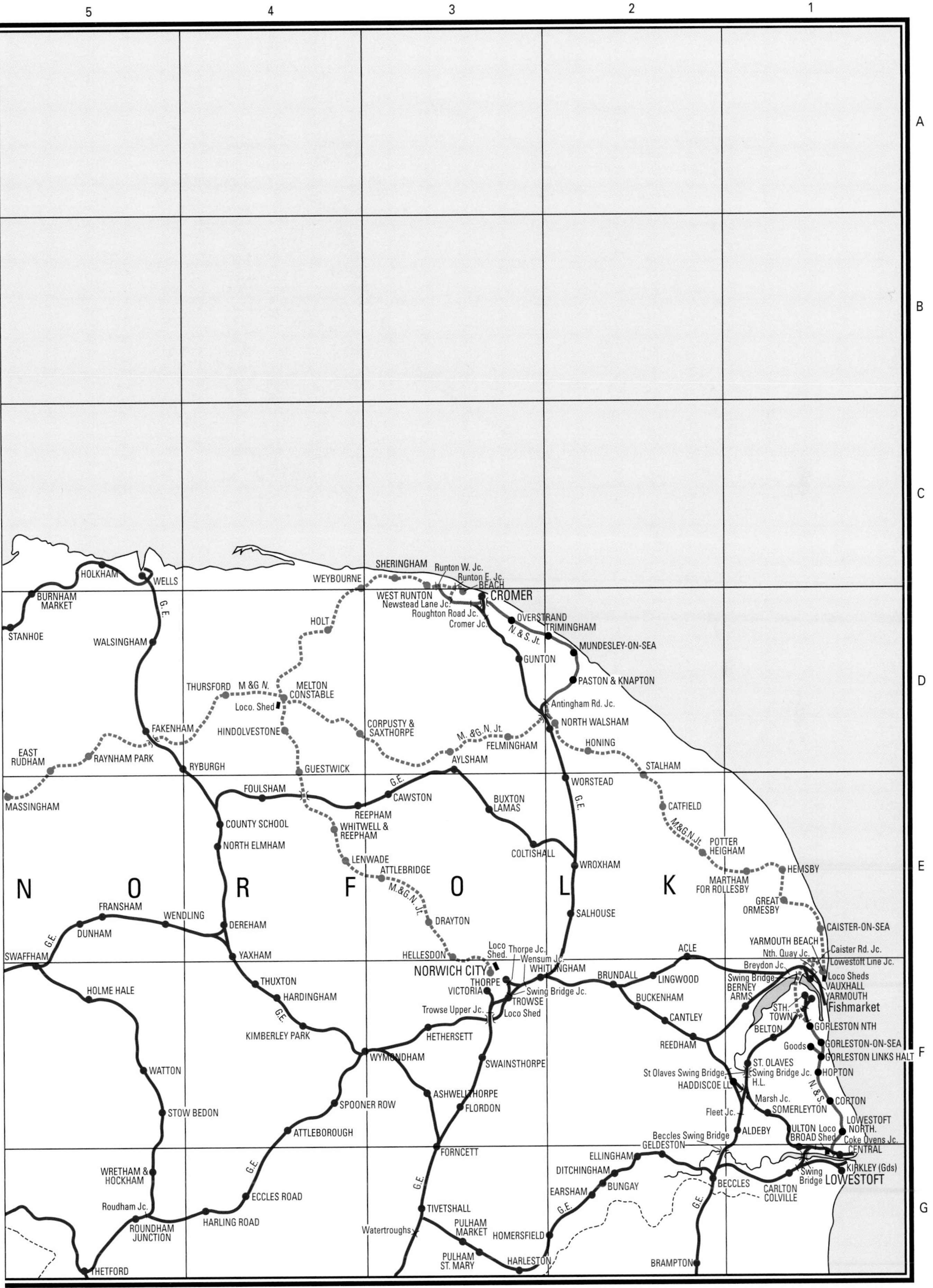
5
4
3
2
1
A
B
C
D
E
F
G
HOLKHAM
WELLS
BURNHAM MARKET
STANHOE
G.E.
WALSINGHAM
WEYBOURNE
SHERINGHAM
Runton W. Jc.
Runton E. Jc.
BEACH
CROMER
WEST RUNTON
Newstead Lane Jc.
Roughton Road Jc.
Cromer Jc.
HOLT
OVERSTRAND
TRIMINGHAM
N. & S. Jt.
MUNDESLEY-ON-SEA
GUNTON
PASTON & KNAPTON
THURSFORD
M &G N.
MELTON CONSTABLE
Loco. Shed
Antingham Rd. Jc.
NORTH WALSHAM
FAKENHAM
HINDOLVESTONE
CORPUSTY & SAXTHORPE
M. &G.N. Jt.
FELMINGHAM
HONING
EAST RUDHAM
RAYNHAM PARK
RYBURGH
GUESTWICK
AYLSHAM
STALHAM
MASSINGHAM
FOULSHAM
G.E.
CAWSTON
REEPHAM
BUXTON LAMAS
WORSTEAD
G.E.
CATFIELD
COUNTY SCHOOL
WHITWELL & REEPHAM
M&G.N.Jt.
POTTER HEIGHAM
NORTH ELMHAM
LENWADE
COLTISHALL
WROXHAM
ATTLEBRIDGE
MARTHAM FOR ROLLESBY
HEMSBY
N O R F O L K
M.&G.N. Jt.
FRANSHAM
WENDLING
DRAYTON
SALHOUSE
GREAT ORMESBY
DUNHAM
DEREHAM
CAISTER-ON-SEA
G.E.
SWAFFHAM
YAXHAM
HELLESDON
Loco Shed.
Thorpe Jc.
Wensum Jc.
YARMOUTH BEACH
Caister Rd. Jc.
Nth. Quay Jc.
Lowestoft Line Jc.
ACLE
Breydon Jc.
NORWICH CITY
WHITLINGHAM
BRUNDALL
LINGWOOD
Swing Bridge
Loco Sheds
VAUXHALL
THORPE
THUXTON
VICTORIA
Swing Bridge Jc.
BERNEY ARMS
YARMOUTH
HOLME HALE
HARDINGHAM
TROWSE
BUCKENHAM
Fishmarket
STH. TOWN
Trowse Upper Jc.
Loco Shed
G.E.
CANTLEY
BELTON
GORLESTON NTH
KIMBERLEY PARK
HETHERSETT
REEDHAM
Goods
GORLESTON-ON-SEA
GORLESTON LINKS HALT
WYMONDHAM
ST. OLAVES
WATTON
SWAINSTHORPE
St Olaves Swing Bridge
Swing Bridge Jc.
H.L.
HOPTON
HADDISCOE L.L.
N & S.
ASHWELLTHORPE
Marsh Jc.
FLORDON
CORTON
SPOONER ROW
SOMERLEYTON
STOW BEDON
Fleet Jc.
LOWESTOFT NORTH.
ALDEBY
ATTLEBOROUGH
Beccles Swing Bridge
ULTON Loco
BROAD Shed
Coke Ovens Jc.
GELDESTON
CENTRAL
FORNCETT
ELLINGHAM
WRETHAM & HOCKHAM
G.E.
DITCHINGHAM
KIRKLEY (Gds)
Swing Bridge
LOWESTOFT
G.E.
BUNGAY
BECCLES
EARSHAM
CARLTON COLVILLE
ECCLES ROAD
G.E.
G.E.
Roudham Jc.
TIVETSHALL
G.E.
ROUNDHAM JUNCTION
HARLING ROAD
PULHAM MARKET
Watertroughs
HOMERSFIELD
PULHAM ST. MARY
HARLESTON
BRAMPTON
THETFORD

Twelve

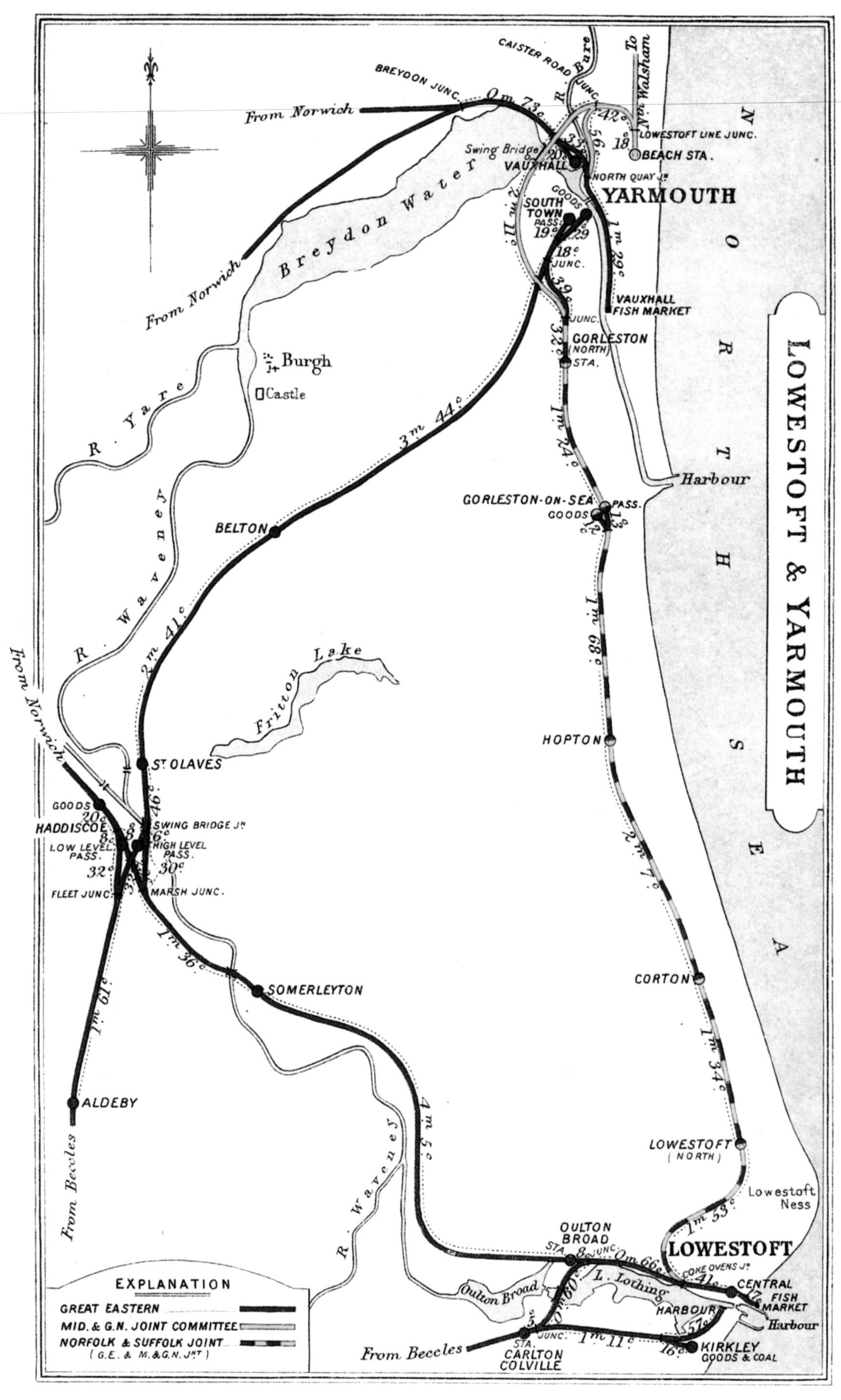

LOWESTOFT & YARMOUTH
NORTH SEA
YARMOUTH
LOWESTOFT
Breydon Water
From Norwich
From Norwich
From Norwich
From Beccles
From Beccles
To Nth Walsham
BREYDON JUNC.
CAISTER ROAD JUNC.
R. Bure
LOWESTOFT LINE JUNC.
BEACH STA.
Swing Bridge
VAUXHALL
NORTH QUAY J^N
GOODS
SOUTH TOWN PASS.
VAUXHALL FISH MARKET
GORLESTON (NORTH) STA.
Harbour
GORLESTON-ON-SEA PASS.
GOODS
BELTON
Burgh
Castle
R. Yare
R. Waveney
Fritton Lake
HOPTON
ST OLAVES
GOODS
HADDISCOE
SWING BRIDGE J^N
LOW LEVEL PASS.
HIGH LEVEL PASS.
FLEET JUNC.
MARSH JUNC.
SOMERLEYTON
CORTON
ALDEBY
LOWESTOFT (NORTH)
Lowestoft Ness
OULTON BROAD STA.
JUNC.
COKE OVENS J^N
CENTRAL
FISH MARKET
Harbour
Oulton Broad
L. Lothing
HARBOUR
JUNC.
CARLTON COLVILLE STA.
KIRKLEY GOODS & COAL
EXPLANATION
GREAT EASTERN
MID. & G.N. JOINT COMMITTEE
NORFOLK & SUFFOLK JOINT (G.E. & M.&G.N. J^NT)

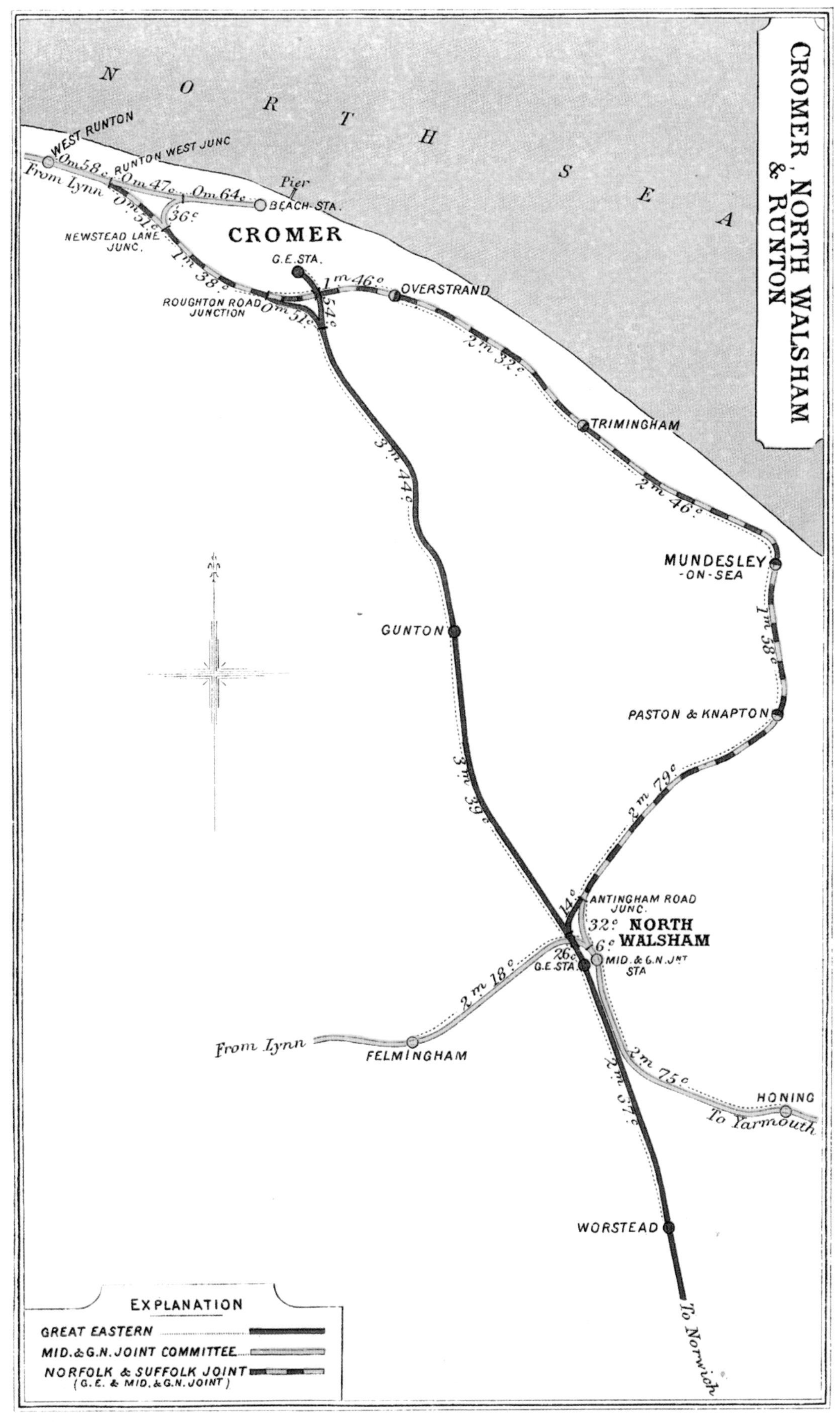

CROMER, NORTH WALSHAM & RUNTON
NORTH SEA
WEST RUNTON
RUNTON WEST JUNC
From Lynn
Pier
BEACH STA.
CROMER
NEWSTEAD LANE JUNC.
G.E. STA.
ROUGHTON ROAD JUNCTION
OVERSTRAND
TRIMINGHAM
MUNDESLEY -ON-SEA
GUNTON
PASTON & KNAPTON
ANTINGHAM ROAD JUNC.
NORTH WALSHAM
G.E. STA.
MID. & G.N. JNT STA
From Lynn
FELMINGHAM
HONING
To Yarmouth
WORSTEAD
To Norwich
EXPLANATION
GREAT EASTERN
MID. & G.N. JOINT COMMITTEE
NORFOLK & SUFFOLK JOINT (G.E. & MID. & G.N. JOINT)

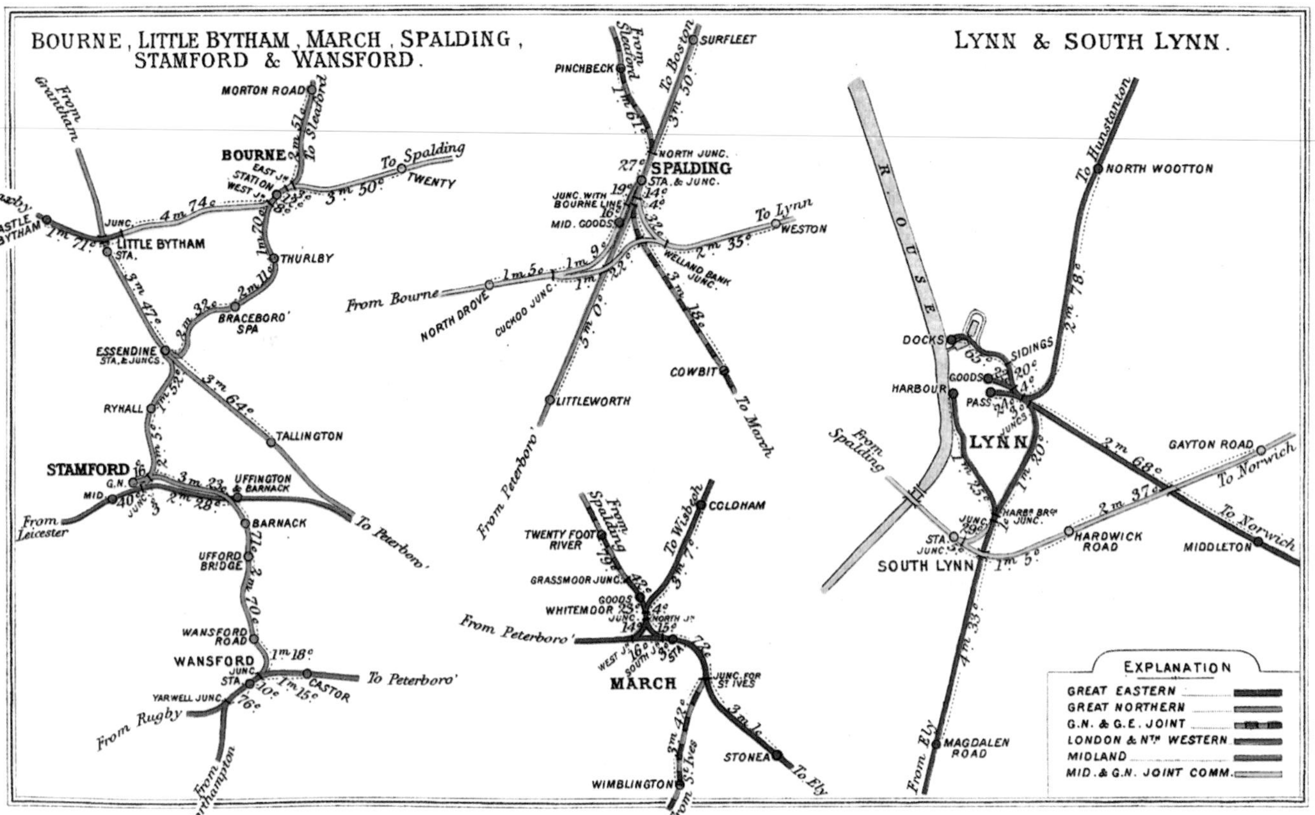

BOURNE, LITTLE BYTHAM, MARCH, SPALDING, STAMFORD & WANSFORD.

LYNN & SOUTH LYNN.

EXPLANATION

GREAT EASTERN
GREAT NORTHERN
G.N. & G.E. JOINT
LONDON & NTH WESTERN
MIDLAND
MID. & G.N. JOINT COMM.

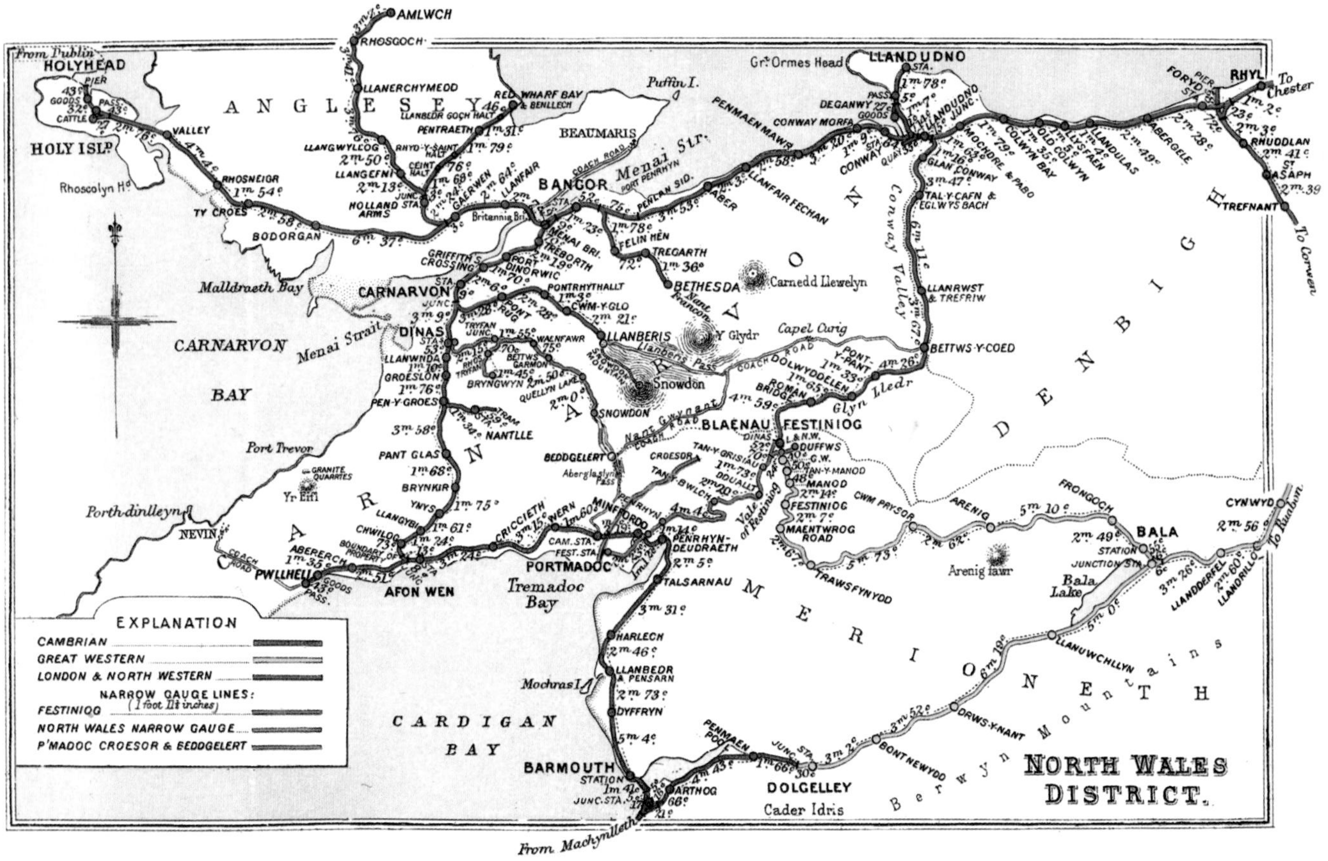

MORTON ROAD, BOURNE, TWENTY, CASTLE BYTHAM, LITTLE BYTHAM STA., THURLBY, BRACEBORO' SPA, ESSENDINE STA. & JUNCS., RYHALL, TALLINGTON, STAMFORD, UFFINGTON & BARNACK, BARNACK, UFFORD BRIDGE, WANSFORD ROAD, WANSFORD, CASTOR, YARWELL JUNC.

SURFLEET, PINCHBECK, SPALDING, WESTON, NORTH DROVE, COWBIT, LITTLEWORTH, COLDHAM, TWENTY FOOT RIVER, GRASSMOOR JUNC., WHITEMOOR, MARCH, STONEA, WIMBLINGTON.

NORTH WOOTTON, DOCKS, HARBOUR, LYNN, GAYTON ROAD, HARDWICK ROAD, MIDDLETON, SOUTH LYNN, MAGDALEN ROAD.

NORTH WALES DISTRICT.

EXPLANATION

CAMBRIAN
GREAT WESTERN
LONDON & NORTH WESTERN
NARROW GAUGE LINES:
FESTINIOG (1 foot 11½ inches)
NORTH WALES NARROW GAUGE
P'MADOC CROESOR & BEDDGELERT

ANGLESEY, CARNARVON, DENBIGH, MERIONETH, CARNARVON BAY, CARDIGAN BAY, Tremadoc Bay, Menai Strait.

AMLWCH, RHOSGOCH, LLANERCHYMEDD, HOLYHEAD, VALLEY, RHOSNEIGR, TY CROES, BODORGAN, LLANGEFNI, HOLLAND ARMS, RED WHARF BAY & BENLLECH, PENTRAETH, BEAUMARIS, LLANFAIR, BANGOR, MENAI BRI., TREBORTH, PORT DINORWIC, GRIFFITHS CROSSING, CARNARVON, PONT RUG, PONTRHYTHALLT, CWM-Y-GLO, LLANBERIS, SNOWDON, BETHESDA, TREGARTH, FELIN HEN, DINAS, TRYFAN JUNC., WAENFAWR, BETTWS GARMON, QUELLYN LAKE, LLANWNDA, GROESLON, PEN-Y-GROES, NANTLLE, PANT GLAS, BRYNKIR, LLANGYBI, CHWILOG, ABERERCH, PWLLHELI, AFON WEN, CRICCIETH, BEDDGELERT, CROESOR, MINFFORDD, PORTMADOC, PENRHYN-DEUDRAETH, TALSARNAU, HARLECH, LLANBEDR & PENSARN, DYFFRYN, BARMOUTH, ARTHOG, PENMAENPOOL, DOLGELLEY, BONTNEWYDD, DRWS-Y-NANT, LLANUWCHLLYN, BALA, FRONGOCH, ARENIG, CWM PRYSOR, TRAWSFYNYDD, MAENTWROG ROAD, FESTINIOG, MANOD, TAN-Y-MANOD, DUFFWS, BLAENAU FESTINIOG, TAN-Y-GRISIAU, DDUALLT, TAN-Y-BWLCH, ROMAN BRIDGE, DOLWYDDELEN, PONT-Y-PANT, BETTWS-Y-COED, LLANRWST & TREFRIW, TAL-Y-CAFN & EGLWYS BACH, GLAN CONWAY, CONWAY, LLANDUDNO, DEGANWY, CONWAY MORFA, PENMAENMAWR, LLANFAIRFECHAN, ABER, COLWYN BAY, OLD COLWYN, LLANDDULAS, ABERGELE, RHYL, FORYD, RHUDDLAN, ST ASAPH, TREFNANT, CYNWYD, LLANDRILLO, LLANDDERFEL.

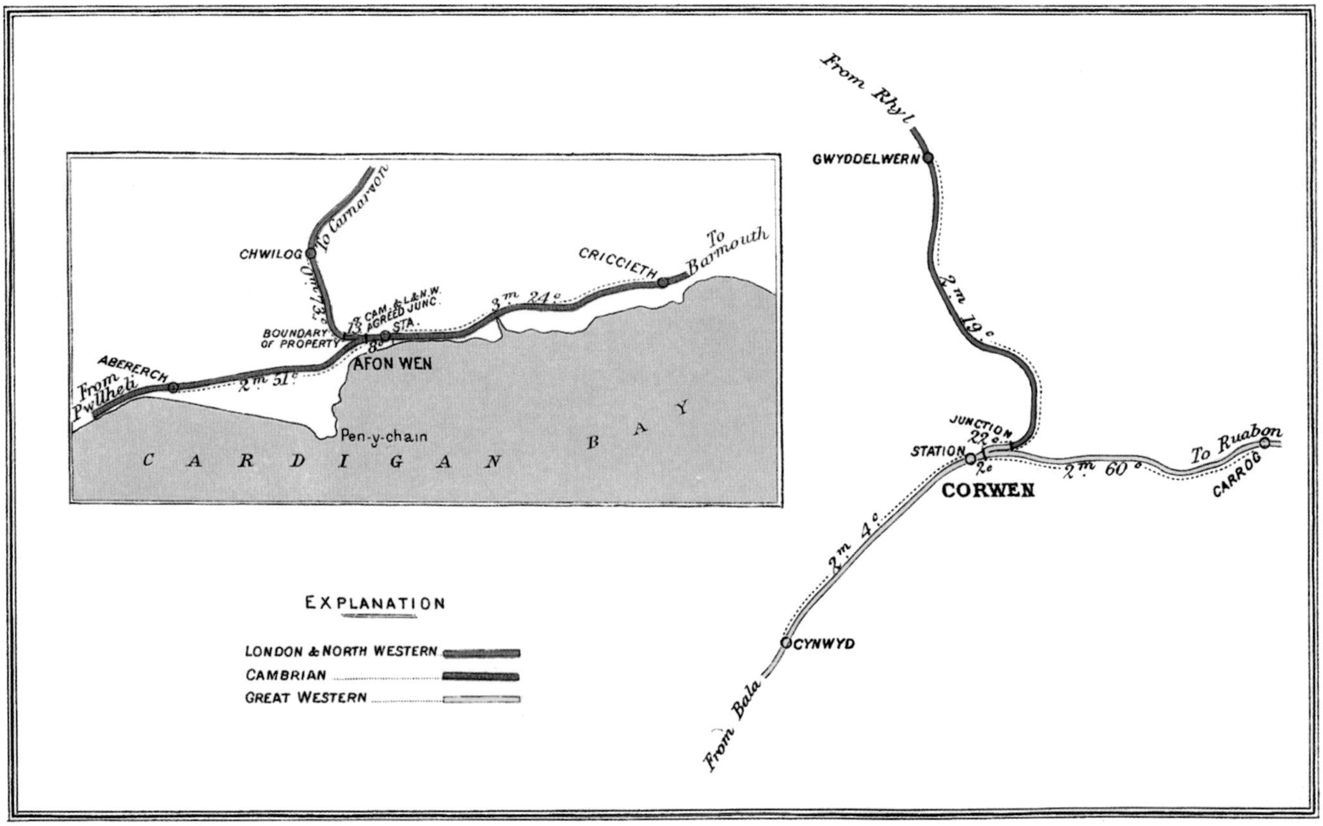

Afon Wen–Corwen

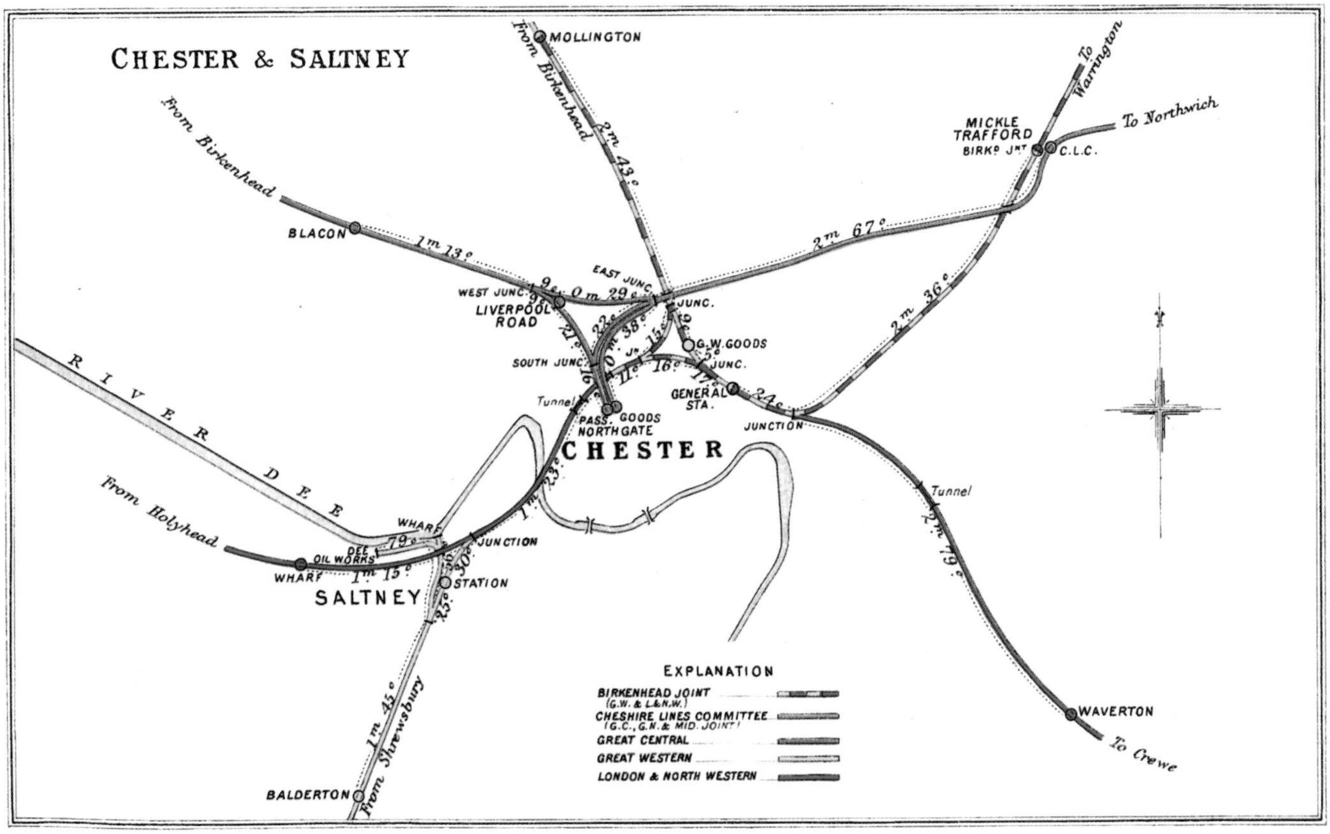

CHESTER & SALTNEY

1 2 3 4 Seven 5

A
B
C
D
E
F
G

Inset

Pier
Loco Shed
HOLYHEAD
VALLEY
Holy Island
L&N.W.
RHOSNEIGR

AMLWCH
RHOSGOCH
LLANERCHYMEDD
ANGLESEY
REDWHARF BAY & BENLLECH
LLANBEDR - GOCH
LLANGWYLLOG
PENTRAETH
RHYD-Y-SAINT
LLANGEFNI
CEINT
RHOSNEIGR
TY CROES
HOLLAND ARMS
BODORGAN
Bodorgan Tuns.
L.& N. W.
LLANFAIR
GAERWEN
Britannia Tubular Bridge
Belmont Tun.
BANGOR
Bangor Tun.
Llandegai Tun.
MENAI BR.
TREBORTH
FELIN HEN
TREGARTH
BETHESDA
ABER
Aber Watertroughs
LLANFAIRFECHAN
PENMAENMAWR
CONWAY MORFA
PORT DINORWIC
GRIFFITHS CROSSING
PONT RUG
PONTRHYTHALLT
CWM-Y-GLO
CARNARVON
TRYFAN JUNC.
WAENFAWR
LLANBERIS
DINAS JUNC.
RHOS TRYFAN
Line closed 1914
BETTWS GARMON
Y Glydr
LLANWNDA
BRYNGWYN
QUELLYN LAKE
SNOWDON MOUNTAIN RLY.
Moel Siabod
GROESLON
SNOWDON
PENYGROES
NANTLLE
NORTH WALES N.G.R.
Snowdon
ROMAN BRIDGE
DOLWYDDELEN
PONT-Y-PANT
CARNARVON
Festiniog Tun.
PANT GLAS
BEDDGELERT
BLAENAU FESTINIOG
DINAS
L & N.W.
DUFFWS
TAN-Y-GRISIAU
FEST.
G.W.
MANOD
CROESOR R.
BRYNKIR
TAN-Y-BWLCH
DDUALLT
FESTINIOG RLY.
FESTINIOG
YNYS
LLANGYBI
PORTMADOC
FEST.
PENRHYNDEUDRAETH
MINFFORDD
CAM.
MAENTWROG RD.
CHWILOG
AFONWEN
WERN (Goods)
PENYCHAIN open 1933
ABERERCH
CRICCIETH
PWLLHELI
TALSARNAU
TRAWSFYNYDD
CAM.
HARLECH
LLANBEDR & PENSARN
DYFFRYN
TALYBONT HALT
CAM.

LLANDUDNO
DEGANWY
LLANDUDNO JUNCTION
COLWYN BAY
Penmaenrhos Tun.
LLYSFAEN
MOCHDRE & PABO
OLD COLWYN
LLANDULAS
ABERGELE
CLAN CONWAY
TAL-Y-CAFN & EGLWYS BACH
L & N.W.
LLANRWST & TREFRIW
DENBIGH
BETTWS-Y-COED
Prestatyn Watertroughs
Foryd Jc.
Pier
FORYD
RHYL
PRESTATYN
RHUDDLAN ROAD
MELIDEN
DYSERTH
RHUDDLAN
ST. ASAPH
TREFNANT
BODFARI
DENBIGH
L & N.W.
LLANRHAIADR
RHEWL
RUTHIN
EYARTH
NANTCLWYD
DERWEN
GWYDDELWERN
CORWEN
G.W.
CYNWYD
ARENIG
G.W.
FRONGOCH
CWM PRYSOR
G.W.
LLANDRILLO
Llandderfel Tun.
LLANDDERFEL
BALA
Bala Lake
BALA JUNC.
MERIONETHSHIRE
G.W.
LLANUWCHLLYN
Rhobell fawr
Aran Benllyn
DRWS-Y-NANT
Aran Mawddwy
BONT NEWYDD
LLANGYNOG
TANAT VALLEY
PENYBONTFAWR
PEDAIR-FFORDD

Thirteen
Fourteen

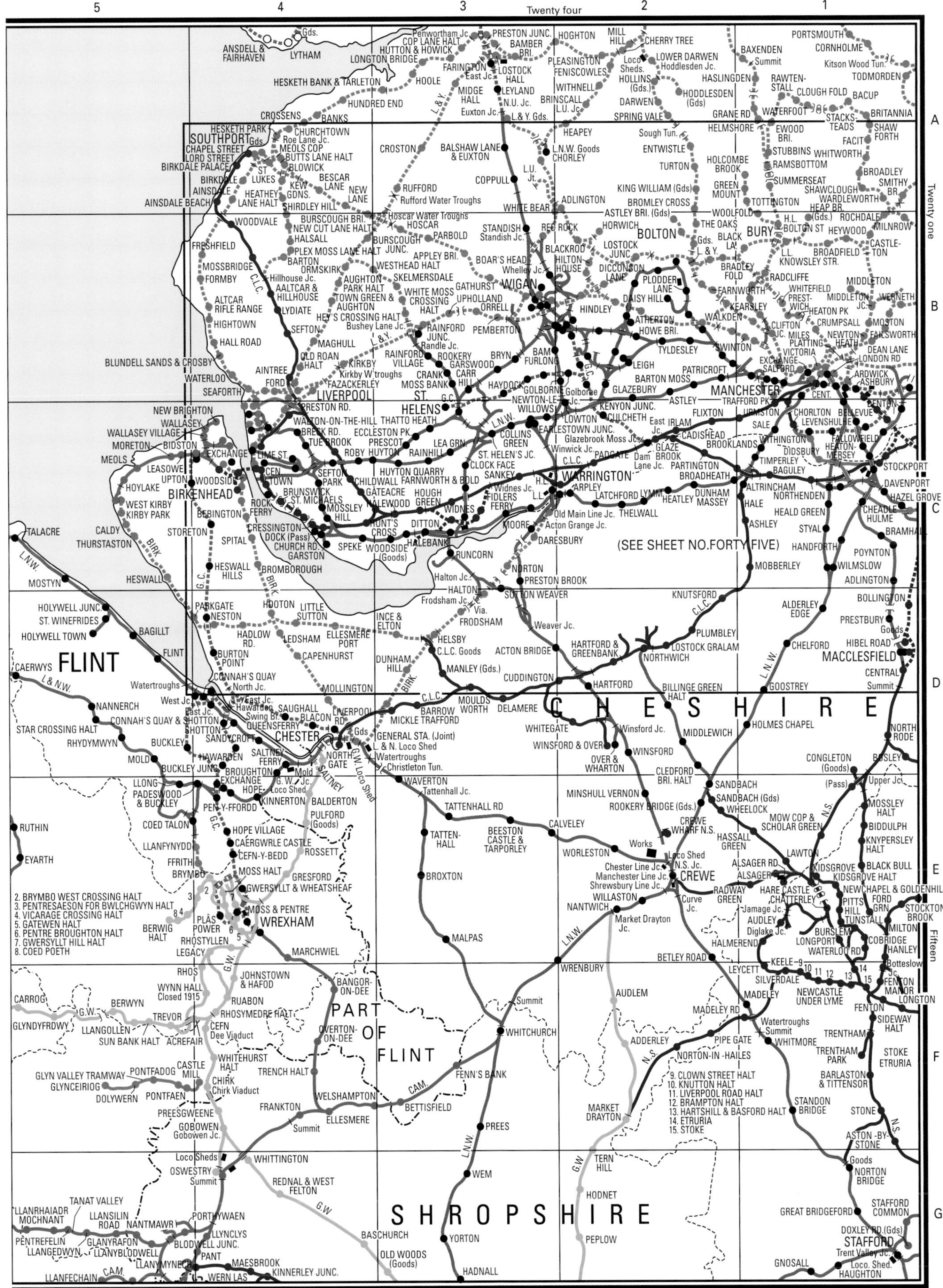

5
4
3
2
1
Twenty four
Twenty one
Fourteen
Fifteen
A
B
C
D
E
F
G
ANSDELL & FAIRHAVEN
LYTHAM
LONGTON BRIDGE
HUTTON & HOWICK
COP LANE HALT
Penwortham Jc.
PRESTON JUNC.
BAMBER BRI.
HOGHTON
MILL HILL
CHERRY TREE
LOWER DARWEN
Hoddlesden Jc.
BAXENDEN
Summit
PORTSMOUTH
CORNHOLME
Kitson Wood Tun.
TODMORDEN
HESKETH BANK & TARLETON
HOOLE
FARINGTON East Jc.
LOSTOCK HALL
LEYLAND
N.U. Jc.
MIDGE HALL
Euxton Jc.
L.& Y. Gds.
PLEASINGTON
FENISCOWLES
WITHNELL
BRINSCALL
L.U. Jc.
HOLLINS (Gds.)
DARWEN
SPRING VALE
HODDLESDEN (Gds)
HASLINGDEN
RAWTENSTALL
CLOUGH FOLD
BACUP
GRANE RD
WATERFOOT
STACKSTEADS
BRITANNIA
HUNDRED END
CROSSENS
BANKS
HESKETH PARK
SOUTHPORT
CHAPEL STREET
LORD STREET
BIRKDALE PALACE
CHURCHTOWN
Roe Lane Jc.
MEOLS COP
BUTTS LANE HALT
BLOWICK
ST. LUKES
BIRKDALE
AINSDALE
KEW GDNS.
BESCAR LANE
NEW LANE
HEATHEY LANE HALT
SHIRDLEY HILL
AINSDALE BEACH
CROSTON
BALSHAW LANE & EUXTON
RUFFORD
Rufford Water Troughs
COPPULL
HEAPEY
L.N.W. Goods
CHORLEY
Sough Tun.
ENTWISTLE
TURTON
HELMSHORE
EWOOD BRI.
STUBBINS
WHITWORTH
FACIT
SHAW FORTH
RAMSBOTTOM
HOLCOMBE BROOK
SUMMERSEAT
BROADLEY
SMITHY BR.
SHAWCLOUGH
WARDLEWORTH
KING WILLIAM (Gds)
GREEN MOUNT
TOTTINGTON
ADLINGTON
BROMLEY CROSS
WHITE BEAR
ASTLEY BRI. (Gds)
WOOLFOLD
THE OAKS
HEAP BR.
ROCHDALE
MILNROW
WOODVALE
BURSCOUGH BRI.
Hoscar Water Troughs
HOSCAR
NEW CUT LANE HALT
HALSALL
PARBOLD
STANDISH
Standish Jc.
RED ROCK
HORWICH
BOLTON
BURY
BOLTON ST
HEYWOOD
CASTLETON
FRESHFIELD
PLEX MOSS LANE HALT
BURSCOUGH JUNC.
APPLEY BRI.
BARTON
ORMSKIRK
WESTHEAD HALT
BOAR'S HEAD
Whelley Jc.
BLACKROD
HILTON HOUSE
LOSTOCK JUNC.
DICCONSON LANE
BRADLEY FOLD
RADCLIFFE
KNOWSLEY STR.
BROADFIELD
MIDDLETON
MOSSBRIDGE
FORMBY
Hillhouse Jc.
AALTCAR & HILLHOUSE
AUGHTON PARK HALT
SKELMERSDALE
GATHURST
WIGAN
PLODDER LANE
FARNWORTH
WHITEFIELD
PRESTWICH
ALTCAR RIFLE RANGE
TOWN GREEN & AUGHTON
WHITE MOSS CROSSING HALT
UPHOLLAND
ORRELL
DAISY HILL
KEARSLEY
HEATON PK
MIDDLETON JC.
WERNETH
HIGHTOWN
LYDIATE
HEY'S CROSSING HALT
Bushey Lane Jc.
RAINFORD JUNC.
Randle Jc.
PEMBERTON
HINDLEY
ATHERTON
HOWE BRI.
WALKDEN
CLIFTON JC.
CRUMPSALL
MOSTON
FAILSWORTH
HALL ROAD
SEFTON
MAGHULL
TYLDESLEY
SWINTON
MILES PLATTING
NEWTON HEATH
DEAN LANE
VICTORIA
BLUNDELL SANDS & CROSBY
OLD ROAN HALT
KIRKBY
RAINFORD VILLAGE
ROOKERY
GARSWOOD
BRYN
BAMFURLONG
LEIGH
PATRICROFT
EXCHANGE
SALFORD
LONDON RD
ARDWICK
ASHBURY
WATERLOO
AINTREE
Kirkby W'troughs
CRANK
CARR HILL
HAYDOCK
GOLBORNE
BARTON MOSS
SEAFORTH
FORD
FAZACKERLEY
MOSS BANK
LIVERPOOL
ST. HELENS
G.C.
NEWTON-LE-WILLOWS
Golborne Jc.
GLAZEBURY
ASTLEY
MANCHESTER
TRAFFORD PK.
CENT.
GORTON
NEW BRIGHTON
PRESTON RD.
KENYON JUNC.
CULCHETH
LOWTON
EARLESTOWN JUNC.
WALLASEY
WALTON-ON-THE-HILL
THATTO HEATH
FLIXTON
URMSTON
CHORLTON
BELLEVUE
WALLASEY VILLAGE
BREK RD.
ECCLESTON PK.
LEA GRN
COLLINS GREEN
Glazebrook Moss Jc.
East Jc.
IRLAM
CADISHEAD
LEVENSHULME
SALE
FALLOWFIELD
MORETON
BIDSTON
EXCHANGE
TUEBROOK
PRESCOT
ROBY
HUYTON
RAINHILL
ST. HELEN'S JC.
Winwick Jc.
PADGATE
Dam Lane Jc.
GLAZEBROOK
BROOKLANDS
WITHINGTON
DIDSBURY
HEATON MERSEY
MEOLS
LIME ST.
LEASOWE
CEN TOWN
CLOCK FACE
C.L.C.
PARTINGTON
TIMPERLEY
BAGULEY
STOCKPORT
UPTON
WOODSIDE
SEFTON PARK
HUYTON QUARRY
FARNWORTH & BOLD
SANKEY
WARRINGTON
BROADHEATH
DAVENPORT
HOYLAKE
BIRKENHEAD
BRUNSWICK
CHILDWALL
GATEACRE
HOUGH GREEN
Widnes Jc.
ARPLEY
LATCHFORD
LYMM
HEATLEY
DUNHAM MASSEY
ALTRINCHAM
NORTHENDEN
HAZEL GROVE
WEST KIRBY
KIRBY PARK
ROCK FERRY
ST. MICHAELS
MOSSLEY HILL
HALEWOOD
WIDNES
FIDLERS FERRY
Old Main Line Jc.
THELWALL
HALE
HEALD GREEN
CHEADLE HULME
BEBINGTON
CRESSINGTON
HUNT'S CROSS
DITTON
MOORE
Acton Grange Jc.
ASHLEY
STYAL
BRAMHALL
TALACRE
CALDY
THURSTASTON
STORETON
SPITAL
DOCK (Pass)
CHURCH RD.
GARSTON
SPEKE
HALEBANK
WOODSIDE (Goods)
DARESBURY
(SEE SHEET NO.FORTY FIVE)
HANDFORTH
POYNTON
BIRK.
RUNCORN
L.N.W.
MOSTYN
HESWALL
HESWALL HILLS
BROMBOROUGH
NORTON
PRESTON BROOK
MOBBERLEY
WILMSLOW
ADLINGTON
Halton Jc.
HALTON
Frodsham Jc.
SUTTON WEAVER
KNUTSFORD
BOLLINGTON
HOLYWELL JUNC.
ST. WINEFRIDES
HOLYWELL TOWN
PARKGATE
NESTON
HOOTON
LITTLE SUTTON
INCE & ELTON
Via.
FRODSHAM
Weaver Jc.
ALDERLEY EDGE
PRESTBURY
Goods
BAGILLT
HADLOW RD.
LEDSHAM
ELLESMERE PORT
HELSBY
C.L.C. Goods
ACTON BRIDGE
HARTFORD & GREENBANK
PLUMBLEY
LOSTOCK GRALAM
NORTHWICH
CHELFORD
HIBEL ROAD
MACCLESFIELD
FLINT
BURTON POINT
CAPENHURST
DUNHAM HILL
MANLEY (Gds.)
CUDDINGTON
CENTRAL
CAERWYS
L & N.W.
CONNAH'S QUAY
North Jc.
Watertroughs
MOLLINGTON
HARTFORD
BILLINGE GREEN HALT
GOOSTREY
Summit
West Jc.
East Jc.
Hawarden Swing Br.
SAUGHALL
BLACON
LIVERPOOL RD
MOULDSWORTH
DELAMERE
BARROW
MICKLE TRAFFORD
C H E S H I R E
NANNERCH
CONNAH'S QUAY & SHOTTON
SHOTTON
QUEENSFERRY
STAR CROSSING HALT
RHYDYMWYN
BUCKLEY
SANDYCROFT
CHESTER
Gds
GENERAL STA. (Joint)
L. & N. Loco Shed
Watertroughs
Christleton Tun.
WHITEGATE
Winsford Jc.
WINSFORD & OVER
OVER & WHARTON
WINSFORD
MIDDLEWICH
HOLMES CHAPEL
NORTH RODE
MOLD
HAWARDEN
SALTNEY FERRY
BROUGHTON
NORTHGATE
G.W. Loco Shed
SALTNEY
Mold Jc.
CONGLETON (Goods)
(Pass)
BOSLEY
Upper Jc.
BUCKLEY JUNC.
EXCHANGE
HOPE
LLONG
PADESWOOD & BUCKLEY
G.W. Jc.
Loco Shed
KINNERTON
WAVERTON
Tattenhall Jc.
CLEDFORD BRI. HALT
MINSHULL VERNON
ROOKERY BRIDGE (Gds.)
SANDBACH
SANDBACH (Gds)
WHEELOCK
MOSSLEY HALT
PEN-Y-FFORDD
BALDERTON
TATTENHALL RD
MOW COP & SCHOLAR GREEN
BIDDULPH
RUTHIN
COED TALON
HOPE VILLAGE
PULFORD (Goods)
TATTENHALL
BEESTON CASTLE & TARPORLEY
CALVELEY
CREWE WHARF N.S.
HASSALL GREEN
KNYPERSLEY HALT
LLANFYNYDD
CAERGWRLE CASTLE
ROSSETT
Works
Loco Shed
N.S. Jc.
LAWTON
EYARTH
FFRITH
CEFN-Y-BEDD
WORLESTON
ALSAGER RD
KIDSGROVE
BLACK BULL
KIDSGROVE HALT
BRYMBO
MOSS HALT
BROXTON
Chester Line Jc.
Manchester Line Jc.
Shrewsbury Line Jc.
CREWE
ALSAGER
HARECASTLE
GRESFORD
GWERSYLLT & WHEATSHEAF
WILLASTON
RADWAY GREEN
CHATTERLEY
NEWCHAPEL & GOLDENHILL
FORD GRN
PITTS HILL
TUNSTALL
STOCKTON BROOK
2. BRYMBO WEST CROSSING HALT
3. PENTRESAESON FOR BWLCHGWYN HALT
4. VICARAGE CROSSING HALT
5. GATEWEN HALT
6. PENTRE BROUGHTON HALT
7. GWERSYLLT HILL HALT
8. COED POETH
MOSS & PENTRE
WREXHAM
NANTWICH
Curve Jc.
Jamage Jc.
AUDLEY
Diglake Jc.
BURSLEM
MILTON
BERWIG HALT
PLAS POWER
RHOSTYLLEN
LEGACY
Market Drayton Jc.
MALPAS
HALMEREND
LONGPORT
WATERLOO RD
COBRIDGE
HANLEY
MARCHWIEL
BETLEY ROAD
KEELE
LEYCETT
SILVERDALE
Botteslow Jc.
FENTON MANOR
LONGTON
RHOS
WYNN HALL Closed 1915
JOHNSTOWN & HAFOD
BANGOR-ON-DEE
WRENBURY
AUDLEM
MADELEY
NEWCASTLE UNDER LYME
FENTON
CARROG
BERWYN
RUABON
RHOSYMEDRE HALT
PART OF FLINT
Summit
MADELEY RD
SIDEWAY HALT
GLYNDYFRDWY
LLANGOLLEN
TREVOR
CEFN
Dee Viaduct
OVERTON-ON-DEE
WHITCHURCH
ADDERLEY
Watertroughs
Summit
WHITMORE
PIPE GATE
TRENTHAM
SUN BANK HALT
ACREFAIR
NORTON-IN-HAILES
TRENTHAM PARK
STOKE
ETRURIA
GLYN VALLEY TRAMWAY
PONTFADOG
CASTLE MILL
WHITEHURST HALT
CHIRK
Chirk Viaduct
TRENCH HALT
FENN'S BANK
CAM.
N.S.
9. CLOWN STREET HALT
10. KNUTTON HALT
11. LIVERPOOL ROAD HALT
12. BRAMPTON HALT
13. HARTSHILL & BASFORD HALT
14. ETRURIA
15. STOKE
BARLASTON & TITTENSOR
GLYNCEIRIOG
DOLYWERN
PONTFAEN
WELSHAMPTON
BETTISFIELD
MARKET DRAYTON
STANDON BRIDGE
STONE
PREESGWEENE
FRANKTON
ELLESMERE
Summit
GOBOWEN
Gobowen Jc.
PREES
ASTON-BY-STONE
Loco Sheds
WHITTINGTON
OSWESTRY
Summit
REDNAL & WEST FELTON
WEM
G.W.
TERN HILL
HODNET
Goods
NORTON BRIDGE
TANAT VALLEY
LLANRHAIADR MOCHNANT
LLANSILIN ROAD
NANTMAWR
PORTHYWAEN
S H R O P S H I R E
GREAT BRIDGEFORD
STAFFORD COMMON
PENTREFELIN
LLANGEDWYN
GLANYRAFON
LLANYBLODWELL
LLYNCLYS
BLODWELL JUNC.
PANT
BASCHURCH
YORTON
PEPLOW
DOXLEY RD (Gds)
STAFFORD
Trent Valley Jc.
Loco. Shed
HAUGHTON
GNOSALL
LLANYMYNECH
MAESBROOK
KINNERLEY JUNC.
WERN LAS
OLD WOODS (Goods)
HADNALL
LLANFECHAIN

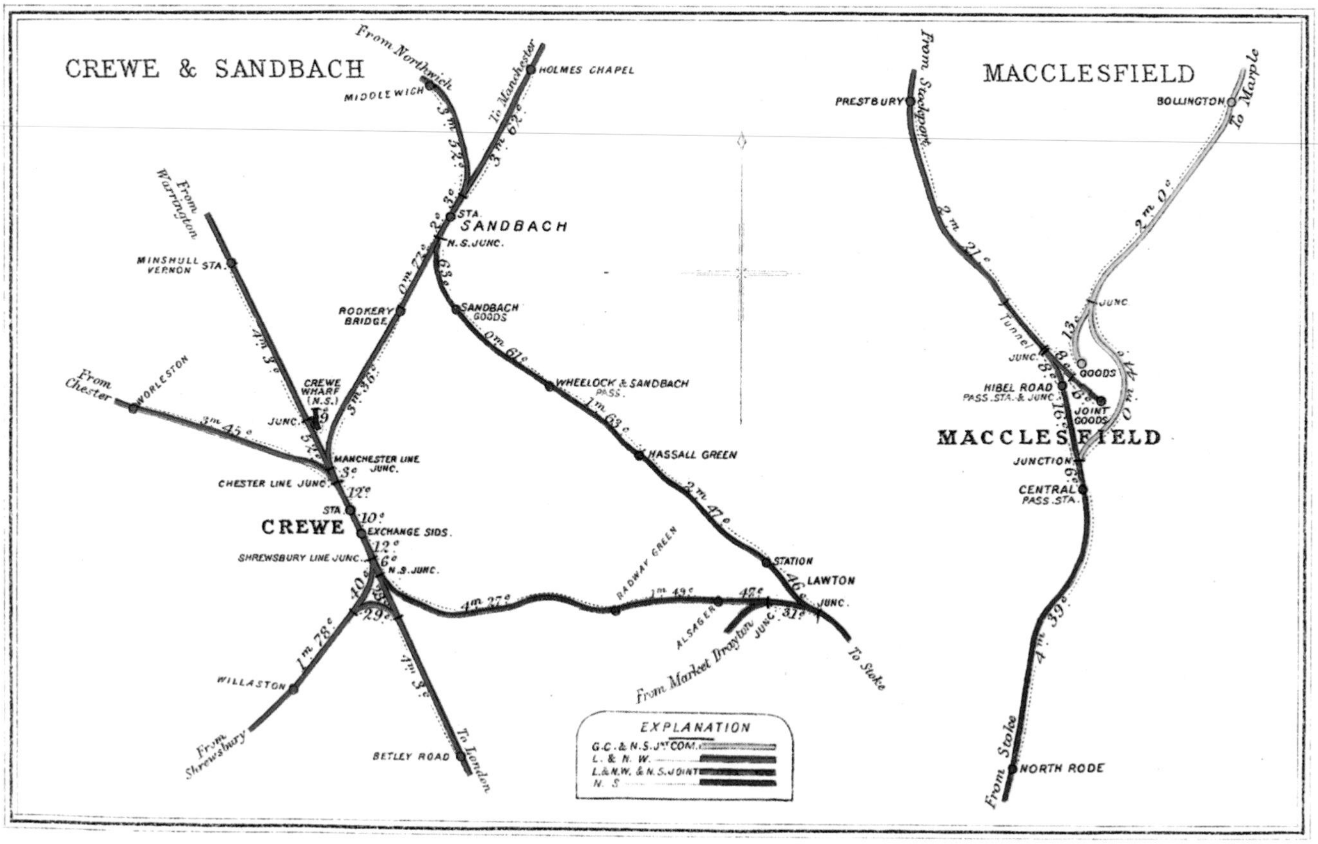

## CREWE & SANDBACH

From Northwich
MIDDLEWICH
HOLMES CHAPEL
To Manchester
SANDBACH
N.S. JUNC.
SANDBACH GOODS
RODKERY BRIDGE
WHEELOCK & SANDBACH PASS.
HASSALL GREEN
From Warrington
MINSHULL VERNON STA.
From Chester
WORLESTON
CREWE WHARF (N.S.)
JUNC.
MANCHESTER LINE JUNC.
CHESTER LINE JUNC.
CREWE
EXCHANGE SIDS.
SHREWSBURY LINE JUNC.
N.S. JUNC.
RADWAY GREEN
ALSAGER
STATION
LAWTON JUNC.
From Market Drayton
To Stoke
WILLASTON
From Shrewsbury
BETLEY ROAD
To London

EXPLANATION

G.C. & N.S. J^t. COM.
L. & N. W.
L. & N. W. & N. S. JOINT
N. S.

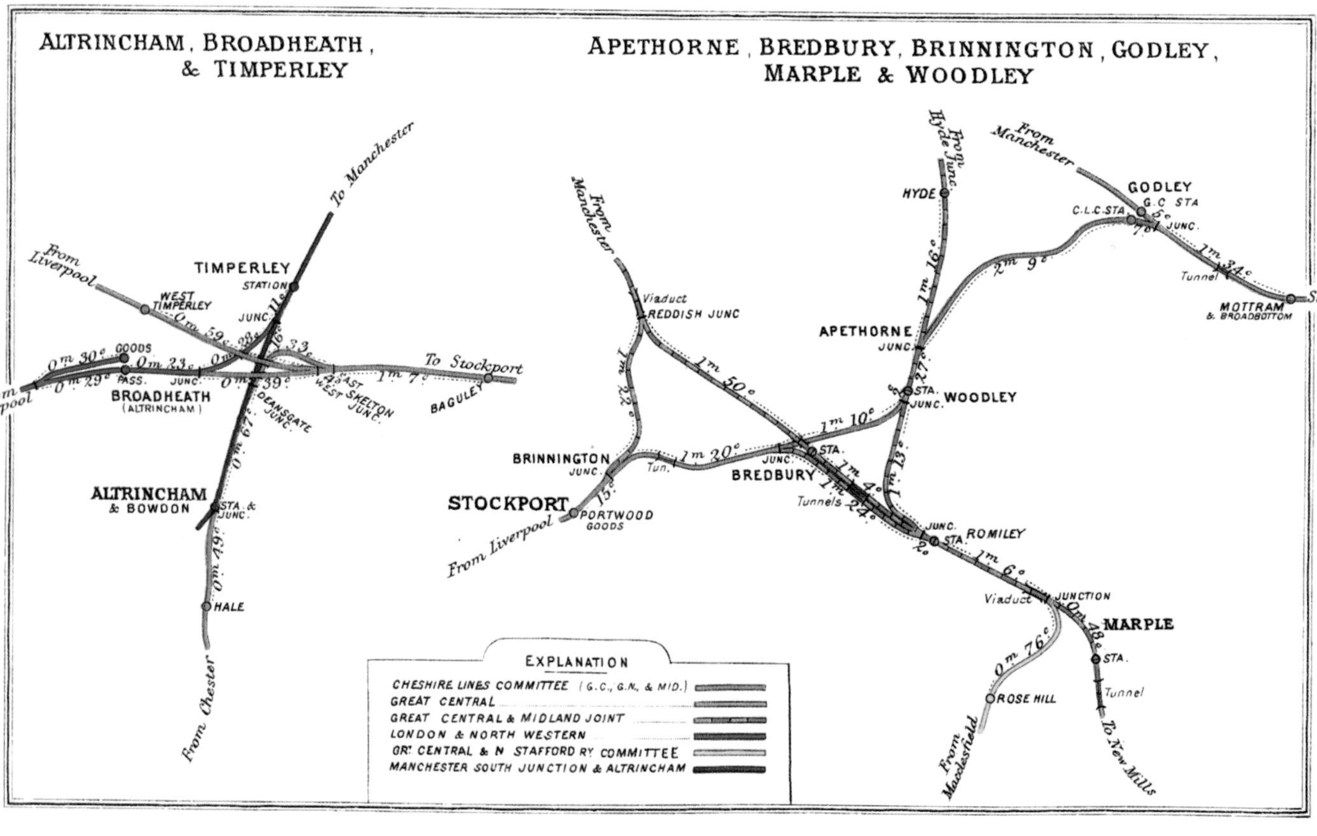

## MACCLESFIELD

From Stockport
PRESTBURY
BOLLINGTON
To Marple
Tunnel
JUNC.
GOODS
HIBEL ROAD PASS. STA. & JUNC.
JOINT GOODS
MACCLESFIELD
JUNCTION
CENTRAL PASS. STA.
From Stoke
NORTH RODE

## ALTRINCHAM, BROADHEATH, & TIMPERLEY

To Manchester
From Liverpool
WEST TIMPERLEY
TIMPERLEY STATION
JUNC.
GOODS
PASS.
BROADHEATH (ALTRINCHAM)
From Liverpool
DEANSGATE JUNC.
EAST WEST SKELTON JUNC.
To Stockport
BAGULEY
ALTRINCHAM & BOWDON
STA. & JUNC.
HALE
From Chester

## APETHORNE, BREDBURY, BRINNINGTON, GODLEY, MARPLE & WOODLEY

From Manchester
Viaduct
REDDISH JUNC
From Hyde Junc.
HYDE
From Manchester
GODLEY
G.C. STA
C.L.C. STA.
JUNC.
Tunnel
MOTTRAM & BROADBOTTOM
To Sheffield
APETHORNE JUNC.
STA. JUNC. WOODLEY
BRINNINGTON JUNC.
Tun.
JUNC.
STA.
BREDBURY
STOCKPORT
PORTWOOD GOODS
From Liverpool
Tunnels
JUNC. STA. ROMILEY
Viaduct
JUNCTION
MARPLE
STA.
Tunnel
ROSE HILL
From Macclesfield
To New Mills

EXPLANATION

CHESHIRE LINES COMMITTEE (G.C., G.N., & MID.)
GREAT CENTRAL
GREAT CENTRAL & MIDLAND JOINT
LONDON & NORTH WESTERN
GR^T. CENTRAL & N. STAFFORD R^Y. COMMITTEE
MANCHESTER SOUTH JUNCTION & ALTRINCHAM

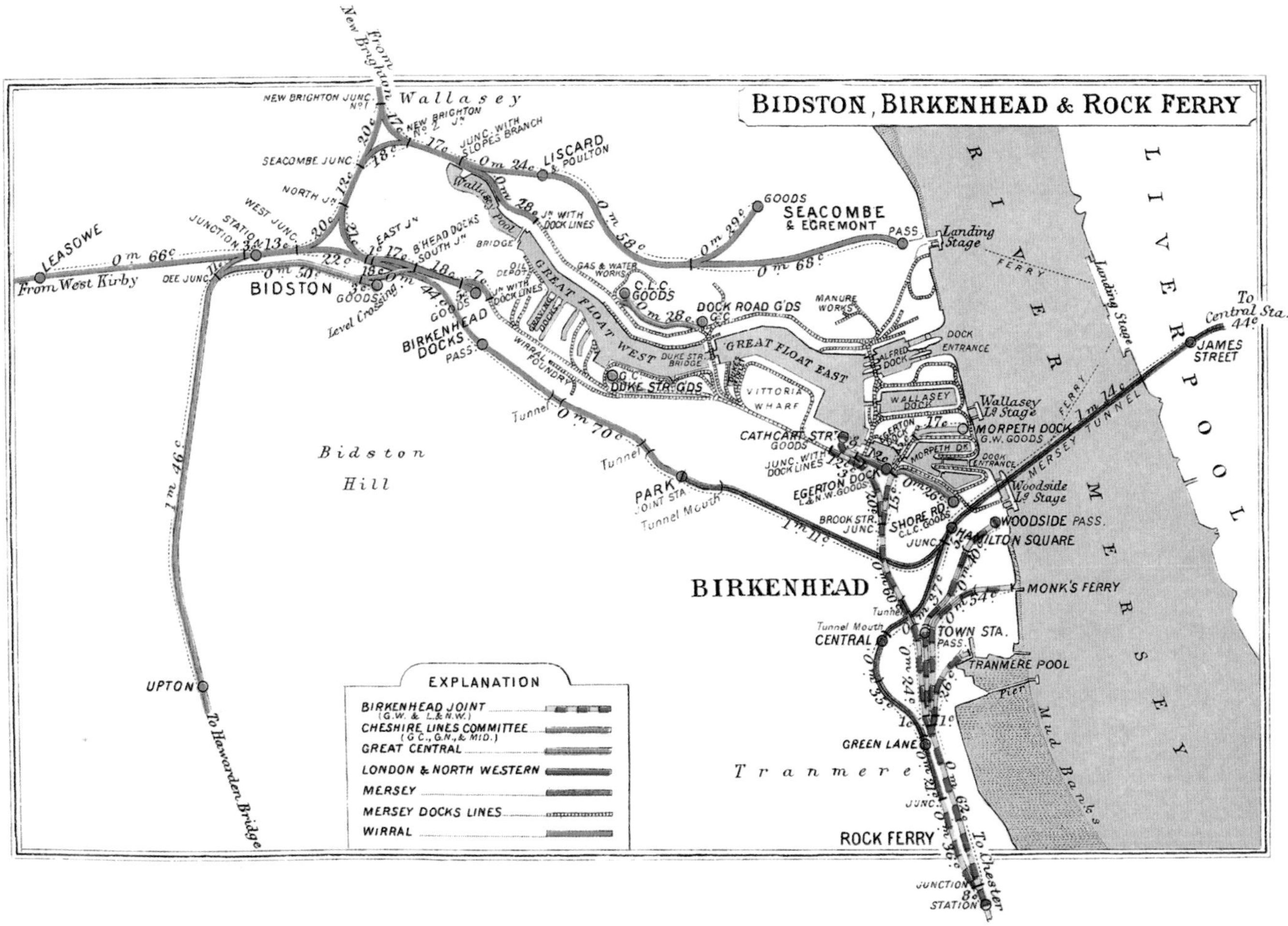

## BIDSTON, BIRKENHEAD & ROCK FERRY

EXPLANATION

- BIRKENHEAD JOINT (G.W. & L.& N.W.)
- CHESHIRE LINES COMMITTEE (G.C., G.N., & MID.)
- GREAT CENTRAL
- LONDON & NORTH WESTERN
- MERSEY
- MERSEY DOCKS LINES
- WIRRAL

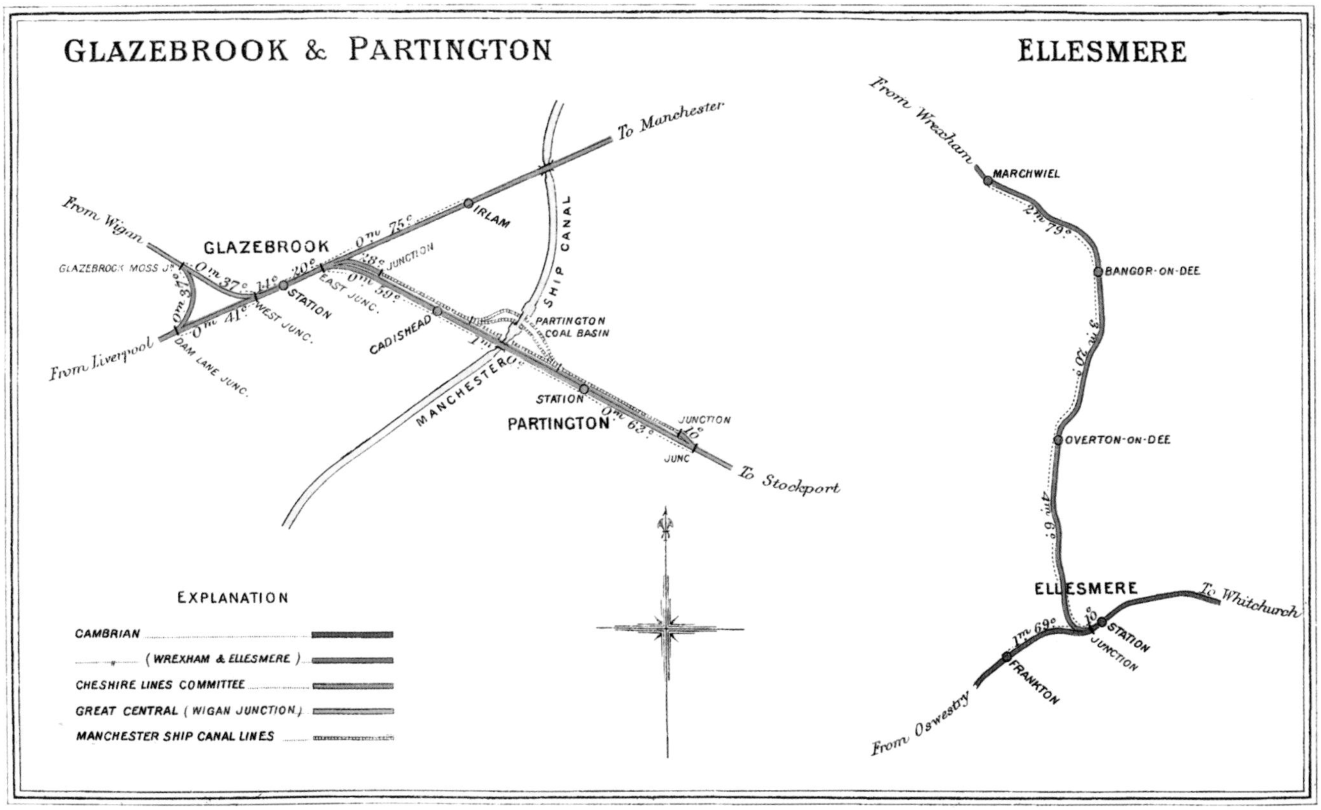

## GLAZEBROOK & PARTINGTON

## ELLESMERE

EXPLANATION

- CAMBRIAN
- (WREXHAM & ELLESMERE)
- CHESHIRE LINES COMMITTEE
- GREAT CENTRAL (WIGAN JUNCTION)
- MANCHESTER SHIP CANAL LINES

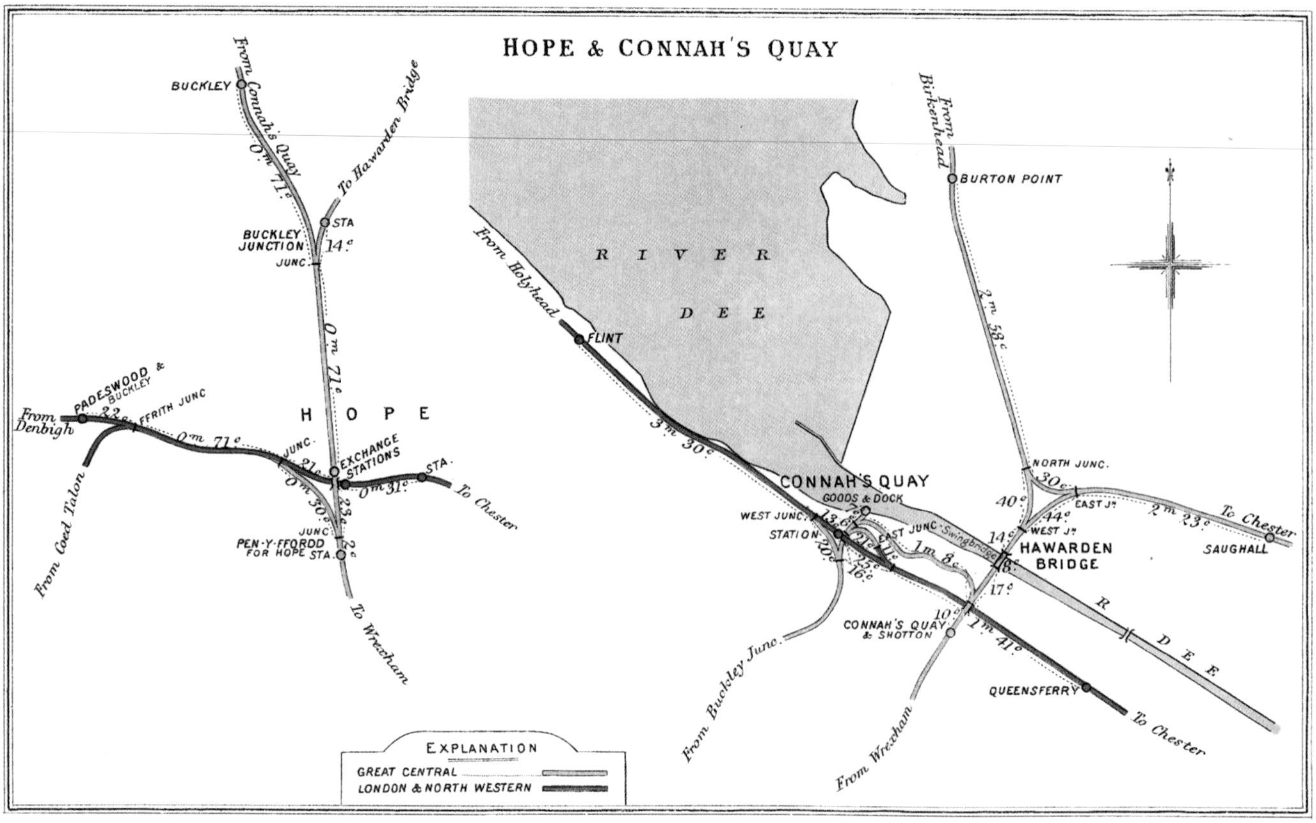
HOPE & CONNAH'S QUAY
From Connah's Quay
BUCKLEY
To Hawarden Bridge
BUCKLEY JUNCTION
STA
JUNC.
HOPE
From Denbigh
PADESWOOD & BUCKLEY
FRITH JUNC
EXCHANGE STATIONS
STA.
To Chester
From Coed Talon
PEN-Y-FFORDD FOR HOPE STA.
JUNC
To Wrexham
From Holyhead
FLINT
RIVER DEE
From Birkenhead
BURTON POINT
NORTH JUNC.
EAST JN
WEST JN
CONNAH'S QUAY
GOODS & DOCK
WEST JUNC.
STATION
EAST JUNC.
Swingbridge
HAWARDEN BRIDGE
To Chester
SAUGHALL
CONNAH'S QUAY & SHOTTON
From Buckley Junc.
QUEENSFERRY
From Wrexham
To Chester
EXPLANATION
GREAT CENTRAL
LONDON & NORTH WESTERN

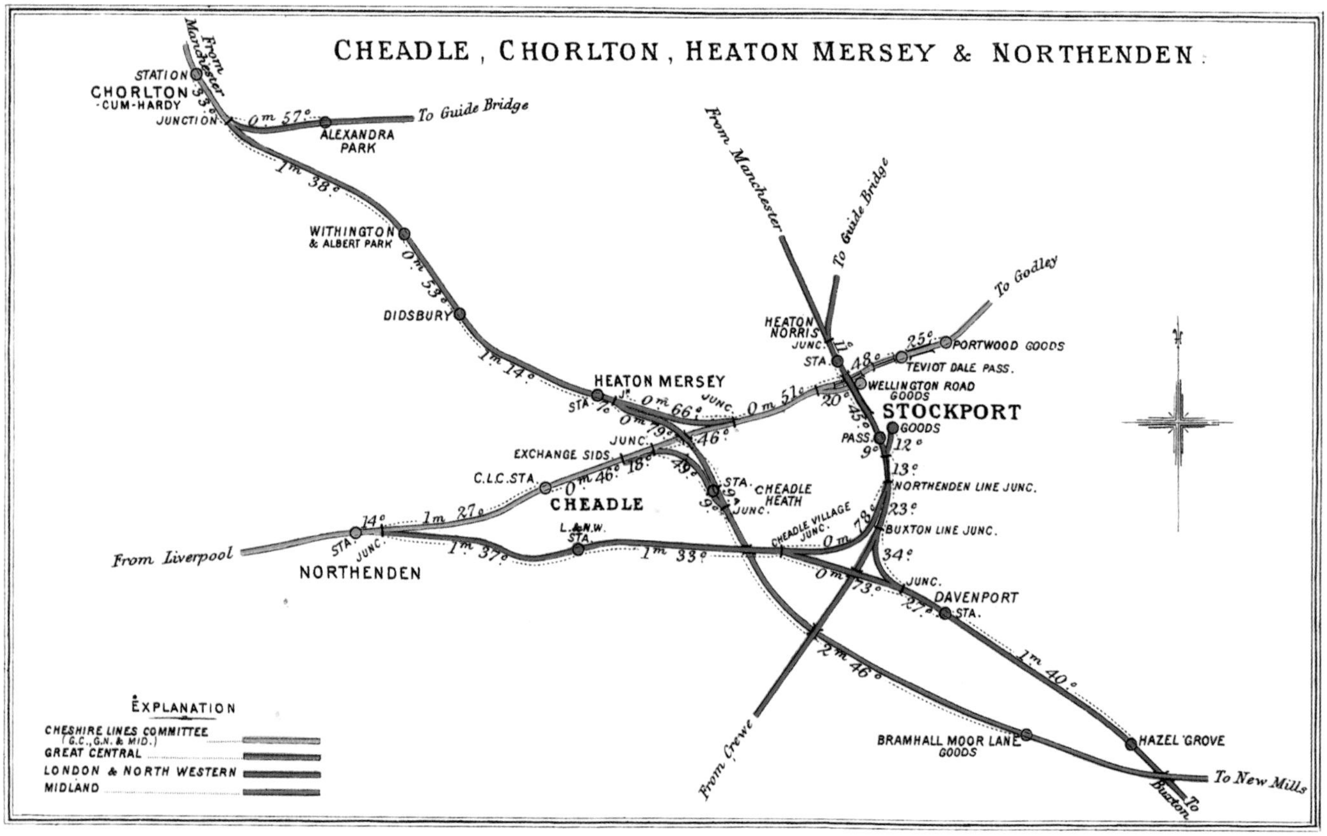
CHEADLE, CHORLTON, HEATON MERSEY & NORTHENDEN
From Manchester
STATION
CHORLTON-CUM-HARDY
JUNCTION
To Guide Bridge
ALEXANDRA PARK
WITHINGTON & ALBERT PARK
DIDSBURY
From Manchester
To Guide Bridge
To Godley
HEATON NORRIS JUNC.
STA.
PORTWOOD GOODS
TEVIOT DALE PASS.
WELLINGTON ROAD GOODS
HEATON MERSEY
STA.
JUNC.
STOCKPORT
GOODS
PASS.
EXCHANGE SIDS
C.L.C. STA.
CHEADLE
STA.
CHEADLE HEATH
JUNC.
NORTHENDEN LINE JUNC.
L.&N.W. STA.
CHEADLE VILLAGE JUNC.
BUXTON LINE JUNC.
From Liverpool
STA.
JUNC.
NORTHENDEN
JUNC.
DAVENPORT
STA.
EXPLANATION
CHESHIRE LINES COMMITTEE (G.C., G.N. & MID.)
GREAT CENTRAL
LONDON & NORTH WESTERN
MIDLAND
From Crewe
BRAMHALL MOOR LANE GOODS
HAZEL GROVE
To New Mills
To Buxton

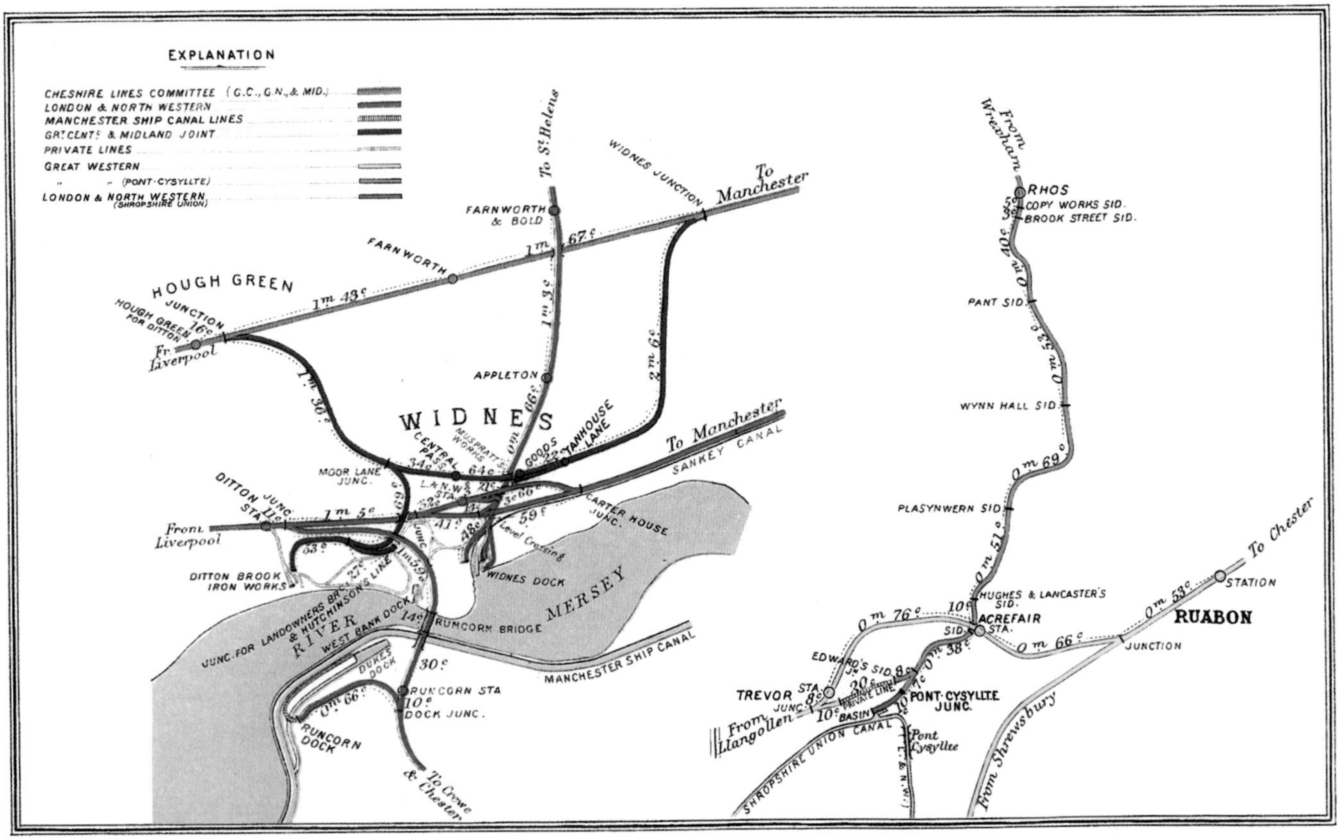

Widnes–Ruabon

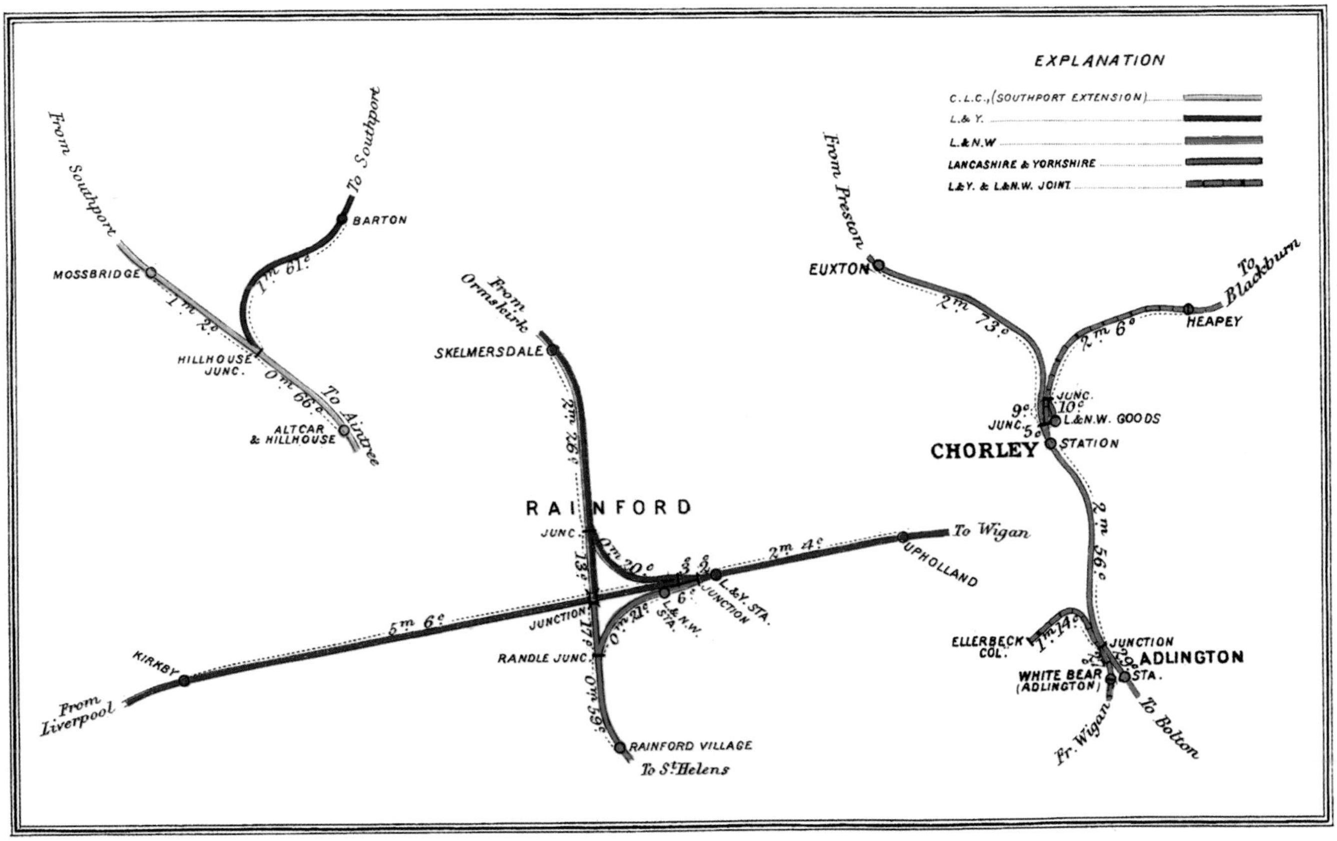

Hillhouse Junc–Rainford–Chorley–Adlington

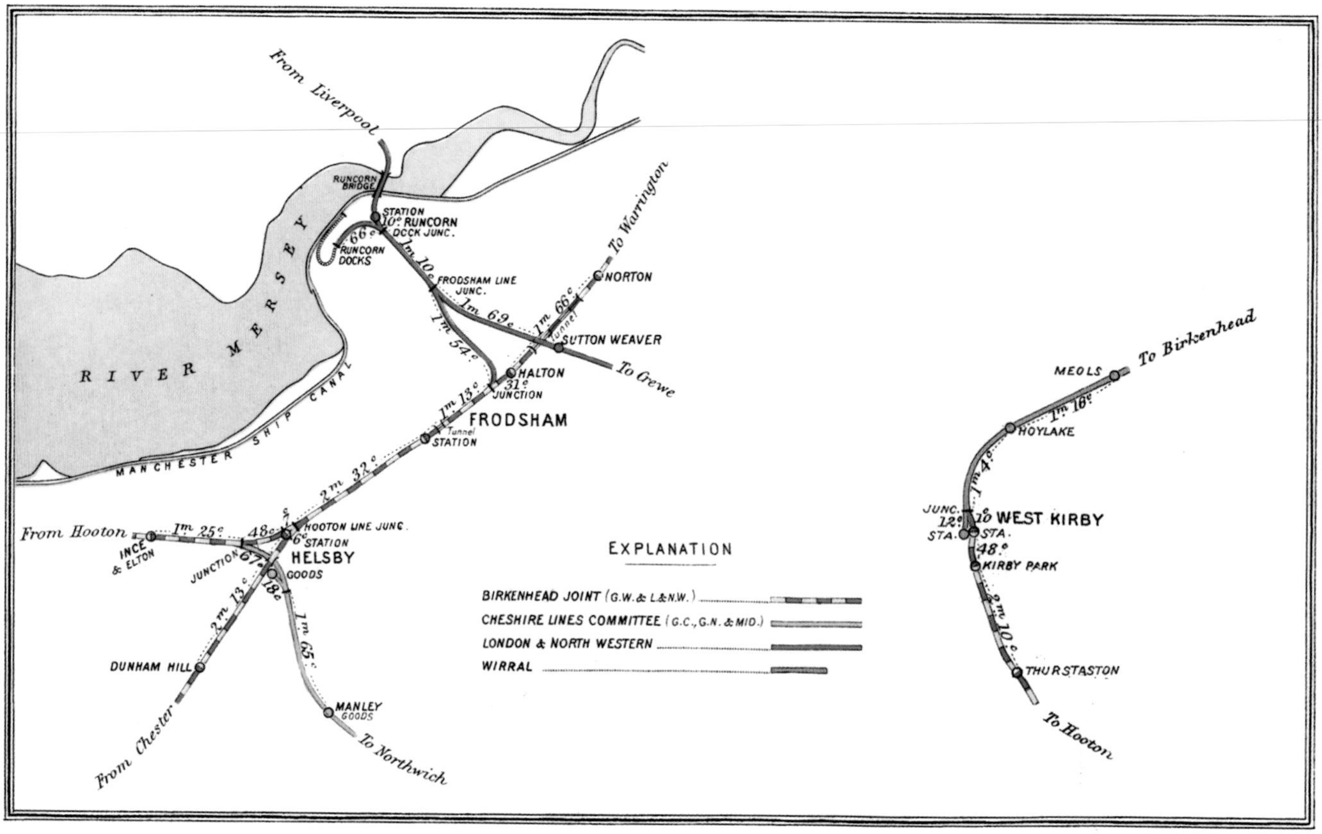

Helsby–Frodsham–West Kirby

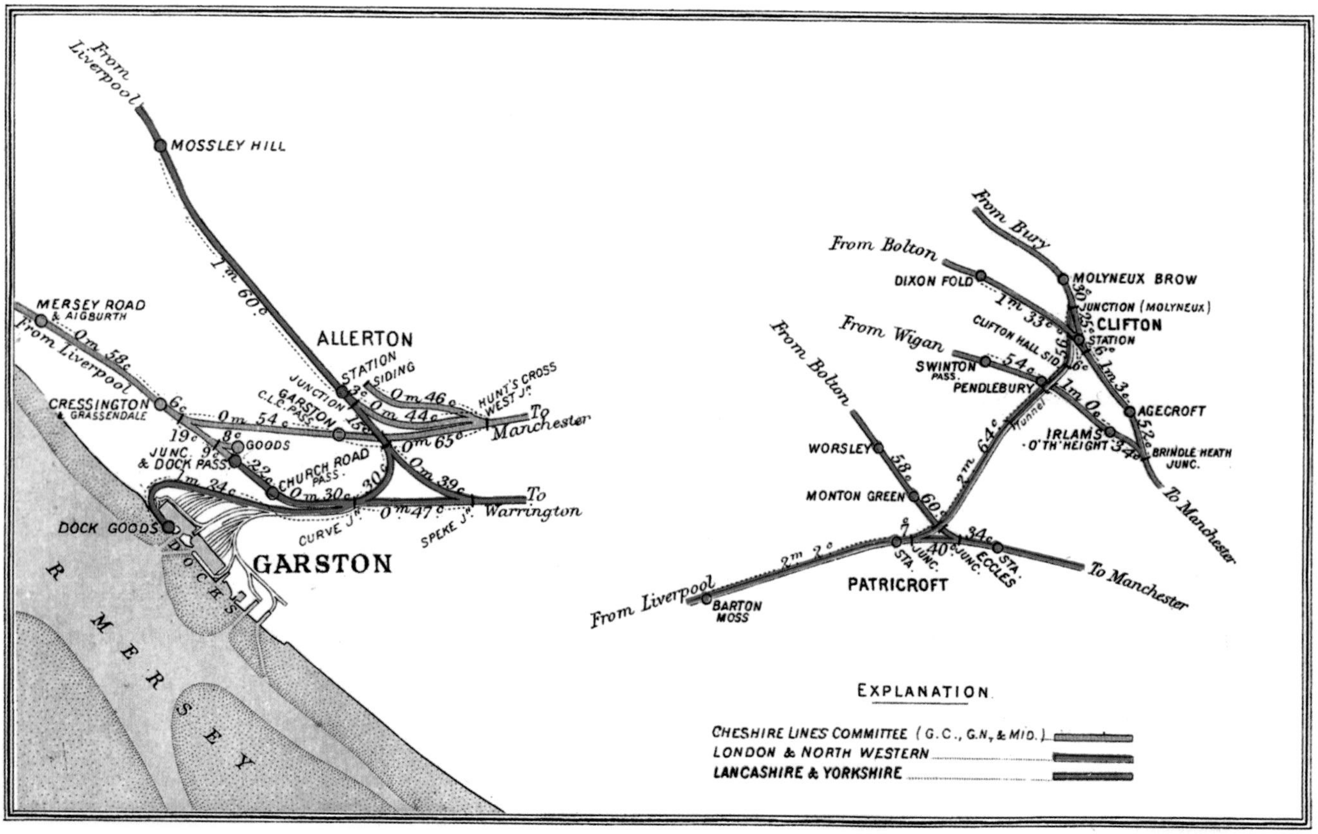

Garston–Allerton–Patricroft–Clifton

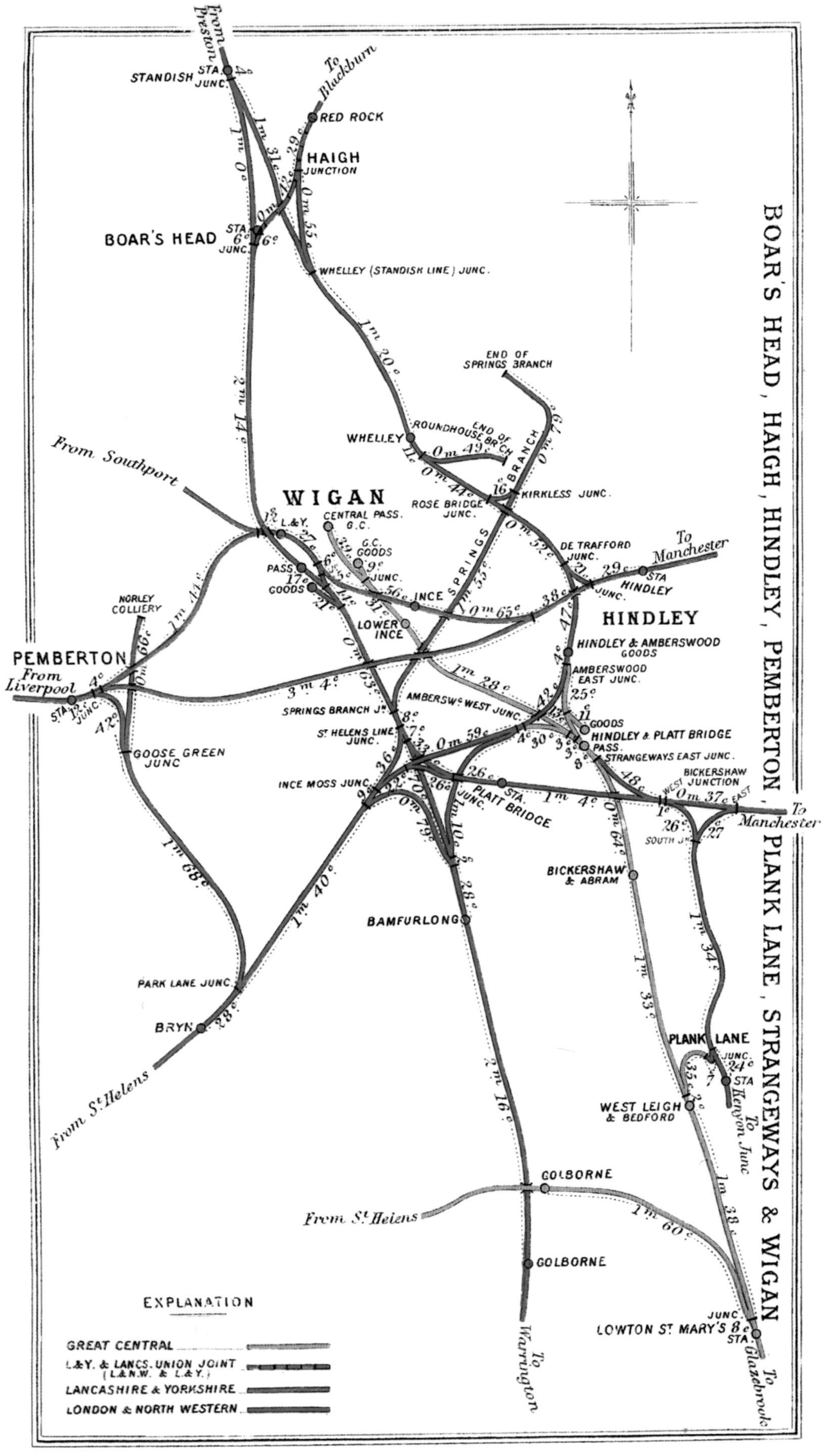
BOAR'S HEAD, HAIGH, HINDLEY, PEMBERTON, PLANK LANE, STRANGEWAYS & WIGAN
From Preston
To Blackburn
STANDISH
RED ROCK
HAIGH
JUNCTION
BOAR'S HEAD
WHELLEY (STANDISH LINE) JUNC.
END OF SPRINGS BRANCH
WHELLEY
ROUNDHOUSE
From Southport
WIGAN
KIRKLESS JUNC.
ROSE BRIDGE JUNC.
CENTRAL PASS. G.C.
G.C. GOODS
DE TRAFFORD JUNC.
To Manchester
HINDLEY
INCE
LOWER INCE
NORLEY COLLIERY
PEMBERTON
From Liverpool
HINDLEY & AMBERSWOOD GOODS
AMBERSWOOD EAST JUNC.
SPRINGS BRANCH JN.
ST. HELENS LINE JUNC.
HINDLEY & PLATT BRIDGE
STRANGEWAYS EAST JUNC.
GOOSE GREEN JUNC
INCE MOSS JUNC.
PLATT BRIDGE
BICKERSHAW JUNCTION
To Manchester
BICKERSHAW & ABRAM
BAMFURLONG
PARK LANE JUNC.
BRYN
From St. Helens
PLANK LANE
WEST LEIGH & BEDFORD
To Kenyon Junc
GOLBORNE
From St. Helens
GOLBORNE
LOWTON ST. MARY'S
To Warrington
To Glazebrook
EXPLANATION
GREAT CENTRAL
L.&Y. & LANCS. UNION JOINT (L.&N.W. & L.&Y.)
LANCASHIRE & YORKSHIRE
LONDON & NORTH WESTERN

## TWENTY ONE

1 2 3 4 5

Twenty eight

REDMIRE
N.E. ASKRIGG
N.E. AYSGARTH
WENSLEY
CONSTABLE BURTON
FINGHALL LANE
LEYBURN
SPENNITHORNE
JERVAULX
CRAKEHALL
AINDERBY
SCRUTON
NORTHALLERTON
South J.c.
Cordio Jcs.
LEEMING BAR
BEDALE
NEWBY WISKE
OTTERINGTON

OLDHAM ROAD
CHARLESTOWN
OLDHAM ROAD (Goods)
STALYBRIDGE
Pass.
Joint Pass.
Joint Goods
PARK PARADE
DUKINFIELD
DUKINFIELD & ASHTON
Crowthorn Jc.
Audenshaw Jc.
GUIDE BRIDGE
Goods
Ashton Moss Jc.
HOOLEY HILL
Denton Jc.

Poppleton Jc.
Bootham Jc.
Severus Jc.
Burton Lane Jc.
Goods
Foss Islands Jc.
North Jc.
Holgate Bridge Jc.
YORK
LAYERTHORPE
FOSS ISLAND (Goods)
Chaloners Whin Jc.

KIRBY MOORSIDE
NAWTON
HELMSLEY
NUNNINGTON
HOVINGHAM SPA
GILLING
COXWOLD

ELSLACK
THORNTON
BARNOLDSWICK
MID.
EARBY
FOULRIDGE
L. & Y.
COLNE
NELSON

MASHAM
TANFIELD
N.E.
PICKHILL
SINDERBY
THIRSK
Pass
Goods
N.E.
MELMERBY
BALDERSBY
TOPCLIFFE

LOFTHOUSE-IN-NIDDERDALE
RAMSGILL
N.V.
WATH-IN-NIDDERDALE
PATELEY BRIDGE

RIPON
SESSAY
PILMOOR
HUSTHWAITE GATE
AMPLEFORTH
SLINGSBY
BRAFFERTON
RASKELF
EASINGWOLD
BOROUGHBRIDGE
ALNE
WORMALD GREEN
TOLLERTON
COPGROVE
FLAXTON
STRENSALL

CARDIGAN RD. (Goods)
LEEDS
(Goods)
(Goods)
(Pass) CENTRAL
ARMLEY
WELLINGTON ST
Geldard Jc.
WELLINGTON
NEW STA.
Wortley Jc.
HOLBECK J.J. H.L.
Three Signal Bri. Jc.
Canal Jc.
Leeds Jc.
HUNSLETT LANE (Goods)
WHITEHALL RD.
Engine Shed Jc.
ARMLEY
Wortley W.
COPLEY HILL
Wortley S. Jc.
FARNLEY & WORTLEY
N.Jc.

GRASSINGTON & THRESHFIELD
MID.
DACRE
BIRSTWITH
RIPLEY VALLEY
DARLEY
RYLSTONE
HAMPSTHWAITE
NIDD BRIDGE
Bilton Road Jc.
Dragon Jc.
N.E.
KNARESBOROUGH
GOLDSBOROUGH
BENINGBROUGH
N.E.
HAXBY
STARBECK
ALLERTON
HAMMERTON
WARTHILL
HOLTBY
HARROGATE
Goods
Loco Shed
WILSTROP SIDING
CATTAL
EARSWICK
MARSTON MOOR
HESSAY
BELL BUSK
GARGRAVE
EMBSAY
Skipton N. Jc.

YORK
Bootham Jc.
Burton Lane Jc.
LAYERTHORPE
MURTON LANE
POPPLETON
Poppleton Jc.
Severus Jc.
Holgate Bridge Jc.
Chaloners Whin Jc.
DUNNINGTON
DUNNINGTON HALT
DUNNINGTON (FOR KEXBY)
ELVINGTON
D.V.

Crimple Jc.
Crimple Tun.
Pannal Jc.
PANNAL
SPOFFORTH
Wetherby W.Jc.
Wetherby E.Jc.
WETHERBY
Goods
BOLTON ABBEY
ADDINGHAM
SKIPTON
ELSLACK
THORNTON
MID.
EARBY
CONONLEY
STEETON & SILSDEN
ILKLEY
BEN RHYDDING
Mid.&N.E.(Otley & Ilkley Jc.)
BURLEY
Milner Wood Jc.
POOL
N.E.
WEETON
COLLINGHAM BRIDGE
THORP ARCH
NEWTON KYME
COPMANTHORPE
Swing Bridge
NABURN
WHELDRAKE

KILDWICK & CROSSHILLS
Worth Valley Bch.Jc.
KEIGHLEY
Goods
MENSTON
OTLEY
ARTHINGTON
Bramhope Tun.
Summit
BARDSEY
TADCASTER
BOLTON PERCY
COTTINGWITH
GUISELEY
ESHOLT
YEADON
THORNER
STUTTON (Goods)
ULLESKELF
ESCRICK
THORGANBY
N.E.

OLDHAM
MUMPS
CENTRAL
OLDHAM WERNETH
L.&N.W.Goods
G.C.Goods
INGROW
DAMEMS
OAKWORTH
GLODWICK ROAD.
HAWORTH
OLDHAM CLEGG STREET
OXENHOPE

INGROW
BINGLEY
Bingley Tun.
BAILDON
THACKLEY
APPERLEY BRI.
CALVERLEY
HORSFORTH
SEE SHEET NO.FORTY TWO
Summit
SCHOLES
CHURCH FENTON
CAWOOD
RICCALL
SKIPWITH & NORTH DUFFIELD
BUBWITHCUM
SALTAIRE
IDLE
NEWLAY
LEEDS
KIRKSTALL
HEADINGLEY
CULLINGWORTH
SHIPLEY
ECCLESHILL
Cross Gates Jc.
N.E.
WILSDEN
FRIZING HALL
BRAMLEY
ARMLEY
MARSH LANE
GARFORTH
MICKLEFIELD
SOUTH MILFORD
WISTOW
SHERBURN-IN-ELMET
CLIFF COMMON
E. Jc.
Barlby Jc.
Swing Bri.
MENTHORPE GATE
DENHOLME
MANNINGHAM
LAISTER-DYKE
STANNINGLEY
W'TON
Loco Shed
CROSS GATE
BRADFORD
Gds.
Hunslet Bch Jc.
HUNSLET
CROSS GATES
HAMBLETON
SELBY
HEMINGBOROUGH
THORNTON
CLAYTON
ARMLEY
PUDSEY(L)
PUDSEY(G)
Stourton Jc.
Milford Jc.
Gasgoigne Wood Jc.
THORP GATES (Gds)
Brayton N. Jc.
Brayton E. Jc.
QUEENSBURY
GT HORTON
DUDLEY HILL
BEESTON
WOODLES-FORD
KIPPAX
MONK FRYSTON
HORTON PARK
BIRKENSHAW
L.&N.W.
CHURWELL
WRESSLE
HOLMFIELD
LOW MOOR
Gds.
GILDERSOME
ROBIN HOOD
ROTHWELL
LEDSTON
BURTON SALMON
BARLOW

STANSFIELD HALL
Hall Royd Jc.
Millwood Tun.
EASTWOOD
Castle Hill Tun.
Horsfall Tun.
TODMORDEN
WALSDEN
Winterbutlee Tun.
Summit Tun.
Weasal Hall Tun.
HEBDEN BRI.
MYTHOLMROYD
ST.PAULS
SOWERBY BRI.
LUDDENDEN FOOT
Watertroughs
TRIANGLE
WHEATLEY
PELLON
OVENDEN
N.BRIDGE
HALIFAX
Bank House Tun.
COPLEY
Milner Royd
GREETLAND
WATSONS CROSSING HALT
RIPPONDEN & BARKISLAND
WEST VALE
ELLAND
STAINLAND
RISHWORTH
Wyke Tun.
WYKE
GOMERSAL
Wyke Jc.
BAILIFF BRI.
LIGHT CLIFFE
LIVERSEDGE
CLIFTON RD.
BRIGHOUSE
COOPER BRI.
Bradley Wood Jc.
BIRSTALL
CLECKHEATON
HECKMONDWYKE
Morley Tun.
MORLEY
ARDSLEY
STANLEY
WOODKIRK
TINGLEY
BATLEY
LOFTHOUSE
ALVERTHORPE
DEWSBURY
FLUSH-DYKE
ALTOFTS
NORMANTON
METHLEY
FRYSTON (Gds)
CASTLEFORD
PONTEFRACT
FERRYBRIDGE (S.&K.)
KNOTTINGLEY
(L&Y&GN)
TEMPLE HIRST
WHITLEY BRIDGE
Gowdall Jc.
Hensall Jc.
CARLTON
Aire Jc.
DRAX
BARMBY
DRAX HALES
AIRMYN
SNAITH
HENSALL
BALNE
MOOR (Gds)
HECK
SNAITH & POLLINGTON
RAWCLIFFE
TANSHELF
L&Y.
PONTEFRACT
FEATHERSTONE
WAKE-FIELD
OAKENSHAW (Gds)
SHARLSTON
OSSETT
HORBURY & OSSETT
CROFTON
HARE PARK
N. Jc.
ACKWORTH
Brackenhill Jc.
WOMERSLEY
KIRK SMEATON
BALNE
SYKEHOUSE
H.&B.
N.E.

LITTLEBOROUGH
SMITHY BRIDGE
Watertroughs
WARDLEWORTH
Rochdale E. Jc.
HILLHOUSE (Gds)
Springwood Jc.
LONGWOOD
GOLCAR
LINTHWAITE (Gds)
SLAITHWAITE
DEIGHTON
MIRFIELD
KIRKHEATON
L.N.W. Jc.
THORNHILL
HUDDERSFIELD
LOCKWOOD
BERRY BROW
Robin Hood Tun.
NETHERTON
FENAY BRI. & LEPTON
KIRKBURTON
L.&N.W.
Crigglestone Tun.
CRIGGLESTONE
MID.
HORBURY JUNC.
SANDAL
NOSTELL
RYHILL
W. Jc.
S. Jc.
G.N.&G.C.Jc.
HEMSWORTH
Brierley Jc.
Royston Jc.
NOTTON & ROYSTON
UPTON
S. ELMSALL
Wrangbrook Jc.
ASKERN
NORTON
MOSS
THORNE
THORNE
Joan Croft Jc.
THORPE-IN-BALNE
Thorne Jc.
G.C.
L.&Y.
H.&B.Jt.

NEW HEY
SHAW & CROMPTON
ROYTON
MARSDEN
Standedge Tun.
Diggle Watertroughs
DIGGLE
DELPH Jc.
SADDLEWORTH
ROYTON JUNC.
DOBCROSS
5 4 3 2 1
OLDHAM WERNETH
6
UPPERMILL
FRIEZLAND
Royal George Tun.
MICKLEHURST (Goods)
Scout Tunnel
OLDHAM PARK BRI.
O.A.&G.
DROYLSDEN
ASHTON
STALEY & MILLBROOK (Goods)
STALYBRIDGE
GUIDE BRIDGE
HYDE JUNC.
Dinting Via.
Denton Jc.
DENTON
NEWTON
HADFIELD
DINTING
GLOSSOP
HYDE
GODLEY JUNCTION
MOTTRAM & BROADBOTTOM
Reddish Jc.
Apethorne Jc.
WOODLEY
Mottram Via.
BREDBURY
ROMILEY
ROSE HILL
STOCKPORT
HIGH LANE
DAVENPORT
MARPLE
STRINES
HAYFIELD
BIRCH VALE
HAZEL GROVE
NEW MILLS

HEALEY HOUSE
HONLEY
BROCKHOLES
STOCKSMOOR
MELTHAM
THONGS BRI.
HOLMFIRTH
SHEPLEY
Thurstonland Tun.
DENBY DALE
SKELMANTHORPE
Cumberworth Tun.
CLAYTON WEST
DARTON
HAIGH
ROYSTON & NOTTON
STAINCROSS
MONK BRETTON
BARNSLEY
SILKSTONE
SUMMER LANE
DODWORTH
SILKSTONE
HAZLEHEAD BRIDGE
Wellhouse Tun.
MOOR END (Gds)
DUNFORD BRIDGE
Woodhead Tun.
PENISTONE
Barnsley Jc.
PILLEY (Gds)
WOODHEAD
BIRDWELL
Thurgoland Tun.
WORTLEY
BIRDWELL
WEST WOOD
DEEPCAR
CROWDEN
1. MOORGATE
2. GREENFIELD
3. GRASSCROFT
4. GROTTON & SPRINGHEAD
5. LEES
6. GLODWICK ROAD
7. MOSSLEY

Gds
Shafton Jc.
MOORTHORPE
MOORHOUSE
HAMPOLE
Askern Jc.
Shaftholme Jc.
Applehurst Jc.
STAINFORTH & HATFIELD
BRAMWITH (Goods)
CUDWORTH
GRIMETHORPE
Hickleton S. Jc.
FRICKLEY
PICKBURN
Adwick Jc.
Skellow Jc.
CARCROFT
Castle Hills Jc.
ARKSEY
BARNBY DUN
Kirk Sandall Jc.
Bentley Jc.
Ardsley Tun.
HOUGHTON
DARFIELD
HICKLETON
D.V.
HARLINGTON
BOLTON ON DEARNE
Dearne Jc.
SPROTBOROUGH
Goods
DONCASTER
Works
Loco Shed
Bally Jc.
WOMBWELL
WOMBWELL
WATH-ON-DEARNE
Wath Rd. Jc.
MEXBORO
DENABY
WARMSWORTH
Low Ellers Jc.
Bessacar Jc.
St. Catherine's Jcs.
Loversall Carr Jc.
FINNINGLEY
G.N.&G.E.Jc.
ELSECAR
WENTWORTH
Tankersley Tun.
SWINTON
KILNHURST
SWINTON
CONISBORO
ROSSINGTON
G.N.

ARKSEY
Kirk Sandall Jc.
YORK RD.
Bentley Jc.
North Jc.
N.Jc.
MARSH GATE (Gds)
DONCASTER
South Jc.
Balby Jc.
CHERRY TREE LANE (Goods)
S.Jc.
Potteric Carr Jc.
Low Ellers Jc.
Hexthorpe Jc.
Hexthorpe
Doncaster Avoiding Line Jc.
Black Carr Jc.
Bessacar Jc.
Black Carr W.
Loversall Carr Jc.
WARMSWORTH (Gds)
Black Carr E.Jc.

CHAPELTOWN
ECCLESFIELD
G.C.
PARKGATE
ROTHERHAM (MASBORO)
PARKGATE & ALDWARKE
G.C.& MID.
Braithwell Jc.
Northern Jc.
TICKHILL & WADWORTH
MISSON (Gds)
HOLMES
ROTHERHAM RD.
ROTHERHAM (WESTGATE)
HELLABY (Gds)
MALTBY
BAWTRY
GC.GN.L.& Y. MID. NE JE
Watertroughs
SCROOBY
WINCOBANK
BRIGHTSIDE
SHEFFIELD VICTORIA
OUGHTY BRIDGE
WADSLEY BRIDGE
TINSLEY
NEEPSEND Tunnel Jc.
CATCLIFFE
GC.H & B & MID
VICTORIA CITY (Gds)
ATTERCLIFFE
DARNALL
Treeton Jc.
TREETON
THURCROFT (Gds)
Southern Jc.
DINNINGTON & N.E.-LAUGHTON (S. YORKS. Jc.)
RANSKILL
QUEENS RD. Gds
POND ST.
WOODHOUSE
WOODHOUSE MILL
Dinnington Jc.
G.N.
MID.

A B C D E F G

Twenty four Inset Twenty

Fifteen Sixteen

## TWENTY TWO

5 Twenty eight 4 3 2 1

A B C D E F G

LEVISHAM
SCALBY
SCARBOROUGH
(Goods)
SCARBOROUGH EXCURSION
Loco Shed
FORGE VALLEY
SINNINGTON
N.E.
PICKERING
THORNTON DALE
EBBERSTON
SNAINTON
WYKEHAM
SAWDON
SEAMER
Seamer Jc.
CAYTON
GRISTHORPE
FILEY
MARISHES ROAD
N.E.
HESLERTON
GANTON
WEAVERTHORPE
KNAPTON
RILLINGTON
BARTON-LE-STREET
AMOTHERBY
HUNMANBY
SPEETON
BEMPTON
FLAMBOROUGH
H I R E
MALTON
Loco Shed
SETTRINGTON
NORTH GRIMSTON
CASTLE HOWARD
HUTTONS AMBO
KIRKHAM ABBEY
WHARRAM
BARTON HILL
Burdale Tun.
BURDALE
SLEDMERE & FIMBER
BRIDLINGTON
Loco. Shed
CARNABY
BURTON AGNES
LOWTHORPE
WETWANG
GARTON
N.E.
NAFFERTON
DRIFFIELD
STAMFORD BRIDGE
SOUTHBURN
FANGFOSS
N.E.
POCKLINGTON
MIDDLETON-ON-THE-WOLDS
BAINTON
HUTTON CRANSWICK
KILNWICK GATE (Goods)
HORNSEA
HORNSEA BRIDGE
NUNBURNHOLME
ENTHORPE
LOCKINGTON
KIPLING COTES
CHERRY BURTON
ARRAM
WASSAND
SIGGLESTHORNE
LONDESBOROUGH
MARKET WEIGHTON
Beverley Jc.
BEVERLEY
WHITEDALE
ELLERBY
EVERINGHAM
N.E.
HOLME
FOGGATHORPE
SKIRLAUGH
HIGH FIELD
SWINE
SOUTH CAVE
H.&B.
LITTLE WEIGHTON
COTTINGHAM
HULL
SUTTON-ON-HULL
STONEFERRY (Goods)
NORTH HOWDEN
NORTH EASTRINGTON
NEWPORT (YORKS)
NORTH CAVE
SANDHOLME
Cottingham Jc.
WILLERBY & KIRK ELLA
MARFLEET
ALEXANDRA DOCKS (Gds)
SOUTH HOWDEN
SOUTH EASTRINGTON
STADDLETHORPE
BROOMFLEET
HEDON
Hessle Road
Hessle Jc.
PARAGON
BROUGH
FERRIBY
HESSLE
KING GEORGE DOCK
RYE HILL
WITHERNSEA
OTTRINGHAM
Swing Br.
GOOLE
SALTMARSHE
N.E.
KEYINGHAM
WHITTON
NEW HOLLAND
WINTERINGHAM
BARTON
BARROW HAVEN
GOXHILL
WINESTEAD (Goods)
PATRINGTON
Marshland Jc.
REEDNESS JUNC.
FOCKERBY
WEST HALTON
EAST HALTON
L&Y&N.E.Jt.
EASTOFT
LUDDINGTON
WINTERTON & THEALBY
THORNTON ABBEY
KILLINGHOLME
WESTERN JETTY
Loco. Shed
Humber Road Jc.
NORMANBY PARK (Goods)
ULCEBY
MEDGE HALL
CROWLE
SCUNTHORPE
APPLEBY
BROCKLESBY
HABROUGH
IMMINGHAM DOCKS (Goods)
GRIMSBY
DOCK
PIER (Pass & Gds)
DOCKS (Goods)
NEW CLEE
CLEETHORPES
MAUDS BRIDGE (Gds)
KEADBY (Goods)
GUNHOUSE WHARF
Loco Shed
G.C.
G.C.
STALLINGBOROUGH
HEALING
Hull to Zeebrugge L.&Y. & N.E. Jnt.
CROWLE
ALTHORPE
GUNNESS (Gds)
FRODINGHAM & SCUNTHORPE
ELSHAM
BARNETBY
GREAT COATES
Gds
G.N. (Gds)
HATFIELD MOOR DEPOT
Keadby Lifting Bridge
Wrawby Jc.
GRIMSBY TOWN
Grimsby to Hamburg, G.C.R.
Grimsby to Rotterdam, G.C.R.
Grimsby to Antwerp, G.C.R.
BELTON
BRIGG
SANDTOFT (Goods)
Kirton Tun.
WEELSBY ROAD & HAINTON ST. HALT
WALTHAM
EPWORTH
HOWSHAM
SCAWBY & HIBALDSTOW
G.C.
L&Y&N.E.Jt.
NORTH KELSEY
HOLTON VILLAGE HALT
PARK DRAIN
HAXEY TOWN
HOLTON LE CLAY
GRAINSBY HALT
MOORTOWN
KIRTON LINDSEY
HAXEY JUNC.
HOLTON
NORTH THORESBY
HAXEY & EPWORTH
NORTHORPE
G.C.
LUDBOROUGH
BLYTON
MISTERTON
STOCKWITH (Goods)
WALKERINGHAM
L I N C O L N
G.N.&G.E. Jt.
UTTERBY HALT
CLAXBY & USSELBY
FOTHERBY HALT
SALTFLEETBY
G.N.
BECKINGHAM
GAINSBOROUGH
MARKET RASEN
LOUTH
GRIMOLDBY
THEDDLETHORPE
South Jc.
North Jc.
G.N.&G.E. Joint
Loco Shed
LEA ROAD
HALLINGTON

Cottingham Jc.
BEVERLEY ROAD
H&B Goods
SCULCOATES
WILMINGTON
STEPNEY
BOTANIC GDNS
Level Crossing
CANNON STR.
L.S.
BURLEIGH STR. (Gds.)
Loco. Shed
PARAGON
SOUTHCOATES
DRYPOOL (Gds.)
KINGSTON STR. (Gds)
Springbank Jcs
NEPTUNE STR. (Gds)
GC
DAIRYCOATS (Goods)
ALBERT DOCKS (Gds.)
Hessle Jc.
ST. ANDREWS DOCK (Goods)
HULL
Loco. Shed
(Docks Omitted)

Sixteen Seventeen

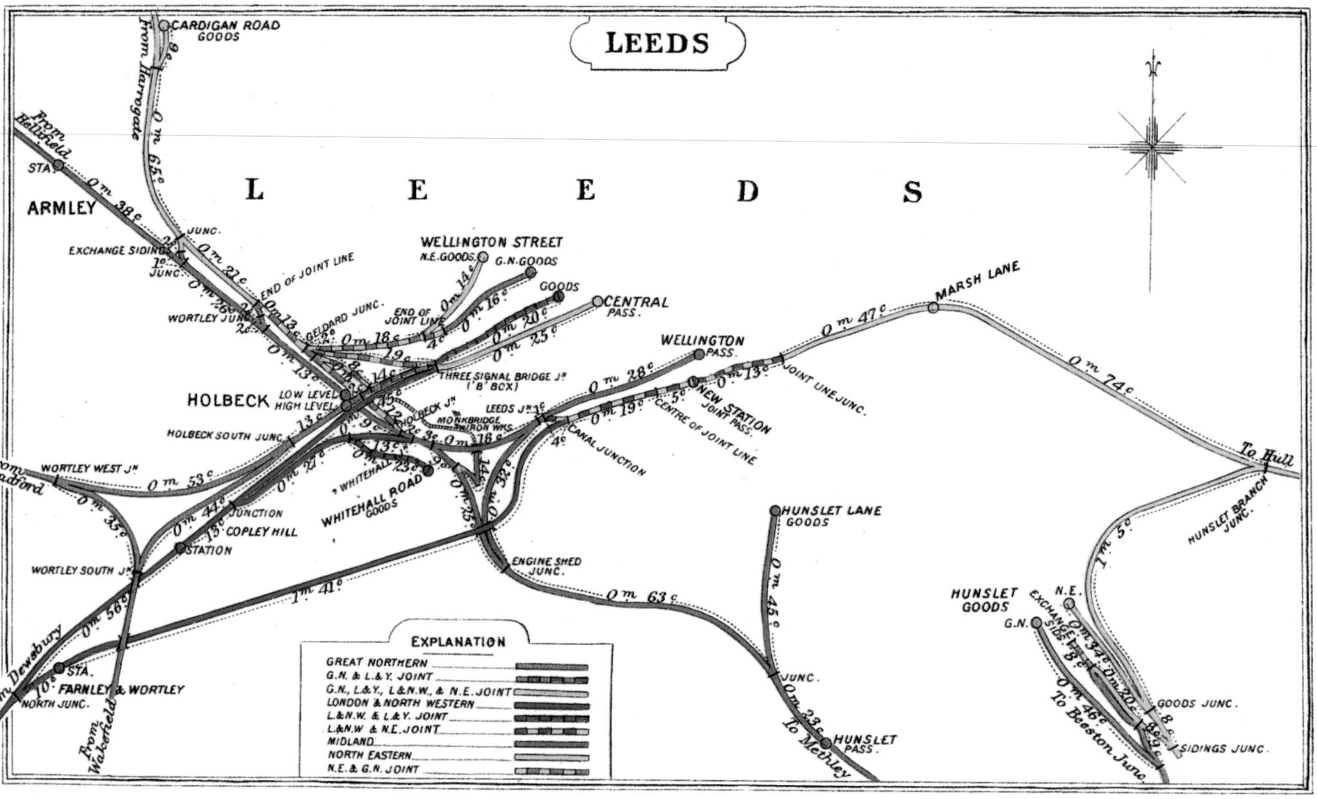
LEEDS
L E E D S
CARDIGAN ROAD GOODS
From Harrogate
From Hellifield
STA.
ARMLEY
EXCHANGE SIDINGS
JUNC.
WORTLEY JUNC.
END OF JOINT LINE
GELDARD JUNC.
END OF JOINT LINE
WELLINGTON STREET
N.E. GOODS
G.N. GOODS
GOODS
CENTRAL PASS.
WELLINGTON PASS.
MARSH LANE
THREE SIGNAL BRIDGE J^N ('B' BOX)
HOLBECK
LOW LEVEL
HIGH LEVEL
HOLBECK J^N
MONKBRIDGE IRON WKS.
LEEDS J^N
NEW STATION JOINT PASS.
CENTRE OF JOINT LINE
JOINT LINE JUNC.
CANAL JUNCTION
HOLBECK SOUTH JUNC.
WORTLEY WEST J^N
From Bradford
WHITEHALL JUNCTION
WHITEHALL ROAD GOODS
COPLEY HILL STATION
WORTLEY SOUTH J^N
ENGINE SHED JUNC.
HUNSLET LANE GOODS
To Hull
HUNSLET BRANCH JUNC.
HUNSLET GOODS
N.E.
G.N.
EXCHANGE SIDS.
GOODS JUNC.
SIDINGS JUNC.
To Beeston Junc.
JUNC.
HUNSLET PASS.
To Methley
From Dewsbury
STA.
FARNLEY & WORTLEY
NORTH JUNC.
From Wakefield
EXPLANATION
GREAT NORTHERN
G.N. & L.& Y. JOINT
G.N., L.&Y., L.&N.W., & N.E. JOINT
LONDON & NORTH WESTERN
L.&N.W. & L.&Y. JOINT
L.&N.W. & N.E. JOINT
MIDLAND
NORTH EASTERN
N.E. & G.N. JOINT

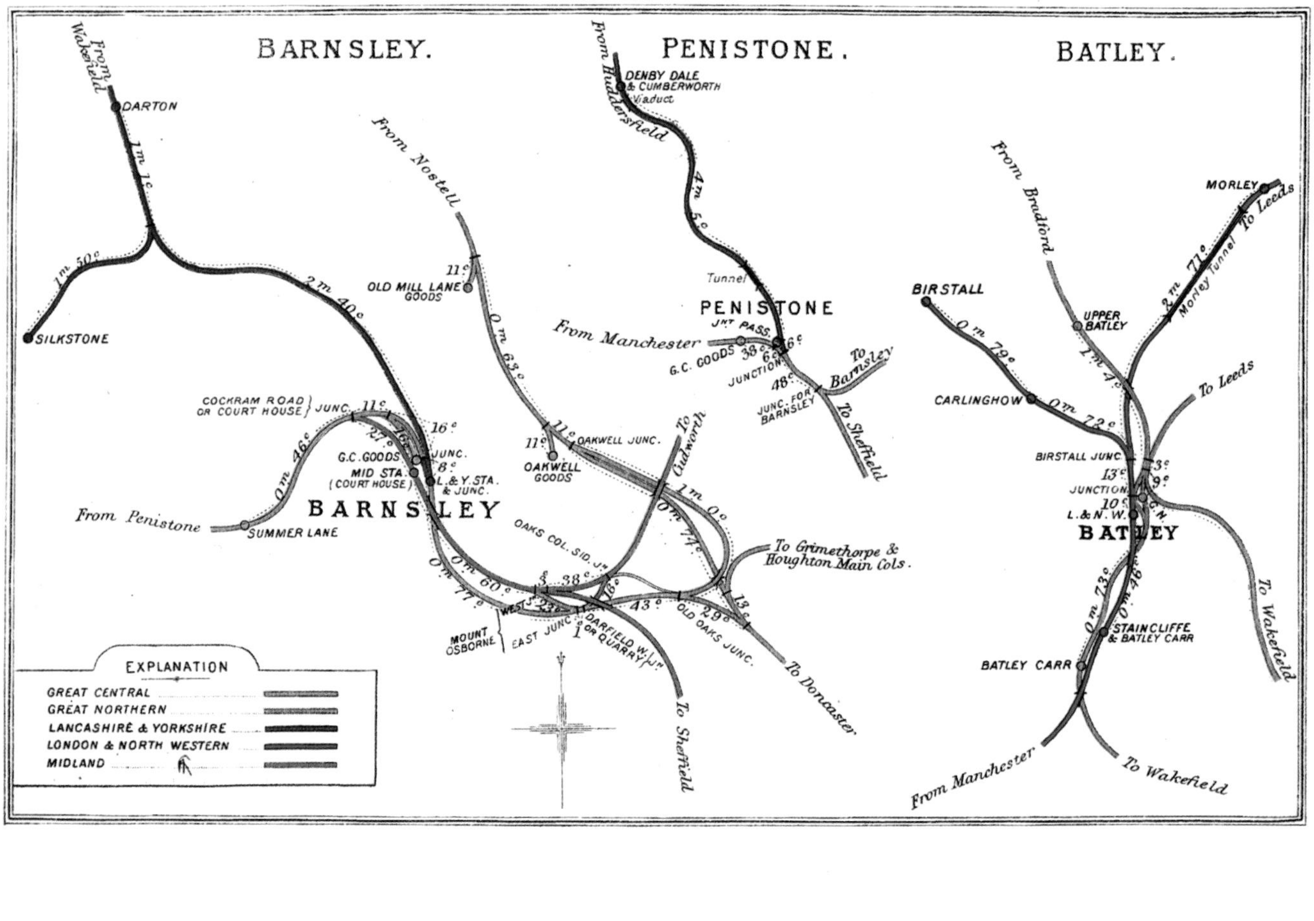
BARNSLEY.
PENISTONE.
BATLEY.
From Wakefield
DARTON
SILKSTONE
From Nostell
OLD MILL LANE GOODS
COCKRAM ROAD OR COURT HOUSE JUNC.
G.C. GOODS
MID STA. (COURT HOUSE)
L. & Y. STA. & JUNC.
From Penistone
SUMMER LANE
BARNSLEY
OAKWELL JUNC.
OAKWELL GOODS
To Cudworth
OAKS COL. SID. J^N
To Grimethorpe & Houghton Main Cols.
MOUNT OSBORNE
WEST
EAST JUNC.
DARFIELD W. OR QUARRY J^N
OLD OAKS JUNC.
To Doncaster
To Sheffield
From Huddersfield
DENBY DALE & CUMBERWORTH Viaduct
Tunnel
PENISTONE
From Manchester
J^NT PASS.
G.C. GOODS
JUNCTION
JUNC. FOR BARNSLEY
To Barnsley
To Sheffield
From Bradford
MORLEY
To Leeds
Morley Tunnel
BIRSTALL
UPPER BATLEY
CARLINGHOW
To Leeds
BIRSTALL JUNC.
JUNCTION
L.&N.W.
G.N.
BATLEY
STAINCLIFFE & BATLEY CARR
BATLEY CARR
To Wakefield
From Manchester
To Wakefield
EXPLANATION
GREAT CENTRAL
GREAT NORTHERN
LANCASHIRE & YORKSHIRE
LONDON & NORTH WESTERN
MIDLAND

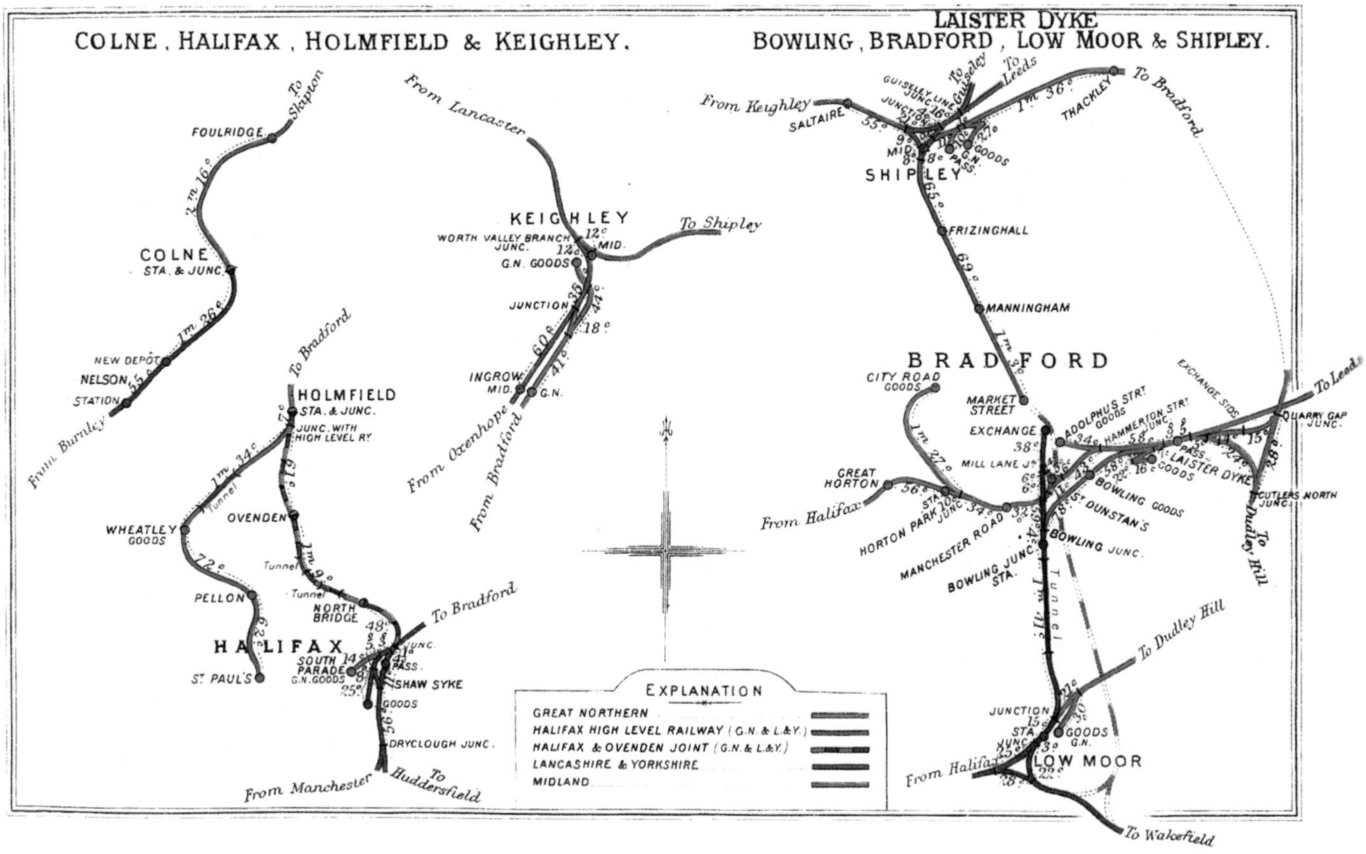
COLNE, HALIFAX, HOLMFIELD & KEIGHLEY.
LAISTER DYKE
BOWLING, BRADFORD, LOW MOOR & SHIPLEY.
To Skipton
FOULRIDGE
COLNE
STA. & JUNC.
NEW DEPÔT
NELSON
STATION
From Burnley
From Lancaster
KEIGHLEY
WORTH VALLEY BRANCH JUNC.
MID.
G.N. GOODS
To Shipley
JUNCTION
INGROW
MID.
G.N.
From Oxenhope
From Bradford
To Bradford
HOLMFIELD
STA. & JUNC.
JUNC. WITH HIGH LEVEL RY.
Tunnel
WHEATLEY
GOODS
OVENDEN
PELLON
NORTH BRIDGE
HALIFAX
SOUTH PARADE
G.N. GOODS
ST. PAUL'S
PASS.
SHAW SYKE
GOODS
DRYCLOUGH JUNC.
To Bradford
From Manchester
To Huddersfield
From Keighley
SALTAIRE
GUISELEY LINE JUNC.
To Guiseley
To Leeds
THACKLEY
To Bradford
SHIPLEY
GOODS
FRIZINGHALL
MANNINGHAM
BRADFORD
CITY ROAD GOODS
MARKET STREET
EXCHANGE
ADOLPHUS STRT GOODS
HAMMERTON STRT JUNC.
EXCHANGE SIDS.
To Leeds
QUARRY GAP JUNC.
MILL LANE JN.
GREAT HORTON
From Halifax
HORTON PARK
MANCHESTER ROAD
BOWLING GOODS
ST. DUNSTAN'S
LAISTER DYKE
GOODS
CUTLERS NORTH JUNC.
To Dudley Hill
BOWLING JUNC.
BOWLING JUNC. STA.
Tunnel
To Dudley Hill
JUNCTION
STA.
GOODS
G.N.
LOW MOOR
From Halifax
To Wakefield
EXPLANATION
GREAT NORTHERN
HALIFAX HIGH LEVEL RAILWAY (G.N. & L.&Y.)
HALIFAX & OVENDEN JOINT (G.N. & L.&Y.)
LANCASHIRE & YORKSHIRE
MIDLAND

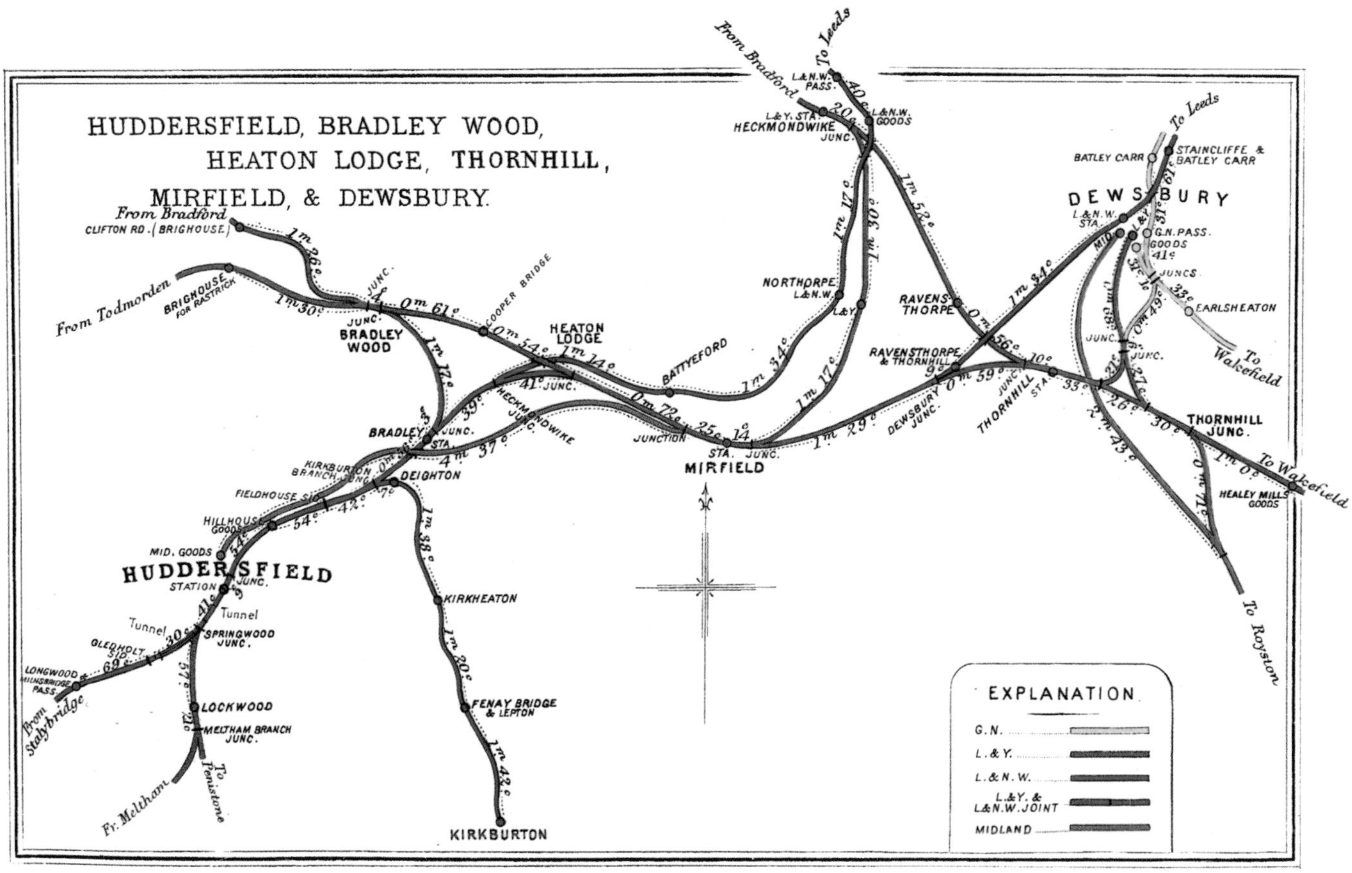
HUDDERSFIELD, BRADLEY WOOD, HEATON LODGE, THORNHILL, MIRFIELD, & DEWSBURY.
From Bradford
To Leeds
L.&N.W. PASS.
L.&Y. STA.
L.&N.W. GOODS
HECKMONDWIKE JUNC.
From Bradford
CLIFTON RD. (BRIGHOUSE)
From Todmorden
BRIGHOUSE FOR RASTRICK
JUNC.
BRADLEY WOOD
COOPER BRIDGE
HEATON LODGE
BATTYEFORD
NORTHORPE
L.&N.W.
L.&Y.
RAVENSTHORPE
RAVENSTHORPE & THORNHILL
DEWSBURY JUNC.
THORNHILL STA.
JUNC.
HECKMONDWIKE JUNC.
BRADLEY
JUNC.
STA.
JUNCTION
STA. JUNC.
MIRFIELD
KIRKBURTON BRANCH JUNC.
DEIGHTON
FIELDHOUSE SIDS.
HILLHOUSE GOODS
MID. GOODS
HUDDERSFIELD
STATION
JUNC.
Tunnel
OLDHOLT SIDS.
SPRINGWOOD JUNC.
LONGWOOD MILNSBRIDGE PASS.
From Stalybridge
LOCKWOOD
MELTHAM BRANCH JUNC.
Fr. Meltham
To Penistone
KIRKHEATON
FENAY BRIDGE & LEPTON
KIRKBURTON
To Leeds
BATLEY CARR
STAINCLIFFE & BATLEY CARR
DEWSBURY
L.&N.W. STA.
MID.
G.N. PASS.
GOODS
JUNCS.
EARLSHEATON
To Wakefield
JUNC.
THORNHILL JUNC.
To Wakefield
HEALEY MILLS GOODS
To Royston
EXPLANATION
G.N.
L.&Y.
L.&N.W.
L.&Y. & L.&N.W. JOINT
MIDLAND

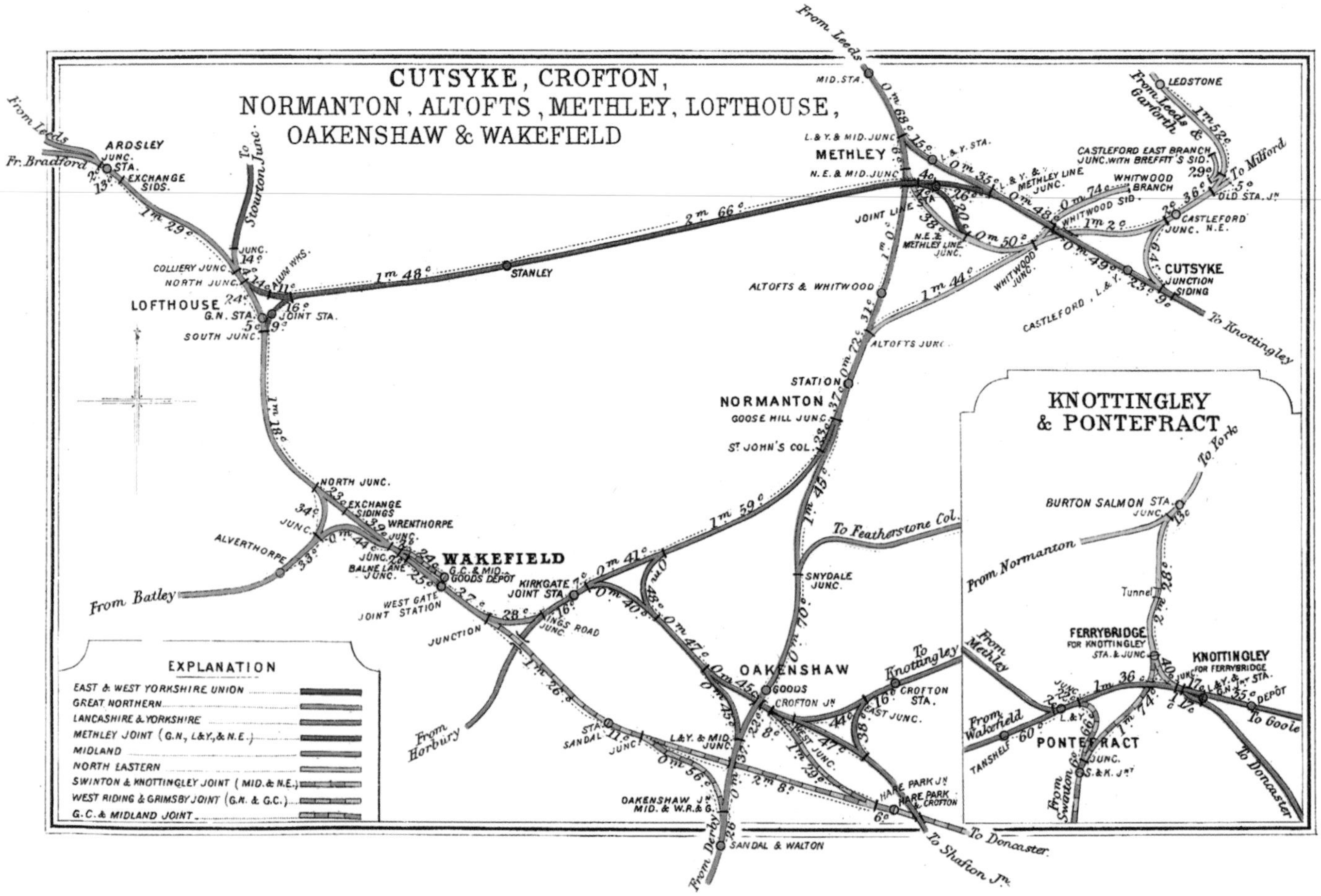
CUTSYKE, CROFTON,
NORMANTON, ALTOFTS, METHLEY, LOFTHOUSE,
OAKENSHAW & WAKEFIELD
From Leeds
Fr. Bradford
ARDSLEY
EXCHANGE SIDS.
To Stourton Junc.
COLLIERY JUNC.
NORTH JUNC.
LOFTHOUSE
G.N. STA.
JOINT STA.
SOUTH JUNC.
STANLEY
METHLEY
MID. STA.
L.& Y. & MID. JUNC.
N.E. & MID. JUNC.
JOINT LINE STA.
ALTOFTS & WHITWOOD
ALTOFTS JUNC.
NORMANTON
STATION
GOOSE HILL JUNC.
ST JOHN'S COL.
LEDSTONE
From Leeds & Garforth
To Milford
CASTLEFORD EAST BRANCH JUNC. WITH BREFFIT'S SID.
OLD STA. JN
WHITWOOD BRANCH
WHITWOOD SID.
CASTLEFORD JUNC. N.E.
CUTSYKE
JUNCTION SIDING
CASTLEFORD, L.& Y.
To Knottingley
NORTH JUNC.
EXCHANGE SIDINGS
WRENTHORPE JUNC.
ALVERTHORPE
From Batley
WAKEFIELD
G.C. & MID. GOODS DEPOT
BALNE LANE JUNC.
WEST GATE JOINT STATION
KIRKGATE JOINT STA.
KINGS ROAD JUNC.
From Horbury
SANDAL
To Featherstone Col.
SNYDALE JUNC.
OAKENSHAW
GOODS
CROFTON JN
CROFTON STA.
EAST JUNC.
To Knottingley
L.& Y. & MID. JUNC.
OAKENSHAW JN MID. & W.R.& G.
HARE PARK JN
HARE PARK & CROFTON
To Doncaster
To Shafton Jn
From Derby
SANDAL & WALTON
EXPLANATION
EAST & WEST YORKSHIRE UNION
GREAT NORTHERN
LANCASHIRE & YORKSHIRE
METHLEY JOINT (G.N., L&Y, & N.E.)
MIDLAND
NORTH EASTERN
SWINTON & KNOTTINGLEY JOINT (MID. & N.E.)
WEST RIDING & GRIMSBY JOINT (G.N. & G.C.)
G.C. & MIDLAND JOINT
KNOTTINGLEY & PONTEFRACT
To York
BURTON SALMON STA.
From Normanton
Tunnel
FERRYBRIDGE FOR KNOTTINGLEY
KNOTTINGLEY FOR FERRYBRIDGE
From Methley
From Wakefield
TANSHELF
PONTEFRACT
To Goole
To Doncaster
From Swinton

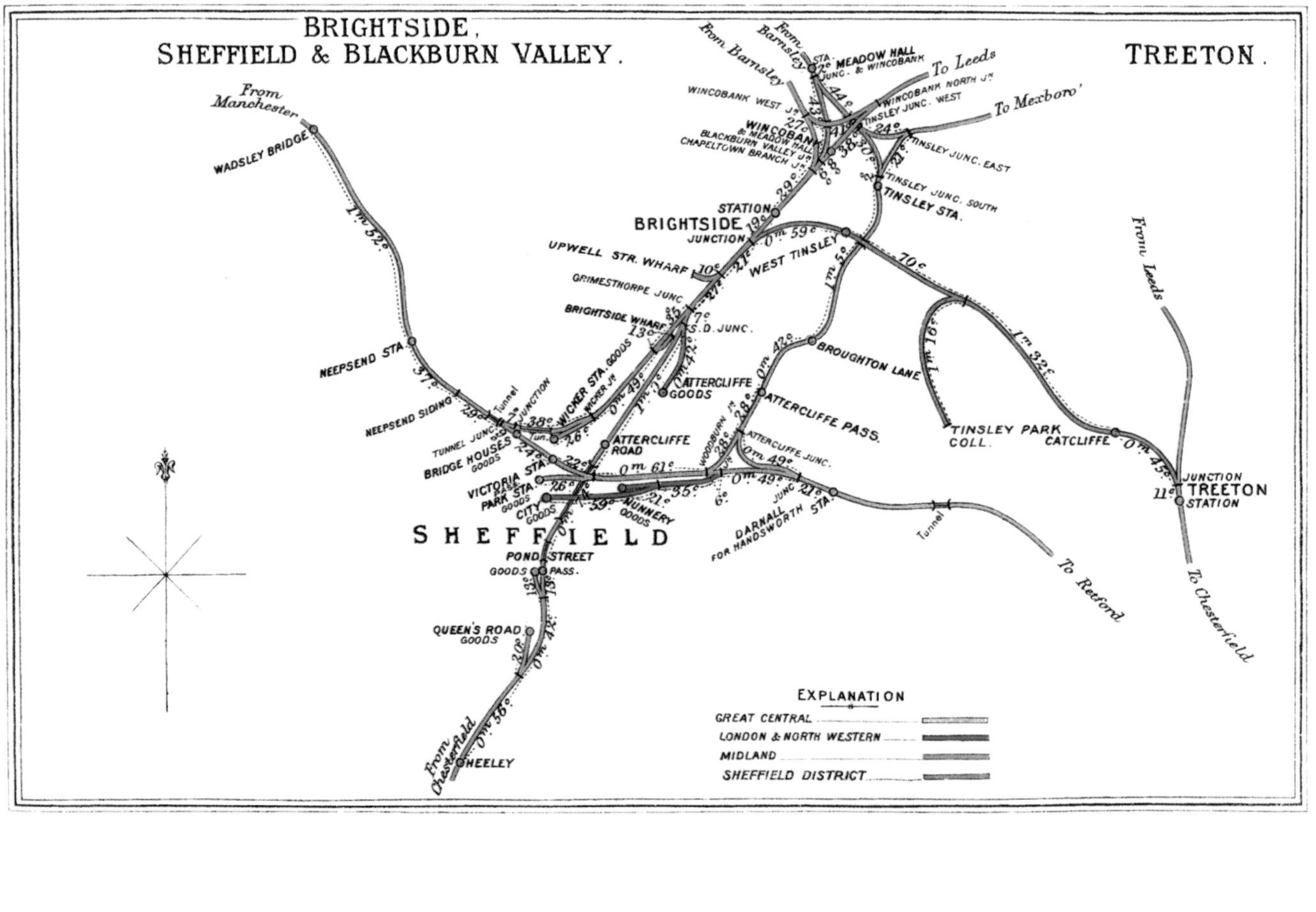
BRIGHTSIDE,
SHEFFIELD & BLACKBURN VALLEY.
TREETON.
From Manchester
WADSLEY BRIDGE
From Barnsley
MEADOW HALL & WINCOBANK
To Leeds
To Mexboro'
WINCOBANK WEST JN
WINCOBANK
TINSLEY JUNC. EAST
TINSLEY JUNC. SOUTH
TINSLEY STA.
BRIGHTSIDE
STATION
JUNCTION
UPWELL STR. WHARF
WEST TINSLEY
GRIMESTHORPE JUNC.
BRIGHTSIDE WHARF
S.D. JUNC.
NEEPSEND STA.
NEEPSEND SIDING
WICKER STA. GOODS
ATTERCLIFFE GOODS
BROUGHTON LANE
ATTERCLIFFE PASS.
TINSLEY PARK COLL.
CATCLIFFE
From Leeds
TUNNEL JUNC.
BRIDGE HOUSES GOODS
ATTERCLIFFE ROAD
VICTORIA STA.
PARK STA. GOODS
CITY GOODS
NUNNERY GOODS
DARNALL FOR HANDSWORTH STA.
JUNCTION
TREETON STATION
Tunnel
To Retford
To Chesterfield
SHEFFIELD
POND STREET
GOODS
PASS.
QUEEN'S ROAD GOODS
From Chesterfield
HEELEY
EXPLANATION
GREAT CENTRAL
LONDON & NORTH WESTERN
MIDLAND
SHEFFIELD DISTRICT

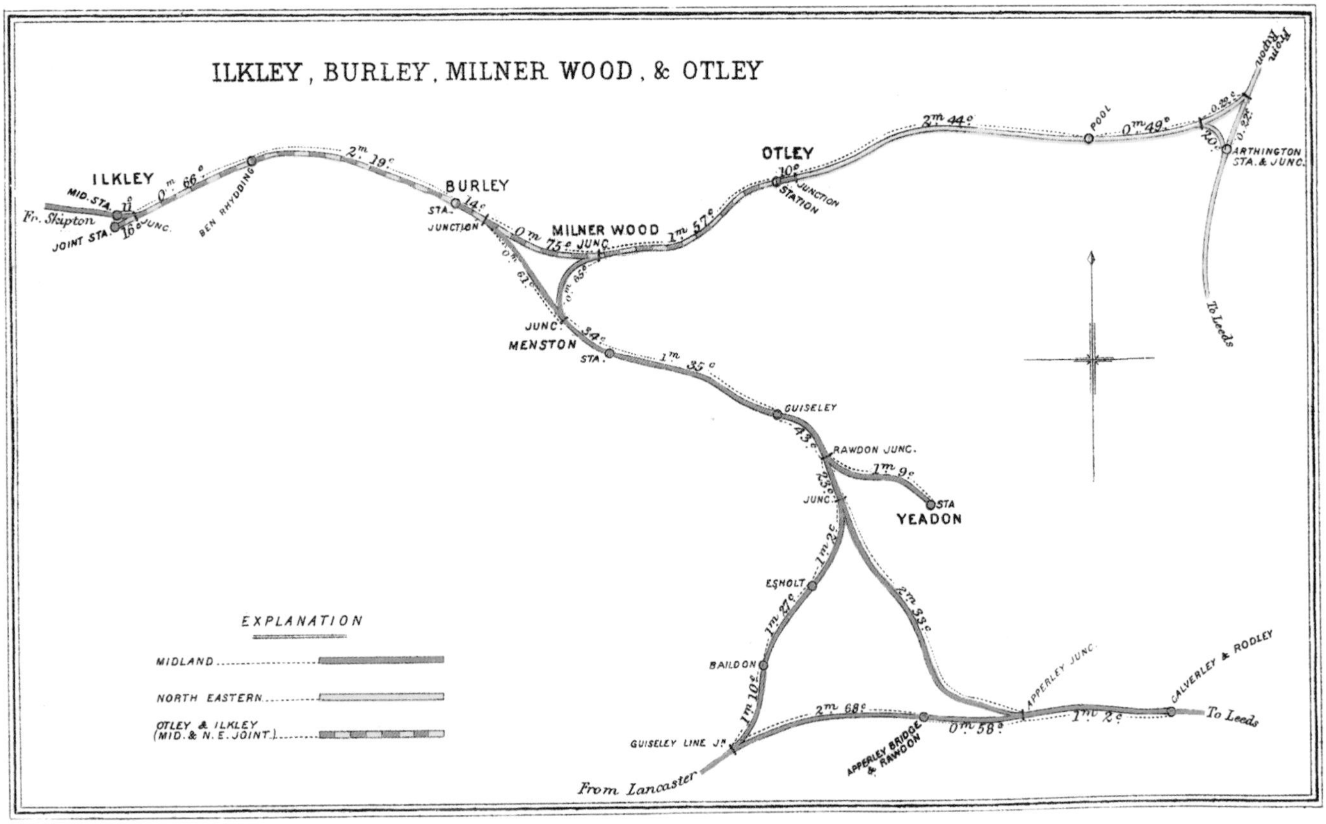

ILKLEY, BURLEY, MILNER WOOD, & OTLEY

EXPLANATION

MIDLAND

NORTH EASTERN

OTLEY & ILKLEY (MID. & N.E. JOINT)

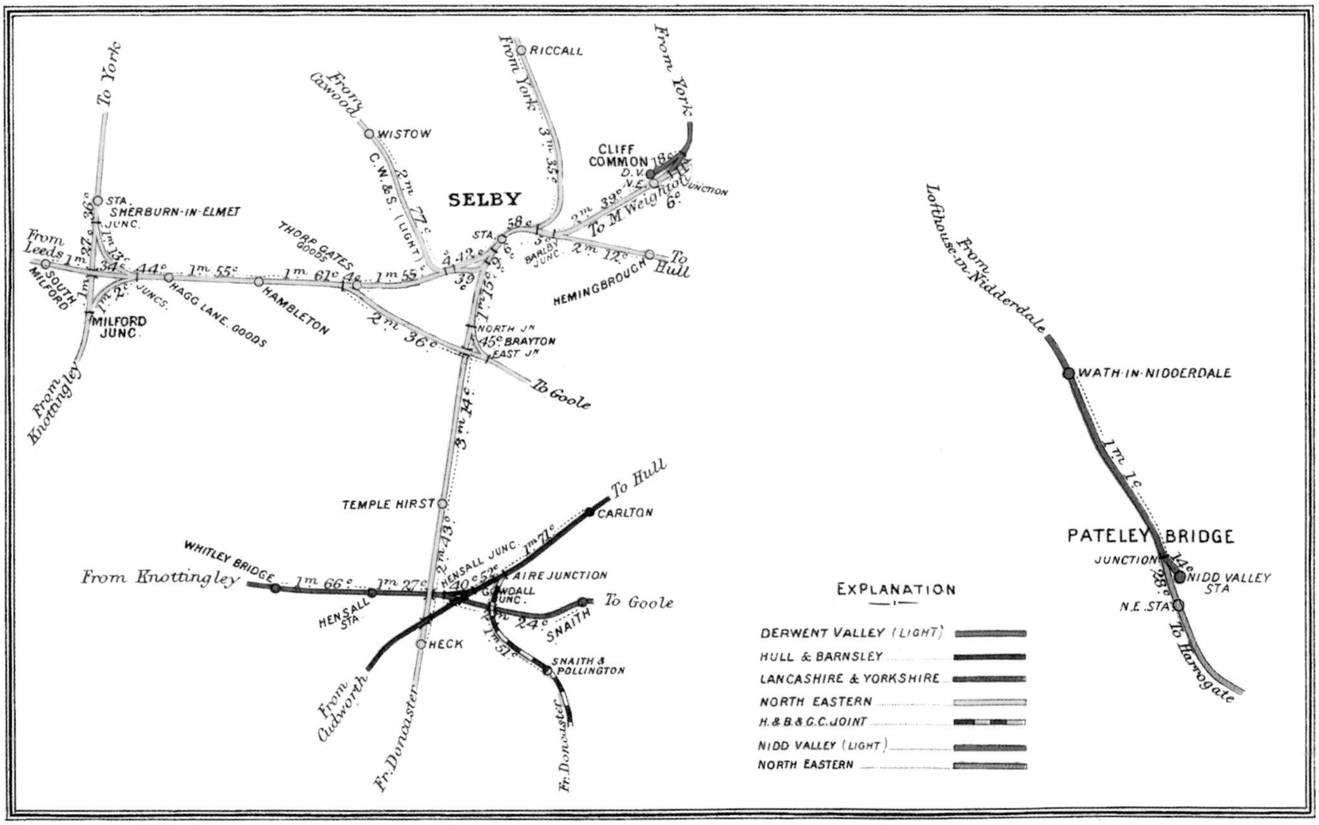

EXPLANATION

DERWENT VALLEY (LIGHT)

HULL & BARNSLEY

LANCASHIRE & YORKSHIRE

NORTH EASTERN

H. & B. & G.C. JOINT

NIDD VALLEY (LIGHT)

NORTH EASTERN

**Selby–Pateley Bridge**

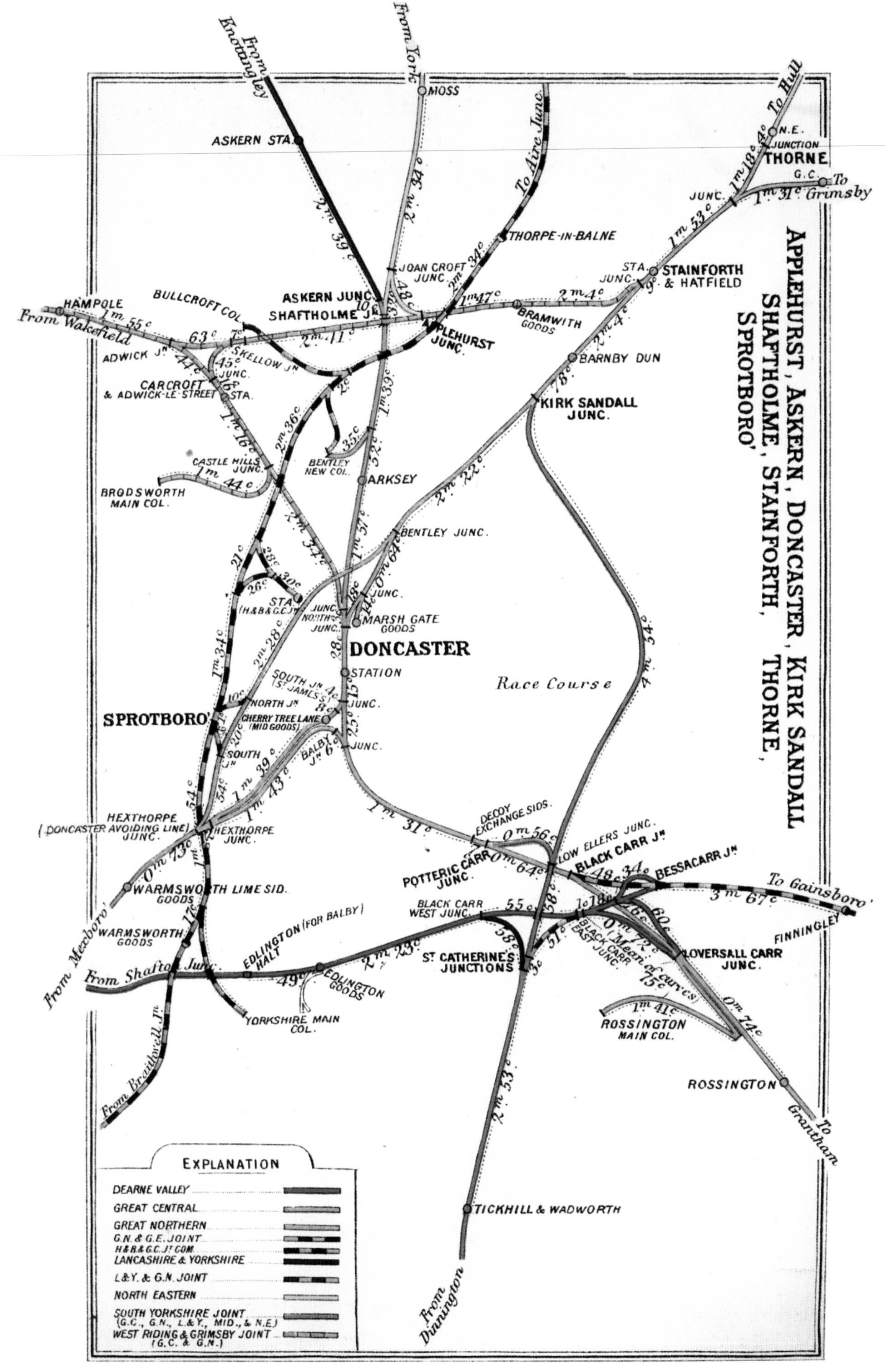
APPLEHURST, ASKERN, DONCASTER, KIRK SANDALL, SHAFTHOLME, STAINFORTH, THORNE, SPROTBORO'
DONCASTER
STATION
Race Course
SPROTBORO'
ASKERN STA.
ASKERN JUNC.
SHAFTHOLME Jn.
APPLEHURST JUNC.
THORPE-IN-BALNE
JOAN CROFT JUNC.
MOSS
From York
From Knottingley
To Aire Junc.
THORNE
N.E. JUNCTION
G.C.
JUNC.
To Hull
To Grimsby
STAINFORTH & HATFIELD
STA. JUNC.
BRAMWITH GOODS
BARNBY DUN
KIRK SANDALL JUNC.
HAMPOLE
From Wakefield
BULLCROFT COL.
ADWICK Jn.
SKELLOW Jn.
CARCROFT & ADWICK-LE-STREET STA.
CASTLE HILLS JUNC.
BRODSWORTH MAIN COL.
BENTLEY NEW COL.
ARKSEY
BENTLEY JUNC.
MARSH GATE GOODS
NORTH JUNC.
STA. (H.&B.&G.C.Jt.)
SOUTH Jn. (ST JAMES')
NORTH Jn.
CHERRY TREE LANE (MID GOODS)
SOUTH Jn.
BALBY Jn.
HEXTHORPE (DONCASTER AVOIDING LINE) JUNC.
HEXTHORPE JUNC.
WARMSWORTH LIME SID. GOODS
WARMSWORTH GOODS
From Mexboro'
From Shafton Jn.
From Braithwell Jn.
EDLINGTON (FOR BALBY) HALT
EDLINGTON GOODS
YORKSHIRE MAIN COL.
DECOY EXCHANGE SIDS.
LOW ELLERS JUNC.
POTTERIC CARR JUNC.
BLACK CARR Jn.
BESSACARR Jn.
To Gainsboro'
BLACK CARR WEST JUNC.
BLACK CARR EAST JUNC.
ST. CATHERINE'S JUNCTIONS
(Mean of curves)
FINNINGLEY
LOVERSALL CARR JUNC.
ROSSINGTON MAIN COL.
ROSSINGTON
To Grantham
TICKHILL & WADWORTH
From Dinnington
EXPLANATION
DEARNE VALLEY
GREAT CENTRAL
GREAT NORTHERN
G.N. & G.E. JOINT
H.&B.&G.C. Jt. COM.
LANCASHIRE & YORKSHIRE
L.&Y. & G.N. JOINT
NORTH EASTERN
SOUTH YORKSHIRE JOINT (G.C., G.N., L.&Y., MID., & N.E.)
WEST RIDING & GRIMSBY JOINT (G.C. & G.N.)

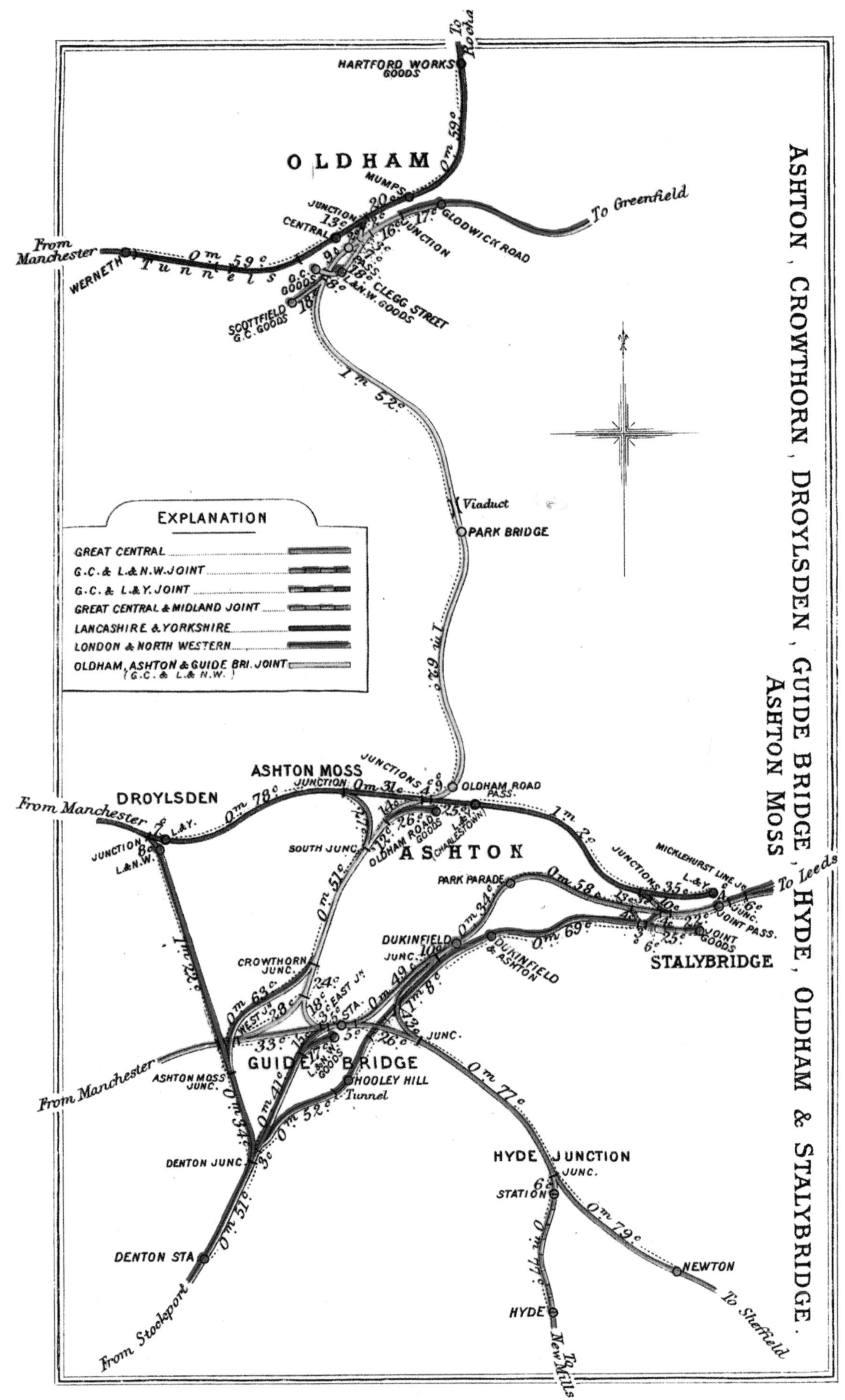
ASHTON, CROWTHORN, DROYLSDEN, GUIDE BRIDGE, HYDE, OLDHAM & STALYBRIDGE.
ASHTON MOSS
OLDHAM
HARTFORD WORKS GOODS
To Rocha
MUMPS
JUNCTION
CENTRAL
GLODWICK ROAD
To Greenfield
From Manchester
WERNETH
Tunnels
CLEGG STREET
L.&N.W. GOODS
SCOTTFIELD G.C. GOODS
Viaduct
PARK BRIDGE
EXPLANATION
GREAT CENTRAL
G.C. & L.&N.W. JOINT
G.C. & L.&Y. JOINT
GREAT CENTRAL & MIDLAND JOINT
LANCASHIRE & YORKSHIRE
LONDON & NORTH WESTERN
OLDHAM, ASHTON & GUIDE BRI. JOINT (G.C. & L.&N.W.)
ASHTON MOSS JUNCTION
DROYLSDEN
From Manchester
OLDHAM ROAD PASS.
ASHTON
SOUTH JUNC.
OLDHAM ROAD GOODS
MICKLEHURST LINE JN.
To Leeds
PARK PARADE
JOINT PASS.
JOINT GOODS
STALYBRIDGE
DUKINFIELD JUNC.
DUKINFIELD & ASHTON
CROWTHORN JUNC.
GUIDE BRIDGE
From Manchester
ASHTON MOSS JUNC.
HOOLEY HILL
Tunnel
DENTON JUNC.
HYDE JUNCTION
STATION
DENTON STA
NEWTON
To Sheffield
HYDE
From Stockport
To New Mills

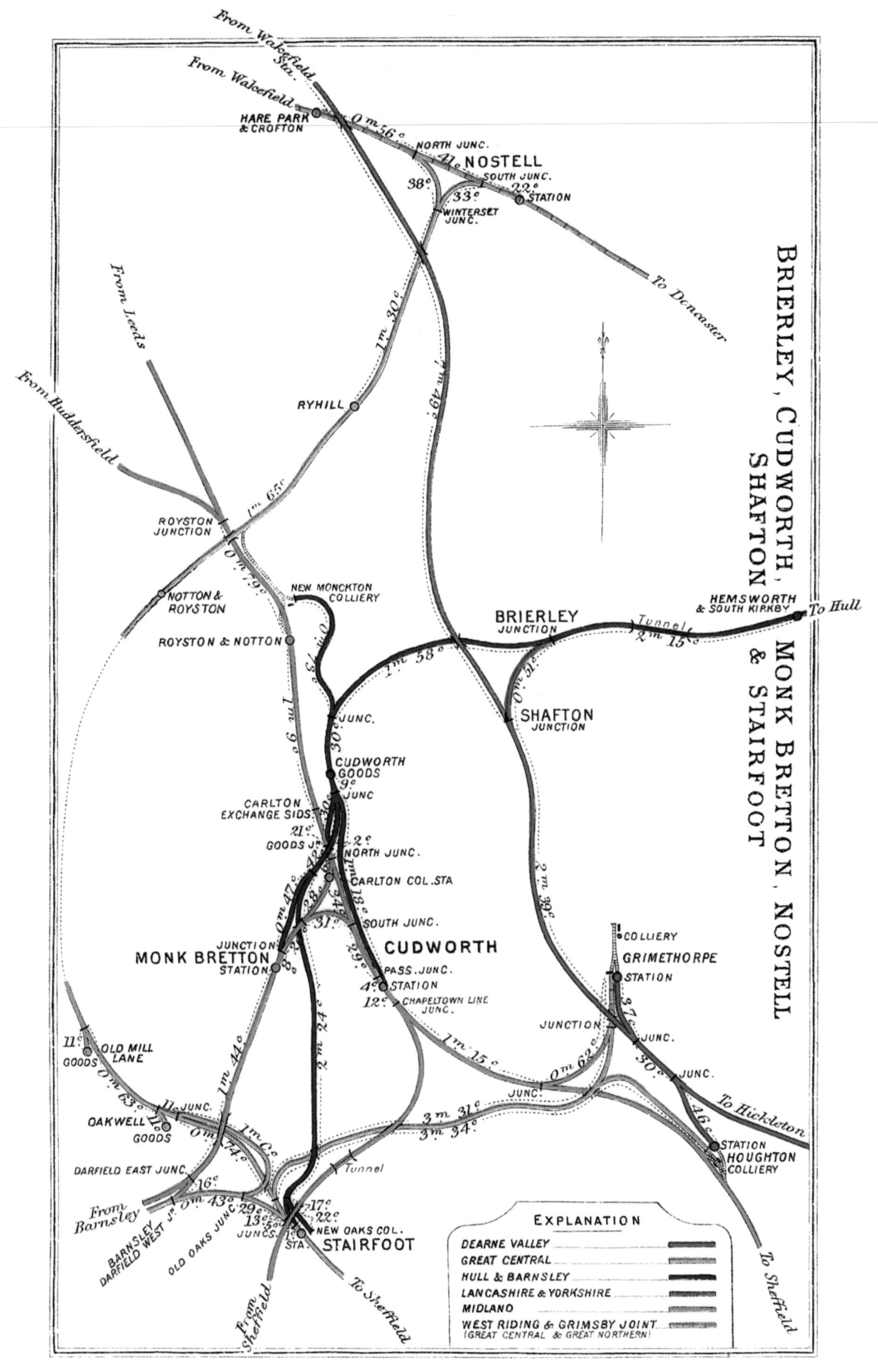
BRIERLEY, CUDWORTH, MONK BRETTON, NOSTELL
SHAFTON & STAIRFOOT
From Wakefield Sta.
From Wakefield
HARE PARK & CROFTON
NORTH JUNC.
NOSTELL
SOUTH JUNC.
STATION
WINTERSET JUNC.
To Doncaster
From Leeds
From Huddersfield
RYHILL
ROYSTON JUNCTION
NOTTON & ROYSTON
ROYSTON & NOTTON
NEW MONCKTON COLLIERY
BRIERLEY JUNCTION
HEMSWORTH & SOUTH KIRKBY
To Hull
Tunnel
SHAFTON JUNCTION
JUNC.
CUDWORTH GOODS
JUNC
CARLTON EXCHANGE SIDS
GOODS JN.
NORTH JUNC.
CARLTON COL. STA
SOUTH JUNC.
JUNCTION
MONK BRETTON STATION
CUDWORTH
PASS. JUNC.
STATION
CHAPELTOWN LINE JUNC.
COLLIERY
GRIMETHORPE STATION
JUNCTION
JUNC.
JUNC.
To Hickleton
OLD MILL LANE GOODS
JUNC.
OAKWELL GOODS
STATION HOUGHTON COLLIERY
DARFIELD EAST JUNC.
Tunnel
From Barnsley
BARNSLEY DARFIELD WEST JN.
OLD OAKS JUNC.
JUNCS.
STA.
NEW OAKS COL.
STAIRFOOT
From Sheffield
To Sheffield
To Sheffield
EXPLANATION
DEARNE VALLEY
GREAT CENTRAL
HULL & BARNSLEY
LANCASHIRE & YORKSHIRE
MIDLAND
WEST RIDING & GRIMSBY JOINT
(GREAT CENTRAL & GREAT NORTHERN)

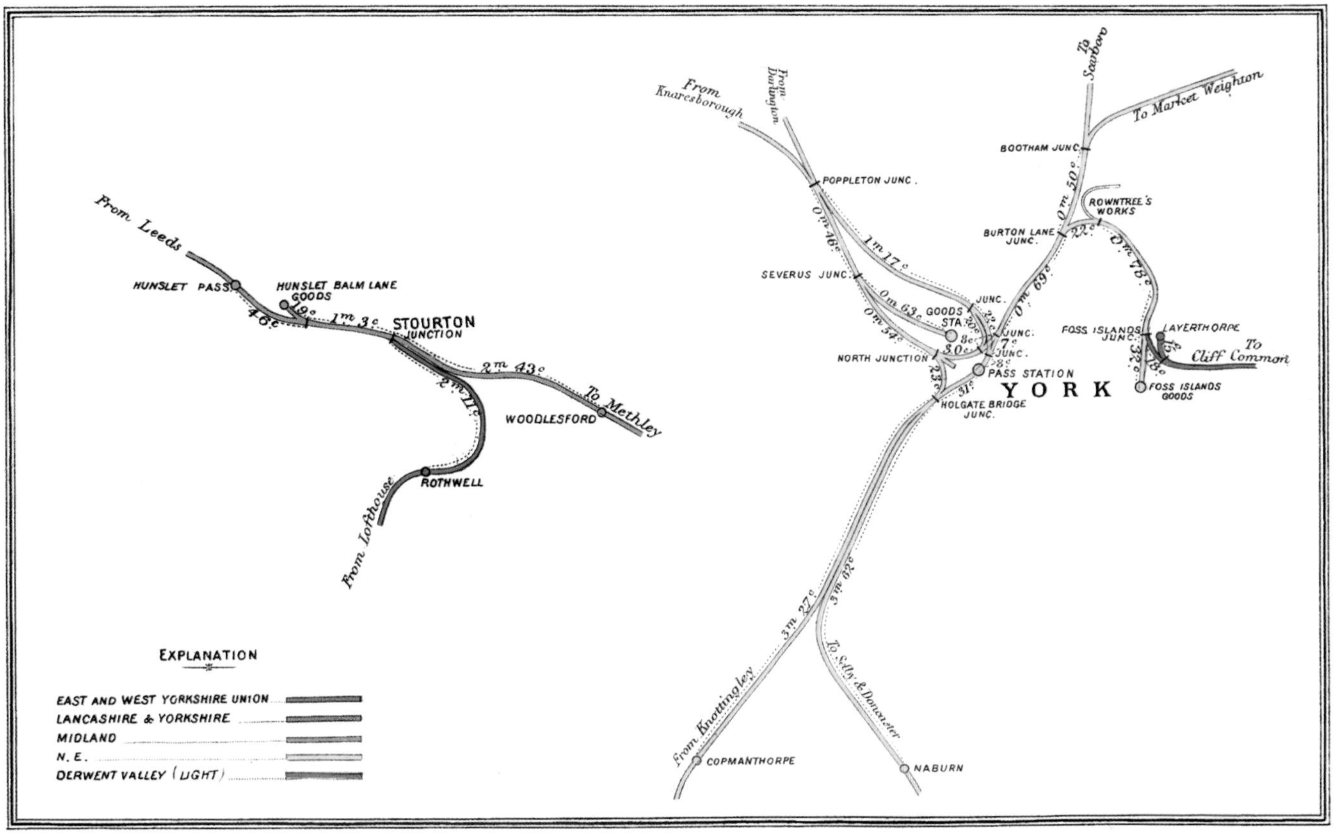

EXPLANATION

- EAST AND WEST YORKSHIRE UNION
- LANCASHIRE & YORKSHIRE
- MIDLAND
- N. E.
- DERWENT VALLEY (LIGHT)

**Stourton–York**

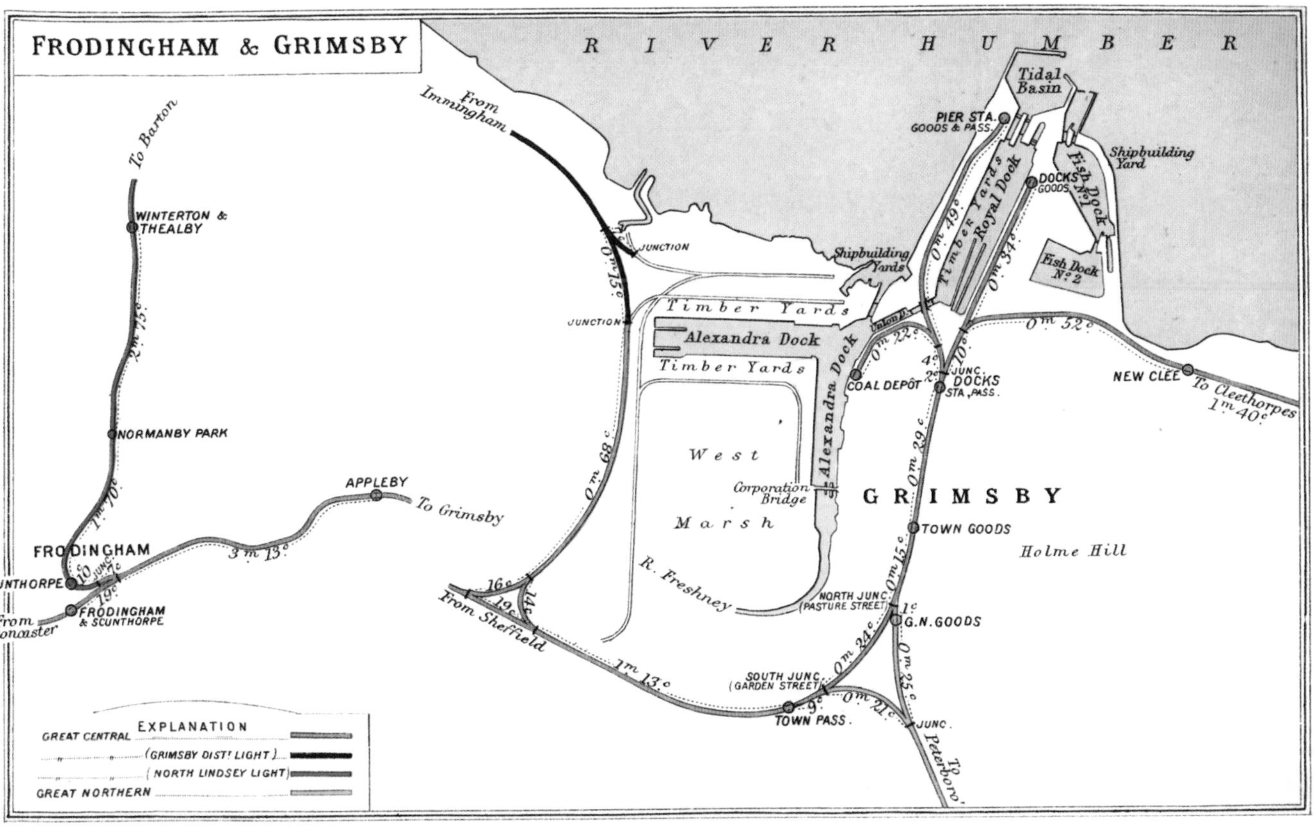

## FRODINGHAM & GRIMSBY

EXPLANATION

- GREAT CENTRAL
- " " (GRIMSBY DIST<sup></sup>. LIGHT)
- " " (NORTH LINDSEY LIGHT)
- GREAT NORTHERN

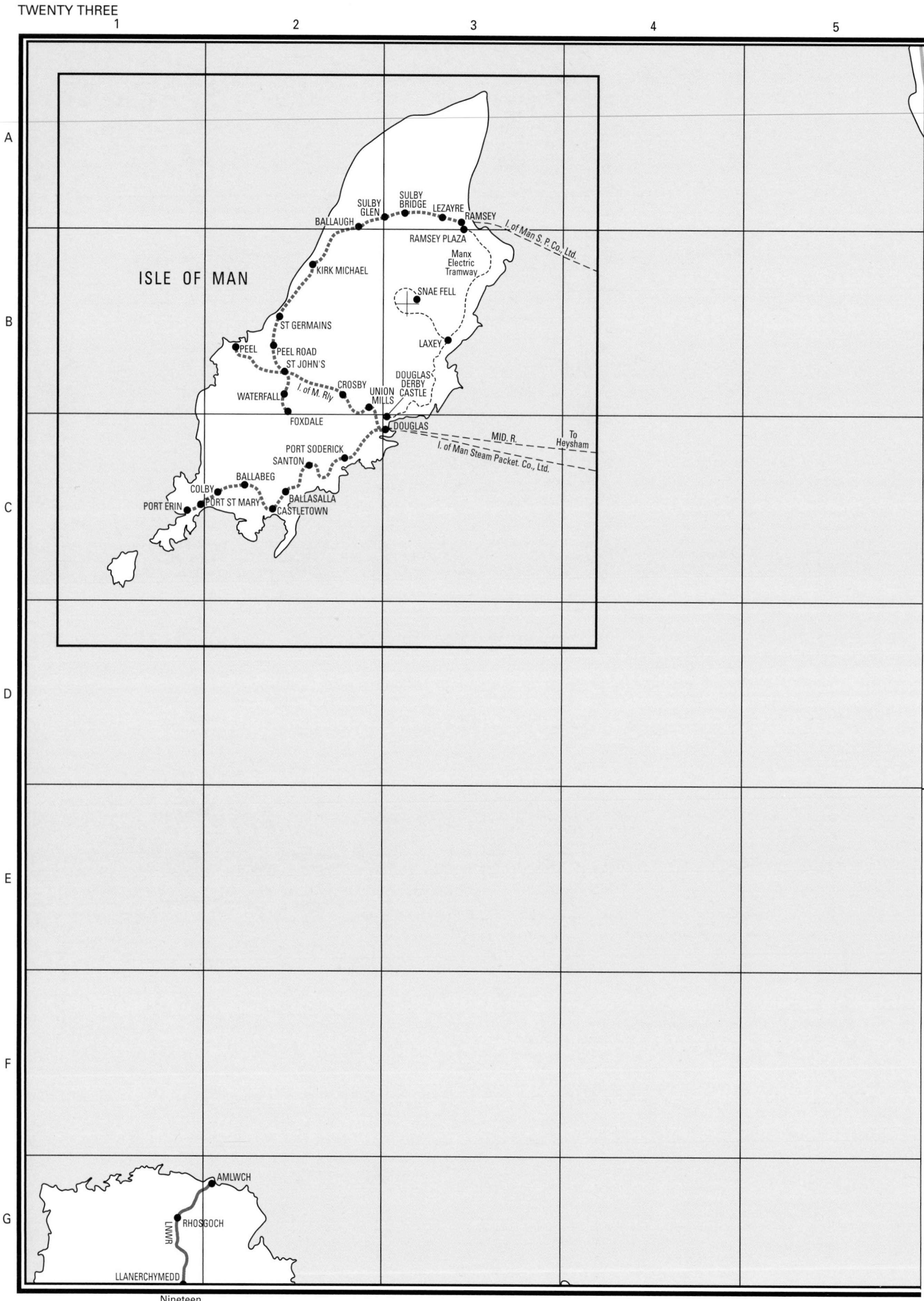

1
2
3
4
5
A
B
C
D
E
F
G
ISLE OF MAN
SULBY GLEN
SULBY BRIDGE
LEZAYRE
RAMSEY
BALLAUGH
RAMSEY PLAZA
I. of Man S. P. Co., Ltd.
KIRK MICHAEL
Manx Electric Tramway
SNAE FELL
ST GERMAINS
LAXEY
PEEL
PEEL ROAD
ST JOHN'S
DOUGLAS DERBY CASTLE
CROSBY
I. of M. Rly
UNION MILLS
WATERFALL
FOXDALE
DOUGLAS
MID. R.
To Heysham
I. of Man Steam Packet. Co., Ltd.
PORT SODERICK
SANTON
BALLABEG
COLBY
BALLASALLA
PORT ERIN
PORT ST MARY
CASTLETOWN
AMLWCH
RHOSGOCH
LNWR
LLANERCHYMEDD
Nineteen

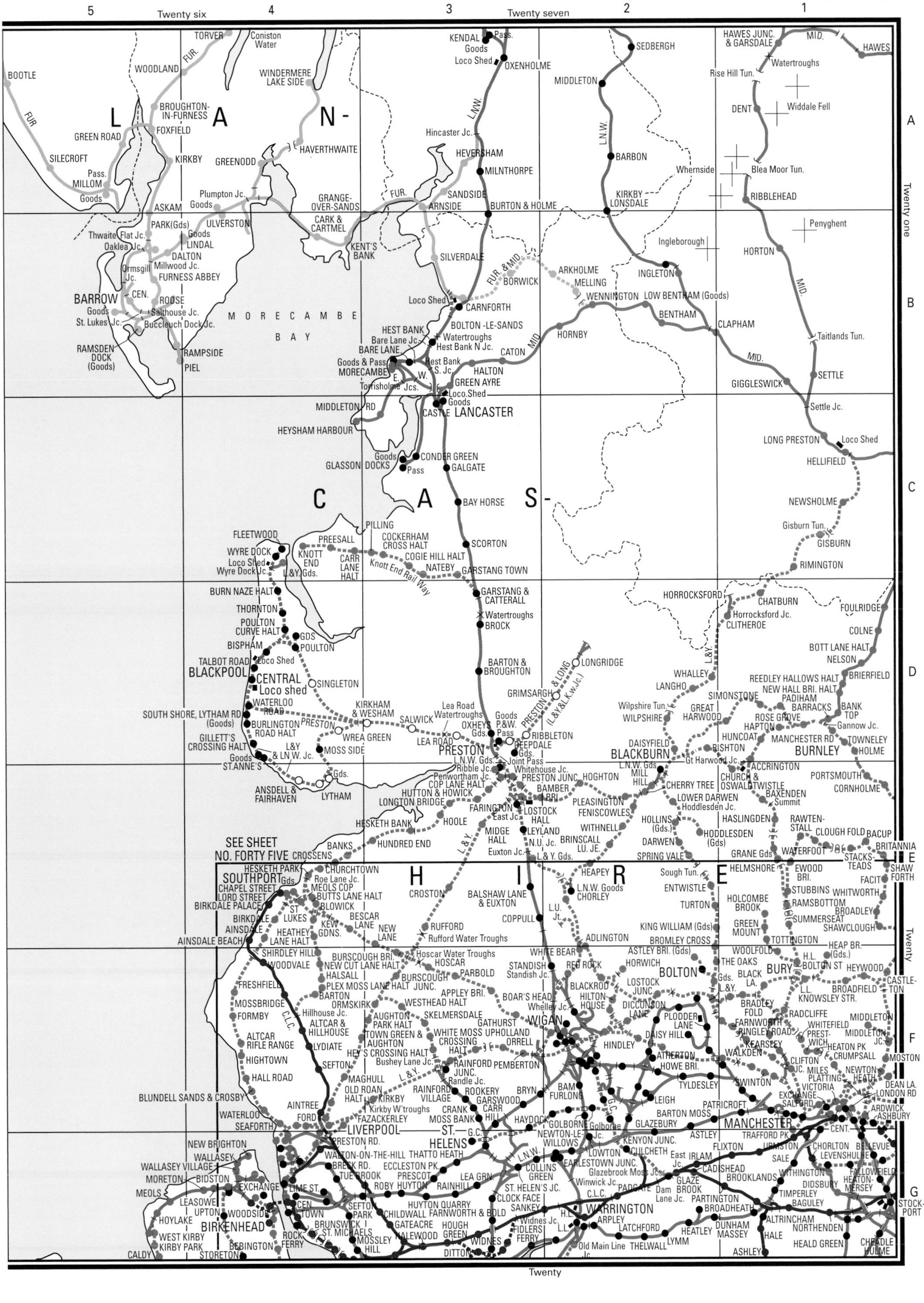

## TWENTY THREE

5 Twenty six 4 3 Twenty seven 2 1

A B C D E F G

Twenty one

Twenty

L A N - C A S - H I R E

TORVER
Coniston Water
WOODLAND
FUR.
BOOTLE
WINDERMERE LAKE SIDE
KENDAL Pass.
Goods
Loco Shed
OXENHOLME
SEDBERGH
HAWES JUNC. & GARSDALE
MID.
HAWES
Watertroughs
Rise Hill Tun.
MIDDLETON
L.N.W.
DENT
Widdale Fell
BROUGHTON-IN-FURNESS
FOXFIELD
GREEN ROAD
HAVERTHWAITE
Hincaster Jc.
SILECROFT
KIRKBY
GREENODD
HEVERSHAM
BARBON
Pass.
MILLOM
Goods
MILNTHORPE
Whernside
Blea Moor Tun.
Plumpton Jc.
Goods
ASKAM
GRANGE-OVER-SANDS
SANDSIDE
ARNSIDE
BURTON & HOLME
KIRKBY LONSDALE
RIBBLEHEAD
PARK (Gds)
ULVERSTON
CARK & CARTMEL
Penyghent
Thwaite Flat Jc.
Oaklea Jc.
Goods
LINDAL
DALTON
KENT'S BANK
Ingleborough
HORTON
Ormsgill Jc.
Millwood Jc.
FURNESS ABBEY
SILVERDALE
FUR. & MID.
ARKHOLME
BORWICK
MELLING
INGLETON
BARROW
CEN.
ROOSE
Goods
St. Lukes Jc.
Salthouse Jc.
Buccleuch Dock Jc.
M O R E C A M B E B A Y
Loco Shed
CARNFORTH
WENNINGTON
LOW BENTHAM (Goods)
BENTHAM
CLAPHAM
HEST BANK
Bare Lane Jc.
BARE LANE
BOLTON-LE-SANDS
Watertroughs
Hest Bank N. Jc.
CATON
HORNBY
Taitlands Tun.
RAMSDEN DOCK (Goods)
RAMPSIDE
PIEL
Goods & Pass
MORECAMBE
E. W.
Hest Bank S. Jc.
HALTON
GREEN AYRE
Torrisholme Jcs.
Loco Shed
Goods
CASTLE LANCASTER
SETTLE
GIGGLESWICK
Settle Jc.
MIDDLETON RD
HEYSHAM HARBOUR
LONG PRESTON
Loco Shed
HELLIFIELD
Goods
CONDER GREEN
GLASSON DOCKS
Pass
GALGATE
BAY HORSE
NEWSHOLME
Gisburn Tun.
GISBURN
PILLING
FLEETWOOD
PREESALL
COCKERHAM CROSS HALT
SCORTON
WYRE DOCK
Loco Shed
Wyre Dock Jc.
KNOTT END
CARR LANE HALT
COGIE HILL HALT
NATEBY
GARSTANG TOWN
RIMINGTON
L.&Y. Gds.
Knott End Rail Way
BURN NAZE HALT
GARSTANG & CATTERALL
HORROCKSFORD
CHATBURN
Horrocksford Jc.
CLITHEROE
FOULRIDGE
THORNTON
Watertroughs
BROCK
COLNE
POULTON CURVE HALT
GDS
POULTON
BISPHAM
BOTT LANE HALT
NELSON
TALBOT ROAD
Loco Shed
BLACKPOOL
CENTRAL
Loco shed
SINGLETON
BARTON & BROUGHTON
LONGRIDGE
PRESTON & LONG. (L&Y&L.N.W.Jc.)
WHALLEY
L.&Y.
BRIERFIELD
LANGHO
REEDLEY HALLOWS HALT
NEW HALL BRI. HALT
WATERLOO ROAD
GRIMSARGH
SIMONSTONE
PADIHAM
BARRACKS
BANK TOP
Wilpshire Tun.
WILPSHIRE
GREAT HARWOOD
ROSE GROVE
Gannow Jc.
SOUTH SHORE, LYTHAM RD (Goods)
KIRKHAM & WESHAM
Lea Road Watertroughs
Goods
P.&W.
SALWICK
OXHEYS
Pass
Gds.
RIBBLETON
HAPTON
BURLINGTON ROAD HALT
PRESTON
WREA GREEN
LEA ROAD
DEEPDALE
Gds.
DAISYFIELD
HUNCOAT
MANCHESTER RD
TOWNELEY
HOLME
GILLETT'S CROSSING HALT
Goods
ST. ANNE'S
L&Y & LN.W. Jc.
MOSS SIDE
PRESTON
L.N.W. Gds.
Joint Pass
Ribble Jc.
Whitehouse Jc.
BLACKBURN
L.N.W. Gds.
RISHTON
Gt Harwood Jc.
ACCRINGTON
BURNLEY
Gds.
Penwortham Jc.
PRESTON JUNC.
HOGHTON
MILL HILL
CHERRY TREE
CHURCH & OSWALDTWISTLE
PORTSMOUTH
CORNHOLME
ANSDELL & FAIRHAVEN
LYTHAM
COP LANE HALT
HUTTON & HOWICK
BAMBER BRI.
LOWER DARWEN
BAXENDEN
Summit
Hoddlesden Jc.
LONGTON BRIDGE
FARINGTON
East Jc.
LOSTOCK HALL
PLEASINGTON
FENISCOWLES
HASLINGDEN
RAWTENSTALL
HOOLE
HOLLINS (Gds.)
HESKETH BANK
MIDGE HALL
LEYLAND
WITHNELL
HODDLESDEN (Gds)
CLOUGH FOLD
BACUP
L&Y.
SEE SHEET NO. FORTY FIVE
BANKS
HUNDRED END
N.U. Jc.
BRINSCALL
LU. JE.
DARWEN
BRITANNIA
CROSSENS
Euxton Jc.
L.& Y. Gds.
SPRING VALE
GRANE Gds
WATERFOOT
STACKSTEADS
HESKETH PARK
CHURCHTOWN
HEAPEY
Sough Tun.
HELMSHORE
EWOOD BRI.
SHAW FORTH
SOUTHPORT
Gds
Roe Lane Jc.
L.N.W. Goods CHORLEY
ENTWISTLE
FACIT
CHAPEL STREET
LORD STREET
MEOLS COP
BUTTS LANE HALT
CROSTON
BALSHAW LANE & EUXTON
STUBBINS
WHITWORTH
BIRKDALE PALACE
BLOWICK
L.U. Jt.
TURTON
HOLCOMBE BROOK
RAMSBOTTOM
BIRKDALE
ST LUKES
BESCAR LANE
COPPULL
BROADLEY
AINSDALE
KEW GDNS.
NEW LANE
RUFFORD
Rufford Water Troughs
KING WILLIAM (Gds)
GREEN MOUNT
SUMMERSEAT
SHAWCLOUGH
HEATHEY LANE HALT
ADLINGTON
BROMLEY CROSS
TOTTINGTON
AINSDALE BEACH
HEAP BR. (Gds.)
SHIRDLEY HILL
BURSCOUGH BRI.
Hoscar Water Troughs
HOSCAR
WHITE BEAR
ASTLEY BRI. (Gds)
WOOLFOLD
H.L.
BOLTON ST
HEYWOOD
WOODVALE
NEW CUT LANE HALT
STANDISH
Standish Jc.
RED ROCK
HORWICH
BOLTON
THE OAKS
BURY
HALSALL
BURSCOUGH JUNC.
PARBOLD
BLACK LA.
CASTLETON
FRESHFIELD
PLEX MOSS LANE HALT
APPLEY BRI.
BLACKROD
LOSTOCK JUNC.
Gds.
L.&Y.
L.L.
BROADFIELD
BARTON
BOAR'S HEAD
HILTON HOUSE
KNOWSLEY STR.
MOSSBRIDGE
ORMSKIRK
WESTHEAD HALT
Whelley Jc.
DICCONSON LANE
BRADLEY FOLD
FORMBY
Hillhouse Jc.
AUGHTON PARK HALT
SKELMERSDALE
GATHURST
WIGAN
PLODDER LANE
RADCLIFFE
MIDDLETON
C.L.C.
ALTCAR & HILLHOUSE
TOWN GREEN & AUGHTON
WHITE MOSS CROSSING HALT
UPHOLLAND
FARNWORTH
WHITEFIELD
ALTCAR RIFLE RANGE
ORRELL
RINGLEY ROAD
PRESTWICH
MIDDLETON JC.
LYDIATE
HEY'S CROSSING HALT
HINDLEY
DAISY HILL
KEARSLEY
HEATON PK
HIGHTOWN
Bushey Lane Jc.
RAINFORD JUNC.
PEMBERTON
ATHERTON
HOWE BRI.
WALKDEN
CLIFTON JC.
CRUMPSALL
MOSTON
SEFTON
Randle Jc.
MILES PLATTING
NEWTON HEATH
HALL ROAD
MAGHULL
L.&Y.
TYLDESLEY
SWINTON
DEAN LA.
OLD ROAN HALT
RAINFORD VILLAGE
ROOKERY
BRYN
BAM FURLONG
VICTORIA
EXCHANGE
LONDON RD
BLUNDELL SANDS & CROSBY
KIRKBY
Kirkby W'troughs
GARSWOOD
CARR HILL
LEIGH
SALFORD
AINTREE
FAZACKERLEY
CRANK
G.C.
PATRICROFT
ARDWICK
WATERLOO
FORD
MOSS BANK
HAYDOCK
BARTON MOSS
ASHBURY
SEAFORTH
LIVERPOOL ST. G.C.
GOLBORNE
Golborne Jc.
GLAZEBURY
MANCHESTER
CENT.
NEWTON-LE-WILLOWS
ASTLEY
TRAFFORD PK
PRESTON RD.
HELENS
KENYON JUNC.
NEW BRIGHTON
WALTON-ON-THE-HILL
THATTO HEATH
LOWTON
CULCHETH
FLIXTON
URMSTON
CHORLTON
BELLEVUE
WALLASEY
L.N.W.
LEVENSHULME
WALLASEY VILLAGE
BRECK RD.
ECCLESTON PK.
EARLESTOWN JUNC.
East Jc.
IRLAM
SALE
FALLOWFIELD
COLLINS GREEN
Glazebrook Moss Jc.
CADISHEAD
MORETON
BIDSTON
TUE BROOK
PRESCOT
LEA GRN.
Winwick Jc.
GLAZEBROOK
BROOKLANDS
WITHINGTON
HEATON-MERSEY
EXCHANGE
LIME ST.
ROBY
HUYTON
RAINHILL
ST. HELEN'S JC.
C.L.C.
PADGATE
Dam Lane Jc.
DIDSBURY
MEOLS
LEASOWE
CEN
SEFTON PARK
HUYTON QUARRY
CLOCK FACE
PARTINGTON
TIMPERLEY
BAGULEY
STOCKPORT
UPTON
WOODSIDE
TOWN
CHILDWALL
FARNWORTH & BOLD
SANKEY
H.L.
WARRINGTON
BROADHEATH
HOYLAKE
BIRKENHEAD
BRUNSWICK
GATEACRE
Widnes Jc.
ARPLEY
ALTRINCHAM
NORTHENDEN
WEST KIRBY
ROCK FERRY
ST. MICHAELS
HALEWOOD
HOUGH GREEN
FIDLERS FERRY
L.L.
LATCHFORD
HEATLEY
DUNHAM MASSEY
HALE
HEALD GREEN
CHEADLE HULME
KIRBY PARK
BEBINGTON
MOSSLEY HILL
WIDNES
Old Main Line Jc.
THELWALL
LYMM
CALDY
STORETON
DITTON
ASHLEY

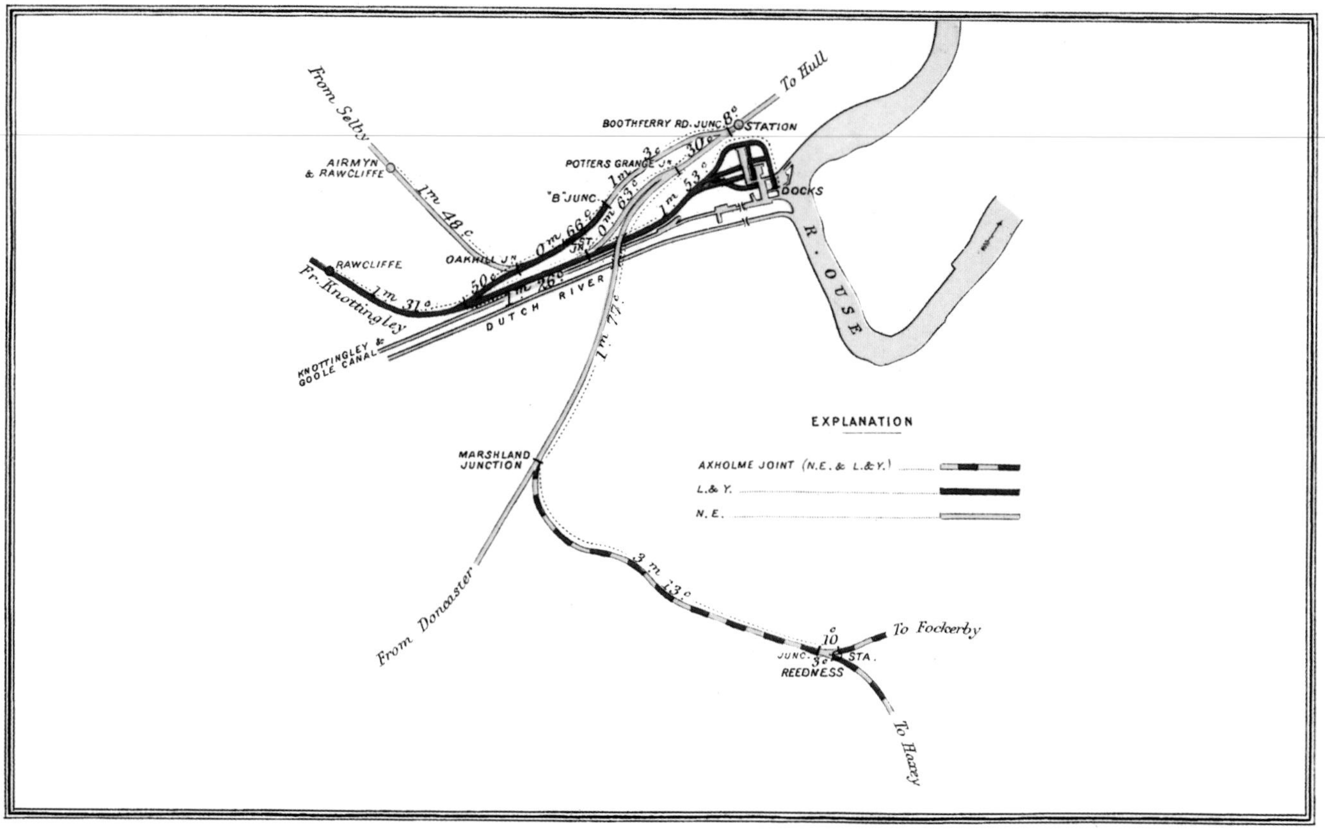

Goole

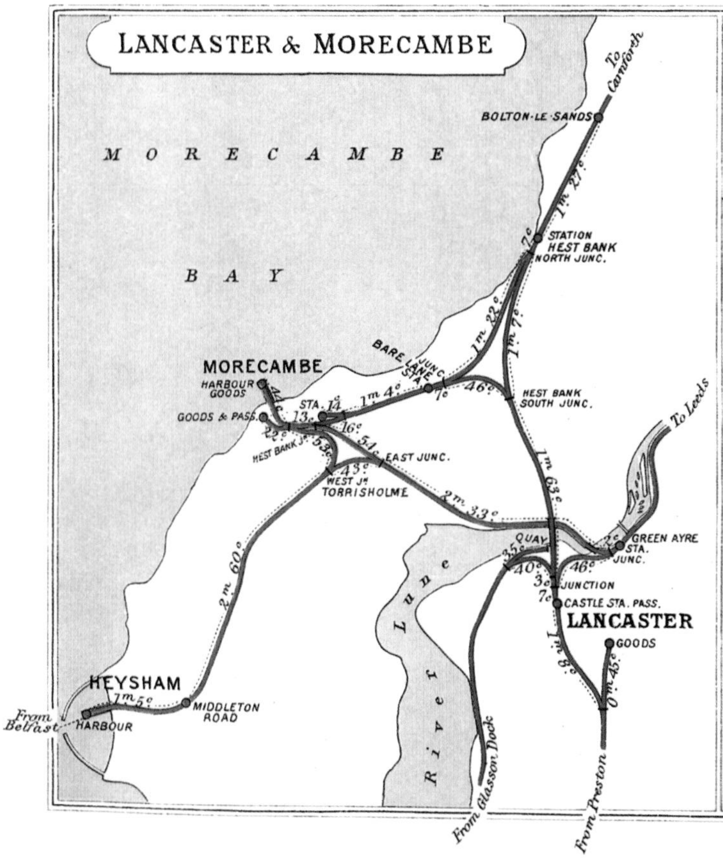

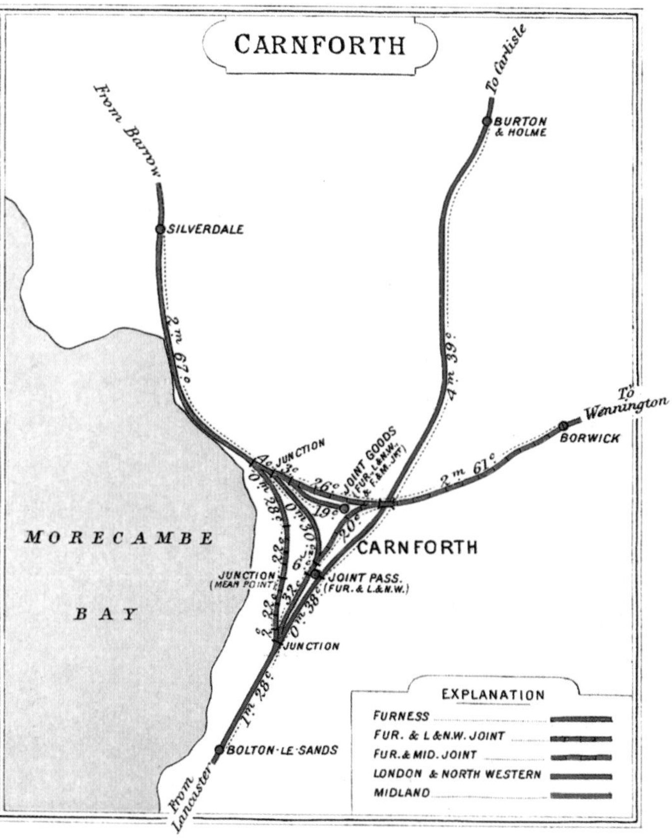

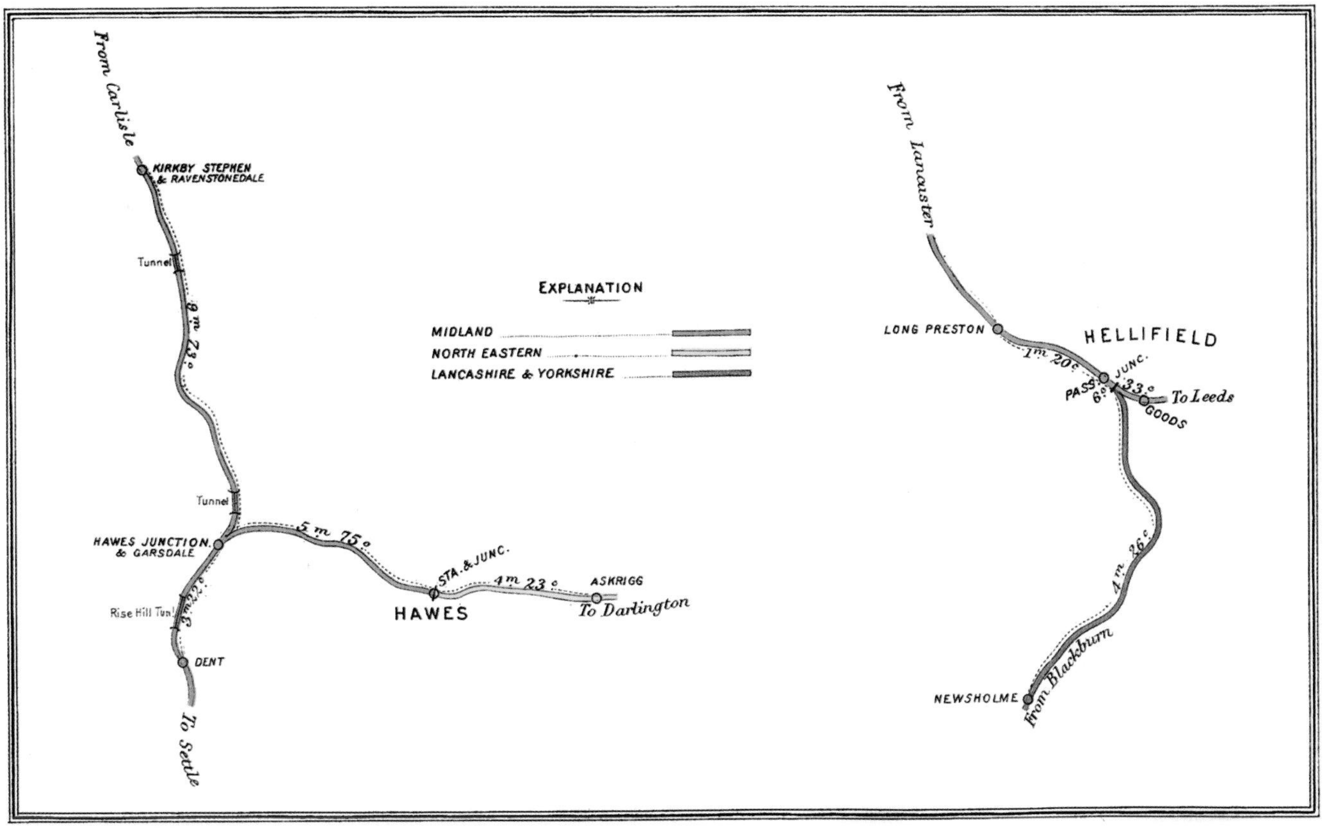

Hawes–Hellifield

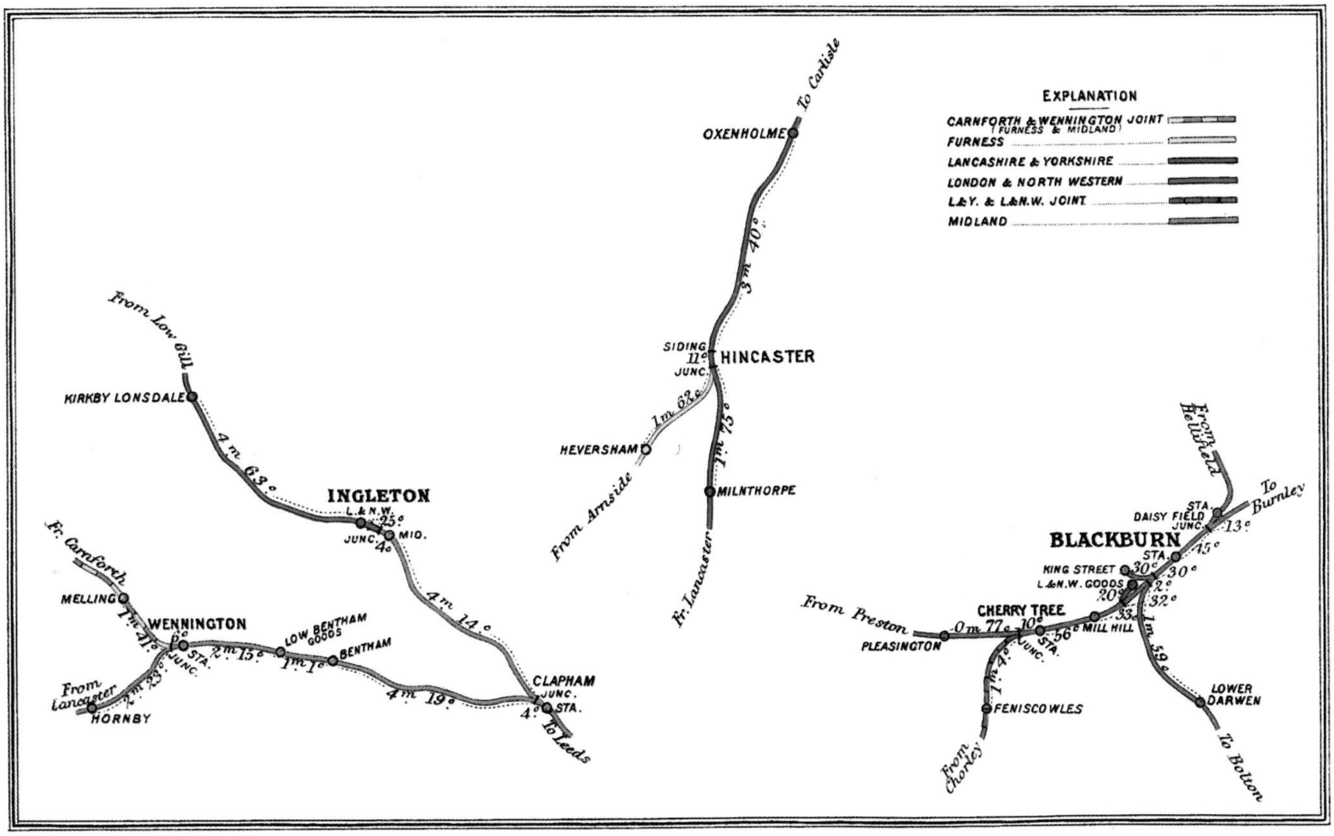

Ingleton–Hincaster–Blackburn

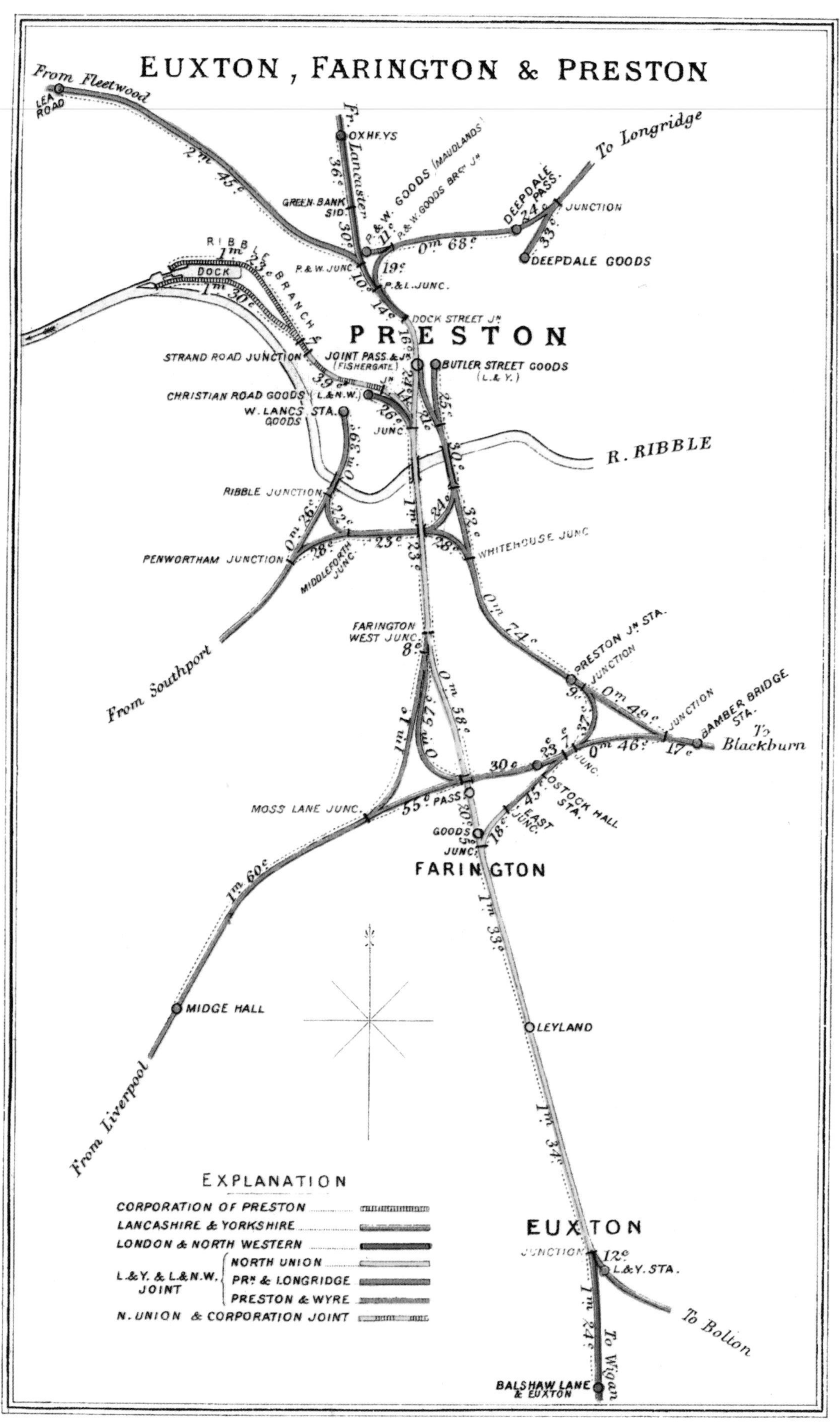

EUXTON, FARINGTON & PRESTON
From Fleetwood
LEA ROAD
Fr. Lancaster
OXHEYS
To Longridge
GREEN BANK SID.
P.&W. GOODS (MAUDLANDS)
P.&W. GOODS BRC^H J^N
DEEPDALE PASS.
JUNCTION
DEEPDALE GOODS
RIBBLE BRANCH
DOCK
P.&W. JUNC.
P.&L. JUNC.
DOCK STREET J^N
PRESTON
STRAND ROAD JUNCTION
JOINT PASS.& J^N (FISHERGATE)
BUTLER STREET GOODS (L.& Y.)
CHRISTIAN ROAD GOODS (L.&N.W.)
W. LANCS. STA. GOODS
JUNC.
R. RIBBLE
RIBBLE JUNCTION
PENWORTHAM JUNCTION
MIDDLEFORTH JUNC.
WHITEHOUSE JUNC.
From Southport
FARINGTON WEST JUNC.
PRESTON J^N STA.
JUNCTION
BAMBER BRIDGE STA.
To Blackburn
LOSTOCK HALL STA.
EAST JUNC.
MOSS LANE JUNC.
PASS.
GOODS
JUNC.
FARINGTON
MIDGE HALL
LEYLAND
From Liverpool
EXPLANATION
CORPORATION OF PRESTON
LANCASHIRE & YORKSHIRE
LONDON & NORTH WESTERN
L.&Y. & L.&N.W. JOINT
NORTH UNION
PR^N & LONGRIDGE
PRESTON & WYRE
N. UNION & CORPORATION JOINT
EUXTON
JUNCTION
L.&Y. STA.
To Bolton
To Wigan
BALSHAW LANE & EUXTON

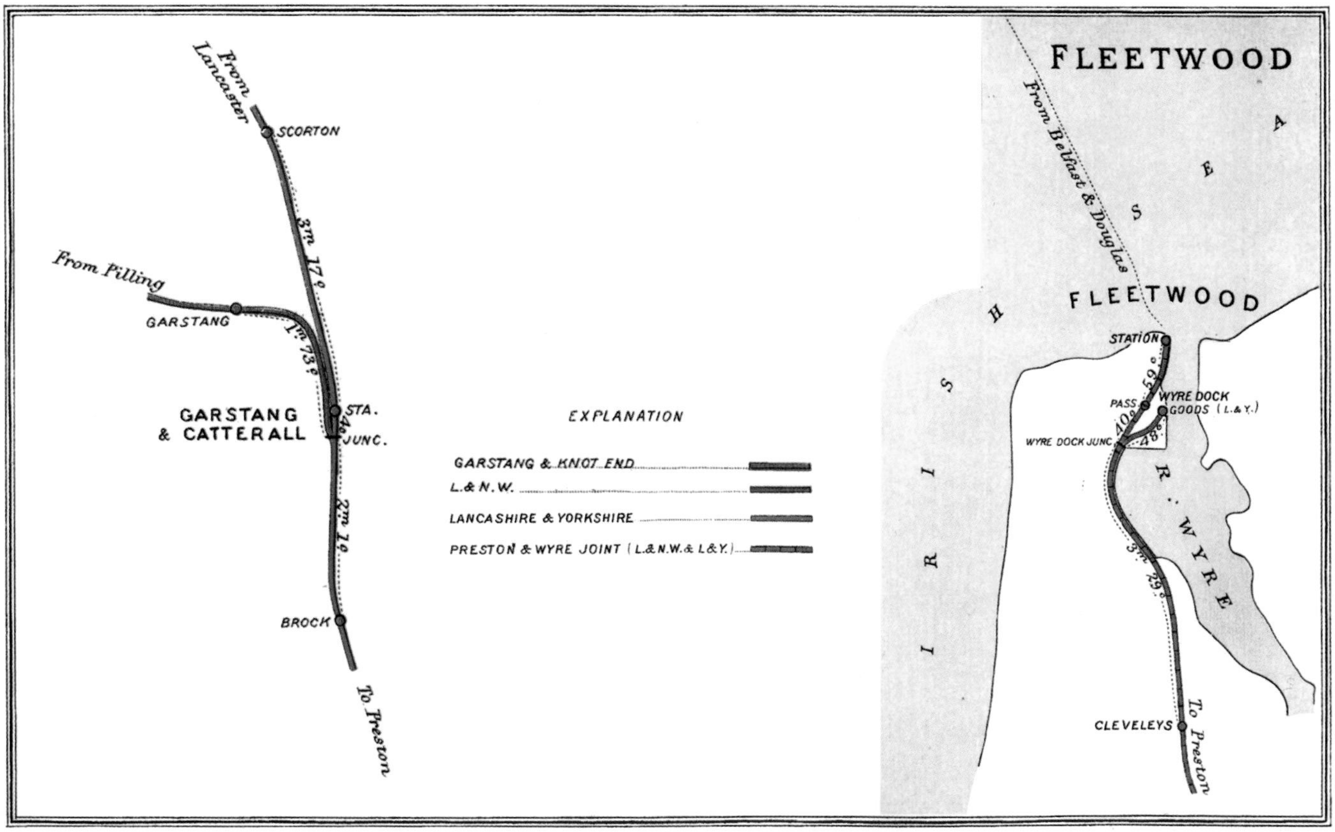

**Garstang & Catterall–Fleetwood**

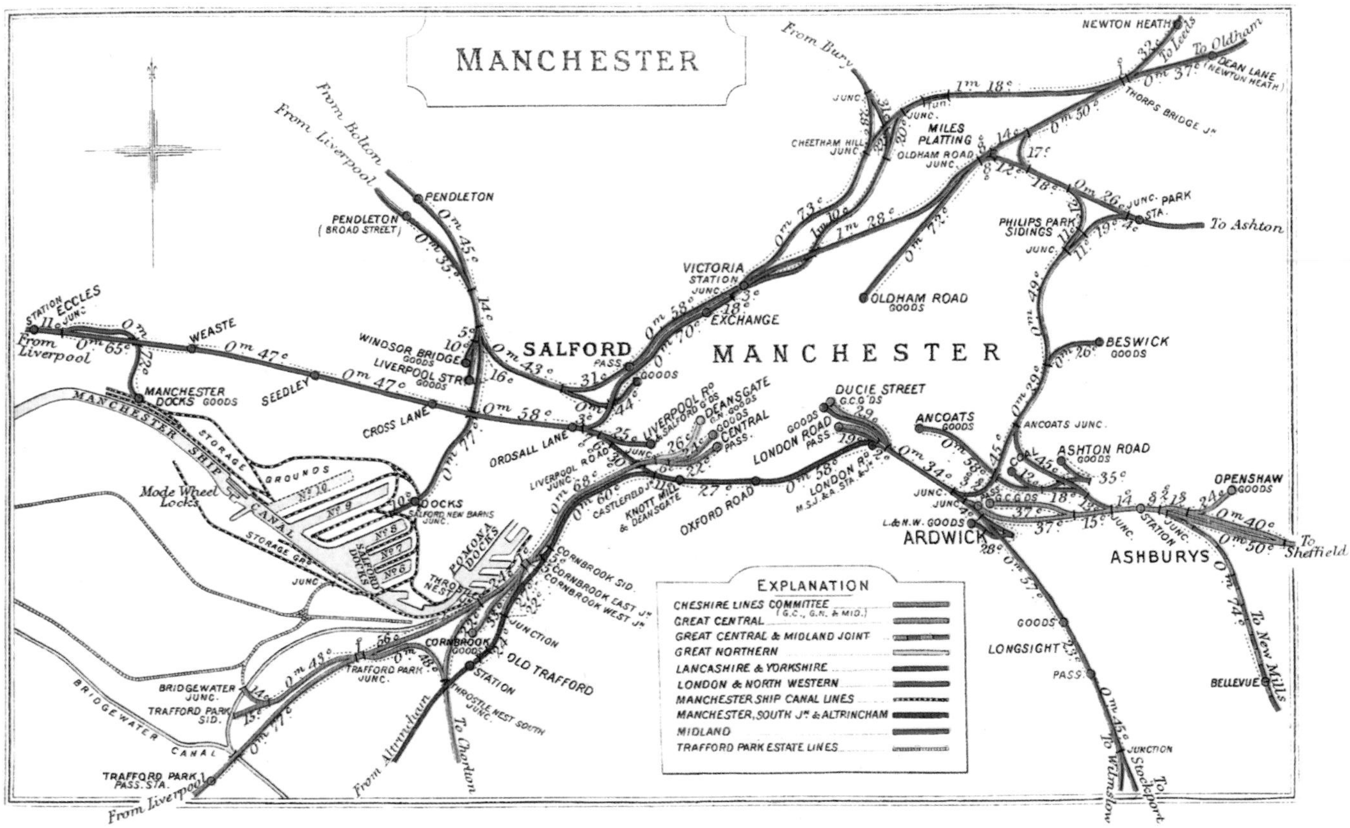

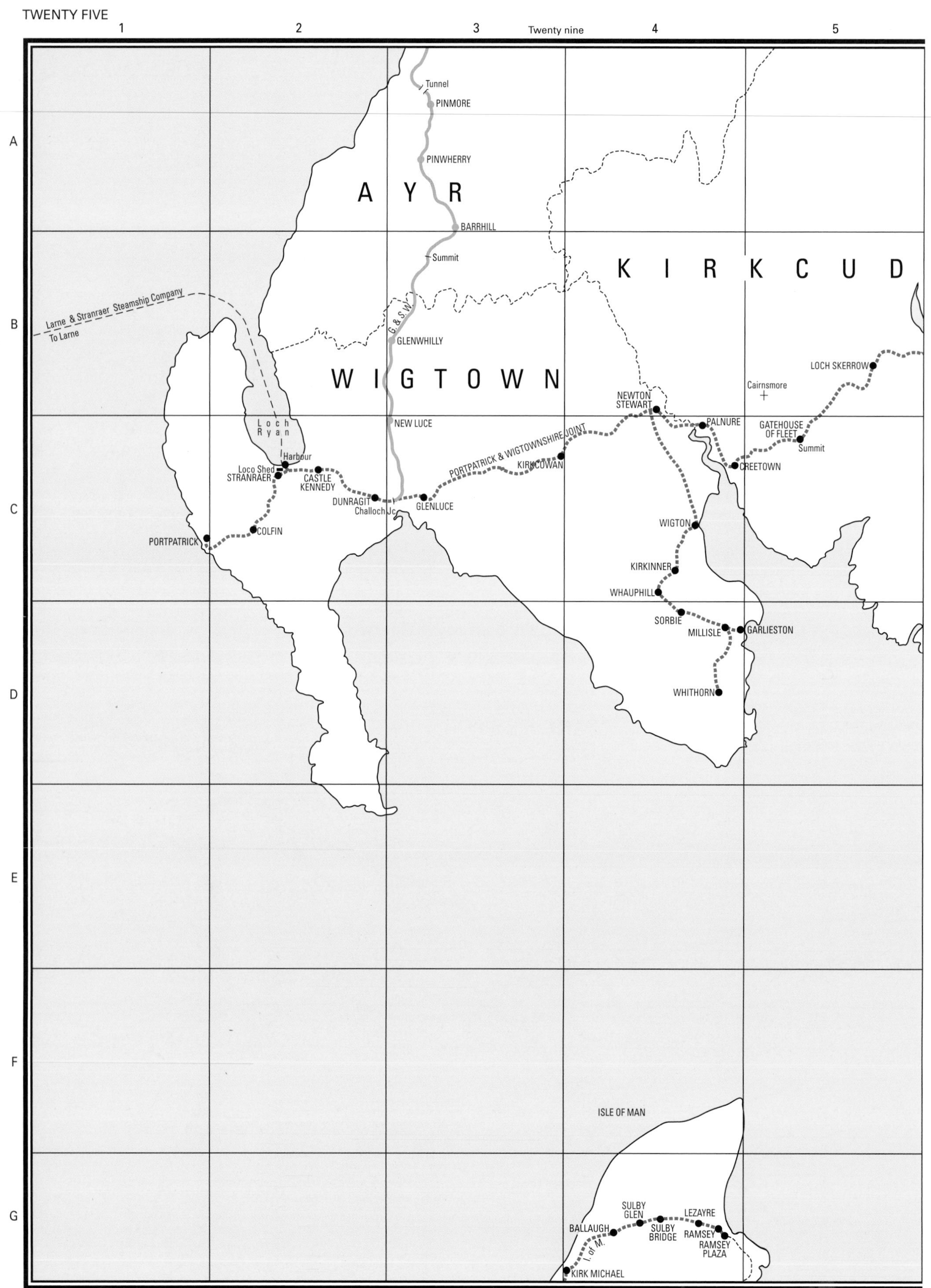
1
2
3
Twenty nine
4
5
A
B
C
D
E
F
G
Tunnel
PINMORE
PINWHERRY
A Y R
BARRHILL
Summit
K I R K C U D
Larne & Stranraer Steamship Company
To Larne
G. & S. W.
GLENWHILLY
W I G T O W N
LOCH SKERROW
Cairnsmore
NEWTON STEWART
Loch Ryan
NEW LUCE
PALNURE
GATEHOUSE OF FLEET
Summit
Harbour
PORTPATRICK & WIGTOWNSHIRE JOINT
KIRKCOWAN
CREETOWN
Loco Shed
STRANRAER
CASTLE KENNEDY
DUNRAGIT
Challoch Jc
GLENLUCE
WIGTON
PORTPATRICK
COLFIN
KIRKINNER
WHAUPHILL
SORBIE
MILLISLE
GARLIESTON
WHITHORN
ISLE OF MAN
SULBY GLEN
LEZAYRE
BALLAUGH
SULBY BRIDGE
RAMSEY
RAMSEY PLAZA
I. of M.
KIRK MICHAEL

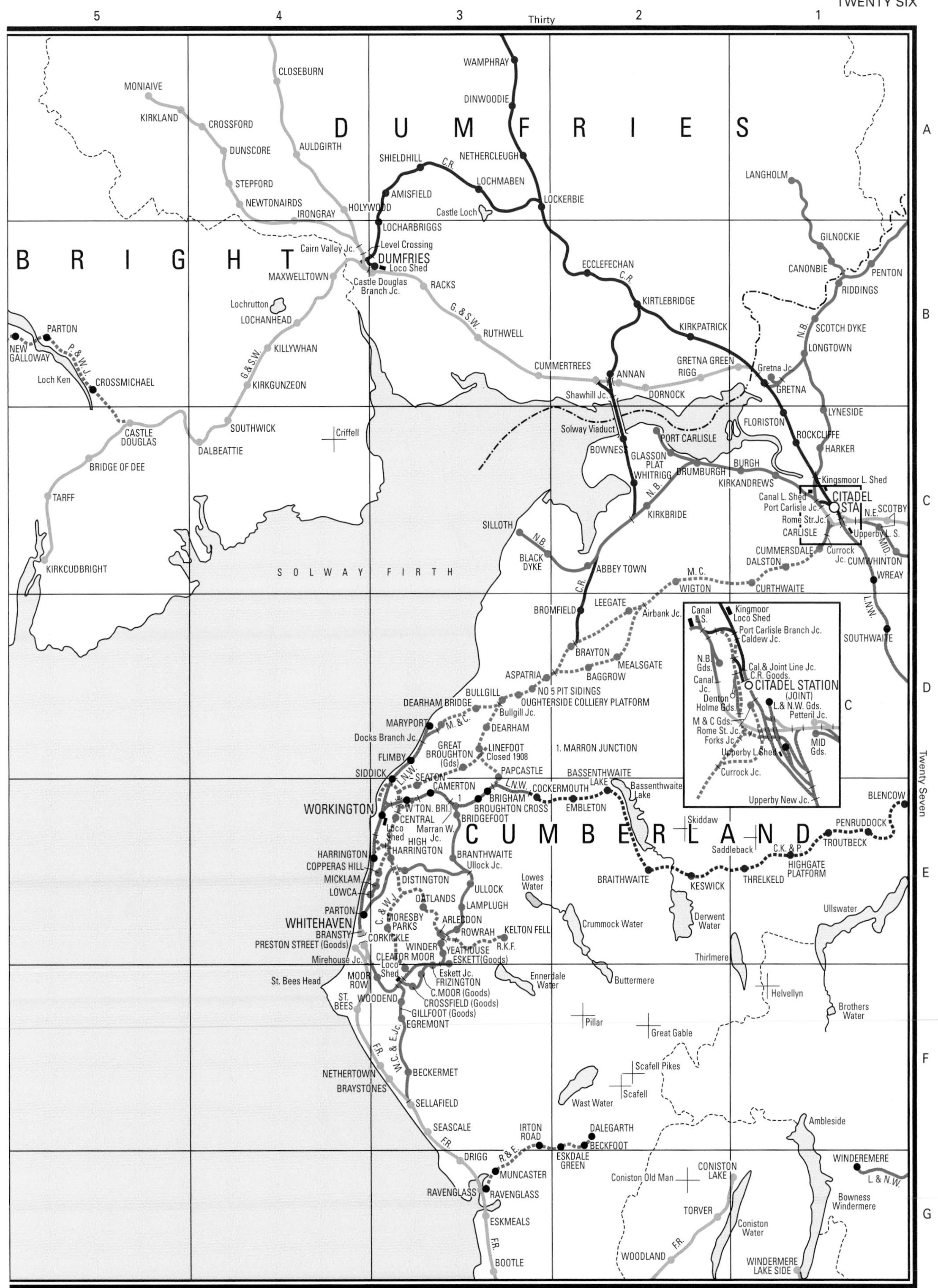
5
4
3
Thirty
2
1
A
B
C
D
E
F
G
DUMFRIES
BRIGHT
CUMBERLAND
SOLWAY FIRTH
Twenty Seven
Twenty four
MONIAIVE
KIRKLAND
CROSSFORD
DUNSCORE
STEPFORD
NEWTONAIRDS
IRONGRAY
CLOSEBURN
AULDGIRTH
HOLYWOOD
WAMPHRAY
DINWOODIE
NETHERCLEUGH
SHIELDHILL
C.R.
LOCHMABEN
AMISFIELD
Castle Loch
LOCKERBIE
LOCHARBRIGGS
Level Crossing
Cairn Valley Jc.
DUMFRIES
Loco Shed
MAXWELLTOWN
Castle Douglas Branch Jc.
RACKS
G. & S.W.
RUTHWELL
Lochrutton
LOCHANHEAD
KILLYWHAN
KIRKGUNZEON
SOUTHWICK
DALBEATTIE
Criffell
PARTON
NEW GALLOWAY
P. & W. J.
Loch Ken
CROSSMICHAEL
CASTLE DOUGLAS
BRIDGE OF DEE
TARFF
KIRKCUDBRIGHT
ECCLEFECHAN
KIRTLEBRIDGE
KIRKPATRICK
CUMMERTREES
ANNAN
Shawhill Jc.
DORNOCK
GRETNA GREEN
RIGG
Gretna Jc.
GRETNA
Solway Viaduct
BOWNESS
GLASSON
PORT CARLISLE
PLAT
WHITRIGG
DRUMBURGH
BURGH
KIRKANDREWS
FLORISTON
ROCKCLIFFE
HARKER
LYNESIDE
LANGHOLM
GILNOCKIE
CANONBIE
PENTON
RIDDINGS
N.B.
SCOTCH DYKE
LONGTOWN
Kingsmoor L. Shed
Canal L. Shed
Port Carlisle Jc.
Rome Str.Jc.
CARLISLE
CITADEL STA
N.E.
SCOTBY
Upperby L. S.
MID
CUMMERSDALE
Currock Jc.
DALSTON
CUMWHINTON
WREAY
KIRKBRIDE
SILLOTH
BLACK DYKE
ABBEY TOWN
M. C.
WIGTON
CURTHWAITE
L.N.W.
SOUTHWAITE
BROMFIELD
LEEGATE
Airbank Jc.
BRAYTON
MEALSGATE
BAGGROW
ASPATRIA
NO 5 PIT SIDINGS
OUGHTERSIDE COLLIERY PLATFORM
BULLGILL
Bullgill Jc.
DEARHAM BRIDGE
DEARHAM
MARYPORT
M. & C.
Docks Branch Jc.
GREAT BROUGHTON (Gds)
LINEFOOT Closed 1908
1. MARRON JUNCTION
FLIMBY
SIDDICK
SEATON
PAPCASTLE
BASSENTHWAITE LAKE
Bassenthwaite Lake
CAMERTON
BRIGHAM
COCKERMOUTH
W'TON. BRI
BROUGHTON CROSS
EMBLETON
WORKINGTON
CENTRAL
Loco Shed
Marron W. Jc.
BRIDGEFOOT
HIGH HARRINGTON
HARRINGTON
COPPERAS HILL
MICKLAM
LOWCA
PARTON
WHITEHAVEN
BRANSTY
PRESTON STREET (Goods)
Mirehouse Jc.
BRANTHWAITE
Ullock Jc.
DISTINGTON
ULLOCK
OATLANDS
C. & W. J.
LAMPLUGH
MORESBY PARKS
ARLECDON
CORKICKLE
ROWRAH
KELTON FELL
WINDER
YEATHOUSE
R.K.F.
CLEATOR MOOR
ESKETT (Goods)
Loco Shed
Eskett Jc.
FRIZINGTON
C.MOOR (Goods)
CROSSFIELD (Goods)
GILLFOOT (Goods)
EGREMONT
St. Bees Head
MOOR ROW
ST. BEES
WOODEND
W.C. & E.Jc.
F.R.
NETHERTOWN
BRAYSTONES
BECKERMET
SELLAFIELD
SEASCALE
DRIGG
R. & E.
IRTON ROAD
ESKDALE GREEN
DALEGARTH
BECKFOOT
MUNCASTER
RAVENGLASS
ESKMEALS
BOOTLE
Skiddaw
Saddleback
C.K. & P.
PENRUDDOCK
TROUTBECK
BLENCOW
BRAITHWAITE
KESWICK
THRELKELD
HIGHGATE PLATFORM
Lowes Water
Crummock Water
Derwent Water
Ullswater
Thirlmere
Buttermere
Ennerdale Water
Helvellyn
Brothers Water
Pillar
Great Gable
Scafell Pikes
Scafell
Wast Water
Ambleside
WINDEREMERE
L. & N.W.
Bowness Windermere
CONISTON LAKE
Coniston Old Man
TORVER
Coniston Water
WOODLAND
WINDERMERE LAKE SIDE
Canal L.S.
Kingmoor Loco Shed
Port Carlisle Branch Jc.
Caldew Jc.
N.B. Gds.
Canal Jc.
Cal.& Joint Line Jc.
C.R. Goods.
CITADEL STATION (JOINT)
Denton Holme Gds.
L.& N.W. Gds.
Petteril Jc.
M & C Gds.
Rome St. Jc.
Forks Jc.
Upperby L.Shed
Currock Jc.
MID Gds.
Upperby New Jc.

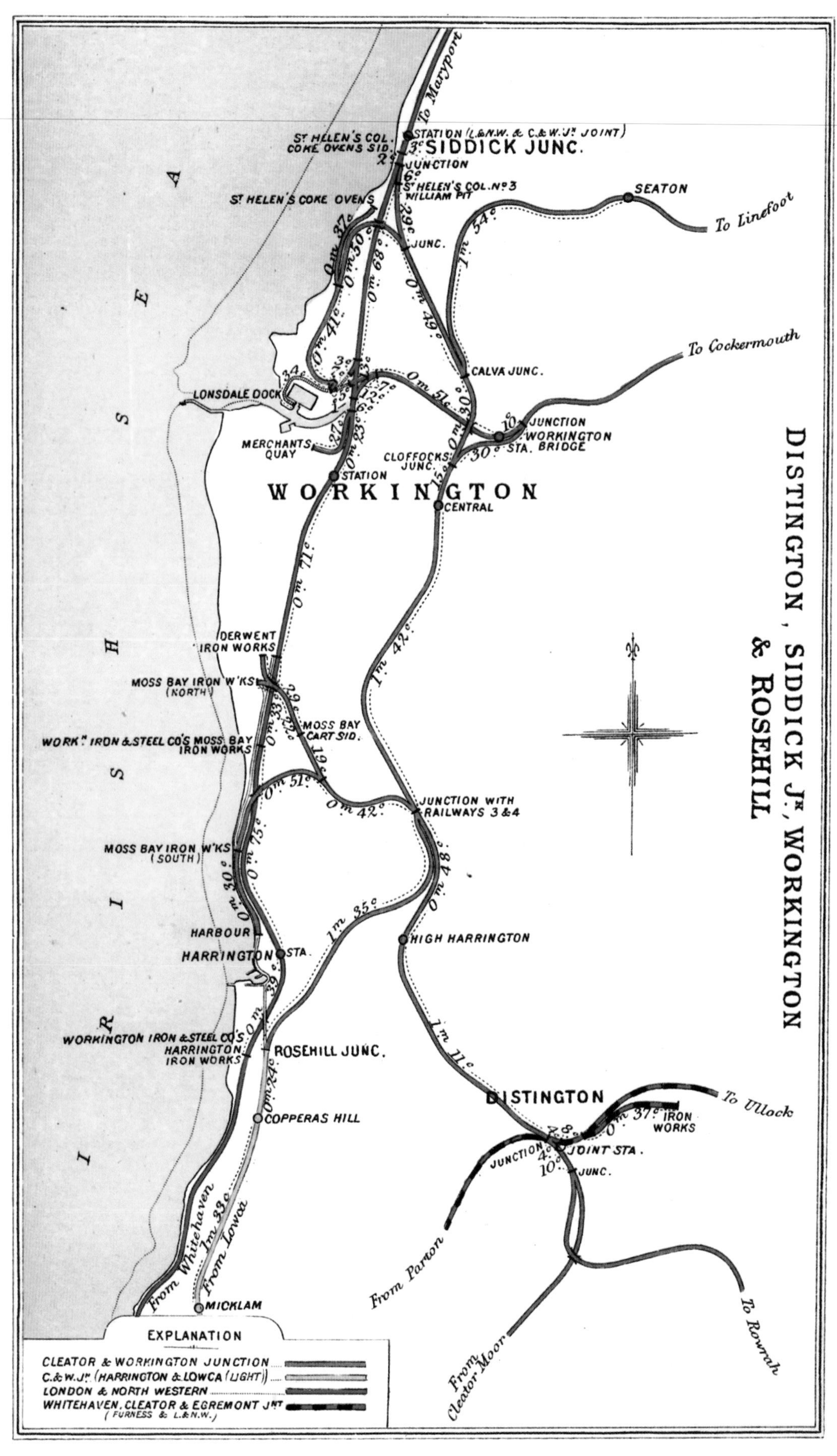

DISTINGTON, SIDDICK Jn., WORKINGTON & ROSEHILL
IRISH SEA
To Maryport
STATION (L.&N.W. & C.&W.Jn. JOINT)
SIDDICK JUNC.
JUNCTION
St. HELEN'S COL. COKE OVENS SID.
St. HELEN'S COL. No 3 WILLIAM PIT
St. HELEN'S COKE OVENS
SEATON
To Linefoot
JUNC.
CALVA JUNC.
To Cockermouth
JUNCTION WORKINGTON STA. BRIDGE
LONSDALE DOCK
MERCHANTS QUAY
CLOFFOCKS JUNC.
STATION
WORKINGTON
CENTRAL
DERWENT IRON WORKS
MOSS BAY IRON W'KS (NORTH)
MOSS BAY CART SID.
WORKn. IRON & STEEL CO'S MOSS BAY IRON WORKS
JUNCTION WITH RAILWAYS 3 & 4
MOSS BAY IRON W'KS (SOUTH)
HARBOUR
HARRINGTON
STA.
HIGH HARRINGTON
WORKINGTON IRON & STEEL CO'S HARRINGTON IRON WORKS
ROSEHILL JUNC.
COPPERAS HILL
DISTINGTON
To Ullock
IRON WORKS
JUNCTION
JOINT STA.
JUNC.
From Parton
From Whitehaven
From Lowca
MICKLAM
From Cleator Moor
To Rowrah
EXPLANATION
CLEATOR & WORKINGTON JUNCTION
C.&W.Jn. (HARRINGTON & LOWCA (LIGHT))
LONDON & NORTH WESTERN
WHITEHAVEN, CLEATOR & EGREMONT Jnt (FURNESS & L.&N.W.)

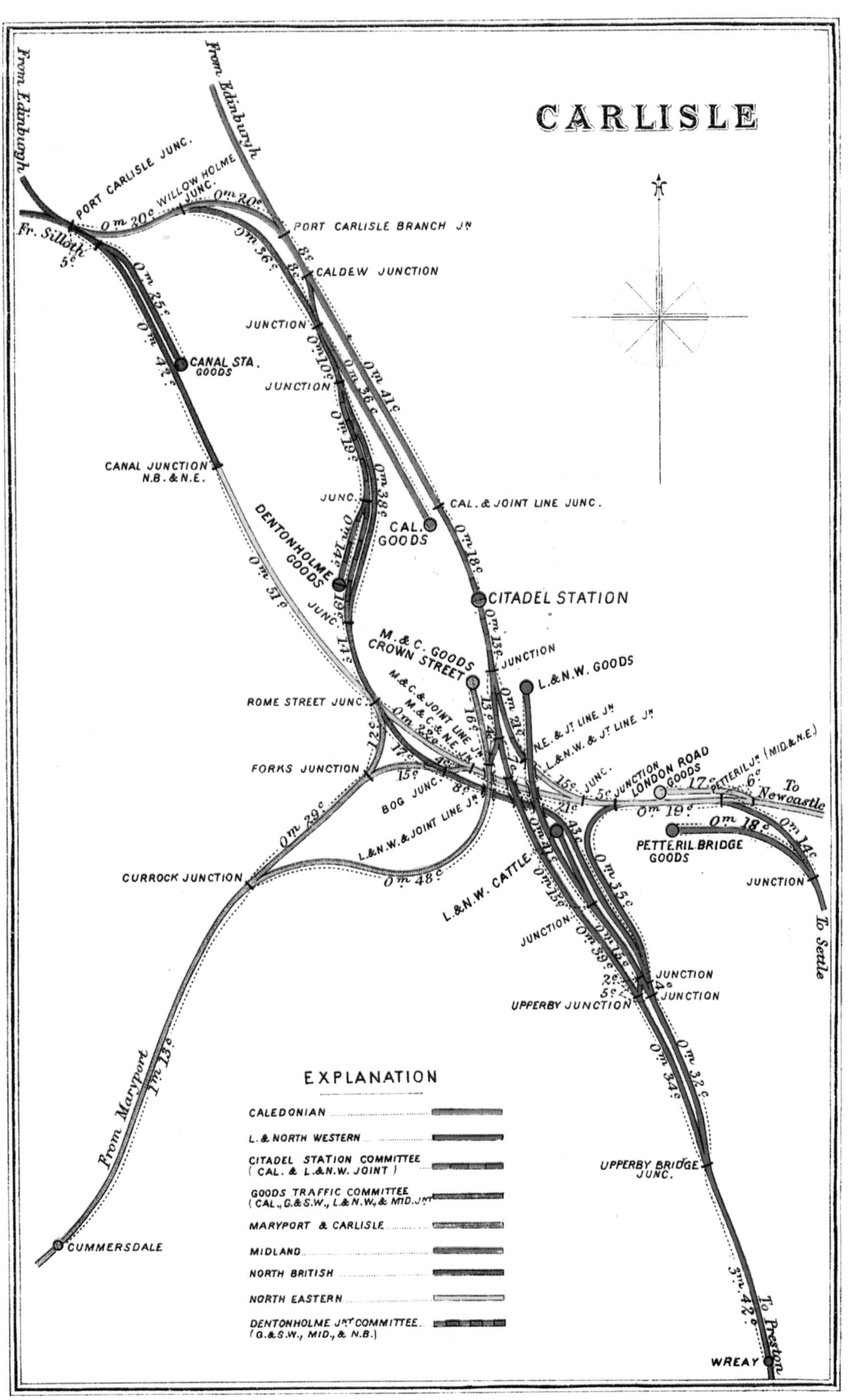
CARLISLE
From Edinburgh
From Edinburgh
PORT CARLISLE JUNC.
WILLOW HOLME JUNC.
Fr. Silloth
PORT CARLISLE BRANCH JN
CALDEW JUNCTION
JUNCTION
CANAL STA. GOODS
JUNCTION
CANAL JUNCTION N.B. & N.E.
JUNC.
CAL. & JOINT LINE JUNC.
CAL. GOODS
DENTONHOLME GOODS
CITADEL STATION
JUNC.
M. & C. GOODS CROWN STREET
JUNCTION
L.&N.W. GOODS
ROME STREET JUNC.
M.&C. & JOINT LINE JN
M.&C. & N.E. JN
N.E. & JT. LINE JN
L.&N.W. & JT. LINE JN
FORKS JUNCTION
BOG JUNC.
JUNC.
JUNCTION
LONDON ROAD GOODS
PETTERIL JN (MID.& N.E.)
To Newcastle
L.&N.W. & JOINT LINE JN
PETTERIL BRIDGE GOODS
CURROCK JUNCTION
L.&N.W. CATTLE
JUNCTION
To Settle
JUNCTION
JUNCTION
JUNCTION
UPPERBY JUNCTION
From Maryport
EXPLANATION
CALEDONIAN
L. & NORTH WESTERN
CITADEL STATION COMMITTEE (CAL. & L.&N.W. JOINT)
GOODS TRAFFIC COMMITTEE (CAL., G.&S.W., L.&N.W., & MID.JNT)
MARYPORT & CARLISLE
MIDLAND
NORTH BRITISH
NORTH EASTERN
DENTONHOLME JNT COMMITTEE (G.&S.W., MID., & N.B.)
UPPERBY BRIDGE JUNC.
CUMMERSDALE
To Preston
WREAY

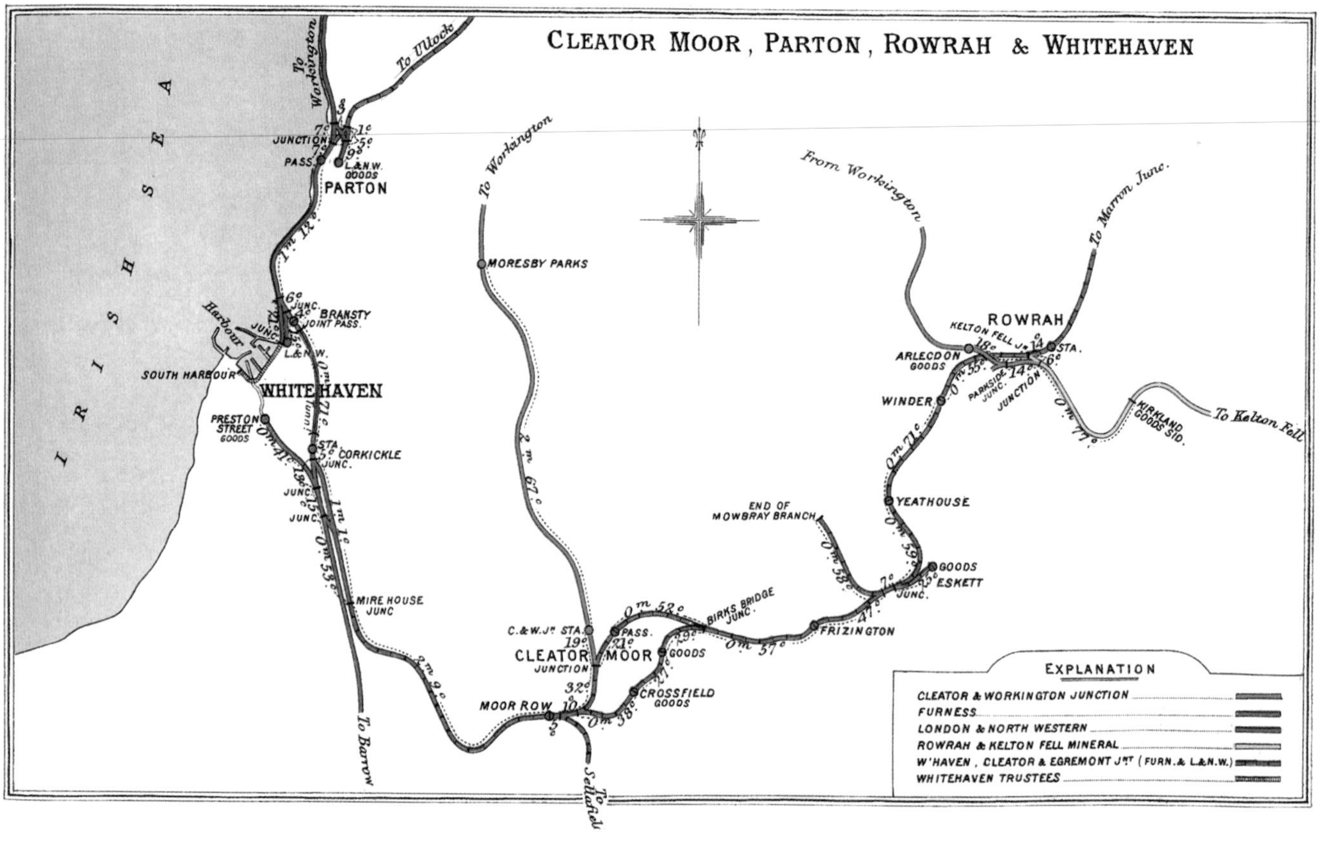
CLEATOR MOOR, PARTON, ROWRAH & WHITEHAVEN
IRISH SEA
To Workington
To Ulock
JUNCTION
PASS.
L.&N.W. GOODS
PARTON
To Workington
From Workington
To Marron Junc.
MORESBY PARKS
ROWRAH
KELTON FELL JN.
STA.
ARLECDON GOODS
PARKSIDE JUNC.
JUNCTION
WINDER
KIRKLAND GOODS SID.
To Kelton Fell
Harbour
BRANSTY JOINT PASS.
L.&N.W.
SOUTH HARBOUR
WHITEHAVEN
PRESTON STREET GOODS
STA.
CORKICKLE JUNC.
YEATHOUSE
END OF MOWBRAY BRANCH
GOODS
ESKETT
JUNC.
MIRE HOUSE JUNC.
BIRKS BRIDGE JUNC.
FRIZINGTON
C.&W.JN. STA.
PASS.
CLEATOR MOOR
JUNCTION
GOODS
CROSSFIELD GOODS
MOOR ROW
To Barrow
To Sellafield
EXPLANATION
CLEATOR & WORKINGTON JUNCTION
FURNESS
LONDON & NORTH WESTERN
ROWRAH & KELTON FELL MINERAL
W'HAVEN, CLEATOR & EGREMONT JNT (FURN. & L.&N.W.)
WHITEHAVEN TRUSTEES

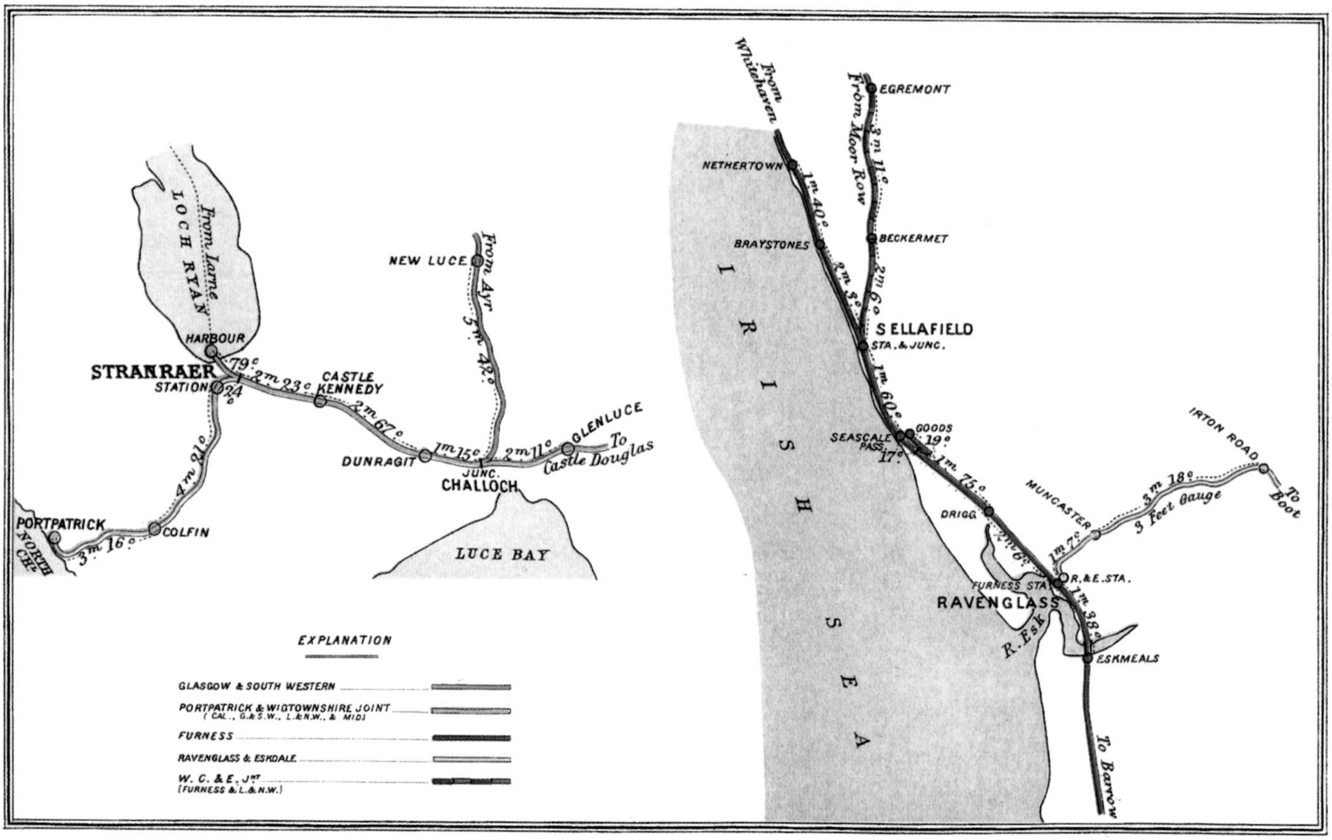
LOCH RYAN
From Larne
HARBOUR
STRANRAER
STATION
CASTLE KENNEDY
NEW LUCE
From Ayr
GLENLUCE
To Castle Douglas
DUNRAGIT
JUNC.
CHALLOCH
LUCE BAY
PORTPATRICK
NORTH CH.
COLFIN
EXPLANATION
GLASGOW & SOUTH WESTERN
PORTPATRICK & WIGTOWNSHIRE JOINT (CAL., G.&S.W., L.&N.W., & MID)
FURNESS
RAVENGLASS & ESKDALE
W. C. & E. JNT (FURNESS & L.&N.W.)
From Whitehaven
EGREMONT
From Moor Row
NETHERTOWN
BECKERMET
BRAYSTONES
IRISH SEA
SELLAFIELD
STA. & JUNC.
SEASCALE PASS.
GOODS
IRTON ROAD
To Boot
MUNCASTER
3 Feet Gauge
DRIGG
R.&E. STA.
FURNESS STA.
RAVENGLASS
R. Esk
ESKMEALS
To Barrow

Stranraer–Ravenglass–Sellafield

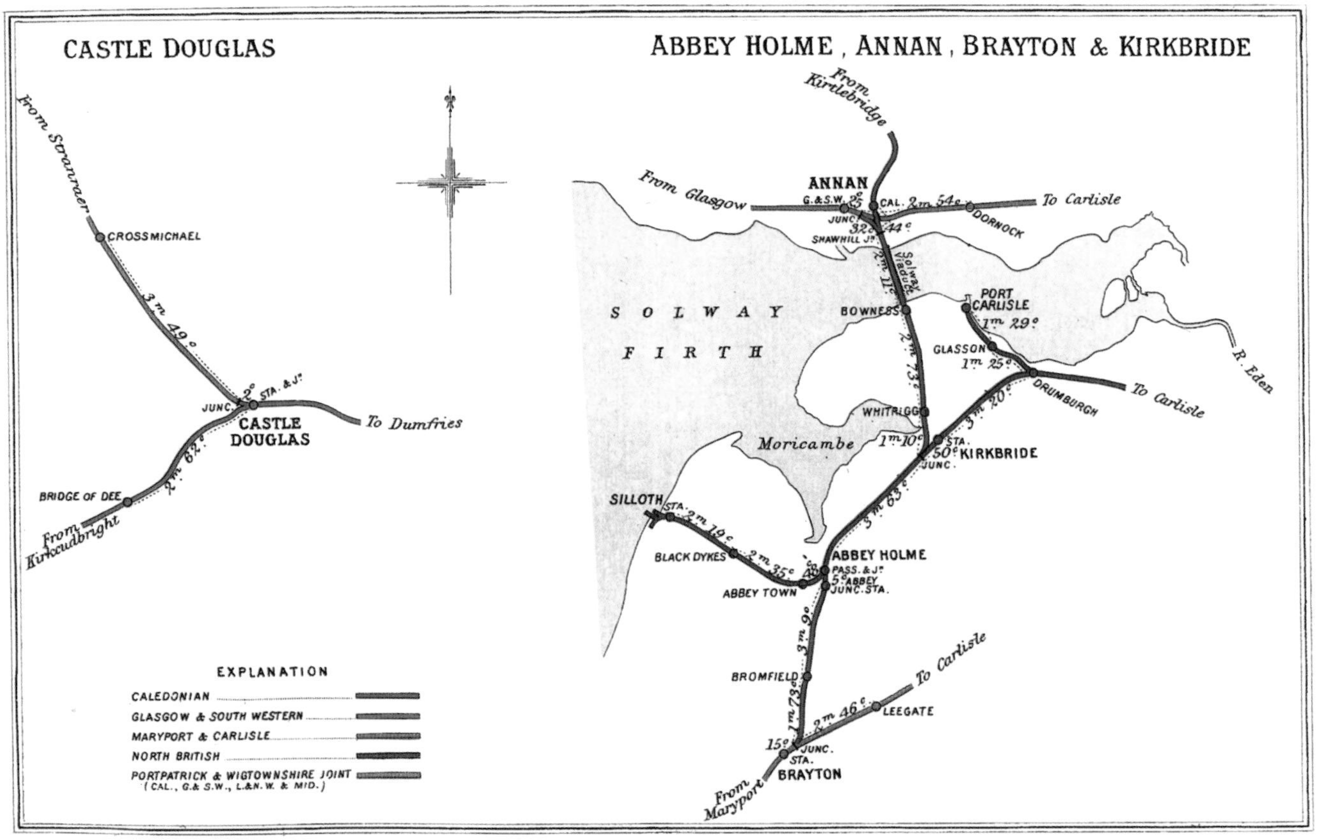

CASTLE DOUGLAS

ABBEY HOLME, ANNAN, BRAYTON & KIRKBRIDE

EXPLANATION

CALEDONIAN

GLASGOW & SOUTH WESTERN

MARYPORT & CARLISLE

NORTH BRITISH

PORTPATRICK & WIGTOWNSHIRE JOINT (CAL., G.& S.W., L.&N.W. & MID.)

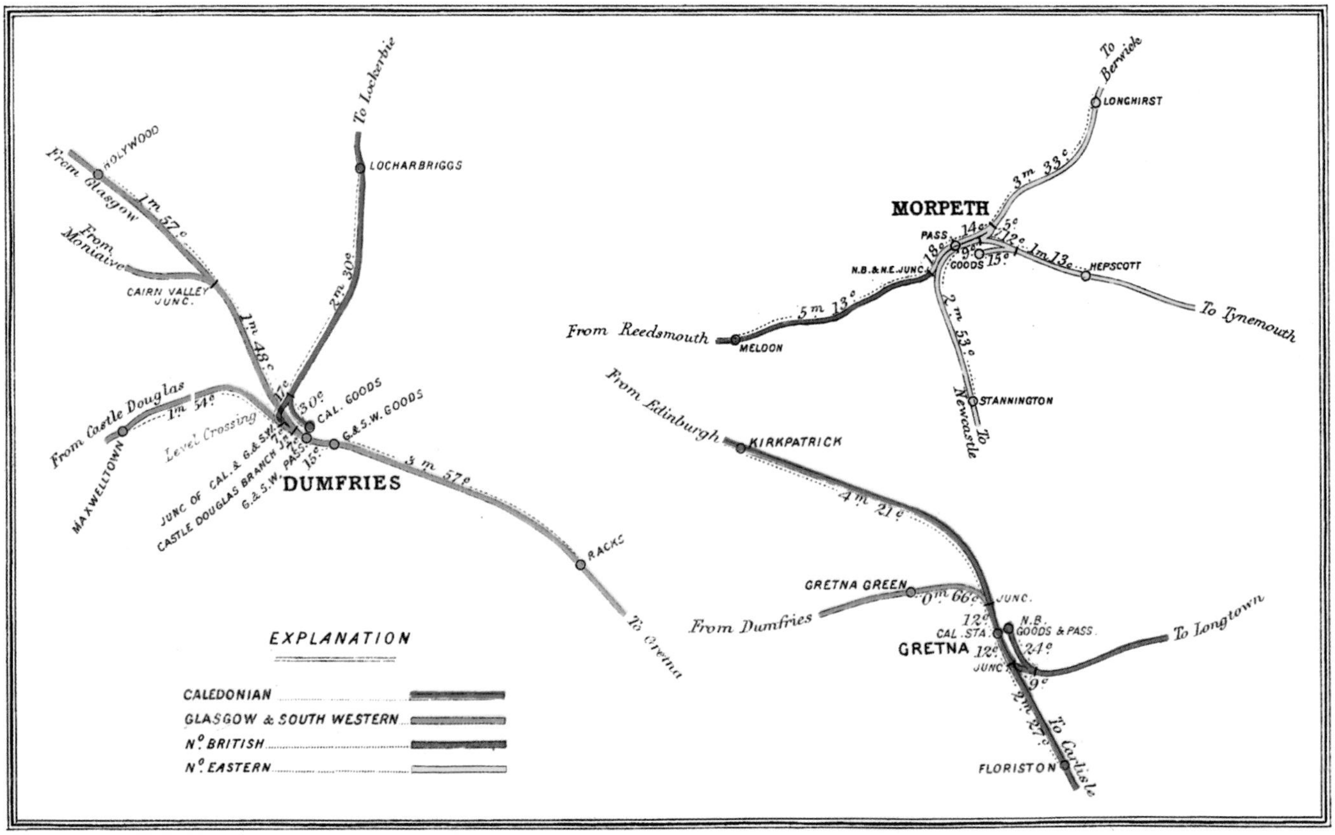

DUMFRIES

MORPETH

GRETNA

EXPLANATION

CALEDONIAN

GLASGOW & SOUTH WESTERN

N° BRITISH

N° EASTERN

**Dumfries–Morpeth–Gretna**

## TWENTY SEVEN

1 2 3 4 5

Thirty one

A B C D E F G

Twenty six

RICCARTON JUNCTION
SAUGHTREE
DEADWATER
N.B.
STEELE ROAD
KIELDER
PLASHETTS
NEWCASTLETON
N. B.
FALSTONE
THORNEYBURN
TARSET
WOODBURN
N.B.
BELLINGHAM
REEDSMOUTH
KERSHOPE FOOT
FONTBURN
EWESLEY
LONG WITTON
SCOTSGAP
KNOWESGATE
MIDDLETON
ANGERTON
MELDON
WIDDRINGTON
LONGHURST
PEGSWOOD
ASHINGTON
NORTH SEATON
MORPETH
HEPSCOTT
N.E.
CHOPPINGTON
BEDLINGTON
STANNINGTON
BEBSIDE

NORTHUMBERLAND

PLESSEY
CRAMLINGTON
PONTELAND
N.E.
ANNITSFORD
CALLERTON
DARRAS HALL
KILLINGWORTH
FOREST HALL
KENTON
COXLODGE
WEST GOSFORTH
SOUTH GOSFORTH
BENTON
LEMINGTON
NEWBURN
HEDDON-ON-THE-WALL
NORTH WYLAM
W. JESMOND
JESMOND
SCOTSWOOD
CENTRAL
WARK
N.B.
BARRASFORD
CHOLLERTON
HUMSHAUGH
FOURSTONES
WALL
HEXHAM
N.E.
GILSLAND
GREENHEAD
HALTWHISTLE
BARDON MILL
HAYDON BRIDGE
Haltwhistle Tunnel
PLENMELLER PARK
LOW ROW
NAWORTH
BRAMPTON TOWN
BRAMPTON JUNC.
FEATHERSTONE PARK
COANWOOD
LAMBLEY
ELRINGTON
LANGLEY
STAWARD
ALLENDALE
CORBRIDGE
Corbridge Tun.
RIDING MILL
STOCKSFIELD
PRUDHOE
WYLAM
RYTON
BLAYDON
SWALWELL
NEWCASTLE
BENSHAM
LOW FELL
ROWLANDS GILL
LAMESLEY
HOW MILL
HEADS NOOK
WETHERAL
BURNSTONES
SLAGGYFORD
HIGH WESTWOOD
LINTZ GREEN
BIRTLEY
EBCHESTER
SHIELD ROW
BEAMISH
PELTON
SHOTLEY BRIDGE
LEADGATE
W. STANLEY (Gds.)
BLACKHILL
CHESTER LE STREET
CONSETT
ANNFIELD PLAIN
KNITSLEY
ROWLEY
PLAWSWORTH
COTEHILL
ARMATHWAITE
Armathwaite Tun.
Baron Wood Tuns.
ALSTON
WASKERLEY (Goods)
BURN HILL
LANCHESTER
WITTON GILBERT
DURHAM
ALDIN GRANGE FOR BEARPARK
PARKHEAD (Goods)
USHAW MOOR
Reilly Mill Jc.
WATERHOUSES
TOW LAW
BRANDON
LAZONBY & KIRKOSWALD
Lazonby Tun.
CALTHWAITE
WEARHEAD
EASTGATE
STANHOPE
ST. JOHN'S CHAPEL
WESTGATE-IN-WEARDALE
FROSTERLEY
BRANCEPETH
CROXDALE
MID.
PLUMPTON
WOLSINGHAM
N.E.
LITTLE SALKELD
HARPERLEY
CROOK
WILLINGTON
SPENNYMOOR
LANGWATHBY
BEECHBURN
HUNWICK
BYERS GREEN

DURHAM

Waste Bank Tun.
Culgaith Tun.
PENRITH
Loco Shed
WITTON-LE-WEAR
WEAR VALLEY JUNC.
COUNDON
ETHERLEY
BISHOP AUCKLAND
CULGAITH
NEW BIGGIN
Red Hills Jc.
Eamont Bri. Jc.
TEMPLE SOWERBY
EVENWOOD
Loco Shed
Eden Valley Jc.
CLIFTON
BUTTERKNOWLE
COCKFIELD
WEST AUCKLAND
SHILDON
KIRKBY THORE
CLIFTON & LOWTHER
CLIBURN
LONG MARTON
MIDDLETON-IN-TEESDALE
MICKLETON
HEIGHINGTON
APPLEBY
ROMALDKIRK

WESTMORLAND

BARNARD CASTLE
BROOMIELAW
WINSTON
COTHERSTONE
N. E.
GAINFORD
Forcett Jc.
Merrybent Jc.
ORMSIDE
N.E.
WARCOP
LARTINGTON
PIERCEBRIDGE
SHAP
Helm Tun.
MUSGRAVE
Stainmore Summit
N.E.
BOWES
BARRAS
Shap Summit
CROSBY GARRETT
FORCETT DEPOT
BARTON (Goods)
L.N.W.
SMARDALE
Belah Viaduct
Loco Shed
KIRKBY STEPHEN & RAVENSTONEDALE
KIRKBY STEPHEN
GAISGILL
RAVENSTONEDALE
Birkett Tun.
MOULTON
Loco Shed
TEBAY
Dillicar Watertroughs
High Seat
Wild Boar Fell
SCORTON
RICHMOND
CATTERICK BRIDGE
Blease Fell
STAVELEY
LOW GILL
Great Shunner Fell
Aisgill Summit
BURNSIDE
GRAYRIGG

YORK

Pass
Baugh Fell
Shotlock Tun.
Moorcock Tun.
Mossdale Head Tun.
KENDAL Gds.
HAWES JUNC. & GARSDALE
Watertroughs
MID.
REDMIRE
SEDBERGH
HAWES
N.E.
LEYBURN
CONSTABLE BURTON
Loco Shed
OXENHOLME
ASKRIGG
WENSLEY
SPENNITHORNE
FINGHALL LANE
CRAKEHALL
AYSGARTH
JERVAULX
Rise Hill Tun.
MIDDLETON
BEDALE

Twenty four

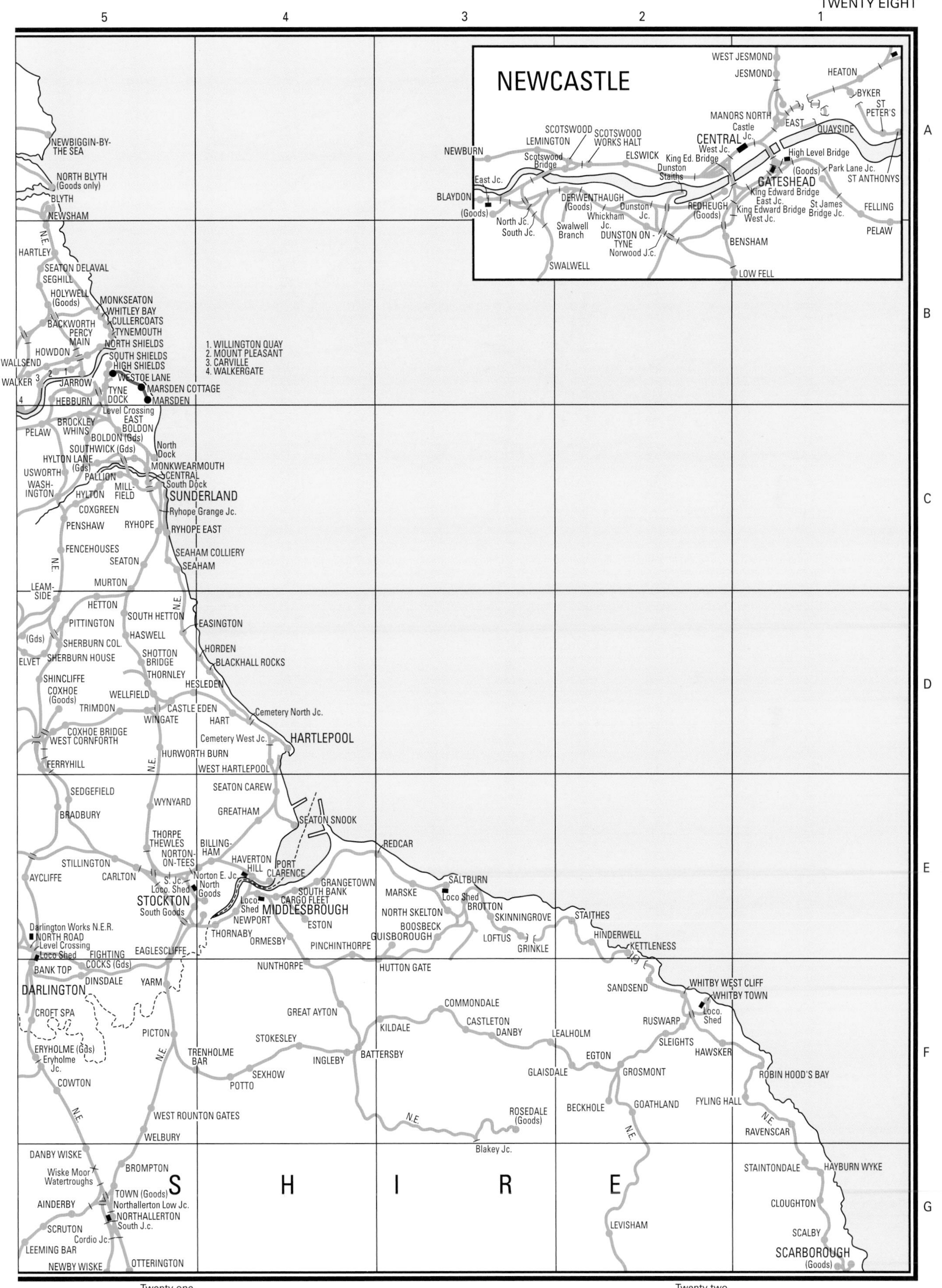
5
4
3
2
1
A
B
C
D
E
F
G
NEWCASTLE
WEST JESMOND
JESMOND
HEATON
BYKER
ST PETER'S
MANORS NORTH
EAST
QUAYSIDE
Castle Jc.
CENTRAL
West Jc.
SCOTSWOOD
SCOTSWOOD WORKS HALT
LEMINGTON
NEWBURN
Scotswood Bridge
ELSWICK
King Ed. Bridge
Dunston Staiths
High Level Bridge
(Goods)
Park Lane Jc.
ST ANTHONYS
GATESHEAD
East Jc.
BLAYDON
(Goods)
DERWENTHAUGH (Goods)
Dunston Jc.
Whickham Jc.
REDHEUGH (Goods)
King Edward Bridge East Jc.
King Edward Bridge West Jc.
St James Bridge Jc.
FELLING
PELAW
North Jc.
South Jc.
Swalwell Branch
DUNSTON ON - TYNE
Norwood J.c.
BENSHAM
SWALWELL
LOW FELL
NEWBIGGIN-BY-THE SEA
NORTH BLYTH (Goods only)
BLYTH
NEWSHAM
N.E.
HARTLEY
SEATON DELAVAL
SEGHILL
HOLYWELL (Goods)
MONKSEATON
WHITLEY BAY
CULLERCOATS
BACKWORTH
TYNEMOUTH
PERCY MAIN
NORTH SHIELDS
HOWDON
WALLSEND
SOUTH SHIELDS
HIGH SHIELDS
1. WILLINGTON QUAY
2. MOUNT PLEASANT
3. CARVILLE
4. WALKERGATE
WALKER
JARROW
WESTOE LANE
TYNE DOCK
MARSDEN COTTAGE
HEBBURN
MARSDEN
Level Crossing
EAST BOLDON
BROCKLEY WHINS
PELAW
BOLDON (Gds)
SOUTHWICK (Gds)
North Dock
HYLTON LANE (Gds)
MONKWEARMOUTH
USWORTH
PALLION
CENTRAL
South Dock
WASHINGTON
MILLFIELD
HYLTON
SUNDERLAND
COXGREEN
Ryhope Grange Jc.
PENSHAW
RYHOPE
RYHOPE EAST
FENCEHOUSES
SEAHAM COLLIERY
SEATON
SEAHAM
LEAMSIDE
MURTON
HETTON
SOUTH HETTON
EASINGTON
PITTINGTON
HASWELL
(Gds)
SHERBURN COL.
HORDEN
SHOTTON BRIDGE
ELVET
SHERBURN HOUSE
BLACKHALL ROCKS
THORNLEY
SHINCLIFFE
HESLEDEN
COXHOE (Goods)
WELLFIELD
TRIMDON
CASTLE EDEN
Cemetery North Jc.
WINGATE
HART
COXHOE BRIDGE
WEST CORNFORTH
Cemetery West Jc.
HARTLEPOOL
HURWORTH BURN
FERRYHILL
WEST HARTLEPOOL
SEATON CAREW
SEDGEFIELD
WYNYARD
GREATHAM
BRADBURY
SEATON SNOOK
THORPE THEWLES
BILLINGHAM
REDCAR
NORTON-ON-TEES
HAVERTON HILL
STILLINGTON
PORT CLARENCE
SALTBURN
AYCLIFFE
CARLTON
Norton E. Jc.
GRANGETOWN
S. Jc.
North Goods
SOUTH BANK
MARSKE
Loco. Shed
Loco Shed
STOCKTON
Loco Shed
CARGO FLEET
BROTTON
South Goods
MIDDLESBROUGH
NORTH SKELTON
SKINNINGROVE
STAITHES
NEWPORT
ESTON
BOOSBECK
Darlington Works N.E.R.
THORNABY
GUISBOROUGH
HINDERWELL
NORTH ROAD
ORMESBY
PINCHINTHORPE
LOFTUS
Level Crossing
GRINKLE
KETTLENESS
Loco Shed
FIGHTING COCKS (Gds)
EAGLESCLIFFE
NUNTHORPE
HUTTON GATE
BANK TOP
DINSDALE
YARM
SANDSEND
DARLINGTON
WHITBY WEST CLIFF
WHITBY TOWN
COMMONDALE
CROFT SPA
GREAT AYTON
CASTLETON
RUSWARP
Loco. Shed
KILDALE
DANBY
LEALHOLM
PICTON
SLEIGHTS
ERYHOLME (Gds)
STOKESLEY
HAWSKER
Eryholme Jc.
TRENHOLME BAR
INGLEBY
BATTERSBY
EGTON
GLAISDALE
GROSMONT
SEXHOW
ROBIN HOOD'S BAY
COWTON
POTTO
ROSEDALE (Goods)
BECKHOLE
GOATHLAND
FYLING HALL
WEST ROUNTON GATES
N.E.
RAVENSCAR
WELBURY
Blakey Jc.
DANBY WISKE
STAINTONDALE
HAYBURN WYKE
Wiske Moor Watertroughs
BROMPTON
S
H
I
R
E
TOWN (Goods)
AINDERBY
Northallerton Low Jc.
CLOUGHTON
NORTHALLERTON
South J.c.
LEVISHAM
SCRUTON
SCALBY
Cordio Jc.
LEEMING BAR
SCARBOROUGH
(Goods)
NEWBY WISKE
OTTERINGTON
Twenty one
Twenty two

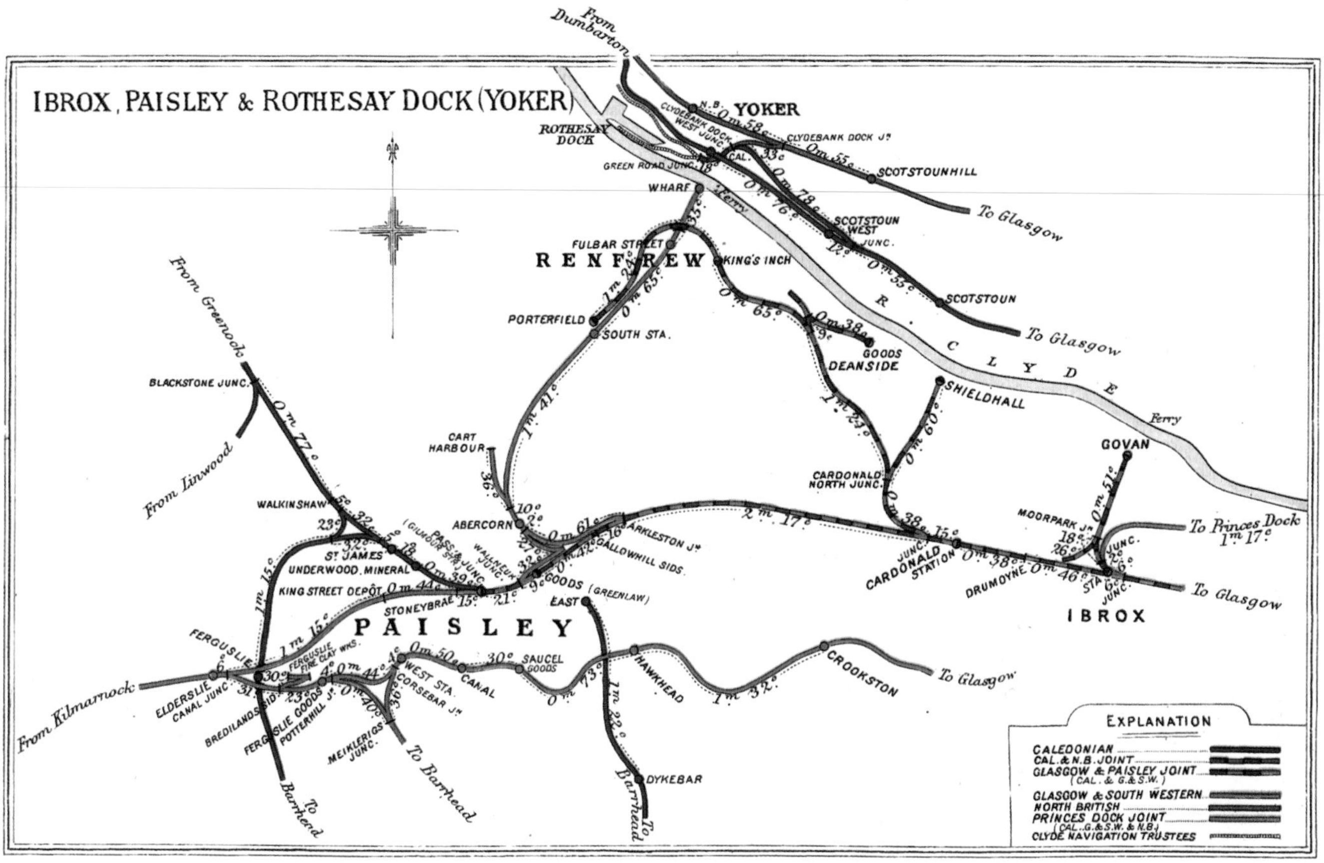

# IBROX, PAISLEY & ROTHESAY DOCK (YOKER)

From Dumbarton
YOKER
N.B.
CLYDEBANK DOCK WEST JUNC.
CLYDEBANK DOCK J.
ROTHESAY DOCK
GREEN ROAD JUNC.
CAL.
SCOTSTOUNHILL
WHARF
Ferry
SCOTSTOUN WEST JUNC.
To Glasgow
FULBAR STREET
RENFREW
KING'S INCH
R. CLYDE
SCOTSTOUN
To Glasgow
PORTERFIELD
SOUTH STA.
GOODS
DEANSIDE
SHIELDHALL
From Greenock
BLACKSTONE JUNC.
From Linwood
CART HARBOUR
CARDONALD NORTH JUNC.
GOVAN
Ferry
WALKINSHAW
ABERCORN
ARKLESTON J.
GALLOWHILL SIDS.
MOORPARK J.
JUNC.
To Princes Dock
ST JAMES
UNDERWOOD MINERAL
(GILMOUR STREET) PASS & JUNC.
WALLNEUK JUNC.
CARDONALD JUNC. STATION
DRUMOYNE
STA. JUNC.
To Glasgow
KING STREET DEPÔT
GOODS
STONEYBRAE
EAST (GREENLAW)
IBROX
PAISLEY
FERGUSLIE
FERGUSLIE FIRE CLAY WKS.
SAUCEL GOODS
CROOKSTON
ELDERSLIE
CANAL JUNC.
WEST STA.
CANAL
HAWKHEAD
To Glasgow
From Kilmarnock
BREDILANDS SID.
FERGUSLIE GOODS
POTTERHILL J.
CORSEBAR J.
MEIKLERIGS JUNC.
To Barrhead
DYKEBAR
To Barrhead
To Barrhead

EXPLANATION
CALEDONIAN
CAL. & N.B. JOINT
GLASGOW & PAISLEY JOINT (CAL. & G.&S.W.)
GLASGOW & SOUTH WESTERN
NORTH BRITISH
PRINCES DOCK JOINT (CAL., G.&S.W. & N.B.)
CLYDE NAVIGATION TRUSTEES

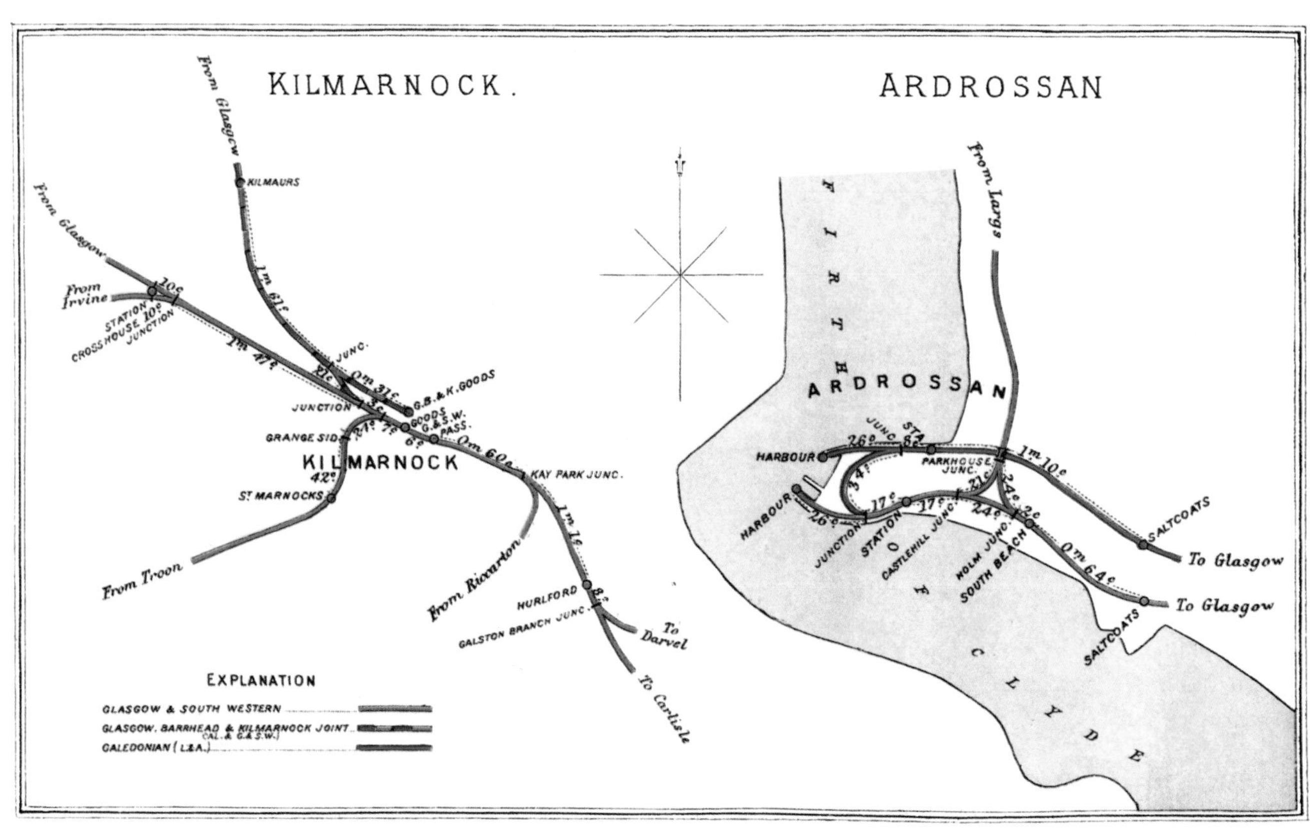

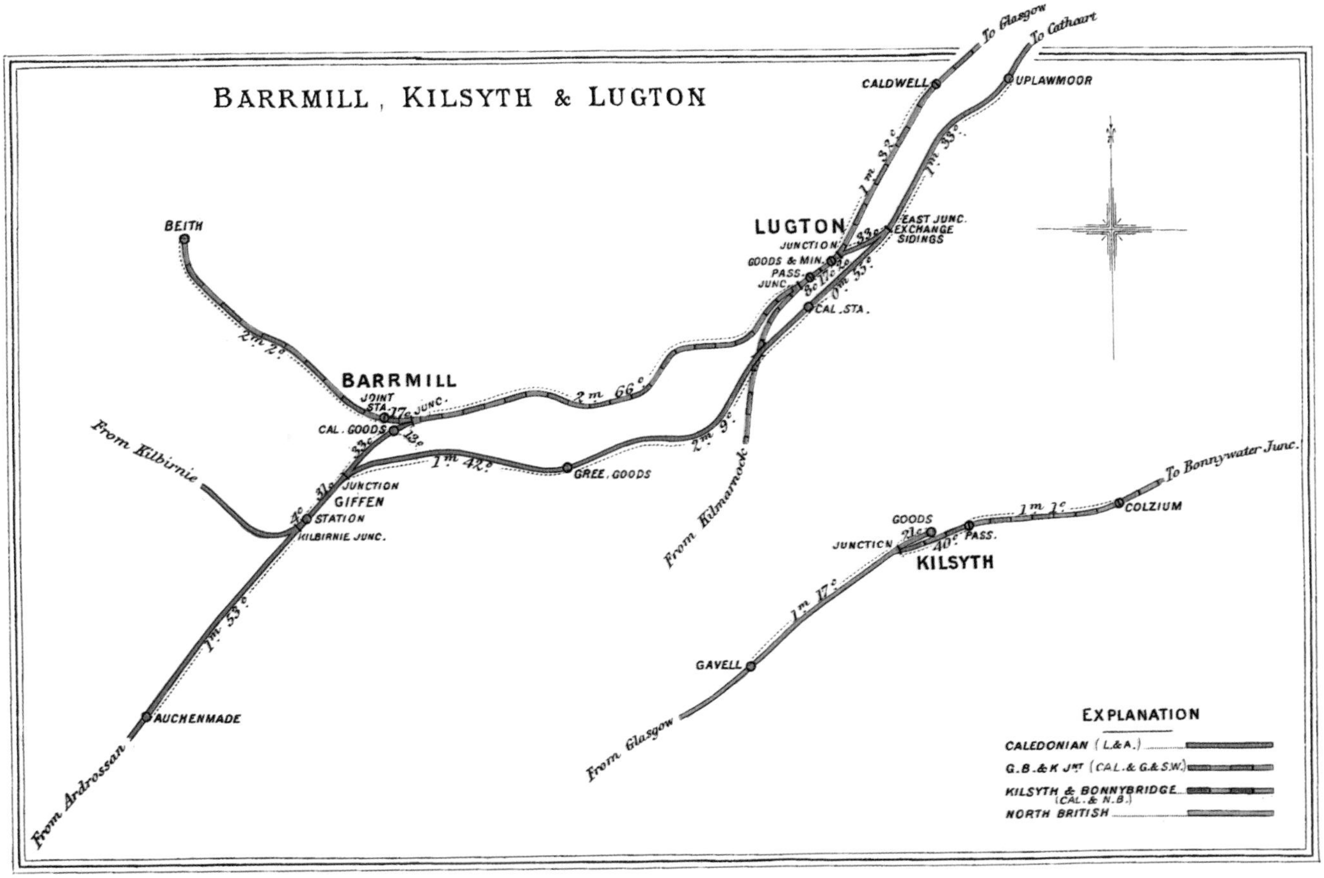

# BARRMILL, KILSYTH & LUGTON

To Glasgow
To Cathcart
CALDWELL
UPLAWMOOR
BEITH
LUGTON
JUNCTION
GOODS & MIN.
PASS.
JUNC.
EAST JUNC.
EXCHANGE SIDINGS
CAL. STA.
BARRMILL
JOINT STA.
JUNC.
CAL. GOODS
From Kilbirnie
JUNCTION
GIFFEN
STATION
KILBIRNIE JUNC.
GREE. GOODS
From Kilmarnock
To Bonnywater Junc.
GOODS
COLZIUM
JUNCTION
PASS.
KILSYTH
GAVELL
AUCHENMADE
From Ardrossan
From Glasgow

EXPLANATION

CALEDONIAN (L.&A.)
G.B.&K. J^NT (CAL.& G.&S.W.)
KILSYTH & BONNYBRIDGE (CAL. & N.B.)
NORTH BRITISH

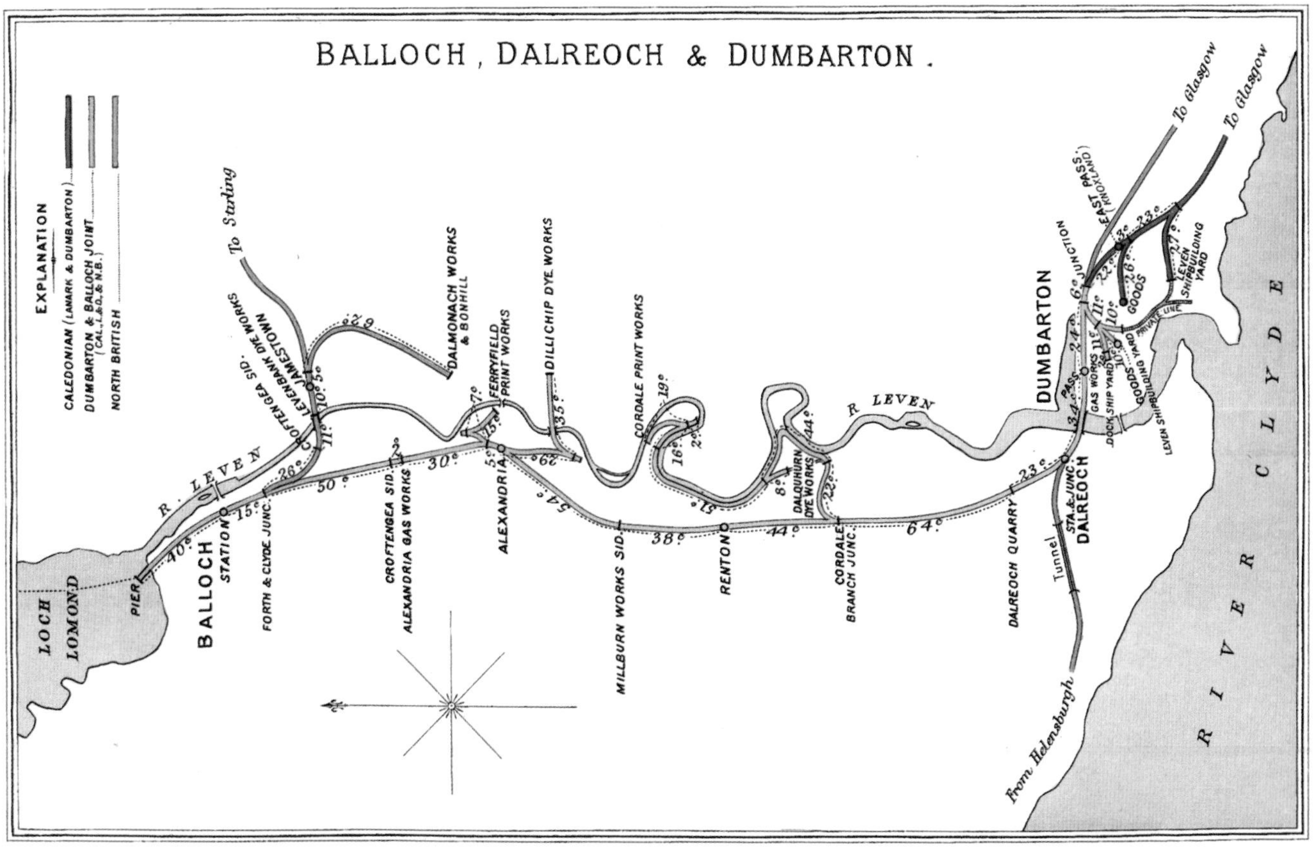

# BALLOCH, DALREOCH & DUMBARTON.

EXPLANATION

CALEDONIAN (LANARK & DUMBARTON)
DUMBARTON & BALLOCH JOINT (CAL. L&D. & N.B.)
NORTH BRITISH

To Sterling
LEVENBANK DYE WORKS
JAMESTOWN
CROFTENGEA SID.
DALMONACH WORKS & BONHILL
FERRYFIELD PRINT WORKS
DILLICHIP DYE WORKS
CORDALE PRINT WORKS
R. LEVEN
LOCH LOMOND
PIER
BALLOCH
STATION
FORTH & CLYDE JUNC.
CROFTENGEA SID.
ALEXANDRIA GAS WORKS
ALEXANDRIA
MILLBURN WORKS SID.
RENTON
DALQUHURN DYE WORKS
CORDALE BRANCH JUNC.
DALREOCH QUARRY
Tunnel
STA. & JUNC.
DALREOCH
From Helensburgh
DUMBARTON
PASS.
GAS WORKS
DOCK SHIP YARD
GOODS YARD
LEVEN SHIPBUILDING YARD
JUNCTION
EAST PASS. (KNOXLAND)
GOODS
LEVEN SHIPBUILDING YARD
PRIVATE LINE
To Glasgow
To Glasgow
RIVER CLYDE

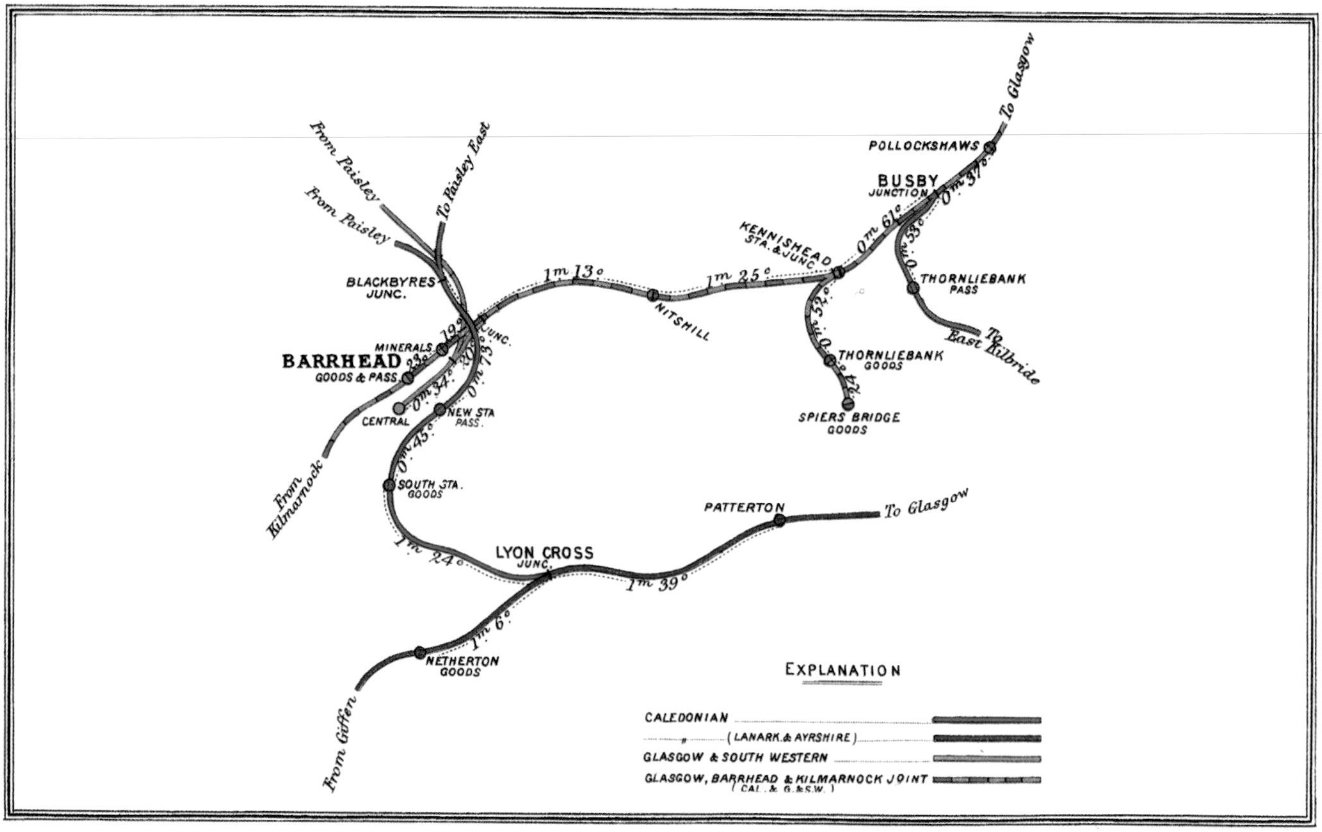

Barrhead–Busby Junc

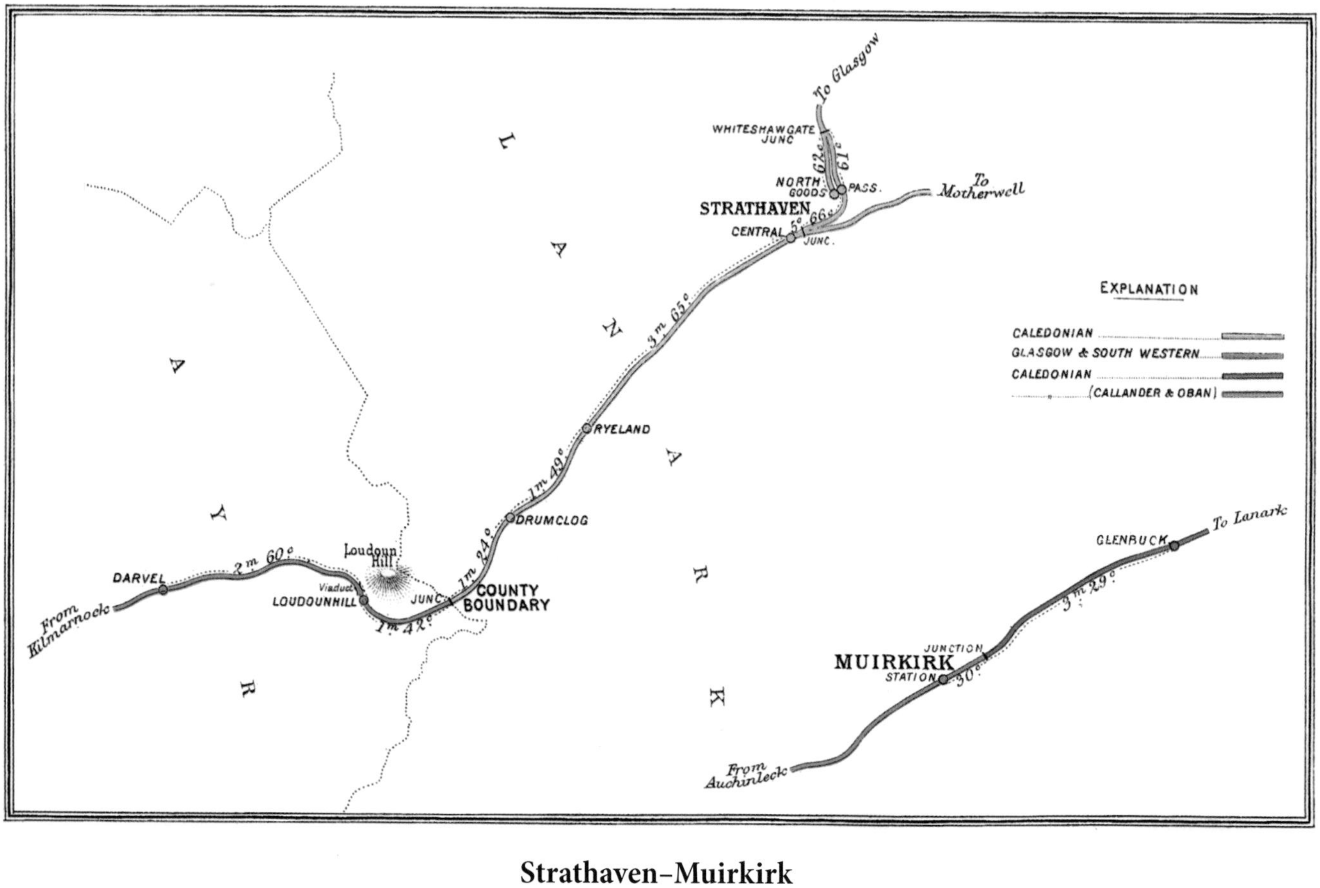

Strathaven–Muirkirk

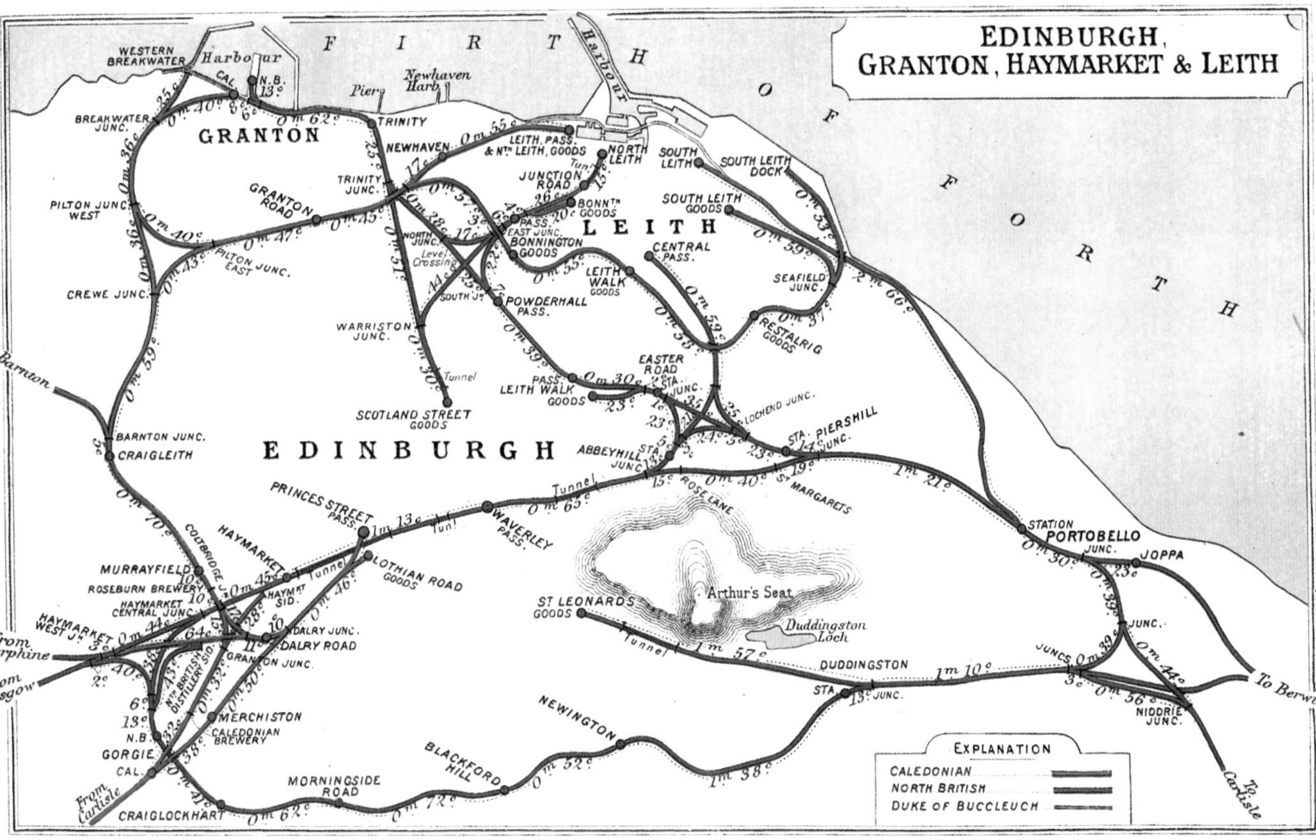
EDINBURGH, GRANTON, HAYMARKET & LEITH
FIRTH OF FORTH
Harbour
Newhaven Harb.
Pier
WESTERN BREAKWATER
GRANTON
TRINITY
NEWHAVEN
LEITH PASS. & Nth LEITH, GOODS
NORTH LEITH
SOUTH LEITH
SOUTH LEITH DOCK
SOUTH LEITH GOODS
BREAKWATER JUNC.
PILTON JUNC. WEST
GRANTON ROAD
TRINITY JUNC.
JUNCTION ROAD
BONNTN GOODS
LEITH
CENTRAL PASS.
BONNINGTON GOODS
EAST JUNC.
NORTH JUNC.
Level Crossing
PILTON JUNC. EAST
CREWE JUNC.
LEITH WALK GOODS
SEAFIELD JUNC.
SOUTH JN
POWDERHALL PASS.
RESTALRIG GOODS
WARRISTON JUNC.
EASTER ROAD STA.
LEITH WALK GOODS
LOCHEND JUNC.
From Barnton
SCOTLAND STREET GOODS
Tunnel
BARNTON JUNC.
CRAIGLEITH
EDINBURGH
ABBEYHILL JUNC.
PIERSHILL JUNC.
ROSE LANE
ST MARGARETS
PRINCES STREET PASS.
WAVERLEY PASS.
STATION
PORTOBELLO JUNC.
JOPPA
HAYMARKET
MURRAYFIELD
ROSEBURN BREWERY
HAYMARKET CENTRAL JUNC.
HAYMKT SID.
LOTHIAN ROAD GOODS
Arthur's Seat
Duddingston Loch
ST LEONARDS GOODS
HAYMARKET WEST JN
From Corstorphine
DALRY JUNC.
DALRY ROAD
GRANTON JUNC.
From Glasgow
NTH BRITISH DISTILLERY SID.
DUDDINGSTON
JUNCS.
JUNC.
NIDDRIE JUNC.
To Berwick
STA. JUNC.
MERCHISTON
CALEDONIAN BREWERY
NEWINGTON
GORGIE
BLACKFORD HILL
EXPLANATION
CALEDONIAN
NORTH BRITISH
DUKE OF BUCCLEUCH
To Carlisle
From Carlisle
MORNINGSIDE ROAD
CRAIGLOCKHART

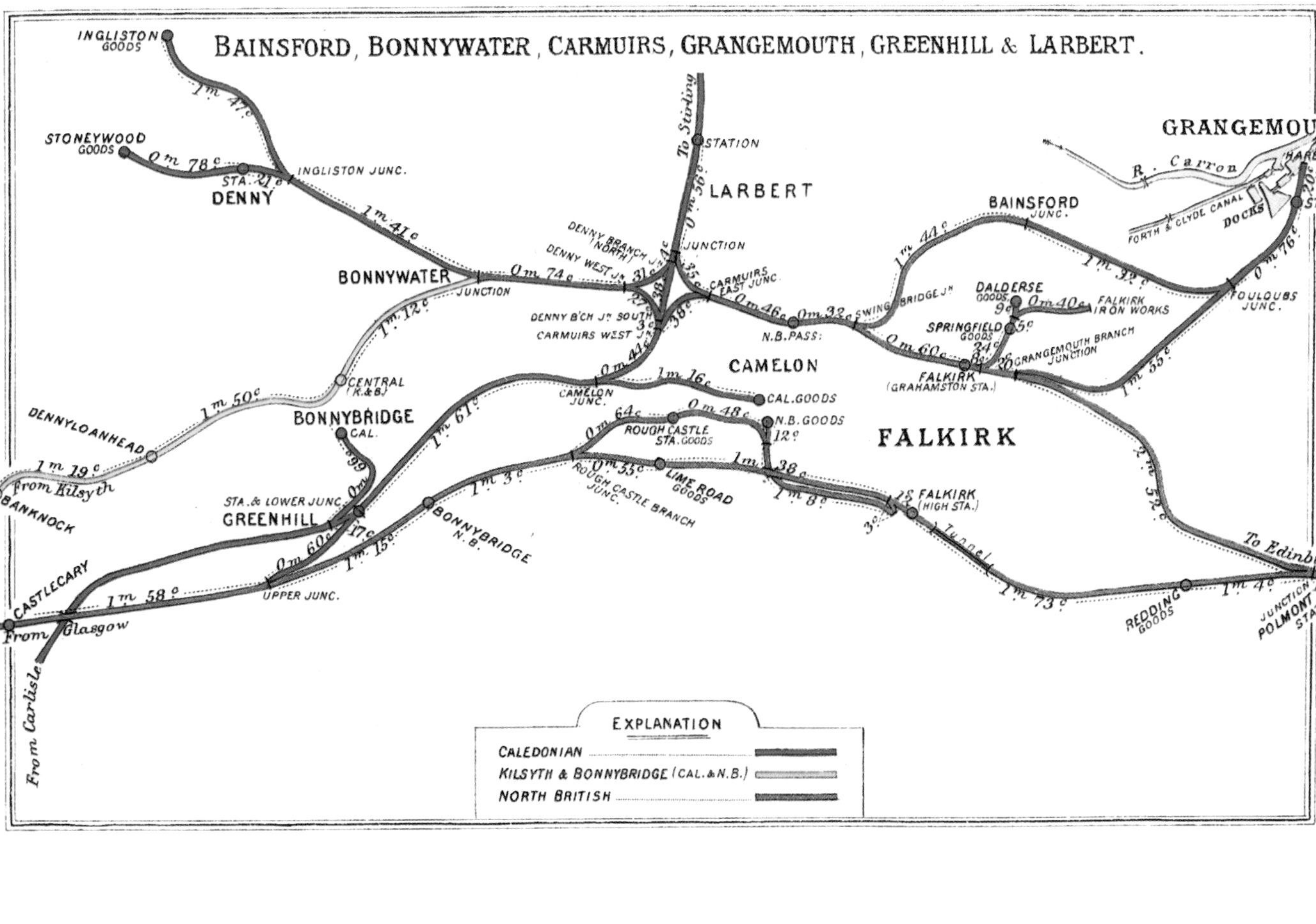
BAINSFORD, BONNYWATER, CARMUIRS, GRANGEMOUTH, GREENHILL & LARBERT.
INGLISTON GOODS
STONEYWOOD GOODS
INGLISTON JUNC.
DENNY
To Stirling
STATION
LARBERT
GRANGEMOUTH
R. Carron
HARBOUR
FORTH & CLYDE CANAL
DOCKS
STA.
BAINSFORD JUNC.
DENNY BRANCH NORTH
DENNY WEST JN
JUNCTION
BONNYWATER
JUNCTION
CARMUIRS EAST JUNC.
SWING BRIDGE JN
DALDERSE GOODS
FALKIRK IRON WORKS
FOULOUBS JUNC.
DENNY B'CH JN SOUTH
CARMUIRS WEST JN
N.B. PASS.
SPRINGFIELD GOODS
GRANGEMOUTH BRANCH JUNCTION
FALKIRK (GRAHAMSTON STA.)
CENTRAL (K.&B.)
CAMELON
CAMELON JUNC.
CAL. GOODS
DENNYLOANHEAD
BONNYBRIDGE CAL.
ROUGH CASTLE STA. GOODS
N.B. GOODS
FALKIRK
From Kilsyth
BANKNOCK
STA. & LOWER JUNC.
GREENHILL
ROUGH CASTLE BRANCH JUNC.
LIME ROAD GOODS
FALKIRK (HIGH STA.)
BONNYBRIDGE N.B.
Tunnel
To Edinburgh
CASTLECARY
UPPER JUNC.
From Glasgow
REDDING GOODS
JUNCTION POLMONT STATION
From Carlisle
EXPLANATION
CALEDONIAN
KILSYTH & BONNYBRIDGE (CAL. & N.B.)
NORTH BRITISH

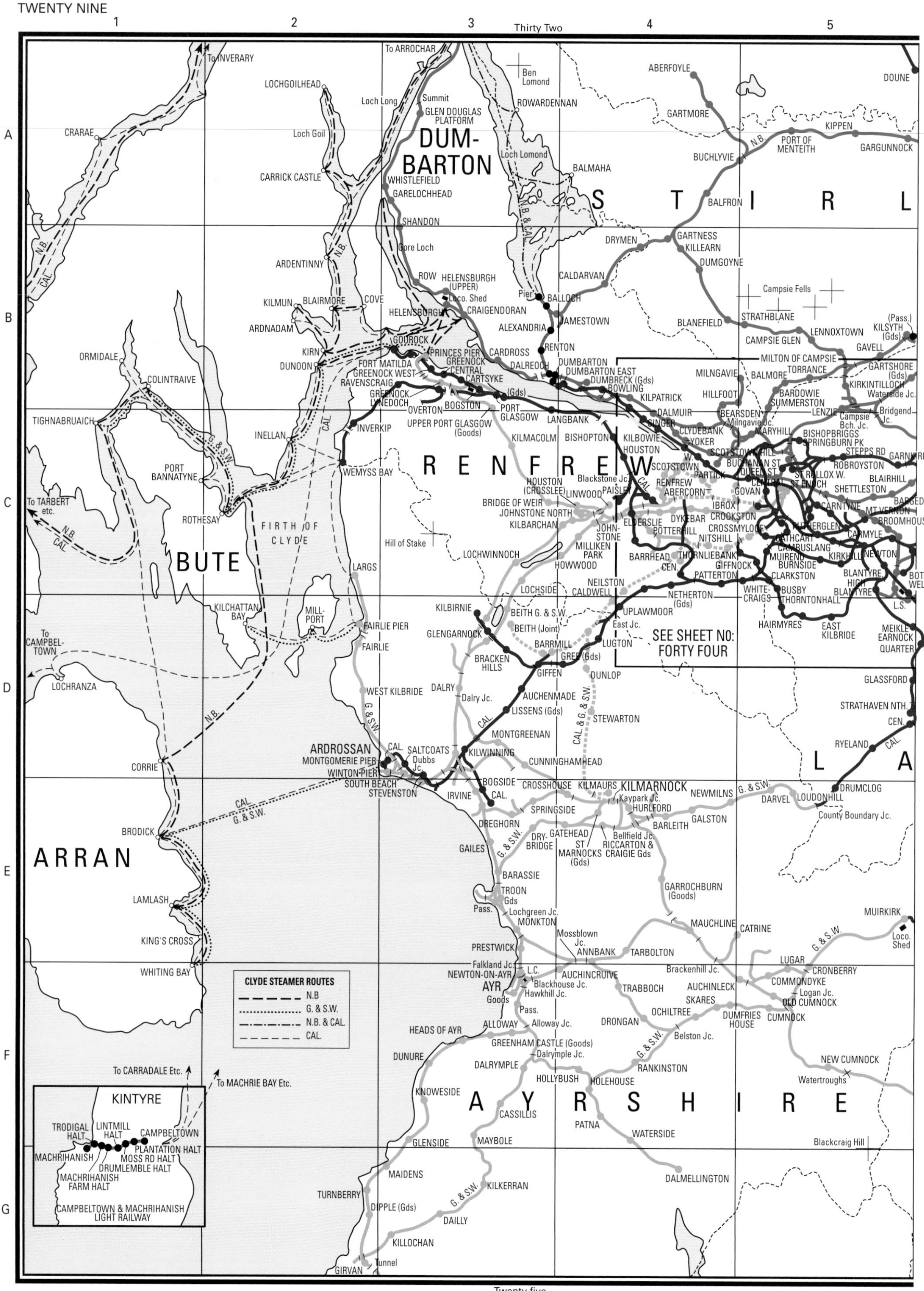
1
2
3
4
5
Thirty Two
A
B
C
D
E
F
G
To INVERARY
To ARROCHAR
Ben Lomond
ABERFOYLE
DOUNE
LOCHGOILHEAD
Loch Long
Summit
GLEN DOUGLAS PLATFORM
ROWARDENNAN
GARTMORE
KIPPEN
CRARAE
Loch Goil
DUM-BARTON
Loch Lomond
PORT OF MENTEITH
GARGUNNOCK
BUCHLYVIE
N.B.
CARRICK CASTLE
WHISTLEFIELD
GARELOCHHEAD
BALMAHA
S T I R L
BALFRON
SHANDON
N.B. & CAL.
DRYMEN
GARTNESS
KILLEARN
DUMGOYNE
Gore Loch
ARDENTINNY
N.B.
CAL.
ROW
HELENSBURGH (UPPER)
Loco. Shed
CALDARVAN
Campsie Fells
Pier
BALLOCH
KILMUN
BLAIRMORE
COVE
HELENSBURGH
CRAIGENDORAN
JAMESTOWN
STRATHBLANE
BLANEFIELD
ARDNADAM
ALEXANDRIA
LENNOXTOWN
KILSYTH (Pass.) (Gds)
CAMPSIE GLEN
GAVELL
KIRN
GOUROCK
PRINCES PIER
CARDROSS
RENTON
ORMIDALE
DUNOON
FORT MATILDA
GREENOCK WEST
GREENOCK CENTRAL
CARTSYKE
DALREOCH
DUMBARTON
DUMBARTON EAST
DUMBRECK (Gds)
MILTON OF CAMPSIE
MILNGAVIE
BALMORE
TORRANCE
GARTSHORE (Gds)
KIRKINTILLOCH
Waterside Jc.
COLINTRAIVE
RAVENSCRAIG
GREENOCK LYNEDOCH
(Gds)
BOWLING
KILPATRICK
HILLFOOT
BARDOWIE
SUMMERSTON
OVERTON
BOGSTON
PORT GLASGOW
DALMUIR
BEARSDEN
Milngavie Jc.
LENZIE
Bridgend Jc.
TIGHNABRUAICH
UPPER PORT GLASGOW (Goods)
LANGBANK
SINGER
CLYDEBANK
YOKER
MARYHILL
Campsie Bch. Jc.
BISHOPBRIGGS
SPRINGBURN PK
INVERKIP
INELLAN
CAL.
G. & S.W.
KILMACOLM
BISHOPTON
KILBOWIE
HOUSTON
SCOTSTOUN
STEPPS RD
GARNKIRK
ROBROYSTON
WEMYSS BAY
R E N F R E W
PORT BANNATYNE
HOUSTON (CROSSLEE)
Blackstone Jc.
PARTICK
BUCHANAN ST
QUEEN ST
CENTRAL
ST ROLLOX W.
ST ENOCH
BLAIRHILL
SHETTLESTON
CAL.
LINWOOD
PAISLEY
RENFREW
ABERCORN
GOVAN
To TARBERT etc.
BRIDGE OF WEIR
IBROX
CARNTYNE
BARGEDDIE
MT VERNON
BROOMHOUSE
ROTHESAY
FIRTH OF CLYDE
JOHNSTONE NORTH
KILBARCHAN
ELDERSLIE
JOHNSTONE
DYKEBAR
CROOKSTON
POTTERHILL
CROSSMYLOOF
RUTHERGLEN
N.B.
CAL.
Hill of Stake
NITSHILL
CATHCART
CARMYLE
MILLIKEN PARK
CAMBUSLANG
BUTE
LOCHWINNOCH
BARRHEAD
THORNLIEBANK
MUIREND
KIRKHILL
NEWTON
HOWWOOD
CEN.
GIFFNOCK
BURNSIDE
BLANTYRE
BOTHWELL
LARGS
PATTERTON
CLARKSTON
HIGH BLANTYRE
NEILSTON
LOCHSIDE
CALDWELL
NETHERTON (Gds)
WHITECRAIGS
BUSBY
THORNTONHALL
L.S.
KILCHATTAN BAY
MILLPORT
KILBIRNIE
BEITH G. & S.W.
UPLAWMOOR
HAIRMYRES
EAST KILBRIDE
MEIKLE EARNOCK
QUARTER
FAIRLIE PIER
BEITH (Joint)
East Jc.
To CAMPBELTOWN
GLENGARNOCK
LUGTON
SEE SHEET NO: FORTY FOUR
FAIRLIE
BARRMILL
BRACKEN HILLS
GREE (Gds)
GIFFEN
LOCHRANZA
DUNLOP
DALRY
WEST KILBRIDE
GLASSFORD
Dalry Jc.
AUCHENMADE
LISSENS (Gds)
G. & S.W.
CAL. & G. & S.W.
CAL.
STEWARTON
STRATHAVEN NTH.
CEN.
N.B.
MONTGREENAN
ARDROSSAN
MONTGOMERIE PIER
CAL.
SALTCOATS
Dubbs Jc.
KILWINNING
CUNNINGHAMHEAD
RYELAND
CAL.
L A
CORRIE
WINTON PIER
SOUTH BEACH
STEVENSTON
IRVINE
BOGSIDE
CAL.
CROSSHOUSE
KILMAURS
KILMARNOCK
NEWMILNS
G. & S.W.
DARVEL
LOUDONHILL
DRUMCLOG
Kaypark Jc.
HURLFORD
County Boundary Jc.
CAL.
G. & S.W.
SPRINGSIDE
BARLEITH
GALSTON
BRODICK
DREGHORN
DRYBRIDGE
GATEHEAD
ST MARNOCKS (Gds)
Bellfield Jc.
RICCARTON & CRAIGIE Gds
ARRAN
GAILES
G. & S.W.
BARASSIE
GARROCHBURN (Goods)
LAMLASH
TROON
Gds
Pass.
Lochgreen Jc.
MONKTON
MAUCHLINE
CATRINE
MUIRKIRK
Mossblown Jc.
KING'S CROSS
PRESTWICK
ANNBANK
TARBOLTON
G. & S.W.
Loco. Shed
WHITING BAY
Falkland Jc.
NEWTON-ON-AYR
L.C.
AUCHINCRUIVE
Brackenhill Jc.
LUGAR
CRONBERRY
COMMONDYKE
CLYDE STEAMER ROUTES
N.B
G. & S.W.
N.B. & CAL.
CAL.
AYR
Goods
Blackhouse Jc.
Hawkhill Jc.
TRABBOCH
AUCHINLECK
SKARES
Logan Jc.
OLD CUMNOCK
Pass.
ALLOWAY
Alloway Jc.
DRONGAN
OCHILTREE
DUMFRIES HOUSE
CUMNOCK
HEADS OF AYR
GREENHAM CASTLE (Goods)
G. & S.W.
Belston Jc.
DUNURE
Dalrymple Jc.
DALRYMPLE
RANKINSTON
NEW CUMNOCK
To CARRADALE Etc.
To MACHRIE BAY Etc.
HOLLYBUSH
HOLEHOUSE
Watertroughs
KINTYRE
KNOWESIDE
A Y R S H I R E
CASSILLIS
TRODIGAL HALT
LINTMILL HALT
CAMPBELTOWN
PATNA
WATERSIDE
PLANTATION HALT
MACHRIHANISH
MOSS RD HALT
DRUMLEMBLE HALT
MACHRIHANISH FARM HALT
GLENSIDE
MAYBOLE
Blackcraig Hill
CAMPBELTOWN & MACHRIHANISH LIGHT RAILWAY
MAIDENS
DALMELLINGTON
TURNBERRY
G. & S.W.
KILKERRAN
DIPPLE (Gds)
DAILLY
KILLOCHAN
GIRVAN
Tunnel
Twenty five

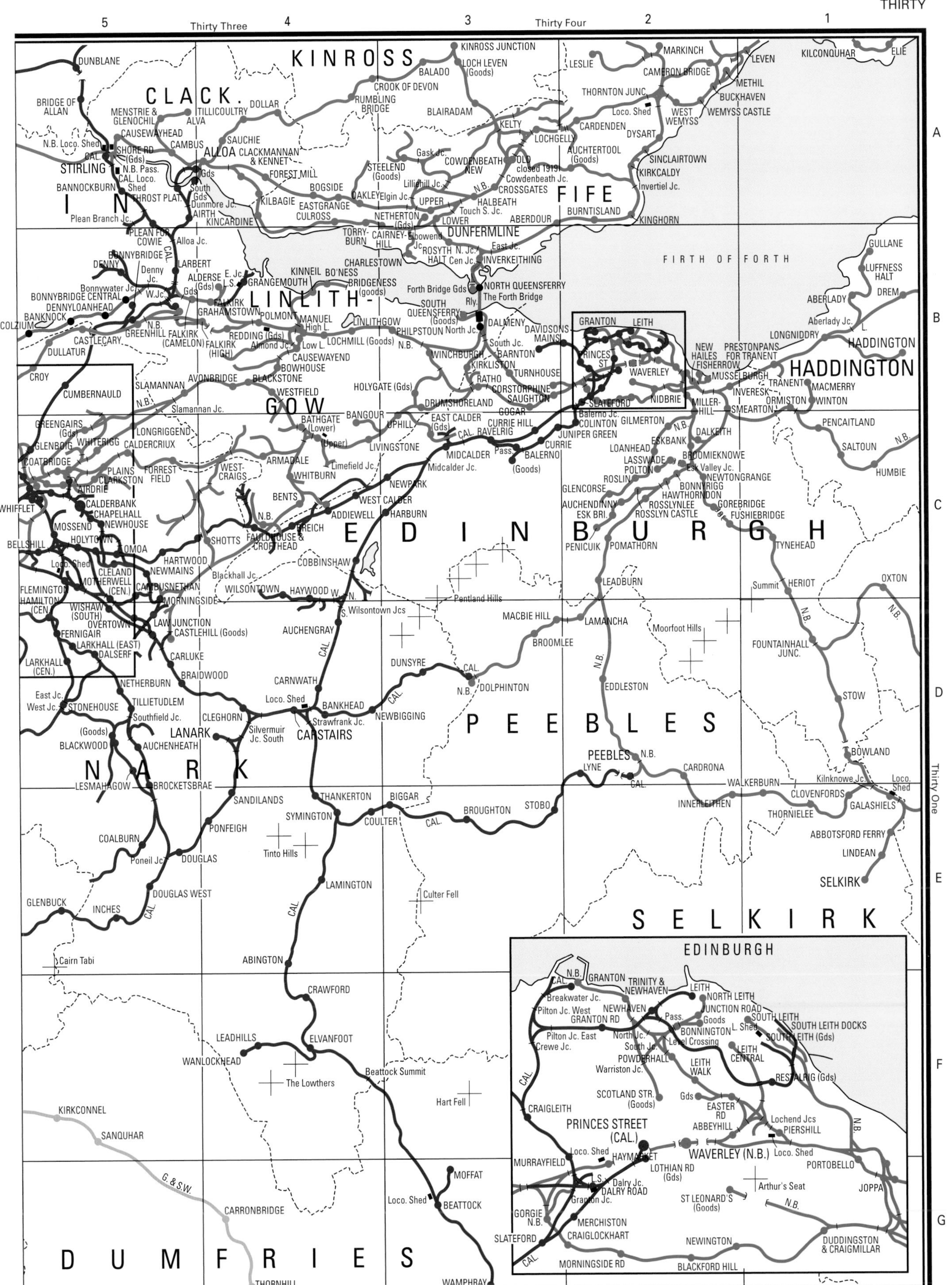
5
Thirty Three
4
3
Thirty Four
2
1
A
B
C
D
E
F
G
Thirty One
Thirty One
KINROSS
CLACK.
FIFE
LINLITH-
GOW
EDINBURGH
PEEBLES
SELKIRK
DUMFRIES
HADDINGTON
FIRTH OF FORTH
DUNBLANE
BRIDGE OF ALLAN
MENSTRIE & GLENOCHIL
TILLICOULTRY
DOLLAR
ALVA
CAUSEWAYHEAD
N.B. Loco. Shed
CAMBUS
SAUCHIE
ALLOA
CLACKMANNAN & KENNET
STIRLING
SHORE RD (Gds)
N.B. Pass.
CAL. Loco. Shed
BANNOCKBURN
THROST PLAT.
FOREST MILL
KILBAGIE
Dunmore Jc.
AIRTH
KINCARDINE
Plean Branch Jc.
PLEAN FOR COWIE
Alloa Jc.
LARBERT
BONNYBRIDGE
DENNY
Denny Jc.
ALDERSE (Gds)
E. Jc.
L.S.
GRANGEMOUTH
Bonnywater Jc.
BONNYBRIDGE CENTRAL
DENNYLOANHEAD
W.Jc.
BANKNOCK
COLZIUM
FALKIRK GRAHAMSTOWN
POLMONT
GREENHILL
FALKIRK (CAMELON)
FALKIRK (HIGH)
CASTLECARY
DULLATUR
REDDING (Gds)
Almond Jc.
MANUEL High L.
Low L.
LINLITHGOW
LOCHMILL (Goods)
CAUSEWAYEND
BOWHOUSE
BLACKSTONE
WESTFIELD
AVONBRIDGE
SLAMANNAN
Slamannan Jc.
CROY
CUMBERNAULD
GREENGAIRS (Gds)
GLENBOIG
WHITERIGG
LONGRIGGEND
CALDERCRUIX
COATBRIDGE
PLAINS
CLARKSTON
FORREST FIELD
WEST-CRAIGS
AIRDRIE
CALDERBANK
CHAPELHALL
NEWHOUSE
WHIFFLET
MOSSEND
HOLYTOWN
BELLSHILL
OMOA
SHOTTS
HARTWOOD
NEWMAINS
CLELAND
MOTHERWELL (CEN.)
CAMBUSNETHAN
MORNINGSIDE
FLEMINGTON
HAMILTON (CEN)
WISHAW (SOUTH)
OVERTOWN
FERNIGAIR
LARKHALL (EAST)
DALSERF
LARKHALL (CEN.)
LAW JUNCTION
CASTLEHILL (Goods)
CARLUKE
BRAIDWOOD
NETHERBURN
TILLIETUDLEM
East Jc.
West Jc.
STONEHOUSE
Southfield Jc.
(Goods)
BLACKWOOD
AUCHENHEATH
LANARK
CLEGHORN
Silvermuir Jc. South
CARSTAIRS
Strawfrank Jc.
Loco. Shed
CARNWATH
BANKHEAD
NEWBIGGING
DUNSYRE
DOLPHINTON
LESMAHAGOW
BROCKETSBRAE
SANDILANDS
PONFEIGH
COALBURN
Poneil Jc.
DOUGLAS
DOUGLAS WEST
GLENBUCK
INCHES
THANKERTON
SYMINGTON
BIGGAR
COULTER
BROUGHTON
STOBO
LYNE
PEEBLES
CARDRONA
Tinto Hills
LAMINGTON
Culter Fell
Cairn Tabi
ABINGTON
CRAWFORD
ELVANFOOT
LEADHILLS
WANLOCKHEAD
The Lowthers
Beattock Summit
Hart Fell
MOFFAT
BEATTOCK
WAMPHRAY
KIRKCONNEL
SANQUHAR
G. & S.W.
CARRONBRIDGE
THORNHILL
KINROSS JUNCTION
LOCH LEVEN (Goods)
BALADO
CROOK OF DEVON
RUMBLING BRIDGE
BLAIRADAM
KELTY
LOCHGELLY
CARDENDEN
LESLIE
MARKINCH
CAMERON BRIDGE
THORNTON JUNC.
Loco. Shed
WEST WEMYSS
WEMYSS CASTLE
METHIL
BUCKHAVEN
LEVEN
KILCONQUHAR
ELIE
DYSART
SINCLAIRTOWN
KIRKCALDY
Invertiel Jc.
AUCHTERTOOL (Goods)
OLD closed 1919
COWDENBEATH
NEW
Cowdenbeath Jc.
CROSSGATES
HALBEATH
Gask Jc.
STEELEND (Goods)
Lilliehill Jc.
OAKLEY
Elgin Jc.
UPPER
BOGSIDE
EASTGRANGE
CULROSS
NETHERTON (Gds)
LOWER
Touch S. Jc.
ABERDOUR
BURNTISLAND
KINGHORN
DUNFERMLINE
TORRY-BURN
CAIRNEY-HILL
Elbowend Jc.
ROSYTH HALT
N. Jc.
Cen Jc.
East Jc.
INVERKEITHING
CHARLESTOWN
KINNEIL
BO'NESS
BRIDGENESS (goods)
Forth Bridge Gds
Rly.
NORTH QUEENSFERRY
The Forth Bridge
SOUTH QUEENSFERRY (Goods)
North Jc.
DALMENY
PHILPSTOUN
N.B.
South Jc.
WINCHBURGH
KIRKLISTON
BARNTON
RATHO
TURNHOUSE
CORSTORPHINE
SAUGHTON
DAVIDSONS MAINS
GRANTON
LEITH
PRINCES ST
WAVERLEY
NIDDRIE
SLATEFORD
Balerno Jc.
COLINTON
JUNIPER GREEN
CURRIE
BALERNO
Pass.
(Goods)
HOLYGATE (Gds)
DRUMSHORELAND
GOGAR
CURRIE HILL
RAVELRIG
EAST CALDER (Gds)
MIDCALDER
Midcalder Jc.
UPHILL
LIVINGSTONE
BANGOUR
BATHGATE (Lower)
(Upper)
ARMADALE
Limefield Jc.
WHITBURN
BENTS
NEWPARK
WEST CALDER
ADDIEWELL
HARBURN
BREICH
FAULDHOUSE & CROFTHEAD
COBBINSHAW
Blackhall Jc.
WILSONTOWN
HAYWOOD
Wilsontown Jcs
AUCHENGRAY
Pentland Hills
MACBIE HILL
LAMANCHA
BROOMLEE
LEADBURN
EDDLESTON
Moorfoot Hills
PENICUIK
POMATHORN
AUCHENDINNY
ESK BRI.
ROSSLYNLEE
ROSSLYN CASTLE
GLENCORSE
ROSLIN
POLTON
LASSWADE
LOANHEAD
ESKBANK
GILMERTON
DALKEITH
BROOMIEKNOWE
Esk Valley Jc.
NEWTONGRANGE
BONNYRIGG
HAWTHORNDON
GOREBRIDGE
FUSHIEBRIDGE
TYNEHEAD
HERIOT
Summit
FOUNTAINHALL JUNC.
STOW
BOWLAND
OXTON
MILLER-HILL
SMEARTON
NEW HAILES
FISHERROW
MUSSELBURGH
PRESTONPANS
FOR TRANENT
INVERESK
TRANENT
ORMISTON
MACMERRY
WINTON
PENCAITLAND
SALTOUN
HUMBIE
LONGNIDDRY
HADDINGTON
Aberlady Jc.
ABERLADY
GULLANE
LUFFNESS HALT
DREM
WALKERBURN
INNERLEITHEN
CLOVENFORDS
THORNIELEE
Kilnknowe Jc.
Loco. Shed
GALASHIELS
ABBOTSFORD FERRY
LINDEAN
SELKIRK
EDINBURGH
CAL.
N.B.
GRANTON
TRINITY & NEWHAVEN
LEITH
NORTH LEITH
Breakwater Jc.
Pilton Jc. West
NEWHAVEN
JUNCTION ROAD
GRANTON RD
Pass.
Goods
SOUTH LEITH
SOUTH LEITH DOCKS
Pilton Jc. East
Crewe Jc.
North Jc.
BONNINGTON
L. Shed
SOUTH LEITH (Gds)
South Jc.
Level Crossing
POWDERHALL
LEITH CENTRAL
Warriston Jc.
LEITH WALK
RESTALRIG (Gds)
SCOTLAND STR. (Goods)
Gds
EASTER RD
Lochend Jcs
CRAIGLEITH
PRINCES STREET (CAL.)
ABBEYHILL
PIERSHILL
Loco. Shed
HAYMARKET
WAVERLEY (N.B.)
Loco. Shed
PORTOBELLO
MURRAYFIELD
LOTHIAN RD (Gds)
L.S.
Dalry Jc.
DALRY ROAD
Arthur's Seat
JOPPA
Granton Jc.
ST LEONARD'S (Goods)
GORGIE N.B.
MERCHISTON
SLATEFORD
CRAIGLOCKHART
NEWINGTON
DUDDINGSTON & CRAIGMILLAR
MORNINGSIDE RD
BLACKFORD HILL

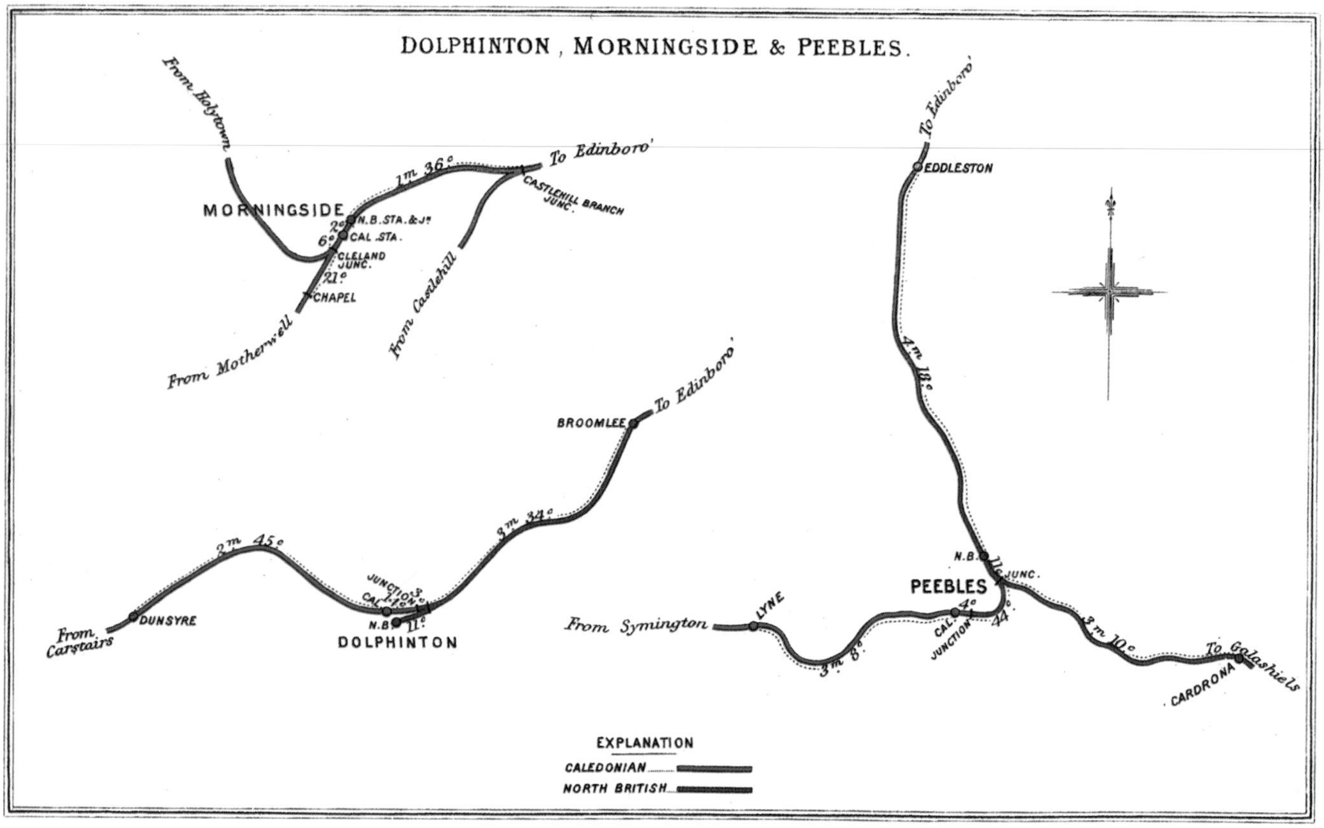

## DOLPHINTON, MORNINGSIDE & PEEBLES.

From Bolytown
To Edinboro'
1m 36c
MORNINGSIDE
N.B. STA. & Jn
CAL. STA.
CASTLEHILL BRANCH JUNC.
CLELAND JUNC.
21c
CHAPEL
From Motherwell
From Castlehill
To Edinboro'
EDDLESTON
4m 18c
BROOMLEE
To Edinboro'
3m 34c
2m 45c
From Carstairs
DUNSYRE
DOLPHINTON
11c
N.B.
PEEBLES
JUNC.
From Symington
LYNE
3m 8c
CAL.
JUNCTION
44c
3m 10c
To Galashiels
CARDRONA

EXPLANATION
CALEDONIAN
NORTH BRITISH

## ALLOA & STIRLING

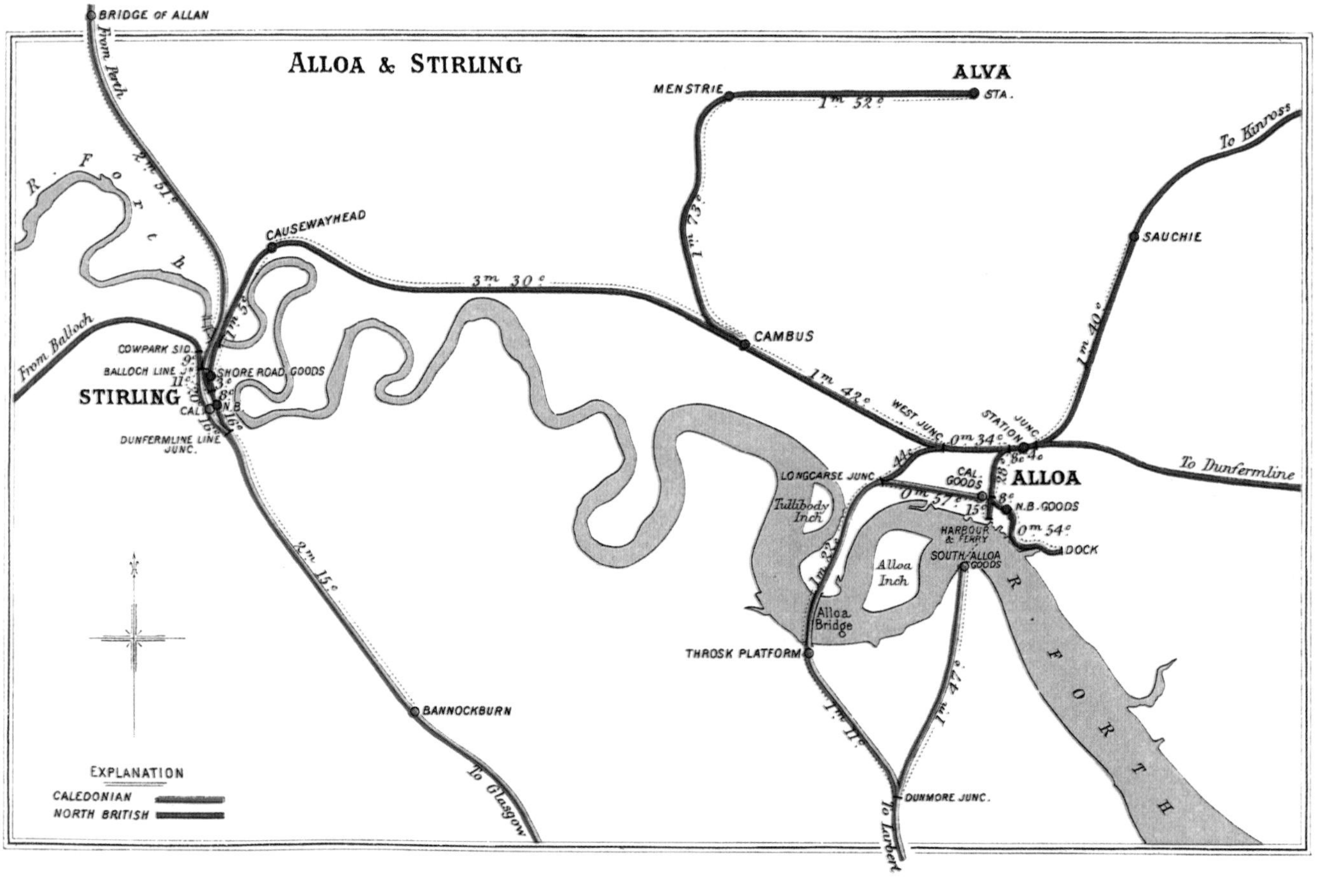

BRIDGE OF ALLAN
From Perth
2m 51c
R. Forth
CAUSEWAYHEAD
3m 30c
MENSTRIE
ALVA
STA.
1m 52c
1m 73c
To Kinross
SAUCHIE
1m 40c
CAMBUS
From Balloch
COWPARK SID.
BALLOCH LINE Jn
SHORE ROAD GOODS
STIRLING
CAL.
N.B.
DUNFERMLINE LINE JUNC.
1m 42c
WEST JUNC.
0m 34c
STATION JUNC.
To Dunfermline
ALLOA
LONGCARSE JUNC.
CAL. GOODS
0m 57c
15c
N.B. GOODS
HARBOUR & FERRY
0m 54c
DOCK
Tullibody Inch
Alloa Inch
SOUTH ALLOA GOODS
R. FORTH
Alloa Bridge
THROSK PLATFORM
2m 15c
BANNOCKBURN
1m 11c
1m 47c
DUNMORE JUNC.
To Larbert
To Glasgow

EXPLANATION
CALEDONIAN
NORTH BRITISH

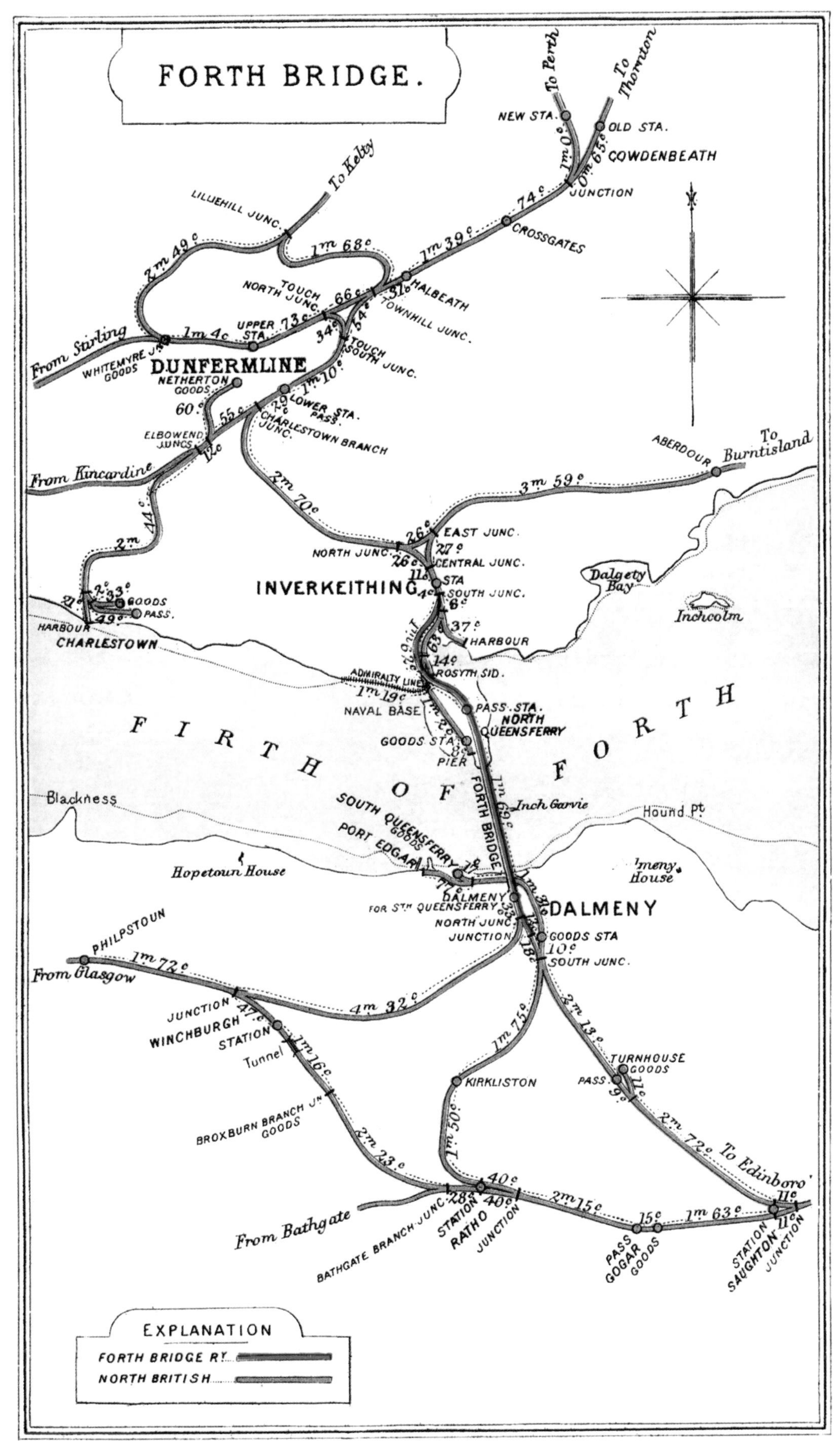

FORTH BRIDGE.
To Perth
To Thornton
NEW STA.
OLD STA.
COWDENBEATH
JUNCTION
To Kelty
LILLIEHILL JUNC.
CROSSGATES
HALBEATH
TOUCH NORTH JUNC.
TOWNHILL JUNC.
TOUCH SOUTH JUNC.
From Stirling
WHITEMYRE JN. GOODS
UPPER STA.
DUNFERMLINE
NETHERTON GOODS
LOWER STA. PASS.
CHARLESTOWN BRANCH JUNC.
ELBOWEND JUNCS
From Kincardine
ABERDOUR
To Burntisland
EAST JUNC.
NORTH JUNC.
CENTRAL JUNC.
INVERKEITHING
STA
SOUTH JUNC.
Dalgety Bay
Inchcolm
GOODS
PASS.
HARBOUR
CHARLESTOWN
HARBOUR
ADMIRALTY LINE
ROSYTH SID.
NAVAL BASE
PASS. STA.
NORTH QUEENSFERRY
GOODS STA.
PIER
FIRTH OF FORTH
FORTH BRIDGE
Blackness
Inch Garvie
Hound Pt.
SOUTH QUEENSFERRY GOODS
PORT EDGAR
Hopetoun House
Dalmeny House
DALMENY
FOR STN QUEENSFERRY
NORTH JUNC.
JUNCTION
GOODS STA
SOUTH JUNC.
PHILPSTOUN
From Glasgow
JUNCTION
WINCHBURGH
STATION
Tunnel
TURNHOUSE GOODS
PASS.
KIRKLISTON
BROXBURN BRANCH JN. GOODS
To Edinboro'
From Bathgate
BATHGATE BRANCH JUNC.
STATION
RATHO
JUNCTION
PASS
GOGAR
GOODS
STATION
SAUGHTON
JUNCTION
EXPLANATION
FORTH BRIDGE RY.
NORTH BRITISH

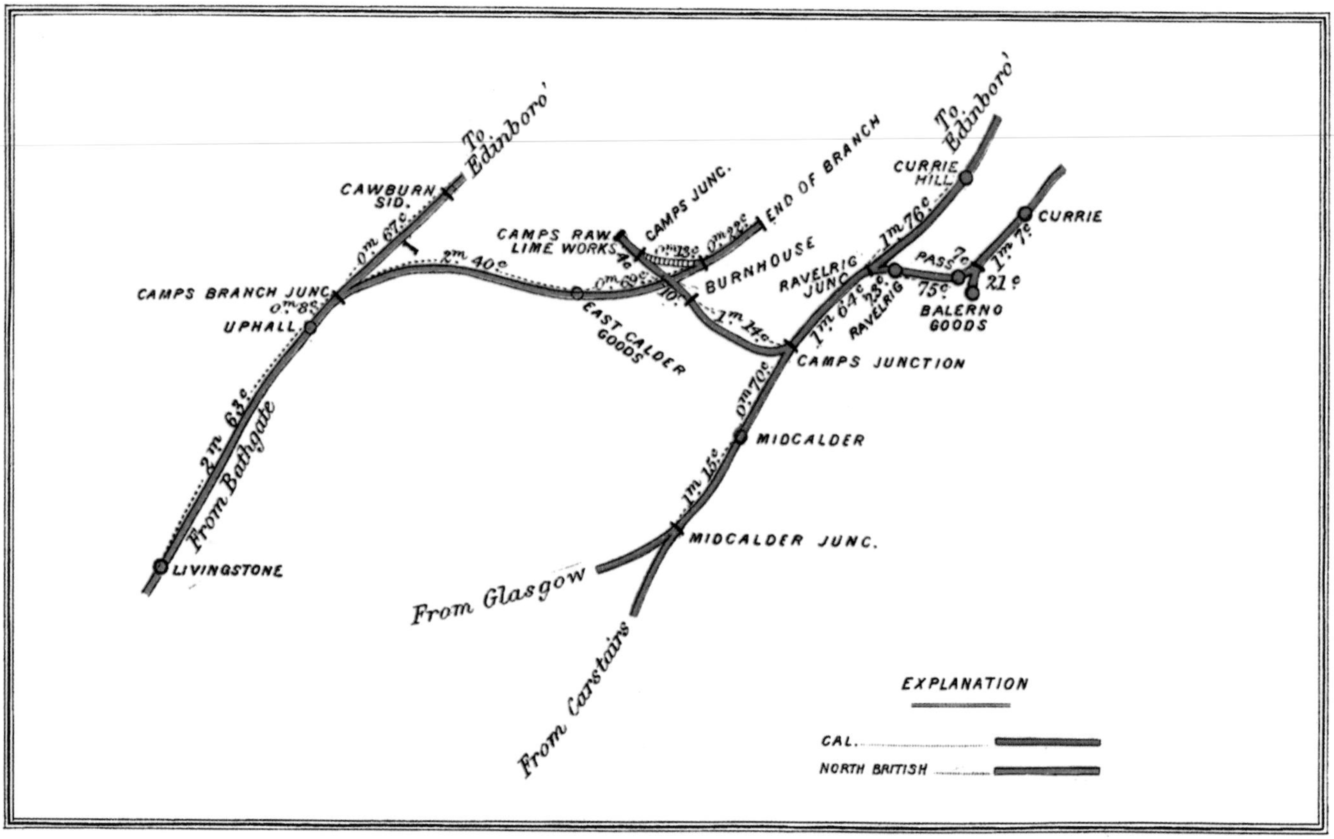

Midcalder

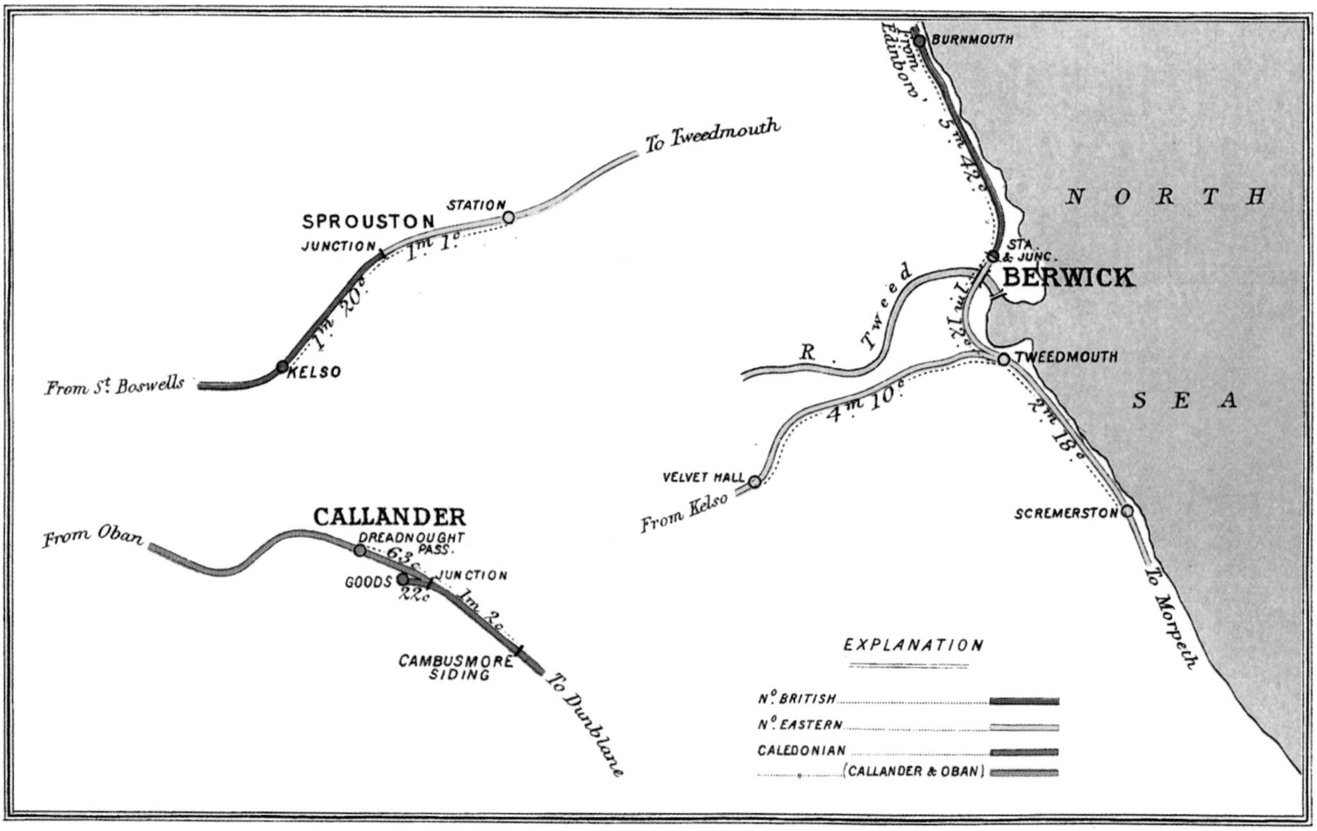

Sprouston–Callander–Berwick

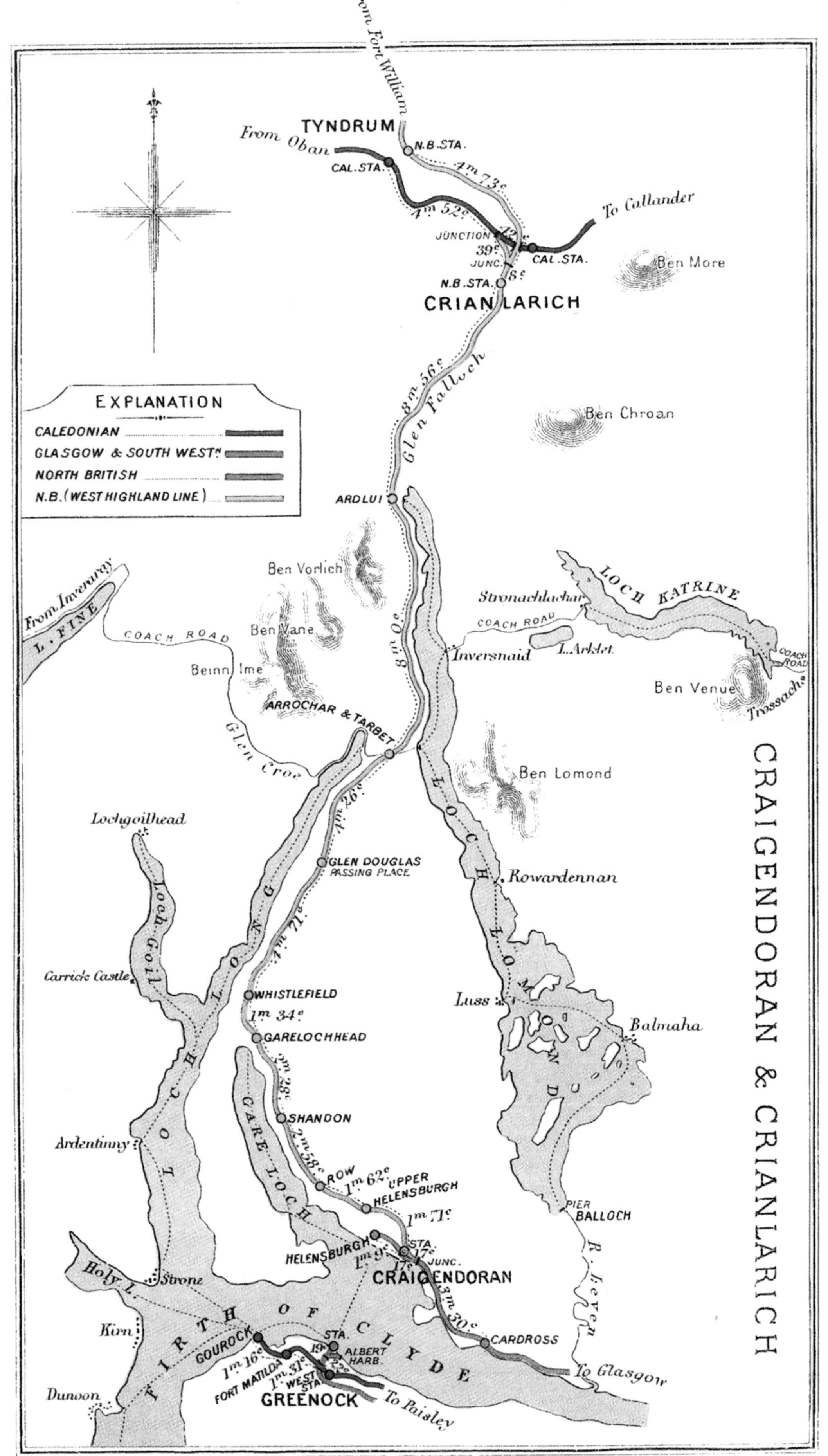
CRAIGENDORAN & CRIANLARICH
EXPLANATION
CALEDONIAN
GLASGOW & SOUTH WESTN.
NORTH BRITISH
N.B. (WEST HIGHLAND LINE)
From Fort William
TYNDRUM
From Oban
N.B. STA.
CAL. STA.
To Callander
JUNCTION
JUNC.
CAL. STA.
N.B. STA.
CRIANLARICH
Ben More
Glen Falloch
Ben Chroan
ARDLUI
Ben Vorlich
Ben Vane
Beinn Ime
From Inveraray
L. FINE
COACH ROAD
LOCH KATRINE
Stronachlachar
L. Arklet
Inversnaid
Ben Venue
Trossachs
ARROCHAR & TARBET
Glen Croe
Ben Lomond
Lochgoilhead
GLEN DOUGLAS PASSING PLACE
Rowardennan
Loch Goil
LOCH LONG
LOCH LOMOND
Carrick Castle
WHISTLEFIELD
Luss
GARELOCHHEAD
Balmaha
GARE LOCH
SHANDON
Ardentinny
ROW
UPPER HELENSBURGH
PIER
BALLOCH
HELENSBURGH
STA.
JUNC.
CRAIGENDORAN
R. Leven
Holy L.
Strone
FIRTH OF CLYDE
Kirn
GOUROCK
STA.
ALBERT HARB.
CARDROSS
To Glasgow
FORT MATILDA
WEST STA.
GREENOCK
To Paisley
Dunoon

1
2
3
4
5
A
B
C
D
E
F
G
Bass Rock
NORTH BERWICK
DIRLETON
EAST FORTUNE
EAST LINTON
DUNBAR
Loco. Shed
N.B.
INNERWICK
COCKBURNSPATH
HADDINGTON
St Abb's Head
GIFFORD
Penmanshiel Tun.
Summit
GRANTSHOUSE
EYEMOUTH
N.B.
RESTON
BURNMOUTH
AYTON
CHIRNSIDE
EDROM
DUNS
N.B.
BERWICK
Royal Border Bridge
TWEEDMOUTH
Loco. Shed
SCREMERSTON
B E R W I C K
MARCHMONT
N.E.
VELVET HALL
NORHAM
N.E.
LAUDER
GORDON
N.B.
GREENLAW
GOSWICK
Holy Island
TWIZELL
BEAL
EARLSTON
CARHAM
COLDSTREAM
SUNILAWS
SMEAFIELD
Thirty
SPROUSTON
N.E.
Sprouston Jc.
MINDRUM
Ravenswood Jc.
N.B.
KELSO
BELFORD
SEAHOUSES
MELROSE
ST BOSWELLS
Eildon Hills
Kelso Jc.
ROXBURGH
KIRKNEWTON
AKELD
LUCKER
NORTH SUNDERLAND
Lucker Watertroughs
N. Sun Lt.
RUTHERFORD
MAXTON
KIRKBANK
WOOLER
NEWHAM
CHATHILL
N.E.
NISBET
BELSES
ILDERTON
CHRISTON BANK
N.B.
JEDFOOT
JEDBURGH
WOOPERTON
HASSENDEAN
R O X B U R G H
HEDGELEY
LITTLE MILL
Loco. Shed
GLANTON
LONGHOUGHTON
HAWICK
ALNWICK
WHITTINGHAM
ALNMOUTH
Loco. Shed
STOBS CAMP
STOBS
EDLINGHAM
WARKWORTH
SHANKEND
AMBLE
N.E.
ROTHBURY
N.B.
ACKLINGTON
BROOMHILL
Whitrope Tun.
Summit
BRINKBURN
Amble Branch Jc.
Peel Fell
CHEVINGTON
SAUGHTREE
RICCARTON JUNC.
DEADWATER
N O R T H U M B E R L A N D
N.B.
FONTBURN HALT
KIELDER
EWESLEY
WIDDRINGTON
Twenty seven

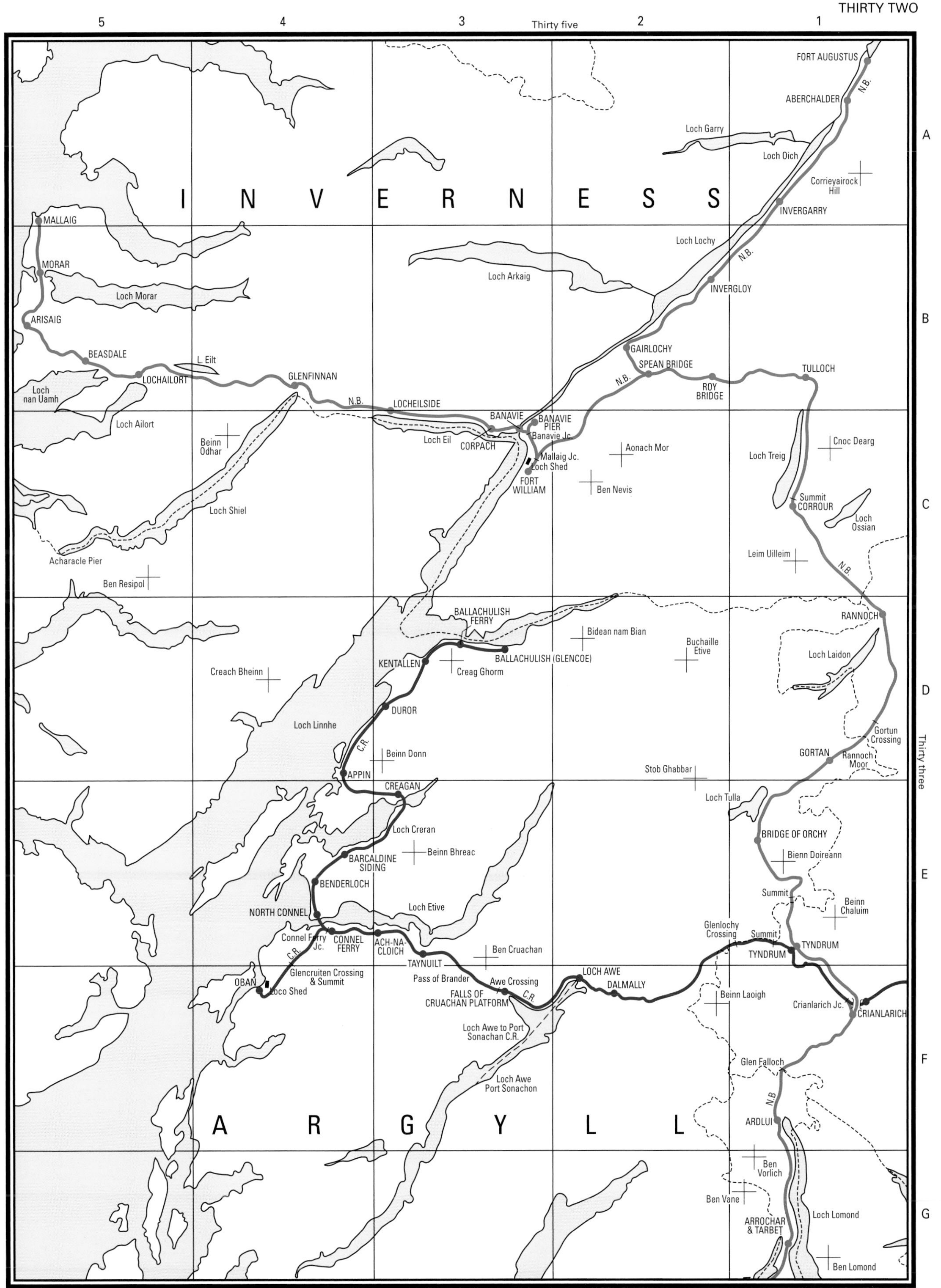

5
4
3
Thirty five
2
1
A
B
C
D
E
F
G
Thirty three
Twenty nine
I N V E R N E S S
A R G Y L L
FORT AUGUSTUS
ABERCHALDER
N.B.
Loch Garry
Loch Oich
Corrieyairock Hill
INVERGARRY
MALLAIG
MORAR
Loch Morar
ARISAIG
BEASDALE
L. Eilt
LOCHAILORT
GLENFINNAN
Loch nan Uamh
Loch Ailort
LOCHEILSIDE
Loch Lochy
Loch Arkaig
INVERGLOY
GAIRLOCHY
SPEAN BRIDGE
ROY BRIDGE
TULLOCH
BANAVIE
BANAVIE PIER
Banavie Jc.
Loch Eil
CORPACH
Mallaig Jc.
Loch Shed
FORT WILLIAM
Aonach Mor
Ben Nevis
Loch Treig
Cnoc Dearg
Summit
CORROUR
Loch Ossian
Beinn Odhar
Loch Shiel
Acharacle Pier
Ben Resipol
Leim Uilleim
BALLACHULISH FERRY
Bidean nam Bian
Buchaille Etive
RANNOCH
KENTALLEN
Creag Ghorm
BALLACHULISH (GLENCOE)
Creach Bheinn
Loch Laidon
DUROR
Loch Linnhe
C.R.
Beinn Donn
APPIN
CREAGAN
Gortun Crossing
GORTAN
Rannoch Moor
Stob Ghabbar
Loch Tulla
Loch Creran
BRIDGE OF ORCHY
BARCALDINE SIDING
Beinn Bhreac
Bienn Doireann
BENDERLOCH
Summit
Beinn Chaluim
NORTH CONNEL
Loch Etive
Connel Ferry Jc.
CONNEL FERRY
ACH-NA-CLOICH
Ben Cruachan
Glenlochy Crossing
TYNDRUM
TAYNUILT
Glencruiten Crossing & Summit
OBAN
Loco Shed
Pass of Brander
Awe Crossing
FALLS OF CRUACHAN PLATFORM
LOCH AWE
DALMALLY
Beinn Laoigh
Crianlarich Jc.
CRIANLARICH
Loch Awe to Port Sonachan C.R.
Glen Falloch
Loch Awe Port Sonachon
ARDLUI
Ben Vorlich
Ben Vane
Loch Lomond
ARROCHAR & TARBET
Ben Lomond

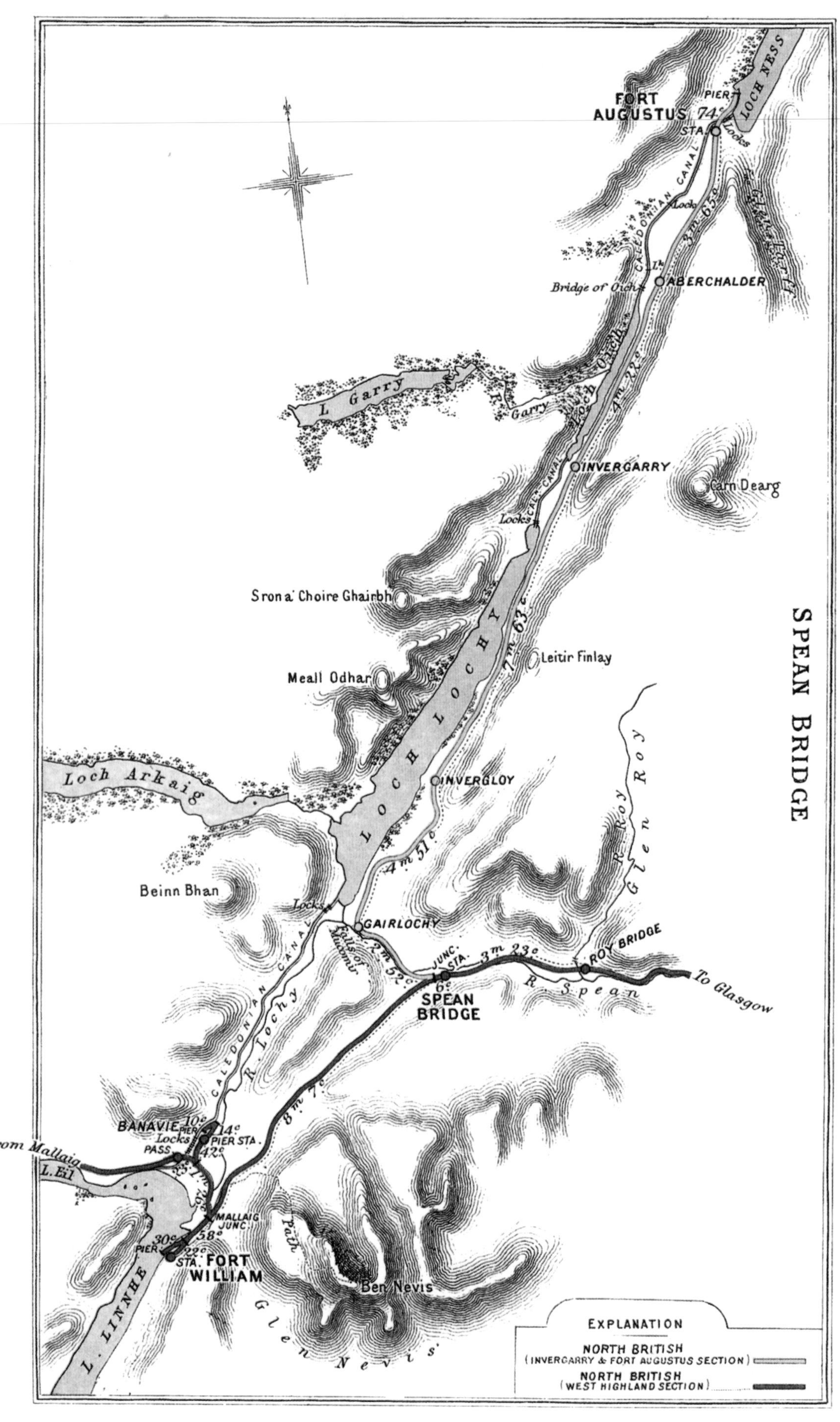


SPEAN BRIDGE

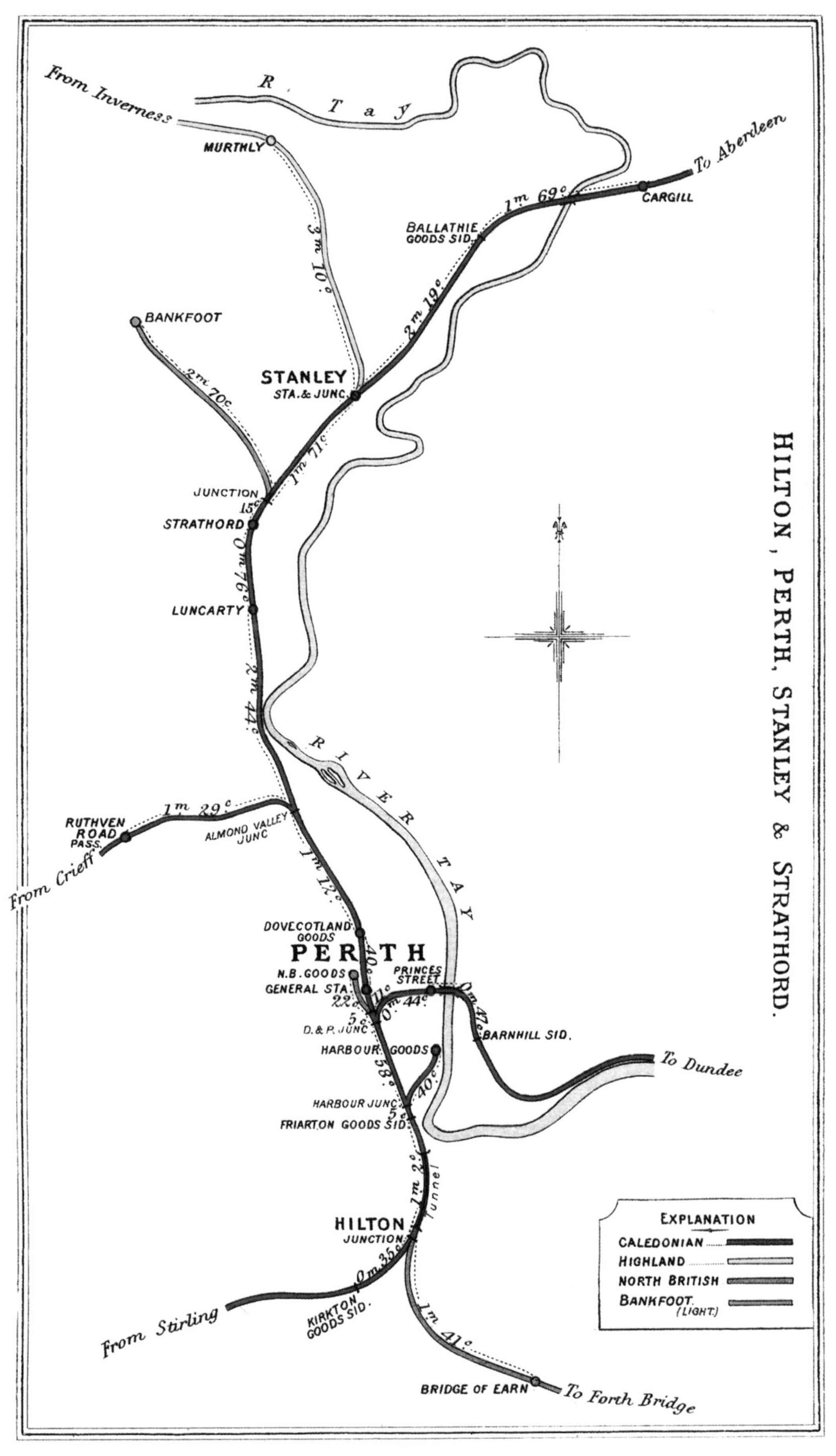
HILTON, PERTH, STANLEY & STRATHORD.
From Inverness
R. Tay
MURTHLY
To Aberdeen
CARGILL
1m 69c
BALLATHIE GOODS SID.
3m 10c
2m 19c
BANKFOOT
STANLEY
STA. & JUNC.
2m 70c
1m 71c
JUNCTION
15c
STRATHORD
0m 76c
LUNCARTY
2m 44c
RIVER TAY
RUTHVEN ROAD PASS.
1m 29c
ALMOND VALLEY JUNC
From Crieff
1m 12c
DOVECOTLAND GOODS
PERTH
N.B. GOODS
GENERAL STA.
PRINCES STREET
0m 44c
0m 47c
D. & P. JUNC
BARNHILL SID.
HARBOUR GOODS
To Dundee
HARBOUR JUNC
FRIARTON GOODS SID.
1m 2c
Tunnel
HILTON
JUNCTION
0m 35c
From Stirling
KIRKTON GOODS SID.
1m 41c
BRIDGE OF EARN
To Forth Bridge
EXPLANATION
CALEDONIAN
HIGHLAND
NORTH BRITISH
BANKFOOT (LIGHT)

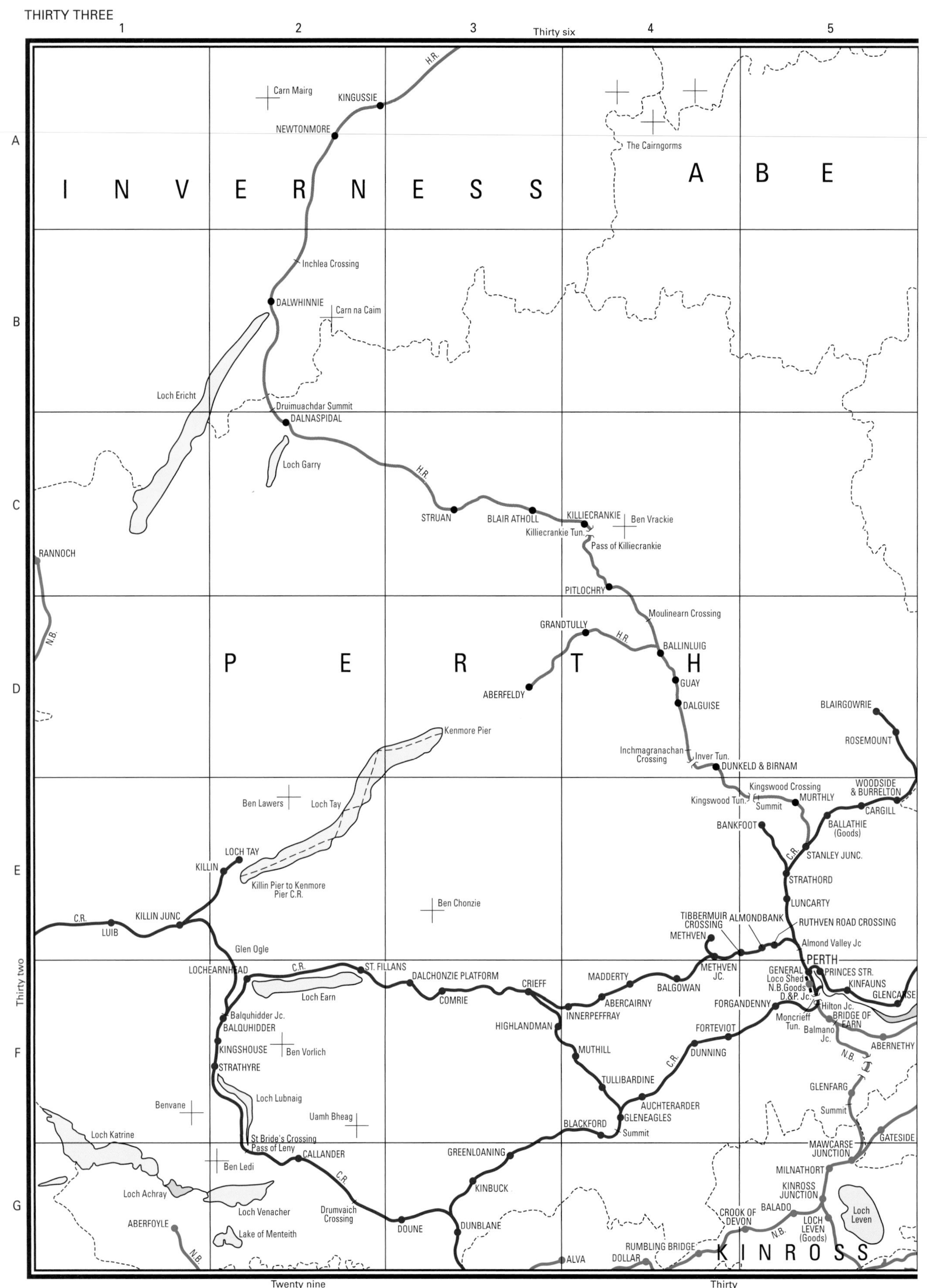

1
2
3
Thirty six
4
5
A
B
C
D
E
F
G
Thirty two
Twenty nine
Thirty
I N V E R N E S S
A B E
P E R T H
K I N R O S S
H.R.
Carn Mairg
KINGUSSIE
NEWTONMORE
The Cairngorms
Inchlea Crossing
DALWHINNIE
Carn na Caim
Loch Ericht
Druimuachdar Summit
DALNASPIDAL
Loch Garry
STRUAN
BLAIR ATHOLL
KILLIECRANKIE
Ben Vrackie
Killiecrankie Tun.
Pass of Killiecrankie
RANNOCH
PITLOCHRY
Moulinearn Crossing
GRANDTULLY
BALLINLUIG
N.B.
ABERFELDY
GUAY
DALGUISE
BLAIRGOWRIE
Kenmore Pier
ROSEMOUNT
Inchmagranachan Crossing
Inver Tun.
DUNKELD & BIRNAM
Kingswood Crossing
WOODSIDE & BURRELTON
Kingswood Tun.
Summit
MURTHLY
CARGILL
Ben Lawers
Loch Tay
BANKFOOT
BALLATHIE (Goods)
C.R.
STANLEY JUNC.
LOCH TAY
KILLIN
Killin Pier to Kenmore Pier C.R.
STRATHORD
LUNCARTY
Ben Chonzie
LUIB
KILLIN JUNC.
TIBBERMUIR CROSSING
ALMONDBANK
RUTHVEN ROAD CROSSING
METHVEN
Almond Valley Jc
Glen Ogle
LOCHEARNHEAD
ST. FILLANS
DALCHONZIE PLATFORM
METHVEN JC.
PERTH
GENERAL
PRINCES STR.
Loco Shed
N.B.Goods
KINFAUNS
D.&P. Jc.
GLENCARSE
Loch Earn
CRIEFF
MADDERTY
BALGOWAN
COMRIE
ABERCAIRNY
FORGANDENNY
Hilton Jc.
Balquhidder Jc.
INNERPEFFRAY
Moncrieff Tun.
BRIDGE OF EARN
BALQUHIDDER
HIGHLANDMAN
FORTEVIOT
Balmano Jc.
KINGSHOUSE
Ben Vorlich
MUTHILL
DUNNING
ABERNETHY
STRATHYRE
TULLIBARDINE
GLENFARG
Loch Lubnaig
Benvane
AUCHTERARDER
Summit
Uamh Bheag
BLACKFORD
GLENEAGLES
Summit
Loch Katrine
St Bride's Crossing
Pass of Leny
CALLANDER
GREENLOANING
MAWCARSE JUNCTION
GATESIDE
Ben Ledi
MILNATHORT
KINBUCK
KINROSS JUNCTION
Loch Achray
Loch Venacher
Drumvaich Crossing
BALADO
Loch Leven
CROOK OF DEVON
ABERFOYLE
DOUNE
DUNBLANE
LOCH LEVEN (Goods)
Lake of Menteith
RUMBLING BRIDGE
ALVA
DOLLAR

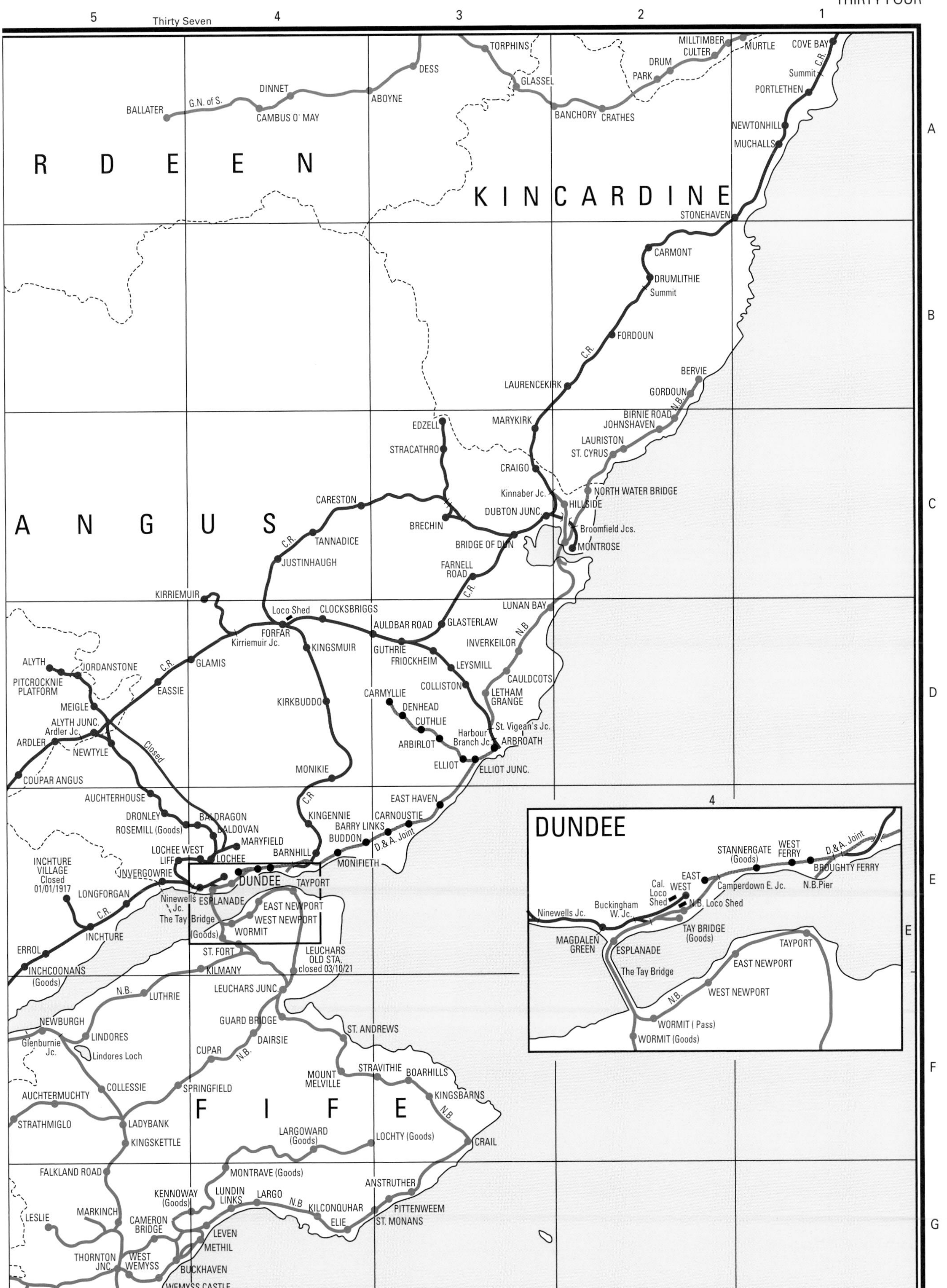
5
Thirty Seven
4
3
2
1
A
B
C
D
E
F
G
BALLATER
G.N. of S.
DINNET
CAMBUS O' MAY
ABOYNE
DESS
TORPHINS
GLASSEL
BANCHORY
CRATHES
PARK
DRUM
MILLTIMBER
CULTER
MURTLE
COVE BAY
Summit
C.R.
PORTLETHEN
NEWTONHILL
MUCHALLS
R D E E N
KINCARDINE
STONEHAVEN
CARMONT
DRUMLITHIE
Summit
FORDOUN
C.R.
LAURENCEKIRK
BERVIE
GORDOUN
N.B.
BIRNIE ROAD
JOHNSHAVEN
LAURISTON
ST. CYRUS
MARYKIRK
EDZELL
STRACATHRO
CRAIGO
Kinnaber Jc.
NORTH WATER BRIDGE
DUBTON JUNC.
HILLSIDE
Broomfield Jcs.
MONTROSE
CARESTON
BRECHIN
BRIDGE OF DUN
A N G U S
C.R.
TANNADICE
JUSTINHAUGH
FARNELL ROAD
C.R.
KIRRIEMUIR
Loco Shed
CLOCKSBRIGGS
FORFAR
Kirriemuir Jc.
KINGSMUIR
AULDBAR ROAD
GLASTERLAW
LUNAN BAY
N.B.
INVERKEILOR
GUTHRIE
FRIOCKHEIM
LEYSMILL
COLLISTON
CAULDCOTS
LETHAM GRANGE
ALYTH
JORDANSTONE
C.R.
GLAMIS
PITCROCKNIE PLATFORM
EASSIE
MEIGLE
KIRKBUDDO
CARMYLLIE
DENHEAD
CUTHLIE
ARBIRLOT
Harbour Branch Jc.
St. Vigean's Jc.
ARBROATH
ELLIOT
ELLIOT JUNC.
ALYTH JUNC.
Ardler Jc.
ARDLER
NEWTYLE
Closed
COUPAR ANGUS
MONIKIE
C.R
AUCHTERHOUSE
DRONLEY
ROSEMILL (Goods)
BALDRAGON
BALDOVAN
MARYFIELD
KINGENNIE
EAST HAVEN
CARNOUSTIE
BARRY LINKS
BUDDON
D.& A. Joint
BARNHILL
MONIFIETH
LOCHEE WEST
LIFF
LOCHEE
INCHTURE VILLAGE Closed 01/01/1917
INVERGOWRIE
DUNDEE
TAYPORT
LONGFORGAN
Ninewells Jc.
ESPLANADE
EAST NEWPORT
C.R.
The Tay Bridge
WEST NEWPORT
INCHTURE
(Goods)
WORMIT
ERROL
ST. FORT
LEUCHARS OLD STA. closed 03/10/21
INCHCOONANS (Goods)
KILMANY
LEUCHARS JUNC.
N.B.
LUTHRIE
NEWBURGH
GUARD BRIDGE
LINDORES
Glenburnie Jc.
Lindores Loch
DAIRSIE
ST. ANDREWS
CUPAR
N.B.
MOUNT MELVILLE
STRAVITHIE
BOARHILLS
KINGSBARNS
N.B.
AUCHTERMUCHTY
COLLESSIE
SPRINGFIELD
F I F E
STRATHMIGLO
LADYBANK
KINGSKETTLE
LARGOWARD (Goods)
LOCHY (Goods)
CRAIL
FALKLAND ROAD
MONTRAVE (Goods)
ANSTRUTHER
KENNOWAY (Goods)
LUNDIN LINKS
LARGO
N.B
KILCONQUHAR
PITTENWEEM
ELIE
ST. MONANS
LESLIE
MARKINCH
CAMERON BRIDGE
LEVEN
METHIL
THORNTON JNC.
WEST WEMYSS
BUCKHAVEN
WEMYSS CASTLE
4
DUNDEE
STANNERGATE (Goods)
WEST FERRY
D.&A. Joint
BROUGHTY FERRY
N.B.Pier
EAST
WEST
Cal. Loco Shed
Camperdown E. Jc.
N.B. Loco Shed
Buckingham W. Jc.
Ninewells Jc.
TAY BRIDGE (Goods)
MAGDALEN GREEN
ESPLANADE
TAYPORT
EAST NEWPORT
The Tay Bridge
N.B.
WEST NEWPORT
WORMIT ( Pass)
WORMIT (Goods)
E

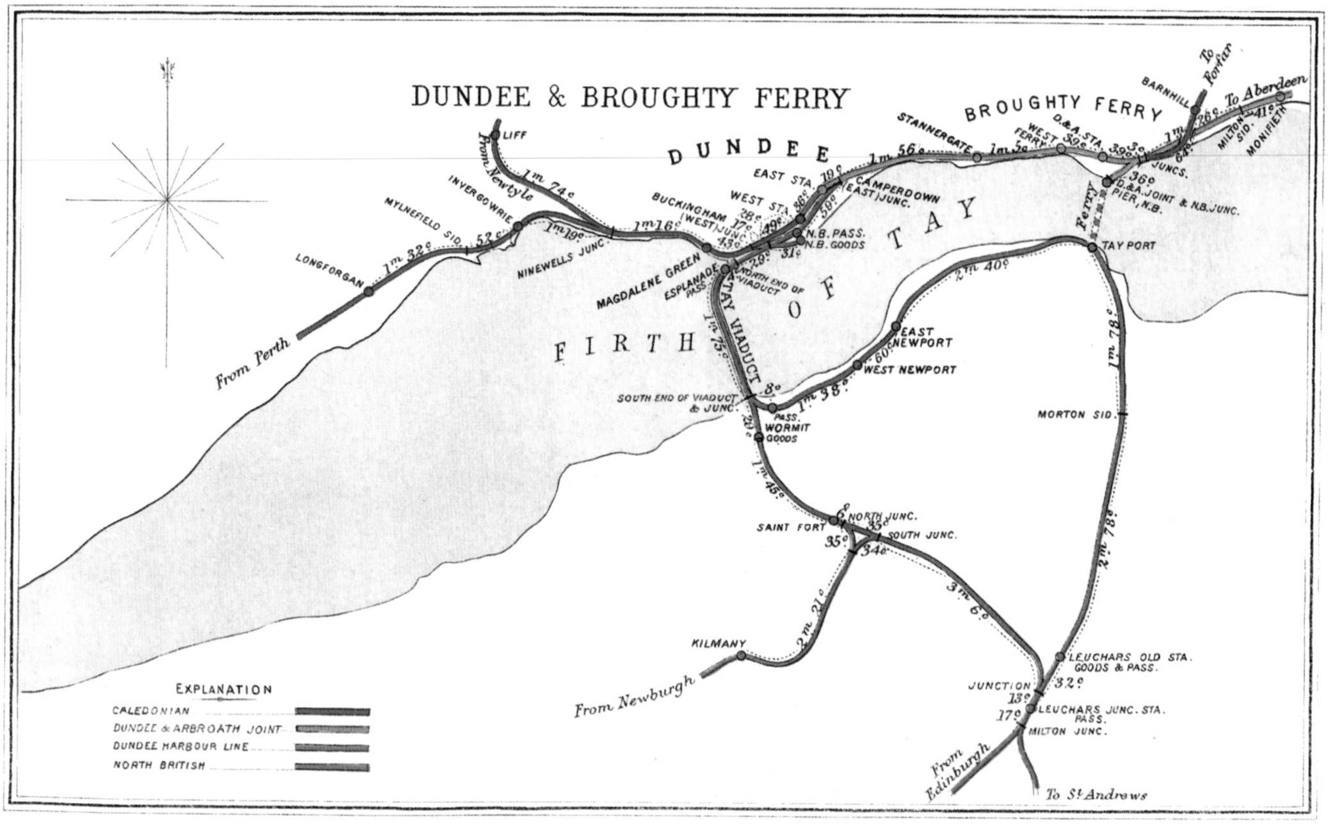

## THIRTY FOUR

## DUNDEE & BROUGHTY FERRY

DUNDEE
BROUGHTY FERRY
FIRTH OF TAY
LIFF
From Newtyle
INVERGOWRIE
MYLNEFIELD SID.
LONGFORGAN
From Perth
NINEWELLS JUNC.
BUCKINGHAM (WEST) JUNC.
WEST STA.
EAST STA.
CAMPERDOWN (EAST) JUNC.
N.B. PASS.
N.B. GOODS
MAGDALENE GREEN
ESPLANADE PASS.
NORTH END OF VIADUCT
TAY VIADUCT
STANNERGATE
WEST FERRY
D.&A. STA.
JUNCS.
D.&A. PIER
D.&A. JOINT & N.B. JUNC.
PIER, N.B.
BARNHILL
To Forfar
To Aberdeen
MILTON SID.
MONIFIETH
Ferry
TAY PORT
EAST NEWPORT
WEST NEWPORT
SOUTH END OF VIADUCT & JUNC.
PASS.
WORMIT GOODS
MORTON SID.
SAINT FORT
NORTH JUNC.
SOUTH JUNC.
KILMANY
From Newburgh
LEUCHARS OLD STA. GOODS & PASS.
JUNCTION
LEUCHARS JUNC. STA. PASS.
MILTON JUNC.
From Edinburgh
To St Andrews

EXPLANATION
CALEDONIAN
DUNDEE & ARBROATH JOINT
DUNDEE HARBOUR LINE
NORTH BRITISH

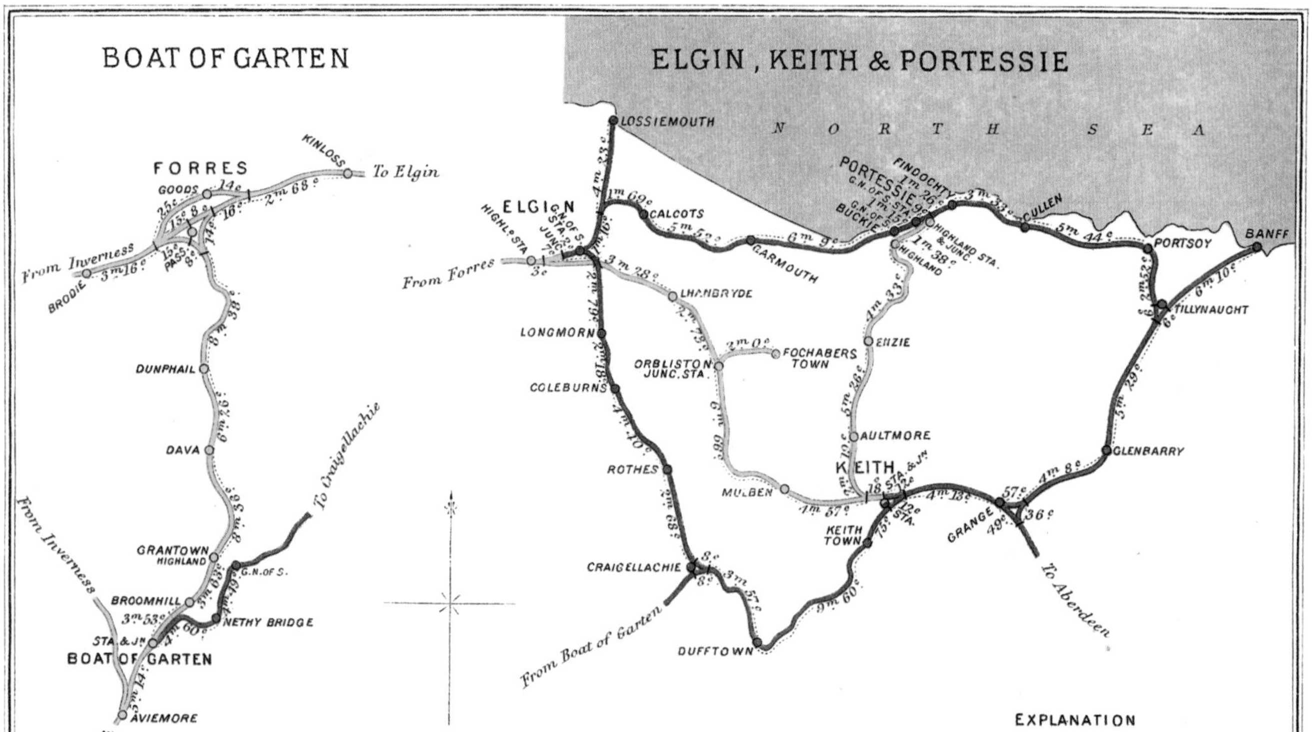

## BOAT OF GARTEN

FORRES
GOODS
PASS.
KINLOSS
To Elgin
From Inverness
BRODIE
DUNPHAIL
DAVA
GRANTOWN HIGHLAND
G.N. OF S.
To Craigellachie
From Inverness
BROOMHILL
NETHY BRIDGE
STA. & JN.
BOAT OF GARTEN
AVIEMORE
From Perth

## ELGIN, KEITH & PORTESSIE

NORTH SEA
LOSSIEMOUTH
ELGIN
HIGHL. STA.
G.N. OF S. STA. & JUNC.
From Forres
CALCOTS
GARMOUTH
LHANBRYDE
LONGMORN
COLEBURNS
ORBLISTON JUNC. STA.
FOCHABERS TOWN
ROTHES
MULBEN
CRAIGELLACHIE
From Boat of Garten
DUFFTOWN
FINDOCHTY
PORTESSIE
G.N. OF S. STA.
BUCKIE
HIGHLAND STA. & JUNC.
HIGHLAND
CULLEN
PORTSOY
BANFF
TILLYNAUGHT
ENZIE
AULTMORE
KEITH
STA. & JN.
KEITH TOWN
GRANGE
GLENBARRY
To Aberdeen

EXPLANATION
GREAT NORTH OF SCOTLAND
HIGHLAND

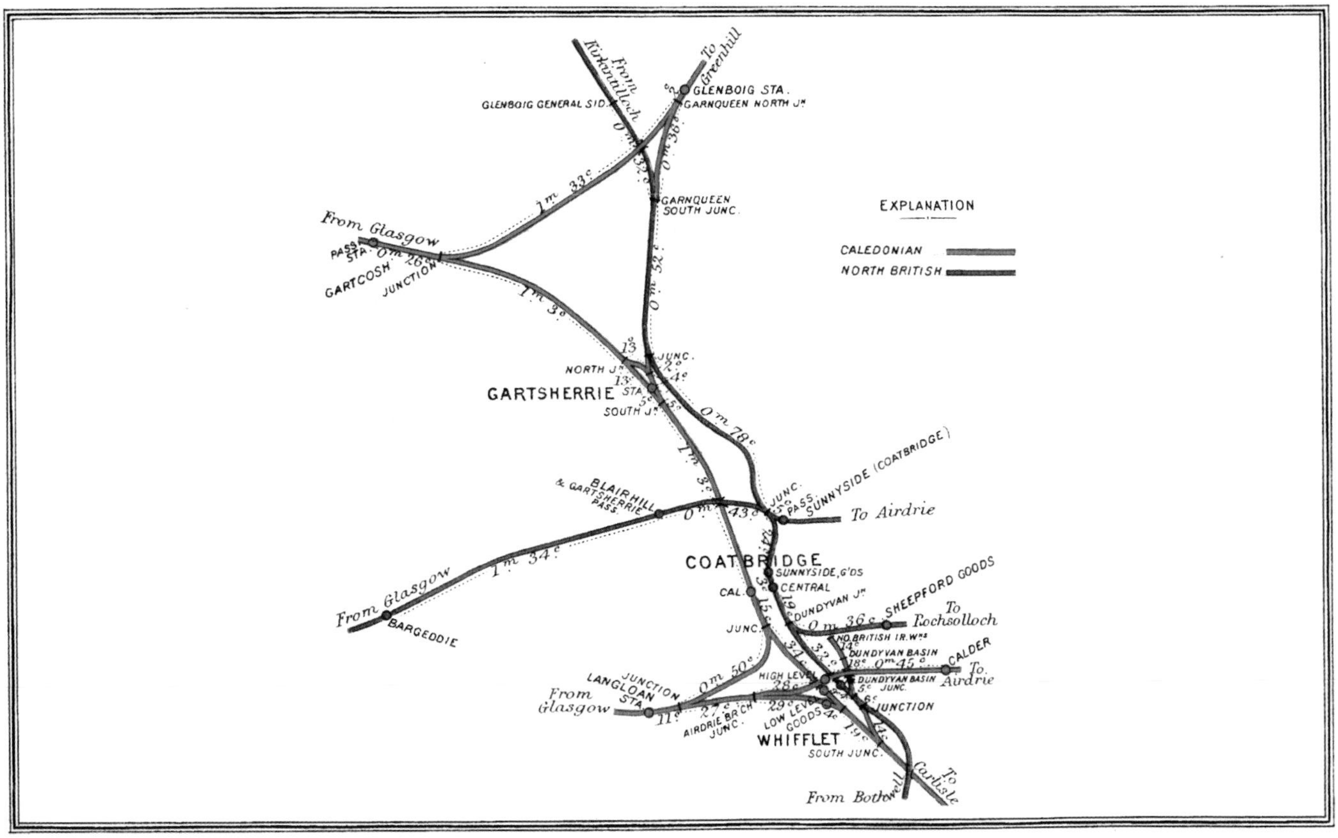

Gartsherrie–Coatbridge–Whifflet

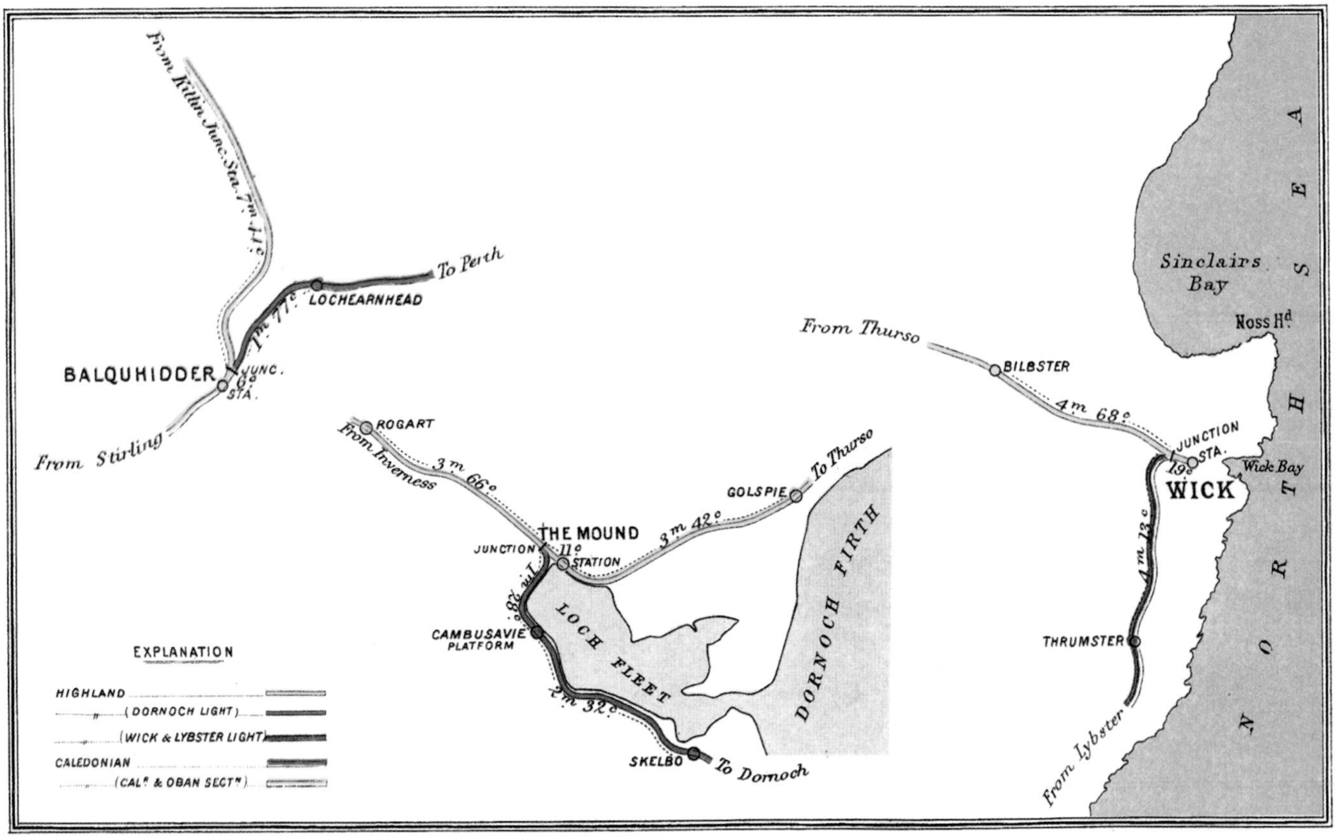

Balquhidder–The Mound–Wick

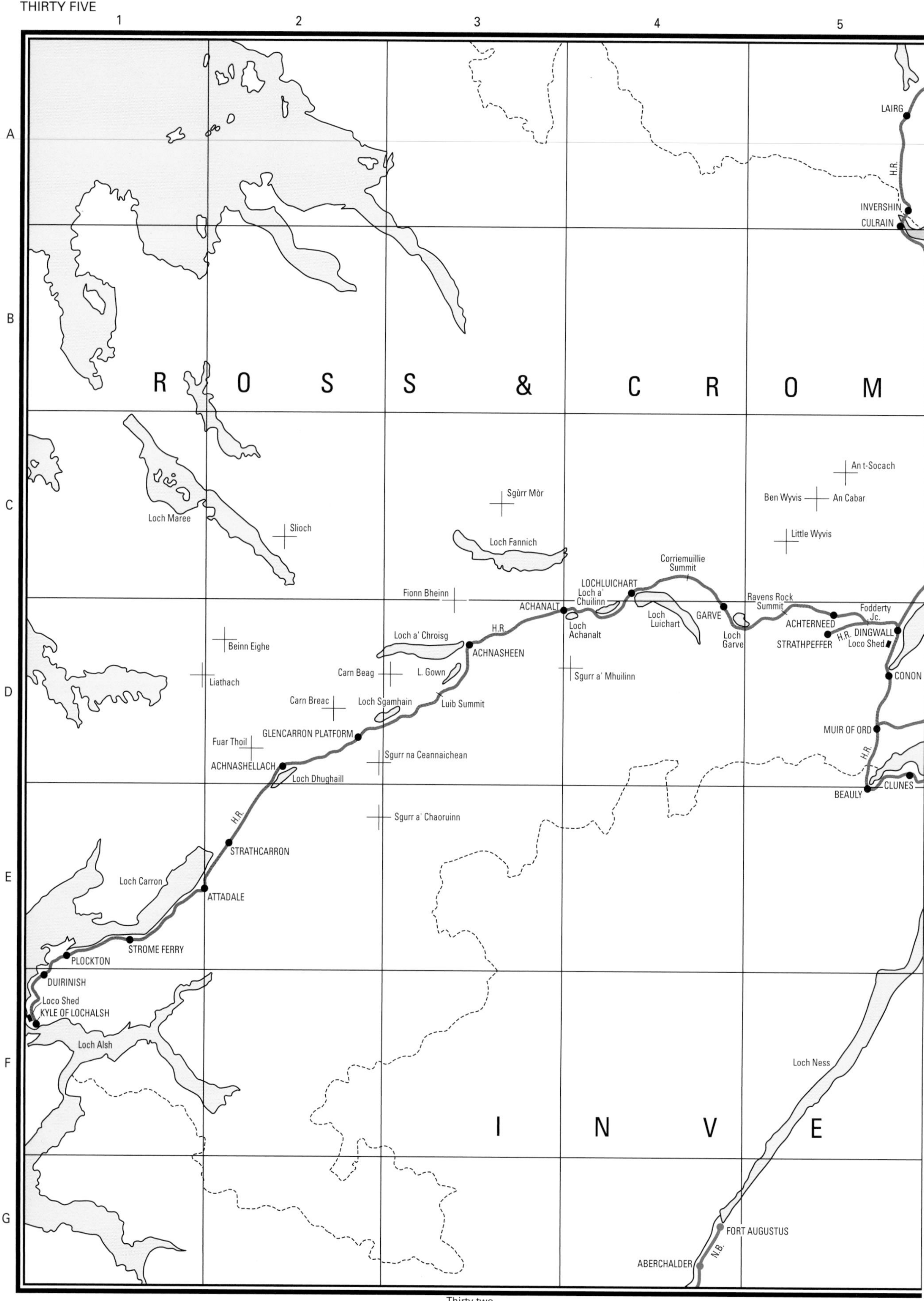
1
2
3
4
5
A
B
C
D
E
F
G
R O S S & C R O M
I N V E
LAIRG
H.R.
INVERSHIN
CULRAIN
An t-Socach
Ben Wyvis
An Cabar
Little Wyvis
Sgùrr Mòr
Loch Maree
Slioch
Loch Fannich
Corriemuillie Summit
LOCHLUICHART
Loch a' Chuilinn
Fionn Bheinn
ACHANALT
Loch Achanalt
Loch Luichart
GARVE
Loch Garve
Ravens Rock Summit
ACHTERNEED
Fodderty Jc.
DINGWALL
STRATHPEFFER
Loco Shed
Loch a' Chroisg
ACHNASHEEN
Beinn Eighe
Liathach
Carn Beag
L. Gown
Sgurr a' Mhuilinn
CONON
Carn Breac
Loch Sgamhain
Luib Summit
MUIR OF ORD
GLENCARRON PLATFORM
Fuar Thoil
Sgurr na Ceannaichean
ACHNASHELLACH
Loch Dhughaill
BEAULY
CLUNES
Sgurr a' Chaoruinn
STRATHCARRON
Loch Carron
ATTADALE
STROME FERRY
PLOCKTON
DUIRINISH
Loco Shed
KYLE OF LOCHALSH
Loch Alsh
Loch Ness
FORT AUGUSTUS
N.B.
ABERCHALDER
Thirty two

5
Thirty eight
4
3
2
1
A
B
C
D
E
F
G
Thirty seven
Thirty three
Summit
Acheilidh Crossing
ROGART
BRORA
H.R.
DUNROBIN (Private)
THE MOUND
GOLSPIE
CAMBUSAVIE PLATFORM
SKELBO
EMBO
DORNOCH
BONAR BRIDGE
Dornoch Firth
EDDERTON
TAIN
A R T Y
FEARN
NIGG
KILDARY
DELNY
ALNESS
INVERGORDON
SHORE
Cromarty Firth
NOVAR
FOULIS
MORAY FIRTH
LOSSIEMOUTH
HOPEMAN
BURGHEAD
COLTFIELD PLATFORM
CALCOTTS
URQUHART
GARMOUTH
SPEY BAY
Loco Shed
G.N. of S.
MOSSTOWIE
ALVES
ELGIN
KINLOSS
LHANBRYDE
BALNACOUL
FOCHABERS TOWN
LONGMORN
ORBLISTON JUNCTION
COLEBURN
BIRCHFIELD PLATFORM
Summit
ORTON
MULBEN
Closed
ROTHES
DANDALEITH
CRAIGELLACHIE
DRUM-MUIR
ABERLOUR
KNOCKANDO
CARRON
DUFFTOWN
FORRES
BRODIE
AULDEARN
NAIRN
FORTROSE
FORT GEORGE
AVOCH
MUNLOCHY
ALLANGRANGE
REDCASTLE
Inverness Firth
GOLLANFIELD JUNC.
DALCROSS
ALLANFEARN
CULLODEN MOOR
M O R A Y
DUNPHAIL
LENTRAN
BUNCHREW
INVERNESS
Loco Sheds
Lochgorm Works H.R.
N A I R N
DAVIOT
DAVA
Dava Summit
BLACKSBOAT
BALLINDALLOCH
ADVIE
Ben Rinnes
MOY
Loch Moy
TOMATIN
Carn Glas
CROMDALE
B A N F F
GRANTOWN-ON-SPEY
GRANTOWN-ON-SPEY
Slochd Summit
Slochd Crossing
BROOMHILL
NETHY BRIDGE
CARR BRIDGE
BOAT OF GARTEN
R N E S S
AVIEMORE
Loch Alvie
Monadhlaith Mountains
KINCRAIG
Loch Insh

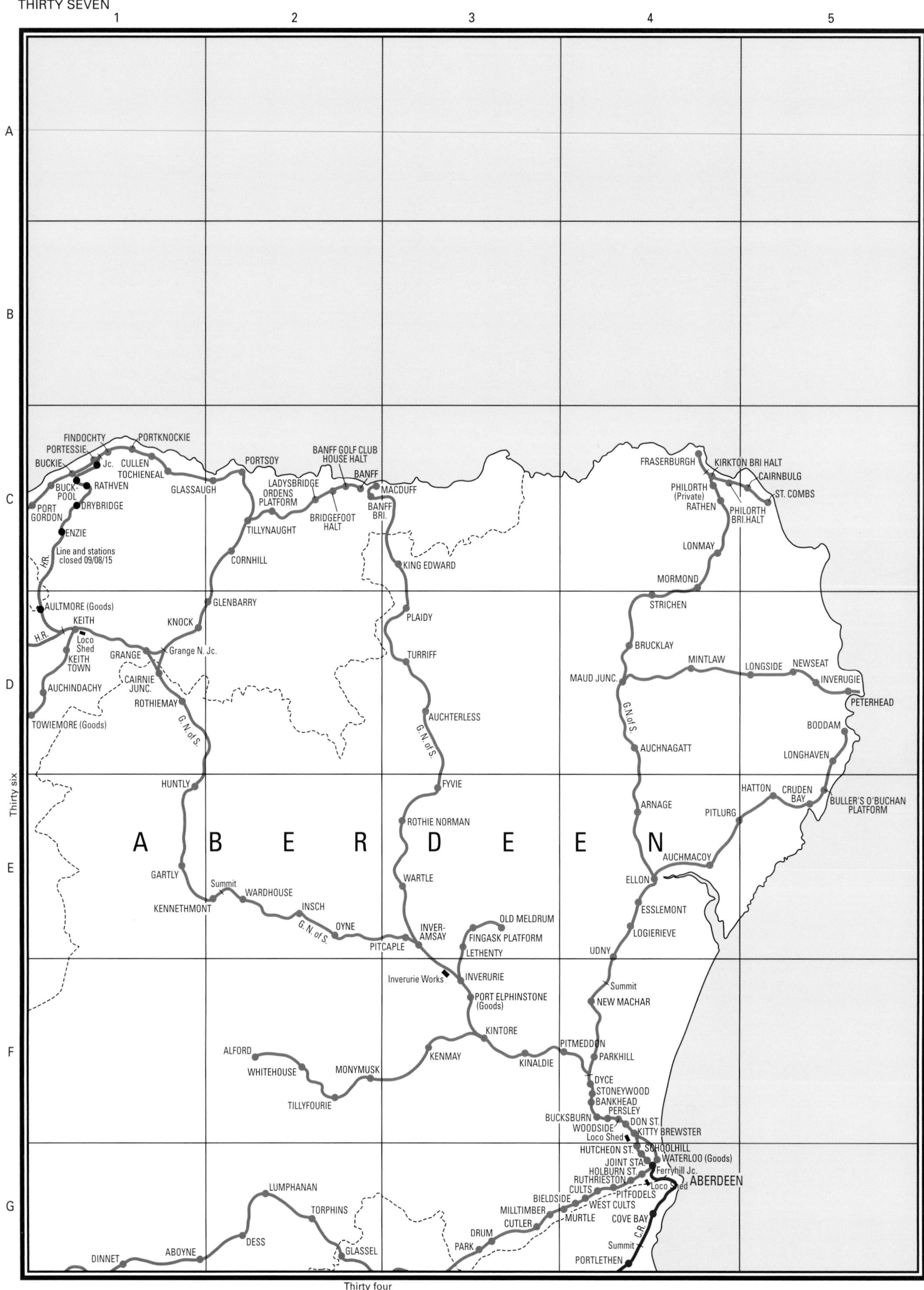
1
2
3
4
5
A
B
C
D
E
F
G
FINDOCHTY
PORTKNOCKIE
PORTESSIE
BUCKIE
Jc.
CULLEN
TOCHIENEAL
BUCK-POOL
RATHVEN
PORT GORDON
DRYBRIDGE
ENZIE
Line and stations closed 09/08/15
H.R.
AULTMORE (Goods)
KEITH
Loco Shed
KEITH TOWN
GRANGE
Grange N. Jc.
CAIRNIE JUNC.
AUCHINDACHY
ROTHIEMAY
TOWIEMORE (Goods)
GLASSAUGH
PORTSOY
TILLYNAUGHT
CORNHILL
GLENBARRY
KNOCK
LADYSBRIDGE
ORDENS PLATFORM
BANFF GOLF CLUB HOUSE HALT
BANFF
BRIDGEFOOT HALT
MACDUFF
BANFF BRI.
KING EDWARD
PLAIDY
TURRIFF
AUCHTERLESS
G.N. of S.
FYVIE
ROTHIE NORMAN
WARTLE
HUNTLY
GARTLY
KENNETHMONT
Summit
WARDHOUSE
INSCH
OYNE
PITCAPLE
INVER-AMSAY
OLD MELDRUM
FINGASK PLATFORM
LETHENTY
Inverurie Works
INVERURIE
PORT ELPHINSTONE (Goods)
KINTORE
KENMAY
KINALDIE
ALFORD
WHITEHOUSE
MONYMUSK
TILLYFOURIE
A B E R D E E N
FRASERBURGH
KIRKTON BRI HALT
CAIRNBULG
ST. COMBS
PHILORTH (Private)
RATHEN
PHILORTH BRI.HALT
LONMAY
MORMOND
STRICHEN
BRUCKLAY
MINTLAW
LONGSIDE
NEWSEAT
INVERUGIE
PETERHEAD
MAUD JUNC.
AUCHNAGATT
BODDAM
LONGHAVEN
HATTON
CRUDEN BAY
BULLER'S O'BUCHAN PLATFORM
PITLURG
ARNAGE
AUCHMACOY
ELLON
ESSLEMONT
LOGIERIEVE
UDNY
Summit
NEW MACHAR
PITMEDDEN
PARKHILL
DYCE
STONEYWOOD
BANKHEAD
PERSLEY
BUCKSBURN
DON ST.
WOODSIDE
KITTY BREWSTER
Loco Shed
SCHOOLHILL
HUTCHEON ST.
WATERLOO (Goods)
JOINT STA.
HOLBURN ST.
Ferryhill Jc.
RUTHRIESTON
ABERDEEN
CULTS
Loco Shed
PITFODELS
BIELDSIDE
WEST CULTS
MILLTIMBER
MURTLE
CUTLER
COVE BAY
DRUM
C.R.
PARK
Summit
PORTLETHEN
LUMPHANAN
TORPHINS
DESS
GLASSEL
ABOYNE
DINNET
Thirty six
Thirty four

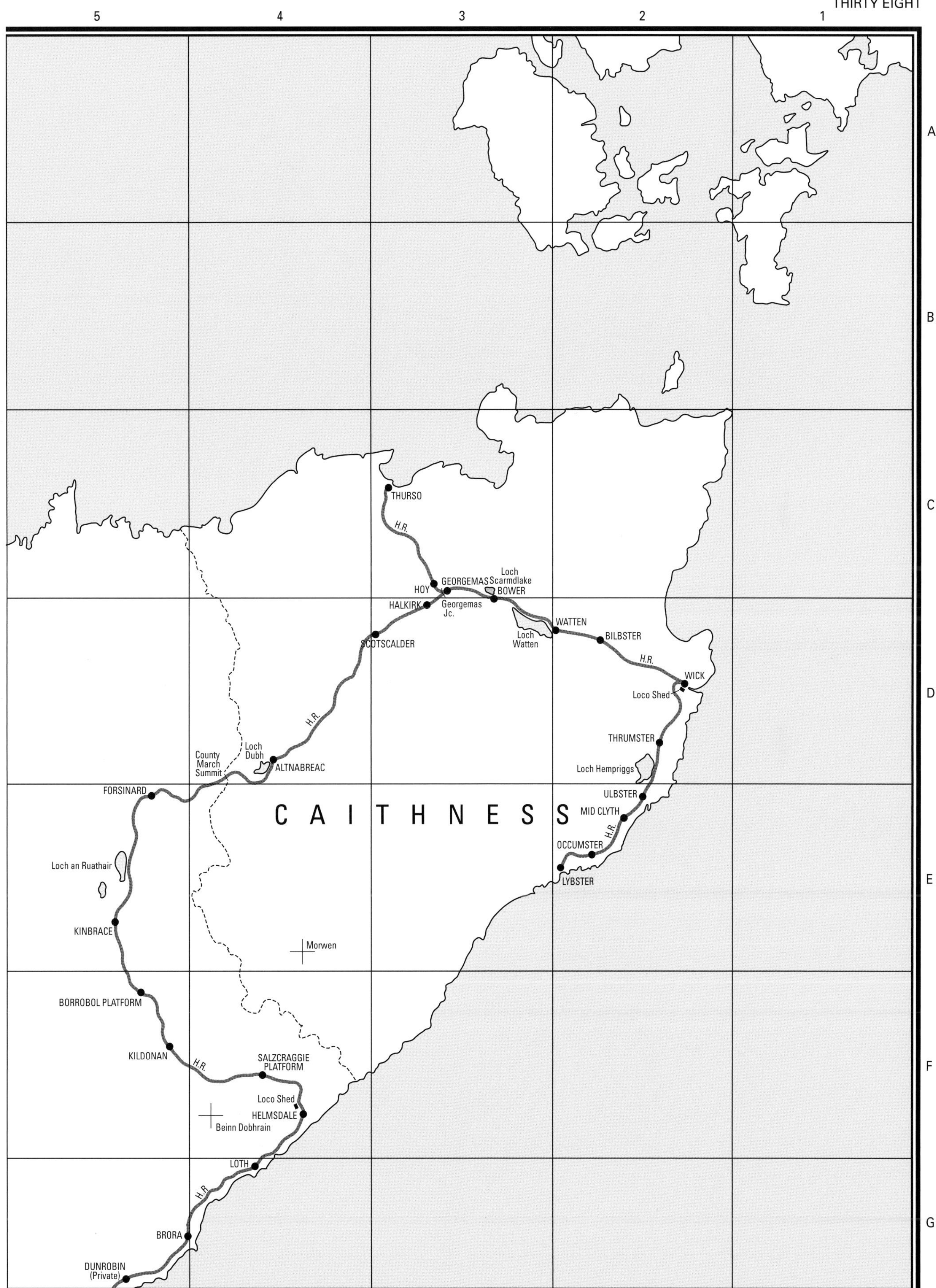
5
4
3
2
1
A
B
C
D
E
F
G
THURSO
H.R.
HOY
GEORGEMAS
Loch Scarmdlake
BOWER
HALKIRK
Georgemas Jc.
WATTEN
Loch Watten
BILBSTER
SCOTSCALDER
H.R.
WICK
Loco Shed
H.R.
THRUMSTER
Loch Dubh
County March Summit
ALTNABREAC
Loch Hempriggs
FORSINARD
ULBSTER
C A I T H N E S S
MID CLYTH
H.R.
OCCUMSTER
LYBSTER
Loch an Ruathair
KINBRACE
Morwen
BORROBOL PLATFORM
KILDONAN
H.R.
SALZCRAGGIE PLATFORM
Loco Shed
HELMSDALE
Beinn Dobhrain
LOTH
H.R.
BRORA
DUNROBIN (Private)

## THIRTY EIGHT

Thirty six

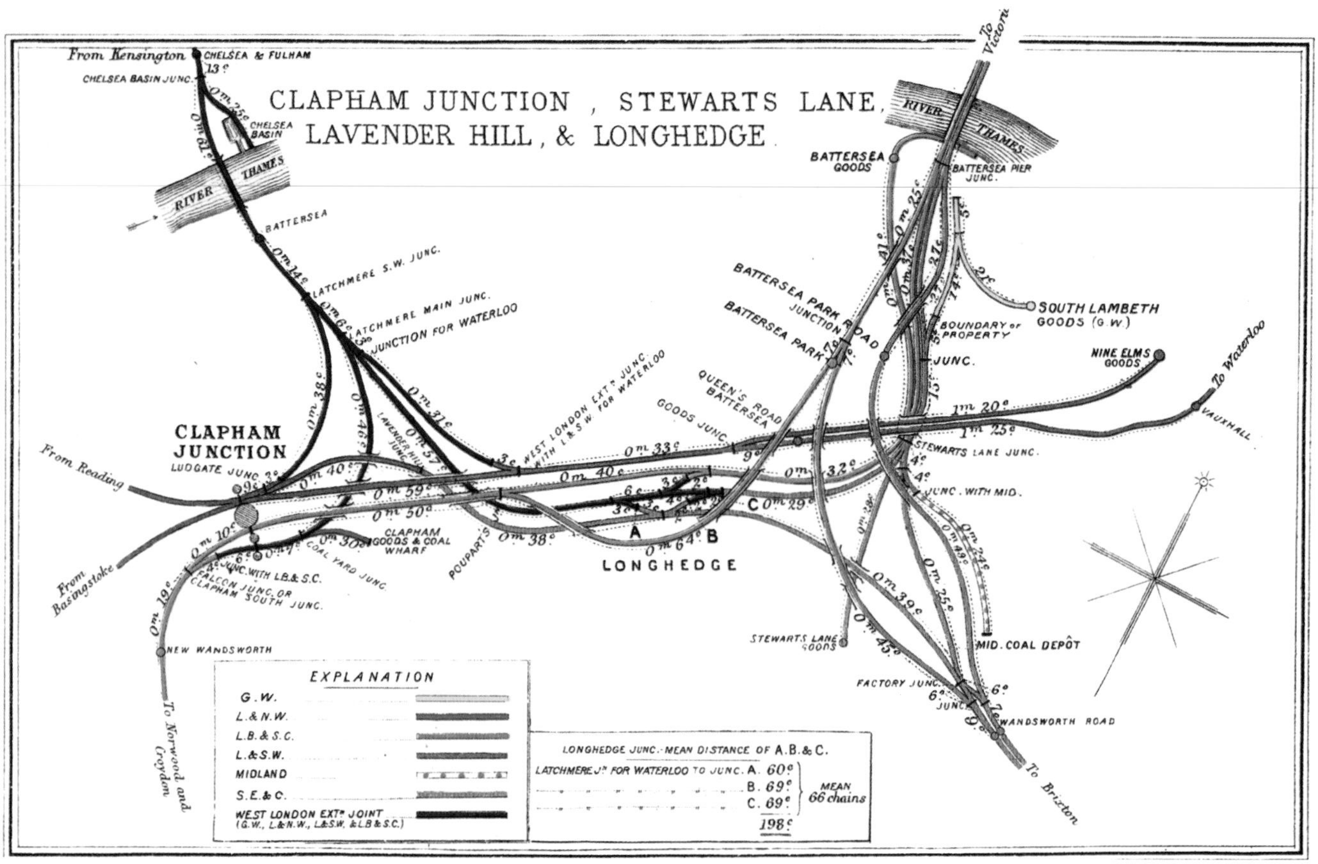

## CLAPHAM JUNCTION, STEWARTS LANE, LAVENDER HILL, & LONGHEDGE

From Kensington
CHELSEA & FULHAM
CHELSEA BASIN JUNC.
CHELSEA BASIN
RIVER THAMES
BATTERSEA
LATCHMERE S.W. JUNC.
LATCHMERE MAIN JUNC.
JUNCTION FOR WATERLOO
CLAPHAM JUNCTION
LUDGATE JUNC.
From Reading
From Basingstoke
LAVENDER HILL JUNC.
WEST LONDON EXT^N JUNC. WITH L.& S.W. FOR WATERLOO
CLAPHAM GOODS & COAL WHARF
COAL YARD JUNC.
JUNC. WITH LB.& S.C.
FALCON JUNC. OR CLAPHAM SOUTH JUNC.
NEW WANDSWORTH
To Norwood and Croydon
POUPARTS
LONGHEDGE
QUEEN'S ROAD BATTERSEA
GOODS JUNC.
BATTERSEA PARK JUNCTION
BATTERSEA PARK ROAD
BATTERSEA PARK
BATTERSEA GOODS
BATTERSEA PIER JUNC.
To Victoria
SOUTH LAMBETH GOODS (G.W.)
BOUNDARY OF PROPERTY
JUNC.
NINE ELMS GOODS
To Waterloo
VAUXHALL
STEWARTS LANE JUNC.
JUNC. WITH MID.
STEWARTS LANE GOODS
MID. COAL DEPÔT
FACTORY JUNC.
JUNC.
WANDSWORTH ROAD
To Brixton

EXPLANATION

| | |
|---|---|
| G.W. | |
| L.& N.W. | |
| L.B.& S.C. | |
| L.& S.W. | |
| MIDLAND | |
| S.E.& C. | |
| WEST LONDON EXT^N JOINT (G.W., L.& N.W., L.& S.W. & L.B.& S.C.) | |

LONGHEDGE JUNC.-MEAN DISTANCE OF A.B.& C.

| | | |
|---|---|---|
| LATCHMERE J^N FOR WATERLOO TO JUNC. A. | 60^c | MEAN 66 chains |
| " " " B. | 69^c | |
| " " " C. | 69^c | |
| | 198^c | |

## EARLS COURT, STUDLAND ROAD, BISHOPS ROAD, ADDISON ROAD, HAMMERSMITH, KENSINGTON, NORTH POLE, SOUTH KENSINGTON, UXBRIDGE ROAD, WESTBOURNE PARK

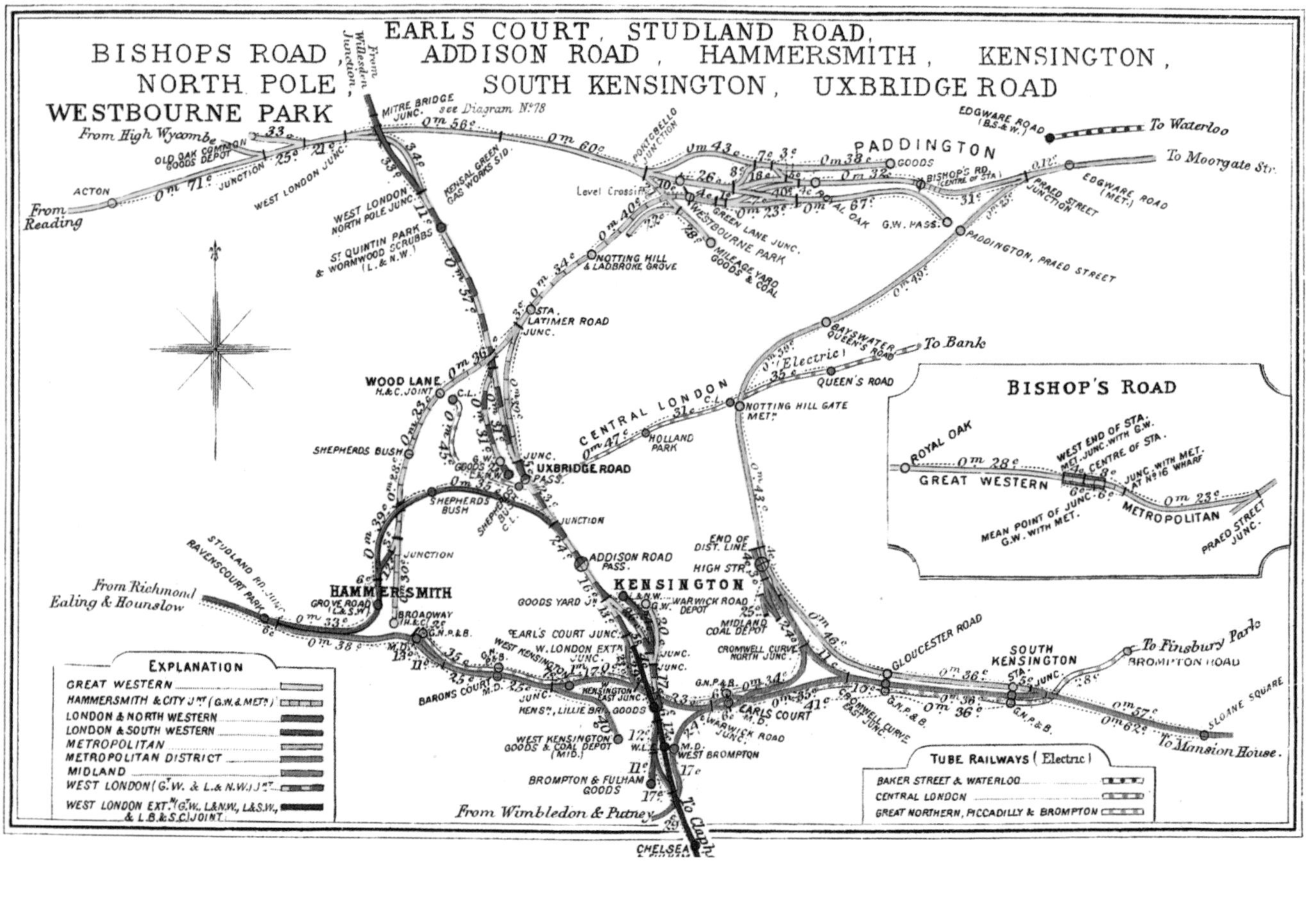

From Willesden Junction
MITRE BRIDGE JUNC. see Diagram N^o 78
From High Wycombe
OLD OAK COMMON GOODS DEPOT
JUNCTION
WEST LONDON JUNC.
ACTON
From Reading
WEST LONDON NORTH POLE JUNC.
KENSAL GREEN GAS WORKS SID.
ST QUINTIN PARK & WORMWOOD SCRUBBS (L.& N.W.)
PORTOBELLO JUNCTION
Level Crossing
PADDINGTON
GOODS
BISHOP'S RD. (CENTRE OF STA.)
ROYAL OAK
G.W. PASS.
GREEN LANE JUNC.
WESTBOURNE PARK
MILEAGE YARD GOODS & COAL
NOTTING HILL & LADBROKE GROVE
PRAED STREET JUNCTION
EDGWARE ROAD (MET.)
PADDINGTON, PRAED STREET
EDGWARE ROAD (B.S.& W.)
To Waterloo
To Moorgate Str.
STA. LATIMER ROAD JUNC.
WOOD LANE H.& C. JOINT
C.L.
SHEPHERDS BUSH
CENTRAL LONDON
HOLLAND PARK
NOTTING HILL GATE MET^R
BAYSWATER QUEEN'S ROAD
(Electric)
To Bank
QUEEN'S ROAD
JUNC.
UXBRIDGE ROAD PASS.
SHEPHERDS BUSH
JUNCTION
ADDISON ROAD PASS.
STUDLAND RD. JUNC.
RAVENSCOURT PARK
From Richmond Ealing & Hounslow
HAMMERSMITH
GROVE ROAD (L.& S.W.)
BROADWAY (H.& C.)
G.N.P.& B.
KENSINGTON
GOODS YARD
L.& N.W. G.W. DEPOT
WARWICK ROAD
END OF DIST. LINE
HIGH STR.
MIDLAND COAL DEPOT
EARL'S COURT JUNC.
W. LONDON EXTN JUNC.
WEST KENSINGTON EAST JUNC.
JUNC.
CROMWELL CURVE NORTH JUNC.
BARONS COURT
M.D.
KENSINGTON LILLIE BR.
KENS^N. LILLIE BR^G. GOODS
EARLS COURT
WARWICK ROAD JUNC.
CROMWELL CURVE EAST JUNC.
GLOUCESTER ROAD
SOUTH KENSINGTON
To Finsbury Park
BROMPTON ROAD
SLOANE SQUARE
To Mansion House
WEST KENSINGTON GOODS & COAL DEPOT (MID.)
W.L.
WEST BROMPTON
BROMPTON & FULHAM GOODS
From Wimbledon & Putney
CHELSEA
To Clapham

BISHOP'S ROAD

ROYAL OAK
GREAT WESTERN
WEST END OF STA. MET. JUNC. WITH G.W.
CENTRE OF STA.
JUNC. WITH MET. AT N^o 16 WHARF
METROPOLITAN
PRAED STREET JUNC.
MEAN POINT OF JUNC. G.W. WITH MET.

EXPLANATION

| | |
|---|---|
| GREAT WESTERN | |
| HAMMERSMITH & CITY J^NT (G.W. & MET^R) | |
| LONDON & NORTH WESTERN | |
| LONDON & SOUTH WESTERN | |
| METROPOLITAN | |
| METROPOLITAN DISTRICT | |
| MIDLAND | |
| WEST LONDON (G^W. & L.& N.W.) J^NT | |
| WEST LONDON EXT^N (G^W., L.& N.W., L.& S.W., & L.B.& S.C.) JOINT | |

TUBE RAILWAYS (Electric)

| | |
|---|---|
| BAKER STREET & WATERLOO | |
| CENTRAL LONDON | |
| GREAT NORTHERN, PICCADILLY & BROMPTON | |

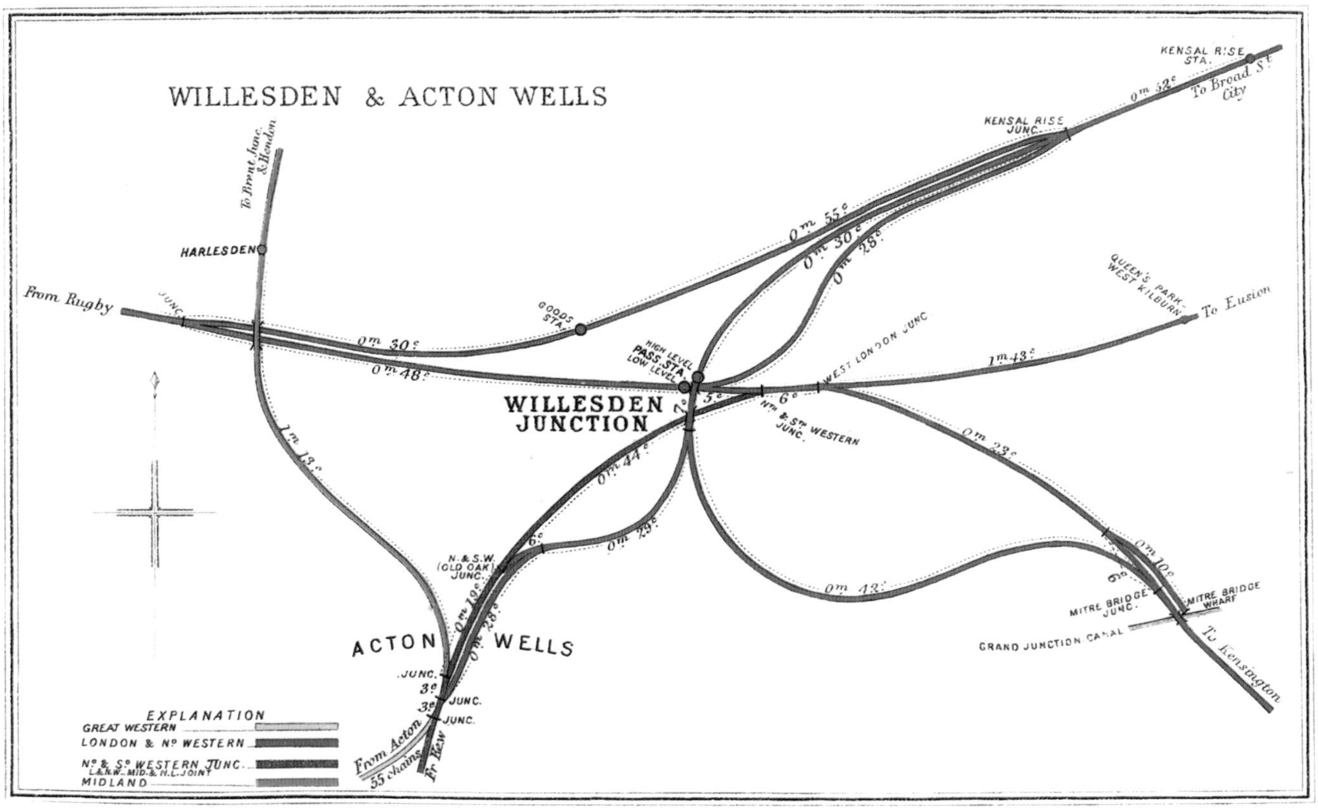

# WILLESDEN & ACTON WELLS

From Rugby
To Brent Junc. & Hendon
HARLESDEN
GOODS STA.
HIGH LEVEL
PASS. STA.
LOW LEVEL
WILLESDEN JUNCTION
WEST LONDON JUNC.
Nth & Sth WESTERN JUNC.
KENSAL RISE JUNC.
KENSAL RISE STA.
To Broad St City
QUEEN'S PARK WEST KILBURN
To Euston
N. & S.W. (OLD OAK) JUNC.
ACTON WELLS
JUNC.
MITRE BRIDGE JUNC.
MITRE BRIDGE WHARF
GRAND JUNCTION CANAL
To Kensington
From Acton 55 chains
Fr. Kew

EXPLANATION

GREAT WESTERN
LONDON & Nº WESTERN
Nº & Sº WESTERN JUNC. L.&N.W., MID. & N.L. JOINT
MIDLAND

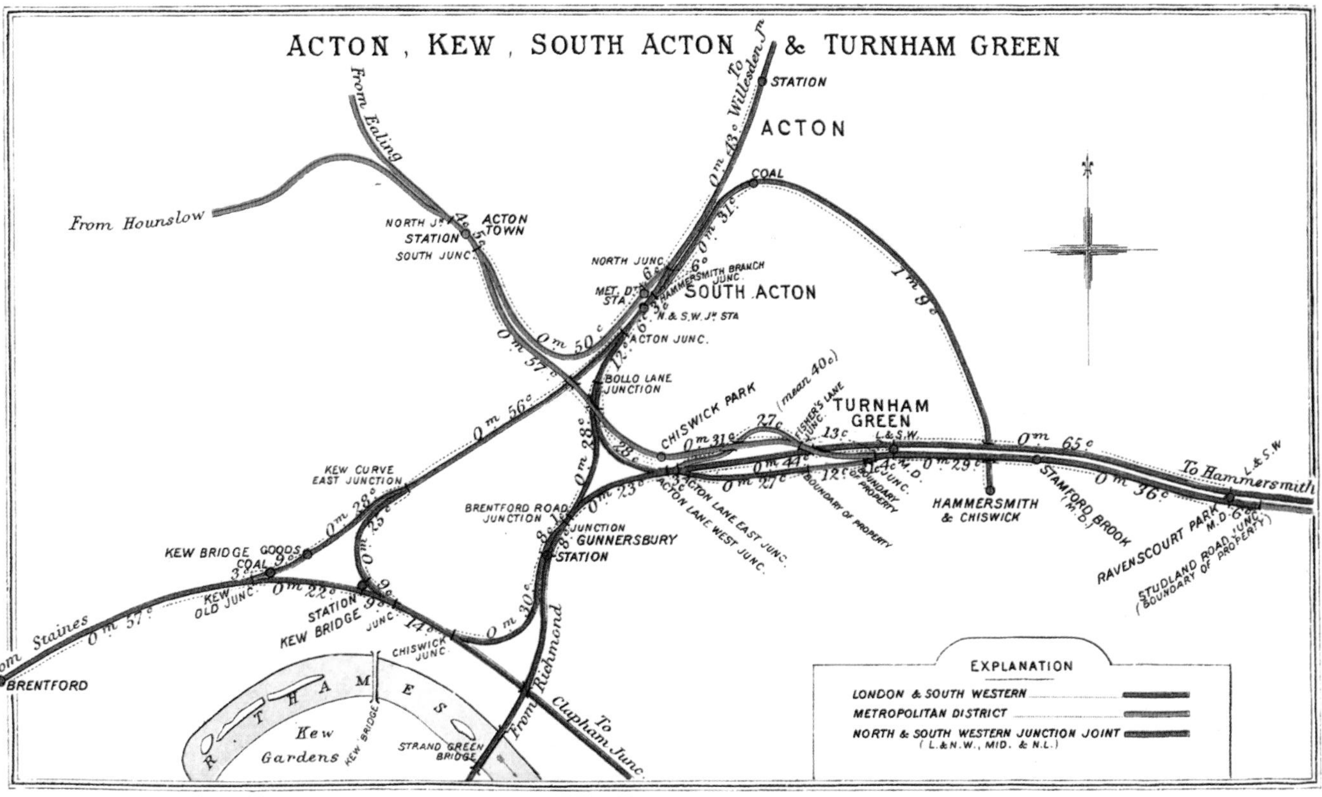

# ACTON, KEW, SOUTH ACTON & TURNHAM GREEN

From Ealing
To Willesden Jn
STATION
ACTON
From Hounslow
NORTH Jn
ACTON TOWN STATION
SOUTH JUNC.
COAL
NORTH JUNC.
HAMMERSMITH BRANCH JUNC.
MET. Dt STA.
SOUTH ACTON
N. & S.W. Jn STA
ACTON JUNC.
BOLLO LANE JUNCTION
CHISWICK PARK
(mean 40c)
FISHER'S LANE JUNC.
TURNHAM GREEN
L.&S.W.
M.D.
JUNC.
BOUNDARY OF PROPERTY
ACTON LANE EAST JUNC.
ACTON LANE WEST JUNC.
HAMMERSMITH & CHISWICK
STAMFORD BROOK (M.D.)
To Hammersmith L.&S.W.
RAVENSCOURT PARK M.D.
STUDLAND ROAD JUNC. (BOUNDARY OF PROPERTY)
KEW CURVE EAST JUNCTION
BRENTFORD ROAD JUNCTION
JUNCTION
GUNNERSBURY STATION
KEW BRIDGE GOODS
COAL
KEW OLD JUNC.
STATION KEW BRIDGE
JUNC.
From Staines
BRENTFORD
CHISWICK JUNC.
R. THAMES
Kew Gardens
KEW BRIDGE
STRAND GREEN BRIDGE
From Richmond
To Clapham Junc.

EXPLANATION

LONDON & SOUTH WESTERN
METROPOLITAN DISTRICT
NORTH & SOUTH WESTERN JUNCTION JOINT (L.&N.W., MID. & N.L.)

## THIRTY NINE

1 2 3 4 5

A B C D E F G

1 Warwick Rd Jc.
2 West Street Jc.
3 SMITHFIELD G.W. Gds
4 WORSHIP STR. (Goods)
5 Minories Jc.
6 ALDGATE EAST
7 HAYDON SQUARE L.N.W. (Goods)
8 GOODMAN'S YARD G.E. (Goods)
9 MINT STR. G.N. (Goods)
10 MINT STR M.R. (Goods)
11 LUDGATE HILL
12 ST PAUL'S S.E. & C.
13 MANSION HOUSE
14 CANNON STREET
15 MONUMENT
16 MARK LANE
17 ST MARY'S
18 WARWICK RD (Goods) L.N.W.
19 WARWICK RD (Goods) G.W.
20 Earls Court Jc.
21 Goods Yard Jc.
22 West London Ext. Jc.
23 KEN. LILLIE BRI. (Gds)
24 TURNHAM GREEN
25 CHISWICK PARK
26 WEST END LANE
27 LADBROKE GROVE
28 WESTBOURNE PARK
29 ROYAL OAK
30 Junction Rd Jc.
31 Highgate Rd Jc.
32 CHALK FARM
33 CAMDEN
34 Hampstead Rd Jc.
35 Kentish Town Jc.
36 CAMDEN TOWN
37 Maiden Lane Jc.
38 St Pancras Jc. (West)
39 KENTISH TOWN
40 St Pancras Jc.
41 North London Incline Jc.
42 ST PANCRAS (Goods)
43 Copenhagen Jc,
44 Copenhagen Tun.
45 MAIDEN LANE (Gds)
46 KINGS CROSS (SUBURBAN)
47 Campbell Road Jc.
48 Upper Abbey Mills Jc.
49 SPITALFIELDS (Goods)
50 Bishopsgate Jc.
51 SPITALFIELDS (Coal)
52 Vallance Road Jc.
53 Borough Market Jc.
54 Metropolitan Jc.
55 Hampstead Tun.
56 St John's WoodTun
57 OLD OAK LANE HALT
58 WEST HAMPSTEAD
59 Primrose Hill Tuns
60 WOOD LANE (WHITE CITY)
61 MAIDEN LANE (Pass.)
62 CALEDONIAN ROAD & BARNSBURY

PINNER
MET. & G.C. Joint
HARROW & WEALDSTONE
L.N.W.
KENTON for NORTHWICK PARK
NORTH HARROW
HARROW-ON-THE-HILL
Gds
North Jc.
South Jc.
MET.
WEST HARROW HALT
RAYNER'S LANE HALT
EASTCOTE HALT
PRESTON ROAD
FINCHLEY (CHURCH END)
G.N.
EAST FINCHLEY
CRANLEY GARDENS
HIGHGATE
HENDON
MID.
Loco. Shed
Brent Jc.
CRICKLEWOOD
SOUTH HARROW
NORTH WEMBLEY
SOUTH HARROW
WEMBLEY PARK
G.W. & G.C. Jt
G.C.
SUDBURY & HARROW RD.
MET. Gds
Rly. Works
Closed 01/10/1902
DUDDING HILL
SUDBURY HILL
WEMBLEY HILL
NEASDEN & K.(Goods)
DOLLIS HILL
KILBURN BRON.
WEST HAMPSTEAD
FINCHLEY RD & FROGNAL
HAMPSTEAD HEATH
GOSPEL OAK
MID.
Haverstock Hill Tun.
Carlton Rd Jc.
NORTHOLT JUNC.
NORTHOLT HALT for WEST END
G.W.
WEMBLEY
Neasden S. Jc.
SUDBURY TOWN
Goods
Loco. Shed
Neasden Jc.
WILLESDEN GREEN
BRONDESBURY
Canfield Place
FINCHLEY RD MET.
SWISS COTTAGE
STONEBRIDGE PARK
Pass
GREENFORD
BRONDESBURY PARK
SOUTH HAMPSTEAD
KILBURN
KENSAL RISE
QUEEN'S PARK WEST KILBURN
Gds
ALPERTON FOR PERIVALE
Goods Pass
HARLESDEN
Goods
Kensal Green Jc.
MARLBOROUGH RD.
L. Shed
PERIVALE HALT
Brent Jc.
NEW
KENSAL GREEN
Kensal Green Tuns
Lords Tun.
ST JOHN'S WOOD ROAD
Loco. Shed
WILLESDEN JUNC.
MAIN
H.L.
West London Jc.
N. & S.W. Jc.
GREAT PORTLAND ST
WESTBOURNE PARK
Portobello Jc.
ROYAL OAK
Goods
CASTLE BAR PARK HALT
BRENTHAM for NTH. EALING
PARK ROYAL
Acton Wells Jc.
Old Oak Jc.
Mitre Bri. Jc.
MITRE BRIDGE (Gds)
Goods
MARYLEBONE
BAKER STREET
Green Lane Jc.
BISHOPS ROAD
Level Crossing
MILEAGE YARD Goods & Coal
PADDINGTON
Pass.
PARK ROYAL & TWYFORD ABBEY
NORTH EALING
DRAYTON GREEN (EALING) HALT
Goods
Loco. Shed
West/ London Jc.
Old Oak Common W. Jc.
Portobello Jc.
Goods
EDGWARE RD
EALING BROADWAY
EALING COMMON
ACTON
EAST ACTON
North Pole Jc.
Level Crossing
Gds
PADDINGTON
PRAED STREET
ST QUINTIN PARK & WORMWOOD SCRUBBS
WEST EALING
ACTON
LATIMER ROAD
BAYSWATER
G.W.
SOUTHALL
Loco. Shed
HANWELL & ELTHORNE
HAMMERSMITH Branch Jc.
Coal
SHEPHERDS BUSH
Uxbridge Rd Jc.
NOTTING HILL GATE
UXBRIDGE ROAD
N. Jc.
ACTON TOWN
N. Jc.
Acton Jc.
STH. ACTON
Bollo Lane Jc.
GOLDHAWK RD
G.W. Gds L.N.W. Gds
HIGH ST KENSINGTON
MET.-DIS.
MET.-DIS.
SOUTH EALING
STAMFORD BROOK
RAVENSCOURT PARK
ADDISON RD
Cromwell Curve North Jc.
SLOANE SQUARE
L.B.S.C.
VICTORIA
S.E. & C.
TRUMPER'S CROSSING (FOR SOUTH HANWELL & OSTERLEY PARK) HALT
NORTHFIELD & LITTLE EALING
Brentford Lane Jc.
Acton Lane Jc.
Studland Rd Jc.
H. & C.
MET.-DIS.
MID. Coal
GLOUCESTER RD
GUNNERSBURY
HAMMERSMITH & CHISWICK
HAMMERSMITH BROADWAY
EARLS COURT
Cromwell Curve East Jc.
STH. KENSINGTON
BOSTON MANOR
Coal
Goods
East Jc.
Old Jc.
BARON'S COURT
WEST KENSINGTON
WEST BROMPTON
KEW BRIDGE
New Jc.
BRENTFORD
MID. Goods
Battersea Wharf
OSTERLEY & SPRING GROVE
CHISWICK & GROVE PARK
BROMPTON & FULHAM L.N.W. Goods
Loco. Shed
HOUNSLOW TOWN
KEW GARDENS
BARNES BRIDGE
WALHAM GREEN
CHELSEA & FULHAM
BATTERSEA PARK
HOUNSLOW BARRACKS
HESTON HOUNSLOW
BRENTFORD
ISLEWORTH
Chelsea Basin Jc.
Chelsea Basin
QUEENS ROAD
PARSONS GREEN
BARNES
BATTERSEA
HOUNSLOW & WHITTON
PUTNEY BRI. & HURLINGHAM
MORTLAKE
Latchmere Jcs
RICHMOND
L.S.W.
L.N.W. Gds
CLAPHAM JUNCTION
PUTNEY
WANDSWORTH TOWN
EAST PUTNEY
Point Pleasant Jc.
Goods
WANDSWORTH COMMON
Hounslow Jc.
ST. MARGARETS
Feltham Jc.
TWICKENHAM
SOUTHFIELDS
L.S.W.
BALHAM & UPPER TOOTING
L.S.W.
Whitton Jc.
EARLSFIELD FOR SUMMERSTOWN
Balham Jc.
Loco. Shed
STRAWBERRY HILL
WIMBLEDON PARK
DURNSFORD ROAD
FULWELL
Closed 01/01/1917 - 27/08/1923
HAYDONS RD
Closed 01/01/1917 - 27/08/1923
TOOTING JUNC.
Gds
WIMBLEDON
'A'
KEMPTON PARK
TEDDINGTON
L.S.W.
Closed 01/01/1917 - 27/08/1923
MERTON ABBEY
HAMPTON
KINGSTON
NORBITON FOR KINGSTON HILL
MERTON PARK
HAMPTON WICK
RAYNES PARK
MORDEN HALT
Goods
Goods
MALDEN for COOMBE
HAMPTON COURT
MITCHAM
THAMES DITTON
MITCHAM JUNC.
SURBITON
Hampton Court Jc.
ESHER
L.S.W.
WORCESTER PARK
HACKBRIDGE

BATTERSEA
W.L.E.
Latchmere S.W. Jc.
Latchmere Main Jc.
Battersea Pier Jc.
Battersea Wharf
SOUTH LAMBETH (Gds)
BATTERSEA PARK
QUEEN'S RD
Longhedge Jc.
CLAPHAM JUNCTION
L.S.W.
Ludgate Jc.
Pouparts Jc.
Stewarts Lane Jc.
L.S.W.
Coal Yard Jc.
FALCON LANE Gds, L.N.W.
Falcon Jc.
NEW WANDSWORTH (Goods)
STEWARTS LANE (Gds)
Factory Jc.
M.R. Coal

A L.B.S.C. & Joint
B WEST LONDON Joint
C WEST LONDON EXTENSION Joint
D HAMMERSMITH & CITY Joint
E EAST LONDON Joint
F WHITECHAPEL & BOW Joint
G L.B.S.C. & S.E. & C. Joint
H NORTH & STH. WESTERN JUNC.
J TOTTENHAM & FOREST GATE
K L.N.W. & MID. Joint
L TOTTENHAM & HAMPSTEAD

**NOTE:**
TO AVOID CONFUSION TUBE RAILWAYS ARE OMITTED AND MET. & MET.-DISTRICT COVERED SECTIONS ARE SHEWN AS SURFACE LINES

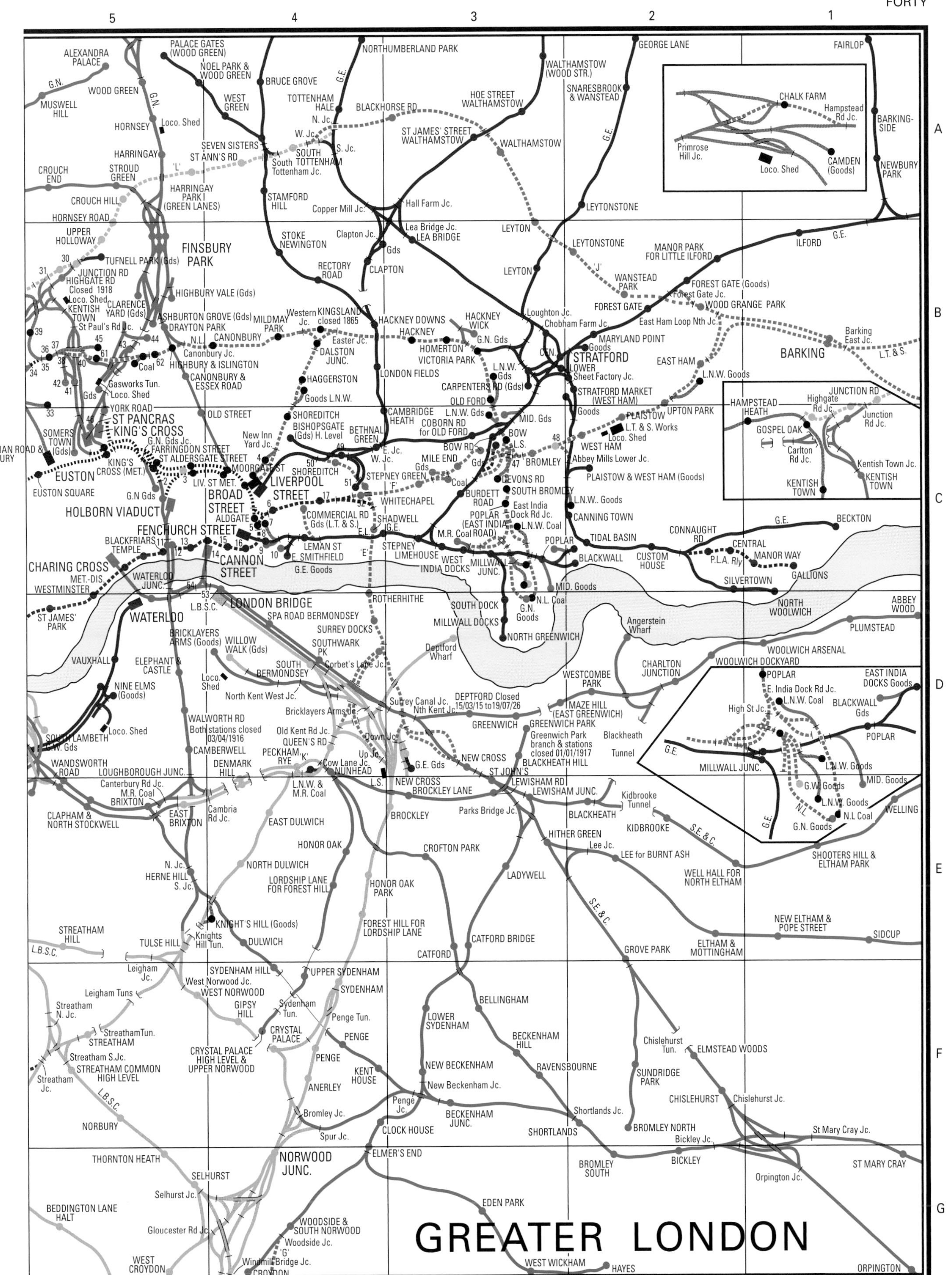
5
4
3
2
1
A
B
C
D
E
F
G
GREATER LONDON
ALEXANDRA PALACE
PALACE GATES (WOOD GREEN)
NOEL PARK & WOOD GREEN
BRUCE GROVE
NORTHUMBERLAND PARK
WALTHAMSTOW (WOOD STR.)
GEORGE LANE
FAIRLOP
MUSWELL HILL
WOOD GREEN
WEST GREEN
TOTTENHAM HALE
BLACKHORSE RD
HOE STREET WALTHAMSTOW
SNARESBROOK & WANSTEAD
HORNSEY
Loco. Shed
N. Jc.
W. Jc.
S. Jc.
ST JAMES' STREET WALTHAMSTOW
WALTHAMSTOW
CHALK FARM
Hampstead Rd Jc.
Primrose Hill Jc.
CAMDEN (Goods)
BARKINGSIDE
NEWBURY PARK
HARRINGAY
SEVEN SISTERS
ST ANN'S RD
SOUTH TOTTENHAM
South Tottenham Jc.
CROUCH END
STROUD GREEN
HARRINGAY PARK (GREEN LANES)
STAMFORD HILL
Copper Mill Jc.
Hall Farm Jc.
LEYTONSTONE
CROUCH HILL
HORNSEY ROAD
UPPER HOLLOWAY
STOKE NEWINGTON
Clapton Jc.
Lea Bridge Jc.
LEA BRIDGE
LEYTON
ILFORD
FINSBURY PARK
TUFNELL PARK (Gds)
JUNCTION RD
HIGHGATE RD Closed 1918
RECTORY ROAD
CLAPTON
MANOR PARK FOR LITTLE ILFORD
WANSTEAD PARK
FOREST GATE (Goods)
Forest Gate Jc.
WOOD GRANGE PARK
FOREST GATE
HIGHBURY VALE (Gds)
KENTISH TOWN
CLARENCE YARD (Gds)
St Paul's Rd Jc.
ASHBURTON GROVE (Gds)
DRAYTON PARK
MILDMAY PARK
Western Jc.
KINGSLAND closed 1865
HACKNEY DOWNS
HACKNEY
HACKNEY WICK
Loughton Jc.
Chobham Farm Jc.
East Ham Loop Nth Jc.
Barking East Jc.
BARKING
L.T. & S.
CANONBURY
Canonbury Jc.
Easter Jc.
DALSTON JUNC.
HOMERTON
G.N. Gds
MARYLAND POINT
STRATFORD
EAST HAM
VICTORIA PARK
HIGHBURY & ISLINGTON
CANONBURY & ESSEX ROAD
LONDON FIELDS
L.N.W. Gds
LOWER Sheet Factory Jc.
L.N.W. Goods
Gasworks Tun.
Loco. Shed
HAGGERSTON
Goods L.N.W.
CARPENTERS RD (Gds)
STRATFORD MARKET (WEST HAM)
JUNCTION RD
HAMPSTEAD HEATH
Highgate Rd Jc.
GOSPEL OAK
Junction Rd Jc.
Carlton Rd Jc.
Kentish Town Jc.
KENTISH TOWN
YORK ROAD
ST PANCRAS
KING'S CROSS
OLD STREET
SHOREDITCH
CAMBRIDGE HEATH
OLD FORD
L.N.W. Gds
COBORN RD for OLD FORD
MID. Gds
Goods
PLAISTOW
UPTON PARK
L.T. & S. Works
Loco. Shed
SOMERS TOWN (Gds)
G.N. Gds Jc.
FARRINGDON STREET
BISHOPSGATE (Gds) H. Level
BETHNAL GREEN
New Inn Yard Jc.
E. Jc.
W. Jc.
BOW RD
BOW
L.S.
WEST HAM
Abbey Mills Lower Jc.
KING'S CROSS (MET.)
ST ALDERSGATE STREET
MOORGATE ST
MILE END
Gds
BROMLEY
EUSTON
LIV. ST MET.
LIVERPOOL STREET
SHOREDITCH
STEPNEY GREEN
Coal
DEVONS RD
PLAISTOW & WEST HAM (Goods)
EUSTON SQUARE
G.N Gds
BROAD STREET
WHITECHAPEL
BURDETT ROAD
SOUTH BROMLEY
L.N.W.. Goods
HOLBORN VIADUCT
ALDGATE
COMMERCIAL RD Gds (L.T. & S.)
SHADWELL
East India Dock Rd Jc.
POPLAR (EAST INDIA ROAD)
L.N.W. Coal
CANNING TOWN
FENCHURCH STREET
M.R. Coal
TIDAL BASIN
CONNAUGHT RD
BECKTON
BLACKFRIARS TEMPLE
LEMAN ST
STEPNEY LIMEHOUSE
POPLAR
CENTRAL
MANOR WAY
CANNON STREET
E. SMITHFIELD
WEST INDIA DOCKS
MILLWALL JUNC.
BLACKWALL
CUSTOM HOUSE
P.L.A. Rly
GALLIONS
CHARING CROSS
G.E. Goods
SILVERTOWN
MET.-DIS.
WATERLOO JUNC.
WESTMINSTER
MID. Goods
N.L. Coal
L.B.S.C.
LONDON BRIDGE
ROTHERHITHE
SOUTH DOCK
G.N. Goods
NORTH WOOLWICH
ABBEY WOOD
ST JAMES' PARK
WATERLOO
SPA ROAD BERMONDSEY
MILLWALL DOCKS
Angerstein Wharf
PLUMSTEAD
SURREY DOCKS
NORTH GREENWICH
BRICKLAYERS ARMS (Goods)
WILLOW WALK (Gds)
SOUTHWARK PK
Deptford Wharf
WOOLWICH ARSENAL
VAUXHALL
ELEPHANT & CASTLE
SOUTH BERMONDSEY
Corbet's Lane Jc.
CHARLTON JUNCTION
WOOLWICH DOCKYARD
WESTCOMBE PARK
Loco. Shed
POPLAR
E. India Dock Rd Jc.
EAST INDIA DOCKS Goods
NINE ELMS (Goods)
North Kent West Jc.
Surrey Canal Jc.
Nth Kent Jc.
DEPTFORD Closed 15/03/15 to 19/07/26
MAZE HILL (EAST GREENWICH)
L.N.W. Coal
High St Jc.
BLACKWALL Gds
Bricklayers Arms Jc.
GREENWICH
GREENWICH PARK
Loco. Shed
WALWORTH RD
Both stations closed 03/04/1916
Old Kent Rd Jc.
Down Jc.
Greenwich Park branch & stations closed 01/01/1917
Blackheath Tunnel
POPLAR
SOUTH LAMBETH
L.W. Gds
QUEEN'S RD
CAMBERWELL
PECKHAM RYE
Up Jc.
G.E. Gds
NEW CROSS
BLACKHEATH HILL
MILLWALL JUNC.
L.N.W. Goods
WANDSWORTH ROAD
LOUGHBOROUGH JUNC.
DENMARK HILL
Cow Lane Jc.
NUNHEAD
ST JOHN'S
MID. Goods
G.W. Goods
Canterbury Rd Jc.
M.R. Coal
L.N.W. & M.R. Coal
L.S.
NEW CROSS
BROCKLEY LANE
LEWISHAM RD
LEWISHAM JUNC.
Kidbrooke Tunnel
L.N.W. Goods
BRIXTON
N.L. Coal
G.N. Goods
WELLING
CLAPHAM & NORTH STOCKWELL
EAST BRIXTON
Cambria Rd Jc.
EAST DULWICH
BROCKLEY
Parks Bridge Jc.
BLACKHEATH
KIDBROOKE
S.E.& C.
HITHER GREEN
HONOR OAK
CROFTON PARK
Lee Jc.
LEE for BURNT ASH
SHOOTERS HILL & ELTHAM PARK
N. Jc.
HERNE HILL
S. Jc.
NORTH DULWICH
LORDSHIP LANE FOR FOREST HILL
HONOR OAK PARK
LADYWELL
WELL HALL FOR NORTH ELTHAM
S.E.& C.
KNIGHT'S HILL (Goods)
FOREST HILL FOR LORDSHIP LANE
NEW ELTHAM & POPE STREET
STREATHAM HILL
TULSE HILL
Knights Hill Tun.
DULWICH
CATFORD BRIDGE
GROVE PARK
ELTHAM & MOTTINGHAM
SIDCUP
L.B.S.C.
CATFORD
Leigham Jc.
SYDENHAM HILL
UPPER SYDENHAM
West Norwood Jc.
WEST NORWOOD
SYDENHAM
Leigham Tuns
Streatham N. Jc.
GIPSY HILL
Sydenham Tun.
Penge Tun.
BELLINGHAM
LOWER SYDENHAM
StreathamTun.
STREATHAM
CRYSTAL PALACE
PENGE
BECKENHAM HILL
Chislehurst Tun.
ELMSTEAD WOODS
Streatham S.Jc.
STREATHAM COMMON HIGH LEVEL
CRYSTAL PALACE HIGH LEVEL & UPPER NORWOOD
PENGE
KENT HOUSE
NEW BECKENHAM
RAVENSBOURNE
Streatham Jc.
New Beckenham Jc.
SUNDRIDGE PARK
ANERLEY
L.B.S.C.
CHISLEHURST
Chislehurst Jc.
Penge Jc.
Bromley Jc.
BECKENHAM JUNC.
Shortlands Jc.
NORBURY
CLOCK HOUSE
SHORTLANDS
BROMLEY NORTH
Spur Jc.
Bickley Jc.
St Mary Cray Jc.
THORNTON HEATH
NORWOOD JUNC.
ELMER'S END
BROMLEY SOUTH
BICKLEY
ST MARY CRAY
SELHURST
Orpington Jc.
Selhurst Jc.
EDEN PARK
BEDDINGTON LANE HALT
WOODSIDE & SOUTH NORWOOD
Gloucester Rd Jc.
Woodside Jc.
'G'
WEST CROYDON
Windmill Bridge Jc.
WEST WICKHAM
HAYES
ORPINGTON
CROYDON (ADDISCOMBE ROAD)
G.N.
G.E.
'L'
'J'
'K'
'F'
'E'
E.L.
CEN.

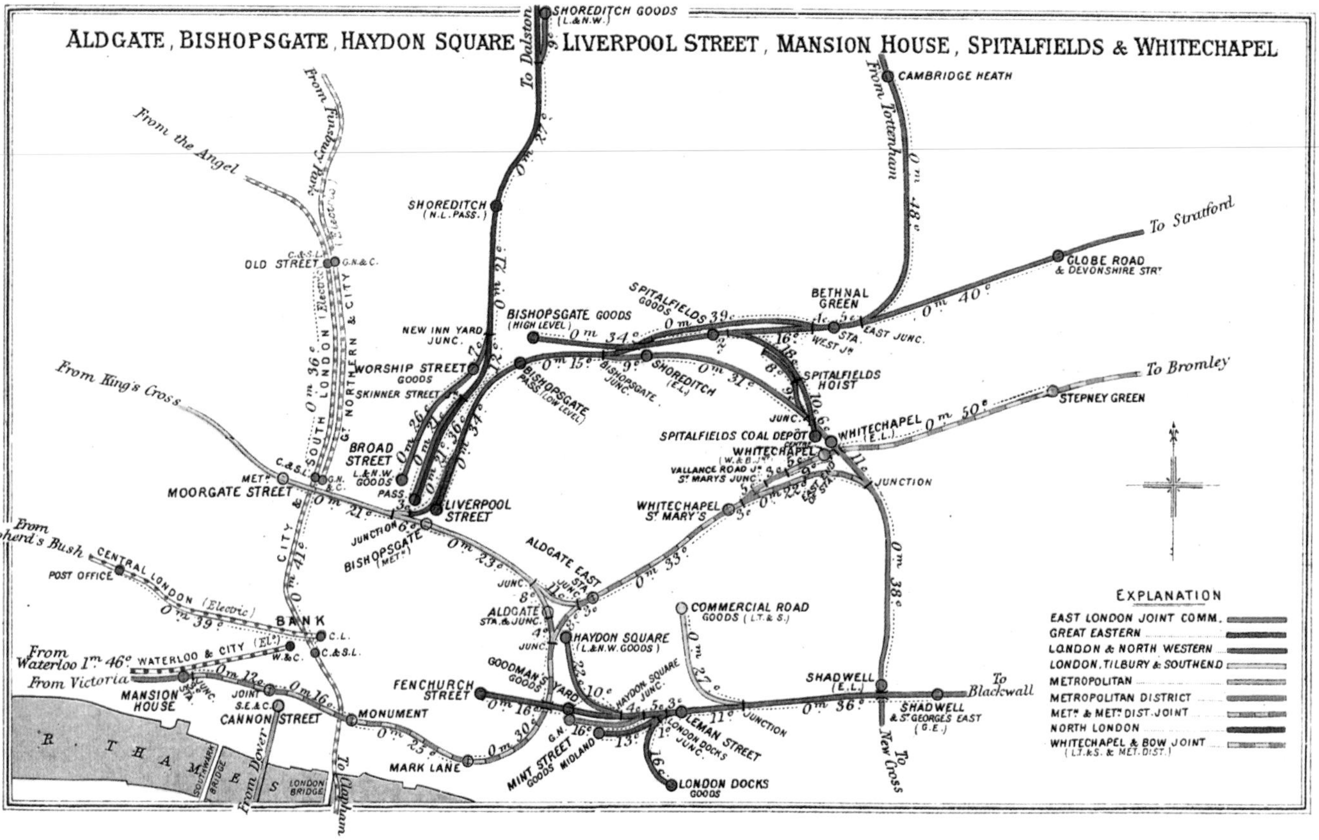
ALDGATE, BISHOPSGATE, HAYDON SQUARE & LIVERPOOL STREET, MANSION HOUSE, SPITALFIELDS & WHITECHAPEL
SHOREDITCH GOODS (L.&N.W.)
To Dalston
CAMBRIDGE HEATH
From Tottenham
From the Angel
From Finsbury Park
SHOREDITCH (N.L. PASS.)
To Stratford
GLOBE ROAD & DEVONSHIRE STRT
OLD STREET
BETHNAL GREEN
SPITALFIELDS GOODS
BISHOPSGATE GOODS (HIGH LEVEL)
NEW INN YARD JUNC.
WORSHIP STREET GOODS
SKINNER STREET
BISHOPSGATE PASS. (LOW LEVEL)
BISHOPSGATE JUNC.
SHOREDITCH (E.L.)
SPITALFIELDS HOIST
To Bromley
STEPNEY GREEN
From King's Cross
CITY & SOUTH LONDON (Electric)
Gt. NORTHERN & CITY
BROAD STREET
L.&N.W. GOODS
SPITALFIELDS COAL DEPOT
WHITECHAPEL (E.L.)
WHITECHAPEL (W.&B.Jt.)
VALLANCE ROAD Jn.
St. MARYS JUNC.
JUNCTION
MOORGATE STREET
LIVERPOOL STREET
WHITECHAPEL St. MARY'S
From Shepherd's Bush
CENTRAL LONDON (Electric)
POST OFFICE
BISHOPSGATE (MET.)
ALDGATE EAST
BANK
COMMERCIAL ROAD GOODS (LT.&S.)
From Waterloo
WATERLOO & CITY (El.)
From Victoria
ALDGATE STA.& JUNC.
HAYDON SQUARE (L.&N.W. GOODS)
MANSION HOUSE
CANNON STREET
MONUMENT
FENCHURCH STREET
GOODMAN'S YARD GOODS
SHADWELL (E.L.)
SHADWELL & St. GEORGES EAST (G.E.)
To Blackwall
LEMAN STREET
MARK LANE
MINT STREET GOODS
LONDON DOCKS GOODS
To New Cross
From Dover
To Clapham
R. THAMES
SOUTHWARK BRIDGE
LONDON BRIDGE
EXPLANATION
EAST LONDON JOINT COMM.
GREAT EASTERN
LONDON & NORTH WESTERN
LONDON, TILBURY & SOUTHEND
METROPOLITAN
METROPOLITAN DISTRICT
METR. & METR. DIST. JOINT
NORTH LONDON
WHITECHAPEL & BOW JOINT (LT.&S. & MET. DIST.)

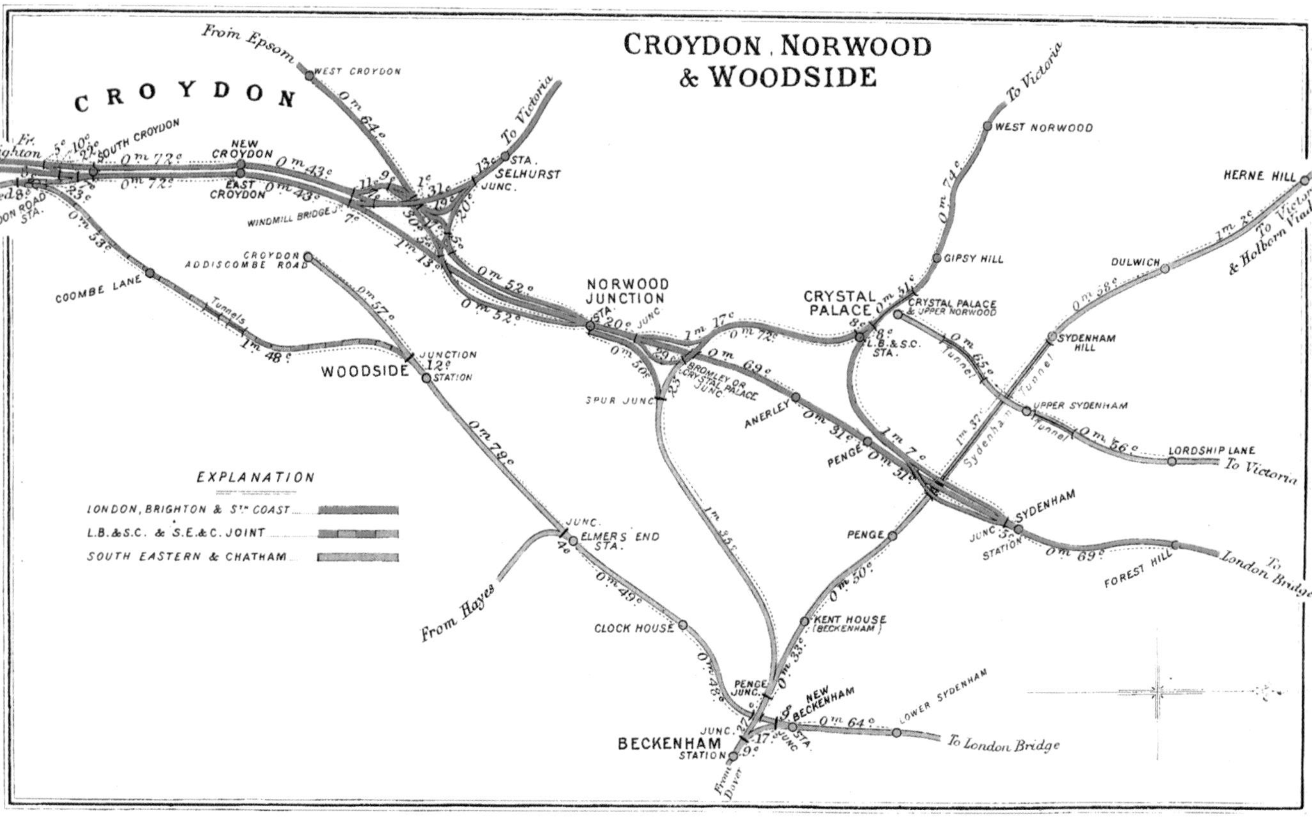
CROYDON, NORWOOD & WOODSIDE
CROYDON
From Epsom
WEST CROYDON
To Victoria
From Brighton
SOUTH CROYDON
NEW CROYDON
EAST CROYDON
Fr. Oxted
SELSDON ROAD STA.
WINDMILL BRIDGE Jn.
SELHURST
WEST NORWOOD
HERNE HILL
To Victoria & Holborn Viaduct
COOMBE LANE
CROYDON ADDISCOMBE ROAD
GIPSY HILL
DULWICH
NORWOOD JUNCTION
CRYSTAL PALACE
CRYSTAL PALACE & UPPER NORWOOD
SYDENHAM HILL
WOODSIDE
SPUR JUNC.
BROMLEY OR CRYSTAL PALACE JUNC.
ANERLEY
UPPER SYDENHAM
PENGE
LORDSHIP LANE
To Victoria
SYDENHAM
EXPLANATION
LONDON, BRIGHTON & Sth. COAST
L.B.&S.C. & S.E.&C. JOINT
SOUTH EASTERN & CHATHAM
ELMERS END STA.
From Hayes
FOREST HILL
To London Bridge
CLOCK HOUSE
KENT HOUSE (BECKENHAM)
PENGE JUNC.
NEW BECKENHAM
LOWER SYDENHAM
BECKENHAM STATION
To London Bridge
From Dover

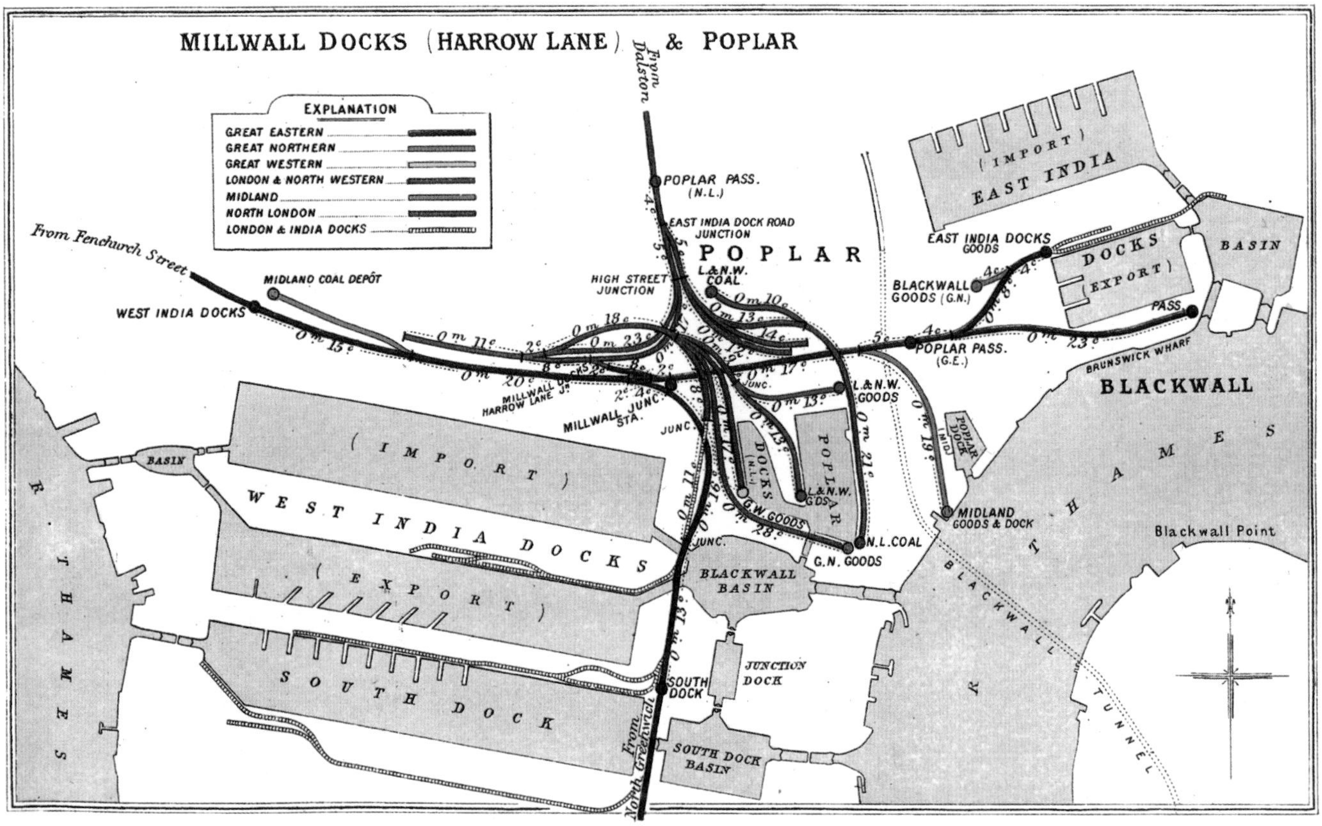

## MILLWALL DOCKS (HARROW LANE) & POPLAR

EXPLANATION

GREAT EASTERN
GREAT NORTHERN
GREAT WESTERN
LONDON & NORTH WESTERN
MIDLAND
NORTH LONDON
LONDON & INDIA DOCKS

From Dalston
POPLAR PASS. (N.L.)
EAST INDIA DOCK ROAD JUNCTION
POPLAR
L.&N.W. COAL
HIGH STREET JUNCTION
From Fenchurch Street
MIDLAND COAL DEPÔT
WEST INDIA DOCKS
MILLWALL DOCKS HARROW LANE J.
MILLWALL JUNC. STA.
JUNC.
L.&N.W. GOODS
DOCKS (N.L.)
POPLAR
L.&N.W. GDS
G.W. GOODS
N.L. COAL
G.N. GOODS
EAST INDIA DOCKS GOODS
BLACKWALL GOODS (G.N.)
POPLAR PASS. (G.E.)
PASS.
BRUNSWICK WHARF
BLACKWALL
(IMPORT) EAST INDIA
DOCKS (EXPORT)
BASIN
POPLAR DOCK (MID.)
MIDLAND GOODS & DOCK
THAMES
Blackwall Point
BLACKWALL TUNNEL
BASIN
(IMPORT)
WEST INDIA DOCKS
(EXPORT)
SOUTH DOCK
BLACKWALL BASIN
JUNCTION DOCK
SOUTH DOCK
SOUTH DOCK BASIN
From North Greenwich
R. THAMES

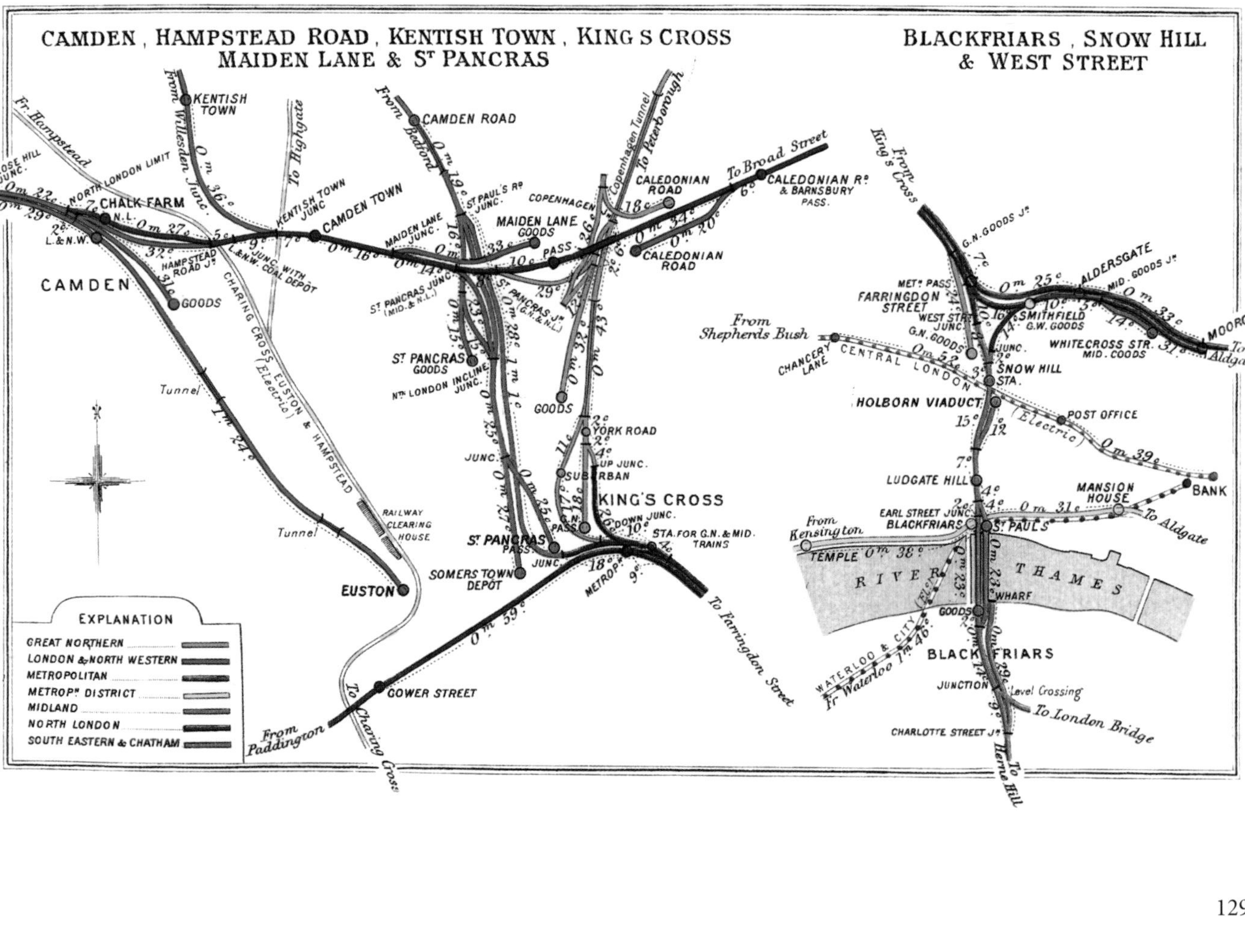

## CAMDEN, HAMPSTEAD ROAD, KENTISH TOWN, KING'S CROSS MAIDEN LANE & ST PANCRAS

KENTISH TOWN
From Willesden Junc.
To Highgate
Fr. Hampstead
PRIMROSE HILL JUNC.
NORTH LONDON LIMIT
From Rugby
CHALK FARM N.L.
L.&N.W.
CAMDEN
HAMPSTEAD ROAD J.
JUNC. WITH L.&N.W. COAL DEPÔT
KENTISH TOWN JUNC.
CAMDEN TOWN
GOODS
CHARING CROSS, EUSTON & HAMPSTEAD (Electric)
Tunnel
Tunnel
RAILWAY CLEARING HOUSE
EUSTON
CAMDEN ROAD
From Bedford
ST PAUL'S RD JUNC.
MAIDEN LANE JUNC.
MAIDEN LANE GOODS
COPENHAGEN
Copenhagen Tunnel
To Peterborough
CALEDONIAN ROAD
PASS.
To Broad Street
CALEDONIAN RD & BARNSBURY PASS.
CALEDONIAN ROAD
ST PANCRAS JUNC. (MID. & N.L.)
ST PANCRAS J. (G.N. & N.L.)
ST PANCRAS GOODS
NTH LONDON INCLINE JUNC.
GOODS
YORK ROAD
UP JUNC.
SUBURBAN
KING'S CROSS
DOWN JUNC.
STA. FOR G.N. & MID. TRAINS
JUNC.
ST PANCRAS PASS.
SOMERS TOWN DEPOT
METROPN
To Farringdon Street
GOWER STREET
From Paddington
To Charing Cross

EXPLANATION

GREAT NORTHERN
LONDON & NORTH WESTERN
METROPOLITAN
METROPN DISTRICT
MIDLAND
NORTH LONDON
SOUTH EASTERN & CHATHAM

## BLACKFRIARS, SNOW HILL & WEST STREET

From King's Cross
G.N. GOODS J.
ALDERSGATE
MID. GOODS J.
METN PASS.
FARRINGDON STREET
WEST STR. JUNC.
SMITHFIELD G.W. GOODS
MOORGATE
To Aldgate
G.N. GOODS
WHITECROSS STR. MID. GOODS
From Shepherds Bush
CHANCERY LANE
CENTRAL LONDON (Electric)
JUNC.
SNOW HILL STA.
HOLBORN VIADUCT
POST OFFICE
LUDGATE HILL
MANSION HOUSE
BANK
To Aldgate
From Kensington
EARL STREET JUNC.
BLACKFRIARS
S. PAUL'S
TEMPLE
RIVER THAMES
WHARF
GOODS
WATERLOO & CITY
Fr. Waterloo
BLACKFRIARS JUNCTION
Level Crossing
To London Bridge
CHARLOTTE STREET J.
To Herne Hill

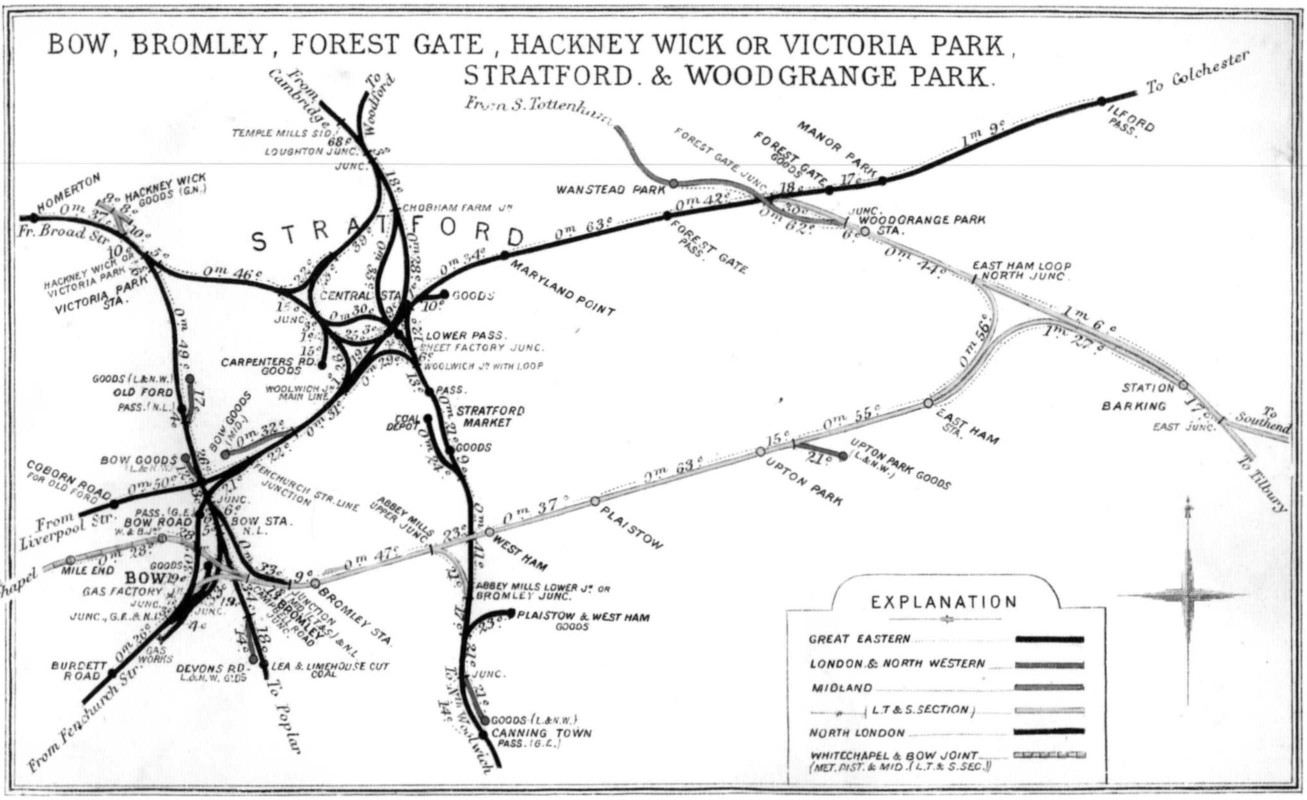
BOW, BROMLEY, FOREST GATE, HACKNEY WICK OR VICTORIA PARK, STRATFORD. & WOODGRANGE PARK.
STRATFORD
To Colchester
ILFORD PASS.
MANOR PARK
FOREST GATE GOODS
WANSTEAD PARK
WOODGRANGE PARK STA.
FOREST GATE PASS.
MARYLAND POINT
EAST HAM LOOP NORTH JUNC.
HOMERTON
HACKNEY WICK GOODS (G.N.)
Fr. Broad Str.
VICTORIA PARK STA.
CENTRAL STA.
GOODS
LOWER PASS.
CARPENTERS RD. GOODS
STRATFORD MARKET
STATION BARKING
EAST JUNC.
To Southend
To Tilbury
EAST HAM STA.
UPTON PARK GOODS (L.&N.W.)
UPTON PARK
PLAISTOW
WEST HAM
BOW GOODS
COBORN ROAD
From Liverpool Str.
BOW ROAD
BOW STA. N.L.
From Whitechapel
MILE END
BOW
GAS FACTORY
BROMLEY STA.
ABBEY MILLS UPPER JUNC.
PLAISTOW & WEST HAM GOODS
BURDETT ROAD
From Fenchurch Str.
DEVONS RD. L.&N.W. GDS
LEA & LIMEHOUSE CUT COAL
To Poplar
GOODS (L.&N.W.)
CANNING TOWN PASS. (G.E.)
EXPLANATION
GREAT EASTERN
LONDON & NORTH WESTERN
MIDLAND
(L.T.& S. SECTION)
NORTH LONDON
WHITECHAPEL & BOW JOINT (MET. DIST. & MID. (L.T.& S. SEC.))

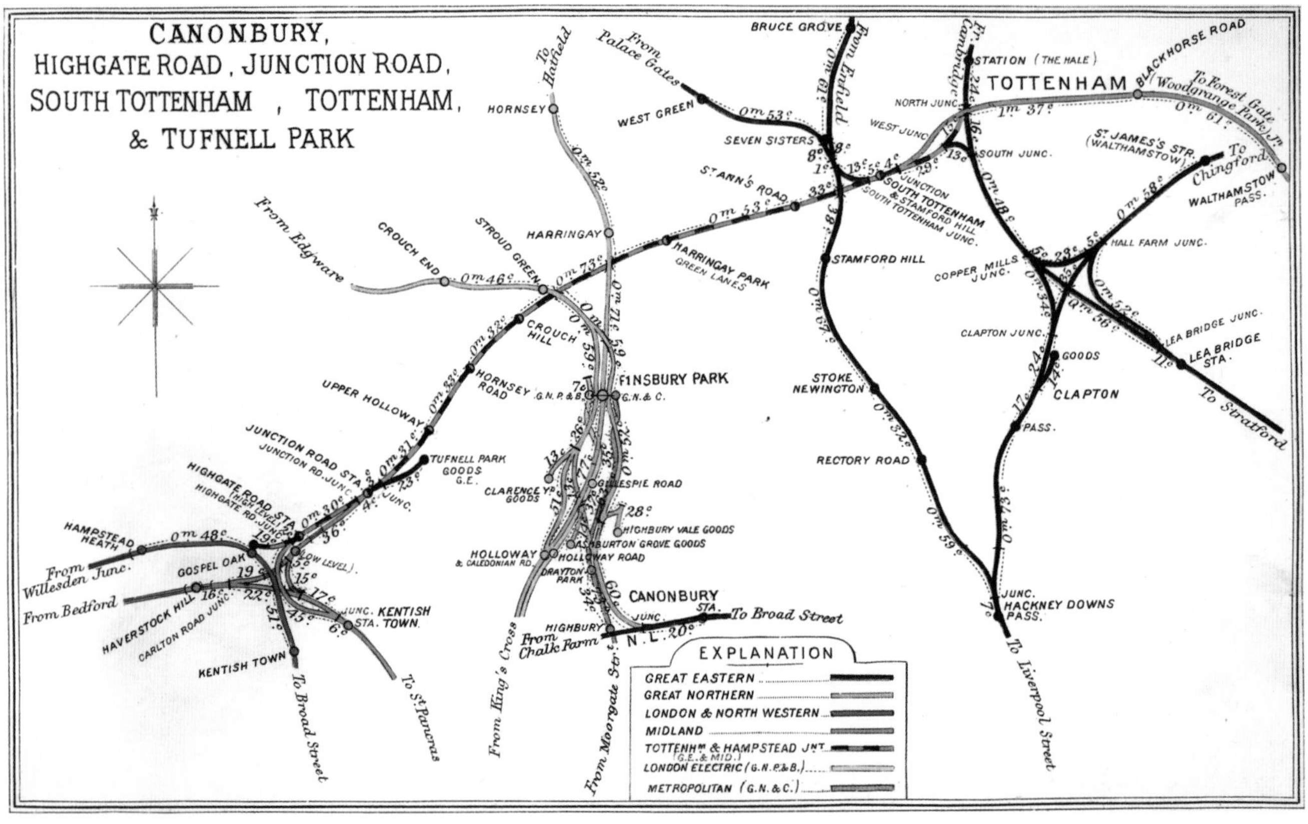
CANONBURY, HIGHGATE ROAD, JUNCTION ROAD, SOUTH TOTTENHAM, TOTTENHAM, & TUFNELL PARK
To Hatfield
From Palace Gates
BRUCE GROVE
From Enfield
STATION (THE HALE)
TOTTENHAM
BLACKHORSE ROAD
To Forest Gate
HORNSEY
WEST GREEN
SEVEN SISTERS
To Chingford
WALTHAMSTOW PASS.
ST. ANN'S ROAD
From Edgware
CROUCH END
STROUD GREEN
HARRINGAY
HARRINGAY PARK GREEN LANES
STAMFORD HILL
HALL FARM JUNC.
COPPER MILLS JUNC.
CROUCH HILL
CLAPTON JUNC.
LEA BRIDGE STA.
UPPER HOLLOWAY
HORNSEY ROAD
FINSBURY PARK
STOKE NEWINGTON
GOODS
CLAPTON
PASS.
To Stratford
JUNCTION ROAD STA.
TUFNELL PARK GOODS G.E.
RECTORY ROAD
HIGHGATE ROAD STA.
GILLESPIE ROAD
HAMPSTEAD HEATH
HIGHBURY VALE GOODS
ASHBURTON GROVE GOODS
From Willesden Junc.
GOSPEL OAK
HOLLOWAY
HOLLOWAY ROAD
From Bedford
DRAYTON PARK
CANONBURY
HAVERSTOCK HILL
KENTISH STA. TOWN
To Broad Street
HIGHBURY
From Chalk Farm
JUNC. HACKNEY DOWNS PASS.
KENTISH TOWN
To Broad Street
To St. Pancras
From King's Cross
From Moorgate Str.
To Liverpool Street
EXPLANATION
GREAT EASTERN
GREAT NORTHERN
LONDON & NORTH WESTERN
MIDLAND
TOTTENHM & HAMPSTEAD JNT (G.E. & MID.)
LONDON ELECTRIC (G.N.P.&B.)
METROPOLITAN (G.N.&C.)

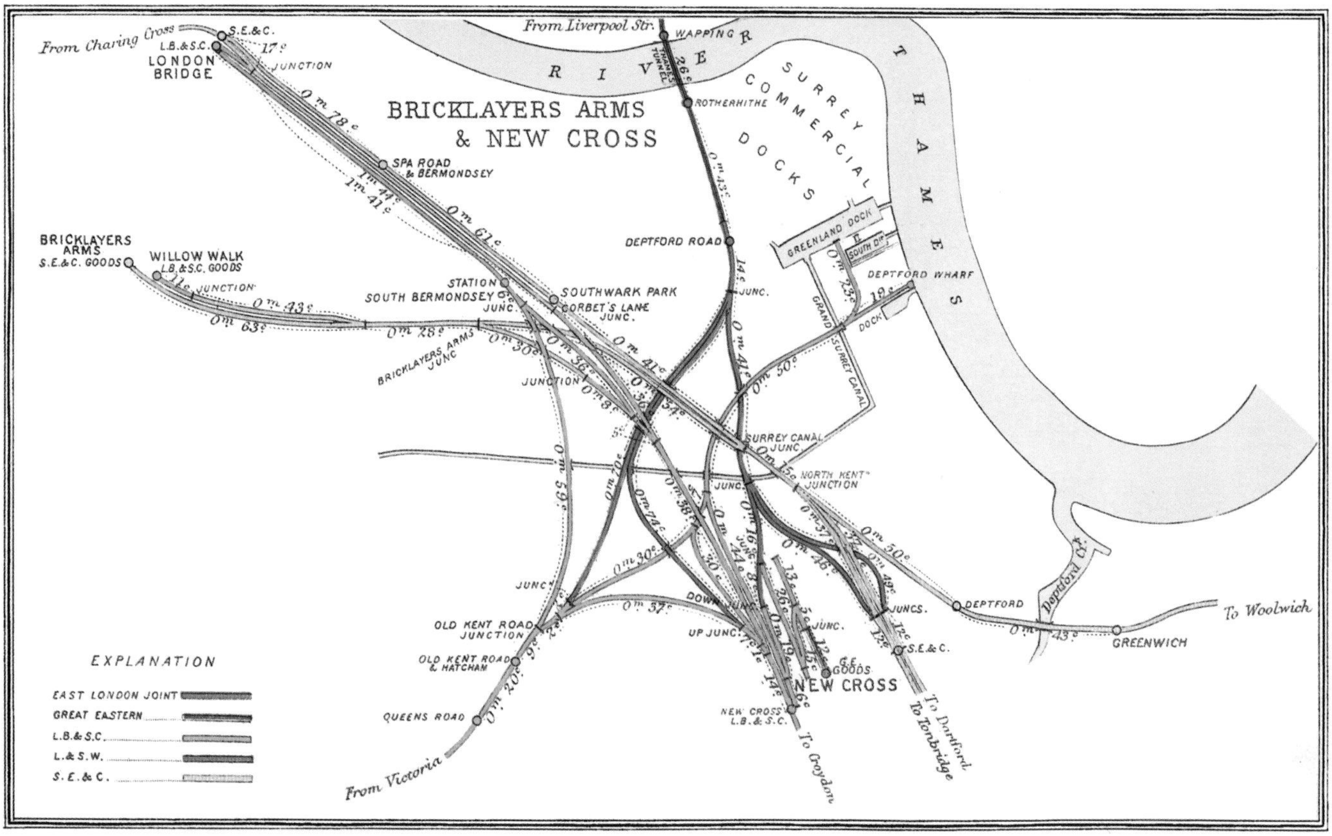

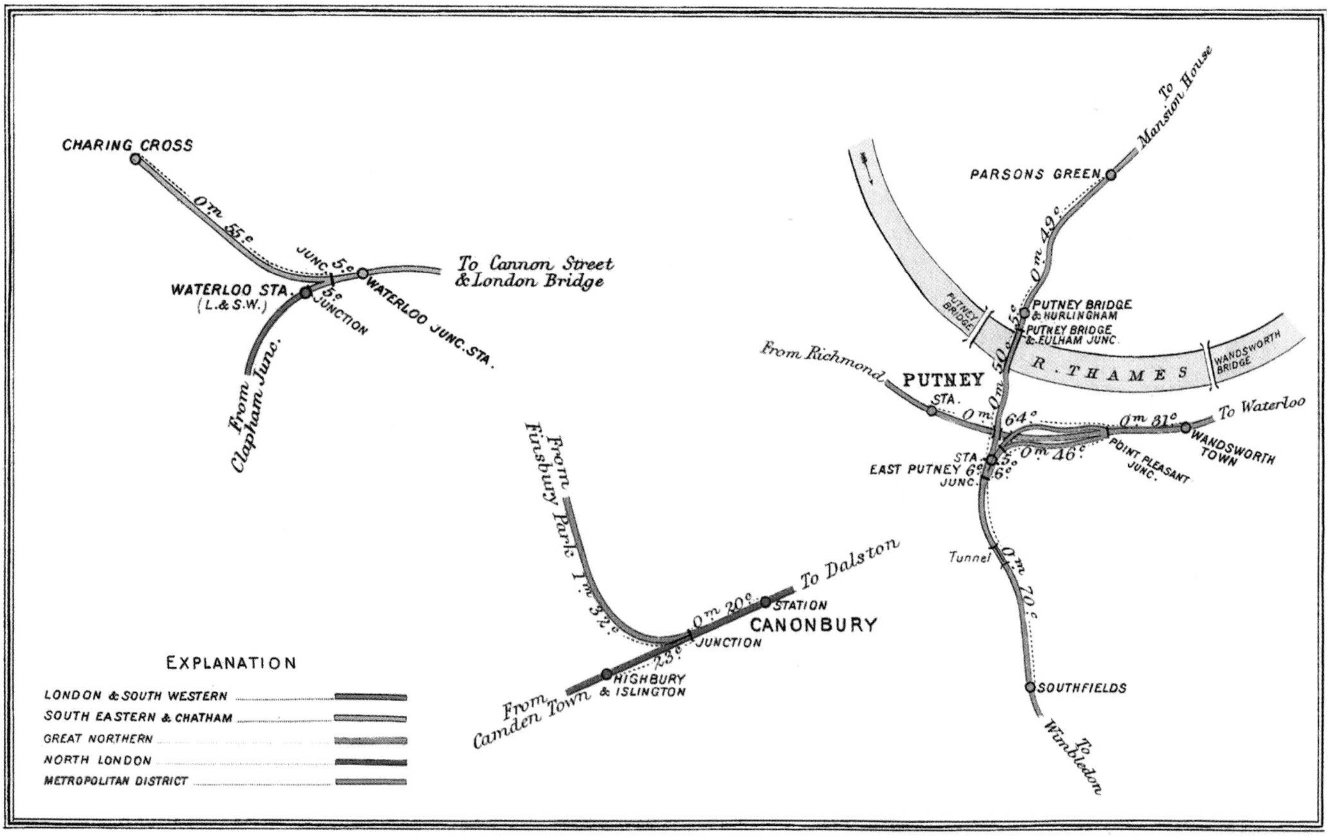

Charing Cross–Waterloo Station–Canonbury–Putney

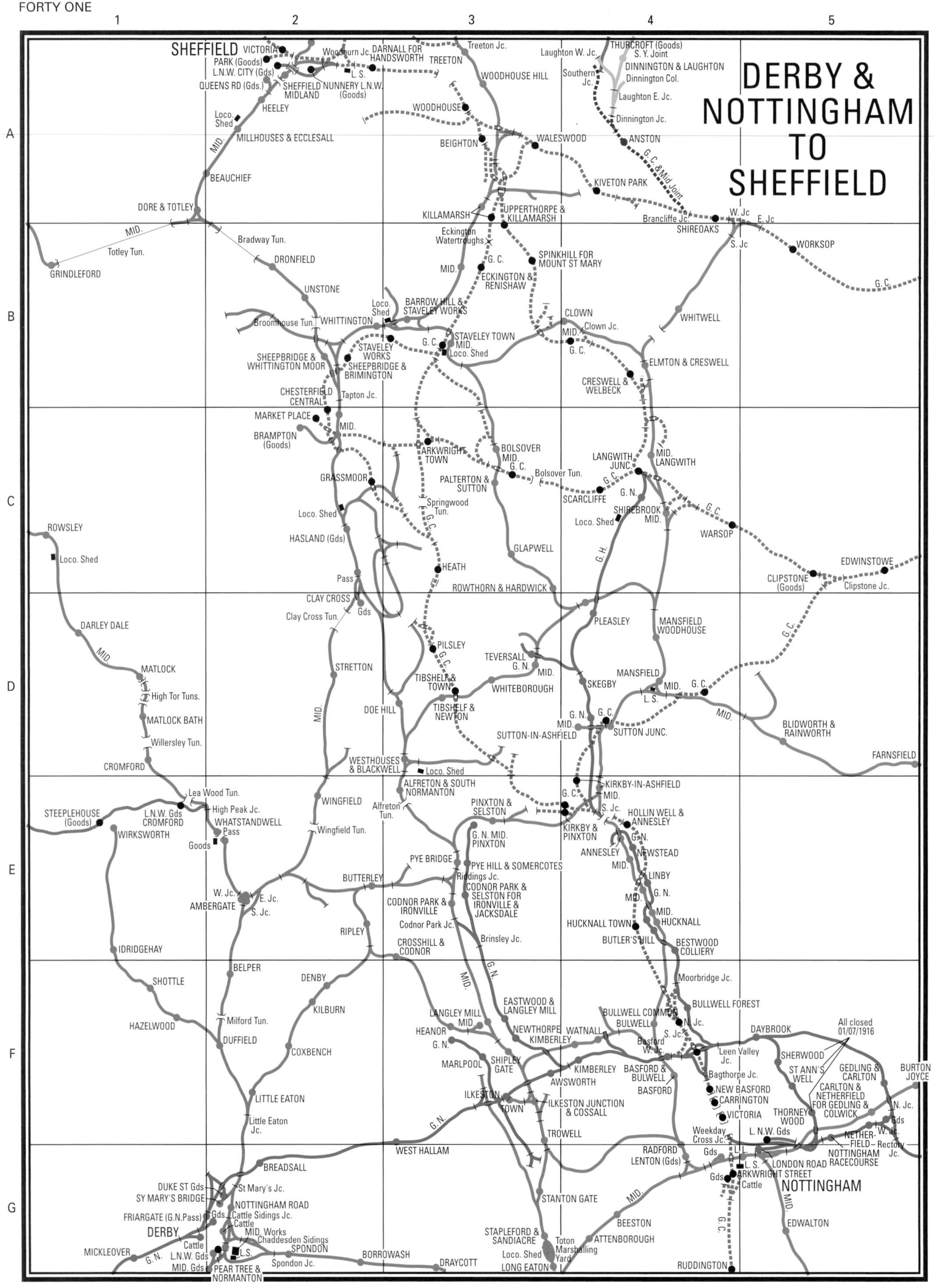
DERBY &
NOTTINGHAM
TO
SHEFFIELD
1
2
3
4
5
A
B
C
D
E
F
G
SHEFFIELD
VICTORIA
PARK (Goods)
L.N.W. CITY (Gds)
QUEENS RD (Gds.)
SHEFFIELD MIDLAND
NUNNERY L.N.W. (Goods)
Woodburn Jc.
DARNALL FOR HANDSWORTH
TREETON
Treeton Jc.
L.S.
WOODHOUSE HILL
WOODHOUSE
HEELEY
Loco. Shed
MILLHOUSES & ECCLESALL
MID.
BEAUCHIEF
DORE & TOTLEY
Totley Tun.
GRINDLEFORD
Bradway Tun.
DRONFIELD
UNSTONE
Laughton W. Jc.
THURCROFT (Goods)
S. Y. Joint
DINNINGTON & LAUGHTON
Dinnington Col.
Southern Jc.
Laughton E. Jc.
Dinnington Jc.
ANSTON
G. C. & Mid. Joint
BEIGHTON
WALESWOOD
KIVETON PARK
KILLAMARSH
UPPERTHORPE & KILLAMARSH
Eckington Watertroughs
Brancliffe Jc.
W. Jc
E. Jc
S. Jc
SHIREOAKS
WORKSOP
G. C.
SPINKHILL FOR MOUNT ST MARY
ECKINGTON & RENISHAW
WHITWELL
BARROW HILL & STAVELEY WORKS
Broomhouse Tun.
WHITTINGTON
CLOWN
Clown Jc.
STAVELEY TOWN
STAVELEY WORKS
Loco. Shed
SHEEPBRIDGE & WHITTINGTON MOOR
SHEEPBRIDGE & BRIMINGTON
ELMTON & CRESWELL
CRESWELL & WELBECK
CHESTERFIELD CENTRAL
Tapton Jc.
MARKET PLACE
BRAMPTON (Goods)
ARKWRIGHT TOWN
BOLSOVER
Bolsover Tun.
LANGWITH JUNC.
LANGWITH
PALTERTON & SUTTON
SCARCLIFFE
GRASSMOOR
Springwood Tun.
SHIREBROOK
WARSOP
ROWSLEY
HASLAND (Gds)
GLAPWELL
EDWINSTOWE
CLIPSTONE (Goods)
Clipstone Jc.
HEATH
Pass
ROWTHORN & HARDWICK
CLAY CROSS
Clay Cross Tun.
Gds
DARLEY DALE
PLEASLEY
MANSFIELD WOODHOUSE
PILSLEY
TEVERSALL
MATLOCK
High Tor Tuns.
MATLOCK BATH
STRETTON
TIBSHELF & TOWN
WHITEBOROUGH
SKEGBY
MANSFIELD
DOE HILL
TIBSHELF & NEWTON
BLIDWORTH & RAINWORTH
Willersley Tun.
SUTTON-IN-ASHFIELD
SUTTON JUNC.
CROMFORD
WESTHOUSES & BLACKWELL
FARNSFIELD
KIRKBY-IN-ASHFIELD
ALFRETON & SOUTH NORMANTON
Lea Wood Tun.
WINGFIELD
Alfreton Tun.
PINXTON & SELSTON
STEEPLEHOUSE (Goods)
L.N.W. Gds CROMFORD
High Peak Jc.
WHATSTANDWELL
KIRKBY & PINXTON
HOLLIN WELL & ANNESLEY
WIRKSWORTH
Wingfield Tun.
G. N. MID. PINXTON
ANNESLEY
NEWSTEAD
PYE BRIDGE
PYE HILL & SOMERCOTES
Riddings Jc.
LINBY
BUTTERLEY
W. Jc.
E. Jc.
S. Jc.
AMBERGATE
CODNOR PARK & IRONVILLE
CODNOR PARK & SELSTON FOR IRONVILLE & JACKSDALE
Codnor Park Jc.
HUCKNALL TOWN
HUCKNALL
RIPLEY
BUTLER'S HILL
BESTWOOD COLLIERY
IDRIDGEHAY
CROSSHILL & CODNOR
Brinsley Jc.
BELPER
DENBY
Moorbridge Jc.
SHOTTLE
KILBURN
BULLWELL FOREST
EASTWOOD & LANGLEY MILL
LANGLEY MILL
Milford Tun.
HAZELWOOD
BULLWELL COMMON
BULWELL
N. Jc.
DAYBROOK
All closed 01/07/1916
DUFFIELD
HEANOR
NEWTHORPE
WATNALL
KIMBERLEY
S. Jc.
Basford W. Jc.
COXBENCH
Leen Valley Jc.
SHERWOOD
MARLPOOL
SHIPLEY GATE
KIMBERLEY
BASFORD & BULWELL
Bagthorpe Jc.
ST ANN'S WELL
GEDLING & CARLTON
BURTON JOYCE
AWSWORTH
BASFORD
CARLTON & NETHERFIELD FOR GEDLING & COLWICK
LITTLE EATON
ILKESTON
TOWN
ILKESTON JUNCTION & COSSALL
NEW BASFORD
CARRINGTON
VICTORIA
THORNEY WOOD
N. Jc.
Little Eaton Jc.
Weekday Cross Jc.
L.N.W. Gds
TROWELL
NETHERFIELD
Rectory Jc.
WEST HALLAM
RADFORD
LENTON (Gds)
LONDON ROAD
NOTTINGHAM RACECOURSE
BREADSALL
ARKWRIGHT STREET
Cattle
NOTTINGHAM
DUKE ST Gds
St Mary's Jc.
SY MARY'S BRIDGE
NOTTINGHAM ROAD
STANTON GATE
FRIARGATE (G.N.Pass)
Cattle Sidings Jc.
DERBY
MID. Works
Chaddesden Sidings
BEESTON
EDWALTON
STAPLEFORD & SANDIACRE
ATTENBOROUGH
MICKLEOVER
L.N.W. Gds
SPONDON
BORROWASH
Toton Marshalling Yard
MID. Gds
Spondon Jc.
DRAYCOTT
LONG EATON
RUDDINGTON
PEAR TREE & NORMANTON
G. N.
G. H.

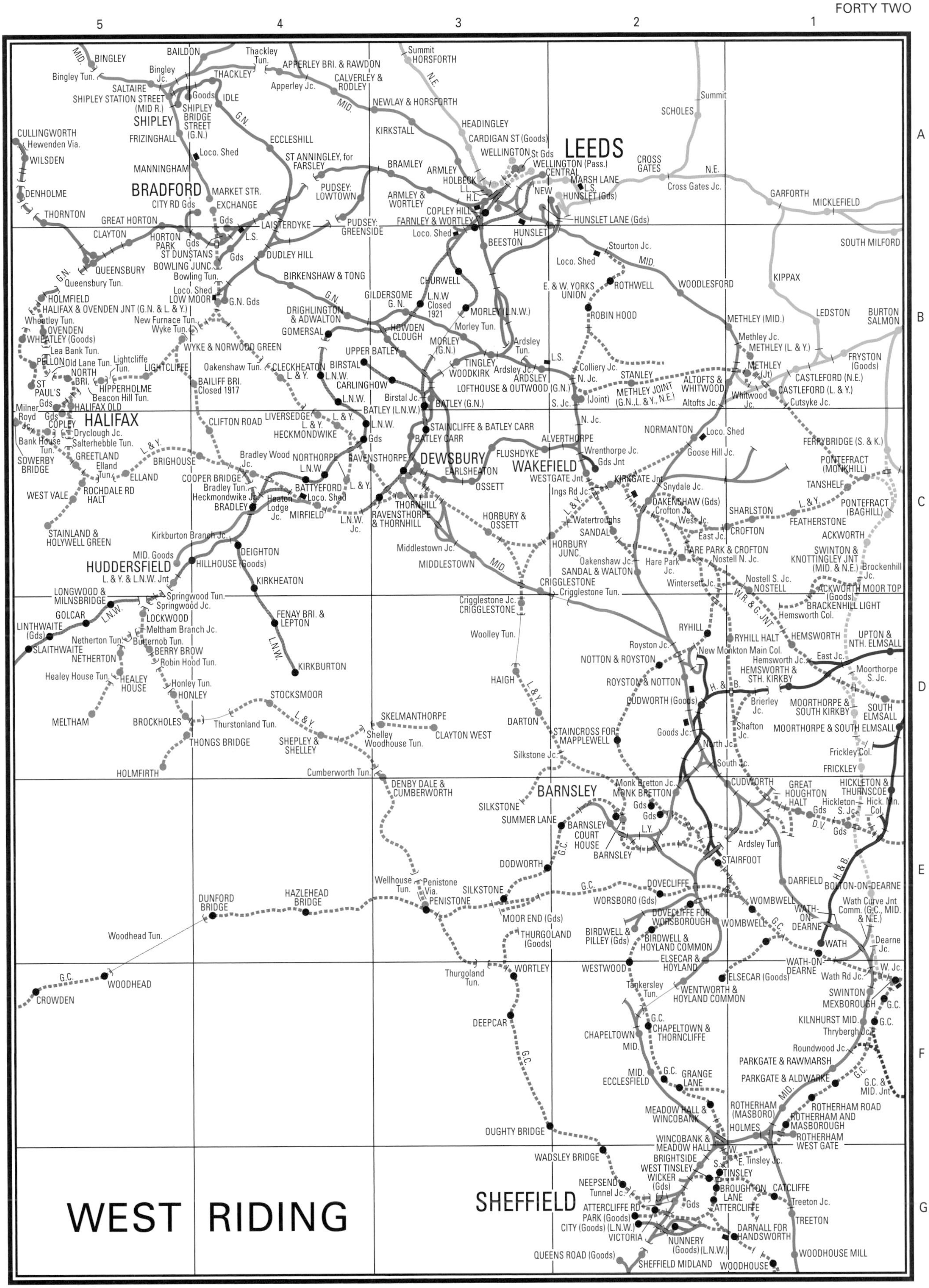

## FORTY TWO

5 4 3 2 1

MID. BINGLEY BAILDON Thackley Tun. APPERLEY BRI. & RAWDON Summit HORSFORTH
Bingley Tun. Bingley Jc. THACKLEY Apperley Jc. CALVERLEY & RODLEY N.E.
SALTAIRE SHIPLEY STATION STREET (MID R.) Goods IDLE MID. NEWLAY & HORSFORTH Summit
SHIPLEY SHIPLEY BRIDGE STREET (G.N.) G.N. SCHOLES
CULLINGWORTH Hewenden Via. FRIZINGHALL ECCLESHILL KIRKSTALL HEADINGLEY
WILSDEN Loco. Shed CARDIGAN ST (Goods) LEEDS A
MANNINGHAM ST ANNINGLEY, for FARSLEY BRAMLEY WELLINGTON St Gds CROSS GATES
ARMLEY WELLINGTON (Pass.) N.E.
BRADFORD MARKET STR. PUDSEY: LOWTOWN HOLBECK CENTRAL MARSH LANE Cross Gates Jc.
DENHOLME CITY RD Gds EXCHANGE ARMLEY & WORTLEY L.L. H.L. NEW L.S. HUNSLET (Gds) GARFORTH MICKLEFIELD
THORNTON COPLEY HILL
GREAT HORTON Gds LAISTERDYKE PUDSEY: GREENSIDE FARNLEY & WORTLEY HUNSLET LANE (Gds)
CLAYTON HORTON PARK Gds L.S. Loco. Shed HUNSLET SOUTH MILFORD
ST DUNSTANS Gds DUDLEY HILL BEESTON Stourton Jc.
QUEENSBURY BOWLING JUNC. Loco. Shed MID.
G.N. Queensbury Tun. Bowling Tun. BIRKENSHAW & TONG CHURWELL ROTHWELL WOODLESFORD KIPPAX
Loco. Shed E. & W. YORKS UNION
HOLMFIELD LOW MOOR G.N. Gds G.N. GILDERSOME G. N. L.N.W Closed 1921
HALIFAX & OVENDEN JNT (G.N. & L. & Y.) DRIGHLINGTON & ADWALTON MORLEY (L.N.W.) ROBIN HOOD METHLEY (MID.) LEDSTON BURTON SALMON B
Wheatley Tun. New Furnace Tun. Wyke Tun. GOMERSAL HOWDEN CLOUGH Morley Tun.
OVENDEN Methley Jc.
WHEATLEY (Goods) WYKE & NORWOOD GREEN UPPER BATLEY MORLEY (G.N.) Ardsley Tun. METHLEY (L. & Y.) FRYSTON (Goods)
Lea Bank Tun. L.S.
PELLON Old Lane Tun. Lightcliffe Tun. LIGHTCLIFFE Oakenshaw Tun. CLECKHEATON L. & Y. BIRSTAL TINGLEY Ardsley Jc. Colliery Jc. METHLEY (Jt) CASTLEFORD (N.E.)
NORTH BRI. WOODKIRK ARDSLEY N. Jc. STANLEY ALTOFTS & WHITWOOD
ST PAUL'S HIPPERHOLME BAILIFF BRI. Closed 1917 L.N.W. CARLINGHOW LOFTHOUSE & OUTWOOD (G.N.) METHLEY JOINT (G.N., L. & Y., N.E.) CASTLEFORD (L. & Y.)
Gds Beacon Hill Tun. Birstal Jc. S. Jc. (Joint) Whitwood Jc. Cutsyke Jc.
Milner Royd Jc. HALIFAX OLD L.N.W. BATLEY (G.N.) Altofts Jc.
Gds HALIFAX CLIFTON ROAD LIVERSEDGE L. & Y. L. & Y. BATLEY (L.N.W.) N. Jc.
COPLEY Dryclough Jc. HECKMONDWIKE L.N.W. STAINCLIFFE & BATLEY CARR NORMANTON Loco. Shed
Bank House Tun. Salterhebble Tun. Gds BATLEY CARR ALVERTHORPE FERRYBRIDGE (S. & K.)
SOWERBY BRIDGE GREETLAND L. & Y. Bradley Wood Jc. NORTHORPE RAVENSTHORPE DEWSBURY FLUSHDYKE Wrenthorpe Jc. Goose Hill Jc. PONTEFRACT (MONKHILL)
Elland Tun. BRIGHOUSE L.N.W. WAKEFIELD Gds Jnt
ELLAND COOPER BRIDGE EARLSHEATON WESTGATE Jnt KIRKGATE Jnt TANSHELF
WEST VALE ROCHDALE RD HALT Bradley Tun. BATTYEFORD L. & Y. OSSETT Ings Rd Jc. Snydale Jc. C
Heckmondwike Jc. Loco. Shed L.N.W. Jc. THORNHILL OAKENSHAW (Gds) SHARLSTON L. & Y. PONTEFRACT (BAGHILL)
BRADLEY Heaton Lodge Jc. MIRFIELD RAVENSTHORPE & THORNHILL HORBURY & OSSETT L. & Y. Crofton Jc. FEATHERSTONE
STAINLAND & HOLYWELL GREEN Kirkburton Branch Jc. Watertroughs West Jc. CROFTON
DEIGHTON Middlestown Jc. SANDAL East Jc. ACKWORTH
MID. Goods HORBURY JUNC. HARE PARK & CROFTON SWINTON & KNOTTINGLEY JNT (MID. & N.E.)
HUDDERSFIELD HILLHOUSE (Goods) MIDDLESTOWN MID. Oakenshaw Jc. Hare Park Jc. Nostell N. Jc. Brockenhill Jc.
L. & Y. & L.N.W. Jnt KIRKHEATON SANDAL & WALTON Wintersett Jc. Nostell S. Jc.
LONGWOOD & MILNSBRIDGE CRIGGLESTONE NOSTELL ACKWORTH MOOR TOP (Goods)
Springwood Tun. Crigglestone Tun. W.R. & G. JNT
GOLCAR L.N.W. Springwood Jc. Crigglestone Jc. CRIGGLESTONE BRACKENHILL LIGHT
LINTHWAITE (Gds) LOCKWOOD FENAY BRI. & LEPTON Hemsworth Col.
Netherton Tun. Meltham Branch Jc. RYHILL
SLAITHWAITE Butternob Tun. Woolley Tun. RYHILL HALT HEMSWORTH UPTON & NTH. ELMSALL
NETHERTON BERRY BROW L.N.W. Royston Jc. New Monkton Main Col.
Robin Hood Tun. NOTTON & ROYSTON Hemsworth Jc. East Jc.
Healey House Tun. HEALEY HOUSE KIRKBURTON HEMSWORTH & STH. KIRKBY Moorthorpe S. Jc.
Honley Tun. HAIGH ROYSTON & NOTTON H. & B. D
HONLEY STOCKSMOOR L. & Y. CUDWORTH (Goods) Brierley Jc. MOORTHORPE & SOUTH KIRBY SOUTH ELMSALL
MELTHAM BROCKHOLES Thurstonland Tun. L. & Y. SKELMANTHORPE DARTON Goods Jc. Shafton Jc.
THONGS BRIDGE SHEPLEY & SHELLEY Shelley Woodhouse Tun. CLAYTON WEST STAINCROSS FOR MAPPLEWELL MOORTHORPE & SOUTH ELMSALL
North Jc. Frickley Col.
HOLMFIRTH Cumberworth Tun. Silkstone Jc. South Jc. FRICKLEY
DENBY DALE & CUMBERWORTH Monk Bretton Jc. CUDWORTH GREAT HOUGHTON HALT HICKLETON & THURNSCOE
BARNSLEY MONK BRETTON Hickleton Hick. Mn. Col.
SILKSTONE Gds Gds S. Jc.
SUMMER LANE BARNSLEY COURT HOUSE L.Y. D.V. Gds
G.C. BARNSLEY Ardsley Tun. H. & B.
DODWORTH STAIRFOOT E
Wellhouse Tun. Penistone Via. DARFIELD BOLTON-ON-DEARNE
DUNFORD BRIDGE HAZLEHEAD BRIDGE SILKSTONE G.C. DOVECLIFFE Wath Curve Jnt Comm. (G.C., MID. & N.E.)
PENISTONE WORSBORO (Gds) WOMBWELL
MOOR END (Gds) DOVECLIFFE FOR WORSBOROUGH WOMBWELL G.C. WATH-ON-DEARNE
Woodhead Tun. THURGOLAND (Goods) BIRDWELL & PILLEY (Gds) BIRDWELL & HOYLAND COMMON WATH Dearne Jc.
ELSECAR & HOYLAND
G.C. WOODHEAD Thurgoland Tun. WORTLEY WESTWOOD ELSECAR (Goods) WATH-ON-DEARNE W. Jc.
CROWDEN Tankersley Tun. WENTWORTH & HOYLAND COMMON Wath Rd Jc.
SWINTON MEXBOROUGH G.C.
DEEPCAR G.C. CHAPELTOWN & THORNCLIFFE KILNHURST MID. G.C.
CHAPELTOWN MID. Thrybergh Jc.
G.C. Roundwood Jc. F
PARKGATE & RAWMARSH
MID. ECCLESFIELD G.C. GRANGE LANE PARKGATE & ALDWARKE G.C. G.C. & MID. Jnt
MEADOW HALL & WINCOBANK ROTHERHAM (MASBORO) MID. ROTHERHAM ROAD
OUGHTY BRIDGE ROTHERHAM AND MASBOROUGH
HOLMES ROTHERHAM WEST GATE
WINCOBANK & MEADOW HALL W.
WADSLEY BRIDGE BRIGHTSIDE S. E. Tinsley Jc.
WEST TINSLEY TINSLEY
NEEPSEND WICKER (Gds) BROUGHTON LANE CATCLIFFE
Tunnel Jc. Gds Treeton Jc. G
SHEFFIELD ATTERCLIFFE RD ATTERCLIFFE
PARK (Goods) TREETON
CITY (Goods) (L.N.W.) DARNALL FOR HANDSWORTH
VICTORIA NUNNERY (Goods) (L.N.W.)
QUEENS ROAD (Goods) SHEFFIELD MIDLAND WOODHOUSE WOODHOUSE MILL

# WEST RIDING

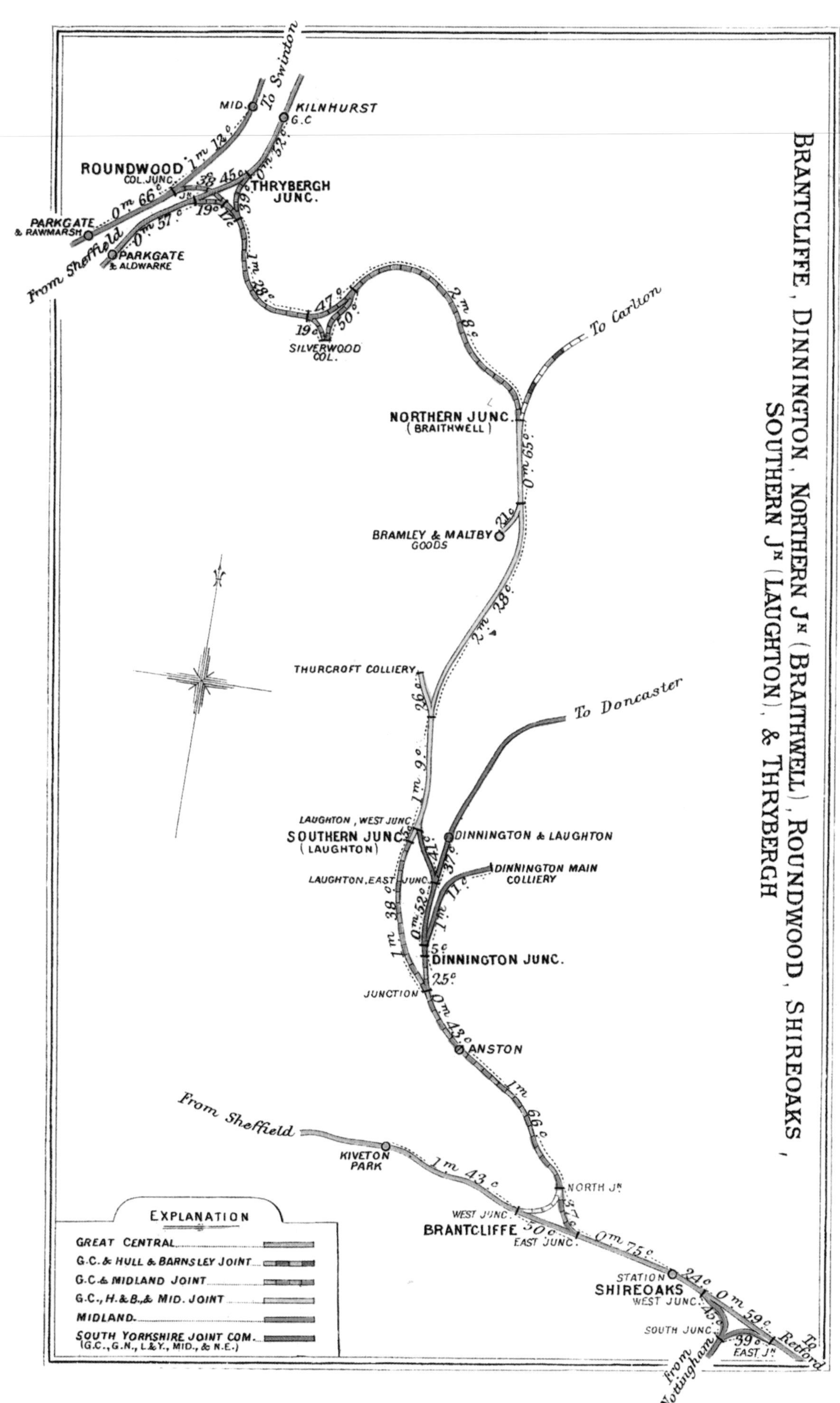
BRANTCLIFFE, DINNINGTON, NORTHERN Jn (BRAITHWELL), ROUNDWOOD, SHIREOAKS, SOUTHERN Jn (LAUGHTON), & THRYBERGH
To Swinton
MID.
KILNHURST
G.C.
ROUNDWOOD
COL. JUNC.
THRYBERGH
JUNC.
PARKGATE
& RAWMARSH
PARKGATE
& ALDWARKE
From Sheffield
SILVERWOOD
COL.
To Carlton
NORTHERN JUNC.
(BRAITHWELL)
BRAMLEY & MALTBY
GOODS
THURCROFT COLLIERY
To Doncaster
LAUGHTON, WEST JUNC.
SOUTHERN JUNC.
(LAUGHTON)
DINNINGTON & LAUGHTON
DINNINGTON MAIN
COLLIERY
LAUGHTON, EAST JUNC.
DINNINGTON JUNC.
JUNCTION
ANSTON
From Sheffield
KIVETON
PARK
NORTH Jn
WEST JUNC.
BRANTCLIFFE
EAST JUNC.
STATION
SHIREOAKS
WEST JUNC.
SOUTH JUNC.
EAST Jn
To Retford
from Nottingham
EXPLANATION
GREAT CENTRAL
G.C. & HULL & BARNSLEY JOINT
G.C. & MIDLAND JOINT
G.C., H.& B., & MID. JOINT
MIDLAND
SOUTH YORKSHIRE JOINT COM.
(G.C., G.N., L.& Y., MID., & N.E.)

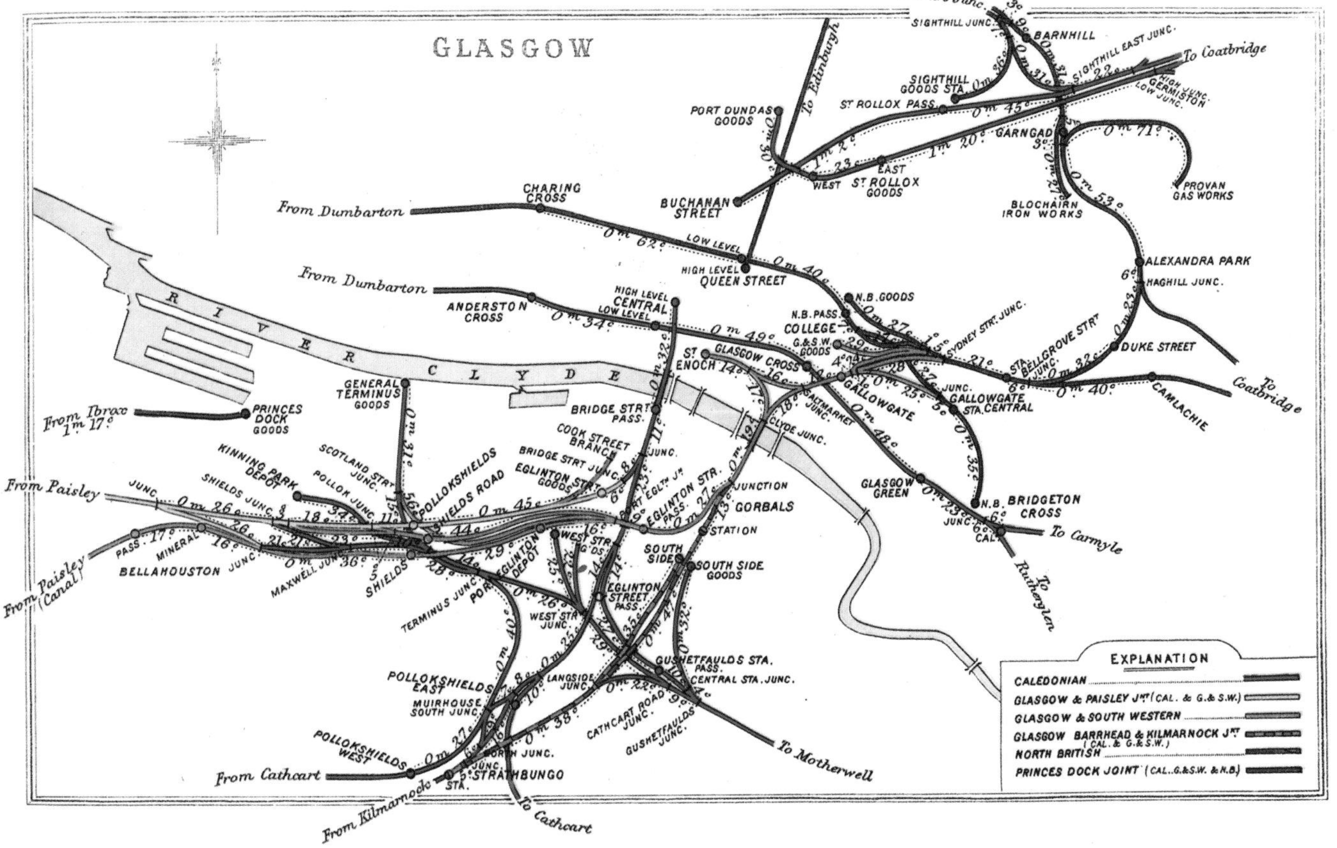

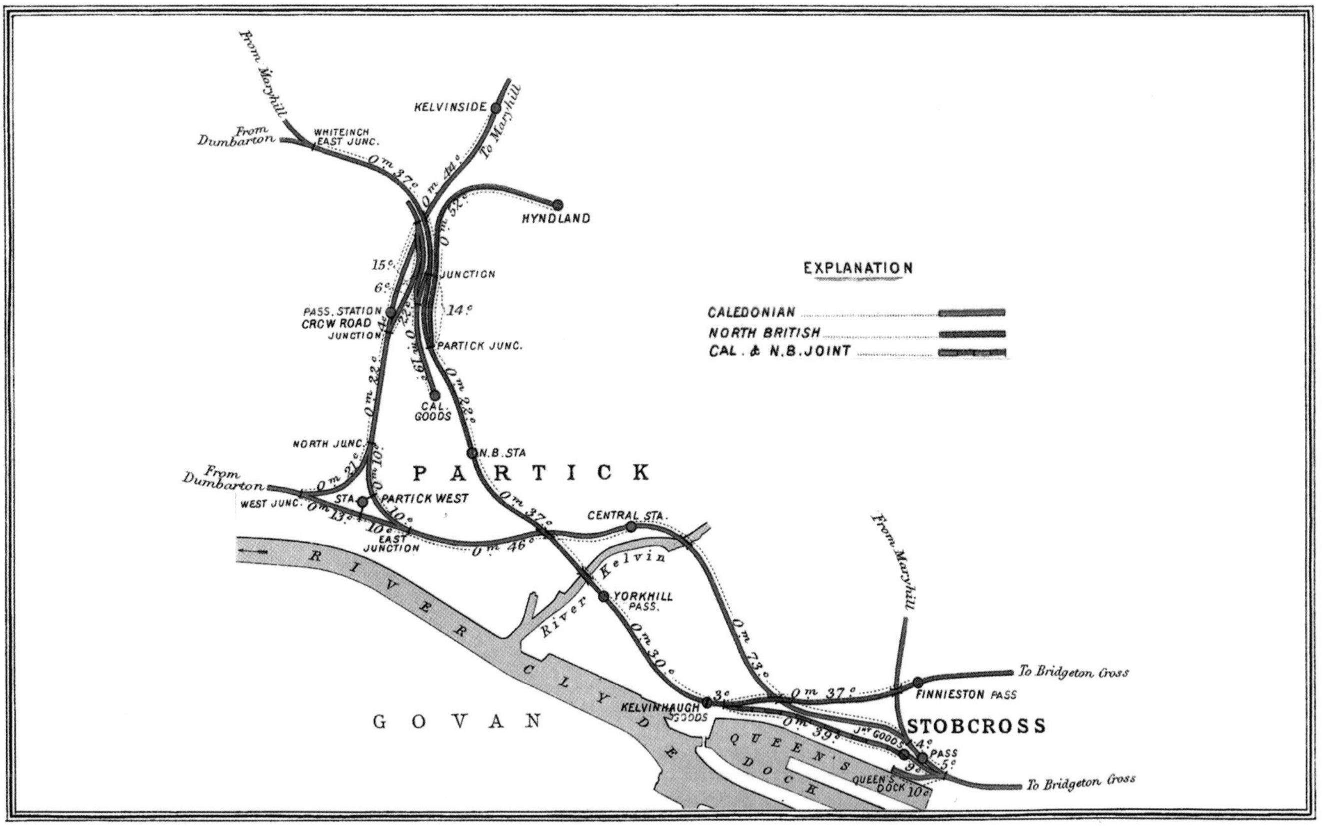

**Partick–Stobcross**

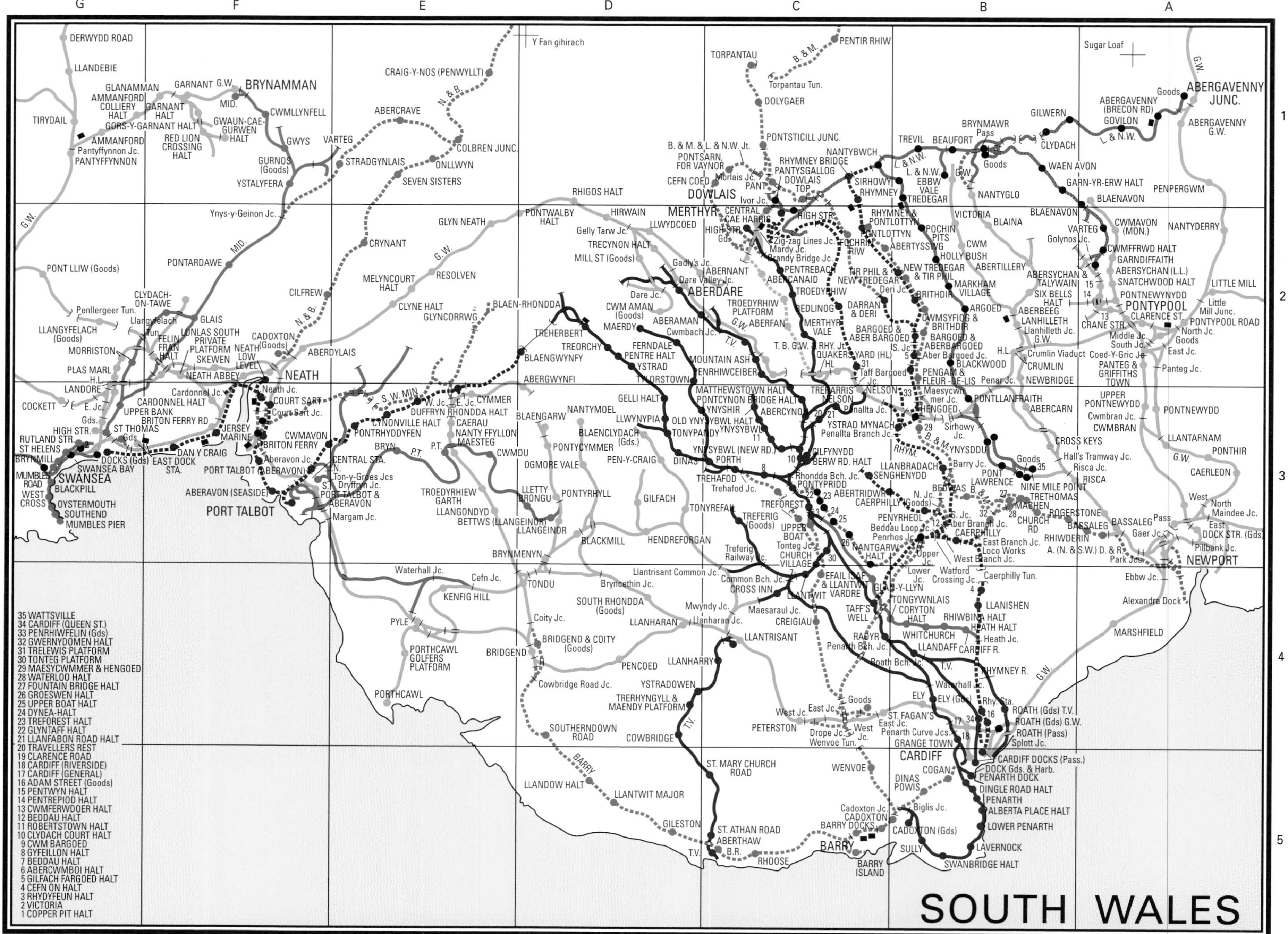
SOUTH WALES
A
B
C
D
E
F
G
1
2
3
4
5
ABERGAVENNY JUNC.
NEWPORT
PONTYPOOL
CARDIFF
BARRY
MERTHYR
DOWLAIS
ABERDARE
BRYNAMMAN
NEATH
PORT TALBOT
SWANSEA
35 WATTSVILLE
34 CARDIFF (QUEEN ST.)
33 PENRHIWFELIN (Gds)
32 GWERNYDOMEN HALT
31 TRELEWIS PLATFORM
30 TONTEG PLATFORM
29 MAESYCWMMER & HENGOED
28 WATERLOO HALT
27 FOUNTAIN BRIDGE HALT
26 GROESWEN HALT
25 UPPER BOAT HALT
24 DYNEA-HALT
23 TREFOREST HALT
22 GLYNTAFF HALT
21 LLANFABON ROAD HALT
20 TRAVELLERS REST
19 CLARENCE ROAD
18 CARDIFF (RIVERSIDE)
17 CARDIFF (GENERAL)
16 ADAM STREET (Goods)
15 PENTWYN HALT
14 PENTREPIOD HALT
13 CWMFFERWDOER HALT
12 BEDDAU HALT
11 ROBERTSTOWN HALT
10 CLYDACH COURT HALT
9 CWM BARGOED
8 GYFEILLON HALT
7 BEDDAU HALT
6 ABERCWMBOI HALT
5 GILFACH FARGOED HALT
4 CEFN ON HALT
3 RHYDYFEUN HALT
2 VICTORIA
1 COPPER PIT HALT

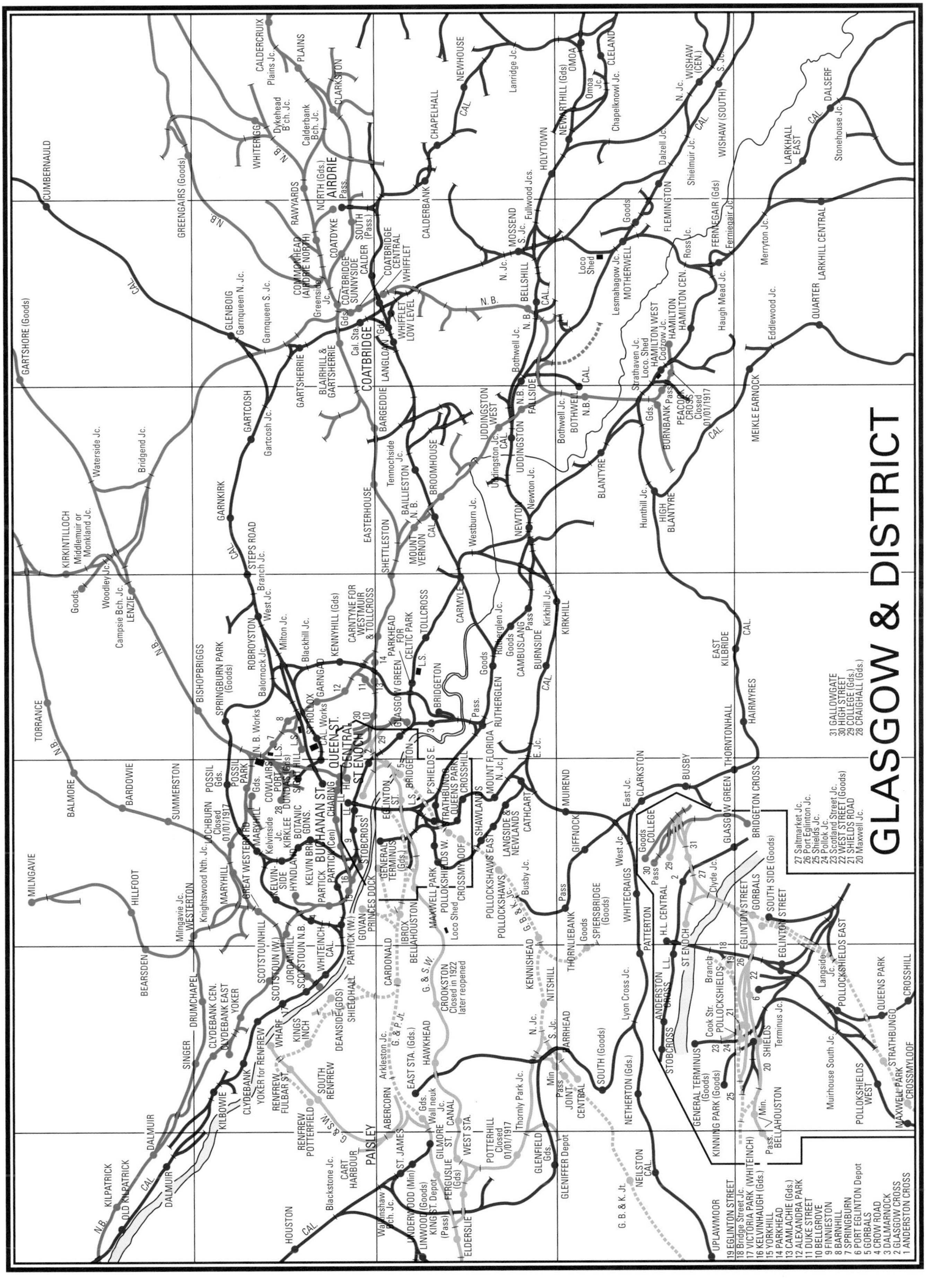

# GLASGOW & DISTRICT

19 EGLINTON STREET
18 Bridge Street Jc.
17 VICTORIA PARK (WHITEINCH)
16 KELVINHAUGH (Gds.)
15 YORKHILL
14 PARKHEAD
13 CAMLACHIE (Gds.)
12 ALEXANDRA PARK
11 DUKE STREET
10 BELLGROVE
9 FINNIESTON
8 BARNHILL
7 SPRINGBURN
6 PORT EGLINTON Depot
5 GORBALS
4 CROW ROAD
3 DALMARNOCK
2 GLASGOW CROSS
1 ANDERSTON CROSS

27 Saltmarket Jc.
26 Port Eglinton Jc.
25 Shields Jc.
24 Pollok Jc.
23 Scotland Street Jc.
22 WEST STREET (Goods)
21 SHIELDS ROAD
20 Maxwell Jc.

31 GALLOWGATE
30 HIGH STREET
29 COLLEGE (Gds.)
28 CRAIGHALL (Gds.)

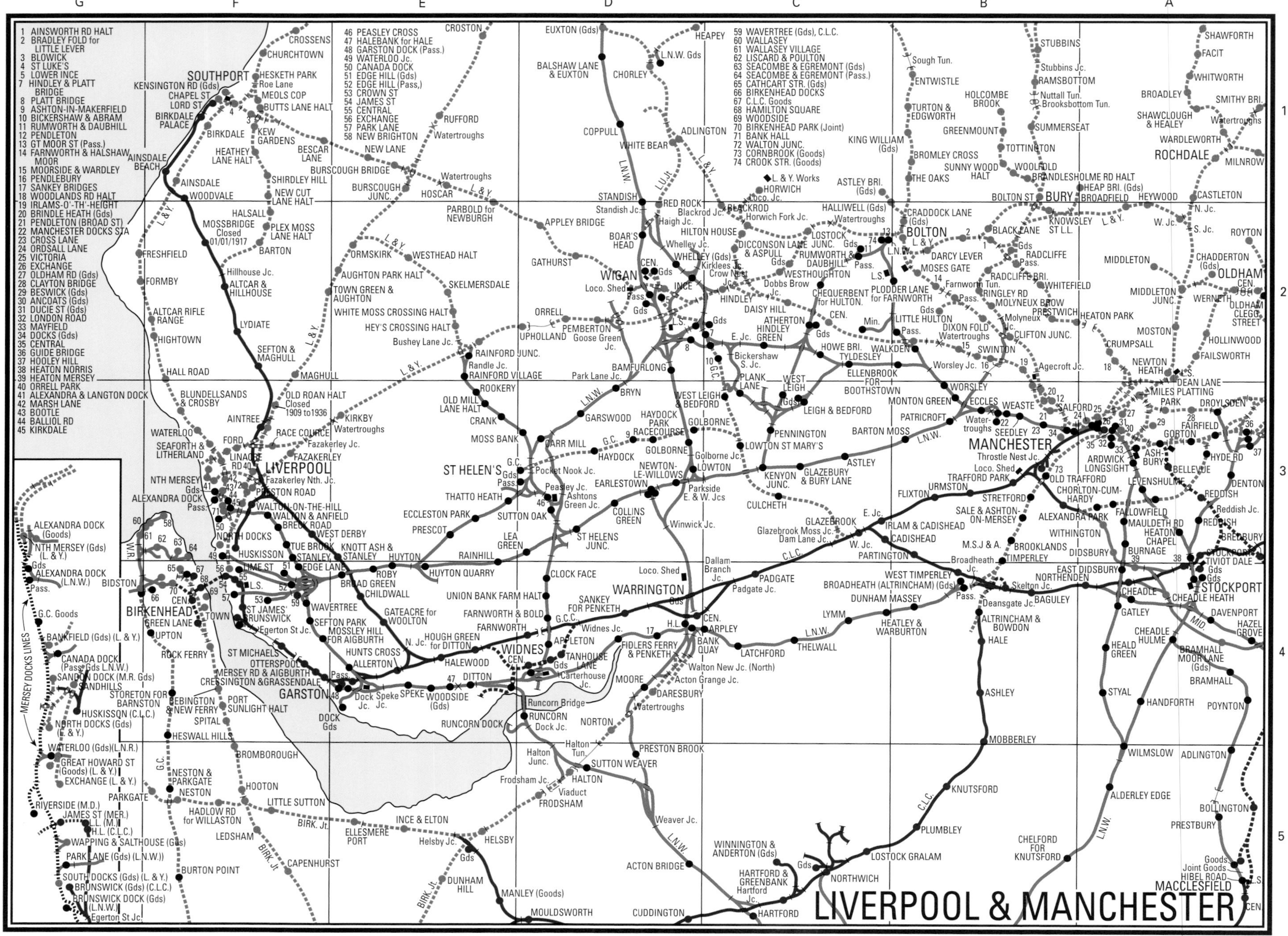
LIVERPOOL & MANCHESTER
1 AINSWORTH RD HALT
2 BRADLEY FOLD for LITTLE LEVER
3 BLOWICK
4 ST LUKE'S
5 LOWER INCE
7 HINDLEY & PLATT BRIDGE
8 PLATT BRIDGE
9 ASHTON-IN-MAKERFIELD
10 BICKERSHAW & ABRAM
11 RUMWORTH & DAUBHILL
12 PENDLETON
13 GT MOOR ST (Pass.)
14 FARNWORTH & HALSHAW MOOR
15 MOORSIDE & WARDLEY
16 PENDLEBURY
17 SANKEY BRIDGES
18 WOODLANDS RD HALT
19 IRLAMS-O'-TH'-HEIGHT
20 BRINDLE HEATH (Gds)
21 PENDLETON (BROAD ST)
22 MANCHESTER DOCKS STA
23 CROSS LANE
24 ORDSALL LANE
25 VICTORIA
26 EXCHANGE
27 OLDHAM RD (Gds)
28 CLAYTON BRIDGE
29 BESWICK (Gds)
30 ANCOATS (Gds)
31 DUCIE ST (Gds)
32 LONDON ROAD
33 MAYFIELD
34 DOCKS (Gds)
35 CENTRAL
36 GUIDE BRIDGE
37 HOOLEY HILL
38 HEATON NORRIS
39 HEATON MERSEY
40 ORRELL PARK
41 ALEXANDRA & LANGTON DOCK
42 MARSH LANE
43 BOOTLE
44 BALLIOL RD
45 KIRKDALE
46 PEASLEY CROSS
47 HALEBANK for HALE
48 GARSTON DOCK (Pass.)
49 WATERLOO Jc.
50 CANADA DOCK
51 EDGE HILL (Gds)
52 EDGE HILL (Pass.)
53 CROWN ST
54 JAMES ST
55 CENTRAL
56 EXCHANGE
57 PARK LANE
58 NEW BRIGHTON
59 WAVERTREE (Gds), C.L.C.
60 WALLASEY
61 WALLASEY VILLAGE
62 LISCARD & POULTON
63 SEACOMBE & EGREMONT (Gds)
64 SEACOMBE & EGREMONT (Pass.)
65 CATHCART STR. (Gds)
66 BIRKENHEAD DOCKS
67 C.L.C. Goods
68 HAMILTON SQUARE
69 WOODSIDE
70 BIRKENHEAD PARK (Joint)
71 BANK HALL
72 WALTON JUNC.
73 CORNBROOK (Goods)
74 CROOK STR. (Goods)
MERSEY DOCKS LINES

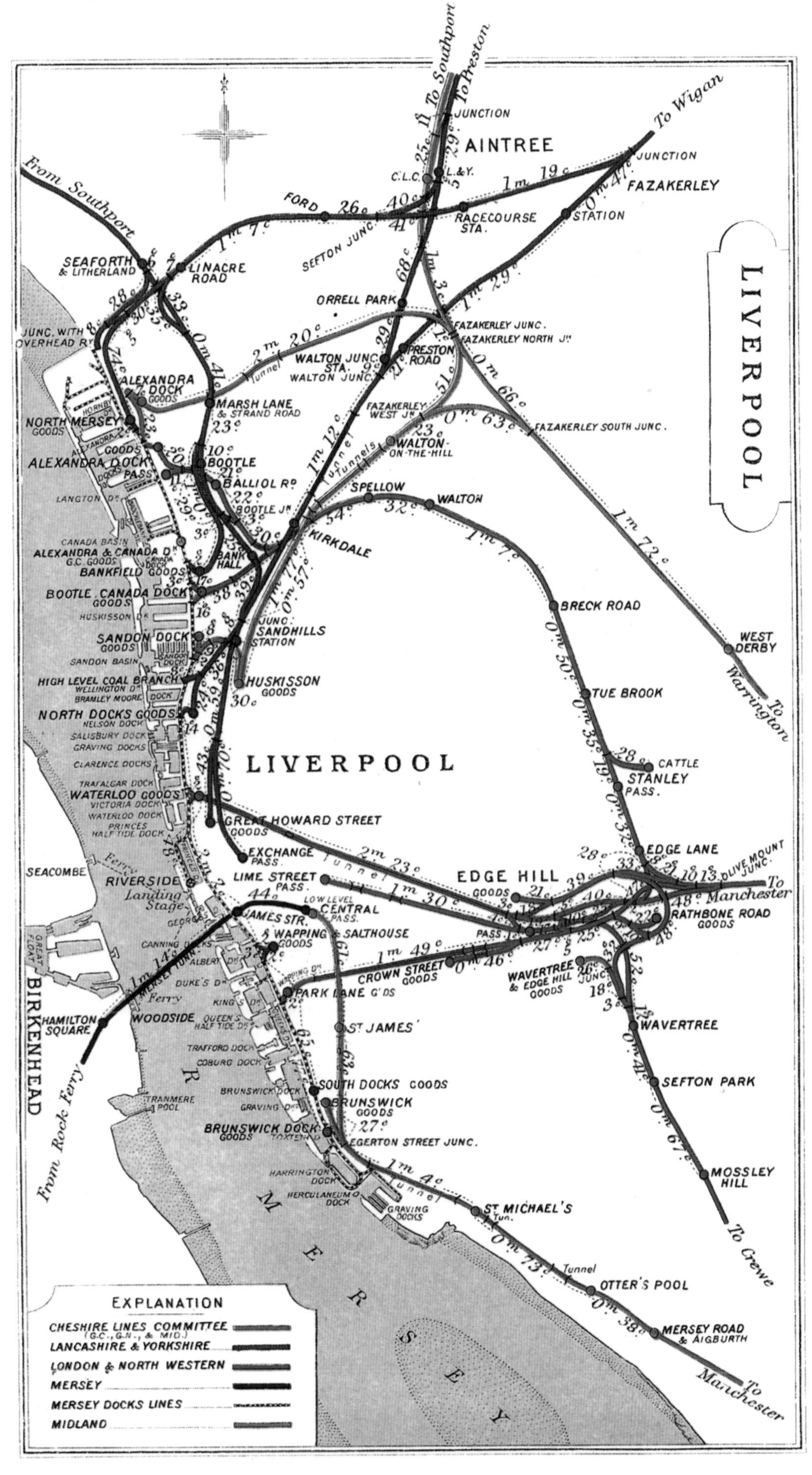
LIVERPOOL
AINTREE
FAZAKERLEY
EDGE HILL
BIRKENHEAD
MERSEY
EXPLANATION
CHESHIRE LINES COMMITTEE (G.C., G.N., & MID.)
LANCASHIRE & YORKSHIRE
LONDON & NORTH WESTERN
MERSEY
MERSEY DOCKS LINES
MIDLAND

## FORTY FIVE

# Gazetteer

This Gazetteer to the Atlas is divided into six parts, in the following order:

1. List of abbreviations used to represent the various companies owning and/or using the various stations, meeting at junctions, etc
2. Index to tunnels named on the maps
3. Index to watertroughs that appear on the maps
4. Index to principal summits named on the maps
5. Index to principal bridges and viaducts marked on the maps
6. Index to stations, junctions, etc

**Stations with dual titles**

Dual titles are only used for stations having the word '&' in such title: they are not cross-indexed and only appear under the first name, e.g. Dunkeld & Birnam only appears under the letter 'D'. In the case of dual titles joined by the word 'for', only the first name is shown.

**Stations sub-titled**

When the sub-title is characteristic, it is indexed in its own right, in addition to the main title, e.g. Norwich is indexed generally under 'N' and also under 'T' as Thorpe (Norwich). Similar entries include the various 'Victorias', Paragon (Hull), Warrior Square (St Leonards), etc. Non-characteristic titles like 'Central', 'Exchange', 'North', 'New', etc, are not directly entered as such, if at all, but when shown they follow the name of the place, e.g. Barnsley (Exchange), Leeds (New).

**Plurality of stations at a single place**

Where two companies each have their own station(s) at any given place, the companies' initials are separated by '&' thus: Bedford, LNW & Mid; Tunbridge Wells, LBSC & SEC. When three or more companies have stations in a place, a comma (,) separates the first two or more, e.g. Cymmer, GW, RSB & SWM.

Joint stations are shown with the initials of the owning partners or of the Joint undertaking if it has a specific name, e.g. Cosham, LBSC&LSWJt.; Ludlow, S&H.

**Ownership and users of stations**

Stations used by more than one company, in so far as passenger traffic is concerned, are shown with the owning company or companies in bolder type, followed by other users shown within brackets, as under (the ramifications of goods workings are too complex to be included):
Aberdeen (Pass), **Cal&GNSJt** (NB)
Branksome, **LSW**(SD)
Crewe, **LNW**(GW/NS)

In some instances, a 'foreign' user has been shown as a matter of interest even though such user may have ceased slightly earlier than 1922. It has also been shown in those cases where an absorbed company appears in its own right on the maps, e.g. Bridgend, **GW**(BRY), the Barry Railway having been absorbed by the GWR prior to the general grouping.

Joint stations used by other companies in addition to the Joint owning partners are shown thus, the joint partners not being individually shown:
Ackworth, **SK**(GN/GC)
Carlisle, **CJC**(G&SW/M&C/Mid/NB/NE)
Knutsford, **CLC**(LNW)

Details of the component partners of all Joint undertakings will be found against the appropriate title in the list of abbreviations.

Joint services using junction or other stations that are purely the property of one or other of the joint partners (the joint line having been terminated at some point thereof) are not shown against such stations unless the Joint Company actually runs its own trains, e.g.:
SD *is* shown against Bath, Broadstone, etc, since the Somerset & Dorset Joint did work trains through between Bath and Bournemouth.
QYM *is not* shown against Quaker's Yard or Merthyr since the Quaker's Yard & Merthyr Joint had no rolling stock or locomotives and was merely a section of the GW and Rhymney joint property lying between Quaker's Yard and Merthyr (GW).
CKP *is* shown against Penrith since the Cockermouth, Keswick & Penrith Company's trains, although worked by the L&NW, nevertheless arrived and departed Penrith in their own right, and were not in any sense 'Joint'.

An exception to this method has been made in the case of the Birkenhead Joint, which, although owning neither rolling stock nor locomotives and whose line terminated at Walton Jc (Warrington), has been shown against certain L&NW stations between Warrington and Manchester Exchange by virtue of the joint service operated between Chester and Manchester, worked variously by L&NW and GW trains.

Line junctions are shown in italics. Those situated on individual companies' lines that can be readily identified by an adjoining or nearby station on the same name are not generally indexed, but those that form a meeting point of two or more companies are shown thus:
*Acton Wells Jc*, NSW/GW/LNW/Mid
*Bopeep Jc*, LBSC/SEC

**Where is it on the map?**

Example from Index: Abermule, Cam, 14B2. Answer: on map 14 in the square found by following section B across until it meets the vertical column No 2.

The assistance of the BTC Archivist, Mr L. C. Johnson, and his staff in making available timetables and other documents of the period is gratefully acknowledged.

# 1 List of Abbreviations

In the case of Joint or Subsidiary Lines with individual titles, the owning or leasing partners or companies are indicated in brackets immediately after the title.

| | |
|---|---|
| AD | Alexandra (Newport & South Wales) Docks & Railway |
| AJ | Axholme Joint (LY and NE) |
| AN | Ashby & Nuneaton Joint (LNW and Midland) |
| BAC | Bere Alston & Calstock Light (PDSW) |
| BC | Bishop's Castle |
| BJ | Birkenhead Joint (GW and LNW) |
| BL | Brackenhill Light |
| BM | Brecon & Merthyr |
| BPGV | Burry Port & Gwendraeth Valley |
| BRY | Barry |
| BWHA | Bideford, Westward Ho! & Appledore |
| Cal | Caledonian |
| Cam | Cambrian |
| Car | Cardiff |
| CE | Clifton Extension (GW and Midland) |
| CJC | (Carlisle) Citadel Station Joint Committee (Cal and LNW) |
| CKP | Cockermouth, Keswick & Penrith |
| CL | Corringham Light |
| CLC | Cheshire Lines Committee (GC, GN and Midland) |
| CM | Campbeltown & Machrihanish Light |
| CMDP | Cleobury Mortimer & Ditton Priors Light |
| CO | Croydon & Oxted Joint (LBSC and SEC) |
| Cor | Corris |
| CRY | Croesor |
| CVH | Colne Valley & Halstead |
| CWJ | Cleator & Workington Junction |
| D&A | Dundee & Arbroath Joint (Cal and NB) |
| D&B | Dumbarton & Balloch Joint (Cal and NB) |
| Dist | Metropolitan District |
| DJ | (Carlisle) Dentonholme Joint Committee (G&SW, Midland and NB) |
| DV | Dearne Valley |
| DVL | Derwent Valley Light |
| Eas | Easingwold |
| ECH | Easton & Church Hope (GW and LSW) |
| EK | East Kent Light |
| EL | East London (GE, LBSC, Met, Met Dist, and SEC) |
| ELB | Edenham & Little Bytham |
| EWY | East & West Yorkshire Union |
| FB | Forth Bridge Railway Co (GN, Midland, NB and NE) |
| Fest | Festiniog |
| Fur | Furness |
| FYN | Freshwater, Yarmouth & Newport |
| GBK | Glasgow, Barrhead & Kilmarnock Joint (Cal and G&SW) |
| GC | Great Central |
| GE | Great Eastern |
| GN | Great Northern |
| GNS | Great North of Scotland |
| G&P | Glasgow & Paisley Joint (Cal and G&SW) |
| G&SW | Glasgow & South Western |
| GTC | (Carlisle) Goods Traffic Committee (Cal, G&SW, LNW and Midland) |
| GV | Gwendraeth Valley |
| GVT | Glyn Valley Tramway |
| GW | Great Western |
| HB | Hull & Barnsley |
| H&C | Hammersmith & City (GW and Met) |
| HHL | Halifax High Level (GN and LY) |
| HJ | Halesowen Joint (GW and Midland) |
| H&O | Halifax & Ovenden Joint (GN and LY) |
| HR | Highland |
| IMR | Isle of Man Railway |
| IW | Isle of Wight Railway |
| IWC | Isle of Wight Central Railway |
| K&B | Kilsyth & Bonnybridge Joint (Cal and NB) |
| KE | Knott End |
| KES | Kent & East Sussex |
| LB | Lynton & Barnstaple |
| LBSC | London, Brighton & South Coast |
| LC | Liskeard & Caradon (GW) |
| LE | London Electric |
| LL | Liskeard & Looe (GW) |
| LM | Llanelly & Mynydd Mawr |
| LNW | London & North Western |
| LOR | Liverpool Overhead |
| LSW | London & South Western |
| LTS | London, Tilbury & Southend |
| LU | Lancashire & Yorkshire & Lancashire Union Joint (LNW and LY) |
| LY | Lancashire & Yorkshire |
| Mawd | Mawddwy Light (Cambrian) |
| M&C | Maryport & Carlisle |
| MDHB | Mersey Docks & Harbour Board |
| ME | Manx Electric |
| Mer | Mersey |
| Met | Metropolitan |
| MGN | Midland & Great Northern Joint (GN and Midland) |
| Mid | Midland |
| MJ | Methley Joint (GN, LY and NE) |
| MSJA | Manchester South Junction & Altrincham (GC and LNW) |
| MSL | Mid-Suffolk Light |
| MSW | Midland & South Western Junction |
| Mum | Swansea & Mumbles |
| NB | North British |

| | |
|---|---|
| N&B | Neath & Brecon |
| NE | North Eastern |
| NL | North London |
| NS | North Staffordshire |
| NSJ | Norfolk & Suffolk Joint (GE and MGN) |
| NSL | North Sunderland Light |
| NSW | North & South Western Junction (LNW, Midland and NL) |
| NU | North Union Joint (LNW and LY) |
| NV | Nidd Valley |
| NWNG | North Wales Narrow Gauge |
| OAGB | Oldham, Ashton-under-Lyne & Guide Bridge (GC and LNW) |
| OAT | Oxford & Aylesbury Tramroad (Met&GCJt) |
| O&I | Otley & Ilkley Joint (Midland and NE) |
| PCB | Portmadoc, Croesor & Beddgelert |
| PDJ | Princes Dock Joint (Cal, G&SW and NB) |
| PDSW | Plymouth, Devonport & South Western Junction |
| PL | Preston & Longridge Joint (LNW and LY) |
| PLA | Port of London Authority |
| PT | Port Talbot Railway and Docks |
| P&W | Portpatrick & Wigtownshire Joint (Cal, G&SW, LNW and Midland) |
| PWY | Preston & Wyre (LNW and LY) |
| QYM | Quaker's Yard & Merthyr Joint (GW and Rhymney) |
| RCT | Rye & Camber Tramway |
| Rhy | Rhymney |
| RKF | Rowrah & Kelton Fell |
| RSB | Rhondda & Swansea Bay |
| SBH | Snailbeach District Railways |
| SD | Somerset & Dorset Joint Committee (LSW and Midland) |
| SEC | South Eastern & Chatham |
| S&H | Shrewsbury & Hereford Joint (GW and LNW) |
| SHD | Sheffield District Railway (GC and Midland) |
| SK | Swinton & Knottingley (Midland and NE) |
| SL | Selsey Light |
| S&M | Shropshire & Montgomeryshire Light |
| SMJ | Stratford-on-Avon & Midland Junction |
| SMR | Snowdon Mountain Railway |
| SSM | South Shields, Marsden & Whitburn Colliery |
| SVW | Severn & Wye Joint (GW and Midland) |
| SWD | Southwold |
| SWM | South Wales Mineral |
| SWN | Shrewsbury & Wellington Joint (GW and LNW) |
| SWP | Shrewsbury & Welshpool Joint (GW and LNW) |
| SYJ | South Yorkshire Joint (GC, GN, LY, Midland and NE) |
| Tal | Talyllyn |
| Tan | Tanat Valley Light (Cambrian) |
| TBJ | Taff Bargoed Joint (GW and Rhymney) |
| TFG | Tottenham & Forest Gate (LTS and Midland) |
| THJ | Tottenham & Hampstead Junction (GE and Midland) |
| TV | Taff Vale |
| Van | Van Light (Cambrian) |
| VR | Vale of Rheidol (Cambrian) |
| VT | Vale of Towy Joint (GW and LNW) |
| WB | Whitechapel & Bow Joint (LTS and Met District) |
| WCE | Whitehaven, Cleator & Egremont Joint (Furness and LNW) |
| WCJ | Wath Curve Joint Committee (GC, Midland and NE) |
| WCP | Weston, Clevedon & Portishead |
| Wir | Wirral |
| WL | West London Joint (GW and LNW) |
| W&L | Welshpool & Llanfair Light (Cambrian) |
| WLE | West London Extension Joint (GW, LNW, LBSC and LSW) |
| WM | Wrexham & Minera Joint (GW and LNW) |
| WP | Weymouth & Portland Joint (GW and LSW) |
| WRG | West Riding & Grimsby Joint (GC and GN) |
| WSC | Woodside & South Croydon (LBSC and SEC) |
| WT | Wantage Tramway |
| WUT | Wisbech & Upwell Tramway |

## 2 Index to Tunnels

| | | |
|---|---|---|
| Abbotscliff | SEC | 6D2 |
| Alderton | GW | 9G3 |
| Alfreton | Mid | 16C4/41E3 |
| Ampthill | Mid | 10C1 |
| Ardsley | Mid | 21F3/42E1 |
| Ardsley | GN | 42B3 |
| Armathwaite | Mid | 27D1 |
| Arnworth | LY | 45B2 |
| Asfordby | Mid | 16E3 |
| Askham | GN | 16A3 |
| | | |
| Balcombe | LBSC | 5E3 |
| Bangor | LNW | 19D2 |
| Bank House | LY | 21E2/42C5 |
| Baron Wood | Mid | 27D1 |
| Beacon Hill | LY | 42B5 |
| Belmont (Bangor) | LNW | 19D2 |
| Betchworth | LBSC | 5D2 |
| Bincombe | GW | 3F3 |
| Bingley | Mid | 21D2/42A5 |
| Birkett | Mid | 27F2 |
| Blackheath | SEC | 40D2 |
| Blaenrhondda | RSB | 7B5/43E2 |
| Blea Moor | Mid | 24A1 |
| Bletchingley | SEC | 5D3 |
| Bodorgan | LNW | 19D1 |
| Bolsover | GC | 41C3 |
| Bopeep | SEC | 6F5 |
| Bowling | LY | 42B4 |
| Box | GW | 3A4 |
| Bradley | LNW | 42C4 |
| Bradway | Mid | 16A5/41B2 |
| Bramhope | NE | 21D3 |
| Brislington | GW | 3A3/8C1 |
| Brooksbottom | LY | 45B1 |
| Broomhouse | Mid | 16A5/41 B2 |
| Brownqueen | GW | 1D3 |
| Buckhorn Weston | LSW | 3D3 |
| Buckshead | GW | 1E1 |
| Burdale | NE | 22B5 |
| Buriton | LSW | 4D2 |
| Butternob | LY | 42D2 |
| | | |
| Caerphilly | Rhy | 43B4 |
| Campden | GW | 9C5 |
| Castle Hill | LY | 21E1 |
| Catesby | GC | 10B4 |
| Charlton | SEC | 6D2 |
| Chatham | SEC | 6B5 |
| Chee Tor | Mid | 15A5 |
| Chilcompton | SD | 3B3/8E1 |
| Chislehurst | SEC | 40F2 |
| Christleton | LNW | 15B1 |
| Clarborough | GC | 16A2 |
| Clay Cross | Mid | 41D2 |
| Clayton | LBSC | 5F3 |
| Combe Down | SD | 3B3/8D1 |
| Copenhagen | GN | 40B5 |
| Corbridge | NE | 27C4 |
| Corby | Mid | 16G1 |
| Cowburn | Mid | 15A5 |
| Cressbrook | Mid | 15A5 |
| Crick | LNW | 10A3 |
| Crigglestone | Mid | 21E3/42D2 |
| Crimple | NE | 21C3 |
| Culgaith | Mid | 27E1 |
| Cumberworth | LY | 21F2/42D3 |
| | | |
| Dainton | GW | 2D3 |
| Devonshire | SD | 3B3/8D1 |
| Dinmore | S&H | 9B1 |
| Dove Holes | Mid | 15A4 |
| | | |
| Elland | LY | 42C5 |
| Elstree | Mid | 11G2 |
| | | |
| Festiniog | LNW | 19E3 |
| Fisherton | LSW | 4C5 |
| Fort Pitt | SEC | 6B5 |
| | | |
| Gas Works (King's Cross) | GN | 40B5 |
| Gillingham (Kent) | SEC | 6B5 |
| Girvan | G&SW | 29G2 |
| Gisburn | LY | 24C1 |
| Glaston | Mid | 16F1 |
| Glenfield | Mid | 16F4 |
| Greet | GW | 9D4 |
| Grimston | Mid | 16E3 |
| Grove | SEC | 5D5 |
| Guston | SEC | 6D2 |
| | | |
| Haddon | Mid | 15B5 |
| Hadley North | GN | 11G2 |
| Hadley South | GN | 11G2 |
| Halton | BJ | 45D5 |
| Hampstead | GC | 39B5 |
| Harbour (Dover) | SEC | 6D2 |
| Hastings | SEC | 6F5 |
| Haverstock Hill | Mid | 39B5 |
| Haywards Heath | LBSC | 5E3 |
| Headstone | Mid | 15B5 |
| Healey House | LY | 42D5 |
| Helm | Mid | 27F2 |
| Hickleton | HB | 42E1 |
| High Tor | Mid | 16B5/41D1 |
| Honiton | LSW | 2A1 |
| Honley | LY | 42D5 |
| Horsfall | LY | 21E1 |
| Hunsbury Hill | LNW | 10B2 |
| Hunting Butts | GW | 9D4 |

| | | |
|---|---|---|
| Inver | HR | 33D4 |
| | | |
| Kensal Green | LNW | 39C4 |
| Kidbrook | SEC | 40E2 |
| Killiecrankie | HR | 33C4 |
| Kilsby | LNW | 10A4 |
| Kingswood | HR | 33E5 |
| Kirton | GC | 22F4 |
| Kitsonwood | LY | 20A1 |
| Knighton | Mid | 16F3 |
| Knights Hill | LBSC | 40E5 |
| | | |
| Lazonby | Mid | 27D1 |
| Lea Bank | H&O | 42B5 |
| Lea Wood | Mid | 16B5/41E1 |
| Leigham | LBSC | 40F5 |
| Lightcliffe | LY | 42B5 |
| Linslade | LNW | 10D1 |
| Litchfield | LSW | 4B3 |
| Litton | Mid | 15A5 |
| Llandegai | LNW | 19D2 |
| Llanderfal | GW | 19F5 |
| Llangyfelach | GW | 43G2 |
| Lord's | GC | 39C5 |
| Lydden | SEC | 6D2 |
| | | |
| Manton | Mid | 16F2 |
| Marley | GW | 2D4 |
| Martello | SEC | 6D2 |
| Merstham | LBSC & SEC | 5C3 |
| Mickleham | LBSC | 5C2 |
| Middle Hill | GW | 3A4 |
| Milford (Derbys) | Mid | 16C5/41F2 |
| Millwood | LY | 21E1 |
| Moncrieff | Cal | 33F5 |
| Moorcock | Mid | 27G2 |
| Morley | LNW | 21E3/42B3 |
| Mossdale Head | Mid | 27G3 |
| Mountfield | SEC | 6E5 |
| Mount Pleasant | SEC | 6F5 |
| | | |
| Netherton | LY | 42D5 |
| New Furnace | LY | 42B4 |
| Northchurch | LNW | 10E1 |
| North Stoke | LBSC | 5F1 |
| Nuttall | LY | 45B1 |
| | | |
| Oakenshaw | LY | 42B4 |
| Old Lane | H&O | 42B5 |
| Ore | SEC | 6F5 |
| | | |
| Pansbourne | GN | 11F2 |
| Patcham | LBSC | 5F3 |
| Peascliffe | GN | 16D1 |
| Penge | SEC | 40F4 |
| Penllergaer | GW | 43G2 |
| Penmaenrhos | LNW | 19D4 |
| Penmanshiel | NB | 31C2 |
| Polhill | SEC | 5C4 |
| Polperro | GW | 1E1 |
| Popham | LSW | 4C3 |
| Potters Bar | GN | 11G2 |
| Preston Hall | SEC | 6C5 |
| Primrose Hill | LNW | 39B5 |
| Priory | SEC | 6D2 |
| | | |
| Queensbury | GN | 42B5 |
| | | |
| Redhill | LBSC | 5C3 |
| Rise Hill | Mid | 24A1/27G2 |
| Robin Hood | LY | 21E2/42D5 |
| Royal George | LNW | 21F1 |
| | | |
| St Anne's Wood | GW | 3A3/8C1 |
| St John's Wood | GC | 39B5 |
| Salterhebble | LY | 42C5 |
| Saltwood | SEC | 6D2 |
| Sandling | SEC | 6D3 |
| Sapperton | GW | 9F4 |
| Saxelby | Mid | 16E3 |
| Scout | LNW | 21F1 |
| Seaton | Mid | 16F1 |
| Selling | SEC | 6C3 |
| Sevenoaks | SEC | 5C4 |
| Severn | GW | 8C2/9F1-G1 |
| Shakespeare | SEC | 6D2 |
| Sharnbrook | Mid | 10B1 |
| Shelley Woodhouse | LY | 42D4 |
| Shillamill | LSW | 1C5 |
| Shillingham | GW | 1D5 |
| Shotlock Hill | Mid | 27G2 |
| Shugborough | LNW | 15E4 |
| Sodbury | GW | 9G3 |
| Somerhill | SEC | 5D5 |
| Sough | LY | 20A2/24E2/24F1/45B1 |
| Spittal | GW | 13G1 |
| Springwood (Derbys) | GC | 41C3 |
| Springwood (Yorks) | LNW&LYJt | 42C5 |
| Standedge | LNW | 21F1 |
| Stanton | Mid | 16D3 |
| Stockingford | Mid | 16F5 |
| Stoke | GN | 16D1 |
| Stowe Hill | LNW | 10B3 |
| Strawberry Hill | SEC | 5D5 |
| Streatham | LBSC | 40F5 |
| Summit (Littleborough) | LY | 21E1 |
| Sydenham | SEC | 40F4 |
| | | |
| Taitlands | Mid | 24B1 |
| Tankersley | Mid | 21F3/42F2 |
| Thackley | Mid | 42A4 |
| Thurgoland | GC | 21F3/42F3 |
| Thurstonland | LY | 21F2/42D4 |

| | | |
|---|---|---|
| Torpantau | B&M | 8A5/14G3/43C1 |
| Totley | Mid | 16A5/41B1 |
| Treverrin | GW | 1D3 |
| Twerton | GW | 3B3/8D1 |
| | | |
| Wadhurst | SEC | 5E5 |
| Waller's Ash | LSW | 4C3 |
| Waste Bank | Mid | 27E1 |
| Watford (Herts) | LNW | 11G1 |
| Watford (Northants) | LNW | 10A3 |
| Weasel Hall | LY | 21E1 |
| Wellhouse | LY | 21F3/42E3 |
| Wells | SEC | 5D5 |
| Welwyn North | GN | 11F2 |
| Welwyn South | GN | 11F2 |
| Wenvoe | BRY | 43C4 |
| Wheatley | HHL | 42B5 |
| Whitehall | GW | 8G5 |
| Whitehouse Farm | GW&GCJt | 5A1/10F2 |
| Whitrope | NB | 31G1 |
| Wickwar | Mid | 8B1/9F2 |
| Willersley | Mid | 16B5/41D1 |
| Wing | Mid | 16F2 |
| Wingfield | Mid | 16C5/41E2 |
| Winsor Hill | SD | 3C2/8E1 |
| Winterbutlee | LY | 21E1 |
| Woodhead | GC | 21F2/42E5 |
| Woolley | LY | 42D3 |
| Wyke | LY | 21E2/42B4 |

## 3 Index to Watertroughs

| | | |
|---|---|---|
| Aber | LNW | 19D3 |
| Aldermaston | GW | 4A3 |
| Aynho | GW | 10C4 |
| | | |
| Brock | LNW | 24D3 |
| | | |
| Castlethorpe | LNW | 10C2 |
| Charlbury | GW | 10D5 |
| Charwelton | GC | 10B4 |
| Chester | LNW | 20D4 |
| Creech (Durston) | GW | 8F3 |
| | | |
| Diggle | LNW | 21F1 |
| Dillicar | LNW | 27F1 |
| | | |
| Eccles | LNW | 45B3 |
| Eckington | GC | 16A4/41B2 |
| Exminster | GW | 2B3 |
| | | |
| Fairwood (Westbury) | GW | 3B4 |
| Ferryside (Carmarthen) | GW | 7A2 |
| Flint | LNW | 20D5 |
| | | |
| Garsdale | Mid | 24A1/27G2 |
| Goring | GW | 4A2/10G3 |
| | | |
| Halebank | LNW | 45E4 |
| Hademore | LNW | 15E5 |
| Haselour | Mid | 15F5 |
| Hest Bank | LNW | 24B3 |
| | | |
| Holbrook Park (Rugby) | LNW | 10A4 |
| Hoscar | LY | 20B3/24F3/45E1 |
| | | |
| Ipswich | GE | 12D3 |
| | | |
| Keynsham | GW | 3A3/8D1 |
| Kirkby | LY | 20B4/24F3/45E3 |
| | | |
| Langley (Knebworth) | GN | 11E2 |
| Lapworth | GW | 9A5 |
| Lea Road (Salwick) | PWY | 24D3 |
| Lostock Jc | LY | 24F2/45C2 |
| Loughborough | Mid | 16E4 |
| Lucker | NE | 31E4 |
| Luddendenfoot | LY | 21E1 |
| Ludlow | S&H | 9A1 |
| | | |
| Magor | GW | 8B2 |
| Melton Mowbray | Mid | 16E2 |
| Moore | LNW | 45D4 |
| Muskham (Newark) | GN | 16B2 |
| | | |
| Newbold (Rugby) | LNW | 10A4 |
| New Cumnock | G&SW | 29F5 |
| | | |
| Oakley | Mid | 10B1/11C1 |
| | | |
| Prestatyn | LNW | 19C5 |
| | | |
| Rufford | LY | 20A3/24E3/45E1 |
| | | |
| Scrooby | GN | 21G5 |
| Smithy Bridge | LY | 21E1/45A1 |
| Sowerby Bridge | LY | 21E1 |
| | | |
| Tivetshall | GE | 12A3/18G3 |
| | | |
| Wakefield | LY | 42C2 |
| Walkden | LY | 45B2 |
| Werrington | GN | 17F2 |
| Whitmore | LNW | 15C3/20F1 |
| Wiske Moor (Northallerton) | NE | 28D5 |

## 4 Index to Summits

| | | |
|---|---|---|
| Aisgill | Mid | 27G2 |
| Amersham | Met&GCJt | 10F1 |
| Beattock | Cal | 30F4 |
| Corriemuille | HR | 35C4 |
| Corrour | NB | 32C1 |
| County March | HR | 38D4 |
| Dainton | GW | 2D3 |
| Dava | HR | 36E3 |
| Desborough | Mid | 10A2/16G2 |
| Druimuachdair | HR | 33B2 |
| Dutchlands | Met&GCJt | 10E2 |
| Elsenham | GE | 11E4 |
| Falahill | NB | 30C1 |
| Glenoglehead | Cal | 33E2 |
| Hewish | LSW | 3E1 |
| Honiton | LSW | 2A2 |
| Ingrave | GE | 5A5 |
| Lickey Incline | Mid | 9A4 |
| Luib | HR | 35D3 |
| Masbury | SD | 3B2/8E1 |
| Mortehoe | LSW | 7E1 |
| Peak Forest | Mid | 15A4 |
| Penmanshiel | NB | 31C2 |
| Raven's Rock | HR | 35D5 |
| Sapperton | GW | 9F4 |
| Shap | LNW | 27F1 |
| Sharnbrook | Mid | 10B1 |
| Shenfield & Hutton | GE | 11G4 |
| Slochd | HR | 36F4 |
| Stainmore | NE | 27F3 |
| Stoke | GN | 16D1 |
| Talerddig | Cam | 14B4 |
| Templecombe | LSW | 8G1 |
| Tyndrum | Cal & NB | 32E1 |
| Wendover | Met&GCJt | 10E2 |
| Whiteball | GW | 8G5 |
| Whitrope | NB | 31G1 |
| Wrangaton | GW | 2D5 |

## 5 Index to Bridges and Viaducts

| | | |
|---|---|---|
| Barmouth | Cam | 13A5 |
| Belah | NE | 27F3 |
| Britannia Tubular Bridge | LNW | 19D2 |
| Chearsley | GW&GCJt | 10E3 |
| Chirk | GW | 20F4 |
| Crumlin | GW | 8B4/43B2 |
| Dee | GW | 20F4 |
| Dinting | GC | 21F1 |
| Forth Bridge | FB | 30B3 |
| Halton | BJ | 15A1/20D3/45D5 |
| Hawarden Swing Bridge | GC | 20D4 |
| Hewenden | GN | 42A5 |
| High Level Bridge (Gateshead) | NE | 28 (inset) |
| King Edward Bridge (Newcastle-on-Tyne) | NE | 28 (inset) |
| Kings Ferry Bridge | SEC | 6B4 |
| Mottram | GC | 21G1 |
| Ouse | LBSC | 5E3 |
| Penistone | LY | 42E3 |
| Royal Albert Bridge (Saltash) | GW | 1D5 |
| Royal Border Bridge | NE | 31C3 |
| Runcorn | LNW | 45D4 |
| Scotswood (Newcastle-on-Tyne) | NE | 28 (inset) |
| Severn | SVW | 8A1/9E2 |
| Solway | Cal | 26B2 |
| Stonehouse | GW | 9E3 |
| Southborough | SEC | 5D5 |
| Tay Bridge | NB | 34E4 |
| Welland | Mid | 16F1 |
| Welwyn | GN | 11F2 |

## 6 Index of Locations

**Note:** The following references are to the original atlas map numbers, not page numbers. Thus Abbey station's reference of 15E1 refers to square E1 in map number 15, which is on page 54. To find the page number for each map, refer to the list on page 5.

Abbey (Shrewsbury), S&M, 15E1
Abbey for West Dereham, GE, 11A5; 17F5
Abbey Foregate Plat, SWN, 15E1
*Abbey Mills Jcs*, LTS & GE, 40C2
Abbey Street (Nuneaton), Mid, 16F5
Abbey Town, NB, 26C2
Abbey Wood, SEC, 5B4; 40D1
Abbeydore, GW, 14F1
Abbeyhill, NB, 30 (inset)
Abbots Ripton, GN, 11B2
Abbotsbury, GW, 3F2
Abbotsford Ferry, NB, 30C1
Abbotsham Road, BWHA, 7F2
*Abbotswood Jc*, Mid/GW, 9C3
*Aber Bargoed Jc*, BM, 43B2
*Aber Branch Jc*, BM/Rhy, 43B3
Aber, LNW, 19D3
Aberaman, TV, 8B5; 43D2
Aberangell, Mawd, 14A4
Aberavon (Seaside), RSB, 7B4; 43F3
*Aberavon Jc*, RSB/PT, 43F3
Aberayron, GW, 13D4
*Aberayron Jc*, GW, 13E5
Aberbargoed & Bargoed, Rhy(BM), 8B4; 43B2
Aberbeeg, GW, 8B4; 43B2
Aberbran, N&B (Mid), 14F4
Abercairny, Cal, 33F4
Abercanaid, QYM, 8A5; 43C2
Abercarn, GW, 8B4; 43B3
Aberchalder, NB, 32A1; 35G4
Abercorn (Paisley), G&SW, 29C4; 44F3
Abercrave, N&B(Mid), 7A4; 43El
Abercwmboi Halt, TV, 43C2
Abercynon, TV, 8B5; 43C3
Aberdare, GW & TV, 8B5; 43D2
Aberdeen (Goods), Cal & GNS, 37G4
Aberdeen (Pass), Cal&GNSJt(NB), 37G4
Aberdour, NB, 30A3
Aberdovey, Cam, 13B5
Aberdylais, GW, 7B4; 43F2
Aberedw, Cam, 14E3
Abererch, Cam, 19F1
Aberfan, QYM, 8B5; 43C2
Aberfeldy, HR, 33D3
Aberffrwd, VR, 14C5
Aberfoyle, NB, 29A4; 33G1
Abergavenny, GW & LNW, 8A3; 43A1
Abergavenny Junc, GW(LNW), 8A3; 43A1
Abergele, LNW, 19D4
Abergwili, LNW, 13G4
Abergwynfi, GW, 7B5; 43D3
Abergynolwyn, Tal, 13B5
*Aberlady Jc*, NB, 30B1
Aberlady, NB, 30B1
Aberllefeni, Cam, 14A5
Aberlour, GNS, 36D1
Abermule, Cam, 14B2
Abernant, GW, 8A5; 43D2
Abernethy, NB, 33F5
Abersychan, GW, 8A4; 43A2
Abersychan & Talywain, LNW(GW), 8A4; 43A2
Aberthaw, BRY & TV, 8D5; 43C5
Abertillery, GW, 8A4; 43B2
Abertridwr, Rhy, 8B4; 43C3
Abertysswg, BM, 43C2
Aberystwyth, Cam&GWJt & VR, 13C5
Abingdon, GW, 10F4
Abington, Cal, 30E4
Aboyne, GNS, 34A4; 37G1
Aby, GN, 17A3
Accrington, LY, 24E1
Ach-na-cloich, Cal, 32E3
Achanalt, HR, 35D4
Acheilidh Crossing, HR, 36A5
Achmacoy, GNS, 37E4
Achnasheen, HR, 35D3
Achnashellach, HR, 35D2
Achterneed, HR, 35D5
Acklington, NE, 31G5
Ackworth, SK(GC/GN), 21 E4; 42C1
Ackworth Moor Top (Goods), BL, 42C1
Acle, GE, 18F2
Acocks Green & South Yardley, GW, 9A5; 15G5
Acrefair, GW, 20F5
Acton, GW & NSW, 5B2; 39C3
Acton Bridge, LNW, 15A1; 20D3; 45D5
*Acton Grange Jc*, BJ/LNW, 15A1; 20C3; 45D4
*Acton Lane Jcs*, LSW/Dist, 39D3
Acton Town, Dist, 39D3
*Acton Wells Jc*, NSW/GW/LNW/Mid, 39C3
Adam Street Goods (Cardiff), Rhy, 43B4
Adderbury, GW, 10C4
Adderley (Salop), GW, 15C2; 20F2
Adderley Park, LNW, 13C4
Addiewell, Cal & NB, 30C4
Addingham, Mid, 21C2
Addison Rd (Kensington), WL(H&C/LBSC/LSW), 39D4
Addlestone, LSW, 5C2
Adisham, SEC, 6C2
Adlestrop, GW, 9D5
Adlington (Ches), LNW(NS), 15A3; 20C1; 45A5
Adlington (Lancs), LY, 20A2; 24F2; 45D1
Admaston, SWN, 15E2
Advie, GNS, 36E2
*Adwick Jc*, WRG, 21F4
Afon Wen, Cam(LNW), 19F1
*Agecroft Jc*, LY, 45B2
Aichengray, Cal, 30D4
Aichnagatt, GNS, 37D4
Ainderby, NE, 21A3; 28G5
Ainsdale, LY (LNW), 20A4; 24F4; 45F1
Ainsdale Beach, CLC, 20A4; 24F4; 45F1
Ainsworth Rd Halt, LY, 45B2
Aintree, LY & CLC, 20B4; 24F4; 45F3
*Airbank Jc*, M&C, 26D2
Airdrie, Cal & NB, 30C5; 44B4
Airdrie North (Goods), NB, 44B4
Airdrie South (Pass), Cal, 44B4
*Aire Jc*, HB/GC&HBJt, 21E5
Airmyn & Rawcliffe, NE, 21E5
Airth, Cal, 30A5
Akeld, NE, 31E3
Akeman Street, GC, 10E3
Albert Dock (Hull), NE, 22A1 (inset)
Albert Road Halt, LSW, 1 (inset)
Alberta Place Halt, TV, 43B5
Albion, LNW, 13B2 (inset)
Albrighton, GW, 15F3
Alcester, Mid(GW), 9B4
Aldeburgh, GE, 12C2
Aldeby, GE, 12A2; 18F1
*Alderbury Jc*, LSW, 4D5
Alderley Edge, LNW, 15A3; 20D1; 45A5
Aldermaston, GW, 4A3
Alderse (Goods), NB, 30B4
Aldersgate Street, Met (Dist/GN/GW/Mid/H&C), 40C5
Aldershot (North Camp) & South Farnborough, SEC, 4B1; 5C1
Aldershot Town, LSW(SEC), 4B1
Aldgate, Met(Dist), 40C4
Aldgate East, Dist&MetJt(H&C), 40C4
Aldin Grange for Bearpark, NE, 27D5
Aldridge, Mid, 15F4
Alexandra Dock (Hull), NE, 22E3
Alexandra Dock (Liverpool), LNW & Mid, 45F3 and inset
Alexandra Dock (Newport), AD, 8C3; 43A4
Alexandra Palace, GN(NL), 40A5
Alexandra Park (Glasgow), NB, 44D4
Alexandra Park (Manchester), GC, 45A3
Alexandria, D&B, 29B3
Alford (Aberdeenshire), GNS, 37F2
Alford (Lincs), GN, 17A3
Alford Halt (Som), GW, 3C2; 8F1
Alfreton & South Normanton, Mid, 16C4; 41E3
Algarkirk, GN, 17D2
All Saints (Clevedon), WCP, 3A1; 8C3
Allanfearn, HR, 36D5
Allangrange, HR, 36D5
*Allbrook Jc*, LSW, 4D3
Allendale, NE, 27C3
*Aller Jc*, GW, 2C3
Allerton (Lancs), LNW & CLC, 45E4
Allerton (Yorks), NE, 21C4
*Alloa Jc*, Cal, 30B5
Alloa, NB(Cal), 30A4
Alloa South (Goods), Cal, 30A5
Alloway, G&SW, 29F3
*Alloway Jc*, G&SW, 29F3
Almeley, GW, 14E1
*Almond Jc*, NB, 30B4
*Almond Valley Jc*, Cal, 33E5
Almondbank, Cal, 33E4
Alne, NE(Eas), 21B4
Alness, HR, 36C5
Alnmouth, NE, 31F5
Alnwick, NE, 31F5
Alperton, Dist, 39B2
Alresford (Essex), GE, 12E4
Alresford (Hants), LSW, 4C3
Alrewas, LNW, 15E5
Alsager, NS, 15C3; 20E1
Alsager Road, NS, 15C3; 20E1
Alsop-en-le-Dale, LNW, 15C5
Alston, NE, 27D2
Altanabreac, HR, 38D4
Altcar & Hillhouse, CLC(LY), 20B4; 24F4; 45F2
Altcar Rifle Range, LY(LNW), 20B4; 24F4; 45F2
Althorne, GE, 6A4; 12G5
Althorp Park, LNW, 10B3

Althorpe, GC, 22F5
Altofts & Whitwood, Mid, 21 E3; 42B1
*Altofts Jc*, Mid/NE, 42B2
Alton (Hants), LSW, 4C2
Alton (Staffs), NS, 15C4
Altrincham & Bowdon, MSJA(CLC), 15A3; 20C1; 24G1; 45B4
Alva, NB, 30A5; 33G3
Alvechurch, Mid, 9A4
Alverstone, IWC, 4F3
Alverthorpe, GN, 21E3; 42C3
Alves, HR, 36C2
Alvescot, GW, 10E5
Alyth Junc, Cal, 34D5
Ambergate, Mid, 16C5; 41G1
*Ambergate East Jc*, Mid, 16C5
*Ambergate South Jc*, Mid, 16C5
*Ambergate West Jc*, Mid, 16C5
Amberley, LBSC, 5F1
Amble, NE, 31F5
*Amble Branch Jc*, NE, 31G5
Amersham, Met&GCJt, 10F1
Amesbury, LSW, 4C5
*Amesbury Jc*, LSW, 4C5
Amisfield, Cal, 26A3
Amlwch, LNW, 19C1
Ammanford, GW, 7A4; 43G1
Ammanford Colliery Halt, GW, 43G1
Amotherby, NE, 22E5
Ampleforth, NE, 21A5
Ampthill, Mid, 10C1; 11D1
Ancaster, GN, 16C1; 17C1
Ancoats (Goods), Mid, 45A3
Anderston Cross, Cal, 44E4; 44F2 (inset)
Andover Junc, LSW(MSW), 4C4
Andover Town, LSW(MSW), 4C4
Andoversford & Dowdeswell, MSW, 9D4
Andoversford, GW(MSW), 9D4
Anerley, LBSC, 40F4
Angel Road, GE, 5A3
Angerstein Wharf, SEC, 40D2
Angerton, NB, 27A4
Angmering, LBSC, 5F2
Annan, G&SW & Cal, 26B2
Annbank, G&SW, 29E4
Annesley, Mid, 41E4 *see also* Hollin Well
Annfield Plain, NE, 27C5
Annitsford, NE, 27B5
Ansdell & Fairhaven, PWY, 20A4; 24E4
Anston, GC&MidJt, 16A4; 41A4
Anstruther, NB, 34G3
*Apethorne Jc*, GC&MidJt/CLC, 21G1
Apperley Bridge & Rawdon, Mid, 21D2; 42A4
*Apperley Jc*, Mid, 42A4
Appin, Cal, 32D4
Appleby (Lincs), GC, 22F4
Appleby (Westmorland), Mid & NE, 27E2
Appledore (Devon), BWHA, 7F2
Appledore (Kent), SEC, 6E4
*Applehurst Jc*, WRG/NE, 21E5
Appleton, LNW, 45D4
Appley Bridge, LY, 20B3; 24F3; 45D2
Arbirlot, D&A, 34D3
Arbroath, D&A, 34D3
*Archcliffe Jc*, SEC, 6D2
Arddleen, Cam, 14A2
Ardingly, LBSC, 5E3
Ardleigh, GE, 12E4
*Ardler Jc*, Cal, 34D5
Ardley, GW, 10D4
Ardlui, NB, 32F1
Ardrossan, G&SW & Cal, 29D3
Ardsley, GN(GC), 21E3; 42B3
*Ardsley Jc*, GN, 42B3
Ardwick, GC, 20B1; 24F1; 45A3
Arenig, GW, 19F4
Argoed, LNW, 8B4; 43B2
Arisaig, NB, 32B5
Arkholme, Fur&MidJt, 24B2
*Arkleston Jc*, G&P/G&SW, 44F3
Arksey, GN(NE), 21F5
Arkwright Street (Nottingham), GC, 16D4; 41G4
Arkwright Town, GC, 16B4; 41C3
Arlecdon, CWJ, 26E3
Arlesey & Shefford Road, GN, 11D2
Arley (Worcs), GW, 9A2
Arley & Fillongley, Mid, 16G5
Armadale, NB, 30C4
Armathwaite, Mid, 27D1
Armitage, LNW, 15E5
Armley & Wortley, GN(LY) & Mid, 21D3 and inset C1; 42A3
Arnage, GNS, 37E4
Arnside, Fur, 24A3
Arpley (Warrington), LNW, 15A2; 20C2; 24G2; 45D4
Arram, NE, 22D4
Arrochar & Tarbet, NB, 32G1
Arthington, NE, 21D3
Arthog, Cam, 13A5
Arundel, LBSC, 5F1
Ascot & Sunninghill, LSW, 4A1; 5B1
Ascott-under-Wychwood, GW, 10D5
Asfordby, Mid, 16E3
Ash, SEC (LSW), 4Bl; 5C1
Ash Green, LSW, 4B1; 5C1
*Ash Jc*, SEC/LSW, 4B1; 5C1
Ash Town, EK, 6C2
Ashbourne, LNW&NSJt, 15C5
Ashburton, GW, 2C4
Ashburton Grove Goods, GN, 40B5
*Ashburton Jc*, GW, 2D4
Ashbury, GC, 20B1; 24F1; 45A3
Ashbury, LSW, 1B5
Ashby Magna, GC, 16G4
Ashby-de-la-Zouch, Mid(LNW), 16E5
Ashchurch, Mid, 9D3
Ashcott, SD, 3C1; 8E2
Ashdon Halt, GE, 11D4
*Ashendon Jcs*, GW&GCJt/GC, 10E3
Ashey, IWC, 4F3
Ashford (Kent), SEC, 6D4
Ashford (Middx), LSW, 5B2
*Ashford Works*, SEC, 6D3
Ashington, NE, 27A5
Ashley (Ches), CLC, 15A3; 20C1, 24G1; 45B4
Ashley & Weston (Northants), LNW, 16F2
Ashley Hill, GW, 8C1 and inset 3F1; 24G1
*Ashley Hill Jc*, GW/Mid, 3G1 (inset)
Ashperton, GW, 9C2
Ashtead, LSW&LBSCJt, 5C2
Ashton (Devon), GW, 2C3
Ashton (Lancs), OAGB, LY, GC & LNW, 21F1 and inset A2; *see also* Dukinfield
Ashton-in-Makerfield, GC, 45D3
*Ashton Jc* (Bristol), GW, 3 (inset)
*Ashton Moss Jcs*, LNW & LY/GC, 21 (inset)
Ashton-under-Hill, Mid, 9C4
*Ashton's Green Jc*, LNW, 45D3
Ashurst, LBSC, 5D4
Ashwater, LSW, 1B5
Ashwell (Rutland), Mid, 16E2
Ashwell & Morden (Cambs), GN, 11D2
Ashwellthorpe, GE, 12A3; 18F3
Askam, Fur, 24B5
Askern, LY(GN), 21E5
*Askern Jc*, GN/LY, 21F5
Askrigg, NE, 21A1; 27G3
Aslockton, GN, 16C2
Aspall & Thorndon, MSL, 12C3
Aspatria, M&C, 26D3
Aspley Guise Halt, LNW, 10C1
Astley, LNW(BJ), 20B2; 24G2; 45C3
Astley Bridge (Goods), LY, 20B2; 24F2; 45C1
Aston (Warwicks), LNW, 13B4; 15G5
Aston Botterell Siding, CMDP, 15G2
Aston-by-Stone, NS, 15D3; 20F1
*Aston Curve Jc*, Mid, 13C4
Aston Rowant, GW, 10F3
Aswarby & Scredingham, GN, 17D1
*Athelney Jc*, GW, 3D1; 8F3
Athelney, GW, 3D1; 8F3
Atherstone, LNW, 16F5
Atherton, LY & LNW, 20B2; 24F2; 45C2
Attadale, HR, 35E2
*Attenborough Jc*, Mid, 16D4
Attenborough, Mid, 16D4; 41G4
Attercliffe, GC, 21G4; 42G2
Attercliffe Road, Mid, 42G2
Attleborough, GE, 12A4; 18F4
Attlebridge, MGN, 18E3
Auchendinny, NB, 30C2
Auchenheath, Cal, 30D5
Auchenmade, Cal, 29D3
Auchincruive, G&SW, 29F4
Auchindachy, GNS, 37D1
Auchinleck, G&SW, 29F5
Auchmacoy, GNS, 37E4
Auchnagatt, GNS, 37D4
Auchterarder, Cal, 33F4
Auchterhouse, Cal, 34E5
Auchterless, GNS, 37D3
Auchtermuchty, NB, 34F5
Auchtertool (Goods), NB, 30A2
*Audenshaw Jc*, OAGB, 21A2 (inset)
Audlem, GW, 15C2; 20F2
Audley, NS, 15C3; 20E1
Audley End, GE, 11E4
Aughengray, Cal, 30D4
Aughton Park Halt, LY, 20B4; 24F3; 45E2
Auldbar Road, Cal, 34D3
Auldearn, HR, 36D3
Auldgirth, G&SW, 26A4
Aultmore, HR, 37D1
Authorpe, GN, 17A3
Aviemore, HR, 36F3
Avoch, HR, 36D5
Avon Lodge, LSW, 4E5
Avonbridge, NB, 30B4
Avoncliff Halt, GW, 3B4
Avonmouth, GW & CE, 3A2; 8C2; 9G1
Avonside Wharf (Goods), Mid, 3 (inset)
Avonwick, GW, 2D4
Awre for Blakeney, GW, 8A1; 9E2
Awsworth, GN, 16C4; 41F3
Axbridge, GW, 3B1; 8E3
Axminster, LSW, 2B1

Aycliffe, NE, 28E5
Aylesbury, GW&GCJt/Met&GCJt, 10E2; LNW, 10E2
*Aylesbury GW&GCJt Comm Jcs*, GW&GCJt, 10E2
*Aylesbury Met&GC Jc*, GW&GCJt,10E2
*Aylesbury North Jc*, GW&GCJt, 10E2
Aylesford, SEC, 6C5
Aylsham, GE & MGN, 18D3
Aynho, GW, 10D4
Aynho Park Plat, GW, 10D4
Ayot, GN, 11F2
Ayr, G&SW, 29F3
Aysgarth, NE, 21A1; 27G4
Ayton, NB, 31C3

Backworth, NE, 28B5
Bacton, GW, 14F1
Bacup, LY, 20A1; 24E1
Badminton, GW, 9G3
Baggrow, M&C, 26D2
Baghill (Pontefract), SK(GC/GN), 21E4; 42C1
Bagillt, LNW, 20D5
Bagshot, LSW, 4A1; 5C1
*Bagthorpe Jc*, GC/GN, 41F4
Baguley, CLC, 20C1; 24G1; 45B4
Bagworth & Ellistown, Mid, 16E4
Baildon, Mid, 21D2; 42A4
Bailey Gate, SD, 3E4
Bailiff Bridge, LY, 21E2; 42B4
Baillieston, Cal, 44C3
Bainton, NE, 22C4
Baker Street, Met(Dist/GW/H&C), 39C5
Bakewell, Mid, 15B5
Bala, GW, 19F4
Bala Junc, GW, 19F4
Balado, NB, 30A3; 33G5
Balcombe, LBSC, 5E3
Baldersby, NE, 21A3
Balderton, GW, 20E4
Baldock, GN, 11E2
Baldovan, Cal, 34E4
Baldragon, Cal, 34E4
Balerno, Cal, 30C3
Balfron, NB, 29A4
Balgowan, Cal, 33F4
Balham & Upper Tooting, LBSC(LNW), 5B3; 39E5
*Balham Jc*, LBSC, 39E5
Ballabeg, IMR, 23C2
Ballachulish, Cal, 32D3
Ballachulish Ferry, Cal, 32D3
Ballasalla, IMR, 23C2
Ballater, GNS, 34A5
Ballathie (Goods), Cal, 33E5
Ballaugh, IMR, 23A2; 25G4
Ballindalloch, GNS, 36E2
Ballingham, GW, 9D1
Ballinluig, HR, 33D4
Balliol Road, LNW, 45F3 *see also* Bootle (Lancs)
Balloch, D&B, 29B3
Balloch Pier, D&B, 29B3
*Bally Jc*, GN/GC, 21F5
*Balmano Jc*, NB, 33F5
Balmore, NB, 29B5; 44E5
Balnacoul, HR, 36C1
Balne, NE, 21E5
Balne Moor (Goods), HB, 21E5
*Balornock Jc*, Cal, 44D4
Balquhidder, Cal, 33F2
*Balquhidder Jc*, Cal, 33F2
Balshaw Lane & Euxton, LNW, 20A3; 24E2; 45D1
Bamber Bridge, LY, 20A3; 24E2
Bamford, Mid, 15A5
Bamfurlong, LNW, 20B2; 24F2; 45D2
Bampton (Devon), GW, 7G5
Bampton (Oxon), GW, 10E5
Banavie, NB, 32C3
*Banavie Jc*, NB, 32C3
Banavie Pier, NB, 32C3
Banbury, GW(GC) & LNW(SMJ), 10C4
*Banbury Jc*, GC/GW, 10C4
*Banbury Line Jc*, GW/Mid, 9D3
Banchory, GNS, 34A3
Banff, GNS, 37C2
Banff Bridge, GNS, 37C2
Banff Golf Club House Halt, GNS, 37C2
Bangor, LNW, 19D2
Bangor-on-Dee, Cam, 20F4
Bangour, NB, 30C4
Bank Hall, LY, 45F3
Bank Quay (Warrington), LNW(BJ) & LNW, 45D4
Bank Top (Burnley), LY, 24D1
Bank Top (Darlington), NE, 28F5
Bankfield (Liverpool) Goods, LY, 45 (inset)
Bankfoot, Cal, 33E5
Bankhead (Aberdeen), GNS, 37F4
Bankhead (Lanark), Cal, 30D4
Banknock, K&B, 30B5
Banks, LY, 20A4; 24E3
Bannister Green Halt, GE, 11E5
Bannockburn, Cal, 30A5
Banstead, LBSC, 5C3
Barassie G&SW, 29E3
Barber's Bridge, GW, 9D2
Barbon, LNW, 24A2
Barcaldine Siding, CR, 32E4
Barcombe, LBSC, 5F4
Barcombe Mills, LBSC, 5F4
Bardney, GN, 17B1
Bardon Hill, Mid, 16E4
Bardon Mill, NE, 27B2
Bardowie, NB, 29B5; 44E5
Bardsey, NE, 21D3
Bare Lane, LNW, 24B3
*Bare Lane Jc*, LNW, 24B3
Bargeddie, NB, 29C5; 44C4
Bargoed & Aberbargoed, BM, 8B4; 43B2
Barham, SEC, 6C2
Barking, LTS(Dist/Mid), 5A4; 40B1
*Barking East Jc*, LTS, 40B1
Barkingside, GE, 40A1
Barkston, GN, 16C1
Barlaston & Tittensor, NS, 15D3; 20F1
*Barlby Jc*, NE, 21D5
Barleith, G&SW, 29E4
Barlow, NE, 21D5
Barmby, HB, 21E5
Barming, SEC, 6C5
Barmouth, Cam, 13A5
*Barmouth Jc*, Cam, 13A5
Barnack, GN, 17F1
Barnard Castle, NE, 27E4
Barnby Dun, GE(NE), 21F5
Barnby Moor & Sutton, GN, 16A3
Barnes, LSW, 5B3; 39E4
Barnes Bridge, LSW, 39D3
Barnetby, GC, 22F3
Barnham, GE, 12B5
*Barnham Jc*, LBSC, 5F1
Barnhill (Dundee), Cal, 34E4
*Barnhill Jc*, NB, 44D4
Barnhurst, SEC, 5B4
Barnsley, GC & LY, 42E2
Barnsley Court House, Mid(GC), 42E2
*Barnsley Jc*, GC, 21F3
Barnstaple, GW, LSW & LB, 7F3
Barnstaple Junction, LSW(GW), 7F3
Barnstaple Town, LSW & LB, 7F3
Barnstone, GN&LNWJt, 16D2
Barnt Green, Mid, 9A4
Barnton, Cal, 30B3
Barnwell, GE, 11C3
Barnwell, LNW, 11A1; 16G1; 17G1
Barons Court, Dist, 39D4
*Barr Road Jc*, GN, 16D1
Barracks, Mid, 24D1
Barras, NE, 27F3
Barrasford, NB, 27B3
Barrhead, GBK, Cal & G&SW, 44F2
Barrhill, G&SW, 25A3
Barrmill, GBK & Cal, 29D3
Barrow, CLC, 15B1; 20D3
Barrow, Fur, 24B5
Barrow Haven, GC, 22E3
Barrow Hill & Staveley Works, Mid, 16A4; 41B3 *see also* Staveley Works
Barrow on Soar & Quorn, Mid, 16E3
Barrs Court (Hereford), S&H(Mid), 9C1
*Barrs Court Jc*, GW, 9C1
*Barrs Court Jc North*, GW, 9C1
Barry, BRY, 8D4; 43C5;
Barry Docks, BRY, 43C5
Barry Island, BRY, 8D4; 43C5
*Barry Jc*, MB/BRY, 8B4; 43B3
Barry Links, D&A, 34E3
Bartlow, GE, 11D4
Barton (Goods) (Hereford), GW, 9C1
Barton (Goods) (Yorks), NE, 27F5
Barton (Lincs), GC, 22E4
Barton & Broughton, LNW, 24D3
Barton & Walton, Mid(LNW), 13A5
Barton Hill, NE, 22B5
Barton-le-Street, NE, 22B5
Barton Moss, LNW, 20B2; 24F2; 45B2
Baschurch, GW, 14A1; 20G4
Basford (Notts), Mid, 41F4
Basford & Bulwell, GN, 16C4; 41F4
Basingstoke, LSW(GW) & GW, 4B3
Bason Bridge, SD, 3B1; 8E3
Bassaleg, GW(LNW), 8C3; 43A3
Bassenthwaite Lake, CKP, 26E2
Bath, GW & Mid(SD), 3A3; 8D1
Bathampton, GW, 3A3
Bathgate, NB, 30C4
Batley, LNW & GN, 21E3; 42B3
Batley Carr, GN, 42C3 *see also* Staincliffe
Battersby, NE, 28F4
Battersea, WLE, 5B3; 39E5 and inset E3
Battersea Park, LBSC, 39D5 and inset E4
*Battersea Pier Jc*, LBSC, 39E4 (inset)
Battle, SEC, 6F5
Battlesbridge, GE, 6A5; 11G5
Battyeford, LNW, 42C4
*Bawtry Jc*, GN, 21G5
Baxenden, LY, 20A1; 24E1
Bay Horse, LNW, 24C3
Baynards, LBSC, 5D2

Bayswater, Met(Dist), 39C5
Bengeworth, Mid, 9C4
Beaconsfield, GW&GCJt, 5A1; 10F1
Beal, NE, 31D4
Bealings, GE, 12D3
Beamish, NE, 27C5
Beanacre Halt, GW, 3A4
Bearley GW, 9B5
Bearsden, NB, 29B4; 44E5
Bearstead & Thurnham, SEC, 6C5
Beasdale, NB, 32B5
Beattock, Cal, 30G3
Beauchief, Mid, 16A5; 41A2
Beaufort, LNW, 8A4; 43B1
Beaulieu Road, LSW, 4E4
Beauly, HR, 35D5
Beaumont's Halt, Mid, 11F1
Bebington & New Ferry, BJ, 20C4; 24G4; 45F4
Bebside, NE, 27A5
Beccles, GE, 12A2; 18G2
*Beccles Swing Bridge*, GE, 12A2; 18F1
Beckenham Hill, SEC, 40F3
Beckenham Junc, SEC, 40F3
Beckermet, WCE, 26F3
Beckfoot, RE, 26F2
Beckford, Mid, 9C4
Beckhole, NE, 28F2
Beckingham, GN&GEJt, 22G5
Beckton, GE, 5B4; 40C1
Bedale, NE, 21A3; 27G5
Beddau Halt, Rhy, 43B3
Beddau Halt, TV, 43C4
*Beddau Loop Jc*, Rhy, 43B3
Beddgelert, NWNG, 19E2
Beddington Lane Halt, LBSC, 40G5
Bedford, Mid & LNW, 10C1; 11D1
*Bedford North Jc*, Mid, 10C1; 11D1
Bedhampton Halt, LBSC, 4E2
Bedlington, NE, 27A5
Bedlinog, TBJ, 8B5; 43C2
Bedminster, GW, 3G1 (inset)
*Bedminster Jc*, GW, 3G1 (inset)
Bedwas, BM, 8B4; 43B3
Bedwellty Pits, LNW, 8A4
Bedworth, LNW, 16G5
Bedwyn, GW, 4A5
Beechburn, NE, 27D5
Beeston (Notts), Mid, 16D4; 41G4
Beeston (Yorks), GN(GC), 21D3; 42B3
Beeston Castle & Tarporley, LNW, 15B1; 20E3
Beeston Tor, NS, 15C5
Beighten, GC, 16A4; 41A3
Beith, G&SW & GBK, 29D3
Bekesbourne, SEC, 6C2
Belford, NE, 31E4
Belgrave & Birstall, GC, 16E3
Bell Busk, Mid, 21C1
Bell Green, LNW, 10A3
Bellahouston, G&SW, 44E3 and inset G1
Belle Vue, GC&MidJt, 20C1; 45A3
*Bellfield Jc*, G&SW, 29E4
Bellgrove, NB, 44D4
Bellingham (Kent), SEC, 40F3
Bellingham (Northumb), NB, 27A3
Bellshill, Cal & NB, 30C5; 44B3
*Bellwater Jc*, GN, 17C3
Belmont (Surrey), LBSC, 5C3
Belper, Mid, 16C5; 41F2
Belses, NB, 31E1
*Belston Jc*, G&SW, 29F4
Belton (Lincs), AJ, 22F5
Belton (Norfolk), GE, 18F1
Beluncle Halt, SEC, 6B5
Belvedere, SEC, 5B4
*Belvoir Jc*, GN, 16D2
Bembridge, IW, 4F2
Bempton, NE, 22B3
Ben Rhydding, O&I, 21C2
Benderloch, Cal, 32E4
Benfleet, LTS, 6A5
Bengeworth, Mid, 9C4
Beningborough, NE, 21C4
Bensham, NE, 27C5; 28 (inset)
Bentham, Mid, 24B2
Bentley (Hants), LSW, 4C1
Bentley (Suffolk), GE, 12D4
*Bentley Jc*, GC, 21F5
Benton, NE, 27B5
Bents, NB, 30C4
Bentworth & Lasham, LSW, 4C2
Benwick Goods, GE, 11A3; 17G3
Bere Alston, LSW/BAC, 1D5
Bere Ferrers, LSW, 1D5
Berkeley, SVW, 8B1; 9F2
Berkeley Road, Mid & SVW, 8B1; 9F2
Berkhamsted, LNW, 10E1
Berkswell, LNW, 9A5
Berney Arms, GE, 18F1
Berrington, GW, 15F1
Berrington & Eye, S&H, 9B1
Berry Brow, LY, 21E2; 42D5
Bervie, NB, 34B2
Berw Road Halt, TV, 43C3
Berwick (Sussex), LBSC, 5F4
Berwick-on-Tweed, NE&NBJt, 31C3
Berwig Halt, GW, 20E5
Berwyn, GW, 20F5
Bescar Lane, LY, 20A4; 24E3; 45F1
Bescot, LNW, 13A3; 15F4
*Bessacarr Jc*, SYJ/DV, 21F5
Bestwood Colliery, GN, 16C4; 41E4
Beswick (Goods), Mid, 45A3
Betchworth, SEC, 5C2
Bethesda, LNW, 19D2
Bethnal Green, GE, 40C4
Betley Road, LNW, 15C2; 20E2
Bettisfield, Cam, 20F3
Bettws (Llangeinor), PT, 7B5; 43D3 *see also* Llangeinor
Bettws Garmon, NWNG, 19E2
Bettws-y-Coed, LNW, 19E4
Beverley, NE, 22D3
*Beverley Jc*, NE, 22D3
Beverley Road (Hull), HB, 22 (inset)
Bewdley, GW, 9A3
Bexhill, LBSC & SEC, 6F5
Bexley, SEC, 5B4
Bexleyheath, SEC, 5B4
Bicester, GW & LNW, 10D3
Bickershaw & Abram, GC, 45C2
*Bickershaw Jcs*, LNW, 45C2
Bickleigh, GW, 2D5
Bickley, SEC, 40G2
*Bickley Jc*, SEC, 40G2
Biddenden, KES, 6D4
Biddulph, NS, 15B3; 20E1
Bideford, LSW & BWHA, 7F2
Bidford-on-Avon, SMJ, 9B5
Bidston (Goods), GC & Wir, 20C4; 24G5; 45F4
Bidston (Pass), Wir(GC), 20C4; 24G5; 45F4
Bieldside, GNS, 37G4
Biggar, Cal, 30E3
Biggleswade, GN, 11D2
*Biglis Jc*, BRY/TV, 8D4; 43B5
Bilbster, HR, 38D2
Billacombe, GW, 2D5
Billericay, GE, 5A5; 11G5
Billing, LNW, 10B2
Billingborough & Horbling, GN, 17D1
Billinge Green Halt, LNW, 15B2; 20D2
Billingham-on-Tees, NE, 28E4
Billingshurst, LBSC, 5E2
Bilson (Goods), GW & SVW, 8A1; 9E2
Bilston, GW, 15F4; 13A1 *see also* Ettingshall Road
*Bilton Road Jc*, NE, 21C3
Binegar, SD, 3B2; 8E1
Bingham, GN, 16C3
Bingham Road (Notts), GN&LNWJt, 16D3
Bingley, Mid, 21D2; 24F1; 42A5
*Bingley Jc*, Mid, 42A5
Binton, SMJ, 9B5
Birch Vale, GC&MidJt, 15A4; 21G1
Birchfield Plat, GNS, 36D1
Birchills, LNW, 15F4
Birchington-on-Sea, SEC, 6B2
Birdbrook, CVH, 11D5
Birdingbury, LNW, 10A4
Birdwell & Hoyland Common, GC, 21F3; 42E2
Birdwell & Pilley (Goods), Mid, 21F3; 42E2
Birkdale, LY(LNW), 20A4; 24E4; 45F1
Birkdale Palace, CLC, 20A4; 24E4; 45F1
Birkenhead, BJ, CLC, GC, GW, LNW, Mer, Wir, 20C4; 24G4; 45F4
Birkenhead Park, Wir, 45F4
Birkenshaw & Tong, GN, 21D2; 42B4
Birmingham (Goods), GW, LNW & Mid, 13 (inset) and 15G4
Birmingham (Pass), GW & LNW&MidJt, 13 (inset) and 15G4
*Birmingham Curve Jc*, Mid, 15E5
Birnie Road, NB, 34C2
*Birstal Jc*, LNW, 42B3
Birstall (Yorks), LNW, 21E2; 42B4
Birstwith, NE, 21C3
Birtley, NE, 27C5
Bishop Auckland, NE, 27E5
Bishop's Castle, BC, 14C1
*Bishop's Castle Railway*, BC, 14C1
Bishop's Cleeve, GW, 9D4
Bishop's Lydeard, GW, 8F4
Bishop's Nympton & Molland, GW, 7F5
Bishops Road, GW&MetJt, 39C2 (inset)
Bishop's Stortford, GE, 11E3
Bishop's Waltham, LSW, 4D3
Bishopbriggs, NB, 29C5; 44D4
Bishopsbourne, SEC, 6C2
Bishopsgate, GE, 40C4
*Bishopsgate Jc*, GE/EL&NL, 40C4
Bishopstone, LBSC, 5G4
Bishopton, Cal, 29C4
Bisley Camp, LSW, 5C1
Bispham, PWY, 24D4
Bittaford Platform, GW, 2D5
Bitterley, S&H, 9A1
Bitterne, LSW, 4E4
Bitton, Mid, 3A3; 8D1
Blaby, LNW, 16F4

Black Bank, GE, 11A4; 17G4
Black Bull, NS, 15C3; 20E1
Black Dog Siding, GW, 3A5
Black Dyke, NB, 26C3
Black Lane (Radcliffe), LY, 20B2; 24F1; 45B2
Blackburn, LY(LNW/Mid), 24D2
Blackford Hill, NB, 30 (inset)
Blackford, Cal, 33F4
Blackfriars, Dist(Met), 40C5
*Blackhall Jc*, NB, 30C4
Blackhall Rocks, NE, 28D4
Blackheath (London), SEC, 5B4; 40E2
Blackheath Hill, SEC, 5B4; 40D3
Blackhill, NE, 27C4
*Blackhill Jc*, Cal, 44D4
Blackhorse Road, TFG, 40A3
*Blackhouse Jc*, G&SW, 29F3
Blackmill, GW, 7B5; 43D3
Blackmoor, LB, 7E4
Blackpill, Mum, 43G3
Blackpool, PWY, 24D4
Blackrod, LY, 20B2; 24F2; 45C2
*Blackrod Jc*, LY, 45C2
Blacksboat, GNS, 36E2
Blackstone, NB, 30B4
*Blackstone Jc*, Cal, 44G4
Blackthorn, GW, 10D3
Blackwall (Goods), GN, 40C3 and inset D1
Blackwall (Pass), GE, 5B4; 40C2
Blackwater (IoW), IWC, 4F3
Blackwater & Camberley, SEC, 4B1 *see also* Camberley & York Town
Blackwell (Worcs), Mid, 9A4
Blackwell Mill Halt, Mid, 15A5
Blackwood (Lanark), Cal, 30D5
Blackwood (Mon), LNW, 8B4; 43B2
Blacon, GC, 20D4
Blaenau Festiniog, LNW, GW & Fest, 19F3
Blaenavon, GW & LNW(GW), 8A4; 43A1
Blaenclydach (Goods), GW, 8B5; 43D3
Blaengarw, GW(PT), 7B5; 43D3
Blaengwynfi, RSB, 7B5; 43D2
Blaenplwyf Halt, GW, 13E5
Blaenrhondda, RSB, 7B5; 43D2
Blagdon, GW, 3B2; 8D2
Blaina, GW, 8A4; 43B2
Blair Atholl, HR, 33C3
Blairadam, NB, 30A3
Blairgowrie, Cal, 33D5
Blairhill & Gartsherrie, NB, 29C5; 44B4 *see also* Gartsherrie
Blake Hall, GE, 11G4
Blake Street, LNW, 15F5
Blakeney (Goods), GW, 8A1; 9E2
Blakesley, SMJ, 10C3
*Blakey Jc*, NE, 28F3
Blandford, SD, 3E4
Blanefield, NB, 29B4
Blankney & Metheringham, GN&GEJt, 16B1; 17B1
Blantyre, Cal, 29C5; 44C2
Blaydon, NE(NB), 27B5 and 28 inset
*Blaydon East Jc*, NE, 28 (inset)
*Blaydon North Jc*, NE, 28 (inset)
*Blaydon South Jc*, NE, 28 (inset)
Bleadon & Uphill, GW, 3B1; 8D3
Blean & Tyler Hill Halt, SEC, 6C3
Bleasby, Mid, 16C3
Bledlow, GW, 10F2
Bledlow Bridge Halt, GW, 10F2
Blencow, CKP, 26E1
Blenheim & Woodstock, GW, 10E4
Bletchington, GW, 10E4
Bletchley, LNW, 10D2
Blidworth & Rainworth, Mid, 16B3; 41D5
Blisworth, LNW & SMJ, 10B3
Blockley, GW, 9C5
Blodwell Junc, Cam, 14A2; 20G5
Blowick, LY, 20A4; 24E4; 45F1
Bloxham, GW, 10C4
Bloxwich, LNW, 15F4
Blue Anchor, GW, 8E5
Blundellsands & Crosby, LY(LNW), 20B4; 24F4; 45F3
Blunham, LNW, 11D1
Blunsdon, MSW, 9F5
Bluntisham, GE, 11B3
Blyth, NE, 28A5
Blythburgh, SWD, 12B2
Blythe Bridge, NS, 15C4
Blyton, GC, 22G5
Boar's Head, LNW & LU, 20B3; 24F2; 45D2
Boarhills, NB, 34F3
Boat of Garten, HR(GNS), 36F3
Boddam, GNS, 37D5
Bodfari, LNW, 19D5
Bodiam, KES, 6E5
Bodmin, GW & LSW, 1D3
Bodmin Road, GW, 1D3
Bodorgan, LNW, 19D1
Bognor, LBSC, 5G1
Bogside (Fife), NB, 30A4
Bogside (Renfrew), Cal & G&SW, 29E3
Bogston, Cal, 29B3
Boldon (Goods), NE, 28C5
Bollington, GC&NSJt, 15A4; 45A5
*Bollo Lane Jc*, LSW/NSW, 39D3
Bolsover, GC & Mid, 16B4; 41C3
Bolton, LY(Mid), LY & LNW, 20B2; 24F1; 45B2
Bolton Abbey, Mid, 21C1
Bolton-le-Sands, LNW, 24B3
Bolton-on-Dearne, SK(GC), 21F4; 42E1
Bolton Percy, NE(LY/GN), 21D4
Bolton Street (Bury), LY, 20B1; 24F1; 45B1
Bonar Bridge, HR, 36B5
Boncath, GW, 13F3
Bo'ness, NB, 30B4
Bonnington, Cal & NB, 30 (inset)
Bonnybridge, Cal, K&B & NB, 30B5
Bonnybridge Central, Cal, K&B & NB, 30B5
Bonnyrigg, NB, 30C2
*Bonnywater Jc*, Cal/K&B, 30B5
Bontnewydd, GW, 14A5; 19G3
Bookham, LSW, 5C2
Boosbeck, NE, 28E3
Boot, RE, 26F2
*Bootham Jc*, NE, 21C5 and inset A4
Bootle (Cumb), Fur, 24A5; 26G3
Bootle (Lancs), LY, 45F3 *see also* Balliol Rd
*Bopeep Jc*, SEC/LBSC, 6F5
Bordesley, GW, 13C4; 15G5
*Bordesley Jc*, GW, 13C4
Bordon, LSW, 4C1
*Borough Market Jc*, SEC, 40C4
Boroughbridge, NE, 21B4
Borrobol Platform, HR, 38F5
Borrowash, Mid, 16D4; 41G2
Borth, Cam, 13C5
Borwick, Fur&MidJt, 24B3
*Boscarne Jc*, LSW/GW, 1D3
Boscombe, LSW, 3F5
Bosham, LBSC, 4E1
Bosley, NS, 15B3; 20D1
Boston, GN, 17C3
Boston Manor, Met & Dist, 39D2
Botanic Gardens (Glasgow), Cal, 44E4
Botanic Gardens (Hull), NE, 22 (inset)
Bothwell, Cal & NB, 29C5; 44C2
*Bothwell Jc*, Cal, 44B3
*Bothwell Jc*, NB, 44C2
Botley, LSW, 4E3
Bott Lane Halt, Mid, 24D1
Bottesford, GN, 16D2
*Bottesford N, E, S & W Jcs*, GN, 16C2
*Botteslow Jc*, NS, 15C3
Bottisham & Lode, GE, 11C4
Boughrood & Llyswen, Cam, 14F3
Boughton, GC, 16B3
*Boultham Jc*, GN&GEJt, 16B1
Bourne, GN(Mid/MGN), 17E1
*Bourne East Jc*, GN, 17E1
Bourne End, GW, 5A1; 10G2
*Bourne West Jc*, GN, 17E1
Bournemouth Central, LSW, 3F5; West, LSW(SD), 3F5
Bournville, Mid, 9A4
Bourton-on-the-Water, GW, 9D5
Bovey for Islington, GW, 2C4
Bow (Devon), LSW, 2B4
Bow (London), NL & LNW, 40C3
Bow Brickhill Halt, LNW, 10D2
Bow Road, WB & GE, 40C3
Bow Street, Cam, 13C5
Bowbridge Crossing Halt, GW, 9E3
Bower, HR, 38C3
Bowes, NE, 27F4
Bowhouse, NB, 30B4
Bowland, NB, 30D1
Bowling, Cal & NB, 29B4
Bowling Junc, LY, 42B4
Bowness, Cal, 26C2
Box, GW, 3A4
Box Hill & Burford Bridge, LBSC, 5C2
Box Hill, SEC, 5C2
Boxford, GW, 4A4
Boxmoor & Hemel Hempsted, LNW, 10E1; 11F1 *see also* Hemel Hempsted
Boyce's Bridge, WUT, 17F4
Braceborough Spa, GN, 17E1
Bracebridge (Goods), GN, 16B1
*Brackenhill Jc* (Ayrshire), G&SW, 29E4
*Brackenhill Jc* (Yorks), SK(GC/GN), 21E4
*Brackenhill Light Railway*, BL, 42D1
Brackenhills, Cal, 9D3
Brackley, LNW, 10C3
Brackley Central, GC, 10C3
Bracknell, LSW, 4A1
Bradbury, NE, 28E5
Bradfield, GE, 12E4
Bradford (Goods), GN, LY, & Mid, 21D2; 42A4
Bradford (Pass), 21D2; 42A4
*Bradford Jcs*, GW, 3B4
Bradford-on-Avon, GW, 3B4
Brading Junc, IW, 4F3
Bradley (Yorks), LNW(LY), 42C4
Bradley Fold, LY, 20B2; 24F1; 45B2
*Bradley Wood Jc*, LY, 21E2; 42C4

Bradnop, NS, 15C4
Bradwell, LNW, 10C2
Brafferton, NE, 21B4
Braidwood, Cal, 30D5
Braintree & Bocking, GE, 11E5
Braithwaite, CKP, 26E2
*Braithwell Jc*, HB&GCJt/GC&Mid&HBJt, 21G5
Bramber, LBSC, 5F2
Brambledown Halt, SEC, 6B4
Bramford, GE, 12D4
Bramhall, LNW(NS), 15A3; 20C1; 45A4
Bramhall Moor Lane (Goods), Mid, 45A4
Bramley (Hants), GW, 4B2
Bramley (Yorks), GN(LY), 21D3; 42A3
Bramley & Wonersh, LBSC, 5D1
Brampford Speke, GW, 2B3
Brampton (Suffolk), GE, 12B2; 18G2
Brampton Goods (Chesterfield), Mid, 16B5; 41C2
Brampton Halt, NS, 20F1
Brampton Junc (Cumb), NE, 27C1
Brampton Town (Cumb), NE, 27C1
Bramwith (Goods), WRG, 21F5
Brancepeth, NE, 27D5
*Brancliffe Jc*, GC/GC&MidJt, 16A4; 41A4
Brandlesholme Road Halt, LY, 45B1
Brandon (Durham), NE, 27D5
Brandon (Norfolk), GE, 11A5; 17G5
Brandon & Wolston, LNW, 10A5
*Brandy Bridge Jc*, TV/GW&TVJt, 43C2
Branksome, LSW(SD), 3F5
Bransford Road, GW, 9B3
Branston (Staffs), Mid, 15E5
Branston & Heighington, GN&GEJt, 16B1; 17B1
*Branston Jc*, Mid, 15E5
Bransty (Whitehaven), Fur&LNWJt, 26E4
Branthwaite, WCE, 26E3
Brasted, SEC, 5C4
Bratton Fleming, LB, 7E3
Braughing, GE, 11E3
Braunston, LNW, 10B4
Braunston & Willoughby, GC, 10B4
Braunton, LSW(GW), 7F3
Braystones, Fur, 26F3
Brayton, M&C(Cal), 26D2
*Brayton East Jc*, NE, 21D5
*Brayton North Jc*, NE, 21D5
Breadsall, GN, 16D5; 41G2
*Breakwater Jc*, Cal, 30 (inset)
Breamore, LSW, 4D5
Brechin, Cal, 34C3
Breck Road, LNW, 20C4; 24G4; 45F3
Brecon, BM (Cam/Mid/N&B), 14F3
*Brecon Curve Jc* (Hereford), GW/Mid, 9C1
Brecon Road (Abergavenny), LNW, 43A1
Bredbury, GC&MidJt, 21G1; 45A3
Bredon (Worcs), Mid, 9C3
Breich, Cal, 30C4
Brent (Devon), GW, 2D4
*Brent Jc* (Cricklewood), Mid, 39B4
*Brent Jc* (Willesden), LNW, 39C3
Brent Knoll, GW, 3B1; 8E3
Brentford, LSW & GW, 5B2; 39D2
*Brentford Lane Jc*, LSW, 39D3
Brentham, GW, 39C2
Brentor, LSW, 1C5
Brentwood & Warley, GE, 5A5
Bretby, Mid, 16E5
Brettell Lane, GW, 15G3
*Breydon Jc*, GE, 18F1
Bricket Wood, LNW, 11G1
Bricklayers Arms Goods, SEC, 40D4
*Bricklayers Arms Jc*, LBSC, 40D4
Bridestowe, LSW, 2B5
Bridge, SEC, 6C3
Bridge of Allan, Cal, 30A5
Bridge of Dee, G&SW, 26C5
Bridge of Dun, Cal, 34C3
Bridge of Earn, NB, 33F5
Bridge of Orchy, NB, 32E1
Bridge of Weir, G&SW, 29C3
Bridge Street (Northampton), LNW, 10B2
*Bridge Street Jc* (Glasgow), Cal/G&P, 44F2 (inset)
Bridgefoot, WCE, 26E3
Bridgefoot Halt, GNS, 37C2
Bridgend, GW(BRY), 7C5; 43D4
Bridgend & Coity (Goods), BRY, 43D4
*Bridgend Jc*, NB, 29B5; 44C5
Bridgeness, NB, 30B4
Bridgeton, Cal, 44D3
Bridgeton Cross, Cal, 44E1
Bridgeton Cross, Cal & NB(G&SW), 44D3
Bridgnorth, GW, 15F2
Bridgwater, GW & SD, 3C1; 8F3
Bridlington, NE, 22B3
Bridport for Lyme Regis, GW, 3F1
Brierfield, LY, 24D1
Brierley Hill, GW, 15G3
*Brierley Jc*, HB/DV, 21E4; 42D1
Brigg, GC, 22F4
Brigham, LNW&M&CJt, 26E3
Brighouse, LY, 21E2; 42C4 *see also* Clifton Road
Brightlingsea, GE, 12F4
Brighton, LBSC, 5F3
Brighton Road (Birmingham), Mid, 13D4
*Brighton Works*, LBSC, 5F3
Brightside, Mid, 21G3; 42G2
Brill & Ludgershall, GW, 10E3
Brill, OAT, 10E3
Brimington, Mid, B2
Brimscombe, GW, 9F3
Brimscombe Bridge Halt, GW, 9F3
Brimsdown, GE, 5A3; 11G3
Brindle Heath (Goods), LY, 45B3
Brinkburn, NB, 31G4
Brinklow, LNW, 10A4
Brinkworth, GW, 9G4
Brinscall, LU, 20A2; 24E2
*Brinsley Jc*, GN 41E3
Brislington, GW, 3A2; 8D1
Bristol, GW/Mid, GW & Mid, 3A2 and inset; 8C1/2
Bristol Road, WCP, 3A1; 8D3
Britannia, LY, 20A1
Brithdiri, Rhy, 8B4; 43B2 *see also* Cwmsyfiog
Briton Ferry Road, GW, 43F3
Briton Ferry, GW, RSB & SWM, 7B4; 43F3
Brixham, GW, 2D3
Brixton, SEC 5B3; 40E5
Brixton Coal Depot, Mid, 40E5
Brixton Road (Devon), GW, 2E5
Brixworth, LNW, 10A2
Broad Clyst, LSW, 2B3
Broad Green, LNW, 20C4; 45E4
Broad Street (London), NL & LNW, 5A3; 40C4
Broad Street (Pendleton), LY, 45B3
Broadfield, LY, 20B1; 24F1; 45A2
*Broadheath Jc*, LNW/CLC, 45B4
Broadheath, LNW, 20C2; 24G2; 45B4
Broadley LY, 20A1; 45A1
Broadstairs, SEC, 6B1
Broadstone, WCP, 3A1; 8D3
*Broadstone Jc*, LSW(SD), 3F5
Broadway, GW, 9C4
Brock, LNW, 24D3
*Brockenhill Jc*, SK(GC/GN)/ind, 42C1
Brockenhurst, LSW, 4E4
Brocketsbrae, Cal, 30D5
Brockford & Wetheringsett, MSL, 12C4
Brockholes, LY, 21F2; 42D5
Brocklesby, GC, 22E3
Brockley, LBSC, 40E3
Brockley Lane, SEC, 40E3
Brockley Whins, NE, 28C5
Brodie, HR, 36D3
Bromborough, BJ, 20C4; 45F5
Bromfield (Cumb), Cal, 26D2
Bromfield (Salop), S&H, 9A1
Bromford Bridge, Mid, 15G5
Bromham & Rowde, GW, 3B5
Bromley (London), LTS(Dist), 40C3
Bromley Cross, LY, 20A2; 24E1; 45B1
*Bromley Jc* (Norwood), LBSC/SEC, 40F4
Bromley North (Kent), SEC, 5B4; 40F2
Bromley South (Kent), SEC, 5B4; 40G2
*Bromley Spur Jc*, SEC/LBSC, 40F4
Brompton (Yorks), NE, 28G5
Brompton & Fulham Goods, LNW, 39D4
Bromsgrove, Mid, 9A4
Bromshall (Goods), NS, 15D4
Bromyard, GW, 9B2
Brondesbury, LNW(NL), 39B4 *see also* Kilburn, Met
Brondesbury Park, LNW(NL), 39B4
Bronwydd Arms, GW, 13G4
Brookland, SEC, 6E4
Brooklands, MSJA(CLC), 20C1; 24G1; 45B3
Brooksby, Mid, 16E3
Brookwood Cemetery (London Necropolis Co), 5C1
Brookwood Cemetery (London Necropolis Co), LSW, 5C1
Brookwood, LSW, 5C1
Broom (Junc), Mid(SMJ), 9B4
Broome, LNW, 14C1
*Broomfield Jc*, Cal/NB, 34C2
Broomfleet, NE(GC), 22E4
Broomhill (Inverness), HR, 36F3
Broomhill (Northumb), NE, 31G5
Broomhouse, NB, 29C5; 44C3
Broomieknowe, NB, 30C2
Broomielaw (Durham), NE, 27E4
Broomlee, NB, 30D3
Brora, HR, 36A4; 38G5
Brotton, NE, 28E3
Brough, NE(GC/LNW), 22E4
Broughton, LNW, 20D4
Broughton (Peebles), Cal, 30E3
Broughton Astley, Mid, 16G4
Broughton Cross, LNW, 26E3
Broughton Gifford Halt, GW, 3B4
Broughton-in-Furness, Fur, 24A5
Broughton Lane, GC, 42G2
Broughty Ferry, D&A, 34E1 (inset)
Browndown Halt, LSW, 4E3
Brownhills, LNW & Mid, 15F4
Broxbourne & Hoddesdon, GE, 11F3
*Broxbourne Jc*, GE, 11F3

Broxton, LNW, 15C1; 20E3
Bruce Grove, GE, 40A4
Brucklay, GNS, 37D4
Brundall, GE, 18F2
Brunswick (Liverpool) Goods, CLC, 20C4; 24G4; 45F4 and inset
Brunswick Dock (Liverpool) Goods, LNW, 45F4 and inset
Bruton, GW, 3C3; 8F1
Brymbo, GW(LNW) & GC, 20E4
Brymbo West Crossing Halt, GW, 20E4
Bryn (Glam), PT, 7B5; 43E3
Bryn (Lancs), LNW, 20B3; 24F2; 45D3
Bryn Teify, GW, 13F4
Brynamman, GW & Mid, 7A4; 43F1
*Bryncethin Jc*, GW, 7C5; 43D4
Brynglas, Tal, 13B5
Bryngwyn (Carnarvon), NWNG, 19E2
Bryngwyn Halt (Montgomery), Cam, 14A2
Brynkir, LNW, 19F2
Brynmawr, LNW(GW), 8A4; 43B1
Brynmenyn, GW, 7C5; 43D3
Brynmill, Mum, 43G3
Bubwith, NE, 21D5
*Buccleuch Dock Jc*, Fur, 24B5
Buchanan Street (Glasgow), Cal, 29C5; 44E4
Buchlyvie, NB, 29A4
Buckden, Mid, 11C2 *see also* Offord
Buckenham, GE, 18F2
Buckfastleigh, GW, 2D4
Buckhaven, NB, 30A2; 34G5
Buckhurst Hill, GE, 5A4
Buckie, GNS & HR, 37C1
Buckingham, LNW, 10D3
*Buckingham West Jc*, Cal, 34E2 (inset)
*Buckland Jc*, SEC, 6D2
Buckley, GC, 20D5 *see also* Padeswood
Buckley Junc, GC, 20D4
Bucknall & Northwood, NS, 15C3
Bucknell, LNW, 14D1
Buckpool, GNS, 37C1
Bucksburn, GNS, 37F4
Buddon, D&A, 34E4
Bude, LSW, 1A4
Budleigh Salterton, LSW, 2C2
Bugle, GW, 1D2
Bugsworth, Mid, 15A4
Buildwas, GW, 15F2
Builth Road, Cam & LNW, 14E3
Builth Wells, Cam, 14E3
Bulford, LSW, 4C5
Bulford Camp, LSW, 4C5
Bulkington, LNW, 16G5
Bullers o' Buchan Platform, GNS, 37E5
Bullgill, M&C, 26D3
*Bullgill Jc*, M&C, 26D3
Bullo Pill, GW, 8A1; 9E2
Bulwell, Mid, 16C4; 41F4 *see also* Basford
Bulwell Common, GC, 16C4; 41F4
Bulwell Forest, GN, 16C4; 41F4
Bunchrew, HR, 36D5
Bungalow Town Halt, LBSC, 5F2
Bungay, GE, 12A2; 18G2
Buntingford, GE, 11E3
Burbage (Goods), GW, 4A5
Burdale, NE, 22B5
Burdett Road, GE(LTS), 40C3
Bures, GE, 12E5
Burgess Hill, LBSC, 5E3
Burgh (Cumb), NB, 26C1
Burgh (Lincs), GN, 17B4
Burghclere, GW, 4B3
Burghead, HR, 36C2
Burleigh Street (Goods) (Hull), HB, 22 (inset)
Burlescombe, GW, 2A2; 8G5
Burlington Road Halt, PWY, 24D4
Burn Hill, NE, 27D4
Burn Naze Halt, PWY, 24D4
Burnage, LNW, 45A3
Burnbank, NB, 44C2
Burneside, LNW, 27G1
Burngullow, GW, 1D2
Burnham (Som), SD, 3B1; 8E3
Burnham Beeches, GW, 5B1
Burnham Market, GE, 18D5
Burnham-on-Crouch, GE, 6A4; 12G5
Burnley, LY, 24D1
Burnmouth, NB, 31C3
Burnside (Westmorland), LNW, 27G1
Burnside, Cal, 29C5; 44D3
Burnstones, NE, 27C2
Burnt House (Goods), GE, 11A3; 17G3
Burnt Mill, GE, 11F3
Burntisland, NB, 30A2
Burrington, GW, 3B2; 8D2
Burry Port, BPGV, 7B2 *see also* Pembrey, GW
Burscough Bridge, LY, 20A4; 24F3; 45E1
Burscough Junc, LY, 20B4; 24F3; 45E1
Bursledon, LSW, 4E3
Burslem, NS, 15C3; 20E1
Burston, GE, 12B3
Burton & Holme, LNW, 24B3
Burton Agnes, NE, 22B3
Burton Joyce, Mid, 16C3; 41F5
*Burton Lane Jc*, NE, 21C5 and inset A4
Burton-on-Trent (Goods), Mid, GN & LNW, 15D5 and inset
Burton-on-Trent (Pass), Mid(GN/LNW/NS), 15D5 and inset
Burton Point, GC, 20D4; 45F5
Burton Salmon, NE(GN), 21E4; 42B1
Burwarton, CMDP, 15G2
Burwell, GE, 11C4
Bury (Lancs), LY, 20B1; 24F1; 45B1/2
Bury St Edmunds, GE, 12C5
Busby, Cal, 29C5; 44E2
*Busby Jc*, Cal/GBK, 44E3
Bush Hill Park, GE, 5A3; 11G3
Bushbury (Goods), LNW, 15F3
*Bushbury Jc*, LNW/GW, 15F3
Bushey & Oxhey, LNW, 5A2; 11G1
*Bushey Lane Jc*, LY, 20B3; 24F3; 45E2
Butler's Hill, GN, 16C4; 41E4
Butterknowle (Goods), NE, 27E4
Butterley, Mid, 16C5; 41E2
Butterton, MS, 15B5
Buttington, Cam & SWP, 14A2
*Butts Jc*, LSW, 4C2
Butts Lane Halt, LY, 20A4; 24E4; 45F1
Buxted, LBSC, 5E4
Buxton, LNW & Mid, 15A4
Buxton Lamas, GE, 18E3
Byers Green, NE, 27D5
Byfield, SMJ, 10B4
Byfleet & Woodham, LSW, 5C1
Byker, NE, 28 (inset)
Bynea (Carmarthenshire), GW, 7B3
Cadbury Road, WCP, 3A1; 8C2
Cadeleigh, GW, 2A3
Cadishead, CLC, 20C2; 24G2; 45C3
Cadoxton, BRY(TV), 8D4; 43B5
Cadoxton Goods (Neath), N&B, 43F2
*Cadoxton Jc*, BR, 43C5
Cae Harris, TBJ, 43C2
Caerau, GW, 7B5; 43E3
Caergwrle Castle, GC, 20E4
Caerleon, GW, 8B3; 43A3
Caerphilly, Rhy(AD), 8C4; 43B3
*Caerphilly East Branch Jc*, BM/RHY, 43B3
*Caerphilly Locomotive Works*, Rhy, 43B3
*Caerphilly Lower Branch Jc*, BM, 43B3
*Caerphilly Upper Branch Jc*, BM/RHY, 43B3
*Caerphilly West Branch Jc*, RHY, 43B3
Caersws, Cam, 14C3
Caerwys, LNW, 20D5
*Cairn Valley Jc*, G&SW, 26B4
Cairnbuig, GNS, 37C5
Cairneyhill, NB, 30A3
Cairnie Junc, GNS, 37D1
Caister-on-Sea, MGN, 18E1
*Caister Road Jc*, MGN, 18F1
Calbourne & Shalfleet, FYN, 4F4
Calcotts, GNS, 36C1
Caldarvan, NB, 29B4
Calder, Cal, 44B4
Calderbank, Cal, 30C5; 44A3
*Calderbank Branch Jc*, NB, 44A4
Caldercruix, NB, 30C5; 44B4
Caldon Low Halt, NS, 15C4
Caldwell, GBK, 29D4
Caldy, BJ, 20C5; 24G5
Caledonian Rd & Barnsbury, NL(LNW), 40B5
Callander, Cal, 33G2
Callerton, NE, 27B5
Callington, BAC, 1C5
Callowland, LNW, 11G1
Calne, GW, 3A5
Calstock, BAC, 1C5
Calthwaite, LNW, 27D1
Calveley, LNW, 15B1; 20E3
Calverley & Rodley, Mid, 21D2; 42A4
Calvert, GC, 10D3
Cam, Mid, 8B1; 9F2
Camber, RCT, 6E4
Camberley & York Town, LSW, 4B1 *see also* Blackwater, SEC
Camborne, GW, 1E5 (inset)
*Cambria Road Jc*, LBSC/SEC, 40E4
Cambridge (Goods), GE, GN, LNW & Mid, 11C3
Cambridge (Pass), GE(GN/LNW/Mid), 11C3
Cambridge Heath, GE, 40C4
Cambus, NB, 30A5
Cambus o' May, GNS, 34A4
Cambusavie Platform, HR, 36A4
Cambuslang, Cal, 29C5; 44D3
Cambusnethan, Cal, 30C5
Camden Goods, LNW, 40C5 and inset A1
Camden Town, NL(LNW), 40B5
Camel's Head Halt, LSW, 1 (inset)
Camelford, LSW, 1B3
Camelon, NB(Cal), 30B5
Camelon (Goods), NB & Cal, 30B5
Cameron Bridge, NB, 30A2; 34G5
Camerton (Cumb), LNW, 26E3
Camerton (Som), GW, 3B3; 8D1
Camlachie (Goods), NB, 44D4

Camp Hill, Mid, 13C4
*Camp Hill Jc*, Mid, 3C4
*Campbell Road Jc*, LTS/WB, 40C3
Campbeltown, CM, 29 (inset)
Campden, GW, 9C5
*Camperdown East Jc*, NB/D&A, 34E2 (inset)
*Campsie Branch Jc*, NB, 29B5; 44D5
Campsie Glen, NB, 29B5
Canada Dock (Liverpool), LNW, 45F3 and inset
Canal (Inverness), HP, 36E5
Canal (Paisley), G&P, 29C4; 44F3
*Canal Jc* (Carlisle), NB, 26C1
Canning Town, GE & LNW, 40C2
Cannock, LNW, 15E4
Cannon Street (Hull), HB, 22 (inset)
Cannon Street (London), SEC & Dist&MetJt, 40C4
Cannon's Marsh (Goods), GW, 3 (inset)
Canonbie, NB, 26B1
Canonbury, NL, 40B4
Canonbury (Essex Road), GN, 40B5
*Canonbury Jc*, GN/NL, 40B5
Canterbury, SEC, 6C3
*Canterbury Road Jc*, SEC, 40E5
Cantley, GE, 18F2
Capel, GE, 12D4
Capel Bangor, VR, 13C5
Capenhurst, BJ, 20D4; 45F5
Carbean, GW, 1D2
Carbis, GW, 1D2
Carbis Bay, GW, 1F4 (inset)
Carcroft, WRG, 21F4
Cardenden, NB, 30A2
Cardiff (Goods), GW, TV, Rhy & LNW, 8C4; 43B4/5
Cardiff (Pass), GW(BRY/TV), Rhy(Car) & TV, 8C4; 43B4/5
Cardiff Docks (Pass), TV, 8C4; 43B5
Cardigan, GW, 13E2
*Cardigan Jc*, GW, 7A1; 13G2
Cardigan Road Goods (Leeds), NE, 42A3
Cardington, Mid, 11D1
Cardonald, G&P, 44F3
Cardonnel Halt, GW, 43F3
*Cardonnel Jc*, GW/RSB, 43F3
Cardrona, NB, 30D2
Cardross, Cal, 29B3
Careston, NB, 34C4
Cargill, Cal, 33E5
Cargo Fleet, NE, 28E4
Carham, NE, 31D2
Carisbrooke Halt, FYN, 4F3
Cark & Cartmel, Fur, 24B4
Carlinghow, LNW, 42B3
Carlisle (Goods), Cal, LNW, M&C, Mid, NB, NE, & DJ, 26C1
Carlisle (Pass), CJC(G&SW/M&C/Mid/NB/NE), 26C1
Carlton (Durham), NE, 28E5
Carlton (Yorks), HB, 21E5
Carlton & Netherfield for Gedling & Colwick, Mid, 16C3; 41F5 *see also* Netherfield, GN
Carlton Colville, GE, 12A1; 18G1
Carlton-on-Trent, GN, 16B2
*Carlton Road Jc*, Mid, 39B5; 40C1 (inset)
Carluke, Cal, 30D5
Carmarthen Junc, GW, 13G4
Carmarthen Town, GW(LNW), 7A2; 13G4
Carmont, Cal, 34B2
*Carmuirs Jcs*, Cal/NB, 30B5
Carmyle, Cal, 29C5; 44D3
Carmyllie, D&A, 34D3
Carn Brea, GW, 1E5 (inset)
Carnaby, NE, 22B3
Carnarvon, LNW, 19D2
Carnforth (Goods), Fur&LNW&MidJt, 24B3
Carnforth (Pass), Fur&LNWJt(Mid), 24B3
Carno, Cam, 14B4
Carnoustie, D&A, 34E3
Carntyne for Westmuir & Tollcross, NB, 29C5; 44D3
Carnwath, Cal, 30D4
Carpenters Road Goods, GE, 40B3
Carr Bridge, HR, 36F3
Carr Lane Halt, KE, 24C4
Carr Mill, LNW, 20B3; 24F3; 45D3
Carrington, GC, 41F4
Carrog, GW, 20F5
Carron, GNS, 36G2
Carronbridge, G&SW, 30G4
Carshalton, LBSC, 5C3
Carstairs, Cal, 30D4
Cart Harbour (Paisley), G&SW, 44G4
*Carterhouse Jc*, LNW, 45D4
Cartsyke, Cal, 29B3
Carville, NE, 28B5
Cassillis, G&SW, 29F3
Castle (Lancaster), LNW(Mid), 24C3
Castle (Northampton), LNW, 10B2
Castle Ashby & Earls Barton, LNW(Mid), 10B2
Castle Bar Park Halt, GW, 39C2
Castle Bromwich, Mid, 15G5
Castle Bytham, Mid(MGN), 16E1; 17E1
Castle Caereinion, W&L, 14B3
Castle Cary (Som), GW, 3C2; 8F1
*Castle Cary Jc*, GW, 3C3; 8F1
Castle Donington & Shardlow, Mid, 16D4
Castle Douglas, G&SW, 26C5
*Castle Douglas Branch Jc*, G&SW, 26B3
Castle Eden, NE, 28D5
*Castle Hills Jc*, WRG, 21F4
Castle Howard, NE, 22B5
*Castle Jc*, NE, 28 (inset)
Castle Kennedy, P&W, 25C2
Castle Mill, GVT, 20F5
Castlecary (Dunbarton), NB, 30B5
Castleford, NE(LY/GN) & LY, 21E4; 42B1
Castlehill (Goods), NB, 30D5
Castlethorpe, LNW, 10C2
Castleton (Lancs), LY, 20B1; 24F1; 45A1
Castleton (Yorks), NE, 28F3
Castletown, IMR, 23C2
Castor, LNW, 11A1; 17F1
Catcliffe, SHD, 21G4; 42G1
Caterham, SEC, 5C3
Catfield, MGN, 18E2
Catford, SEC, 40E3
Catford Bridge, SEC, 40E3
Cathcart, Cal, 29C5; 44E3
Cathcart Street (Birkenhead), BJ, 45F4
Cathcart Street (Greenock), Cal, 29B3
Caton, Mid, 24B3
Catrine, G&SW, 29E5
Cattal, NE, 21C4
Catterick Bridge, NE, 27F5
*Cattewater Jc*, GW/LSW, 1 (inset)
*Cattle Sidings Jc*, Mid, 41G2
Cauldcots, NB, 34D3
Causeland, LL, 1D4
Causewayend, NB, 30B4
Causewayhead, NB, 30A5
Cavendish, GE, 11D5
Cawood, NE, 21D5
Cawston, GE, 18E3
Caythorpe, GN, 16C1
Cayton, NE, 22A3
Cefn, GW, 20F4
Cefn Coed, BM&LNWJt, 8A5; 43C1
*Cefn Jc*, GW/PT, 7C5; 43E4
Cefn On Halt, Rhy, 43B4
Cefn-y-bedd, GC, 20E4
Ceint, LNW, 19D2
*Cemetery North Jc*, NE, 28D4
*Cemetery West Jc*, NE, 28D4
Cemmaes, Mawd, 14B4
Cemmes Road, Cam, 14B5
Central (Royal Albert Docks), PLA(GE), 40C2
Cerist, Van, 14C4
Cerney & Ashton Keynes, MSW, 9F4
Chacewater, GW, 1E1 and inset E5
Chadderton (Goods), LY, 45A2
Chaddesden Sidings, Mid, 41G2
Chalcombe Road Platform, GC, 10C4
Chalder, SL, 4E1
Chalfont & Latimer, Met&GCJt, 10F1
Chalford, GW, 9F3
Chalk Farm, NL, 39B5; 40A1 (inset)
*Challoch Jc*, P&W, 25C3
Challow, GW, 10F5
*Chaloners Whin Jc*, NE, 21C5 and inset A5
Chandlers Ford, LSW, 4D4
Chapel Lane, S&M, 14A1
Chapel Street (Southport), LY(LNW), 20A4; 24E4; 45F1
Chapel-en-le-Frith, Mid & LNW, 15A4
Chapelhall, Cal, 30C5; 44A3
*Chapelknowle Jc*, Cal, 44A2
Chapelton, LSW, 7F3
Chapeltown, Mid, 21F3; 42F2
Chapeltown & Thorncliffe, GC, 21F3; 42F2
Chappel & Wakes Colne, GE(CVH), 12E5
Chard, GW&LSWJt, 3E1
Chard Junc, LSW, 2A1; 3E1
Charfield, Mid, 8B1; 9F2
Charing, SEC, 6C4
Charing Cross (Glasgow), NB, 44E4
Charing Cross (London), SEC & Dist(Met), 5B3; 40C5
Charlbury, GW, 10D5
Charlestown (Ashton), LY(LNW), 21A2 (inset)
Charlestown (Fife), NB, 30B3
Charlton Halt (Oxon), LNW, 10E4
Charlton Junc (Kent), SEC, 5B4; 40D2
Charlton Kings, GW(MSW), 9D4
Charlton Mackrell, GW, 3D2; 8F2
Chartham, SEC, 6C3
Chartley, GN, 15D4
Charwelton, GC, 10B4
Chatburn, LY, 24D1
Chatham, SEC, 6B5
Chathill, NE(NSL), 31E5
Chatteris, GN&GEJt, 11A3; 17G3
Chatterley, NS, 15C3; 20E1
Cheadle (Ches), CLC & LNW, 20C1; 45A4
Cheadle (Staffs), NS, 15C4
Cheadle Heath, Mid, 43A4
Cheadle Hulme, LNW(NS), 15A3; 24G1; 45A4
Cheam, LBSC, 5C3

Checker House, GC, 16A3
Cheddar, GW, 3B1; 8E2
Cheddington, LNW, 10E1
Cheddleton, NS, 15C4
Chedworth, MSW, 9E4
Cheesewring Quarry, LC, 1C4
Chelfham, LB, 7F3
Chelford for Knutsford, LNW, 15A3; 20D1; 45B5
Chellaston & Swarkstone, Mid, 16D5
Chelmsford, GE, 11F5
Chelsea & Fulham, WLE, 5B3; 39D5
*Chelsea Basin Jc*, WLE, 39D5
Chelsfield, SEC, 5C4
Cheltenham, GW, Mid & Mid(MSW), 9D4
Cheltenham Race Course, GW, 9D4
Cheltenham South & Leckhampton, GW(MSW), 9D4
Chepstow, GW, 8B2; 9F1
Chequerbent for Hulton, LNW, 45C2
Cheriton Halt, SEC, 6D2
Cherry Burton, NE, 2D4
Cherry Tree, LY(LNW), 20A2; 24E2
Chertsey, LSW, 5B1
Chesham, Met&GCJt, 10F1
Cheshunt, GE, 11G3
Chester, CLC, GC & LNW, 20D4
*Chester Jc*, LNW, 15C2; 20E2
Chester-le-Street, NE, 27C5
Chester North Gate, CLC, 20D4
Chester Road, LNW, 15F5
Chesterfield Central, GC, 41B2
Chettisham, GE, 11B4
Chevening Halt, SEC, 5C4
Chevington, NE, 31G5
Chichester, LBSC & SL, 4E1
Chigwell Lane, GE, 11G3
Chigwell, GE, 5A4
Chilcompton, SD, 3B3; 8E1
Childwall, CLC, 20C4; 24G3; 45E5
Chilham, SEC 6C3
Chilsworthy, BAC, 1C5
Chiltern Green, Mid, 11F1
Chilworth & Albury, SEC, 5D1
Chingford, GE, 5A4, 11G3
Chinley, Mid, 15A5
*Chinley East Jc*, Mid, 15A4
*Chinley North Jc*, Mid, 15A4
*Chinley South Jc*, Mid, 15A4
Chinnor, GW, 10F2
Chippenham, GW, 3A4
*Chippenham Jc*, GE, 11C4
Chipping Norton, GW, 10D5
Chipping Sodbury, GW, 8C1; 9G2
Chipstead, SEC, 5C3
Chirk, GW & GVT, 20F4
Chirnside, NB, 31C3
Chiseldon & Chenies, MSW, 11G1
Chiselhurst, SEC, 40F2
*Chiselhurst Jc*, SEC, 40F2
Chislet Colliery Halt, SEC, 6C2
Chiswick & Grove Park, 39D3
Chittening Factory Platform, GW, 8C2; 9G1
*Chobham Farm Jc*, GE, 40B3
Chollerton, NB, 27B3
Cholsey & Moulsford, GW, 10C4
Choppington, NE, 27A5
Chorleywood & Chenies, Met&GCJt, 5A1; 10F1
Chorlton, CLC, 20C1
Chorlton, LNW, 24G1
Chorlton-cum-Hardy, CLC, 45B3
Christchurch, LSW, 4F5
Christon Bank, NE, 31E5
Christow, GW, 2B4
Christs Hospital (West Horsham), LBSC, 5E2
Chudleigh, GW, 2C3
Church & Oswaldtwistle, LY, 24E1
Church Fenton, NE(GC/GN/LY), 21D4
Church Road (Garston), LNW, 20C4
Church Road (Mon), BM, 8B4; 43B3
Church Road (Warwicks), Mid, 13C3; 15G4
Church Stretton, S&H, 14B4
Church Village, TV, 8C5; 43C3
Churchbury, GE, 5A3; 11G3
Churchdown, GW&Mid, 9D3
Churchill & Blakedown, GW, 9A3
Churchtown, LY, 20A4; 24E4; 45F1
Churn, GW, 10G4
Churston, GW, 2D3
Churwell, LNW, 21D3; 42B3
Chwilog, LNW, 19F1
Chwilog, LNW, 19F1
Cilfrew, N&B, 7B4; 43F2
Cilfynydd, TV, 8B5; 43C3
Ciliau-Aeron, GW, 13E4
Cilmery, LNW, 14E3
Cinderford, GW & SVW, 8A1; 9E2
Cirencester, GW & MSW, 9F4
*City Basin Jc* (Exeter), GW, 2B3
City Road Goods (Bradford), GN, 42A4
Clackmannan & Kennet, NB, 30A4
Clacton-on-Sea & Southcliff, GE, 12F3
Clandon, LSW, 5C1
Clapham (Yorks), Mid, 24B1
Clapham & North Stockwell (London), SEC(LBSC), 40E5
Clapham Junc (London), LSW, LBSC(LNW) & WLE, 5B3; 39E5 and inset F3
Clapton, GE, 40B4
*Clapton Jc*, GE, 40B4
Clapton Road, WCP, 3A1; 8C2
*Clarbeston Jc*, GW, 13G1
Clarbeston Road, GW, 13G1
*Clarborough Jc*, GC, 16A2
Clare, GE, 11D5
Clarence Road (Cardiff), GW(BRY/TV), 43B4
Clarence Street (Pontypool), GW, 43A2
Clarence Yard Goods, GN, 40B5
Clarkston (Lanark), NB, 30C5; 44A4
Clarkston (Renfrew), Cal, 29C5; 44E2
Clatford, LSW(MSW), 4C4
Claverdon, GW, 9B5
Claxby & Usselby, GC, 22G3
Clay Cross, Mid, 16B5; 41C; 2D2
Claydon (Bucks), LNW, 10D3
Claydon (Suffolk), GE, 12D4
Claygate & Claremont, LSW, 5C2
Claypole, GN, 16C2
Clayton, GN, 21D2; 42B5
Clayton Bridge, LY, 45A3
Clayton West, LY, 21F3; 42D3
Cleator Moor, WCE & CWJ, 26E3
Cleckheaton, LY & LNW, 21E2; 42B4
Cledford Bridge Halt, LNW, 15B2; 20D2
Clee Hill, S&H, 9A1
Cleethorpes, GC, 22F2
Cleeve, Mid, 9D3
Clegg Street (Oldham), OAGB(LY), 21D1 (inset); 45A2
Cleghorn, Cal, 30D4
Cleland, Cal, 30C5; 44A2
Clenchwarton, MGN, 17E4
Cleobury Mortimer, GW & CMDP, 9A2
Cleobury North Crossing, CMDP, 15G2
Cleobury Town, CMDP, 9A2
Clevedon, GW & WCP, 3A1; 8D3
Clevedon (All Saints), 3A1; 10F1
Clevedon East, WCP, 3A1; 8D3
Cliburn, NE, 27E1
Cliddesden, LSW, 4B2
Cliff Common, NE & DVL, 21D5
Cliffe, SEC, 6B5
Clifford, GW, 14E2
Clifton (Derbys), NS, 15C5
Clifton (Westmorland), NE, 27E1
Clifton & Lowther, LNW, 27E1
Clifton Bridge, GW, 3A2 and inset
Clifton Down, CE, 3 (inset); 3A2; 8C2
Clifton Junc (Lancs), LY, 20B1; 24F1; 45B2
Clifton Maybank (Goods), GW, 3E2; 8G2
*Clifton Maybank Jc*, GW, 3D2
Clifton Mill, LNW, 10A4
Clifton-on-Trent, GC, 16B2
Clifton Road (Brighouse), LY, 21E2; 42C4
Clipston & Oxendon, LNW, 10A3; 16G3
Clipstone (Goods), GC, 16B3; 41C5
*Clipstone Jc*, GC/ind, 16B3; 41C5
Clitheroe, LY(Mid), 24D1
Clock Face, LNW, 20C3; 24G3; 45D4
Clock House, SEC, 40F4
Clocksbriggs, Cal, 34D4
Closeburn, G&SW, 26A4
Clough Fold, LY, 20A1; 24E1
Cloughton, NE, 28G1
Clovenfords, NB, 30E1
Clown, GC & Mid, 16A4; 41B4
*Clown Jc*, GC/Mid, 41B4
Clown Street Halt, NS, 20F1
Clunes, HR, 35D5
Clutton, GW, 3B3; 4D1
Clydach (Brecknock), LNW, 8A4; 43B1
Clydach Court Halt, TV, 43C3
Clydach-on-Tawe, Mid & GW, 7B4; 43F2
*Clyde Jc*, G&SW, 44E2 (inset)
Clydebank, Cal, 29C4; 44F4
Clydebank Central, NB, 44F4
Clydebank East, NB, 29C4; 44F4
Clynderwen, GW, 13G2
Clyne Halt, GW, 43E2
Clyst St Mary & Digby Halt, LSW, 2C3
*Coal Yard Jc* (Clapham), LNW/WLE, 39E4 (inset)
Coalbrookdale, GW, 15F2
Coalburn, Cal, 30E5
Coaley Junc, Mid, 8B1; 9E2
Coalpit Heath, GW, 8C1; 9G2
Coalport, GW & LNW, 15F2
Coalville, Mid & LNW, 16E4
Coanwood, NE, 27C2
Coatbridge, Cal & NB, 30C5; 44B4
Coatbridge Sunnyside, NB, 44B4
Coatdyke, NB, 44B4
Coates (Glos), GW, 9F4
Cobbinshaw, Cal, 30C4
Cobham for Stoke d'Abernon, LSW, 5C2
Coborn Road, GE, 40C3
Cobridge, NS, 15C3; 20E1
Cockburnspath, NB, 31B2
Cockerham Cross Halt, KE, 24C3

Cockermouth, LNW&CKPJt (M&C), 26E3
Cockett, GW, 7B3; 43G3
Cockfield (Durham), NE, 27E4
Cockfield (Suffolk), GE, 12C5
Cocking, LBSC, 4D1
*Cockley Brake Jc*, LNW/SMJ, 10C2
Codford, GW, 3C5
Codnor Park, GN, 16C4; 41E3
Codnor Park & Selston for Ironville & Jacksdale, Mid, 16C4; 41E3
*Codnor Park Jc*, Mid/GN, 41E3
Codsall, GW, 15F3
*Codzow Jc*, Cal, 44B2
Coed Poeth, GW, 20E5
Coed Talon, LNW, 20E5
*Coed-y-Gric Jc*, GW, 8B3; 43A2
Cogan, BRY, 8C4; 43B5
Cogie Hill Halt, KE, 24C3
*Cogload Jc*, GW, 8F3
*Coity Jc*, GW/BRY, 7C5; 43D4
*Coke Ovens Jc*, GE/NSJ, 12A1; 18F1
Colbren Junc, N&B(Mid), 7A5; 43E1
Colby, IMR, 23C2
Colchester, GE, 12E4
Cold Norton, GE, 12G5
Coldham, GE, 17F3
*Coldham Lane Jc*, GE, 11C3
Coldstream, NE, 31D3
Cole Green, GN, 11F2
Cole, SD, 3C3; 8F1
Coleburn, GNS, 36D1
Coleford for Staurton, SVW & GW, 8A1; 9E1
*Coleford Jc*, LSW, 2B4
Colehouse Lane, WCP, 3A1; 8D3
Coleshill, Mid, 15G5
Colfin, P&W, 25C2
Colinton, Cal, 30C2
College Goods (Glasgow), G&SW, 44D4 and inset E2
Collessie, NB, 34F5
*Colliery Jc*, EWY/GN, 42B2
Collingbourne, MSW, 4B5
Collingham, Mid, 16B2
Collingham Bridge, NE, 21C4
Collins Green, LNW, 20C3; 24G2; 45D3
Colliston, Cal, 34D3
Colnbrook, GW, 5B1; 10G1
Colne, Mid, 24D1
Colne, LY&MidJt, 21 (inset)
Coltfield Platform, HR, 36C2
Coltishall, GE, 18E3
Colwall, GW, 9C2
Colwich, LNW&NSJt, 15E4
Colwyn Bay, LNW, 19D4
Colyford, LSW, 2B1
Colyton, LSW, 2B1
Colzium, K&B, 30B5
Combe Hay Halt, GW, 3B3; 8D1
Combpyne, LSW, 2B1
Commercial Road Goods, LTS, 40C4
*Common Branch Jc*, TV, 43C4
Commondale, NE, 28F3
Commondyke, G&SW, 29F5
Commonhead (Airdrie North), NB, 44B4
Compton, GW, 10G4
Comrie, Cal, 33F3
Conder Green, LNW, 24C3
Condover, S&H, 15F1
Congleton, NS(LNW), 15B3; 20D1
*Congleton Upper Jc*, NS, 15B3; 20E3
Congresbury, GW, 3A1; 8D3
Coningsby, GN, 17C2
Conisborough, GC(Mid), 21F4
Coniston, Fur, 26G1
Connah's Quay, LNW, 20D4
Connah's Quay & Shotton, GC, 20D4
*Connah's Quay East Jc*, GC, 20D4
*Connah's Quay North Jc*, GC, 20D4
Connaught Road, PLA(GE), 40C2
Connel Ferry, Cal, 32E4
*Connel Ferry Jc*, Cal, 32E4
Conon, HR, 35D5
Cononley, Mid, 21C1
Consall, NS, 15C4
Consett, NE, 27C4
Constable Burton, NE, 21A2; 27G5
Conway Morfa, LNW, 19D3
Conwil, GW, 13G4
Cook Street Branch, G&SW, 44F2 (inset)
Cookham, GW, 5A1; 10G2
Cooksbridge, LBSC, 5F4
Coombe, LL, 1D4
Coombe Lane, WSC, 5C3
Cooper Bridge, LY, 21E2; 42C4
Cop Lane Halt, LY, 20A3; 24E3
*Copenhagen Jc*, GN, 40B5
Copgrove, NE, 21B3
Copley, LY, 21E2; 42C5
Copley Hill, LNW, 42A3
Copmanthorpe, NE(GN), 21C5
*Copper Mill Jc*, GE, 40A4
Copper Pit Halt, GW, 43G2
Copperas Hill, CWJ, 26E3
Copplestone, LSW, 2A4
Coppull, LNW, 20A3; 24E2; 45D1
*Copyhold Jc*, LBSC, 5E3
*Corbet's Lane Jc*, LBSC/SEC, 40D4
Corbridge, NE(NB), 27C4
Corby (Lincs), ON, 16D1; 17E1
*Cordio Jc*, ME, 21A3; 28G5
Corfe Castle, LSW, 3G5
*Corfe Mullen Jc*, SD, 3F5
Corkickle (Whitehaven), Fur, 26E4
Cornbrook Goods, CLC, 45B3
Cornhill, GNS, 37C2
Cornholme, LY, 20A1; 21E1
Cornwood, GW, 2D5
Corpach, NB, 32C3
Corpusty & Saxthorpe, MGN, 18D4
Corringham, CL, 6A5
*Corringham Light Railway*, CL, 6A5
Corris, Cor, 14B5
Corrour, NB, 32C1
Corsham, GW, 3A4
Corstorphine, NB, 30B3
Corton, NSJ, 12A1; 18F1
Corwen, GW(LNW), 19F5
Coryates, GW, 3F3
Coryton, CL, 6A5
Coryton (Devon), GW, 1C5
Coryton Halt (Glam), Car, 43B4
Cosham, LSW&LBSCJt, 4E2
*Cosham Jc*, LBSC/LSW, 4E2
Cossington, SD, 3C1; 8E3
Cotehill, Mid, 27C1
Cotham, GN, 16C2
Cotherstone, NE, 27E4
Coton Hill (Goods), GW, 15E1
Cottam, GC, 16A2
Cottesmore, Mid, 16E1
Cottingham, NE, 22D3
*Cottingham Jc*, NE, 22D3; 22A2 (inset)
Cottingwith, DVL, 21D5
Coughton, Mid, 9B4
Coulsdon & Cane Hill, SEC, 5C3
Coulsdon & Smitham Downs, LBSC, 5C3
Coulter, Cal, 30E4
Coundon, NE, 27E5
Coundon Road, LNW, 10A5
Counter Drain, MGN, 17E2
Countesthorpe, Mid, 16F3
*County Boundary Jc*, Cal/G&SW, 29E5
County School, GE, 18E4
Coupar Angus, Cal, 34D5
Court Sart, RSB, 7B4; 43F3
*Court Sart Jc*, SWM, 43F3
Cove Bay, Cal, 34A1; 37G4
Coventry, LNW, 10A5
*Cow Lane Jc*, LBSC/SEC, 40D4
Cowbit, GN&GEJt, 17E2
Cowbridge, TV, 8C5; 43D4
*Cowbridge Road Jc*, BRY/GW, 43D4
Cowden, LBSC, 5D4
*Cowdenbeath Jc*, NB, 30A3
Cowdenbeath New, NB, 30A3
Cowes, IWC, 4F3
Cowlairs, NB, 44D4
Cowley, GW, 5A2; 10G1
*Cowley Bridge Jc*, GW/LSW, 2B3
Cowton, NE, 28F5
Coxbench, Mid, 16C5; 41F2
Coxgreen, NE, 28C5
Coxhoe (Goods), NE, 28D5
Coxhoe Bridge, NE, 28D5
Coxlodge, NE, 27B5
Coxwold, NE, 21A4
Craddock Lane (Bolton) Goods, LY, 45B2
Cradley Heath & Cradley, GW, 15G2
Cradoc, N&B (Mid), 14F4
Craig-y-Nos (Penwyllt), NAB(Mid), 7A5; 43E1
Craigellachie, GNS, 36D1
Craigendoran, NB, 29B3
Craigendoran Pier, NB, 29B3
Craighall Goods, NB, 44E4
Craigleith, Cal, 30 (inset)
Craiglockhart, NB, 30 (inset)
Craigo, Cal, 34C3
Crail, NB, 34F3
Crakehall, NE, 21A3; 27G5
Cramlington, NE, 27B5
Cranbrook, SEC, 6D5
Crane Street (Pontypool), GW, 8B4; 43A2
*Crane Street Jc*, LNW/Mid, 15E3 (inset)
Cranford (Northants), Mid, 10A1
Crank, LNW, 20B3; 24F3; 45E3
Cranleigh, LBSC, 5D2
Cranley Gardens, GN(NL), 39A5
Cranmore, GW, 3C3; 8E1
Cransley, Mid, 10A2
Crathes, GNS, 34A2
Craven Arms & Stokesay, S&H(BC), 14C1
Crawford, Cal, 30F4
Crawley, LBSC, 5D3
Cray, N&B(Mid), 14G4
Crayford, SEC, 5B4
Creagan, Cal, 32E3
Credenhill, Mid, 9C1; 14F1

Crediton, LSW, 2B4
*Creech Jc*, GW, 8F4
Creetown, P&W, 25C4
Creigiau, BRY, 8C5; 43C4
Cressage, GW, 15F1
Cressing, GE, 11F5
Cressington & Grassendale, CLC, 20C4; 45F4
Cresswell (Staffs), NS, 15D4
Creswell & Welbeck, GC, 16B4; 41B3
Crew Green, S&M, 14A1
Crewe, LNW(GW/NS), 15C2; 20E2
*Crewe Jc*, Cal, 30 (inset)
*Crewe North-South Jc*, LNW, 20E2
Crewe Wharf (Goods), NS, 15B2; 20E2
*Crewe Works*, LNW, 15B2; 20E2
Crewkerne, LSW, 3E1
Crews Hill, GN, 11G2
*Crianlarich Jc*, NB/Cal, 32F1
Crianlarich, Cal & NB, 32F1; 33F1
Criccieth, Cam, 19F2
Cricklade, GW, 9F4
Cricklewood, Mid, 5A3; 39B4
Crieff, Cal, 33F3
Criggion, S&M, 14A2
Crigglestone, LY & Mid, 21E3; 42C3/D3
*Crigglestone Jc*, LY, 42D3
*Crimple Jc*, NE, 21C3
*Croesor Railway*, CRY, 19F2
Croft, LNW, 16F4
Croft Spa, NE, 28F5
Crofton, LY, 21E4; 42C1 *see also* Hare Park
*Crofton Jc*, LY/WRG, 42C2
Crofton Park, SEC, 40E3
Cromdale, GNS, 36E2
Cromer, GE, 18D3
Cromer Beach, MGN, 18D3
*Cromer Jc*, GE, 18D3
Cromford, Mid & LNW, 16B5; 41D1/E1
*Cromwell Curve Jcs*, Dist, 39D5
Cronberry, G&SW, 29E5
Crook, NE, 27D5
Crook of Devon, NB, 30A3; 33G4
Crook Street (Bolton) Goods, LNW, 45C2
Crookston, G&SW, 29C4; 44F3
Cropredy, GW, 10C4
Crosby (IoM), IMR, 23B2
Crosby Garrett, Mid, 27F2
Cross Gates (Yorks), NE, 21D3; 42A2
*Cross Gates Jc*, NE, 21D3; 42A2
Cross Hands, GW & LM, 7A3
Cross Hill, GBK, 44 (inset)
Cross Inn, TV, 8C5; 43C4
Cross Keys, GW, 8B4; 43B3
Cross Lane, LNW(BJ), 45B3
Crossens, LY, 20A4; 24E4; 45F1
Crossfield (Goods), WCE, 26F3
Crossford, G&SW, 26A4
Crossgates (Fife), NB, 30A3
Crosshill, Cal, 44E3 and inset F1
Crosshill & Codnor, Mid, 16C4; 41F3
Crosshouse, G&SW, 29E4
Crossmichael, P&W, 26B5
Crossmyloof, GBK, 29C5; 44E3 and inset F1
Croston, LY, 20A3; 24E3; 45E1
Crouch End, GN(NL), 40A5
Crouch Hill, THJ(LTS), 40A5
*Crow Nest Jc*, LY, 45C2
Crow Park, GN, 16B2
Crow Road, Cal, 44E4
Crowborough & Jarvis Brook, LBSC, 5E5
Crowcombe, GW, 8F4
Crowden, GC, 21F2; 42F5
*Crowhorn Jc*, GC, 21A2 (inset)
Crowhurst, SEC, 6F5
*Crowhurst Jc*, LBSC/CO, 5D4
Crowle, AJ, 22E5
Crowle, GC, 22F5
Crown Street (Liverpool) Goods, LNW, 45F4
*Crowthorn Jc*, LNW/OAGB, 21A2 (inset)
Croxall, Mid, 15E5
Croxdale, NE, 27D5
Croxley Green, LNW, 5A2; 11G1
Croy, NB, 30B1
Croydon (Addiscombe Road), SEC, 40G4
*Cruckmeole Jc*, SWP, 14A1
Cruckton, S&M, 14A1
Cruden Bay GNS, 37E5
Crudgington, GW, 15E2
Crumlin, GW, 8B4; 43B2
Crumpsall, LY, 20B1; 24F1; 45A2
Crymmych Arms, GW, 13F2
Crynant, N&B, 7A5; 43E2
Crystal Palace, LBSC(LNW), 5B3; 40F4
Crystal Palace High Level & Upper Norwood, SEC, 5B3; 40F4
*Cuckoo Jc*, MGN, 17E2
Cuddington, CLC, 15D2; 20D2; 45D5
Cudworth, Mid(HB/LY) & HB, 21F3/4; 42D2/E2
Cuffley & Goff's Oak, GN, 11G2
Culcheth, GC, 20C2; 24G2; 45C3
Culgaith, Mid, 27E1
Culham, GW, 10F4
Culkerton, GW, 9F3
Cullen, GNS, 37C1
Cullercoats, NE, 28B5
Cullingworth, GN, 21D1; 42A5
Culloden Moor, HR, 36D4
Cullompton, GW, 2A2
Culmstock, GW, 2A2; 8G5
Culrain, HR, 35A5
Culross, NB, 30A4
Culter, GNS, 34A2; 37G3
Cults, GNS, 37G4
Culworth, GC, 10C4
*Culworth Jc*, GC, 10C4
Cumbernauld, Cal, 30B5; 44B5
Cummersdale, M&C, 26C1
Cummertrees, G&SW, 26B3
Cumnock, G&SW, 29F5
Cumwhinton, Mid, 26C1
Cunninghamhead, G&SW, 29D3
Cupar, NB, 34F4
Currie, Cal, 30C3
Currie Hill, Cal, 30C3
*Currock Jc*, MC, 26C1 and inset
*Curry Rivell Jc*, GW, 3D1; 8F3
Curthwaite, M&C, 26C1
*Curve Jc (Crewe)*, LNW, 20E2
Curzon Street, LNW, 13C4
*Curzon Street Jc*, LNW/Mid, 13C4
Custom House, GE, 40C2
Cuthlie, D&A, 34D3
Cutler, GNS, 34A2; 37G3
Cutler's Green Halt, GE, 11E4
*Cutsyke Jc*, LY/NB, 42B1
Cuxton, SEC, 5B5
Cwm, GW, 8A4; 43B2
Cwm Bargoed, TBJ, 43C2
Cwm Blawd, LM, 7A3
Cwm Mawr, BPGV, 7A3
Cwm Prysor, GW, 19F4
Cwm-y-Glo, LNW, 19E2
Cwmaman, GW, 8B5; 43D2
Cwmavon (Glam), RSB, 7B4; 43F3
Cwmavon (Mon), GW, 8A4; 43A2
Cwmbran, GW, 8B3; 43A3
*Cwmbran Jc*, GW, 43A3
Cwmdu, PT, 7B5; 43E3
Cwmffrwd Halt, GW, 43A2
Cwmffrwdoer Halt, GW, 43A2
Cwmllynfell, Mid, 7A4; 43F1
Cwmsyfiog & Brithdir, BM, 43B2 *see also* Brithdir
Cyfronydd, W&L, 14B3
Cymmer, GW, RSB & SWM, 7B5; 43E3
Cynghordy, LNW, 14F5
Cynheidre, LM, 7A3
Cynonville Halt, RSB, 43E3
Cynwyd, GW, 19F5

Dacre, NE, 21B2
Dagenham, LTS, 5A4
Dagenham Dock, LTS, 5A4
Daggons Road, LSW, 3E5
Dailly, G&SW, 29G3
Daimler Halt, LNW, 10A5
Dairsie, NB, 34F4
Dairycoates (Goods), HB, 22 (inset)
Daisy Bank, GW, 13A1
Daisy Hill, LY, 20B2; 24F2; 45C2
Daisyfield, LY, 24D2
Dalbeattie, G&SW, 26C4
Dalchonzie Platform, Cal, 33F3
Dalcross, HR, 36D4
Dalegarth, RE, 26F2
Dalguise, HR, 33D4
Dalkeith, NB, 30C2
*Dallam Branch Jc*, LNW, 45D4
Dallow Lane Wharf, LNW, 15D5 (inset)
Dalmally, Cal, 32F2
Dalmarnock, Cal, 44D3
Dalmellington, G&SW, 29G4
Dalmeny, NB, 30B3
Dalmuir, Cal & NB, 29B4; 44G5
Dalnaspidal, HR, 33C2
Dalreoch, D&B, 29B3
Dalry, G&SW, 29D3
*Dalry Jc*, Cal, 30 (inset)
*Dalry Jc*, G&SW, 29D3
Dalry Road, Cal, 30 (inset)
Dalrymple, G&SW, 29F3
*Dalrymple Jc*, G&SW, 29F3
Dalserf, Cal, 30D5; 44A1
Dalston (Cumb), M&C, 26C1
Dalston Junc (London), NL(LNW), 40B4
Dalton, Fur, 24B4
Dalwhinnie, HR, 33B2
*Dalzell Jc*, Cal, 44A2
*Dam Lane Jc*, CLC, 20C2; 24G2; 45C3
Damems, Mid, 21D1
Dan-y-Graig, RSB, 7B4; 43F3
Danby, NE, 28F3
Danby Wiske, NE, 28G5
Dandaleith, GNS, 36D1
Danzey for Tanworth, GW, 9A5
Darcy Lever, LY, 45B2
*Dare Jc*, GW, 43D2
*Dare Valley Jc*, TV, 43D2

Daresbury, BJ, 15A1; 20C3; 45D4
Darfield, Mid, 21F4; 42E1
Darlaston, LNW, 13A2; 15F4
Darley, NE, 21C2
Darley Dale, Mid, 16B5; 41D1
Darlington, NE, 28F5
*Darlington Works*, NE, 28F5
Darnall for Handsworth, GC, 16A3; 21G4; 41A2; 42G1
Darran & Deri, Rhy(BM), 8B4; 43C2
Darras Hall, NE, 27B5
Darsham, GE, 12B2
Dartford, SEC, 5B5
*Dartmouth (ferry service for Kingswear)*, GW, 2E3
Darton, LY, 21F3; 42D3
Darvel, G&SW, 29E5
Darwen, LY(Mid), 20A2; 24E2
Datchet, LSW, 5B1; 10G1
Dauntsey, GW, 9G4
Dava, HR, 36E3
Davenport, LNW, 15A3; 20C1; 21G1; 45A4
Daventry, LNW, 10B3
Davidson's Mains, Cal, 30B2
Daviot, HR, 36E4
Dawlish, GW, 2C3
Dawlish Warren, GW, 2C3
*Day's Bridge Jc*, GW, 3 (inset)
Daybrook, GN, 16C3; 41F5
Dduallt, Fest, 19F3
Deadwater, NB, 27A1; 31G1
Deal, SEC, 6C1
Dean, LSW, 4D5
Dean Lane, LY, 20B1; 24F1; 45A2
*Deansgate Jc* (Altrincham), CLC/MSJA, 45B4
Deanside (Goods), G&P, 44F4
Dearham Bridge, M&C, 26D3
Dearham, M&C, 26D3
*Dearne Jc*, SK, 21F4; 42E1
Deepcar, GC, 21F3; 42F3
Deepdale, PL & PWY, 24D3
Deepfields & Coseley, LNW, 13A1; 15F4
Deeping St James, GN, 17F2
Defford, Mid, 9C3
Defiance, GW, 1D5
Deganwy, LNW, 19C3
Deighton, LNW, 21E2; 42C4
Delabole, LSW, 1C3
Delamere, CLC, 15B1; 20D3
Delny, HR, 36C5
Delph, LNW, 21F1
Denaby, DV & HB, 21F4
Denbigh, LNW, 19D5
Denby Dale & Cumberworth, LY, 21F3; 42E3
Denby, Mid, 16C5; 41F2
Denham, GW&GCJt, 5A1; 10G1
Denham Golf Club Platform, GW&GCJt, 5A1; 10F1
Denhead, D&A, 34D3
Denholme, GN, 21D2; 42A5
Denmark Hill, LBSC(SEC), 40E4
Denny, Cal, 30B5
*Denny Jc*, Cal/K&B, 30B5
Dennyloanhead, K&B, 30 B5
Denstone Crossing, NS, 15C5
Dent, Mid, 24A1
Denton (Lancs), LNW(LY), 20C1; 21G1; 45A3
*Denton Jc*, LNW, 21G1
Denton Siding, GN, 16D2
Denver, GE, 11A4; 17F4
Deptford, SEC, 40D3
Deptford Wharf, LBSC, 40D3
Derby, Mid(LNW/NS) & GN, 16D5; 41G2
Derby Road (Ipswich), GE, 12D3
Dereham, GE, 18E4
*Deri Jc*, BM/Rhy, 8B4; 43C3
Derry Ormond, GW, 13E5
Dersingham, GE, 17D5
Derwen, LNW, 19E5
Derwenthaugh (Goods), NE, 28 (inset)
Derwydd Road, GW(LNW), 7A4; 13G5; 43G1
Desborough & Rothwell, Mid, 10A2; 16G2
Desford, Mid, 16F4
Dess, GNS, 34A3; 37G2
Detton Road Siding, CMDP, 9A2
Devil's Bridge, VR, 14C5
Devizes, GW, 3B5
Devonport, GW & LSW, 1D5 and inset
*Devonport Jc*, GW/LSW, 1A1 (inset)
Devons Road, NL & LNW, 40C3
Devynock & Sennybridge, N&B(Mid), 14F4
Dewsbury, GN, LNW, LY & Mid, 21E3; 42C3
Dicconson Lane & Aspull, LY, 20B2; 24F2; 45C2
Didcot, GW, 10F4
*Didcot N & E Jcs*, GW, 10F5
*Didcot West Curve Jc*, GW, 10F4
Didsbury, Mid, 20C1; 24G1; 45A3
Digby, GN&GEJt, 17C1
Diggle, LNW, 21F1
*Diglake Jc*, NS, 15C3; 20E1
Dinas (Merioneth), Fest, 19F3
Dinas (Rhondda), TV, 43D3
Dinas Junc (Carnarvon), LNW & NWNG, 19E2
Dinas Mawddwy, Mawd, 14A4
Dinas Powis, BRY, 8D4; 43B5
Dingestow, GW, 8A2; 9E1
Dingle Road Halt, TV, 43B5
Dingwall, HR, 35D5
Dinmore, S&H, 9B1
Dinnet, GNS, 34A4; 37G1
Dinnington & Laughton, SYJ, 16A4; 21G4; 41A4
Dinnington Colliery, SYJ, 41A4
*Dinnington Jc*, SYJ/GC&MidJt, 16A4; 21C4; 41A4
*Dinnington South Jc*, SYJ/GC&MidJt, 16A4
Dinsdale, NE, 28F5
Dinting, GC, 21G1
Dinton, LSW, 3C5
Dinwoodie, Cal, 26A3
Dipple (Goods), G&SW, 29G2
Dirleton, NB, 31B1
Disley, LNW, 15A4
Diss, GE, 12B4
Distington, WCE&CWJJt, 26E3
Ditchford, LNW, 10A1
Ditchingham, GE, 12A2; 18G2
Ditton, LNW, 15A1; 20C3; 24G3; 45E4
Ditton Priors, CMDP, 15G1
Dixon Fold, LY, 45B2
*Dobbs Brow Jc*, LY, 45C2
*Dock Jc (Ely)*, GE, 11B4
Dock Street (Newport) Goods, GW, 43A3
Docking, GE, 17D5
*Docks Branch Jc* (Maryport), LNW, 26D3
Doddington & Harby, GC, 16B2
Dodworth, GC, 21F3; 42E3
Doe Hill, Mid, 16B4; 41D3
Dogdyke, GN, 17C2
Dolau, LNW, 14D3
Doldowlod, Cam, 14D4
Dolgelley, GW(Cam), 14A5
Dolgoch, Tal, 13B5
Dollar, NB, 30A4; 33G4
Dollis Hill, Met, 39B4
Dolphinton, Cal & NB, 30D3
Dolwen, Cam, 14C4
Dolwyddelen, LNW, 19E3
Dolygaer, BM, 8A5; 43C1
Dolyhir, GW, 14E2
Dolywern, GVT, 20F5
Don Street, GNS, 37F4
Doncaster (Goods), GN, GC & Mid, 21F5 and inset G2
Doncaster (Pass), GN(GC/GE/LY/Mid/NE) & GC&HBJt, 21F5 and inset G2
*Doncaster Works*, GN, 21F5
Donington-on-Bain, GN, 17A2
Donington Road, GN&GEJt, 17D2
Donisthorpe, AN, 16E5
Donnington, LNW, 15E2
Dorchester, GW & LSW, 3F3
*Dorchester Jc*, GW/WP, 3F3
Dore & Totley, Mid, 16A5; 41A1
*Dore South Jc*, Mid, 16A5
Dorking, LBSC & SEC, 5C2
Dormans, LBSC, 5D4
Dornoch, HR, 36B4
Dornock, G&SW, 26B2
Dorrington, S&H, 14B1; 15F1
Dorstone, GW, 14F1
Doublebois, GW, 1D4
Douglas (IoM), IMR & ME, 23C2
Douglas (Lanark), Cal, 30E5
Douglas Derby Castle (IoM), MER, 23B3
Douglas West, Cal, 30E5
Doune, Cal, 33G3
Dousland, GW, 2C5
Dove Holes, LNW, 15A4
*Dove Jc*, NS/GN, 15D5
Dovecliffe, GC, 42E2
Dovecliffe for Worsborough, LY, 42E1
Dover, SEC, 6D2
Dover Marine, SEC, 6D2
Dover Priory, SEC, 6D2
Dovercourt Bay, GE, 12E3
Dovey Junc, Cam, 14B5
Dowlais, BM, LNW & TBJ, 8A5; 43C2
Dowlais Top, BM, 8A5; 43C1
Dowlow Halt, LNW, 15B5
Downfield Crossing Halt, GW, 9E3
Downham, GE, 17F4
Downton, LSW, 4D5
Doxey Rd (Goods), GN, 15E3
*Dragon Jc*, NE, 21C3
Drax, HB, 21E5
Drax Hales, NE, 21E5
Draycott (Derbys), Mid, 16D4; 41G3
Draycott (Som), GW, 3B2; 8 E2
Drayton (Norfolk), MGN, 18E3
Drayton (Sussex), LBSC, 4E1; 5F1
Drayton Green (Ealing) Halt, GW, 39C1
*Drayton Jc*, LNW/GN&LNWJt, 16G2
Drayton Park, GN, 40B5
Dreghorn, G&SW, 29E3
Drem, NB(NE), 30B1
Driffield, NE, 22C4
Drigg, Fur, 26F3

Drighlington & Adwalton, GN, 42B4
Droitwich, GW(Mid), 9B3
Droitwich Road (Goods), Mid, 9B3
Dronfield, Mid, 16A5; 41B2
Drongan, G&SW, 29F4
Dronley, Cal, 34E5
*Drope Jc*, BRY, 43C4
Droxford, LSW, 4D2
Droylsden, LY & LNW, 21F1 and inset A2; 45A3
Drum, GNS, 34A2; 37G3
Drumburgh, NB, 26C2
Drumchapel, NB, 44F4
Drumclog, Cal, 29E5
Drumlemble Halt, CM, 29 (inset)
Drumlithie, Cal, 34B2
Drummuir, GNS, 36D1
Drumshoreland, NB, 30B3
Drumvaich Crossing, Cal, 33G2
Drws-y-Nant, GW, 14A5; 19G4
Drybridge (Ayrshire), G&SW, 29E3; 37C1
Drybrook Road, SVW, 8A1; 9E2
*Dryclough Jc*, LY, 42C5
*Dryffryn Jc*, GW, 43E3
Drymen, NB, 29B4
Drypool (Goods), NE, 22 (inset)
Drysllwyn, LNW, 7A3; 13G5
*Dubbs Jc*, G&SW, 29D3
Dubton Junc, Cal, 34C3
Ducie Street Goods (Manchester), GC, 45A3
Dudbridge, Mid, 9E3
Dudding Hill Goods, Mid, 39B4
Duddingston & Craigmillar, NB, 30 (inset)
Dudley, GW, LNW(GW) & Mid, 13B2; 15G4
Dudley Hill, GN, 21D2; 42B4
Dudley Port, LNW, 13B2; 15G4
Dudworth (Goods), HB, 42D2
Duffield, Mid, 16C5; 41F2
Duffryn Rhondda Halt, RSB, 43E3
Dufftown, GNS, 36E1
Duffws, Fest, 19F3
Duirinish, HR, 35F1
Duke Street (Derby) Goods, GN, 41G2
Duke Street (Glasgow), NB, 44D4
Dukeries Junc, GN & GC, 16B2
Dukinfield, GC, 21A2 (inset)
Dukinfield & Ashton, LNW, 21A2 (inset)
Dulingham, GE, 11C4
Dullator, NB, 30B5
Dulverton, GW, 7F5
Dulwich, SEC, 40E4
Dumbarton, D&B, 29B3
Dumbarton (East), Cal, 29B4
Dumbreck (Goods), NB, 29B4
Dumfries, G&SW(Cal), G&SW & Cal, 26B3
Dumfries House, G&SW, 29F4
Dumgoyne, NB, 29B4
Dunball, GW, 3C1; 8E3
Dunbar, NB(NE), 31BI
Dunblane, Cal, 30A5; 33G3
Dunbridge, LSW, 4D4
Dunchurch, LNW, 10A4
Dundee (East), D&A, 34E4
Dundee (Tay Br), NB, 34E4
Dundee (West), Cal, 34E4
Dunfermline, NB, 30A3
Dunford Bridge, GC, 21F2; 42E4
Dungeness, SEC, 6E3
Dunham, GE, 18E5
Dunham Hill, BJ, 15A1; 20D3; 45E5
Dunham Massey, LNW, 15A2; 20C2; 24G2; 45B4
Dunhampstead (Goods), Mid, 9B3
Dunkeld & Birnham, HR, 33D4
Dunkerton, GW, 3B3; 8D1
Dunkerton Colliery Halt, GW, 3B3; 8D1
Dunlop, GBK, 29D4
Dunmere Halt, LSW, 1D3
*Dunmore Jc*, Cal, 30A5
Dunmow, GE, 11E4
Dunning, Cal, 33F4
Dunnington, DVL, 21C5
Dunnington Halt, DVL, 21C5
Dunphail, HR, 36D3
Dunragit, P&W, 25C2
Dunrobin (private), HR, 36A4; 38G5
Duns, NB, 31C2
*Dunsbear* (workmen), SR, 1A5
Dunscore, G&SW, 26A4
Dunsland Cross, LSW, 1A5
Dunstable (Goods), GN & LNW, 10D1; 11E1
Dunstable (Pass), GN(LNW) & LNW(GN), 10D1; 11E1
Dunstable Church Street, GN, 10D1; 11E1
Dunstall Park, GW, 15F3
Dunster, GW, 8E5
*Dunston Jc*, NE, 28 (inset)
Dunston-on-Tyne, NE, 28 (inset)
Dunston Staiths, NE 28 (inset)
Dunsyre, Cal, 30D3
Dunton Green, SEC, 5C4
Dunure, G&SW, 29F3
Dunvant, LNW, 7B3
Durham, NE, 27D5
*Durham Ox Jc* (Lincoln), GN/GC, 16B1 and inset; 17B1
Durley Halt, LSW, 4D3
Durnsford Road, 39F5
Duror, Cal, 32D3
Dursley, Mid, 8B1; 9F2
Durston, GW, 3D1; 8F3
Dyce, GNS, 37F4
*Dyffryn Jc*, PT, 43E3
Dyffryn, Cam, 13A5; 19G2
Dyke Junc Halt, LBSC, 5F3
Dykebar, Cal, 29C4
*Dykehead Branch Jc*, NB, 44A4
Dymock, GW, 9D2
Dynea Halt, AD, 43C3
Dysart, NB, 30A2
Dyserth, LNW, 19D5

Eaglescliffe, NE, 28E5
Ealing Broadway, GW, Dist & LE, 5B2; 39C2
Ealing Common, Dist, 39C3
*Eamont Bridge Jc*, LNW/NE, 27E1
Earby, Mid, 21C1
Eardington, GW, 15G2
Eardisley, Mid(GW), 14E2
Earith Bridge, GE, 11B3
Earlestown, LNW(BJ), 20C3; 24G2; 45D3
Earley, SEC(LSW), 4A2
Earls Colne, CVH, 12E5
Earls Court, Dist(LNW), 39D5
*Earls Court Jc*, Dist/WL/WLE, 39D4
Earlsfield for Summerstown, LSW, 5B3; 39E5
Earlsheaton, GN, 42C3
Earlston, NB, 31D1
Earlswood, LBSC, 5D3
Earlswood Lakes, GW, 9A5
Earsham, GE, 12A2; 18G2
Earswick, NE, 21C5
Easington, NE, 28D5
Easingwold, Eas, 21B4
Eassie, Cal, 34D5
East Acton, GW, 39C3
East Anstey, GW, 7F5
East Barkwith, GN, 17A2
East Boldon, NE, 28C5
East Brixton, LBSC, 40E5
East Budleigh, LSW, 2B2
East Calder (Goods), NB, 30C3
East Croydon, LBSC(SEC/LNW), 5C3
East Didsbury, LNW, 45A4
East Dulwich, LBSC, 40E4
East Farleigh, SEC, 6C5
East Finchley, GN(NL), 5A3; 39A5
East Fortune, NB, 31B1
East Garston, GW, 4A4; 10G5
*East Gate Jc* (Colchester), GE, 12E5
East Grinstead, LBSC, 5D4
East Halton, GC, 22E3
East Ham, LTS(Dist/Mid), 40B2
*East Ham Loop North Jc*, LTS, 40B2
East Horndon, LTS, 5A5
*East India Dock Road Jc*, NL, 40D1 (inset); 40C3
East India Docks Goods, GE, 40C2 and inset D1
*East Jc* (Colwich), LNW, 15E4
*East Kent Light Railway*, EK, 6C2
East Kilbride, Cal, 29D5; 44D2
East Langton, Mid, 16F3
East Leake, GC, 16D4
East Linton, NB, 31B1
East Malling Halt, SEC, 6C5
East Minster-on-Sea, SEC, 6B4
East Newport, NB, 34E4
East Norton, GN&LNWJt, 16F2
East Putney, LSW(Dist), 39E4
East Rudham, MGN, 18D5
East Smithfield Goods, GE, 40C4
East Southsea, LSW&LBSCJt, 4E2
East Street (Bridport), GW, 3F1
*East Suffolk Jc*, GE, 12D3
East Sussex Mental Platform, LBSC, 5F5
East Ville, GN, 17C3
East Winch, GE, 17E5
Eastbourne, LBSC, 5G5
Eastbury, GW, 4A4; 10G5
Eastchurch, SEC, 6B4
Eastcote, Met(Dist), 39Bl
Easter Road (Goods), NB, 30 (inset)
Easterhouse, NB, 44C3
Eastgate, NE, 27D3
Eastgrange, NB, 30A4
Easthaven, D&A, 34E3
Eastleigh & Bishopstoke, LSW(GW), 4D3
*Eastleigh South Jc*, LSW, 4D3
*Eastleigh Works*, LSW, 4D3
Eastoft, AJ, 22E5
Easton, ECH, 3G3
Easton Court, S&H, 9A1
Easton Lodge, GE, 11E4
Eastry, EK, 6C2
Eastry South, EK, 6C2
Eastwood (Yorks), LY, 21E1
Eastwood & Langley Mill, GN, 41F3 *see also* Langley Mill
Eaton, BC, 14C1
Ebberston, NE, 22A4

*Ebbw Jc* (Newport, Mon), GW, 8C3; 43A4
Ebbw Vale, GW & LNW, 8A4; 43B1
Ebchester, NE, 27C4
Ebdon Lane, WCP, 3A1; 8D3
Ebley Crossing Halt, GW, 9E3
Ecclefechan, Cal, 26B2
Eccles, LNW(BJ), 45B3
Eccles Road, GE, 12A4; 18G4
Ecclesfield, Mid & GC, 21G3; 42F2
Eccleshill, GN, 21D2; 42A4
Eccleston Park, LNW, 20C3; 24G3; 45E3
Eckington (Worcs), Mid, 9C3
Eckington & Renishaw, GC & Mid, 16A4; 41B3
Ecton, NS, 15B5
Edale, Mid, 15A5
Edderton, HR, 36B5
Eddleston, NB, 30D2
*Eddlewood Jc*, Cal, 44B1
Eden Park, SEC, 5B3; 40G3
*Eden Valley Jc*, LNW/NE, 27E1
Edenbridge, LBSC & SEC, 5D4
Edenbridge Town, LBSC, 5D4
*Edenham & Little Bytham Railway*, ELB, 16E1
Edge Hill, LNW, 45F4
Edge Lane, LNW, 45F4
Edgebold, S&M, 14A1; 15E1
Edgware, GN, 5A2
Edgware Road, Met(Dist/GW/H&C), 39C5
Edinburgh, Cal & NB, 30B2 and inset
Edington & Bratton, GW, 3B4
Edington Junc, SD, 3C1; 8E3
Edlingham, NE, 31F4
Edlington (Goods), DV, 21G2 (inset)
Edmondthorpe & Wymondham, Mid(MGN), 16E2
Edrom, NB, 31C2
Edwalton, Mid, 16D3; 41G5
Edwinstowe, GC, 16B3; 41C5
Edzell, Cal, 34C3
Efail Isaf, BRY, 8C5; 43C4
Effingham Junc, LSW, 5C2
*Egerton Street Jc*, CLC, 45F4 and inset G5
Eggesford, LSW, 2A5; 7G4
Egginton, NS&GNJt, 16D5
Egham, LSW, 5B1
Eglinton Street, Cal, GAP & G&SW, 44E3 and inset F1
Egloskerry, LSW, 1B4
Egremont (Cumberland), WCE, 26F3
Egton, NE, 28F2
*Elbowend Jc*, NB, 30B3
Elburton Cross, GW, 2E5
Elderslie, G&SW, 29C4; 44G3
Elephant & Castle, SEC, 40D5
Elford, Mid, 15E5
Elgin, GNS & HR, 36C2
*Elgin Jc* (Fife), NB, 30A3
Elham, SEC, 6D2
Elie, NB, 30A1; 34G4
Elland, LY, 21E2; 42C5
*Elland Jc*, LY, 42C5
Ellenbrook for Boothtown, LNW, 45B2
Ellerby, NE, 22D3
Ellesmere, Cam, 20F4
Ellesmere Port, BJ, 20D4; 45E5
Ellingham, GE, 12A2; 18G2
Elliot, Cal, 34D3
Elliot Junc, D&A, 34D3
Ellon, GNS, 37E4
Elmbridge, WUT, 17F4
Elmers End, SEC, 5B3; 40G4
Elmesthorpe, LNW(Mid), 16F4
Elmore Halt, LSW, 4E3
Elmstead Woods, SEC, 40F2
Elmswell, GE, 12C4
Elmton & Creswell, Mid, 16A4; 41B4 *see also* Creswell, GC
Elrington, NE, 27C3
Elsecar (Goods), GC, 42F2
Elsecar & Hoyland Common, Mid, 21F3; 42F2 *see also* Wentworth
Elsenham, GE, 11E4
Elsham, GC, 22F4
Elslack, Mid, 21C1
Elsted, LSW, 4D1
Elstree, Mid, 5A2; 11G2
Elswick, NE(NB), 28 (inset)
Eltham & Mottingham, SEC, 5B4; 40E2
Elton (Northants), LNW, 11A1; 17G1
Elton & Orston (Notts), GN, 16C2
Elvanfoot, Cal, 30F4
Elvet, NE, 28D5
Elvington (Kent), EK, 6C2
Elvington (Yorks), DVL, 21C5
Ely (Cambs), GE, 11B4
Ely (Glam), GW(BRY) & TV, 8C4; 43B4
Embleton, CKP, 26E2
Embo, HR, 36A4
Embsay, Mid, 21C1
Emerson Park Halt, LTS, 5A5
Emneth, GE, 17F4
Emsworth, LBSC, 4E1
*Enborne Jc*, GW, 4A3
Enderby, LNW&MidJt, 16F4
Endon, NS, 15C4
Enfield, GN, 5A3; 11G2
Enfield Lock, GE, 11G3
Enfield Town, GE, 5A3; 11G3
Enthorpe, NE, 22C4
Entwistle, LY, 20A2; 24E2; 45B1
Enzie, HR, 37C1
Epping, GE, 11G3
Epsom, LSW & LBSC, 5C2;
Epsom Downs, LBSC, 5C3
Epworth, AJ, 22F5 *see also* Haxey, GN&GEJt
Erdington, LNW, 15F5
Eridge, LBSC, 5D5
Erith, SEC, 5B4
Errol, Cal, 34E5
Erwood, GW, 14F3
Eryholme (Goods), NE, 28F5
*Eryholme Jc*, NE, 28F3
Escrick, NE, 21D5
Esgairgeiliog, Corris, 14B5
Esher & Claremont, LSW, 5B2; 39G1
Esholt, Mid(NE), 21D2
*Esk Valley Jc*, NB, 30C2
Eskbank, NB, 30C2
Eskbridge, NB, 30C2
Eskdale Green, RE, 26F2
Eskett (Goods), WCE, 26E3
*Eskett Jc*, WCE, 26E3
Eskmeals, Fur, 26G3
Esplanade (Dundee), NB, 34E4
Esplanade (Ryde, IoW), LSW&LBSCJt(IW/IWC), 4F3
Essendine, GN, 16E1; 17E1
Esslemont, GNS, 37E4
Eston, NE, 28E4
Etchingham, SEC, 6E5
Etherley, NE, 27E5
Etruria, NS, 15C3; 20F1
Ettingshall Rd & Bilston, LNW, 15F4 *see also* Bilston, GW
Ettington, SMJ, 10C5
Etwall, GN, 16D5
Euston, LNW, 5A3; 40C5
Euston Square, Met(Dist/GW/H&C), 40C5
Euxton (Goods), LY, 20A3; 24E2; 45D1 *see also* Balshaw Lane
*Euxton Jc*, LNW/LY, 20A3; 24E3
Eveningham, NE, 22D5
Evenwood, NE, 27E5
Evercreech (New), SD, 3C3; 8E1
Evercreech Junc, SD, 3C3; 8F1
Evershot, GW, 3E2
Evesham, GW & Mid, 9C4
Ewell, LSW & LBSC, 5C3
Ewesley, NB, 27A4; 31G4
Ewood Bridge, LY, 20A1; 24E1
Exchange (Liverpool), LY, 45F4 and inset G5
Exeter, GW(LSW), GW & LSW, 2B3
Exminster, GW, 2B3
Exmouth, LSW, 2C2
*Exmouth Jc*, LSW, 2B3
Eyarth, LNW, 19E5; 20E5
Eydon Road Platform, GC, 10C4
Eye (Suffolk), GE, 12B3
Eye Green, MGN, 17F2
Eyemouth, NB, 31C3
Eynsford, SEC, 5C5
Eynsham, GW, 10E4
Eythorne, EK, 6C2

Facit, LY, 20A1; 24E1; 45A1
*Factory Jc*, SEC, 39F4 (inset)
Failsworth, LY, 20 B1; 45A2
Fairbourne, Cam, 13A5
Fairfield, GC, 45A3
Fairford, GW, 9F5
Fairlie, G&SW, 29D2
Fairlie Pier, G&SW, 29D2
Fairlop, GE, 5A4; 40A1
Fakenham, GE & MGN, 18D5
*Falcon Jc*, LBSC, 39F2 (inset)
Falcon Lane Goods, LNW, 39F3 (inset)
Falkirk, NB & Cal, 30B4
Falkirk (High), NB, 30B4
Falkirk Grahamstown, NB, 30B4
*Falkland Jc*, G&SW, 29F3
Falkland Road, NB, 34G5
Fallowfield, GC, 20C1; 24G1; 45A3
Falls of Cruachan Platform, CR, 32F3
Fallside, Cal, 44C3
Falmer, LBSC, 5F3
Falmouth, GW, 1F1
Falstone, NB, 27A2
Fambridge, GE, 6A4; 12G5
Fangfoss, NE, 22C5
Fareham, LSW, 4E3
Faringdon (Berks), GW, 10F5
Farington (Lancs), NU, 20A3; 24E3
Farlington, LBSC, 4E2
Farnborough, LSW & SEC, 4B1
Farncombe, LSW, 5D1
Farnell Road, Cal, 34C3
Farnham, LSW, 4C1

*Farnham Jc*, LSW, 4B1
Farningham Road & Sutton-at-Hone, SEC, 5B5
Farnley & Wortley, LNW, 21D3 and inset; 42A3
Farnsfield, Mid, 16B3; 41D5
Farnworth, CLC, 45D4
Farnworth & Bold, LNW, 20C3; 24G3; 45D4
Farnworth & Halshaw Moor, LY, 20B2; 24F1; 45B2
Farringdon (Goods) (Hants), LSW, 4C2
Farringdon Street, Met(Dist/GN/GW/Mid/H&C), 40C5
Farthinghoe, LNW(SMJ), 10C4
Fauldhouse & Crofthead, Cal & NB, 30C4
Faversham, SEC, 6C3
*Faversham Jc*, SEC, 6C3
Fawkham for Hartley & Longfield, SEC, 5B5
Fawley (Hereford), GW, 9D1
Fay Gate, LBSC, 5D3
Fazakerley, LY, 20B4; 24G4; 45F3
*Fazakerley Jc*, LY, 45F3
*Fazakerley North Jc*, LY, 45F3
Fearn, HR, 36B4
Featherstone, LY, 21E4; 42C1
Featherstone Park, NE, 27C2
*Feeder Bridge Jc*, GW, 3 (inset)
Felin Fach, GW, 13E5
Felin Foel, LM, 7B3
Felin Fran Halt, GW, 7B4; 43F2
Felin Hen, LNW, 19D2
Felixstowe, GE, 12E3
Felling, NE, 28 (inset)
Felmingham, MGN, 18D3
Felstead, GE, 11E5
Feltham, LSW, 5B2
*Feltham Jc*, LSW, 39E1
Fenay Bridge & Lepton, LNW, 21E2; 42D4
Fencehouses, NE, 28C5
Fenchurch Street, GE(LTS), 5B3; 40C4
Fencote, GW, 9B1
Feniscowles, LU, 20A2; 24E2
Fenn's Bank, Cam, 15D1; 20F3
Fenny Bentley (Goods), LNW, 15C5
Fenny Compton, GW & SMJ, 10B4
Fenny Stratford, LNW, 10D2
Fenton, NS, 15C3; 20F1
Fenton Manor, NS, 15C3; 20F1
Ferguslie (Paisley) Goods, Cal & G&SW, 44G3
Ferndale, TV, 8B5; 43D2
Fernhill Heath, GW(Mid), 9B3
Ferniegair (Goods), Cal, 30D5; 44B2
*Ferniegair Jc*, Cal, 4B2
Ferriby, NE(GC), 22E4
Ferry (Cambs), MGN, 17E3
Ferry (Sussex), SL, 4F1
Ferrybridge for Knottingley, SK(GC/GN), 21E4; 42C1 *see also* Knottingley
Ferryhill (Durham), NE, 28D5
*Ferryhill Jc* (Aberdeen), Cal/GNS, 37G4
Ferryside, GW, 7A2
Festiniog, GW, 19F3
*Festiniog Railway*, Fest, 19F3
Ffairfach, GW(LNW), 13G5
Ffridd Gate, Cam, 14B5
Ffrith, WM, 20E4
Fidlers Ferry & Penketh, LNW, 15A1; 20C3; 24G3; 45D4
Fighting Cocks (Goods), NE, 28F5
Filey, NE, 22A3
Filleigh, GW, 7F4
Filton Junc, GW, 8Cl; 9G1
Finchley (Church End), GN(NL), 5A3; 39A5
Finchley Road, Met & Mid, 39B5
Finchley Road & Frognal, LNW(NL), 39B5
Findochty, GNS, 37C1
Finedon, Mid, 10A2
Fingask Platform, GNS, 37E3
Finghall Lane, NE, 21A2; 27G5
Finmere, GC, 10D3
Finnieston, NB, 44E4
Finningham, GE, 12C4
Finningley, GN&GEJt, 21F5
Finsbury Park, GN(NL), 5A3; 40B5
Firsby, GN, 17B3
*Firsby South Jc*, GN, 17B3
Fish Ponds, Mid, 3A3; 8C1
Fishbourne Halt, LBSC, 4E1
Fisherrow (Goods), NB, 30B2
Fishersgate Halt, LBSC, 5F3
Fishguard & Goodwick, GW, 13F1
Fishguard Harbour, GW, 13F1
Fiskerton, Mid, 16C3
Fittleworth, LBSC, 5E1
Five Ways (Staffs), LNW, 15E4
Five Mile House, GN, 17B1
Fladbury, GW, 9C4
Flamborough, NE, 22B3
Flax Bourton, GW, 3A2; 8D2
Flaxton, NE, 21B5
Flecknoe, LNW, 10B4
Fledborough, GC, 16B2
Fleet (Hants), LSW, 4B1
Fleet (Lincs), MGN, 17E3
*Fleet Jc*, GE, 12A2; 18F1
Fleetwood, PWY & LY, 24C4
Flemington, Cal, 30C5; 44A2
Fletton (Goods), GN, 11A2; 17G2
Flimby, LNW, 26D3
Flint, LNW, 20D5
Flitwick, Mid, 10D1; 11E1
Flixton, CLC, 20C2; 45B3
Flordon, GE, 12A3; 18F3
Floriston, Cal, 26C1
Flushdyke, GN, 21E3; 42C3
Fochabers Town, HR, 36C1
Fochriw, BM, 8A5; 43C2
Fockerby, AJ, 22E5
*Fodderty Jc*, HR, 35D5
Foggathorpe, NE, 22D5
Foleshill, LNW, 10A5
Foley Park Halt, GW, 9A3
Folkestone, SEC Central, 6D2; Harbour, 6D2; Junction, 6D2
Fontburn Halt, NB, 27A4; 31G4
Forcett Depot, NE, 27F5
*Forcett Jc*, NE, 27E5
Ford & Crossgates (Salop), S&M, 14A1
Ford (Devon), LSW & GW, 1D5 and inset
Ford (Lancs), LY, 20B4; 24G4; 45F3
Ford Bridge, S&H, 9B1
Ford Green, NS, 15C3; 20E1
Ford Junc (Sussex), LBSC, 5F1
Forden, Cam, 14B2
Fordham, GE, 11B4
Fordingbridge, LSW, 4E5
Fordoun, Cal, 34B2
Foregate Street (Worcester), GW, 9B3
Forest Gate, GE, 40B2
*Forest Gate Jc*, GE/LTS, 40B2
Forest Hall, NE, 27B5
Forest Hill, LBSC, 40E4
Forest Mill, NB, 30A4
Forest Row, LBSC, 5D4
Forfar, Cal, 34D4
Forgandenny, Cal, 33F5
Forge Mills, Mid, 15F5
Forge Valley, NE, 22A4
Formby, LY(LNW), 20B4; 24F4; 45G2
Forncett, GE, 12A3; 18G3
Forres, HR, 36D3
Forrestfield, NB, 30C5
Forsinard, HR, 38E5
Fort Augustus, NB, 32A1; 35G4
Fort Brockhurst, LSW, 4E3
Fort George, HR, 36D4
Fort Gomer Halt, LSW, 4E3
Fort Matilda, Cal, 29B3
Fort William, NB, 32C3
Forteviot, Cal, 33F4
Fortrose, HR, 36D5
Forty Hill, GE, 11G3
Foryd, LNW, 19C5
*Foryd Jc*, LNW, 19C5
Foryd Pier, LNW, 19C5
Foss Cross, MSW, 9E4
*Foss Island Jc*, NE, 21A4 (inset)
Foss Islands (Goods), NE, 21A4 (inset)
Fotherby Halt, GN, 17A3; 22G2
Foulis, HR, 36C5
Foulridge, Mid, 21 (inset); 24D1
Foulsham, GE, 18E4
Fountain Bridge Halt, BM(Rhy), 43B3
Fountainhall Junc, NB, 30D1
Four Ashes, LNW, 15E3
Four Crosses, Cam, 14A2
Four Oaks, LNW, 15F5
Fourstones, NE, 27B3
Fowey, GW, 1D3
Foxdale, IMR, 23B2
Foxfield, Fur, 24A5
*Foxhall Jc*, GW, 10F4
Foxton, GE(GN), 11D3
Framlingham, GE, 12C3
Frankton, Cam, 20F4
Fransham, GE, 18E5
Frant, SEC, 5D5
Fraserburgh, GNS, 37C4
Fratton, LSW&LBSCJt, 4E2
Fremington, LSW, 7F3
French Drove, GN&GEJt, 17F3
Freshfield, LY(LNW), 20B4; 24F4; 45G2
Freshford, GW, 3B3
Freshwater, FYN, 4F4
Friargate (Derby), GN, 16D5; 41G2
Friary (Plymouth), LSW, 1 (inset)
*Friary Jc*, GW/LSW, 1 (inset)
*Friary N, S & W Jcs*, GW, 1 (inset)
Frickley, SK(GC), 21F4; 42D1
Frickley Colliery, SK(GC), 42D1
Friden (Goods), LNW, 15B5
Friezland, LNW, 21F1
Frimley, LSW, 4B1; 5C1
Frinton-on-Sea, GE, 12E3
Friockheim, Cal, 34D3
Frisby, Mid, 16E3
Frittenden Road, KES, 6D5
Fritwell & Somerton, GW, 10D4
Frizinghall, Mid, 21D2; 42A5
Frizington, WCE, 26F3

Frocester, Mid, 9E3
Frodingham & Scunthorpe, GC, 22F4 *see also* Scunthorpe
Frodsham, BJ, 15A1; 20D3; 45D5
*Frodsham Jc*, BJ/LNW, 15A1; 20D3; 45D5
Frome, GW, 3C3
Frongoch, GW, 19F4
Frosterley, NE, 27D4
Fryston (Goods), NE, 21E4; 42B1
Fulbar Street (Renfrew), G&SW, 44F4
Fulbourne, GE, 11C4
Fullerton, LSW(MSW), 4C4
*Fullwood Jcs*, Cal, 44B3
Fulwell (Middx), LSW, 5B2; 39F1
Fulwell & Westbury (Bucks), LNW, 10D3
Furness Abbey, Fur, 24B5
Furness Vale, LNW, 15A4
Fushiebridge, NB, 30C2
Fyling Hall, NE, 28F1
Fyvie, GNS, 37E3

*Gadly's Jc*, GW/TV, 8A5; 43D2
*Gaer Jc*, GW, 43A3
Gaerwen, LNW, 19D2
Gailes, G&SW, 29E3
Gailey, LNW, 15E3
Gainford, NE, 27E5
Gainsborough, GC & GN&GEJt, 16A2; 22G5
*Gainsborough N & S Jcs*, GC/GN&GEJt, 16A2; 22G5
Gairlochy, NB, 32B2
Gaisdale, NE, 28F2
Galashiels, NB, 30E1
Galgate, LNW, 24C3
Gallions, PLA(GE), 40C1
Gallowgate, G&SW, 44 (inset)
Galston, G&SW, 29E4
*Galton Jc*, GW, 13C2
Gamlingay, LNW, 11D2
*Gannow Jc*, LY, 24D1
Ganton, NE, 22A4
Gara Bridge, GW, 2D4
Garelochhead, NB, 29A3
Garforth, NE, 21D4; 42A1
Gargrave, Mid, 21C1
Gargunnock, NB, 29A5
Garlieston, P&W, 25D4
Garmouth, GNS, 36C1
Garn-yr-erw, LNW(GW), 43B1
Garnant, GW, 7A4; 43F1
Garnant Halt, GW, 43F1
Garndiffaith, LNW, 43A2
Garneddwen, Cor, 14A5
Garngad, NB, 44D4
Garnkirk, Cal, 29C5; 44C4
*Garnqueen North Jc*, Cal, 44B4
*Garnqueen South Jc*, Cal/NB, 44B4
Garrochburn (Goods), G&SW, 29E4
Garstang & Catterall, LNW(KE), 24D3
Garstang Town, KE, 24D3
Garston, CLC & LNW, 20C4; 45E4
Garston Dock, LNW, 20C4; 45E4
Garswood, LNW, 20B3; 24F3; 45D3
Gartcosh, Cal, 44C4
*Gartcosh Jc*, Cal, 44C4
Garth, LNW, 14E4
Garth Road, Van, 14C4
Gartly, GNS, 37E1
Gartmore, NB, 29A4
Gartness, NB, 29B4
Garton, NE, 22C4
Gartsherrie Cal, 44B4 *see also* Blairhill
Gartshore (Goods), NB, 29B5; 44B5
Garve, HR, 35C4
*Gascoigne Wood Jc*, NE, 21D4
*Gask Jc*, NB, 30A3
*Gasworks Jc*, LSW, 3F5
Gateacre, CLC, 20C4; 24G3; 45E4
Gatehead, G&SW, 29E4
Gatehouse-of-Fleet, P&W, 25C5
Gateshead, NE, 28 (inset)
Gateside, NB, 33F5
Gatewen Halt, GW, 20E4
Gathurst, LY, 20B2; 24F3; 45D2
Gatley, LNW, 45A4
Gatwick Racecourse, LBSC, 5D3
Gavell, NB, 29B5
Gayton Road, MGN, 17E5
Geddington, Mid, 16G2
Gedling & Carlton, GN, 16C3; 41F5
Gedney, MGN, 17E3
Geldeston, GE, 12A2; 18G2
Gelli Halt, TV, 43D3
*Gelly Tarw Jc*, GW, 8A5; 43D2
General Terminus Goods (Glasgow), Cal, 44E3 and inset F2
George Lane, GE, 5A4; 40A2
Georgemas, HR, 38C3
*Georgemas Jc*, HR, 38C3
Gerrards Cross, GW&GCJt, 5A1; 10F1
Gidea Park, GE, 5A4;
Giffen, Cal, 29D3
Giffnock, Cal, 44E2
Gifford, NB, 31C1
Giggleswick, Mid, 24B1
Gildersome, GN & LNW, 21D3; 42B3
Gileston, BRY, 8D5; 43D5
Gilfach, GW, 8B5; 43D3
Gilfach Fargoed Halt, Rhy, 43B2
Gillett's Crossing Halt, PWY, 24D4
Gillfoot (Goods), WCE, 26
Gilling, NE, 21A5
Gillingham (Dorset), LSW, 3D4
Gillingham (Kent), SEC, 6B5
Gilmerton, NB, 30C2
Gilmour Street (Paisley), G&P, 44G3
Gilnockie, NB, 26B1
Gilsland, NE, 27B1
Gilwern, LNW, 8A4; 43B1
Gipsy Hill, LBSC(LNW), 40F4
Girvan, G&SW, 29G2
Gisburn, LY, 24C1
Glais, Mid, 7B4; 43F2
Glaisdale, NE, 28F2
Glaisgill, NE, 27F2
Glamis, Cal, 34D5
Glan Conway, LNW, 19D4
Glan-y-Llyn, Car, 43C4
Glanamman, GW, 7A4; 43F1
Glandyfi, Cam, 14B5
Glanrafon, VR, 13C5
Glanrhyd, VT, 14G5
Glanton, NE, 31F4
Glanyrafon, Tan, 14A2; 20G5
Glapwell, Mid, 16B4; 41C3
Glasbury-on-Wye, Mid, 14F2
Glasgow (Goods), Cal, GBK, G&P, G&SW, & NB, 29 –; 44 –
Glasgow (Pass), Cal, G&SW & NB, 29 –; 44 –
Glasgow Cross, Cal, 44D4 and inset E2
Glasgow Green, Cal, 44D3 and inset E2
Glassaugh, GNS, 37C2
Glassel, GNS, 34A3; 37G2
Glassford, Cal, 29D5
Glasson Dock, LNW, 24C3
Glasson Plat, NB, 26C2
Glasterlaw, Cal, 34D3
Glastonbury & Street, SD, 3C2; 8E2
Glazebrook & Bury Lane, CLC, 20C2; 45C3
*Glazebrook Moss Jc*, CLC/GC, 20C2; 24G2; 45C3
Glazebury, LNW(BJ), 20B2; 24G2; 45C3
Glemsford, GE, 12D5
Glen Douglas Platform, 29A3
Glen Parva, LNW, 16F4
Glenbarry, GNS, 37D1
Glenboig, Cal, 30C5; 44B4
Glenbuck, Cal, 30E5
*Glenburnie Jc*, NB, 34F5
Glencarron Platform, HR, 35D2
Glencarse, Cal, 33F5
Glencorse, NB, 30C2
*Glencruiten Crossing*, Cal, 32E4
Glendon & Rushton, Mid, 10A2; 16G2
*Glendon South Jc*, Mid, 10A2; 16A2
Gleneagles, Cal, 33F4
Glenfarg, NB, 33F5
Glenfield (Leicester), Mid, 16F4
Glenfield Goods (Paisley), Cal, 44G3
Glenfinnan, NB, 32B4
Glengarnock, G&SW & Cal, 29D3
Gleniffer (Goods), G&SW, 44G2
Glenluce, P&W, 25C3
Glenside, G&SW, 29F3
Glenwhilly, G&SW, 25B2
Glodwick Road (Oldham), LNW(GC), 21F1 and inset D1
Glodwick Road, LNW, 21D1
Glogue, GW, 13F3
Glossop, GC, 21G1
Gloucester, GW & Mid, 9E3
Gloucester Road (London), Dist & Met(Dist), 39D5
Glyn Abbey, BPGV, 7A2
Glyn Neath, GW, 7A5; 43E2
*Glyn Valley Tramway*, GVT, 20F5
Glynceiriog, GVT, 20F5
Glyncorrwg, SWM, 43E2
Glynde, LBSC, 5F4
Glyndyfrdwy, GW, 20F5
Glyntaff Halt, AD, 43C3
Gnosall, LNW, 15E3; 20G2
Goathland, NE, 28F2
Gobowen, GW, 20F4
*Gobowen Jc*, 20F4
Godalming, LSW, 5D1
Godley, GC & CLC, 21G1
Godmanchester, GN&GEJt(Mid), 11B2
Godshill, IWC, 4G3
Godstone, SEC, 5D3
Godwin's Halt, Mid, 10G1; 11F1
Gogar, NB, 30B3
Golant, GW, 1D3
Golborne, LNW & GC, 20B2; 24F2; 45D3
*Golborne Jc*, LNW, 20B2; 24F1; 45D3
Golcar, LNW, 21E2; 42D5
Golden Grove, LNW, 13G5
Golden Hill Platform (Pembroke), GW, 7D2

Goldhawk Road, H&C, 39D4
Goldsborough, NE, 21C4
Golf Club Platform, LBSC, 5F3
Golfa, W&L, 14B2
Gollanfield Junc, HR, 36D4
Golspie, HR, 36A4
*Golynos Jc*, GW/LNW, 43A2
Gomersal, LNW, 21E2; 42B4
Gomshall & Shere, SEC, 5D2
Goole, NE(GC/LY), 22E5
Goonbell Halt, GW, 1E1
Goonhavern Halt, GW, 1D1
*Goose Green Jc*, LNW, 45D2
*Goose Hill Jc*, Mid/LY, 42C2
Goostrey, LNW, 15B3; 20D1
Gorbals, GBK, 44E3 and inset E1
Gordon, NB, 31D1
Gordon Hill, GN(NL), 11G2
Gordoun, NB, 34B2
Gorebridge, NB, 30C2
Goring & Streatley, GW, 10G3
Goring-by-Sea, LBSC, 5F2
Gorleston Links Halt, GE, 18F1
Gorleston North, NSJ, 18F1
Gorleston-on-Sea, NSJ, 18F1
Gors-y-Garnant Halt, GW, 43G1
Gorseinon, LNW, 7B3
Gortan, NB, 32D1
Gortan Crossing, NB, 32D1
Gorton, GC, 45A3
Gosberton GN&GEJt, 17D2
Gosford Green, LNW, 10A5
Gospel Oak, LNW(NL) & THJ, 39B5; 40C1 (inset)
Gosport, LSW, 4E2
Goswick, NE, 31D4
Gotham, GC, 16D4
*Gotham Jc*, GC, 16D4
Gotherington, GW, 9D4
Goudhurst, SEC, 6D5
Gourock, Cal, 29B3
Govan, G&P, 29C4; 44E4
Govilon, LNW, 8A4; 43A1
*Gowdall Jc*, HB, 21E5
Gowerton, LNW, 7B3
Goxhill, GC, 22E3
Grace Dieu Halt, LNW, 16E4
Grafham, Mid, 11B1
Grafton & Burbage, MSW, 4B5
*Grafton Jc*, GW/MSW, 4B5
Grahamston (Falkirk), NB(Cal), 30B4
Grain Crossing Halt, SEC, 6B4
Grainsby Halt, GN, 22F2
Grampound Road, GW, 1E2
Grandborough Road, Met&GCJt, 10D3
Grandtully, HR, 33D4
Grane Road (Goods), LY, 20A1; 24E1
Grange, GNS, 7D1
Grange Court, GW, 8A1; 9E2
Grange Lane, GC, 42F2
*Grange North Jc*, GNS, 37D1
Grange-over-Sands, Fur, 24B3
Grange Road, LBSC, 5D3
Grangemouth, Cal(NB), 30B4
Grangetown (Glam), TV(BRY), 8C4; 43C4
Grangetown (Yorks), NE, 28
Grantham, GN, 16D1
Granton, Cal & NB, 30B2 and inset
*Granton Jc*, Cal/NB, 30 (inset)
Granton Road, Cal, 30 (inset)
Grantown-on-Spey, HR & GNS, 36F3
Grantshouse, NB, 31C2
Grasscroft, LNW, 21F1
Grassington & Threshfield, Mid, 21B1
Grassmoor, GC, 16B5; 41C2
*Grassmoor Jc*, GE/GN&GEJt, 11A3; 17F3
Grateley, LSW, 4C5
Gravel Hill, GW, 1D1
Gravelly Hill, LNW, 15F5
Graveney (Goods), SEC, 6C3
Gravesend Central, SEC, 5B5
Gravesend West Street, SEC, 5B5
Grayrigg, LNW, 27G1
Grays, LTS, 5B5
Great Alne, GW, 9B5
Great Ayton, NE, 28F4
Great Barr, LNW, 13B3; 15F4
*Great Barr/Perry Barr North Jc*, LNW, 13B3
Great Bentley, GE, 12E4
Great Bridge, GW & LNW, 13B2 (inset)
Great Bridgeford, LNW(NS), 15D3; 20G1
Great Broughton (Goods), CWJ, 26D3
Great Chesterford, GE, 11D4
Great Coates, GC, 22F2
Great Dalby, GN&LNWJt, 16E2
Great Eastern Goods (Smithfield), GE, 40C4
Great Glen, Mid, 16F3
Great Harwood, LY, 24D1
*Great Harwood Jc*, LY, 24D2
Great Haywood Halt, NS, 15E4
Great Horton, GN, 21D2; 42A5
Great Houghton, DV, 42E1
Great Howard Street (Liverpool) Goods, LY, 45 (inset)
Great Linford, LNW, 10C2
Great Longstone for Ashford, Mid, 15B5
Great Malvern, GW(Mid), 9C3
Great Missenden, Met&GCJt, 10F2
Great Moor Street (Bolton), LNW, 45C2
Great Ormesby, MGN, 18E1
Great Ponton, GN, 16D1
Great Portland Street, Met(Dist/GW/H&C), 39C5
Great Shefford, GW, 4A4; 10G5
Great Somerford, GW, 9G4
Great Western Road (Glasgow), NB, 44E4
Greatham, NE, 28E4
Gree (Goods), Cal, 29D4
Green Ayre (Lancaster), Mid, 24B3
Green Lane, Mer, 45F4
*Green Lane Jc*, GW, 39C1 (inset)
Green Road, Fur, 24A5
Green's Siding, GW, 14F2
Greenfield, LNW, 21F1
Greenford, GW, 5A2; 39B1
Greengairs (Goods), NB, 30C5; 44A5
Greenham Castle (Goods), G&SW, 29F3
Greenhead, NE, 27B2
Greenhill, Cal, 30B5
Greenhithe, SEC, 5B5
Greenlaw, NB, 31D2
Greenloaning, Cal, 33G3
Greenmount, LY, 20A1; 24E1; 45B1
Greenock, Cal & G&SW, 29B3
Greenock West, Cal, 29B3
Greenodd, Fur, 24A4
Greenside (Pudsey), GN, 21D2; 42A4
*Greenside Jc* (Coatbridge), NB, 44B4
Greenwich, SEC, 5B4; 40D3
Greenwich Park, SEC, 40D3
Greetland, LY, 21E2; 42C5
*Greetwell Jc*, GN/GN&GEJt, 16B1; 17B1
*Grendon Underwood Jc*, GC, 10D3
Gresford, GW, 20E4
Gresley, Mid(LNW), 16E5
Gretna, Cal & NB, 26B1
Gretna Green, G&SW, 26B1
*Gretna Jc*, NB, 26B1
Gretton (Northants), Mid, 16F1
Gretton Hall (Glos), GW, 9D4
Griffith's Crossing, LNW, 19D2
Grimes Hall & Wythall Halt, GW, 9A5
Grimes Hill Platform, GW, 9A5
Grimethorpe, Mid&GCJt & DV, 21F4
Grimoldby, GN, 17A3; 22G1
Grimsargh, PL, 24D2
Grimsby Docks, GC(GN), GC & GN, 22F2
Grimsby Town, GC(GN), GC & GN, 22F2
Grimston, Mid, 16E3
Grimston Road, MGN, 17E5
Grimstone & Frampton, GW, 3F3
Grindleford, Mid, 16A5; 41B1
Grindley, GN, 15D4
Grindon, NS, 15C5
Grinkle, NE, 28E3
Gristhorpe, NE, 22A3
Groeslon, LNW, 19E2
Groeswen Halt, AD, 43C3
Grogley Halt, LSW, 1D2
Groombridge, LBSC, 5D5
Grosmont, NE, 28F2
Grotton, LNW, 21F1
Grove Ferry, SEC, 6C2
*Grove Jc*, SEC/LBSC, 5D5
Grove Park, SEC, 5B4; 40E2
Grovesend, LNW, 7B3
Guard Bridge, NB, 34F4
Guay, HR, 33D4
Guestwick, MGN, 18D4
Guide Bridge, GC(LNW) & LNW, 21A2 (inset); 45A3
*Guild Street Jc*, Mid, 15D5
Guildford, LSW(LBSC&SEC), 5C1
Guisborough, NE, 28E3
Guiseley, Mid(NE), 21D2
Gullane, NB, 30B1
Gunheath, GW, 1D2
Gunhouse Wharf, GC, 22F5
Gunnersbury, LSW(Dist/NL), 39D3
Gunness (Goods), GC, 22F5
Gunnislake, BAC, 1C5
Gunton, GE, 18D3
Gurnos (Goods), Mid, 7A4; 43F1
Guthrie, Cal, 34D3
Guyhirne, GN&GEJt, 17F3
Gwaun-cae-Gurwen Halt, GW, 43F1
Gwernydomen Halt, BM(Rhy), 43B3
Gwersyllt & Wheatsheaf, GC, 20E4
Gwersyllt Hill Halt, GW, 20E4
Gwinear Road, GW, 1(inset)
Gwyddelwern, LNW, 19F5
Gwys, Mid, 7A4; 43F1
Gyfeillon Halt, TV, 43C3
Gypsy Hill, LBSC, 40F4

Habrough, GC, 22E3
Hackbridge, LBSC, 39G5
Hackney Downs, GE, 5A3; 40B4
Hackney, NL, 40B3

Hackney Wick Goods, GN, 40B3
Haddenham (Bucks), GW&GCJt, 10E3
Haddenham (Cambs), GE, 11B3
Haddington, NB, 30B1
Haddiscoe, GE, 12A2; 18F1
Hadham, GE, 11F3
Hadleigh, GE, 12D4
Hadley, LNW, 15E2
Hadley Wood, GN(NL), 11G2
Hadlow Road, BJ, 20D4; 45F5
Hadnall, LNW, 15E1; 20G3
Hadneld, GC, 21G1
Haggerston, NL, 40B4
Hagley, GW, 9A3
Hagley Road, LNW, 13C3
Haigh, LY, 21F3; 42D3
*Haigh Jc*, LNW/LU, 20B3; 24F2; 45D2
Hailsham, LBSC, 5F5
Hairmyres, Cal, 29D5; 44D1
Halbeath, NB, 30A3
Hale, CLC(LNW), 20C1; 24G1; 45B4
Halebank, LNW, 15A1; 20C3; 45E4
Halesowen, GW(Mid), 9A4; 15G4
Halesworth, GE & SWD, 12B2
Halewood, CLC, 15A1; 20C3; 24G3; 45E4
Halifax, LY(GN), LY, HO, HHL & GN, 21E2; 42B5/C5
Halkirk, HR, 38D3
*Hall Farm Jc*, GE, 40A3
Hall Green, GW, 9A5; 15G5
Hall Road, LY(LNW), 20B4; 24F4; 45F2
*Hall Royd Jc*, LY, 21E1
Hallaton, GN&LNWJt, 16F2
Hallatrow, GW, 3B3; 8D1
Halling, SEC, 6C5
Hallington, GN, 17A2; 22G2
Halliwell (Goods), LY, 45B1
*Halls Tramway Jc*, GW, 8B4; 43B3
Halmerend, NS, 15C3; 20E1
Halsall, LY, 20B4; 24F4; 45F2
Halstead (Essex), CVH, 11E5
Halton (Ches), BJ, 15A1; 20D3; 45D5
Halton (Lancs), Mid, 24B3
Halton, Mid, 24B3
Halton Holgate, GN, 17B3
*Halton Jc* (Ches), LNW, 15A1; 20C3; 45D5
Haltwhistle, NE, 27B2
Halwill Junc & Beaworthy, LSW, 1B5
Ham Bridge Halt, LBSC, 5F2
Ham Lane, WCP, 3A1; 8D3
Ham Mill Crossing Halt, GW, 9F3
Ham Street & Orlestone, SEC, 6D4
Hambleton, NE, 21D5
Hamilton Square (Birkenhead), Mer, 45F4
Hamilton, Cal & NB, 30D5; 44B2
Hammersmith & Chiswick, NSW, 39D3
*Hammersmith Branch Jcs*, GW & NSW, 39D3
Hammersmith Broadway, Dist & H&C, 39D4
Hammerton, NE, 21C4
Hammerwich, LNW, 15F4
Hampden Park, LBSC, 5F5
Hampole, WRG, 21F4
Hampstead Heath, LNW(NL), 39B5; 40C1 (inset)
Hampstead Norris, GW, 4A3; 10G4
*Hampstead Road Jc*, LNW, 40A1 (inset)
Hampsthwaite, NE, 21C3
Hampton, LSW, 5B2; 39F1
Hampton Court, LSW, 5B2; 39G2
*Hampton Court Jc*, LSW, 5B2, 9G1
Hampton-in-Arden, LNW & Mid, 9A5; 15G5
Hampton Loade, GW, 15G2
Hampton Wick, LSW, 39F2
Hamworthy (Goods), LSW, 3F5
Hamworthy Junc, LSW, 3F5
Handborough, GW, 10E4
Handforth, LNW, 15A3; 20C1; 45A4
Handsworth & Smethwick, GW, 13B3
*Handsworth Jc*, LNW, 13B3
Handsworth Wood, LNW, 13B3
Hanley, NS, 15C3; 20E1
Hannington, GW, 9F5
Hanwell & Elthorne, GW, 5B2; 39C2
Hanwood, SWP, 9A4; 14A1; 15E1
Hapton, LY, 24D1
Harborne, LNW, 13C3; 15G4
*Harborne Jc*, LNW, 13C3
*Harbour Branch Jc* (Arbroath), Cal/NB, 34D3
Harburn, Cal, 30C3
Harby & Stathern, GN&LNWJt, 16D2
*Hardham Jc*, LBSC, 5F1
Hardingham, GE, 18F4
Hardwick Road (Goods), MGN, 17E5
Hare Park & Crofton, WRG, 21E3; 42C2 *see also* Crofton
*Hare Park Jc*, 42C2
Harecastle, NS, 15C3; 20E1
Haresfield, Mid, 9E3
Hareston, GE, 12B3; 18G3
Harker, NB, 26C1
Harlech, Cam, 19F2
Harlesden, LNW(LE) & Mid, 39B3
Harlesford, GE, 12C2
Harling Road, GE, 12A4; 18G4
Harlington (Beds), Mid, 10D1; 11E1
Harlington (Yorks), DV, 21F4
Harlow, GE, 11F3
Harmston, GN, 16B1
Harold Wood, GE, 5A5
Harpenden, Mid & GN, 11F1
*Harpenden Jc*, Mid, 11F1
Harperley, NE, 27D4
Harpur Hill, LNW, 15B4
Harrietsham, SEC, 6C4
Harringay, GN(NL), 40A5
Harringay Park, THJ(LTS), 40A5
Harrington, LNW, 26E3
Harringworth, Mid, 16F1
Harrogate, NE(Mid/GN), 21C3
Harrow & Wealdstone, LNW(LE), 5A2; 39A2
Harrow-on-the-Hill, Met&GCJt, 5A2; 39A2
Harston, GE(GN), 11D3
Hart, NE, 28D4
Hartfield, LBSC, 5D4
Hartford, LNW, 15B2; 20D2; 45C5
Hartford & Greenbank, CLC(LNW), 15B2; 20D2; 45C5
*Hartford Jc*, CLC/LNW, 45C5
Hartington, LNW, 15B5
Hartlebury, GW, 9A3
Hartlepool, NE, 28D4
Hartley, NE, 28B5
Harton Road, GW, 15G1
Harts Hill, GW, 15G3
Hartshill & Basford Halt, NS, 20F1
Hartwood, Cal, 30C5
Harty Road Halt, SEC, 6B3
Harvington, Mid, 9C4
Harwich, GE, 12E3
Hasland (Goods), Mid, 16B5; 41C2
Haslemere, LSW, 4C1
Haslingden, LY, 20A1; 24E1
Hassall Green, NS, 15B3; 20E1
Hassendean, NB, 31F1
Hassocks, LBSC, 5F3
Hassop, Mid, 15B5
Hastings, SEC(LBSC), 6F5
Haswell, NE, 28D5
Hatch, GW, 3D1; 8G3
Hatch End, LNW(LE), 5A2
Hatfield (Herts), GN, 11F2
Hatfield Moor Depot, AJ, 22F5
Hatfield Peverel, GE, 11F5
*Hatherley Curve Jc*, GW, 9D3
Hathern, Mid, 16D4
Hathersage, Mid, 15A5
Hatton (Aberdeen), GNS, 37E5
Hatton (Warwicks), GW, 9B5
*Haugh Mead Jc*, Cal, 44B2
Haughley, GE & MSL, 12C4
Haughton, LNW, 15E3; 20G1
Havant, LBSC(LSW), 4E2
Haven Street, IWC, 4F3
Havenhouse, GN, 17B4
Haverfordwest, GW, 7C2
Haverhill, GE & CVH, 11D5
Haverthwaite, Fur, 24A4
Haverton Hill, NE, 28E4
Hawarden, GC, 20D4
Hawes, Mid&NEJt, 27G3
Hawes Junction & Garsdale, Mid(NE), 24A1; 27G2
Hawick, NB, 31F1
Hawkesbury Lane, LNW, 16G5
Hawkhead, G&SW, 44F3
*Hawkhill Jc*, G&SW, 29F3
Hawkhurst, SEC, 6E5
Haworth, Mid, 21D1
Hawsker, NE, 28F2
Hawthornden, NB, 30C2
Haxby, NE, 21C5
Haxey & Epworth, GN&GEJt, 22F5
Haxey Junc, AJ, 22F5
Haxey Town, AJ, 22F5
Hay, Mid(GW), 14F2
Hayburn Wyke, NE, 28G1
Haydock, GC, 20B3; 24F3; 45D3
Haydock Park Racecourse, GC, 45D3
Haydon Bridge, NE, 27B3
Haydon Square Goods, LNW, 40C4
Haydons Road, LBSC&LSWJt, 39F5
Hayes (Kent), SEC, 5C4; 40G2
Hayes & Harlington (Middx), GW, 5B2
Hayfield, GC&MidJt, 15A4; 21G1
Hayle, GW, 1E4 (inset)
Hayling Island, LBSC, 4E2
Haymarket (Edinburgh), NB, 30 (inset)
Haywards Heath, LBSC, 5E3
Haywood, Cal, 30C4
Hazel Grove, LNW & Mid, 15A4; 20C1; 21G1; 45A4
Hazelwell, Mid, 9A4
Hazelwood, Mid, 16C5; 41F1
Hazlehead Bridge, GC, 21F2; 42E4
Heacham, GE, 17D5
Headcorn, SEC & KES, 6D5
Headingley, NE, 21D3; 42A3
Heads Nook, NE, 27C1
Heads of Ayr, G&SW, 29F3

Heald Green, LNW, 15A3; 20C1; 24G1; 45A4
Healey House, LY, 21F2; 42D5
Healing, GC, 22F2
Heanor, Mid & GN, 16C4; 41F3
Heap Bridge (Goods), LY, 20B1; 24F1; 45A1
Heapey, LU, 20A2; 24E2; 45D1
Heath (Derbys), GC, 16B4; 41C3
Heath Halt (Glam), Car, 43B4
*Heath Jc*, Rhy/Car, 8C4; 43B4
Heath Park Halt, Mid, 10E1; 11F1
*Heath Town Jc*, LNW, Mid, 15E3 (inset)
Heather & Ibstock, AN, 16E5
Heathey Lane Halt, LY, 20A4; 24E4; 45F1
Heathfield (Devon), GW, 2C4
Heathfield (Sussex), LBSC, 5E5
Heatley & Warburton, LNW, 15A1; 20C2; 24G2; 45C4
Heaton, NE, 28 (inset)
Heaton Chapel, LNW, 45A3
*Heaton Lodge Jc*, LY/LNW, 42C4
Heaton Mersey, Mid, 20C1; 24G1; 45A4
Heaton Norris, LNW, 45A3
Heaton Park, LY, 20B1; 24F1; 45A2
Hebburn, NE, 28B5
Hebden Bridge, LY, 21E1
Heck, NE, 21E5
Heckington, GN, 17C2
Heckmondwike, LY & LNW, 21E2; 42C4
*Heckmondwike Jc*, LNW, 42C4
Heddon-on-the-Wall, NE, 27B5
Hedgeley, NE, 31F4
Hednesford, LNW, 15E4
Hedon, NE, 22E3
Heeley, Mid, 16A5; 41A2
Heighington (Durham), NE, 27E5
Hele & Bradninch, GW, 2A3
Helensburgh, NB, 29B3
Helensburgh Upper, NB, 29B3
Hellaby (Goods), GC&Mid&HBJt, 21G4
Hellesdon, MGN, 18F3
Hellifield, Mid(LY) & Mid, 24C1
Hellingly, LBSC, 5F5
Helmdon, GC & SMJ, 10C3
Helmsdale, HR, 38F4
Helmshore, LY, 20A1; 24E1
Helmsley, NE, 21A5
Helpringham, GN&GEJt, 17D1
Helpston, Mid, 17F1
Helsby, BJ & CLC, 15A1; 20D3; 45E5
Helston, GW, 1F5 (inset)
Hemel Hempsted, Mid, 10E1; 11F1 *see also* Boxmoor
Hemingborough, NE, 21D5
Hemsby, MGN, 18E1
Hemsworth, WRG, 21E4; 42D1
Hemsworth & South Kirkby, HB, 21E4; 42D1
Hemsworth Colliery, BL, 42D1
*Hemsworth Jc*, HB/WRG, 42D1
Hemyock, GW, 2A2; 8G4
Henbury, GW, 8C2; 9G1
Hendon, Mid, 5A3; 39A4
Hendreforgan, GW, 8B5; 43D3
Henfield, LBSC, 5F2
Hengoed, GW & Rhy, 8B4; 43B3 *see also* Maesycwmmer
Henham Halt, GE, 11E4
Heniarth, W&L, 14B3
Henley-in-Arden, GW, 9B5
Henley-on-Thames, GW, 10G2
Henllan, GW, 13F4
Henlow, Mid, 11E1
*Hensall Jc*, LY&GNJt/H&B, 21E5
Hensall, LY, 21E5
Henstridge, SD, 3D3; 8G1
Henwick (Worcs), GW, 9B3
Hepscott, NE, 27A5
Hereford (Goods), S&H, GW & Mid, 9C1
Hereford (Pass), S&H(Mid), 9C1
Heriot, NB, 30C1
Hermitage, GW, 4A3
Herne Bay, SEC, 6B2
Herne Hill, SEC, 5B3; 40E5
Herriard, LSW, 4C2
Hertford, GN & GE, 11F2
Hertford Cowbridge, GN, 11F2
Hertingfordbury, GN, 11F2
Hesketh Bank & Tarleton, LY, 20A3; 24E3
Hesketh Park, LY, 20A4; 24E4; 45F1
Hesleden, NE, 28D5
Heslerton, NE, 22A4
Hessay, NE, 21C4
Hessle, NE(GC), 22E4
*Hessle Road Jc*, NE, 22E3; 22A2 (inset)
Hest Bank, LNW, 24B3
*Hest Bank N & S Jcs*, LNW, 24B3
Heston Hounslow, Met & Dist, 39D1
Heswall, BJ, 20C5
Heswall Hills, GC, 20C4; 45F4
Hethersett, GE, 18F3
Hetton, NE, 28D5
Hever, LBSC, 5D4
Heversham, Fur, 24A3
Hexham, NE(NB), 27B3
*Hexthorpe Jc*, GC, 21G2
Heyford, GW, 10D4
Heys Crossing Halt, LY(LNW), 20B3; 24F3; 45E2
Heysham Harbour, Mid, 24C3
Heytesbury, GW, 3C4
Heywood, LY, 20B1; 24F1; 45A1
Hibel Road (Macclesfield), LNW(NS), 15A3; 20D1; 45A5
Hickleton & Thurnscoe, HB, 21F4; 42E1
*Hickleton South Jc*, SK/DV, 21F4; 42E1
High Barnet, GN(NL), 5A3
High Blantyre, Cal, 29C5; 44C2
High Field, NE, 22D5
High Halden Road, KES, 6D4
High Halstow Halt, SEC, 6B5
High Harrington, CWJ, 26E3
High Lane, GC&NSJt, 15A4; 21G1
*High Level Bridge* (Gateshead), NE, 28 (inset)
*High Peak Jc*, Mid/LNW, 16C5; 41E1
High Rocks Halt, LBSC, 5D5
High Shields, NE, 28B5
High Street (Glasgow), NB, 44D4 and inset E2
High Westwood, NE, 27C4
High Wycombe, GW&GCJt, 10F2
Higham (Kent), SEC, 6B5
Higham (Suffolk), GE, 11C5
Higham Ferrers, Mid, 10A1
Higham-on-the-Hill, AN, 16F5
Highams Park, GE, 5A4
Highbridge, GW & SD, 3B1; 8E3
Highbury & Islington, NL(LNW), 40B5
Highbury Vale Goods, GN, 40B5
Highclere, GW, 4B3
Higher Buxton, LNW, 15A4
Highgate, GN(NL), 5A3; 39A5
Highgate Platform, CKP, 26E1
Highgate Road, Mid(LTS) & THJ, 40B5
*Highgate Road Jc*, Mid/THJ(LTS), 40C1 (inset)
Highlandman, Cal, 33F3
Highley, GW, 9A2; 15G2
Hightown, LY(LNW), 20B4; 24F4; 45F2
Highworth, GW, 9F5
Hildenborough, SEC, 5D5
Hilgay, GE, 11A4; 17F4
Hill End, GN, 11F2
Hillfoot, NB, 29B4; 44E5
Hillhouse Goods (Yorks), LNW, 21E2; 42C4
*Hillhouse Jc* (Lancs), LY/CLC, 20B4; 24F4; 45F2
Hillington, MGN, 17E5
Hillside (Kincard), NB, 34C2
Hilton House, LY, 20B2; 24F2; 45C2
*Hilton Jc*, Cal/NB, 33F5
*Hincaster Jc*, LNW/Fur, 24A3
Hinckley, LNW(Mid), 16F4
Hinderwell, NE, 28E2
Hindley, LY, 20B2; 24F2; 45C2
Hindley & Amberswood (Goods), LNW, 45D2
Hindley & Platt Bridge, GC, 20B2; 24F2; 45D2 *see also* Platt Bridge
Hindley Green, LNW, 45C2
Hindlow, LNW, 15B5
Hindolvestone, MGN, 18D4
Hinton (Glos), Mid, 9C4
Hinton Admiral, LSW, 4F5
Hipperholme, LY, 42B5
Hirwain, GW, 8A5; 43D2
Histon, GE(Mid), 11C3
Hitchin, GN(Mid), GN & Mid, 11E2
Hither Green, SEC, 40E3
Hixon, NS, 15D4
Hockerill Halt, GE, 11E4
Hockley (Birmingham), GW, 13C3; 15G4
Hockley (Essex), GE, 6A5
*Hoddesdon Jc*, LY(LNW), 20A2; 24E2
Hoddlesdon (Goods), LY, 20A2; 24E1
Hodnet, GW, 15D2; 20G2
Hoe Street (Walthamstow), GE, 40A3
Hoghton, LY, 20A2; 24E2
Holbeach, MGN, 17E3
Holbeck, GN(LY/GC) & Mid(NE), 21C2 (inset); 42A3
Holborn Viaduct, SEC, 5B3; 40C5
Holburn Street, GNS, 37G4
Holcombe Brook, LY, 20A1; 24E1; 45B1
Holehouse, G&SW, 29F4
*Holes Bay Jc*, LSW, 3F5
*Holgate Bridge Jc*, NE, 21C5 and inset A4
Holkham, GE, 18C5
Holland Arms, LNW, 19D1
Holland Road Halt, LBSC, 5F3
Hollin Well & Annesley, GC, 41E4
Hollingbourne, SEC, 6C5
Hollins (Goods), LY, 20A2; 24E2
Hollinswood (Goods), GW, 15E2
Hollinwood, LY, 45A2
Holly Bush (Mon), LNW, 8A4; 43B2
Hollybush (Ayr), G&SW, 29F4
Holme (Hunts), GN, 11A2; 17G2
Holme (Lancs), LY, 24D1
Holme (Yorks), NE, 22D5
Holme Hale, GE, 18F5
Holme Lacy, GW, 9C1
Holmes, Mid, 21G4; 42F1
Holmes Chapel, LNW, 15B3; 20D1

Holmfield, H&O, 21D2; 42B5
Holmfirth, LY, 21F2; 42D5
Holmsley, LSW, 4E5
Holmwood, LBSC, 5D2
Holsworthy, LSW, 1A4
Holt (Norfolk), MGN, 18D4
Holt Junc, GW, 3B4
Holtby, NE, 21C5
Holton, GC, 22F3
Holton-le-Clay, GN, 22F2
Holton Village Halt, GN, 22F2
Holwell (Goods), Mid, 16E3
Holygate (Goods), NB, 30B3
Holyhead, LNW, 19B2
Holytown, Cal, 30C5; 44A3
Holywell (North) Goods, NE, 28B5
Holywell Junc, LNW, 20D5
Holywell Town, LNW, 20D5
Holywood, G&SW, 26A4
Homersfield, GE, 12A3; 18G3
Homerton, NL, 40B3
Honeybourne, GW, 9C5
*Honeybourne Line Jc*, GW/Mid, 9D3
Honing, MGN, 18D2
Honington, GN, 16C1
Honiton, LSW, 2A2
Honley, LY, 21F2; 42D5
Honor Oak, SEC, 40E4
Honor Oak Park, LBSC, 40E4
*Hoo Jc*, SEC, 6B5
Hook, LSW, 4B2
Hook Norton, GW, 10D5
Hookagate, S&M, 15E1
Hoole, LY, 20A3; 24E3
Hooley Hill, LNW, 21A2 (inset); 45A3
Hooton, BJ, 20D4; 45F5
Hope (Derbys), Mid, 15A5
Hope & Pen-y-ffordd, LNW, 20E4
Hope Exchange (Flint), GC & LNW, 20E4
Hope Village, GC, 20E4
Hopeman, HR, 36C2
Hopton, NSJ, 12A1; 18F1
Hopton Heath, LNW, 14C1
Horbury & Ossett, LY, 21E3; 42C3 *see also* Ossett, GN
Horbury Junc, LY, 21E3; 42C2
Horden, NE, 28D4
Horderley, BC, 14C1
Horeb, LM, 7A3
Horham, MSL, 12B3
Horley, LBSC, 5D3
Hornby, Mid, 24B2
Horncastle, GN, 17B2
Hornchurch, LTS, 5A5
Horninglow, NS(GN), 15C5 (inset)
*Horninglow Jc*, NS, 15D5
Horninglow Wharf, Mid, 15D5 (inset)
Hornsea, NE, 22C2
Hornsea Bridge, NE, 22C2
Hornsey, GN(NL), 40A5
Hornsey Road, THJ(LTS), 40B5
Horrabridge, GW, 1C5
Horringford, IWC, 4F3
Horrocksford, LY, 24D1
*Horrocksford Jc*, LY, 24D1
Horsebridge, LSW(MSW), 4C4
Horsehay & Dawley, GW, 15F2
Horsforth, NE, 21D3; 42A3 *see also* Newlay
Horsham, LBSC, 5E2
Horsley, LSW, 5C2
*Horsleyfield Jc*, GW/LNW, 13B2
Horsmonden, SEC, 6D5
Horsted Keynes, LBSC, 5E3
Horton, Mid, 24B1
Horton Park, GN, 21D2; 42B5
Horwich, LY, 20B2; 24F2; 45C1
*Horwich Fork Jc*, LY, 45C2
Hoscar, LY, 20B3; 24F3; 45E1
Hothfield, SEC, 6D4
Hotwells, CE, 3 (inset)
Hough Green, CLC, 15A1; 20C3; 24G3; 45E4
Hougham, GN, 16C1
Hounslow & Whitton, LSW & Dist, 5B2; 39D1/E1
Hounslow Barracks, Dist & Met, 39D1
*Hounslow Jc*, LSW, 39E1
Houston (Crosslee), Cal & G&SW, 29C4; 44G4
Hove, LBSC, 5F3
Hovingham Spa, NE, 21B5
How Mill, NE, 27C1
Howden Clough, GN, 42B3
Howdon, NE, 28B5
Howe Bridge, LNW, 20B2; 24F2; 45C2
Howsham, GC, 22F3
Howwood, G&SW, 29C4
Hoy, HR, 38C3
Hoylake, Wir, 20C5; 24G5
Hubbert's Bridge, GN, 17C2
Hucknall, Mid & GN, 16C4; 41E4
Hucknall Town, GC, 16C4, 41E4
Huddersfield, LNW&LYJt & Mid, 21E2; 42C5
Hugglescote, AN, 16E4
Hull, NE(GC/LNW/LY), NE & HB, 22D3/E3 and inset
Hullavington, GW, 9G3
Hulme End, NS, 15B5
*Humber Rd Jc* (Coventry), LNW, 10A5
*Humber Rd Jc* (Lincs), GC, 22E3
Humberstone, GN, 16F3
Humberstone Road, Mid, 16F3
Humbie, NB, 30C1
Humshaugh, NB, 27B3
Huncoat, LY, 24D1
Hundred End, LY, 20A4; 24E3
Hungerford, GW, 4A4
Hunmanby, NE, 22B3
Hunnington, HJ, 9A4; 15G4
Hunslet (Goods), GN & NE, 21D3; 42A2
Hunslet (Pass), Mid(LY), 21D3; 42B2
*Hunslet Branch Jc*, NE, 21D3
Hunslet Lane (Goods), Mid, 21D3 and inset C2; 42A2
Hunstanton, GE, 17D5
Hunston, SL, 4E1
Hunt's Cross, CLC, 20C4; 45E4
*Hunthill Jc*, Cal, 44C2
Huntingdon, GN, GN&GEJt & Mid, 11B2
Huntly, GNS, 37E1
Hunwick, NE, 27D5
Hurdlow, LNW, 15B5
Hurlford, G&SW, 29E4
Hurn, LSW, 4E5
Hurst Green Halt, CO, 5C4
*Hurst Green Jc*, LBSC/CO, 5C4
Hurstbourne, LSW, 4B4
Hurworth Burn, NE, 28D5
Husborne Crawley Halt, LNW, 10C1
Huskisson (Liverpool), CLC, 45F3 and inset
Husthwaite Gate, NE, 21B4
Hutcheon Street, GNS, 37F4
Hutton (Lancs) & Howick, LY, 20A3; 24E3
Hutton Cranswick, NE, 22C4
Hutton Gate, NE, 28E3
Huttons Ambo, NE, 22B5
Huyton, LNW, 20C3; 24G3; 45E4
Huyton Quarry, LNW, 20C3; 24G3; 45E4
Hyde, GC&MidJt, 21G1
Hyde Junc, GC&MidJt, 21G1
Hyde Road, GC, 45A3
Hykeham, Mid, 16B1
Hylton, NE, 28C5
Hylton Lane (Goods), NE, 28C5
Hyndland, NB, 44E4
Hythe (Essex), GE, 12E4
Hythe (Kent), SEC, 6D3

Ibrox, G&P, 29C4; 44E3
Icknield Port Road, LNW, 13C3
Ide, GW, 2B3
Idle, GN, 21D2; 42A4
Idridgehay, Mid, 16C5; 41E1
Ifield Halt, LBSC, 5D3
Ilderton, NE, 31E4
Ilford, GE, 5A4; 40B1
Ilfracombe, LSW(GW), 7E3
Ilkeston, GN, 16C4; 41F3
Ilkeston Junc & Cossall, Mid, 16C4; 41F3
Ilkeston Town, Mid, 16C4; 41F3
Ilkley, Mid & O&I, 21C2
Ilminster, GW, 3D1; 8G3
Immingham, GC, 22E3
Immingham Dock (Goods), GC, 22E2
Ince (Lancs), LY, 45D2 *see also* Lower Ince
Ince & Elton, BJ, 20D3; 45E5
Inchcoonans (Goods), Cal, 34E5
Inches, Cal, 30E5
Inchlea Crossing, HR, 33B2
Inchmagranachan Crossing, HR, 33D4
Inchture, Cal, 34E5
Inchture Village, Cal, 34E5
Ingatestone, GE, 11G4
Ingersby, GN, 16F3
Ingestre, GN, 15D4 *see also* Weston (Staffs)
Ingham, GE, 12B5
Ingleby, NE, 28F4
Ingleton, Mid(LNW), 24B2
Ingrow, Mid & GN, 21D1
*Ings Road Jc*, LY/GN, 42C2
Innerleithen, NB, 30E2
Innerpeffray, Cal, 33F4
Innerwick, NB, 31B2
Insch, GNS, 37E2
Instow, LSW, 7F3
Inveramsay, GNS, 37E3
Inveresk, NB, 30B2
Invergarry, NB, 32A2
Invergloy, NB, 32B2
Invergordon, HR, 36C5
Invergowrie, Cal, 34E5
Inverkeilor, NB, 34D3
Inverkeithing, NB, 30B3
Inverkip, Cal, 29C2
Inverness, HR, 36E5
Invershin, HR, 35A5
Inverugie, GNS, 37D5
Inverurie, GNS, 37F3
Inworth, GE, 12F5
Ipstones, NS, 15C4

Ipswich, GE, 12D3
Irchester, Mid, 10B1
*Irchester Jc*, Mid, 10B1
Irlam & Cadishead, CLC, 20C2; 24G2; 45C3
Irlams-o'th-Height, LY, 45B2
Iron Acton, Mid, 8C1; 9G2
Iron Bridge & Broseley, GW, 15F2
Irongray, G&SW, 26A4
Irthlingborough, LNW, 10A1
Irton Road, RE, 26F3
Irvine, G&SW & Cal, 29E3
Isfield, LBSC, 5F4
Isham & Burton Latimer, Mid, 10A2
Isleham, GE, 11B4
Isleworth, LSW, 39D2
Islip, LNW, 10E4
Itchen Abbas, LSW, 4C3
*Itchingfield Jc*, LBSC, 5E2
*Ivor Jc*, BM/LNW, 43C1
Ivybridge, GW, 2D5

*Jamage Jc*, NS, 15C3; 20E1
James Street, Mer, 45G5 (inset)
Jamestown, NB, 29B3
Jarrow, NE, 28B5
Jedburgh, NB, 31E1
Jedfoot, NB, 31E1
Jersey Marine, RSB, 7B4; 43F3
Jervaulx, NE, 21A2; 27G5
Jesmond, NE, 27B5, 28 (inset)
*Joan Croft Jc*, NE, 21F5
John o' Gaunt, GN&LNWJt, 16E2
Johnshaven, NB, 34C2
Johnston, GW, 7C1
Johnstone, G&SW, 29C4
Johnstone North, G&SW, 29C4
Johnstown & Hafod, GW, 20F4
Jones' Drove (Goods), GE, 11A3; 17G3
Joppa, NB, 30 (inset)
Jordanhill, NB, 44E4
Jordanstone, Cal, 34D5
Junction Road (London), THJ(LTS), 40B5 and inset C1
Junction Road, NB, 30 (inset)
Junction Road (Sussex), KES, 6E5
*Junction Road Jc*, Mid/THJ(LTS), 40C1 (inset)
Juniper Green, Cal, 30C3
Justinhaugh, Cal, 34C4

*Kaypark Jc*, G&SW, 29E4
Keadby (Goods), GC, 22F5
Kearsley, LY, 20B2; 24F1; 45B2
Kearsney, SEC, 6D2
Keele, NS, 15C3; 20F1
Kegworth, Mid, 16D4
Keighley, Mid(GN), Mid & GN, 21D1
Keinton Mandeville, GW, 3D2; 8F2
Keith, GNS & HR, 37D1
Keith Town, GNS, 37D1
Kelmarsh, LNW, 10A2
Kelmscott & Langford, GW, 9F5; 10F5
Kelso, NB(NE), 31E2
*Kelso Jc*, NB, 31E1
Kelston, Mid, 3A3; 8D1
Kelton Fell, RKF, 26E3
Kelty, NB, 30A3
Kelvedon, GE, 12F5
Kelvedon Low Level, GE, 12F5
Kelvin Bridge, Cal, 44E4
Kelvinhaugh (Goods), Cal&NBJt, 44E4
Kelvinside, Cal, 44E4
*Kelvinside Jc*, Cal, 44E4
Kemble Junc, GW, 9F4
Kemp Town, LBSC, 5F3
Kempston & Elstow Halt, LNW, 10C1; 11D1
Kempston Hardwick Halt, LNW, 10C1; 11D1
*Kempston Rd Jc*, Mid, 10C1; 11D1
Kempton Park, LSW, 39F1
Kemsing, SEC, 5C5
Kendal, LNW(Fur), 24A3; 27G1
Kenfig Hill, GW, 7C5; 43E4
Kenilworth, LNW, 10A5
*Kenilworth Jc*, LNW, 10A5
Kenley, SEC, 5C3
Kenmay, GNS, 37F3
Kennethmont, GNS, 37E2
Kennett, GE, 11C5
*Kennington Jc* (Oxon), GW, 10E4
Kennishead, GBK, 44E3
Kennoway (Goods), NB, 34G5
Kennybill, (Goods), Cal, 44D4
Kensal Green, LNW(LE), 39C4
*Kensal Green Jc*, LNW, 39B4
Kensal Rise, LNW(NL), 39B4
Kensington (Addison Rd), WL(H&C/LBSC/LSW), 5B3; 39D4
Kensington High Street (Coal), Mid, 39D5
Kensington High Street (Pass), Dist & Met(Dist), 39D5
Kensington Road Goods (Southport), LY, 45F1
*Kent & East Sussex Light Railway*, KES, 6E4
Kent House, SEC, 40F4
Kentallen, Cal, 32D3
Kentish Town, Mid(LTS/GE) & LNW(NL), 5A3; 40B5 and inset C1
*Kentish Town Jc*, Mid, 40C1 (inset)
Kenton (Middx), LNW(LE), 39A2
Kenton (Northumb), NE, 27B5
Kenton (Suffolk), MSL, 12C3
Kenton for Northwick Park, LNW, 39A2
Kents Bank, Fur, 24B3
Kenyon Junc, LNW(BJ), 20C2; 24G2; 45C3
Kerne Bridge, GW, 8A2; 9D1
Kerry, Cam, 14C2
Kershope Foot, NB, 27A1
Keswick, CKP, 26E2
Ketley, GW, 15E2
*Ketley Jc*, GW/LNW, 15C2; 20E2
Kettering, Mid, 10A2
*Kettering Jc*, Mid, 10A2
Kettleness, NE, 28E2
Ketton, Mid(LNW), 16F1; 17F1
Kew Bridge, LSW(NL), 39D3
Kew Gardens (Lancs), LY, 20A4; 24E4; 45F1
Kew Gardens (London), LSW(Dist/NL), 39D3
Keyham (Devonport), GW, 1D5 and inset
Keyingham, NE, 22E2
*Keymer Jc*, LBSC, 5E3
Keynsham, GW, 3A3; 8D1
Kibworth, Mid, 16F3
Kidbrooke, SEC, 40E2
Kidderminster, GW, 9A3
Kidlington, GW, 10E4
Kidsgrove, NS, 15C3; 20E1
Kidsgrove Halt, NS, 15C3; 20E1
Kidwelly, GW, 7A2
Kielder, NB, 27A1; 31G1
Kilbagie, NB, 30A4
Kilbarchan, G&SW, 29C4
Kilbirnie, Cal & G&SW, 29D3
Kilbowie, Cal, 29C4; 44F4
Kilburn (Derbys), Mid, 16C5; 41F2
Kilburn & Brondesbury (Met), 39B4
Kilburn & Maida Vale, LNW(NL), 39B5
Kilconquhar, NB, 30A1; 34G4
Kildale, NE, 28F3
Kildary, HR, 36C4
Kildonan, HR, 38F5
Kildwick & Crosshills, Mid, 21C1
Kilgerran, GW, 13F3
Kilgetty, GW, 7D3
Kilkerran, G&SW, 29G3
*Kilknowe Jc*, NB, 30D1
Killamarsh, GC & Mid, 16A4; 41A3 *see also* Upperthorpe
Killay, LNW, 7B3
Killearn, NB, 29B4
Killiecrankie, HR, 33C4
Killin, Cal, 33E2
Killin Junc, Cal, 33E1
Killingholme, GC, 22E3
Killingworth, NE, 27B5
Killochan, G&SW, 29G3
Killywhan, G&SW, 26B4
Kilmacolm, G&SW, 29C3
Kilmany, NB, 34E4
Kilmarnock, G&SW & GBK, 29E4
Kilmaurs, G&SW, 29D4
Kilnhurst, Mid & GC, 21 F4; 42F1
Kilnwick Gate (Goods), NE, 22C4
Kilpatrick, NB, 29B4; 44G5
Kilsby & Crick, LNW, 10A4
Kilsyth, K&B & NB, 29B5
Kilwinning, G&SW & Cal, 29D3
Kimberley Park, GE, 18F4
Kimberley, GN & Mid, 16C4; 41F4
Kimbolton, Mid, 11B1
*Kimbridge Jc*, LSW, 4D4
Kinaldie, GNS, 37F3
Kinbrace, HR, 38E5
Kinbuck, Cal, 33G3
Kincardine, NB, 30A4
Kincraig, HR, 33A3; 36G4
Kineton, SMJ, 10C5
Kinfauns, Cal, 33F5
King Edward, GNS, 37C3
King George Dock (Goods) (Hull), NE&HBJt, 22E3
King Street Goods (Paisley), G&SW, 44G3
King William (Goods), LY, 20A2; 24E1; 45B1
King's Cross, GN & Met(Dist/GW/GN/Mid/H&C), 5A3; 40C5
King's Inch, G&P, 44F4
King's Langley & Abbot's Langley, LNW, 11G1
King's Lynn, GE(MGN), 17E4
King's Norton, Mid, 9A4
King's Sutton, GW, 10C4
King's Worthy, GW, 4C3
King's Heath, Mid, 9A4; 15G4
Kingennie, Cal, 34E4
Kingham, GW, 9D5
Kinghorn, NB, 30A2
Kingsbarns, NB, 34F3
Kingsbridge, GW, 2E4
Kingsbury, Mid, 15F5
Kingscliffe, LNW, 11A1; 16F1; 17F1
Kingscote, LBSC, 5D4

Kingshouse, Cal, 33F2
Kingskerswell, GW, 2D3
Kingskettle, NB, 34F5
Kingsland, (Hereford), GW, 14D1
Kingsland, NL, 40B4
*Kingsland Eastern Jc*, NL, 40B4
*Kingsland Western Jc*, NL, 40B4
Kingsley & Froghall, NS, 15C4
Kingsley Halt, LSW, 4C1
Kingsmuir, Cal, 34D4
Kingston (Surrey), LSW, 5B2; 39F2
Kingston (Sussex) (Goods), LBSC, 5F3
Kingston Crossing Halt, GW, 10F3
Kingston Road, WCP, 3A1; 8D3
Kingston Street (Hull) (Goods), NE, 22 (inset)
Kingswear, GW, 2D3
Kingswood & Burgh Heath, SEC, 5C3
*Kingswood Crossing*, HR, 33E5
*Kingswood Jc*, GW, 3 (inset)
Kingthorpe, GN, 17B1
Kington, GW, 14E2
Kingussie, HR, 33A2
Kinloss, HR, 36C2
*Kinnaber Jc*, Cal/NB, 34C3
Kinneil, NB, 30B4
Kinnerley Junc, S&M, 14A1
Kinnersley, Mid, 14E1
Kinnerton, LNW, 20E4
Kinning Park Goods, Cal, 44F2 (inset)
Kinross Junc, NB, 30A3; 33G5
Kintbury, GW, 4A4
Kintore, GNS, 37F3
Kipling Cotes, NE, 22D4
Kippax, NE, 21D4; 42B1
Kippen, NB, 29A5
Kirby Cross, GE, 12E3
Kirby Moorside, NE, 21A5
Kirby Muxloe, Mid, 16F4
Kirby Park, BJ, 20C5; 24G5
Kirk Michael, IMR, 23B2; 25G4
*Kirk Sandall Jc*, GC/SYJ, 21F5 and inset
Kirk Smeaton, HB, 21E4
Kirkandrews, NB, 26C1
Kirkbank, NB, 31E2
Kirkbride, NB, 26C2
Kirkbuddo, Cal, 34D4
Kirkburton, LNW, 21E2; 42D4
*Kirkburton Branch Jc*, LNW, 42C4
Kirkby (in-Furness), Fur, 23A4
Kirkby (Lancs), Fur, 24A5
Kirkby (Lancs), LY, 20B4; 24F3; 45E3
Kirkby & Pinxton, GC, 16C4; 41E4 *see also* Pinxton
Kirkby-in-Ashfield, Mid &GC, 16C4; 41E4
Kirkby Lonsdale, LNW, 24B2
Kirkby Stephen, NE, 27F2
Kirkby Stephen & Ravenstonedale, Mid, 27F2
Kirkby Thore, NE, 27E2
Kirkcaldy, NB, 30A2
Kirkconnel, G&SW, 30F5
Kirkcowan, P&W, 25C3
Kirkcudbright, G&SW, 26C5
Kirkdale, LY, 45F3
Kirkgate (Wakefield), LY&GNJt, 21E3; 42C2
Kirkgunzeon, G&SW, 26B4
Kirkham & Wesham, PWY, 24D3
Kirkham Abbey, NE, 22B5
Kirkheaton, LNW, 21E2; 42C4
Kirkhill, Cal, 29C5; 44D3
*Kirkhill Jc*, Cal, 44D3
Kirkinner, P&W, 25C4
Kirkintilloch, NB, 29B5; 44C5
Kirkland, G&SW, 26A5
Kirklee, Cal, 44E4
Kirkley (Goods), GE, 12A1; 18G1
Kirklington & Edingley, Mid, 16B3
Kirkliston, NB, 30B3
Kirknewton, NE, 31E3
Kirkpatrick, Cal, 26B2
Kirkstall, Mid, 21D3; 42A3
Kirriemuir, Cal, 34D4
*Kirriemuir Jc*, Cal, 34D4
Kirtlebridge, Cal, 26B2
Kirton, GN, 17D2
Kirton Bridge Halt, GNS, 37C4
Kirton Lindsey, GC, 22F4
Kittybrewster, GNS, 37F4
Kiveton Park, GC, 16A4; 41A4
Knapton (Yorks), NE, 22B4
Knaresborough, NE, 21C3
Knebworth, GN, 11F2
Knight's Hill Goods, LNW, 40E4
Knighton, LNW, 14D2
*Knighton Jcs*, Mid, 16F3
*Knighton South Jc*, LNW/Mid, 16F3
*Knightswood North Jc*, NB, 44E4
Knightwick, GW, 9B2
Knitsley, NE, 27C5
Knock, GNS, 37D1
Knockando, GNS, 36E2
Knockholt, SEC, 5C4
Knott End, KE, 24C4
Knottingley for Ferrybridge, LY&GNJt, 21E4; 42C1 *see also* Ferrybridge
Knotty Ash & Stanley, CLC, 45E3 *see also* Stanley (Lancs)
Knowesgate, NB, 27A4
Knoweside, G&SW, 29F3
Knowle & Dorridge, GW, 9A5
Knowle Platform, LSW, 4D3
Knowlton, EK, 6C2
Knowsley Street (Bury), LY, 20B1; 24F1; 45B2
Knucklas, LNW, 14D2
Knutsford, CLC(LNW), 15A2; 20D2; 45B5
Knutton Halt, NS, 20F1
Knypersley Halt, NS, 15B3; 20E1
Kyle of Lochalsh, HR, 35F1

Lacock Halt, GW, 3A4
Ladmanlow (Goods), LNW, 15B4
Ladybank, NB, 34F5
Ladysbridge, GNS, 37C2
Ladywell, SEC, 40E3
Laindon, LTS, 5A5
Laira Halt, GW, 1 (inset)
*Laira Jc* (Plymouth), GW, 1 (inset)
Lairg, HR, 35A5
Laisterdyke, GN(LY), 21D2; 42A4
Lakenheath, GE, 11A5; 17G5
Lamancha, NB, 30D2
Lambley, NE, 27C2
Lambourn, GW, 4A4; 10G5
Lamesley, NE, 27C5
Lamington, Cal, 30E4
Lampeter, GW, 13E5
Lamphey, GW, 7D2
Lamplugh, WCE, 26E3
Lamport, LNW, 10A2
Lanark, Cal, 30D4
Lancaster, LNW(Mid), LNW & Mid, 24C3
Lanchester, NE, 27D5
Lancing, LBSC, 5F2
Landore, GW, 7B4; 43G3
Langbank, Cal, 29B3
Langford (Som), GW, 3B2; 8D2
Langford (Essex), GE, 12F5
Langho, LY, 24D2
Langholm, NB, 26A1
Langley (Bucks), GW, 5B1
Langley (Northumb), NE, 27C3
Langley Green & Rood End, GW, 13C2; 15G4
*Langley Jc*, GN, 11E2
Langley Mill, Mid, 41F3 *see also* Eastwood, GN
Langloan, Cal, 44B3
Langport (East and West), GW, 3D1; 8F3
Langrick, GN, 17C2
Langside & Newlands, Cal, 44E3
*Langside Jc*, Cal/GBK, 44F1 (inset)
Langston, LBSC, 4E2
Langwathby, Mid, 27D1
Langwith, Mid, 16B4; 41C4
Langwith Junc, GC(GN), 16B4; 41C4
Langworth, GC, 16A1; 17A1
*Lanridge Jc*, Cal, 44A3
Lansdown (Cheltenham), Mid(MSW), 9D3
Lapford, LSW, 2A4
Lapworth, GW, 9A5
Larbert, Cal(NB), 30B5
Largo, NB, 34G4
Largoward (Goods), NB, 34F4
Largs, G&SW, 29C2
Larkhall (Central), Cal, 30D5; 44B1
Larkhall (East), Cal, 30D5; 44A1
Lartington, NE, 27E4
Lasswade, NB, 30C2
Latchford, LNW, 15A2; 20C2; 24G2; 45C4
Latchley, BAC, 1C5
*Latchmere Jcs*, WLE, 39E5 and inset E3
Latimer Road, H&C, 39C4
Lauder, NB, 31D1
*Laughton East Jc*, SYJ, 41A4
*Laughton West Jc*, SYJ, 41A4
Launceston, LSW & GW, 1B4
Launton, LNW, 10D3
Laurencekirk, Cal(NB), 34B2
Lauriston, NB, 34C2
Lavant, LBSC, 4E1
Lavenham, GE, 12D5
Lavernock, TV, 8D4; 43B5
Laverton Halt, GW, 9C4
Lavington, GW, 3B5
Law Junc, Cal, 30D5
Lawley Bank, GW, 15E2
Lawley Street (Goods), Mid, 13C4
Lawrence Hill, GW, 3 (inset)
*Lawrence Hill Jc*, Mid, 3G1 (inset)
Lawton, NS, 15B3; 20E1
Laxey, ME, 23B3
Laxfield, MSL, 12B3
Layerthorpe, DVL, 21C5 and inset A5
Lazonby & Kirkoswald, Mid, 27D1
Lea, GN&GEJt, 16A2
Lea Bridge, GE, 5A3; 40B3
*Lea Bridge Jc*, GE, 40B3
Lea Green, LNW, 20C3; 24G3; 45D3
Lea Road (Gainsborough), GN&GEJt, 16A2; 22G5
Lea Road (Preston), PWY, 24D3

Leadburn, NB, 30C2
Leadenham, GN, 16C1
Leadgate, NE, 27C5
Leadhills, Cal, 30F4
Leagrave, Mid, 10D1; 11E1
Lealholm, NE, 28F3
Leamington Spa, GW & LNW, 10B5
Leamside, NE, 28D5
Leasowe, Wir, 20C5; 24G5
Leatherhead, LSW & LBSC, 5C2
Leaton, GW, 14A1; 15E1
Lechlade, GW, 9F5
Ledbury, GW, 9C2
Ledsham, BJ, 20D4; 45F5
Ledston, NE, 21E4; 42B1
Lee (Kent), SEC, 5B4; 40E2
*Lee Jc*, SEC, 40E2
Lee-on-the-Solent, LSW, 4E3
Leebotwood, S&H, 14B1; 15F1
Leeds (Goods), GN, LNW&LYJt, Mid & NE, 21B2 (inset); 42A2/3
Leeds (Pass), Central: GN, LY, LNW, NE; New: LNW&NEJt; Wellington: Mid(LY), 21B2 (inset); 42A2/3
Leegate, M&C, 26D2
Leek, NS, 15C4
Leeming Bar, NE, 21A3; 28G5
*Leen Valley Jc*, GN, 16C3; 41F4
Lees, LNW, 21F1
Legacy, GW, 20E4
Legbourne Road, GN, 17A3
Leicester (Goods), Mid, GC, GN & LNW, 16F3
Leicester (Pass), Mid(LNW/MGN), GC &GN, 16F3
*Leicester Jc* (Burton-on-Trent), Mid, 15E5 and inset
Leigh (Staffs), NS, 15D4
Leigh & Bedford, LNW, 20B2; 24F2; 45C3
Leigh Court, GW, 9B3
Leigh-on-Sea, LTS, 6A5
*Leigham Jc*, LBSC, 40E5
Leighton Buzzard, LNW, 10D1
Leiston, GE, 12C2
Leith, Cal & NB, 30B2 and inset
Leith Central, NB, 30 (inset)
Leith Walk (Goods), Cal, 30 (inset)
Lelant, GW, 1E4 (inset)
Leman Street, GE, 40C4
Lemington, NE, 27B5
Lenham, SEC, 6C4
Lennoxtown, NB, 29B5
Lenton (Goods), Mid, 16D4; 41G4
Lentran, HR, 36D5
Lenwade, MGN, 18E4
Lenzie, NB, 29B5; 44D5
Leominster, S&H, 9B1
*Leominster Jc* (Worcester), GW, 9B3
Leslie, NB, 30A1; 34G5
Lesmahagow, Cal, 30D5
*Lesmahagow Jc*, Cal, 44B2
Letchworth, GN, 11E2
Letham Grange, NB, 34D3
Lethenty, GNS, 37E3
Letterston, GW, 13F1
*Letterston Jc*, GW, 13F1
Leuchars Junc, NB, 34F4
Leuchars Old, NB, 34E4
Leven, NB, 30A1; 34G4
Levenshulme, LNW, 20C1; 24G1; 45A3
Leverton, GC, 16A2
Levisham, NE, 22A5; 28G2
Lewes, LBSC, 5F4
Lewes Road, LBSC, 5F3
Lewisham Junc, SEC, 40E3
Lewisham Road, SEC, 40E3
Lewknor Bridge Halt, GW, 10F3
Leyburn, NE, 21A2; 27G5
Leycett, NS, 15C3; 20F1
Leyland, NU, 20A3; 24E3
Leysdown, SEC, 6B3
Leysmill, Cal, 34D3
Leyton, GE & TFG, 40B3
Leytonstone, GE & TFG, 5A4; 40A2/B2
Lezayre, IMR, 23A3; 25C4
Lhanbryde, HR, 36C1
Lichfield (City), LNW, 15E5
Lichfield (Trent Valley), LNW, 15E5
Lidlington, LNW, 10C1
Liff, Cal, 34E5
Lifford, Mid, 9A4
Lifton, GW, 1B5
Lightcliffe, LY, 21E2; 42B5
Lightmoor Platform, GW, 15F2
Lilbourne, LNW, 10A4
Lillie Bridge Goods, WLE, 39D4
*Lilliehill Jc*, NB, 30A3
Lime Street (Liverpool), LNW, 20C4; 24G4; 45F4
*Limefield Jc*, Cal, 30C4
Limehouse, GE, 40C3
Limpley Stoke, GW, 3B3
Linacre Road, LY, 45F3
Linby, Mid & GN, 16C4; 41E4
Lincoln (Goods), GC, GN & Mid, 16B1 and inset
Lincoln (Pass), GN(GC/GE) & Mid, 16B1 and inset
Lindal, Fur, 24B4
Lindean, NB, 30E1
Lindores, NB, 34F5
Linefoot, MC, 26D3
Lingfield, LBSC, 5D4
Lingwood, GE, 18F2
Linley, GW, 15F2
Linlithgow, NB, 30B4
Linthwaite (Goods), LNW, 21E2; 42D5
Lintmill Halt, CM, 29 (inset)
Linton, GE, 11D4
Lintz Green, NE, 27C5
Linwood (Goods), Cal, 29C4; 44G3
Lion's Holt Halt, LSW, 2C3
Liphook, LSW, 4D1
*Lipson Jc*, GW, 1 (inset)
Lipson Vale Halt, GW, 1 (inset)
Liscard & Poulton, Wir(GC), 45F3
Liskeard, GW & LL, 1D4
Liss, LSW, 4D1
Lissens (Goods), Cal, 29D3
Litchfield (Hants), GW, 4B3
Little Bytham, GN, 16E1; 17E1
*Little Bytham Jc*, Mid/MGN, 16E1; 17E1
Little Eaton, Mid, 16C5; 41F2
*Little Eaton Jc*, Mid, 16C5; 41F2
Little Hulton, LY, 45B2
Little Kimble, GW&GCJt, 10E2
Little Mill, GW, 8B3; 43A2
*Little Mill Jc*, GW, 8B3; 43A2
Little Mill, NE, 31F5
Little Salkeld, Mid, 27D1
Little Somerford, GW, 9G4
Little Steeping, GN, 17B3
Little Sutton, BJ, 20D4; 45F5
Little Weighton, HB, 22D4
Littleborough, LY, 21E1
Littleham, LSW, 2C2
Littlehampton, LBSC, 5G1
*Littlehampton Jc*, LBSC, 5F1
Littlehaven Halt, LBSC, 5E2
Littlemore, GW, 10F4
Littleport, GE, 11A4; 17G4
Littleton & Badsey, GW, 9C4
Littleworth, GN, 17E2
Liverpool (Goods), CLC, GC, LNW, LY & Mid, 20 –; 24 –; 45 –
Liverpool (Pass), Central: CLC & Mer; Exchange: LY(Mid); Lime Street: LNW, 20 –; 24 –; 45 –
Liverpool Road (Chester), GC, 20D4
Liverpool Road Halt, NS, 20F1
Liverpool Street (London), GE & Met(Dist/GW/H&C), 5A3; 40C4
Liversedge, LNW & LY, 21E2; 42B4/C4
Livingston, NB, 30C4
Llanaber Halt, Cam, 13A5
Llanarthney, LNW, 13G5
Llanbadarn, VR, 13C5
Llanbedr & Pensarn, Cam, 19G2
Llanbedr Goch, LNW, 19C2
Llanberis, LNW & SM, 19E2
Llanbethery Halt, TV, 43C5
Llanbister Road, LNW, 14D2
Llanbradach, Rhy, 8B4; 43B3
Llanbrynmair, Cam, 14B4
Llandaff, TV, 8C4; 43B4
Llandderfel, GW, 19F5
Llandebie, GW(LNW), 7A3; 43G1
Llandenny, GW, 8A3
Llandilo, GW(LNW), 13G5
Llandilo Bridge, LNW, 13G5
Llandinam, Cam, 14C3
Llandovery, VT, 14F5
Llandow Halt, BRY, 43D5
Llandre, Cam, 13C5
Llandrillo, GW, 19F5
Llandrindod Wells, LNW, 14D3
Llandrinio Road, S&M, 14A2
Llandudno, LNW, 19C3
Llandudno Junc, LNW, 19D4
Llandulas, LNW, 19D4
Llandyssil, GW, 13F4
Llanelly, GW & LM(BPGV), 7B3
Llanelly Queen Victoria Road, LM, 7B3
Llanerch-Ayron Halt, GW, 13D4
Llanerchymedd, LNW, 19C1
Llanfabon Road Halt, TV, 43C3
Llanfair, LNW, 19D2
Llanfair Caereinion, W&L, 14B3
Llanfairfechan, LNW, 19D3
Llanfalteg, GW, 13G2
Llanfechain, Cam, 14A2; 20G5
Llanfyllin, Cam, 14A3
Llanfynydd, WM, 20E4
Llanfyrnach, GW, 13F3
Llangadock, VT, 14F5
Llangammarch Wells, LNW, 14E4
Llangedwyn, Tan, 14A2; 20G5
Llangefni, LNW, 19D1
Llangeinor, GW, 7B5; 43D3 *see also* Bettws
Llangennech, GW, 7B3
Llanglydwen, GW, 13G2

Llangollen, GW, 20F5
Llangonoyd, GW, 7B5; 43E3
Llangunllo, LNW, 14D2
Llangwyllog, LNW, 19C1
Llangybi (Cardigan), GW, 13E5
Llangybi (Carnarvon), LNW, 19F1
Llangyfelach, GW, 7B4; 43G2
Llangyfelach (Goods), GW, 43G2
Llangynog, Tan, 19G5
Llanharan, GW, 8C5; 43D4
Llanharry, TV, 8C5; 43C4
Llanhilleth, GW, 8B4; 43B2
*Llanhilleth Jc*, GW, 43B2
Llanidloes, Cam, 14C4
Llanilar, GW, 13D5
Llanishen, Rhy, 8C4; 43B4
Llanmorlais, LNW, 7B3
Llanpumpsaint, GW, 13F4
Llanrhaiadr, LNW, 19E5
Llanrhaiadr Mochnant, Tan, 14A3; 20G5
Llanrhystyd Road, GW, 13C5
Llanrwst & Trefriw, LNW, 19E4
Llansamlet, GW, 7B4
Llansantffraid, Cam, 14A2
Llansilin Road, Tan, 14A2; 20G5
Llantarnam, GW, 8B3 ; 43A3
Llantrisant, GW(TV) & TV, 8C5; 43C4
*Llantrisant Common Jc*, TV/GW, 43C4
Llantwit Major, BRY, 8D5; 43D5
Llanuwchllyn, GW, 19G4
Llanvihangel (Mon), GW, 8A3; 14G1
Llanwern, GW, 8B3
Llanwit, TV, 8C5; 43C4
Llanwnda, LNW, 19E2
Llanwrda, VT, 14F5
Llanwrtyd Wells, LNW, 14E4
Llanyblodwell, Tan, 14A2; 20G5
Llanybylher, GW, 13F5
Llan-y-Cefn, GW, 13G2
Llanymynech, Cam & S&M, 14A2; 20G4
Lletty Brongu, PT, 7B5; 43D3
Llong, LNW, 20E5
Llwydcoed, GW, 8A5; 43D2
Llwyn Gwern, Corris, 14B5
Llwyngwril, Cam, 13A5
Llwynypia, TV, 8B5; 43D3
Llynclys, Cam, 14A2; 20G4
Llysfaen, LNW, 19D4
Loanhead, NB, 30C2
Loch Awe, Cal, 32F2
Loch Leven (Goods), NB, 30A3; 33G5
Loch Skerrow, P&W, 25B5
Loch Tay, Cal, 33E2
Lochailort, NB, 32B5
Lochanhead, G&SW, 26B4
Locharbriggs, Cal, 26A3
Lochburn, NB, 44E4
Lochearnhead, Cal, 33F2
Lochee, Cal, 34E4
Lochee West, Cal, 34E4
Locheilside, NB, 32B3
*Lochend Jcs*, NB, 30 (inset)
Lochgelly, NB, 30A3
Lochgorm Works, HR, 36E5
*Lochgreen Jc*, G&SW, 29E3
Lochluichart, HR, 35C4
Lochmaben, Cal, 26A3
Lochmill, NB, 30B4
Lochmill (Goods), NB, 30B4
Lochside, G&SW, 29C3
Lochty Goods, NB, 34F4
Lochwinnoch, G&SW, 29C3
Lockerbie, Cal, 26A3
Lockington, NE, 22C4
Lockwood, LY, 21E2; 42D5
Loddington, Mid, 10A2
Loddiswell, GW, 2E4
Lodge Hill, GW, 3B2; 8E2
Lofthouse & Outwood, GN(GC) & MJ, 21E3; 42B2
Lofthouse-in-Nidderdale, NV, 21B2
Loftus, NE, 28E3
*Logan Jc*, G&SW, 29F5
Logiereve, GNS, 37E4
Login, GW, 13G2
Londesborough, NE, 22D5
London, 5 –; 39 –; 40 –
London Bridge, LBSC & SEC, 5B3; 40D4
London Fields, GE, 40B4
London Road (Guildford), LSW, 5C1
London Road (Manchester), LNW(NS), GC & MSJA, 20B1; 24F1; 45A3
London Road (Nottingham), GN(LNW), 41G5
London Road (Brighton), LBSC, 5F3
*London Road Jc* (Derby), Mid, 16D5
Long Buckby, LNW, 10B3
Long Clawson & Hose, GN&LNWJt, 16D2
Long Eaton, Mid, 16D4; 41G3
Long Marston, GW, 9C5
Long Marton, Mid, 27E2
Long Melford, GE, 12D5
Long Preston, Mid, 24C1
Long Road, GW, 9C5
Long Stanton, GE(Mid), 11C3
Long Stow (Goods), Mid, 11B1
Long Sutton (Lincs), MGN, 17E3
Long Sutton & Pitney (Som), GW, 3D1; 8F2
Long Witton, NB, 27A4
Longcliffe (Goods), LNW, 15C5
Longdown, GW, 2B3
Longfield Halt for Rindon & Westwood, SEC, 5B5
Longford & Exhall, LNW, 10A5; 16G5
Longforgan, Cal, 4E5; 34E5
Longhaven, GNS, 37D5
*Longhedge Jc*, WLE/SEC, 39E3 (inset)
Longhope, GW, 8A1; 9E2
Longhoughton, NE, 31F5
Longhurst, NE, 27A5
Longmorn, GNS, 36D2
Longniddry, NB, 30B1
Longparish, LSW, 4C4
Longport, NS, 15C3; 20E1
Longridge, PL, 24D2
Longriggend, NB, 30C5
Longside, GNS, 37D5
Longsight, LNW, 45A3
Longton, NS, 15C3; 20F1
Longton Bridge, LY, 20A3; 24E3
Longtown, NB, 26B1
Longville, GW, 15F1
*Longville Jc*, LNW/GN, 11A1; 17F2
Longwood & Milnsbridge, LNW, 21E2; 42D5
Lonlas South Private Platform, Mid, 43F2
Lonmay, GNS, 37C4
Looe, LL, 1D4
Lord Street (Southport), CLC, 20A4; 24E3; 45F1
Lord's Bridge, LNW, 11C3
Lordship Lane for Forest Hill, SEC, 40E4
Lossiemouth, GNS, 36C1
Lostock Gralam, CLC, 15A2; 20D2; 45C5
Lostock Hall, LY, 20A3; 24E3
Lostock Junc, LY, 20B2; 24F2; 45C2
Lostwithiel, GW, 1D3
Loth, HR, 38G4
Lothian Road (Goods), Cal, 30F2 (inset)
Loudounhlll, G&SW, 29E5
Loudwater, GW, 5A1; 10F2
Loughborough, Mid, GC & LNW, 16E4
Loughborough Junc, SEC, 40E5
Loughor, GW, 7B3
Loughton, GE, 5A4; 11G3
*Loughton Jc*, GE, 40B3
Louth, GN, 17A3; 22G2
*Loversall Carr Jc*, GN/DV, 21F5
Low Bentham (Goods), Mid, 24B2
*Low Ellers Jc*, SYJ, 21F2
Low Fell, NE, 27C5 and 28 (inset)
Low Gill, LNW, 27G1
Low Moor, LY(GN), LY & GN, 21E2; 42B4
Low Row, NE, 27C1
Low Street, LTS, 5B5
Lowca, CWJ, 26E3
Lowdham, Mid, 16C3
Lower Darwen, LY, 20A2; 24E2
Lower Edmonton, GE, 5A3
Lower Ince, GC, 45D2 *see also* Ince (Lancs)
Lower Penarth, TV, 8D4; 43B5
Lower Sydenham, SEC, 40F3
Lowesby, GN, 16F2
Lowestoft, GE(MGN), 12A1; 18G1
*Lowestoft Line Jc*, MGN, 18F1
Lowestoft North, NSJ, 12A1; 18F1
Lowthorpe, NE, 22C3
Lowton, LNW, 20C2; 24G2; 45D3
Lowton St Mary's, GC, 45C3
Lowtown (Pudsey), GN, 21D2; 42A4
Lubenham, LNW, 16G3
Lucas Terrace, GW, 1 (inset)
Lucker, NE, 31E4
Luckett, BAC, 1C5
Ludborough, GN, 22G2
Luddendenfoot, LY, 21E1
Luddington, AJ, 22E5
*Ludgate Jc*, LSW, 39E3 (inset)
Ludgershall (Wilts), MSW, 4B5
Ludlow, S&H, 9A1
Luffenham, Mid(LNW), 16F1
Luffness Halt, NB, 30B1
Lugar, G&SW, 29F5
Lugton, Cal & GBK, 29D4
Luib, Cal, 33E1
Lumphanan, GNS, 37G2
Lunan Bay, NB, 34D3
Luncarty, Cal(HR), 33E5
Lundin Links, NB, 34G4
Lunlas South Private Platform, GW, 43F2
Lustleigh, GW, 2C4
Luthrie, NB, 34F5
Luton, Mid & GN(LNW), 11E1
Luton Hoo, GN, 11F1
Lutterworth, GC, 10 A4; 16G4 *see also* Ullesthorpe
Luxulyan, GW, 1D3
Lybster, HR, 38E2
Lydbrook Junc, GW & SVW, 8A2; 9E1
Lydd, SEC, 6E3
Lydford, LSW & GW, 1C5
Lydham Heath, BC, 14C1

Lydiate, CLC, 20B4; 24F4; 45F2
Lydney, GW, 8B1; 9F2
Lydney Junc, SVW, 8B1; 9E2
Lydney Town, SVW, 8A1; 9E2
Lydstep, GW, 7D2
Lye, GW, 9A3; 15G3
Lyghe Halt, SEC, 5D5
Lyme Regis, LSW, 3F1
Lyminge, SEC, 6D3
*Lymington Jc*, LSW, 4D4
Lymington Pier, LSW, 4F4
Lymington Town, LSW, 4F4
Lymm, LNW, 20C2; 24G2; 45C4
Lympstone, LSW, 2C3
Lyndhurst Road, LSW, 4E4
Lyne, Cal, 30D2
Lynedoch, G&SW, 29B3
Lyneside, NB, 26B1
Lynton, LB, 7E4
*Lyon Cross Jc*, Cal, 44F2
Lyonshall, GW, 14E1
Lytham, PWY, 20A4; 24E4

Mablethorpe, GN, 17A4
Macbie Hill, NB, 30D3
Macclesfield (Goods), LNW&NSJt & GC&NSJt, 15A3; 20D1; 45A5
Macclesfield Central, NS, 15A3; 20D1; 45A5
Macclesfield, Hibel Road, LNW(NS), 15A3; 20D1; 45A5
Macduff, GNS, 37C2
Machen, BM(Rhy), 8B4; 43B3
Machrihanish, CM, 29 (inset)
Machrihanish Farm Halt, CM, 29 (inset)
Machynlleth, Cam & Cor, 14B5
Macmerry, NB, 30B1
Madderty, Cal, 33F4
Madeley (Salop), GW, 15F2
Madeley (Staffs), LNW, 15C3; 20F1
*Madeley Jc*, GW, 15E2
Madeley Market, LNW, 15F2
Madeley Road, NS, 15C3; 20F1
Maenclochog, GW, 13F2
Maentwrog Road, GW, 19F3
Maerdy, TV, 8B5; 43D2
*Maesaraul Jc*, TV/GW, 43C4
Maesbrook, S&M, 14A2; 20C4
Maesteg, GW & PT, 7B5, 43E3
Maesycrugiau, GW, 13F4
Maesycwmmer & Hengoed, BM, 43B3 *see also* Hengoed
*Maesycwmmer Jc*, BM/GW, 43B3
Magdalen Green (Dundee), Cal, 34E2 (inset)
Magdalen Road, GE, 17F4
Maghull, LY, 20B4; 24F4; 45F2 *see also* Sefton
Magor, GW, 8C3
Maiden Lane (Goods), LNW, 40B5
Maiden Lane (Pass), NL, 40B5
Maiden Newton, GW, 3F2
Maidenhead, GW, 4A1; 5B1; 10G2
Maidens, G&SW, 29G3
Maidstone, SEC, 6C5
*Maindee Jcs*, GW, 8B3; 43A3
Malden, LSW, 5B3; 39F3
Maldon East & Heybridge, GE, 12F5
Maldon West, GE, 12F5
Malins Lee, LNW, 15E2
Mallaig, NB, 32A5
*Mallaig Jc*, NB, 32C3
Malling, SEC, 5C5
Mallwyd, Mawd, 14A4
Malmesbury, GW, 9F3
Malpas, LNW, 15C1; 20E3
Maltby, SYJ, 21G4
Malton, NE, 22B5
Malvern Link, GW, 9C3
Malvern Road (Cheltenham), GW, 9D4
Malvern Wells, GW & Mid, 9C3
Manchester (Goods), CLC, GC, GN, LNW, LY & Mid, 20 –; 24 –; 45 –
Manchester (Pass), 20 –; 24 –; 45 –; Central: CLC Exchange: LNW(BJ); London Road: LNW(NS), GC & MSJA; Victoria: LY(LNW/Mid), 20B1; 24F1; 45A3
Manchester Docks, LY, 45B3
*Manchester Line Jc*, LNW, 15C2; 20E2
Manchester Road (Burnley), LY, 24D1
Manea, GE, 11A3; 17G4
Mangotsfield, Mid, 3A3; 8C1; 9G2
Manley Goods, CLC, 15B2; 20D3; 45E5
Manningham, Mid(NE), 21D2; 42A4
Manningtree, GE, 12E4
*Manningtree N & E Jcs*, GE, 12E4
Manod, GW, 19F3
Manor Park for Little Ilford, GE, 40E2
Manor Way, PLA(GE), 40C1
Manorbier, GW, 7D2
Manors, NE, 28 (inset)
Mansfield, Mid(GC) & GC, 16B4; 41D4
Mansfield Woodhouse, Mid(GC), 16B4; 41D4
Mansion House, Dist(Met), 40C5
Manton, Mid, 16F2
Manuel, NB, 30B4
Marazion, GW, 1F4 (inset)
March, GE, 11A3; 17F3
*March N, S & W Jcs*, GE, 11A3; 17F5
Marchington, NS(GN), 15D5
Marchmont, NB, 31D2
Marchwiel, Cam, 20E4
Marden, SEC, 6D5
Mardock, GE, 11F3
*Mardy Jc*, GW/GW&TVJt, 43C2
*Marefield N, S & W Jcs*, GN/GN&LNWJt, 16F2
Marfleet, NE, 22D3
*Margam Jc*, GW/PT, 7B4; 43F3
Margaretting Halt, GE, 11G5
Margate, SEC, 6B1
Marishes Road, NE, 22A5
Mark Lane, Dist&MetJt, 40C4
Mark's Tey, GE, 12E5
Market Bosworth, AN, 16F5
Market Drayton, GW(NS), 15D2; 20F2
*Market Drayton Jc* (Nantwich), LNW/GW, 15C2; 20E2
*Market Drayton Jc* (Wellington), SWN/GW, 15E2
Market Harborough, LNW & Mid, 16G2
Market Place (Chesterfield), GC, 16B5; 41C2
Market Rasen, GC, 17A1; 22G3
Market Street (Bradford), Mid(NE), 42A4
Market Weighton, NE, 22D4
Markham Village, LNW, 43B2
Markinch, NB, 30A2; 34G5
Marlborough, GW & MSW, 4A5
Marlborough Road, Met, 39B5
Marlow, GW, 10G2
Marlpool, GN, 16C4; 41F3
Marple, GC&MidJt, 21G1 *see also* Rose Hill
*Marron West Jc*, LNW/WCE, 26E3
Marsden (Durham), SSM, 28B5
Marsden (Yorks), LNW, 21F1
Marsden Cottage, SSM, 28B5
Marsh Brook, S&H, 14C1; 15G1
*Marsh Farm Jc*, S&H/GW, 14C1; 15G1
Marsh Gate (Goods), GC, 21G2 (inset)
Marsh Gibbon & Poundon, LNW, 10D3
*Marsh Jc*, GE, 12A1; 18F1
Marsh Lane (Lancs), LY, 45F3
Marsh Lane (Yorks), NE, 21D3; 42A2
Marsh Mills, GW, 2D5
Marshfield, GW, 8C3; 43A4
*Marshland Jc*, NE/AJ, 22E5
Marske, NE, 28E3
Marston Gate, LNW, 10E2
Marston Green, LNW, 15G5
Marston Magna, GW, 3D2; 8G1
Marston Moor, NE, 21C4
Martham, MGN, 18E1
Martock, GW, 3D2; 8G2
Marton, LNW, 10A5
*Marton Jc*, LNW, 10B5
Maryfield (Dundee), Cal, 34E4
Maryhill, Cal & NB, 29C5; 44E4
Marykirk, Cal, 34C3
Maryland Point, GE, 40B2
Marylebone, GC, 5A3; 39C5
Maryport, M&C(LNW), 26D3
Marytavy & Blackdown, GW, 1C5
Masbury, SD, 3C2; 8E1
Masham, NE, 21A3
Massingham, MGN, 18E5
Matlock, Mid, 16B5; 41D1
Matlock Bath, Mid, 16B5; 41D1
Matthews Town Halt, TV, 43C3
Mauchline, G&SW, 29E4
Maud Junc, GNS, 37D4
Maud's Bridge (Goods), GC, 22F5
Mauldeth Road, LNW, 45A3
Mawcarse Junc, NB, 33G5
Maxton, NB, 31E1
Maxwell Park, Cal, 44E3 and inset
Maxwelltown, G&SW, 26B4
May Hill (Monmouth), GW, 8A2; 9E1
Maybole, G&SW, 29F3
Mayfield (Manchester), LNW, 45A3
Mayfield (Sussex), LBSC, 5E5
Maze Hill (East Greenwich), SEC, 40D3
Meadow Hall & Wincobank, GC, 42F2 *see also* Wincobank
Mealsgate, M&C, 26D2
Measham, AN, 16E5
Medge Hall, GC, 22F5
Medina Wharf, IWC, 4F3
Medina Wharf (Goods), IWC, 4F3
Medstead, LSW, 4C2
Meigle, Cal, 34D5
Meikle Earnock, Cal, 29D5; 44B1
Meir, NS, 15C4
Melangoose Mill, GW, 1D2
Melbourne, Mid, 16D5
Melcombe Regis, WP, 3G3
Meldon, NB, 27A5
*Meldon Jc*, LSW, 2B5
Meldreth & Melbourn, GN, 11D3
Meledor Mill, GW, 1D2
Meliden, LNW, 19C5
Melksham, GW, 3A4
Melling, Fur&MidJt, 24B2

Mellis, GE, 12B4
Mells Road, GW, 3B3; 8E1
Melmerby, NE, 21A3
Melrose, NB, 31E1
Meltham, LY, 21F2; 42D5
*Meltham Branch Jc*, LY, 42D5
Melton, GE, 12D3
Melton Constable, MGN, 18D4
*Melton Jc*, Mid, 16E2
Melton Mowbray, Mid(MGN) & GN&LNWJt, 16E2
Melverley, S&M, 14A1
Melyncourt Halt, GW, 43E2
Menai Bridge, LNW, 19D2
Mendlesham, MSL, 12C4
Menheniot, GW, 1D4
Menston, Mid(NE), 21D2
Menstrie & Glenochil, NB, 30A5
Menthorpe Gate, NE, 21D5
Meole Brace, S&M, 14B1; 15E1
Meols, Wir, 20C5
Meols Cop, LY, 20A4; 24E4; 45F1
Meopham, SEC, 5B5
Merchiston, Cal, 30 (inset)
*Merrybent Jc*, NE, 27E5
*Merryton Jc*, Cal, 44B1
Mersey Road & Aigburth, CLC, 45F4
Merstham, SEC, 5C3
Merstone, IWC, 4F3
Merthyr, GW(BM/LNW/TV) & TV, 8A5; 43C2
Merthyr Vale, TV, 8B5; 43C2
Merton Abbey, LBSC&LSWJt, 39F5
Merton Park, LBSC&LSWJt, 39F4
Methil, NB, 30A2; 34G4
Methley, Mid(LY), LY & MJ, 21E4; 42B1
*Methley Jc*, GN&LY&NEJt/LY/Mid, 42B1
Methven, Cal, 33E4
*Methven Jc*, Cal, 33E4
*Metropolitan Jc*, SEC, 40C5
Mexborough, GC(Mid), 21F4
Micheldever, LSW, 4C3
Micklam, CWJ, 26E3
Mickle Trafford, BJ & CLC, 15B1; 20D3
Micklefield, NE, 21D4; 42A1
Micklehurst (Goods), LNW, 21F1
Mickleover, GN, 16D5; 41G1
Mickleton, NE, 27E4
Mid Clyth, HR, 38E2
*Mid Suffolk Light Railway*, MSL, 12B3; 12C3
Midcalder, Cal, 30C3
*Midcalder Jc*, Cal, 30B3
Middle Drove, GE, 17F4
Middle Stoke Halt, SEC, 6B5
*Middlemuir Jc*, NB, 44C5
Middlesbrough, NE, 28E4
Middlestown, Mid, 42C3
*Middlestown Jc*, Mid, 42C3
Middleton (Lancs), LY, 20B1; 24F1; 45A2
Middleton (Norfolk), GE, 17E5
Middleton (Northumb), NE, 27A4
Middleton (Salop), S&H, 9A1
Middleton (Westmorland), LNW, 24A2; 27G1
Middleton-in-Teesdale, NE, 27E3
Middleton Junc, LY, 20B1; 45A2
Middleton-on-the-Wolds, NE, 22C4
Middleton Road Goods (Heysham), Mid, 24C3
Middletown, SWP, 14A2
Middlewich, LNW, 20D2
Middlewood, LNW & GC&NSJt, 15A4
Midford, SD, 3B3; 8D1
Midford Halt, GW, 3B3; 8D1
Midge Hall, LY, 20A3; 24E3
Midgham, GW, 4A3
Midhurst, LBSC, 5E1
Midhurst, LSW, 4D1; 5E1
Midsomer Norton & Welton, GW & SD, 3B3; 8E1
Midville, GN, 17C3
Milborne Port, LSW, 3D3; 8G1
Milcote, GW, 9B5
Mildenhall, GE, 11B5
Mildmay Park, NL, 40B4
Mile End, WB, 40C3
Miles Platting, LY, 20B1; 24F1; 45A3
Milford (Surrey), LSW, 5D1
Milford & Brocton, LNW, 15E4
Milford Haven, GW, 7D1
*Milford Jc* (Wilts), LSW, 4D5
*Milford Jc* (Yorks), NE, 21D4
Milkwall for Clearwell, SVW, 8A2; 9E1
Mill Hill (IoW), IWC, 4F3
Mill Hill (Lancs), LY(LNW), 20A2; 24E2
Mill Hill (Middx), Mid & GN, 5A3
Mill Houses, Mid, 16A5
Mill Road Halt, GE, 11E4
Mill Street Goods (Aberdare), GW, 8A5; 43D2
Millbay (Plymouth), GW, 1D5 and inset
Millbrook (Beds), LNW, 10C1; 11D1
Millbrook (Hants), LSW(MSW), 4E4
Millerhill, NB, 30B2
Miller's Dale, Mid, 15A5
*Millers Dale Jc*, Mid, 15A5
Millfield, NE, 28C5
Millhouses & Ecclesall, Mid, 16A5; 41A2
Milliken Park, G&SW, 29C4
Millisle, P&W, 25D4
Millom, Fur, 24A5
Milltimber, GNS, 37G3
Millwall Docks, GE, 40D3
Millwall Junc, GE, 40C3 and inset D1
*Millwood Jc*, Fur, 24B5
Milnathort, NB, 33G5
*Milner Royd Jc*, LY, 21E1; 42C5
*Milner Wood Jc*, Mid/O&I, 21C2
Milngavie, NB 29B4; 44E5
*Milngavie Jc*, NB, 29C4; 44E5
Milnrow, LY, 20B1; 45A1
Milnthorpe, LNW, 24A3
Milton (Staffs), NS, 15C3; 20E1
Milton Halt, GW, 10C4
*Milton Jc* (Glasgow), Cal, 44D4
Milton of Campsie, NB, 29B5
Milton Road, WCP, 3A1; 8D3
Milverton (Som), GW, 8F4
Milverton (Warwick), LNW, 10B5
Mindrum, NE, 31E3
Minehead, GW, 8E5
Minety & Ashton Keynes, GW, 9F4
Minffordd, Cam & Fest, 19F2
Minions, LC, 1C4
*Minories Jc*, Met/Dist, 40C4
Minshull Vernon, LNW, 15B2; 20E2
Minster (Thanet), SEC, 6C2
*Minster 'B' Jc*, SEC, 6C2
*Minster East Jc*, SEC, 6C2
*Minster West Jc*, SEC, 6C2
Minster-On-Sea (Sheppey), SEC, 6B4
Minsterley, SWP, 14B1
Mint Street Goods, GN & Mid, 40C4
Mintlaw, GNS, 37D4
*Mirehouse Jc*, Fur, 26F3
Mirfield, LY(LNW), 21E2; 42C4
Mislingford (Goods), LSW, 4E3
Misson (Goods), GN, 21G5
Misterton, GN&GEJt, 22G5
Mistley, GE, 12E4
Mitcham, LBSC, 5B3; 39G5
Mitcham Junc, LBSC, 5B3; 39G5
Mitcheldean Road, GW, 9D2
Mitchell & Newlyn Halt, GW, 1D1
Mithian Halt, GW, 1D1
Mitre Bridge Goods, LNW, 39C4
*Mitre Bridge Jc*, LNW, 39C3
Moat Lane Junc, Cam, 14C3
Mobberley, CLC, 20C1; 15A3; 45B5
Mochdre & Pabo, LNW, 19D4
Moffat, Cal, 30G3
Moira, Mid, 16E5
Mold, LNW, 20E5
*Mold Jc*, LNW, 20D4
Mollington, BJ, 20D4
Molyneux Brow, LY, 45B2
*Molyneux Jc*, LY/LNW, 45B2
Moniaive, G&SW, 26A5
Monifieth, D&A, 34E4
Monikie, Cal, 34D4
Monk Bretton, Mid, 21F3; 42E2
*Monk Bretton Jc*, Mid/HB, 42E2
Monk Fryston, NE(LY/GN), 21D4
Monkhill (Pontefract), LY(NE), 21E4; 42C1
*Monkland Jc*, NB, 44C5
Monks Lane Halt, LBSC, 5C4
Monkseaton, NE, 28B5
Monkton, G&SW, 29E3
Monkton & Came Halt, GW, 3F3
Monkton Combe, GW, 3B3; 8D1
Monkwearmouth, NE, 28C5
Monmore Green, LNW, 15F3
Monmouth, GW, 8A2; 9E1
Monsal Dale, Mid, 15B5
Montacute, GW, 3D2; 8G2
Montgomerie Pier (Ardrossan), Cal, 29D3
Montgomery, Cam, 14B2
Montgreenan, G&SW, 29D3
Monton Green, LNW, 45B3
Montpelier, CE, 3 (inset)
Montrave (Goods), NB, 34G4
Montrose, NB & Cal, 34C2
Monument, Dist&MetJt, 40C4
Monument Lane, LNW, 13C3
Monymusk, GNS, 37F2
Moor End (Goods), GC, 21F3; 42E3
Moor Row, WCE, 26F3
Moor Street Wharf (Burton-on-Trent), LNW, 15D5 (inset)
*Moorbridge Jc*, GN/GC, 16C4; 41F4
Moore, LNW, 15A1; 20C3; 45D4
Moorfields Goods (Hereford), Mid, 9C1
Moorgate, LNW, 21F1
Moorgate Street, Met(Dist/GN/GW/H&C/Mid), 40C4
Moorhampton, Mid, 14E1
Moorhouse & South Elmsall, HB, 21F4; 42 D1
Moorside & Wardley, LY, 45B2
*Moorswater Jc*, LL/LC, 1D4
Moorthorpe & South Elmsall, SK(GC), 21F4; 42D1
*Moorthorpe South Jc*, SK(GC), 42D1

Moortown, GC, 22F3
Morar, NB, 32B5
Morchard Road, LSW, 2A4
Morcott, LNW, 16F1
Morden Halt (Surrey), LBSC, 39F5
Morebath, GW, 8F5
Morecambe, Mid & LNW, 24B3
Moresby Parks, CWJ, 26E3
Moreton (Ches), Wir, 20C5; 24G4
Moreton (Dorset), LSW, 3F3
Moreton-in-Marsh, GW, 9D5
Moreton-on-Lugg, S&H, 9C1
Moretonhampstead, GW, 2B4
*Morlais Jc*, BM/LNW, 8A5; 43C1
Morley, LNW & GN, 21E3; 42B3
Mormond, GNS, 37C4
Morningside Road, NB, 30 (inset)
Morningside, Cal & NB, 30C5
Morpeth, NE(NB), 27A5
Morriston, GW & Mid, 7B4; 43G2
Mortehoe, LSW(GW), 7E3
Mortimer, GW, 4A2
Mortlake, LSW, 5B2; 39E3
Morton Pinkney, SMJ, 10C4
Morton Road, GN, 17E1
Moseley, Mid, 15G4
Moses Gate, LY, 45B2
Moss (Denbigh) & Pentre, GC, 20E4
Moss (Yorks), NE, 21E5
Moss Bank, LNW, 20B3; 24F3; 45D3
Moss Halt (Denbigh), GW, 20E4
Moss Road Halt, CM, 29 (inset)
Moss Side, PWY, 24D4
*Mossblown Jc*, G&SW, 29E4
Mossbridge, CLC, 20B4; 24F4; 45F2
Mossend, Cal, 30C5; 44B3
Mossley Halt, NS, 15B3; 20E1
Mossley, LNW, 21F1
Mossley Hill for Aigburth, LNW, 20C4; 24G4; 45F4
Mosstowie, HR, 36C2
Moston, LY, 20B1; 24F1; 45A2
Mostyn, LNW, 20C5
Motherwell, Cal, 30C5; 44B2
Mottisfont, LSW(MSW), 4D4
Mottram & Broadbottom, GC, 21G1
Mouldsworth, CLC, 15B2; 20D3; 45D5
Moulinearn Crossing, HR, 33D4
Moulton (Lincs), MGN, 17E3
Moulton (Yorks), NE, 27F5
Mount Florida, Cal, 44E3
*Mount Gould Jc*, GW, 1 (inset)
Mount Hawke Halt, GW, 1E1
Mount Melville, NB, 34F4
Mount Pleasant, NE, 28B5
Mount Pleasant Road Halt, LSW, 2C3
Mount Vernon, Cal & NB, 29C5; 44C3
Mountain Ash, GW & TV, 8B5; 43C2
Mow Cop & Scholar Green, NS, 15B3; 20E1
Moy, HR, 36E4
Much Wenlock, GW, 15F2
Muchalls, Cal, 34A1
Muir of Ord, HR, 35D5
Muirend, Cal, 29C5; 44E2
*Muirhouse South Jc*, Cal, 44F1 (inset)
Muirkirk, G&SW(Cal), 29E5
Mulben, HR, 36D1
Mumbles Pier, Mum, 7B3; 43G3
Mumbles Road, LNW & Mum, 7B3; 43G3
Mumby Road, GN, 17A4
Mumps (Oldham) LY, 21D1 (inset)
Muncaster, RE, 26G3
Mundesley-on-Sea, NSJ, 18D2
Munlochy, HR, 36D5
Murrayfield, Cal, 30 (inset)
Murrow, GN&GEJt & MGN, 17F3
Murthly, HR, 33E5
Murtle, GNS, 37G4
Murton, NE, 28C5
Murton Lane, DVL, 21C5
Musgrave, NE, 27F2
Musselburgh, NB, 30B2
Muswell Hill, GN(NL), 5A3; 40A5
Muthill, Cal, 33F4
Mutley, GW(LSW), 1A2 (inset)
*Mwyndy Jc*, GW, 43C4
Mynydd-y-Garreg (Goods), GV, 7A2
*Myrtle Hill Jc*, GW, 13G4
Mytholmroyd, LY, 21E1

Naburn, NE, 21C5
Nafferton, NE, 22C3
Nailsea & Backwell, GW, 3A2; 8D2
Nailsworth, Mid, 9F3
Nairn, HR, 36D4
Nancegollan, GW, 1F5 (inset)
Nannerch, LNW, 20D5
Nanstallon Halt, LSW, 1D3
Nantclwyd, LNW, 19E5
Nantgaredig, LNW, 13G4
Nantgarw Halt, AD & Car, 43C3
Nantlle, LNW, 19E2
Nantmawr, Cam, 20G5
Nantwich, LNW(GW), 15C2; 20E2
Nantybwch, LNW, 8A4; 43C1
Nantybwch, Rhy, 9A5; 43C1
Nantyderry, GW, 8A3; 43A2
Nantyffyllon, GW, 7B5; 43E3
Nantyglo, GW, 8A4; 43B1
Nantymoel, GW, 7B5; 43D3
Nantyronen, VR, 14C5
Napsbury, Mid, 11G1
Napton & Stockton, LNW, 10B4
Narberth, GW, 7C3
Narborough (Leics), LNW, 16F4
Narborough (Norfolk), GE, 17E5
Nassington, LNW, 11A1; 16F1; 17F1
Nast Hyde Halt, GN, 11F2
Nateby, KE, 24D3
Navenby, GN, 16B1; 17C1
Naworth, NE, 27C1
Nawton, NE, 21A5
Neasden & Kingsbury, Met, 5A2; 39B4
*Neasden Jc*, GC/Mid, 39B3
Neasden Railway Works, LNW, 39B3; 36E5
Neath, GW, GW(N&B), RSB & N&B, 7B4; 43F2
Neath Abbey, GW, 7B4; 43F2
*Neath Jc*, RSB, 43F3
Neath Low Level, RSB, 43F2
Needham, GE, 12C4
*Needingworth Jc*, GN&GEJt/GE, 11B3
Neen Sollars, GW, 9A2
Neepsend, GC, 21G3; 42G2
Neilston, GBK & Cal, 29C4; 44G2
Nelson (Glam), TV, 8B4; 43C3
Nelson (Lancs), LY, 21B1 (inset); 24D1
Neptune Street (Goods) (Hull), HB, 22 (inset)
Nesscliff & Pentre, S&M, 14A1
Neston & Parkgate, GC, 20D4; 45F5
Neston, BJ, 20D4; 45F5
Netherburn, Cal, 30D5
Nethercleugh, Cal, 26A3
Netherfield, GN(LNW), 16C3; 41F5 *see also* Carlton, Mid
Netherton Goods (Fife), NB, 30A3
Netherton Goods (Renfrew), Cal, 29C4; 44F2
Netherton (Staffs), GW, 13B1; 15G4
Netherton (Yorks), LY, 21E2; 42D5
Nethertown, Fur, 26F3
Nethy Bridge, GNS, 36F3
Netley, LSW, 4E3
New Barnet, GN(NL), 5A3; 11G2
New Basford, GC, 41F4
New Beckenham, SEC, 40F3
*New Beckenham Jc*, SEC, 40F3
New Biggin, Mid, 27E1
New Bolingbroke, GN, 17C3
New Brighton, Wir, 20C4; 24G4; 45F3
New Clee, GC, 22F2
New Cross (Goods), GE, 40D3
New Cross (Pass), LBSC(EL) & SEC(EL), 40D3
New Cumnock, G&SW, 29F5
New Cut Lane Halt, LY, 20B4; 24F4; 45F1
New Eltham & Pope Street, SEC, 5B4; 40E1
New England Sidings, GN, 11A2; 17F2
New Galloway, P&W, 26B5
New Hailes, NB, 30B2
New Hall Bridge Halt, LY, 24D1
New Hey, LY, 21F1
New Holland, GC, 22E3
*New Inn Yard Jc*, NL/LNW, 40C4
New Lane, LY, 20A4; 24F3; 45E1
New Luce, G&SW, 25B2
New Machar, GNS, 37F4
New Mills (Derbys), LNW, Mid & GC&MidJt, 15A4; 21G1
New Milton, LSW, 4F5
New Monkton Main Colliery, WRG, 42D1
New Radnor, GW, 14E2
New Road (Ynysybwl), TV, 43C3
New Romney & Littlestone-on-Sea, SEC, 6E3
New Street (Birmingham), LNW&MidJt, 13C3; 15G4
New Tredegar & Tir Phil, BM, 8A4; 43B2 *see also* Tir Phil
New Wandsworth, LBSC, 39F2 (inset)
Newark, GN & Mid, 16C2
Newarthill (Goods), Cal, 44A2
Newbiggin-by-the-Sea, NE, 28A5
Newbigging, Cal, 30D4
Newbridge (Mon), GW, 43B2
Newbridge-on-Wye, Cam, 14E3
Newburgh, NB, 34F5
Newburn, NE, 27B5; 28 (inset)
Newbury, GW, 4A3
Newbury (West Fields) Halt, GW, 4A3
Newbury Park, GE, 40A1
Newbury Racecourse, GW, 4A3
Newby Wiske, NE, 21A3; 28G5
Newcastle Emlyn, GW, 13F3
Newcastle-on-Tyne, NE(NB) & NE, 27B5/C5; 28 (inset)
Newcastle-under-Lyme, NS, 15C3; 20F1
Newcastleton, NB, 27A1
Newchapel & Goldenhill, NS, 15C3; 20E1
Newchurch, IWC, 4F3
Newent, GW, 9D2

Newham (Northumb), NE, 31E5
Newham Goods (Truro), GW, 1E1
Newhaven (Leith), Cal, 30 (inset)
Newhaven Harbour (Sussex), LBSC, 5F4
Newhaven Town (Sussex), LBSC, 5F4
Newhouse, Cal, 30C5; 44A3
Newick & Chailey, LBSC, 5E4
Newington (Edinburgh), NB, 30 (inset)
Newington (Kent), SEC, 6B4
Newland, GW, 8A2; 9E1
Newlay & Horsforth, Mid, 21D3; 42A3
Newmains, Cal, 30C5
Newmarket Warren Hill, GE, 11C4
Newmilns, G&SW, 29E4
Newnham, GW, 8A1; 9E2
Newnham Bridge, GW, 9A2
Newpark, Cal, 30C3
Newport (East Riding), HB, 22D5
Newport (Essex), GE, 11E4
Newport (IoW), IWC(FYN) & FYN, 4F3
Newport (Mon) (Alexandra Dock), AD, 8C3; 43A4
Newport (Mon), GW(LNW/BM) & GW, 8B3; 43A3
Newport (North Riding), NE, 28E4
Newport (Salop), LNW, 15E2
Newport Pagnell, LNW, 10C2
Newquay, GW, 1D1
Newseat, GNS, 37D5
Newsham, NE, 28A5
Newsholme, LY, 24C1
Newstead, Mid & GN, 16C4; 41E4
*Newstead Lane Jc*, MGN/NSJ, 18D3
Newthorpe, GN, 41F3
Newton (Ches), GC, 21G1
Newton (Lanarks), Cal, 29C5; 44C3
Newton Abbot, GW, 2C3
Newton Heath, LY, 20B1; 24F1; 45A2
*Newton Jc*, NB, 44C3
Newton Kyme, NE, 21D4
Newton-le-Willows, LNW(BJ), 20C3; 24G2; 45D3
Newton-on-Ayr, G&SW, 29F3
Newton Poppleford, LSW, 2B2
Newton Road, LNW, 13B3; 15F4
Newton St Cyres, LSW, 2B3
Newton Stewart, P&W, 25B4
Newton Tony, LSW, 4C5
Newtonairds, G&SW, 26A4
Newtongrange, NB, 30C2
Newtonhill, Cal, 34A1
Newtonmore, HR, 33A2
Newtown (Mon), Cam, 14C3
Newtyle, Cal, 34D5
Neyland, GW, 7D2
Nidd Bridge, NE, 21C3
Niddrie, NB, 30B2
Nigg, HR, 36B4
Nine Elms Goods, LSW, 40D5
Nine Mile Point, LNW, 8B4; 43B3
*Nine Wells Jc*, Cal, 34E4 and inset G2
Ningwood, FYN, 4F4
Nisbet, NB, 31E1
Nitshill, GBK, 29C4; 44F3
No 5 Pet Sidings, M&C, 26D3
Nocton & Dunston, GN&GEJt, 16B1; 17B1
Noel Park & Wood Green, GE, 40A5
Norbiton for Kingston Hill, LSW, 5B2; 39F3
Norbury (Surrey), LBSC, 40F5
Norbury & Ellaston, NS, 15C5
Norham, NE, 31D3
Normacot, NS, 15C3
Norman's Bay Halt, LBSC, 5F5
Normanby Park (Goods), GC, 22E4
Normanton (Yorks), Mid(LY/NE), 21E4; 42C2
North Berwick, NB, 31B1
North Blyth (Goods), NE, 28A5
North Bridge (Halifax), H&O, 21E2; 42B5
North Camp & Ash Vale, LSW, 4B1; 5C1 *see also* Aldershot (North Camp)
North Cave, HB, 22D4
North Connel, Cal, 32E4
North Docks (Liverpool), LY, 45F3 and inset
North Drove, MGN, 17E2
North Dulwich, LBSC, 40E4
North Ealing, Dist, 39C3
North Eastrington, HB, 22D5
North Elmham, GE, 18E4
North Greenwich, GE, 40D3
North Grimston, NE, 22B5
North Harrow, Met&GCJt, 5A2; 39A1
North Hayling, LBSC, 4E2
North Howden, NE, 22D5
*North Jc* (Derby), Mid, 16D5
North Kelsey, GC, 22F3
*North Kent Jc*, SEC, 40D3
*North Kent West Jc*, SEC, 40D4
North Leith, NB, 30 (inset)
*North Maindee Jc*, GW, 8B3; 43A3
North Mersey (Goods), LY, 45F3 and inset
*North Pole Jc*, GW/LNW/WL, 39C4
*North Quay Jc* (Yarmouth), MGN, 18F1
North Queensferry, FB, 30B3
North Road (Darlington), NE, 28E5
North Road (Plymouth), GW&LSWJt, 1D5 and inset
North Rode, NS, 15B3; 20D1
North Seaton, NE, 27A5
North Shields, NE, 28B5
North Skelton, NE, 28E3
*North Staff Jc*, Mid/NS, 15D5 (inset)
North Sunderland, NSL, 31E5
North Tawton, LSW, 2B5
North Thoresby, GN, 22F2
*North Wales Narrow Gauge Railway*, NWNG, 19E2
North Walsham, GE & MGN, 18D2
North Water Bridge, NB, 34C2
North Weald, GE, 11G4
North Wembley, LNW(LE), 39B2
North Woolwich, GE, 5B4; 40D1
North Wootton, GE, 17E5
North Wylam, NE, 27B5
Northallerton, NE, 21A3; 28G5
*Northallerton Low Jc*, NE, 28G5
*Northallerton South Jc*, NE, 21A3; 28G5
Northam (Devon), BWHA, 7F2
Northam (Hants), LSW(GW), 4E4
Northampton, LNW & Mid, 10B2
Northenden, CLC(LNW), 20C1; 24G1; 45A4
*Northern Jc*, GC&MidJt/GC&Mid&HBJt, 21G4
Northfield, Mid, 9A4
Northfield & Little Ealing, Met & Dist, 39D2
Northfleet, SEC, 5B5
Northgate (Chester), CLC, 20D4
Northiam, KES, 6E5
Northolt Halt for West End, GW, 39B1
Northolt Junc, GW&GCJt, 5A2; 39B1
Northorpe (Lincs), GC, 22G4
Northorpe (Yorks), LNW & LY, 42C4
Northumberland Park, GE, 40A4
Northwich, CLC(LNW), 15A2; 20D2; 45C5
Northwood (Middx), Met&GCJt, 5A2
Norton (Ches), BJ, 15A1; 20C3; 45D4
Norton (Yorks), LY(GN), 21E5
Norton Bridge, LNW(NS) & NS, 15D3; 20G1
Norton Fitzwarren, GW, 8F4
Norton-in-Hales, NS, 15D2; 20F2
Norton Junc, GW, 9B3
Norton-on-Tees, NE, 28E5
Norwich, GE & MGN, 18F3
*Norwood Jc* (Newcastle-on-Tyne), NE, 28 (inset)
Norwood Junc (Surrey), LBSC(SEC & LNW), 5B3; 40G4
Nostell, WRG, 21E4; 42C1
*Nostell N, S, E & W Jcs*, GC & GC/WRG, 21E4
Notgrove, GW, 9D4
Notting Hill Gate, Met(Dist), 39C4
Nottingham (Goods), Mid, GC, GN & LNW, 16C/D; 41G4/5
Nottingham (Pass), Mid, GC&GNJt & GN(LNW), 16C/D; 41G4/5
Nottingham Road, (Derby), Mid, 16D5; 41G2
Notton & Royston, GC, 21F3; 42D2 *see also* Royston, Mid
Novar, HR, 36C5
Nunburnholme, NE, 22C5
Nuneaton (Abbey Street), Mid, 16F5
Nuneaton (Trent Valley), LNW, 16F5
Nunhead, SEC, 40D4
Nunnery (Goods) (Sheffield), LNW, 41A2; 42G2
Nunnington, NE, 21A5
Nunthorpe, NE, 28E4
Nursling, LSW(MSW), 4D4
Nutbourne Halt, LBSC, 4E1
Nutfield, SEC, 5D3
Nysddu, LNW, 8B4; 43B3

Oakamoor, NS, 15C4
Oakengates, GW & LNW, 15E2
Oakenshaw (Goods), Mid, 21E4; 42C2
*Oakenshaw Jc*, LY/Mid, 42C2
Oakham, Mid, 16E2
Oakington, GE(Mid), 11C3
Oakle Street, GW, 8A1; 9E2
*Oaklea Jc*, Fur, 24B5
Oakleigh Park, GN(NL), 5A3; 11G2
Oakley (Beds), Mid, 10B1; 11C1
Oakley (Fife), NB, 30A4
Oakley (Hants), LSW, 4B3
*Oakley Jc*, Mid, 10C1; 11D1
Oakworth, Mid, 21D1
Oatlands, WCE, 26E3
Oban, Cal, 32F4
Occumster, HR, 38E2
Ochiltree, G&SW, 29F4
Ockendon, LTS, 5A5
Ockley for Capel, LBSC, 5D2
Oddington Halt, LNW, 10E4
Offord & Buckden, GN, 11C2
Ogbourne, MSW, 4A5
Ogmore Vale, GW, 7B5; 43D3
Okehampton, LSW, 2B5
Old Colwyn, LNW, 19D4
Old Cumnock, G&SW, 29F5
Old Dalby, Mid, 16E3
Old Ford, NL, 40B3
Old Hill, GW, 13C1; 15G4

*Old Kent Rd Jc*, LBSC, 40D4
Old Kilpatrick, Cal, 29B4; 44G5
Old Leake, GN, 17C3
*Old Main Line Jc*, BJ/LNW, 15A1; 20C3; 24G2
Old Meldrum, GNS, 37E3
Old Mill Lane Halt, LNW, 45E3
Old North Road, LNW, 11C2
*Old Oak Common West Jc*, GW, 39C3
*Old Oak Jc*, LNW/NSW, 39C3
Old Oak Lane Halt, GW, 39C3
Old Roan Halt, LY, 20B4; 24F4; 45F3
Old Street, GN, 40C5
Old Trafford, MSJA(CLC), 45B3
Old Woods (Goods), 15E1; 20G3
Old Ynysybwl Halt, TV, 43C3
Oldbury (Goods & Pass), GW, 13B2; 15G4
Oldbury & Bromford Lane, LNW, 13B2
Oldham, OAGB, LY, LNW, & GC, 21F1 and inset D1; 45A2
Oldham Clegg Street, OAGB, 21D1
Oldham Road (Ashton) (Goods), LNW, 21A2 (inset)
Oldham Road (Ashton) (Pass), OAGB(LY), 21A2 (inset)
Oldham Road (Manor) (Goods), LY, 45A3
Oldham Werneth, LY, 21D1
Ollerton, GC, 16B3
Olney, Mid, 10B2
Olton, GW, 9A5; 15G5
Omoa, Cal, 30C5; 44A2
*Omoa Jc*, Cal, 44A2
Ongar, GE, 11G4
Onibury, S&H, 9A1; 14C1
Onllwyn, N&B, 7A5; 43E1
Orbliston Junc, HR, 36D1
Ordens Platform, GNS, 37C2
Ordsall Lane, LNW(BJ), 45B3
Ore, SEC, 6F5
Oreston, LSW, 1 (inset)
Ormesby, NE, 28E4
Ormiston, NB, 30B1
*Ormsgill Jc*, Fur, 24B5
Ormside, Mid, 27E2
Ormskirk, LY(LNW), 20B4; 24F3; 45E2
Orpington, SEC, 5B4; 40G1
*Orpington Jc*, SEC, 40G1
Orrell, LY, 20B3; 24F3; 45D2
Orrell Park, LY, 45F3
Orton, HR, 36D1
Orton Waterville, LNW, 11A1; 17F2
Orwell, GE, 12D3
Ossett, GN, 21E3; 42C3 *see also* Horbury
Osterley & Spring Grove, Dist, 5B2; 39D2
Oswestry, GW & Cam, 20G4
Otford, SEC, 5C5
Otley, O&I, 21D2
*Otley & Ilkley Jc* (Mid/NE(O&I), 21C2
*Otley & Ilkley (Mid & NE) Jc*, Mid/Mid & NE, 21C2
Otterham, LSW, 1B3
Otterington, NE, 21A3; 28G5
Otterspool, CLC, 45F4
Ottery St Mary, LSW, 2B2
Ottringham, NE, 22E2
Oughterside Colliery Platform, M&C, 26D3
Oughty Bridge, GC, 21G3; 42F3
Oulton Broad, GE, 12A1; 18G1
Oundle, LNW, 11A1; 16G1
Outwell Basin, WUT, 17F4
Outwell Village, WUT, 17F4
Ovenden, H&O, 21E2; 42B5
Over & Wharton, LNW, 15B2; 20D2 *see also* Winsford & Over
*Over Jc*, GW, 9D3
Overstrand, NSJ, 18D3
Overton (Hants), LSW, 4B3
Overton (Renfrew), Cal, 29B3
Overton-on-Dee, Cam, 20F4
Overtown, Cal, 30D5
Oxenholme, LNW(Fur), 24A3; 27G1
Oxenhope, Mid, 21D1
Oxford, GW, 10E4
Oxford (Rewley Road), LNW, 10E4
Oxford Road Halt (Oxon), LNW, 10E4
Oxheys (Goods), LNW, 24D3
Oxshott & Fair Mile, LSW, 5C2
Oxted & Limpsfield, CO, 5C4
Oxton, NB, 30C1
Oyne, GNS, 37E2
Oystermouth, Mum, 43G3

Padbury, LNW, 10D3
Paddington, GW, 5B3; 39C5 and inset C3 *see also* Bishops Road *and* Praed Street
Paddock Wood, SEC, 5D5
Padeswood & Buckley, LNW, 20E4 *see also* Buckley
Padgate, CLC, 20C2; 24G2; 45C4
*Padgate Jc*, CLC, 45C4
Padiham, LY, 24D1
Padstow, LSW, 1C2
Paignton, GW, 2D3
Paisley, G&P, Cal & G&SW, 29C4; 44F3
Palace Gates (Wood Green), GE, 5A3; 40A5
Pallion, NE, 28C5
Palmers Green, GN(NL), 5A3
Palnure, P&W, 25B4
Palterton & Sutton, Mid, 16B4; 41C3
Pampisford, GE, 11D4
Pandy, GW, 14G1
Pangbourne, GW, 4A2; 10G3
Pannal, NE, 21C3
*Pannal Jc*, NE, 21C3
Pant (Glam), BM, 8A5; 43C1
Pant (Salop), Cam, 14A2; 20G4
Pant Glas, LNW, 19E1
Panteg & Griffithstown, GW, 8B3; 43A2
*Panteg Jc*, GW, 8B3; 43A2
Pantydwr, Cam, 14D4
Pantyffynnon, GW(LNW), 7A3; 43G1
Pantysgallog, BM, 43C1
Papcastle, M&C, 26D3
Par, GW, 1D3
Paragon (Hull), NE(GC/LNW/LY), 22E3
Parbold, LY, 20B3; 24F3; 45E1
Parham, GE, 12C2
Park (Aberdeen), GNS, 34A2; 37G3
Park (Barrow) (Goods), Fur, 24B5
Park (Birkenhead), Wir&MerJt, 45F4
Park (Kincard), GNS, 37G3
Park (Manchester), LY, 45A3
Park (Sheffield) (Goods), GC, 41A2; 42G2
Park Bridge, OAGB, 21F1
Park Drain, GN&GEJt, 22F5
*Park Jcs* (Newport, Mon), GW, 43A3
Park Lane Goods (Liverpool), LNW, 45F4 and inset
*Park Lane Jc* (Lancs), LNW, 45D3
*Park Lane Jc* (Gateshead), NE, 28 (inset)
Park Parade (Ashton), GC, 21A2 (inset)
Park Royal, GW, 39C3
Park Royal & Twyford Abbey, Dist, 39C3
Park Street & Frogmore, LNW, 11G1
Parkend, SVW, 8A1; 9F2
Parkeston Quay, GE, 12E3
Parkgate (Ches), BJ, 20D4; 45F5 *see also* Neston
Parkgate & Aldwarke (Yorks), GC, 21G4; 42F1
Parkgate & Rawmarsh (Yorks), Mid, 21G4; 42F1
Parkhead for Celtic Park (Glasgow), Cal & NB, 44D3
Parkhead (Goods), NE, 27D4
Parkhill, GNS, 37F4
*Parks Bridge Jc*, SEC, 40E3
*Parkside Jcs*, LNW, 45D3
Parkstone, LSW(SD), 3F5
Parracombe, LB, 7E4
Parsley Hay, LNW, 15B5
Parsons Green, Dist, 39D4
Partick, Cal & NB, 29C4; 44E4
Partick Central, NB, 44E4
Partick West, Cal, 44E4
Partington, CLC, 20C2; 24G1; 45B3
Parton (Cumb), LNW, 26E4
Parton (Kirkcud), G&SW, 26B5
Partridge Green, LBSC, 5E2
Paston & Knapton, NSJ, 18D2
Patchway, GW, 8C1; 9G1
Pateley Bridge, NE & NV, 21B2
Patna, G&SW, 29F4
Patney & Chirton, GW, 3B5
Patricroft, LNW(BJ), 20B2; 24F1; 45B3
Patrington, NE, 22E2
Patterton, Cal, 29C4; 44E2
Paulton Halt, GW, 3B3; 8D1
Peacock Cross, NB, 44B2
Peak Forest for Peak Dale, Mid, 15A5
Peakirk GN, 17F2
Pear Tree & Normanton, Mid, 16D5: 41G2
Peasley Cross, LNW, 45D3
*Peasley Jc*, LNW, 45D3
*Peasmarsh Jc*, LSW/LBSC, 5D1
Peckham Rye, LBSC(SEC), 40D4
Peckham Rye Coal Depot, LNW&MidJt, 40D4
Pedair Ffordd, Tan, 14A3; 19G5
Pedbrook, GW, 8A2; 9E1
Peebles, NB & Cal, 30D2
Peel, IMR, 23B2
Peel Road, IMR, 23B2
Pegswood, NE, 27A5
Pelaw, NE, 28C5 and inset
Pellon, HHL, 21E2; 42B5
Pelsall, LNW, 15F4
Pelton, NE, 27C5
Pemberton, LY, 20B3; 24F3; 45D2
Pembrey, BPGV, 7B2
Pembrey & Burry Port, GW, 7B2
Pembridge, GW, 14E1
Pembroke, GW, 7D2
Pen Mill (Yeovil), GW, 3D2; 8G2
Pen-y-ffordd, GC, 20E4
Pen-y-graig, GW, 8B5; 43D3
*Penallta Branch Jc*, Rhy, 43B3
*Penallta Jc*, GW/Rhy, 43V3
Penally, GW, 7D3
*Penar Jc*, GW, 43B3
Penarth, TV, 8D4; 43B5
*Penarth Branch Jc*, TV, 43C4

*Penarth Curve Jc*, GW/TV, 8C4
Penarth Dock TV, 8C4; 43B5
Pencader, GW, 13F4
Pencaitland, NB, 30C1
Penclawdd, LNW, 7B3
Pencoed, GW, 8C5; 43D4
Pendlebury, LY, 45B2
Pendleton, LY, 45B3
Pendleton (Broad Street), LY, 45B3
Pendre, Tal, 13B5
Pengam & Fleur-de-lis (Mon), BM, 8B4; 43B2
Penge, LBSC & SEC, 40F4
*Penge Jc*, SEC, 40F3
Penicuik, NB, 30C2
Penistone, GC&LYJt, 21F3; 42E3
Penkridge, LNW, 15E3
Penmaenmawr, LNW, 19D3
Penmaenpool, Cam, 14A5
Pennington, LNW, 45C3
Penns, Mid, 15F5
Penpergwm, GW, 8A3; 43A1
Penrhiwceiber, GW & TV, 8B5; 43C2
Penrhiwfelin Goods, Rhy, 43B3
*Penrhos Jc*, Rhy/BRY/AD, 43B3
Penrhyndeudraeth, Cam & Fest, 19F2
Penrith, LNW(CKP/NE), 27E1
Penruddock, CKP, 26E1
Penryn, GW, 1F1
Pensford, GW, 3A2; 8D1
Penshaw, NE, 28C5
Penshurst, SEC, 5D4
Pentir Rhiw, BM, 8A5; 14G3; 43C1
Penton, NB, 26B1
Pentraeth, LNW, 19D2
Pentre Broughton Halt, GW, 20E4
Pentre Halt, TV, 43D2
Pentrebach, TV, 8A5; 43C2
Pentrecourt Platform, GW, 13F4
Pentrefelin, Tan, 14A2; 20G5
Pentrepiod Halt, GW, 43A2
Pentresaeson Halt, GW, 20E4
Pentwyn Halt, GW, 43A2
*Penwithers Jc*, GW, 1E1
*Penwortham Jc*, LY, 20A3; 24E3
Penybont, LNW, 14D3
Penybontfawr, Tan, 14A3; 19G5
Penychain, Cam, 19F1
Penygroes, LNW, 19E1
Penyrheol, Rhy, 8B4; 43B3
Penzance, GW, 1F4 (inset)
Peplow, GW, 15E2; 20G2
Percy Main, NE, 28B5
Perivale Halt, GW, 39C2
Perranporth, GW, 1D1
Perranwell, GW, 1E1
Perry Barr, LNW, 13B3; 15G4
Pershore, GW, 9C4
Persley, GNS, 37F4
Perth (General) (Pass), Cal(NB/HR), 33F5
Perth (Goods), Cal & NB, 33F5
Perth (Princes Street), Cal, 33F5
Peterborough, GE(LNW/Mid) & GN(Mid/MGN/GE), 11A2; 17F2
*Peterborough Jc*, LNW&GEJt, 11A2
Peterchurch, GW, 14F1
Peterhead, GNS, 37D5
Petersfield, LSW, 4D2
Peterston, GW 8C5; 43C4
*Petteril Jc* (Carlisle), NE/Mid, 26 (inset)
Petworth, LBSC, 5E1
Pevensey & Westham, LBSC, 5F5
Pevensey Bay Halt, LBSC, 5F5
Pewsey, GW, 4B5
Philorth (private), GNS, 37C4
Philorth Bridge Halt, GNS, 37C4
Philpstoun, NB, 30B3
Pickburn, HB, 21F4
Pickering, NE, 22A5
Pickhill, NE, 21A3
Picton, NE, 28F5
Piddington, Mid, 10B2
Piel, Fur, 24B4
Pier Head (Ryde, IoW), LBSC&LSWJt(IW/IWC), 4F3
Piercebridge, NE, 27E5
Piershill, NB, 30 (inset)
Pill, GW, 3A2; 8C2; 9G1
*Pillbank Jc*, GW, 43A3
Pilling, KE, 24C3
Pilmoor, NE, 21B4
Pilning, GW, 8C2; 9G1
Pilsley, GC, 16B4; 41D3
*Pilton Jcs*, Cal, 30 (inset)
Pinchbeck, GN&GEJt, 17E2
Pinchinthorpe, NE, 28E4
Pinged, BPGV, 7A2
Pinhoe, LSW, 2B3
Pinmore, G&SW, 25A3
Pinner, Met&GCJt, 5A2; 39A1
Pinwherry, G&SW, 25A3
Pinxton & Selston, Mid, 16C4; 41E3
Pinxton, GN, 16C4; 41E3 *see also* Kirkby, GC
Pipe Gate, NS, 15C2; 20F2
*Pirbright Jc*, LSW, 4B1; 5C1
Pitcaple, GNS, 37E3
Pitcrocknie Platform, CR, 34D5
Pitfodels, GNS, 37G4
Pitlochry, HR, 33C4
Pitlurg, GNS, 37E4
Pitmedden, GNS, 37F4
Pitsea, LTS, 6A5
Pitsford & Brampton, LNW, 10B2
Pittenweem, NB, 34G3
Pittington, NE, 28D5
Pitts Hill, NS, 15C3; 20E1
Plaidy, GNS, 37D3
*Plains Jc*, NB, 44A4
Plains, NB, 30C5; 44A4
Plaistow, LTS(Dist), 40C2
Plank Lane, LNW, 45C3
Plantation Halt, CM, 29 (inset)
Plas Marl, GW, 7B4; 43G2
Plas Power, GW & GC, 20E4
Plashetts, NB, 27A2
Platt Bridge, LNW, 45D2 *see also* Hindley
Plawsworth, NE, 27C5
Plealey Road, SWP, 14B1
*Plean Branch Jc*, Cal, 30A5
Plean for Cowie, Cal, 30A5
Pleasington, LY, 20A2; 24E2
Pleasley, Mid & GN, 16B4; 41D4
Plenmeller Halt, NE, 27C2
Plessey, NE, 27B5
Plex Moss Lane Halt, LY, 20B4; 24F4; 45F2
Plockton, HR, 35E1
Plodder Lane, LNW, 20B2; 24F2; 45C2
Plowden, BC, 14C1
Pluckley, SEC, 6D4
Plumley CLC, 15A2; 20D2; 45B5
Plumpton (Cumb), LNW, 27D1
Plumpton (Sussex), LBSC, 5F3
*Plumpton Jc*, Fur, 24A4
Plumstead, SEC, 40D1
Plumtree, Mid, 16D3
Plym Bridge Platform, GW, 2D5
Plymouth, GW(LSW), GW & LSW, 1D5 and inset
Plymouth North Road, GW, 1 (inset)
Plympton, GW, 2D5
Plymstock, LSW(GW), 1 (inset)
Pochin Pits, LNW, 43B2
*Pocket Nook Jc*, LNW, 45D3
Pocklington, NE, 22C5
*Point Pleasant Jc*, LSW, 39E5
Pokesdown, LSW, 4F5
Polegate, LBSC, 5F5
Polesworth, LNW, 16F5
*Pollok Jc*, G&SW/G&P, 44F1 (inset)
Pollokshaws, GBK, 44E3
Pollokshaws East, Cal, 44E3 and inset F1
Pollokshields East, Cal, 44E3 and inset F1
Pollokshields West, Cal, 44E3 and inset F1
Polmont, NB, 30B4
Polsham, SD, 3C2; 8E2
Polsloe Bridge Halt, LSW, 2B3
Polton, NB, 30C2
Pomathorn, NB, 30C2
Pond Street (Sheffield) (Goods), Mid, 16A5; 21G3
Pond Street (Sheffield) (Pass), Mid(HB/NE/LY), 16A5; 21G3
Ponder's End, GE, 5A3; 11G3
*Poneil Jc*, Cal, 30E5
Ponfeigh, Cal, 30E4
Pont Lawrence, LNW, 8B4; 43B3
Pont Llanio, GW, 13E5
Pont Rug, LNW, 19D2
Pont Yates, BPGV, 7A3
Pontardawe, Mid, 7A4; 43F2
Pontardulais, GW&LNWJt, 7A3
Pontcynon Bridge Halt, TV, 43C3
Pontdolgoch, Cam, 14B3
Pontefract (Baghill), SK(GC/GN), 21E4; 42C1
Pontefract (Monkhill), LY(NE), 21E4; 42C1
Ponteland, NE, 27B5
Pontesbury, SWP, 14B1
Pontfadog, GVT, 20F5
Pontfaen, GVT, 20F5
Ponthenry, BPGV, 7A3
Ponthir, GW, 8B3; 43A3
Pontllanfraith, GW & LNW, 8B4; 43B3
Pontlliw (Goods), GW, 7B3; 43G2
Pontlottyn, Rhy, 43C2 *see also* Rhymney, BM
Pontnewydd, GW, 8B3; 43A3
Pontnewynydd, GW, 43A2
Pontrhyddfen, RSB, 43E3
Pontrhythallt, LNW, 19D2
Pontrilas, GW, 14G1
Pontsarn for Vaynor, BM&LNWJt, 8A5; 43C1
Pontsticill Junc, BM, 8A5; 43C1
Pontwalby Halt, GW, 43E2
Pontyberem, BPGV, 7A3
Pontycymmer, GW(PT), 7B5; 43D3
Pont-y-Pant, LNW, 19E3
Pontypool, GW, 8B3; 43A2
*Pontypool East Jc*, GW, 43A2
*Pontypool Middle Jc*, GW, 43A2
*Pontypool North Jc*, GW, 43A2
Pontypool Road, GW, 8B3; 43A2

*Pontypool South Jc*, GW, 43A2
Pontypridd, TV(AD) & BRY, 8B5; 43C3
Pontyrhyll, GW(PT), 7B5; 43D3
Pool-in-Wharfedale, NE, 21C3
Pool Quay, Cam, 14A2
Poole, LSW(SD), 3F5
Poplar (East India Road) Tidal Basin, GE, 40C2
Poplar (Goods), GN, GW, LNW, Mid & NL, 40C3/D3 and inset D1/E1
Poplar (Pass), GE & NL, 40C3 and inset D1
Poppleton, NE, 21C4
*Poppleton Jc*, NE, 21C5 and inset A4
Port Carlisle, NB, 26C2
*Port Carlisle Branch Jc*, Cal, 26C1 and inset
Port Clarence, NE, 28E4
Port Dinorwic, LNW, 19D2
Port Dundas (Goods) (Glasgow), Cal & NB, 44E4
Port Eglington Depot, G&SW, 44F1 (inset)
Port Elphinstone (Goods), GNS, 37F3
Port Erin, IMR, 23C1
Port Glasgow, Cal, 29B3
Port Gordon, GNS, 37C1
Port Isaac Road, LSW, 1C3
Port Meadow Halt, LNW, 10E4
Port of Menteith, NB, 29A5
Port St Mary, IMR, 23C1
Port Soderick, IMR, 23C2
Port Sunlight (Goods), BJ, 45F4
Port Talbot (Aberavon), RSB, 7B4; 43F3
Port Talbot (Central), PT, 7B4; 43F3
Port Talbot & Aberavon, GW(PT), 7B4; 43F3
Port Victoria, SEC, 6B4
Portbury, GW, 3A2; 8C2; 9G1
Portchester, LSW, 4E2
*Portcreek Jc*, LSW/LBSC, 4E2
Porterfield (Renfrew), G&P, 44F4
Portesham, GW, 3F2
Portessie, GNS, 37C1
Porth, TV(BRY), 8B5; 43C3
Porthcawl, GW, 7C5; 43E4
Porthcawl Golfers Platform, GW, 43E4
Porthywaen, Tan, 14A2; 20G5
Portishead, GW & WCP, 3A2; 8C2; 9G1
Portishead South Portbury Road, WCP, 3A2; 8C2
Portknockie, GNS, 37C1
Portland, WP, 3G3
Portlethen, Cal, 34A1; 37G4
Portmadoc, Cam, Fest & PCB, 19F2
Portobello, NB, 30 (inset)
*Portobello Jc*, GW, 39C5 and inset C1
Porton, LSW, 4C5
Portpatrick, P&W, 25C1
Portreath, GW, 1E5 (inset)
Portskewett, GW, 8B2; 9F1
Portslade, LBSC, 5F3
Portsmouth (Yorks), LY, 20A1; 21E1
Portsmouth Arms, LSW, 7G3
Portsmouth Harbour, LSW&LBSCJt, 4E2
Portsmouth Town (Hants), LSW&LBSCJt, 4E2
Portsoy, GNS, 37C2
Possil Goods, Cal, 44E4
Possilpark, NB, 44E4
Postland, GN&GEJt, 17E2
Potter Hanworth, GN&GEJt, 16B1; 17B1
Potter Heigham, MGN, 18E2
Potterhill (Paisley), G&SW, 29C4; 44 G3
Potters Bar, GN(NL), 11G2
Potto, NE, 28F4
Potton, LNW, 11D2
Poulton (Lancs), PWY, 24D4
Poulton Curve Halt, PWY, 24D4
*Pouparts Jc*, LBSC, 39E3 (inset)
Powderhall, NB, 30 (inset)
Powerstock, GW, 3F2
Poynton, GC&NSJt, 15A4
Poynton, LNW(NS), 15A3; 20C1; 45A4
Praed Street, Met(Dist), 39C5 *see also* Paddington
Praze, GW, 1E5 (inset)
Prees, LNW, 15D1; 20F3
Preesall, KE, 24C4
Preesgweene, GW, 20F4
Prescot, LNW, 20C3; 24G3; 45E3
Prescott Siding, CMDP, 9A2; 15G2
Prestatyn, LNW, 19C5
Prestbury, LNW(NS), 15A3; 20D1; 45A5
Presteign, GW, 14D2
Presthope, GW, 15F1
Preston (Goods), LNW, LY, PL & PWY, 24E3
Preston (Pass), NU & LY, 24D3
Preston Brook, LNW, 15A1; 20C3; 45D5
Preston Junc, LY, 20A3; 24E3
Preston Park, LBSC, 5F3
Preston Platform, GW, 2D3
Preston Road (Middx), Met, 39A3
Preston Road (Lancs), LY, 20C4; 24G4; 45F3
Preston Street Goods (Whitehaven), Fur, 26E4
Prestonpans for Tranent, NB, 30B1
Prestwich LY, 20B1; 24F1; 45B2
Prestwick, G&SW, 29E3
Priestfield, GW, 13A1
*Primrose Hill Jc*, LNW, 40A2 (inset)
Princes Dock (Glasgow), PDJ, 44E3
Princes End, GW, 13A1; 15F4
Princes Pier (Greenock), G&SW, 29B3
Princes Risborough, GW&GCJt, 10F2
Princes Street (Edinburgh), Cal, 30B2 and inset
Princes Street (Perth), Cal, 33F5
Princetown, GW, 2C5
Priory (Dover), SEC, 6D2
Priory Road, Wells (Som), SD, 3C2; 8E2
Prittlewell, GE, 6A4
Privett, LSW, 4D2
Probus & Ladock Platform, GW, 1E2
*Proof House Jc*, LNW/Mid, 13C4
Prudhoe, NE(NB), 27B4
Pudsey Greenside, GN, 21D2; 42A4
Pudsey Lowtown, GN, 21D2; 42A4
Pulborough, LBSC, 5E1
Pulford (Goods), GW, 20E4
Pulham Market, GE, 12B3; 18G3
Pulham St Mary, GE, 12B3; 18G3
Puncheston, GW, 13F1
Purfleet, LTS, 5B5
Purfleet Rifle Range, LTS, 5B5
Purley, LBSC(SEC), 5C3
Purley Oaks, LBSC, 5C3
Purton, GW, 9F4
Putney, LSW, 5B3; 39E4
Putney Bridge, Dist, 39E4
Puxton & Worle, GW, 3B1; 8D3
Pwllheli, Cam, 19F1
Pye Bridge, Mid, 16C4; 41E3
Pye Hill & Somercotes, GN, 16C4; 41E3
*Pye Wipe Jc* (Lincoln), GC/GN/GN&GEJt, 16B1 and inset
Pyle, GW, 7C5; 43E4
Pylle, SD, 3C2; 8E1
Pylle Hill Goods (Bristol), GW, 3 (inset)
*Quainton & Aylesbury Tramroad*, OAT, 10E3
Quainton Road, Met&GCJt & OAT, 10E3
*Quainton Road Jc*, GC/Met&GCJt, 10E3
Quaker's Drove (Goods), GE, 11A3; 17F3
Quaker's Yard (High Level), GW(Rhy), 8B5; 43C2
Quaker's Yard (Low Level), GW&TVJt, 8B5; 43C2
Quarter, Cal, 29D5; 44B1
Queen Street (Cardiff), TV, 8C4; 43B4
Queen Street (Exeter), LSW, 2B3
Queen Street (Glasgow), NB, 29C5; 44E4
Queen's Park (Glasgow), Cal, 44E3 and inset F1
Queen's Park, West Kilburn, LNW(NL/LE), 39B5
Queen's Road (Battersea), LSW, 39D5 and inset E4
Queen's Road (Peckham), LBSC, 40D4
Queens Road Goods (Sheffield), Mid, 16A5; 21G3; 41A2; 42G2
Queenborough, SEC, 6B4
Queensbury, GN, 21D2; 42B5
Queensferry, LNW, 20D4
Quellyn Lake, NWNG, 19E2
Quintrel Downs Platform, GW, 1D1
Quorn & Woodhouse, GC, 16E4 *see also* Barrow-on-Soar
Quy, GE, 11C4

Racks, G&SW, 26B3
Radcliffe, LY, 20B1; 24F1; 45B2 *see also* Black Lane
Radcliffe Bridge, LY, 45B2
Radcliffe-on-Trent, GN(LNW), 16D3
Radford & Timsbury Halt, GW, 3B3; 8D1
Radford, Mid, 16D4; 41G4
Radipole Halt, GW, 3G3
Radlett, Mid, 11G1
Radley, GW, 10F4
Radstock, GW & SD, 3B3; 8E1
Radway Green, NS, 15C2; 20E1
Radyr, TV, 8C4; 43C4
Raglan, GW, 8A3
*Rainbow Hill Jc* (Worcester), GW, 9B3
Rainford Junc, LY(LNW) & LNW, 20B3; 24F3; 45E2
Rainford Village, LNW, 20B3; 24F3; 45E2
Rainham (Essex), LTS, 5A4
Rainham (Kent), SEC, 6B5
Rainhill, LNW, 20C3; 24G3; 45E3
Rampside, Fur, 24B4
Ramsbottom, LY, 20A1; 24E1; 45B1
Ramsden Dock, Fur, 24B5
Ramsey (Hunts), GN, 11A2/B2; 17G2
Ramsey (IoM), IMR & ME, 23A3; 25G4
Ramsey High Street (Hunts), GN&GEJt, 11B2
Ramsey Plaza (IoM), MER, 23A3; 25G4
Ramsgate Harbour, SEC, 6B1
Ramsgate Town, SEC, 6B1
Ramsgill, NV, 21B2
*Randle Jc*, LNW, 20B3; 24F3; 45E2
Rankinston, G&SW, 29F4
Rannoch, NB, 32C1; 33D1
Ranskill, GN, 16A3; 21G5
Raskelf, NE, 21B4
Ratby, Mid, 16F4
Ratgoed Quarry, Cor, 14A5
Rathen, GNS, 37C4
Ratho, NB, 30B3
Rathven, GNS, 37C1
Rauceby, GN, 16C1; 17C1
Raunds, Mid, 10A1; 11B1
Ravelrig Halt, Cal, 30C3

Raven Square, W&L, 14B2
Ravenglass, Fur & RE, 26G3
Ravensbourne, SEC, 40F3
Ravenscar, NE, 28F1
Ravenscourt Park, LSW(Dist), 39D4
Ravenscraig, Cal, 29B3
Ravensthorpe, LY, 42C4
Ravensthorpe & Thornhill, LNW, 42C3 *see also* Thornhill
Ravenstonedale, NE, 27F2 *see also* Kirkby Stephen
*Ravenstone Wood Jc*, Mid/SMJ, 10B2
Ravenswood Jc, NB, 31E1
Rawcliffe, LY, 21E5 *see also* Airmyn
Rawtenstall, LY, 20A1; 24E1
Rawyards, NB, 44A4
Raydon Wood, GE, 12D4
Rayleigh, GE, 6A5
Rayne, GE, 11E5
Rayner's Lane, Met(Dist), 39B1
Raynes Park, LSW, 5B3; 39F4
Raynham Park, MGN, 18D5
Reading, GW & SEC(LSW), 4A2
Reading West, GW, 4A2
Rearsby, Mid, 16E3
*Rectory Jc*, GN, 16D3; 41F5
Rectory Road, GE, 40B4
*Red Hill Jc* (Hereford), GW/LNW, 9C1; 14F1
*Red Hills Jc*, (Penrith), CKP/NE, 27E1
Red House, Van, 14C4
Red Lion Crossing Halt, GW, 43F1
*Red Posts Jc*, LSW/MSW, 4C4
Red Rock, LU, 20B3; 24F2; 45D2
Red Wharf Bay & Benllech, LNW, 19C2
Redbourn, Mid, 11F1
Redbridge, LSW(MSW), 4E4
Redcar, NE, 28E4
Redcastle, HR, 36D5
Redding (Goods), NB, 30B4
Reddish, LNW(LY) & GC&MidJt, 21G1; 45A3
*Reddish Jc*, GC&MidJt, 45A3
Redditch, Mid, 9B4
Redheugh (Goods), NE, 28 (inset)
Redhill (Surrey), SEC(LBSC), 5C3
Redland, CE, 3 (inset)
Redmile, GN&LNWJt, 16D2
Redmire, NE, 21A1; 27G4
Rednal & West Felton, GW, 20G4
Redruth, GW, 1E5 (inset)
*Redruth Jc*, GW, 1E5 (inset)
Reedham (Norfolk), GE, 18F2
Reedley Hallows Halt, LY, 24D1
Reedness, AJ, 22E5
Reedsmouth, NB, 27A3
Reepham (Lincs), GC, 16A1; 17B1
Reepham (Norfolk), GE, 18E4 *see also* Whitwell
Reigate, SEC, 5C3
*Relly Mill Jc*, NE, 27D5
Renfrew, G&P & G&SW, 29C4; 44F4
Renton, D&B, 29B3
Repton & Willington, Mid(LNW), 16D5
Resolven, GW, 7A5; 43E2
Restalrig (Goods), Cal, 30 (inset)
Reston, NB, 31C3
Retford (Goods), GN & GC, 16A3
Retford (Pass), GN(GC), 16A3
*Retford N & S Jcs*, GC/GN, 16A3
Rhayader, Cam, 14D4
Rheidol Falls, VR, 14C5
Rhewl, LNW, 19E5
Rhigos, Halt, GW, 43D1
Rhiwbina Halt, Car, 43B4
Rhiwderin, BM, 8B4; 43A3
Rhiwfron, VR, 14C5
*Rhondda Branch Jc*, TV, 43C3
Rhoose, BRY, 8D5; 43C5
Rhos (Denbigh), GW, 20F4
Rhos Tryfan, NWNG, 19E2
Rhosgoch, LNW, 19C1; 23G1
Rhosneigr, LNW, 19D1
Rhostyllen, GW, 20E4
Rhosymedre Halt, GW, 20F4
Rhuddlan, LNW, 19D5
Rhuddlan Road, LNW, 19C5
Rhydowen, GW, 13F3
Rhydyfelin Halt, AD & Car, 43C3
Rhydymwyn, LNW, 20D5
Rhydyronen, Tal, 13B5
Rhyd-y-Saint, LNW, 19D2
Rhyl, LNW, 19C5
Rhymney, Rhy, 8A5; 43B4; 43C2
Rhymney & Pontlottyn, BM, 8A4; 43C1
Rhymney Bridge, LNW&RhyJt & LNW, 8A5; 43C1
*Ribble Jc*, LY, 24E3
Ribblehead, Mid, 24A1
Ribbleton, PL, 24D2
Riccall, NE, 21D5
Riccarton & Craigie, G&SW, 29E4
Riccarton Junc, NB, 27A1; 31G1
Richmond (Surrey), LSW(Dist/NL), 5B2; 39E3
Richmond (Yorks), NE, 27F5
Rickmansworth, Met&GCJt & LNW, 5A2; 10F1
Riddings, NB, 26B1
*Riddings Jc*, Mid, 41E3
Ridgmont, LNW, 10C1
Riding Mill, NE(NB), 27C4
Rifle Range Halt, GW, 9A3
Rifle Range Platform, LSW, 1C2
Rigg, G&SW, 26B2
Rillington, NE, 22B5
Rimington, LY, 24C1
Ringley Road, LY, 20B1; 24F1; 45B2
Ringstead & Addington, LNW, 10A1
Ringwood, LSW, 4E5
Ripley, Mid, 16C5; 41E2
Ripley Valley, NE, 21C3
Ripon, NE, 21B3
Rippingale, GN, 17D1
Ripple, Mid, 9C3
Ripponden & Barkisland, LY, 21E1
Risca, GW(LNW), 8B4; 43B3
*Risca Jc*, GW, 43B3
Rishton, LY, 24D1
Rishworth, LY, 21E1
Riverside (Cardiff), GW(BRY/TV), 43B4
Riverside (Liverpool), MDHB(LNW), 45 (inset)
Roade, LNW, 10C2
*Roade Jc*, LNW/SMJ, 10C2
Roath (Goods), GW & TV, 8C4; 43B4
Roath (Pass), GW, 8C4; 43B4
*Roath Branch Jc*, TV, 43B4
*Roath Dock Jc*, TV/Car, 8C4
Robertsbridge, SEC(KES), 6E5
Robertstown Halt, TV, 43C3
Robin Hood, EWY, 21E3; 42B2
Robin Hood's Bay, NE, 28F1
Robroyston, Cal, 29C5; 44D4
Roby, LNW, 20C4; 24G3; 45E4
Rocester, NS, 15D5
Rochdale, LY, 20A1; 45A1
*Rochdale East Jc*, LY, 21E1
Rochdale Road Halt, LY, 42C5
Roche, GW, 1D2
Rochester, SEC, 6B5
*Rochester Bridge Jc*, SEC, 6B5
Rochester Bridge, SEC, 6B5
Rochford, GE, 6A4
Rock Ferry, BJ(Mer), 20C4; 24G4
Rockcliffe, Cal, 26C1
Rockingham, LNW, 16F2
Rodmarton Platform, GW, 9F3
Rodwell, WP, 3G3
*Roe Lane Jc*, LY, 20A4; 24E4; 45F1
Roffey Road Halt, LBSC, 5E2
Rogart, HR, 36A5
Rogate for Harting, LSW, 4D1
Rogerstone, GW, 8B4; 43A3
Rolleston Junc, Mid, 16C2
Rolleston-on-Dove, NS(GN), 15D5
Rollright Halt, GW, 10D5
Rolvenden, KES, 6E4
Romaldkirk, NE, 27E4
Roman Bridge, LNW, 19E3
Roman Road (Woodnesborough), EK, 6C2
*Rome Street Jc* (Carlisle), M&C/NE, 26C1 and inset
Romford, GE & LTS, 5A4
Romiley, GC&MidJt, 21G1
Romsey, LSW(MSW), 4D4
Rookery Bridge (Goods), LNW, 15B2; 20E2
Rookery, LNW, 20B3; 24F3; 45E3
Roose, Fur, 24B5
Ropley, LSW, 4C2
Rose Grove, LY, 24D1
Rose Hill, GC&NSJt, 21G1 *see also* Marple
Rosebush, GW, 13F2
Rosedale (Goods), NE, 28F3
Rosemill (Goods), Cal, 34E4
Rosemount, Cal, 33D5
Rosherville, SEC, 5B5
Roskear, GW, 1E5 (inset)
Roslin, NB, 30C2
*Ross Jc* (Lanarks), Cal, 44B2
Ross-on-Wye, GW, 9D1
Rossett, GW, 20E4
Rossington, GN, 21F5
Rosslyn Castle, NB, 30C2
Rosslynlee, NB, 30C2
Rosyth Halt, NB, 30B3
Rothbury, NB, 31G4
Rotherfeld & Mark Cross, LBSC, 5E5
Rotherham & Masborough, GC, 21G4; 42F1
Rotherham (Masborough), Mid(NE/LY), 21G4; 42F1
Rotherham Road, GC, 21G4; 42F1
Rotherham Westgate, Mid, 21G4; 42F1
Rotherhithe, EL, 40D4
*Rotherwas Jc* (Hereford), GW/LNW, 9C1
Rothes, GNS, 36D1
Rothie Norman, GNS, 37E3
Rothiemay, GNS, 37D1
Rothley, GC, 16E4
Rothwell (Yorks), EWY, 21D3; 42B2
Rotton Park Road, LNW, 13C3
Roudham Junc, GE, 12A5; 18G5
*Roughton Road Jc*, GE/NSJ, 18D3
Round Oak, GW, 15G3
*Roundwood Jc*, Mid/GC&MidJt, 42F1

Row, NB, 29B3
Rowden Mill, GW, 9B2
Rowfant, LBSC, 5D3
Rowland's Castle, LSW, 4E2
Rowlands Gill, NE, 27C5
Rowley, NE, 27C4
Rowley Regis & Blackheath, GW, 13C2; 15G4
Rowrah, WCE, 26E3
Rowsley, Mid, 16B5; 41C1
Rowthorn & Hardwick, Mid, 16B4; 41C3
Roxburgh, NB, 31E2
Roy Bridge, NB, 32B2
Royal Oak, GW(H&C), 39C5 and inset C1
Roydon, GE, 11F3
Royston (Herts), GN, 11D3
Royston & Notton, Mid, 21F3; 42D2 *see also* Notton, GC
*Royston Jc*, Mid, 21E3; 42D2
Royton, LY, 21F1; 45A2
Royton Junc, LY, 21F1
Ruabon, GW, 20F4
Rubery, HJ, 9A4
Ruddington, GC, 16D4; 41G4
Rudgwick, LBSC, 5E2
Rudyard (Horton), NS, 15B4
Rudyard Lake, NS, 15B4
Rufford, LY, 20A3; 24E3; 45E1
Rugby, LNW(Mid) & GC, 10A4
Rugeley (Trent Valley), LNW, 15E4
Rugeley Town, LNW, 15E4
Ruislip & Ickenham, GW&GCJt, 10G1
Ruislip, Met(Dist), 5A2
Rumbling Bridge, NB, 30A4; 33G4
Rumworth & Daubhill, LNW, 45C2
Runcorn, LNW, 15A1; 20C3; 45D4
Runcorn Dock, LNW, 45E4
Runnymede (Goods), GW, 5B1
Runnymede Range, GW, 5B1
*Runton E & W Jcs*, MGN/NSJ, 18D3
Rushbury, GW, 15G1
Rushcliffe Halt, GC, 16D4
Rushden, Mid, 10B1
Rushey Platt (Goods), MSW, 9G5
Rushton (Staffs), NS, 15B4
Ruskington, GN&GEJt, 17C1
Ruspidge, GW, 8A1; 9E2
Ruswarp, NE, 28F2
Rutherford, NB, 31E1
Rutherglen, Cal, 29C5; 44D3
*Rutherglen Jc*, Cal, 44D3
Ruthern Bridge, LSW, ID2
Ruthin, LNW, 19E5; 20E5
Ruthrieston, GNS, 37G4
Ruthven Road Crossing, Cal, 33E5
Ruthwell, G&SW, 26B3
Rutland Street (Swansea), Mum, 7B4; 43G3
Ryburgh, GE, 18D5
Ryde (Esplanade), LBSC&LSWJt(IW/IWC), 4F3
Ryde (Pier Head), LBSC&LSWJt(IW/IWC), 4F3
Ryde (St John's Road), IW & LBSC&LSWJt(IWC), 4F3
Ryde Locomotive Works, IW, 4F3
Rye, SEC & RCT, 6E4
*Rye & Camber Tramway*, RCT, 6C3
Rye Harbour, SEC, 6E4
Rye Hill, NE, 22E2
Rye House, GE, 11F3
*Ryecroft Jc*, LNWR/Mid, 15F4
Ryeford, Mid, 9E3
Ryeland, Cal, 29 D5
Ryhall, GN, 16E1; 17F1
Ryhill, GC, 21E3; 42D2
Ryhill Halt, LY, 42D1
Ryhope, NE, 28C5
Ryhope East, NE, 28C5
*Ryhope Grange Jc*, NE, 28C5
Rylstone, Mid, 21C1
Ryston, GE, 11A4; 17F4
Ryton, NE(NB), 27B5

Saddleworth, LNW, 21F1
Saffron Walden, GE, 11D4
St Agnes, GW, 1E1
St Albans, Mid, LNW(GN) & GN, 11F1
St Albans London Road, LNW, 11F1
St Andrew's Dock (Goods) (Hull), NE, 22 (inset)
St Andrews, NB, 34F4
*St Andrew's Jc*, Mid, 13C4
St Ann's Road, THJ(LTS), 40A4
St Ann's Well, GN, 16C3; 41F5
St Anne's Park, GW, 8C1
*St Annes Park Jc*, GW, 3A3 and inset G1
St Annes-on-the-Sea, PWY, 24E4
St Anthonys, NE(NB), 28 (inset)
St Asaph, LNW, 19D5
St Athan Road, TV, 8D5; 43C5
St Austell, GW, 1D2
St Bees, Fur, 26F4
St Blazey, GW, 1D3
St Boswells, NB, 31E1
St Botolph's, GE, 12E4
St Briavels & Llandogo, GW, 8A2; 9E1
St Bride's Crossing, Cal, 33G2
St Budeaux Platform, GW, 1D5
St Budeaux, LSW, 1D5
*St Catherine's Jcs*, SYJ/LY/GN&LYJt, 21F5
St Clears, GW, 7A1; 13G3
St Columb Road, GW, 1D2
St Combs, GNS, 37C5
St Cyrus, NB, 34C2
St David's (Exeter), GW(LSW), 2B3
*St Dennis Jc*, GW, 1D2
St Denys, LSW(GW), 4D4
St Devereux, GW, 14F1
St Dunstans, GN, 42B4
St Enoch (Glasgow), G&SW, 29C5; 44E4 and inset E2
St Erth, GW, 1F4 (inset)
St Fagans, GW(BRY) & BRY, 8C4; 43C4
St Fillans, Cal, 33F2
St Fort, NB, 34E4
St Germains, IMR, 23B2
St Germans, GW, 1D5
St Harmons, Cam, 14D4
St Helens (Glam), Mum, 43G3
St Helens (IoW), IW, 4F2
St Helens (Lancs), LNW & GC, 20C3; 24G3; 43D3
St Helens Junc, LNW, 20C3; 24G3; 45D3
St Ives (Cornwall), GW, 1E4 (inset)
St Ives (Hunts), GN&GEJt(Mid), 11B2
St James (Cheltenham), GW, 9D4
St James (Liverpool), CLC, 45F4
St James (Paisley), Cal, 44G3
*St James's Bridge Jc*, NE, 28 (inset)
St James's Park, Dist(Met), 40D5
St John's (IoM), IMR, 22B2
St John's (London), SEC, 40E3
St John's Chapel, NE, 27D3
St John's Road (Ryde, IoW), IW & LBSC&LSWJt(IWC), 4F3
St John's Wood Road, Met, 39C5
St Kew Highway, LSW, 1C2
St Keyne, LL, 1D4
St Lawrence, IWC, 4G3
St Leonards (Edinburgh) (Goods), NB, 30 (inset)
St Leonards (Sussex), SEC, LBSC & SEC(LBSC), 6F5
St Luke's (Southport), LY, 20A4; 24E4; 45F1
*St Luke's Jc* (Barrow), Fur, 24B5
St Margaret's (Herts), GE, 11F3
St Margaret's (Middx), LSW, 39E2
*St Margarets Jc*, LBSC, 5D4
St Marnocks (Goods), G&SW, 29E4
St Mary Church Road, TV, 8C5; 43C5
St Mary Cray, SEC, 5B4; 40G1
*St Mary Cray Jc*, SEC, 40F1
St Mary's (Hunts), GN, 11A2; 17G2
St Mary's (London), Dist&MetJt(H&C), 40C4
St Mary's Bridge Goods (Derby), Mid, 41G2
St Mary's Crossing Halt, GW, 9F3
*St Marys Jc*, Mid, 41G2
St Michael's, CLC, 20C4; 24G4; 45F4
St Monan's, NB, 34G3
St Neots, GN, 11C2
St Olaves, GE, 18F1
*St Olaves Jc*, GE, 18F1
St Olaves Swing Bridge, GE, 12A2; 18F1
St Pancras (Goods), Mid, 40B5
St Pancras (Pass), Mid(LTS/GE), 5A3; 40C5
*St Pancras Jcs*, NL/Mid & NL/GN, 40B5
St Paul's (Halifax), HHL, 21E2; 42B5
St Paul's (London), SEC, 40C5
*St Paul's Road Jc*, Mid, 40B5
St Peter's, NE, 28 (inset)
St Philip's (Bristol), Mid, 3 (inset)
St Philip's Marsh (Bristol)(Goods), GW, 3 (inset)
St Quintin Park & Wormwood Scrubbs, WL, 39C4
St Rollox, Cal, 29C5; 44D4
St Thomas (Exeter), GW, 2B3
St Thomas (Swansea), Mid, 43G3
*St Vigean's Jc*, D&A/Cal/NB, 34D3
St Winifrides, LNW, 20D5
Sale & Ashton-on-Mersey, MSJA(CLC), 20C1; 24G1; 45B3
Salehurst Halt, EK, 6E5
Salford Priors, Mid, 9B4
Salford, LY(Mid), 20B1; 24F1; 45A3
Salfords Goods, LBSC, 5D3
Salhouse, GE, 18E2
Salisbury, LSW(GW), LSW & GW, 4C5
Salt, GN, 15D4
Saltaire, Mid, 21D2; 42A5
Saltash, GW, 1D5
Saltburn, NE, 28E3
Saltcoats, G&SW & Cal, 29D3
Saltfleetby, GN, 17A3; 22G1
Saltford, GW, 3A3; 8D1 *see also* Kelston
*Salthouse Jc*, Fur, 24B5
Saltley, Mid, 13B4; 15G5
*Saltley Jc*, Mid, 13C3
*Saltmarket Jc*, G&SW, 44E2 (inset)
Saltmarshe, NE(GC), 22E5
Saltney, GW, 20D4
Saltney Ferry, LNW, 20D4
Saltoun, NB, 30C1
Salwick, PWY, 24D3
Salzcraggie Plat, HR, 38F4

Sampford Courtenay, LSW, 2B5
Sandal & Walton, Mid, 21E3; 42C2
Sandal, WRG, 21E3; 42C2
Sandbach, LNW & NS, 15B2; 20E2
Sandbach (Wheelock), NS, 15B2; 20E2
Sanderstead, CO, 5C3
Sandford & Banwell, GW, 3B1; 8D3
Sandgate, SEC, 6D2
Sandhills, LY, 45 (inset)
Sandholme, HB, 22D5
Sandhurst Halt, SEC, 4B1
Sandilands, Cal, 30E4
Sandling Junc, SEC, 6D3
Sandon, NS, 15D4
Sandon Dock (Goods), Mid, 45G4 (inset)
Sandown, IW, 4F3
Sandplace, LL, 1D4
Sandsend, NE, 28F2
Sandside, Fur, 24A3
Sandtoft (Goods), AJ, 22F5
Sandwich, SEC, 6C2
Sandwich Road, EK, 6C2
Sandy, GN & LNW, 11D2
Sandy Lodge, Met&GCJt, 5A2
Sandycroft, LNW, 20D4
Sankey Bridges, LNW, 45D4
Sankey for Penketh, CLC, 20C3; 24G3; 45D4
Sanquhar, G&SW, 30F5
Santon, IMR, 23C2
Sarnau, GW, 7A2; 13G3
Sarsden Halt, GW, 10D5
Sauchie, NB, 30A4
Saughall, GC, 20D4
Saughton, NB, 30B3
Saughtree, NB, 27A1; 31G1
Saundersfoot, GW, 7D3
Saunderton, GW&GCJt, 10F2
Savernake, GW, 4A5
Sawbridgeworth, GE, 11F3
Sawdon, NE, 22A4
Sawley, Mid, 16D4
Sawley Junc, Mid, 16D4
Saxby, Mid(MGN), 16E2
Saxham & Risby, GE, 11C5
Saxilby, GN, 16A1
Saxmundham, GE, 12C2
*Saxondale Jc*, GN/LNW, 16C3
Scafell Halt, Cam, 14C3
Scalby, NE, 22A4; 28G1
Scalford, GN&LNWJt, 16E2
Scarborough, NE, 22A3; 28G1
Scarborough Excursion, NE, 22A3; 28G1
Scarcliffe, GC, 16B4; 41C4
Scawby & Hibaldstow, GC, 22F4
Scholes, NE, 21D3; 42A2
Schoolhill, GNS, 37G4
Scopwick & Timberland, GN & GE, 17C1
Scorrier, GW, 1E1 and inset E5
Scorton (Lancs), LNW, 24C3
Scorton (Yorks), NE, 27F5
Scotby, Mid & NE, 26C1
Scotch Dyke, NB, 26B1
Scotland Street (Goods), NB, 30 (inset)
*Scotland Street Jc*, G&SW/Cal, 44F2 (inset)
Scotscalder, HR, 38D3
Scotsgap, NB, 27A4
Scotstoun, Cal, 29C4; 44F4
Scotstoun West, Cal, 29C4; 44F4
Scotstounhill, NB, 29C4; 44F4
Scotswood, NE(NB), 27B5
Scotswood Works Halt, NE(NB), 27B5; 28 (inset)
Scremerston, NE, 31D4
Scrooby, GN, 21G5
Scruton, NE, 21A3; 28G5
Sculcoates, NE & HB, 22 (inset)
Scunthorpe, GC, 22F4 *see also* Frodingham
Sea Mills, CE, 3A2; 8C2; 9G1
Seacombe & Egremont, Wir(GC), 45F3
Seacroft, GN, 17B4
Seaford, LBSC, 5G4
Seaforth & Litherland, LY(LNW/LOR), 20B4; 24G4; 45F3
Seaham Colliery, NE, 28C5
Seaham, NE, 28C5
Seahouses, NSL, 31E5
Seamer, NE, 22A3
*Seamer Jc*, NE, 22A3
Seascale, Fur, 26F3
Seaton (Cumb), CWJ, 26D3
Seaton (Devon), LSW, 2B1
Seaton (Durham), NE, 28C5
Seaton (Rutland), LNW, 16F1
Seaton Carew, NE, 28E4
Seaton Delaval, NE, 28B5
Seaton Junc (Devon), LSW 2B1
Seaton Snook, NE, 28E4
Sedbergh, LNW, 24A2; 27G2
Sedgebrook, GN, 16D2
Sedgefield, NE, 28E5
Sedgeford, GE, 17D5
*Sedgley Jc*, LNW, 13B1
Seedley, LNW(BJ), 45B3
Seend, GW, 3B4
Seer Green Halt for Beaconsfield Golf Club, GW&GCJt, 5A1; 10F1
Sefton & Maghull, CLC, 20B4; 24F4; 45F2 *see also* Maghull
Sefton Park, LNW, 20C4; 24G4, 45F4
Seghill, NE, 28B5
Selby, NE(GN/GE/LNW), 21D5
*Selby East Jc*, NE, 21D5
Selby Swing Bridge, NE, 21D5
Selham, LBSC, 5E1
Selhurst, LBSC, 5B3; 40G5
*Selhurst Jc*, LBSC, 40G5
Selkirk, NB, 30E1
Sellafield, Fur, 26F3
Selling, SEC, 6C3
Selly Oak, Mid, 9A4; 15G4
Selsdon Road, CO/WSC, 5C3
Selsey, SL, 4F1
Selsey Bridge, SL, 4F1
*Selsey Light Railway*, SL, 4E1
Semington Halt, GW, 3B4
Semley, LSW, 3D4
Senghenydd, Rhy, 8B4; 43C3
*Serridge Jc*, SVW, 8A1; 9E2
Sessay, NE, 21B4
Settle, Mid, 24B1
*Settle Jc*, Mid, 24C1
Settrington, NE, 22B5
Seven Hills Halt, GE, 12B5
Seven Kings, GE, 5A4
Seven Sisters (Glam), N&B, 7A5; 43E1
Seven Sisters (Middx), GE, 5A3; 40A4
Seven Stars, W&L, 14B2
Sevenoaks Bat & Ball, SEC, 5C4
Sevenoaks Tub's Hill, SEC, 5C4
Severn Beach, GW, 9G1
Severn Bridge, SVW, 8A1; 9E2
Severn Tunnel Junc, GW, 8B2; 9F1
*Severus Jc*, NE, 21A4 (inset); 21C5
Sexhow, NE, 28F4
Shackerstone, AN, 16F5
Shadwell, GE & EL, 40C4
*Shaftholme Jc*, GN/NE, 21F5
*Shafton Jc*, LY/DV, 21F4; 42D1
Shalford, SEC, 5D1
*Shalford Jc*, LSW/SEC, 5D1
Shandon, NB, 29A3
Shankend, NB, 31F1
Shanklin, IW, 4G3
Shap, LNW, 27F1
Shapwick, SD, 3C1; 8E3
Sharlston, LY, 21E4; 42C1
Sharnal Street, SEC, 6B5
Sharnbrook, Mid, 10B1; 11C1
Sharpness, SVW, 8B1; 9F2
Shaugh Bridge Platform, GW, 2D5
Shaw & Crompton, LY, 21F1
Shawclough & Healey, LY, 20A1; 24E1; 45A1
Shawford & Twyford, LSW(GW), 4D3
Shawforth, LY, 20A1; 24E1; 45A1
*Shawhill Jc*, Cal, 26B2
Shawlands, Cal, 44E3
Sheepbridge, Mid, 16A5; 41B2
Sheepbridge & Whittington Moor, GC, 16A5; 41B2
Sheerness Dockyard, SEC, 6B4
Sheerness East, SEC, 6B4
Sheerness-on-Sea, SEC, 6B4
*Sheet Factory Jc*, GE, 40B2
*Sheet Stores Jc*, Mid, 16D4
Sheffield (Goods), GC, LNW, Mid & SHD, 16A5; 21G3; 41A2; 42G2
Sheffield (Pass), GC(LY) & Mid(NE/LY), 16A5; 21G3; 41A2; 42G2
Sheffield Midland, Mid, 41A2
Sheffield Park, LBSC, 5E4
Shefford, Mid, 11D1
Shelford, GE, 11D3
*Shelwick Jc*, S&H/GW, 9C1
Shenfield & Hutton, GE, 5A5; 11G4
Shenstone, LNW, 15F5
Shenton, AN, 16F5
Shepherds, GW, 1D1
Shepherds Bush, H&C, 39C4
Shepherd's Well, SEC & EK, 6D2
Shepley & Shelley, LY, 21F2; 42D4
Shepperton, LSW, 5B2
Shepreth, GN, 11D3
*Shepreth Branch Jc*, GE, 11C3
Shepshed, LNW, 16E4
Shepton Mallet, GW, 3C2; 8E1
Shepton Mallett (Charlton Road), SD, 3C3; 8E1
Sherborne, LSW, 3D3; 8G1
Sherburn Colliery, NE, 28D5
Sherburn House, NE, 28D5
Sherburn-in-Elmet, NE(GN), 21D4
Sheringham, MGN, 18D3
Sherwood, GN, 16C3; 41F5
Shettleston, NB, 29C5; 44C3
Shide, IWC, 4F3
Shield Row, NE, 27C5
Shieldhall Goods, G&P, 44F4
Shieldhill, Cal, 26A3
Shields, G&SW, 44F1 (inset)

*Shields Jc*, Cal/G&P/G&SW, 44F1 (inset)
Shields Road, G&P, 44F1 (inset)
*Shielmuir Jc*, Cal, 44A2
Shifnal, GW, 15E2
Shildon, NE, 27E5
Shillingstone, SD, 3E4
Shilton, LNW, 10A5; 16G5
Shincliffe, NE, 28D5
Shiplake, GW, 10G2
Shipley Bridge Street, GN, 42A5
Shipley Gate, Mid, 16C4; 41F3
Shipley Station Street, Mid(NE) & GN, 21D2; 42A5
Shippea Hill, GE, 11B4
Shipston-on-Stour, GW, 9C5
Shipton, GW, 10D5
Shirdley Hill, LY, 20A4; 24F4; 45F1
Shirebrook, Mid(GC) & GN, 16B4; 41C4
Shirehampton, CE, 8A2; 9G1
Shireoaks, GC(Mid), 16A4; 41A4
Shirley, GW, 9A5
Shobhall Wharf, Mid, 15D5 (inset)
Shoeburyness, LTS, 6A4
Sholing, LSW, 4E3
Shooters Hill & Eltham Park, SEC, 40E1
Shore (Invergordon), HR, 36C5
Shore Road Goods (Stirling), NB, 30A5
Shoreditch (Goods), LNW, 40C4
Shoreditch (Pass), EL & NL, 40C4
Shoreham (Kent), SEC, 5C4
Shoreham-by-Sea (Sussex), LBSC, 5F3
Shorncliffe Camp, SEC, 6D2
Short Heath (Clark's Lane), Mid, 15F4
Shortlands, SEC, 5B4; 40F2
*Shortlands Jc*, SEC, 40F2
Shotley Bridge, NE, 27C4
Shottle, Mid, 16C5; 41F1
Shotton, LNW, 20D4 *see also* Connah's Quay
Shotton Bridge, NE, 28D5
*Shotton E & W Jcs*, GC, 20D4
Shotts, Cal & NB, 30C4
Shrawardine, S&M, 14A1
Shrewsbury (Goods), S&H, GW, LNW & S&M, 15E1
Shrewsbury (Pass), S&H & S&M, 15E1
*Shrewsbury Line Jc*, LNW, 15C2; 20E2
Shrewsbury West, S&M, 14A1; 15E1
Shrivenham, GW, 9F5
Shrub Hill (Worcester), GW&MidJt, 9B3
Shustoke, Mid, 16G5
Sible & Castle Hedingham, CVH, 11E5
Sibley's for Chickney & Broxted, GE, 11E4
Sibsey, GN, 17C3
Sidcup, SEC, 5B4; 40E1
Siddick, LNW&CWJJt, 26D3
Sideway Halt, NS, 20F1
Sidlesham, SL, 4F1
Sidley, SEC, 6F5
Sidmouth, LSW, 2B2
*Sidmouth Junc*, LSW, 2B2
Sigglesthorne, NE, 22D3
Sight Hill (Goods), NB, 44D4
Sileby, Mid, 16E3
Silecroft, Fur, 24A5
Silian Halt, GW, 13E5
Silkstone, GC, 21F3; 42E3
Silkstone Colliery, LY, 21F3; 42E3
*Silkstone Jc*, LY, 42D2
Silloth, NB, 26C3
Silverdale (Lancs), Fur, 24B3
Silverdale (Staffs) NS, 15C3; 20F1
*Silvermuir Jc South*, Cal, 30D4
Silverton, GW, 2A3
Silvertown, GE, 40C2
Simonstone, LY, 24D1
*Sincil Jc*, GN/GN&GEJt, 16B1; 17B1 (inset)
Sinclairtown, NB, 30A2
Sinderby, NE, 21A3
Sindlesham & Hurst Halt, SEC, 4A1
Singer, NB, 29C4; 44F4
Singleton (Lancs), PWY, 24D4
Singleton (Sussex), LBSC, 4E1
Sinnington, NE, 22A5
Sirhowy, LNW, 8A4; 43B1
*Sirhowy Jc*, LNW/GW, 43B3
Sittingbourne, SEC, 6C4
Six Bells Halt, GW, 43B2
Six Mile Bottom, GE, 11C4
Skares, G&SW, 29F4
Skegby, GN, 16B4; 41D4
Skegness, GN, 17B4
Skelbo, HR, 36A4
Skellingthorpe, GC, 16B1
*Skellow Jc*, WRG, 21F4
Skelmanthorpe, LY, 21F3; 42D3
Skelmersdale, LY(LNW), 20B3; 24F3; 45E2
*Skelton Jc*, CLC, 45B4
Skewen, GW, 7B4; 43F2
Skinningrove, NE, 28E3
Skipton, Mid, 21C1
*Skipton North Jc*, Mid, 21C1
Skipwith & North Duffield, DVL, 21D5
Skirlaugh, NE, 22D3
Slades Green, SEC, 5B4
Slaggyford, NE, 27C2
Slaithwaite, LNW, 21E2; 42D5
Slamannan, NB, 30B5
*Slamannan Jc*, NB, 30B5
Slateford, Cal, 30B2 and inset
Sleaford, GN(GN&GEJt), 16C1; 17C1
*Sleaford East Jc* (Boston), GN, 17D3
*Sleaford N & S Jcs*, GN&GEJt, 17C1
Sledmere & Fimber, NE, 22B4
Sleights, NE, 28F2
Slinfold, LBSC, 5E2
Sling, SVW, 8A2; 9E1
Slingsby, NE, 21B5
Sloane Square, Dist(Met), 39D5
Slochd Crossing, HR, 36F4
Slough, GW, 5B1; 10G1
Small Heath, GW, 15G5
*Smallbrook Jc*, IW/IWC, 4F3
Smallford, GN, 11F2
Smardale, NE, 27F2
Smeafield, NE, 31D4
Smeaton, NB, 30B2
Smeeth, SEC, 6D3
Smeeth Road, GE, 17F4
Smethwick, LNW, 13B2 *see also* Handsworth
Smethwick Junc, GW, 13B2
Smitham, SEC, 5C3
Smithfield Goods, GW, 40C5
Smithy Bridge, LY, 20A1; 45A1
Snae Fell, ME, 23B3
Snailbeach, SBH, 14B1
*Snailwell Jc*, GE, 11C4
Snainton, NE, 22A4
Snaith, LY, 21E5
Snaith & Pollington, GC&HBJt, 21E5
Snape (Goods), GE, 12C1
*Snape Jc*, GE, 12C2
Snapper, LB, 7F3
Snaresbrook & Wanstead, GE, 5A4; 40A2
Snarestone, AN, 16E5
Snatchwood Halt, GW, 43A2
Snell's Nook Halt, LNW, 16E4
Snettisham, GE, 17D5
Snodland, SEC, 6C5
Snowdon, NWNG & SM, 19E2
*Snowdon Mountain Railway*, SM, 19E2
Snow Hill (Birmingham), GW, 13C3; 15G4
Snelland, GC, 17A1
*Snydale Jc*, Mid, 42C2
*Soap Works Jc* (Soho), LNW, 13C2
Soham, GE, 11B4
Soho, LNW, 13C2; 15G4
Soho & Winson Green, GW, 13C3; 15G4
*Soho East Jc*, LNW, 13C3
Soho Goods, LNW, 13C3
Soho Pool, LNW, 13B3
*Soho Pool Jc*, LNW, 13B3
Soho Road, LNW, 13B3; 15G4
Sole Street, SEC, 5B5
Solihull, GW, 9A5
Somerleyton, GE, 12A1; 18F1
Somers Town Goods, Mid, 40C5
Somerset Road, Mid, 13D3; 15G4
Somersham, GN&GEJt, 11B3
Somerton (Som), GW, 3D2; 8F2
Sorbie, P&W, 25C4
South Acton, NSW & Dist, 39C3
South Bank, NE, 28E4
South Beach (Ardrossan), G&SW, 29D3
South Bermondsey, LBSC, 40D4
South Bromley, LNW, 40C3
South Canterbury, SEC, 6C3
South Caradon, LC, 1C4
South Cave, HB, 22D4
South Dock (Millwall), GE, 40D3
South Docks Goods (Liverpool), LY, 45 (inset)
South Ealing, Dist, 39D2
South Eastrington, NE, 22D5
South Elmsall, WRG, 21F4; 42 D1 *see also* Moorhouse
South Farnborough, LSW, 5C1 *see also* Aldershot North Camp
South Gosforth, NE, 27B5
South Hampstead, LNW, 39B5
South Harrow, Dist, 5A2; 39B1
South Harrow, GC, 39B2
South Hetton, NE, 28D5
South Howden, HB, 22E5
South Kensington, Dist & Met(Dist), 39D5
South Lambeth Goods, GW, 39E4 (inset); 40D5
*South Leicester Jc*, LNW/Mid, 16F5
South Leigh, GW, 10E5
South Leith, NB, 30 (inset)
South Leith (Goods), NB, 30 (inset)
South Leith Docks, Cal, 30 (inset)
South Lynn, MGN, 17E4
South Milford, NE, 21D4; 42B1
South Molton, GW, 7F4
South Molton Road, LSW, 7G4
South Queensferry (Goods), NB, 30B3
South Renfrew, G&SW, 44F4
South Rhondda (Goods), GW, 8C5; 43D4
South Shields, NE & SSM, 28B5

South Shore Goods (Blackpool), PWY, 24D4
South Side Goods (Glasgow), Cal & GBK, 44, Inset E1
South Street Halt, SEC, 6B3
South Tottenham, THJ(LTS), 40A4
*South Tottenham Jc*, GE, 40A4
South Town (Yarmouth), GE, 18F1
South Willingham & Hainton, GN, 17A2
South Witham, Mid(MGN), 16E1
Southall, GW, 5B2; 39C1
Southam & Long Itchington, LNW, 10B4
Southam Road & Harbury, GW, 10B5
Southampton (Town), LSW(GW/MSW), 4E4
Southampton (West), LSW(MSW), 4E4
Southborough, SEC, 5D5
Southbourne Halt, LBSC, 4E1
Southburn, NE, 22C4
Southcoates, NE, 22 (inset)
*Southcote Jc*, GW, 4A2
Southease & Rodmell Halt, LBSC, 5F4
Southend (Glam), Mum, 43G3
Southend-on-Sea, LTS & GE, 6A4
Southend-on-Sea for Westcliff & Thorpe Bay, GE, 6A4
*Southerham Jc*, LBSC, 5F4
*Southern Jc*, SYJ, 16A4; 21G4; 41A4
Southerndown Road, BRY, 7C5; 43D4
*Southfield Jc*, Cal, 30D5
Southfields, LSW(Dist), 39E4
Southfleet, SEC, 5B5
Southill, Mid, 11D1
Southminster, GE, 12G5
Southport, LY(LNW), LY & CLC, 20A4; 24E4; 45F1
Southrey, GN, 17B1
Southwaite, LNW, 26D1
Southwark Park, SEC, 40D4
Southwater, LBSC, 5E2
Southwell, Mid, 16C3
Southwick (Durham) Goods, NE, 28C5
Southwick (Kircud), G&SW, 26C4
Southwick (Sussex), LBSC, 5F3
Southwold, SWD, 12B1
*Southwold Railway*, SWD, 12B1
Sowerby Bridge, LY, 21E1; 42C5
Spa Road Bermondsey, SEC, 40D4
Spalding, GN(GE/MGN) & Mid, 17E2
*Spalding North Jc*, GN/GN&GEJt, 17E3
*Spalding South Jc*, GN/MGN, 17E3
Sparkford, GW, 3D2; 8F1
Sparrowlee, NS, 15C5
Spean Bridge, NB, 32B2
Speech House Road, SVW, 8A1; 9E1
Speen, GW, 4A3
Speeton, NE, 22B3
Speke, LNW, 20C4; 45E4
*Speke Jc*, LNW, 45E4
Spennithorne, NE, 21A2; 27G5
Spennymoor, NE, 27D5
Spetchley (Goods), Mid, 9B3
Spetisbury, SD, 3E4
Spey Bay, GNS, 36C1
Spiersbridge (Goods), GBK, 44E2
Spilsby, GN, 17B3
Spink Hill for Mount St Mary, GC, 16A4; 41B3
Spital, BJ, 20C4; 45F4
Spitalfields Goods, GE, 40C4
*Splott Jc*, TV, 43B4
Spofforth, NE, 21C3
Spon Lane, LNW, 13B2; 15G4
Spondon, Mid, 16D5; 41G2
*Spondon Jc*, Mid, 16D5, 41G2
Spooner Row, GE, 12A4; 18F4
Spratton, LNW, 10A3
Spring Vale, LY, 20A2; 24E2
*Springbank Jcs* (Hull), HB, 22 (inset)
Springburn Park (Goods), Cal, 29C5; 44D4
Springburn, NB, 44D4
Springfield, NB, 34F5
Springside, G&SW, 29E3
*Springwood Jc*, LNW&LYJt/LNW/LY, 21E2; 42D5
Sprotborough, HB, 21F4
Sprouston, NE, 31E2
*Sprouston Jc*, NB/NE, 31E2
Stacksteads, LY, 20A1; 24E1
Staddlethorpe, NE(GC/LNW), 22E5
Stafford, LNW(NS/GN), 15E3; 20G1
Stafford Common, GN, 15D3; 20G1
*Stafford Jc*, LNW/SWN, 15E2
Staincliffe & Batley Carr, LNW, 42C3 *see also* Batley Carr
Staincross for Mapplewell, GC, 21F3; 42D2
Staines, LSW & GW, 5B1
*Staines Jc*, LSW, 5B1
Stainforth & Hatfield, GC(NE), 21F5
Stainland & Holywell Green, LY, 21E2; 42C5
Staintondale, NE, 28G1
Stairfoot, GC, 42E2
Staithes, NE, 28E2
Stalbridge, SD, 3D3; 8G1
Staley & Millbrook (Goods), LNW, 21F1
Stalham, MGN, 18E2
Stallingborough, GC, 22F2
Stalybridge, GC&LNWJt & LY, 21F1 and inset A2
Stamford, Mid(LNW) & GN, 16F1; 17F1
Stamford Bridge (Yorks), NE, 22C5
Stamford Brook, (LSW(Dist), 39D4
Stamford Hill, GE, 40A4
*Stammerham Jc*, LBSC, 5E2
Stanbridgeford, LNW, 10D1
Standish (Lancs), LNW, 20B3; 24F2; 45D1
*Standish Jc* (Glos), GW/Mid, 9E3
*Standish Jc* (Lancs), LNW, 20B3; 24F3; 45D2
Standon, GE, 11E3
Standon Bridge, LNW, 15D3; 20F1
Stane Street Halt, GE, 11E4
Stanford-le-Hope, LTS, 5A5
Stanhoe, GE, 18D5
Stanhope, NE, 27D4
Stanley (Lancs), LNW, 45F3 *see also* Knotty Ash
Stanley (Yorks), MJ, 21E3; 42B2
Stanley Bridge Halt, GW, 3A4
Stanley Junc (Perth), Cal(HR), 33E5
Stanmore, LNW, 5A2
Stanner, GW, 14E2
Stannergate (Goods), D&A, 34E1 (inset)
Stanningley, GN(LY), 21D2; 42A4
Stannington, NE, 27A5
Stansfield Hall, LY, 21E1
Stansted, GE, 11E4
Stanton, GW, 9F5
Stanton Gate, Mid, 16D4; 41G3
Staple, EK, 6C2
Staple Hill, Mid, 3A3; 8C1; 9G2
Stapleford & Sandiacre (Notts), Mid, 16D4; 41G3
Staplehurst, SEC, 6D5
Stapleton Road, GW, 3 (inset); 8C1
Starbeck, NE, 21C3
Starcross, GW, 2C3
Staveley (Westmorland), LNW, 27G1
Staveley Town (Derbys), GC & Mid, 16A4; 41B3
Staveley Works, GC, 16A4; 41B3 *see also* Barrow Hill
Staverton (Devon), GW, 2D4
Staverton Halt (Wilts), GW, 3B4
Staward, NE, 27C3
Stechford, LNW, 15G5
Steele Road, NB, 27A1
Steelend (Goods), NB, 30A3
Steens Bridge, GW, 9B1
Steeplehouse (Goods), LNW, 16C5; 41E1
Steer Point, GW, 2E5
Steeton & Silsden, Mid, 21C1
*Stenson Jc*, Mid, 16D5
Stepford, G&SW, 26A4
Stepney (Hull), NE, 22 (inset)
Stepney (London), GE(LTS), 40C3
Stepney Green, WB, 40C3
Stepps Road, Cal, 29C5; 44C4
Stevenage, GN, 11E2
Stevenston, G&SW & Cal, 29D3
Steventon, GW, 10F4
Stewarton, GBK, 29 D4
Stewarts Lane Goods, SEC, 39E4 (inset)
*Stewarts Lane Jc*, SEC, 39E4 (inset)
Steyning, LBSC, 5F2
Stickney, GN, 17C3
Stillington, NE, 28E5
Stirchley, GW, 15F2
Stirling, Cal & NB, 30A5
Stixwould, GN, 17B2
Stobcross, Cal & Cal&NBJt, 44E4
Stobo, Cal, 30E3
Stobs, NB, 31F1
Stobs Camp, NB, 31F1
Stockbridge, LSW(MSW), 4C4
Stockcross & Bagnor, GW, 4A4
Stockingford, Mid, 16F5
Stockport, LNW(NS/LY) & CLC, 20C1; 21G1; 45A4
Stocksfield, NE(NB), 27C4
Stocksmoor, LY, 21F2; 42D4
Stockton (Durham), NE, 28E5
Stockton Brook, NS, 15C3; 20E1
Stockwith (Goods), GN&GEJt, 22G5
Stogumber, GW, 8F5
Stoke (Suffolk), GE, 11D5
Stoke Bruern (Goods), SMJ, 10C3
Stoke Canon, GW, 2B3
Stoke Edith, GW, 9C2
Stoke Ferry, GE, 11A4; 17F5
Stoke Golding, AN, 16F5
Stoke Mandeville, Met&GCJt, 10E2
Stoke Newington, GE, 40B4
Stoke-on-Trent, NS(LNW), 15C3; 20F1
Stoke Works (Goods), Mid, 9B4
Stoke Works (Pass), GW(Mid), 9B4
Stokesley, NE, 28F4
Stone, NS, 15D3; 20F1
Stone Cross Halt, LBSC, 5F5
*Stone Cross Jc*, LBSC, 5F5
Stone Crossing Halt, SEC, 5B5
Stonea, GE, 11A3; 17G3
Stonebridge Park, LNW(LE), 39B3
Stoneferry (Goods), NE, 22D3
Stonehaven, Cal(NB), 34A2
Stonehouse (Glos), GW & Mid, 9E3

Stonehouse (Lanarks), Cal, 30D5
*Stonehouse Jcs*, Cal, 44A1
Stonehouse Pool, LSW, 1 (inset)
Stoneywood (Aberdeen), GNS, 37F4
Storeton for Barnston, GC, 20C4; 24G4; 45F4
Stottesdon, CMDP, 9A2; 15G2
Stoulton, GW, 9C3
Stourbridge, GW, 9A3; 15G3
Stourbridge Junc, GW, 9A3; 15G3
Stourport, GW, 9A3
*Stourton Jc*, Mid/EWY, 21D3; 42B2
Stow (Midlothian), NB, 30D1
Stow (Norfolk), GE, 17F4
Stow Bedon, GE, 12A5; 18F5
Stow-on-the-Wold, GW, 9D5
Stow Park, GN&GEJt, 16A2
Stowmarket, GE, 12C4
Stracathro, Cal, 34C3
Stradbroke, MSL, 12B3
Stranraer, P&W, 25C2
Strata Florida, GW, 14D5
Stratford, GE, 5A4; 40B3
Stratford Market, GE, 40B2
Stratford-on-Avon, GW & SMJ, 9B5
Strathaven (Central and North), Cal, 29D5
*Strathaven Jc*, Cal, 44C2
Strathblane, NB, 29B5
Strathbungo, GBK, 44E3 and inset F1
Strathcarron, HR, 35E2
Strathmiglo, NB, 34F5
Strathord, Cal(HR), 33E5
Strathpeffer, HR, 35D5
Strathyre, Cal, 33F2
Stratton, GW, 9F5
Stravithie, NB, 34F3
Strawberry Hill, LSW, 5B2; 39E2
*Strawfrank Jc*, Cal, 30D4
Streatham, LBSC, 5B3; 40F5
Streatham Common, LBSC, 40F5
Streatham Hill, LBSC(LNW), 40E5
*Streatham Jc*, LBSC, 40F5
*Streatham North Jc*, LBSC, 40F5
*Streatham South Jc*, LBSC, 40F5
Streetly, Mid, 15F5
Strensall, NE, 21B5
Stretford, MSJA(CLC), 45B3
Stretford Bridge, BC, 14C1
*Stretford Bridge Jc*, BC/GW&LNWJt, 14C1
Stretham, GE, 11B4
Stretton (Derbys), Mid, 16B5; 41D2
Stretton & Clay Mills (Staffs), NS(GN), 15C5 (inset)
*Stretton Jc*, LNW/NS, 15C5 (inset)
Stretton-on-Fosse, GW, 9C5
Strichen, GNS, 37C4
Strines, GC&MidJt, 15A4; 21G1
Strome Ferry, HR, 35E1
Strood, SEC, 6B5
Stroud, GW & Mid, 9E3
Stroud Green, GN(NL), 40A5
Struan, HR, 33C3
Stubbins, LY, 20A1; 24E1; 45B1
*Stubbins Jc*, LY, 45B1
*Studland Road Jc*, LSW/Dist, 39D4
Studley & Astwood Bank, Mid, 9B4
Sturmer, GE, 11D5
Sturminster Newton, SD, 3E3
Sturry, SEC, 6C2
Sturton, GC, 16A2
Stutton (Goods), NE, 21D4
Styal, LNW, 15A3; 20C1; 45A4
Suckley, GW, 9B2
Sudbrook (Goods), GW, 8B2; 9F1
Sudbury (Staffs), NS(GN), 15D5
Sudbury (Suffolk), GE, 12D5
Sudbury & Harrow Road, GC, 39B2
Sudbury Hill, Dist, 39B2
Sudbury Town, Dist, 39B2
Sugar Loaf, LNW, 14E4
Sulby Bridge, IMR, 23A3; 25G4
Sulby Glen, IMR, 23A3; 25G4
Sully, TV, 8D4; 43B5
Summer Lane, GC, 21F3; 42E2
Summerseat, LY, 20A1; 24E1; 45B1
Summerston, NB, 29B5; 44E5
Sunbank Halt, GW, 20F5
Sunbury, LSW, 5B2
Sunderland, NE, 28C5
Sundridge Park, SEC, 40F2
Sunilaws, NE, 31D2
Sunningdale, LSW, 5B1
Sunnywood Halt, LY, 45B1
Surbiton, LSW, 5B2; 39G2
Surfleet, GN, 17D2
*Surrey Canal Jc*, SEC, 40D3
Surrey Docks, EL, 40D4
Sutton (Cambs), GE, 11B3
Sutton (Surrey), LBSC, 5C3
Sutton Bingham, LSW, 3E2
Sutton Bridge, MGN, 17E4
*Sutton Bridge Jc*, MGN, 17E3
Sutton Coldfield, LNW, 15F5
Sutton-in-Ashfield, Mid, GC& GN, 16B4; 41D4
Sutton Junc, Mid, 16B4; 41D4
Sutton Oak, LNW, 45D3
Sutton-on-Hull, NE, 22D3
Sutton-on-Sea, GN, 17A4
Sutton Park, Mid, 15F5
Sutton Scotney, GW, 4C3
Sutton Weaver, LNW, 15A1; 20D3; 45D5
Swadlincote, Mid, 16E5
Swaffham, GE, 18F5
Swaffhamprior, GE, 11C4
Swainsthorpe, GE, 18F3
Swalwell, NE, 27C5; 28 (inset)
*Swalwell Branch Jc*, 28 (inset)
Swan Village, GW, 13B2; 15F4
Swanage, LSW, 3G5
Swanbourne, LNW, 10D2
Swanbridge Halt, TV, 43B5
Swanley, SEC, 5B4
Swannington, Mid, 16E4
Swansea, GW, LNW, Mid, RSB & Mum, 7B4; 43G3
Swansea Bay, LNW, 7B4; 43G3
Swanwick, LSW, 4E3
Swavesey, GE(Mid), 11B3
Sway, LSW, 4E5
Swaythling, LSW(GW), 4D4
Swimbridge, GW, 7F4
Swinderby, Mid, 16B2
Swindon, GW, 9G5
Swindon Town, MSW, 9G5
Swindon Works, GW, 9G5
Swine, NE, 22D3
Swineshead, GN, 17D2
*Swing Bridge Jc* (St Olaves), GE, 18F1
*Swing Bridge Jc* (Trowse), GE, 18F3
Swinton (Lancs), LY, 20B2; 24F1; 45B2
Swinton (Yorks), Mid(NE) & GC, 21F4; 42F1
Swiss Cottage, Met, 39B5
Sydenham, LBSC, 40F4
Sydenham Hill, SEC, 40F4
Sykehouse, GC&HBJt, 21E5
*Sykes Jc*, GC/GN&GEJt, 16A2
Sylfaen, W&L, 14B2
Symington, Cal, 30E4
Symonds Yat, GW, 8A2; 9E1
Syston, Mid(MGN), 16E3
*Syston N, S & E Jcs*, Mid, 16E3

Tadcaster, NE, 21D4
Tadworth & Walton-on-Hill, SEC, 5C3
*Taff Bargoed Jc*, GW/TBJ, 43C3
Taffs Well, TV(Rhy), 8C4; 43C4
Tain, HR, 36B4
Takeley, GE, 11F4
Talacre, LNW, 20C5
Talbot Road (Blackpool), PWY, 24D4
Talerddig, Cam, 14B4
Talgarth, Cam(Mid), 14F3
Talley Road, VT, 13G5
Tallington, GN, 17F1
Talsarn Halt, GW, 13E5
Talsarnau, Cam, 19F2
Talybont Halt, Cam, 13A5; 19G2
Talybont-on-Usk, BM, 14G3
Tal-y-Cafn & Eglwysbach, LNW, 19D4
Talyllyn Junc, BM(Mid/Cam), 14G3
Tamerton Foliot, LSW, 1D5
Tamworth, LNW & Mid, 15F5
*Tanat Valley Railway*, Tan, 19G5; 20G5
Tanfield, NE, 21A3
Tanhouse Lane, GC&MidJt(CLC), 45D4
Tankerton Halt, SEC, 6B3
Tannadice, Cal, 34C4
Tanshelf, LY, 21E4; 42C1
Tan-y-Bwlch, Fest, 19F3
Tan-y-Grisiau, Fest, 19F3
Taplow, GW, 5B1; 10G2
*Tapton Jc*, Mid, 16B5; 41B2
Tarbolton, G&SW, 29E4
Tarff, G&SW, 26C5
Tarset, NB, 27A2
Tattenhall, LNW, 15B1; 20E3
*Tattenhall Jc*, LNW, 15B1; 20E3
Tattenhall Road, LNW, 15B1; 20E3
Tattenham Corner, SEC, 5C3
Tattershall, GN, 17C2
Taunton, GW, 8F4
Tavistock, LSW & GW, 1C5
*Tavistock Jc*, GW, 2D5
Tay Bridge (Dundee), NB, 34 (inset)
Taynuilt, Cal, 32E3
Tayport, NB, 34E4
Tean, NS, 15D4
Tebay, LNW&NEJt, 27F1
Teddington, LSW, 5B2; 39F2
Teigngrace, GW, 2C3
Teignmouth, GW, 2C3
Temple Hirst, NE, 21E5
Temple Meads (Bristol), GW&MidJt, 3A2 and inset; 8C2
Temple Sowerby, NE, 27E1
Temple, Dist(Met), 40C5
Templecombe, LSW&SDJt & SD, 3D3; 8G1
Templecombe Lower Platform, SD, 3D3; 8G1
Templeton, GW, 7C3

Tempsford, GN, 11C2
Tenbury Wells, S&H, 9A1
Tenby, GW, 7D3
*Tennochside Jc*, NB, 44C3
Tenterden St Michael's, KES, 6D4
Tenterden Town, KES, 6D4
Tern Hill, GW, 15D2; 20G2
Terrington, MGN, 17E4
Teston Crossing Halt, SEC, 6E5
Tetbury, GW, 9F3
Teversall, Mid & GN, 16B4; 41D3
Tewkesbury, Mid, 9D3
Teynham, SEC, 6C4
Thackley, GN, 21D2; 42A4
Thame, GW, 10E3
Thames Ditton, LSW, 5B2; 39G2
Thames Haven, LTS, 6A5
Thankerton, Cal, 30E4
Thatcham, GW, 4A3
Thatto Heath, LNW, 20C3; 24G3; 45E3
Thaxted, GE, 11E4
The Dyke, LBSC, 5F3
The Hale Halt, GN, 5A2
The Lodge Halt, GW, 20E4
The Mound, HR, 36A4
The Oaks, LY, 20B2; 24F2; 45B1
Theale, GW, 4A2
Theddingworth, LNW, 16G3
Theddlethorpe, GN, 17A3; 22G1
Thelwall, LNW, 15A2; 20C2; 24G2; 45C4
Theobalds Grove, GE, 11G3
Thetford, GE, 12B5; 18G5
Thetford Bridge, GE, 12B5
Theydon Bois, GE, 11G3
*Thingley Jc*, GW, 3A4
Thirsk, NE, 21A4
Thongs Bridge, LY, 21F2; 42D5
Thorganby, DVL, 21D5
Thorington, GE, 12E4
Thornaby, NE, 28E4
Thornbury, Mid, 8B1; 9F2
Thorne, GC & NE(GC), 21E5
Thorner, NE, 21D3
Thorney, MGN, 17F2
Thorneyburn, NB, 27A2
Thorneywood, GN, 41F5
Thornfalcon, GW, 8F4
Thornhill (Dumfries), G&SW, 30G4
Thornhill (Yorks), LY, 21E3; 42C3 *see also* Ravensthorpe
Thornielee, NB, 30E1
Thornley, NE, 28D5
Thornliebank (Goods), GBK, 29C5; 44F2
Thornliebank (Pass), Cal, 29C5; 44E2
*Thornly Park Jc*, G&SW, 44G3
Thornton (Lancs), PWY, 24D4
Thornton (Yorks), GN, 21D2; 42A5
Thornton (Yorks), Mid, 21C1
Thornton Abbey, GC, 22E3
Thornton Dale, NE, 22A5
Thornton Heath, LBSC, 5B3; 40G5
Thornton-in-Craven, Mid, 21C1
Thornton Junc, NB, 30A2; 34G5
Thorntonhall, Cal, 29D5; 44E2
Thorp Arch, NE, 21C4
Thorp Gates (Goods), NE, 21D5
Thorpe (Northants), LNW, 10A1; 11B1
Thorpe (Norwich), GE, 18F3
Thorpe Bay, LTS, 6A4
Thorpe Cloud, LNW, 15C5
Thorpe Culvert, GN, 17B4
Thorpe-in-Balne, GC&HBJt, 21F5
*Thorpe Jc*, GE, 18F3
Thorpe-le-Soken, GE, 12E3
Thorpe-on-the-Hill, Mid, 16B1
Thorpe Thewles, NE, 28E5
Thorpness Halt, GE, 12C2
Thor's Cave, NS, 15B5
Thorverton, GW, 2A3
Thrapston, LNW & Mid, 10A1, 11B1
Three Bridges, LBSC, 5D3
Three Cocks Junc, Cam(Mid), 14F2
Three Counties, GN, 11E2
Threlkeld, CKP, 26E1
Thringstone Halt, LNW, 16E4
Throsk Platform, Cal, 30A5
*Throstle Nest Jc*, CLC, 45B3
Thrumster, HR, 38D2
*Thrybergh Jc*, GC/GC&MidJt, 42F1
Thurcroft (Goods), GC/Mid&HBJt, 16A4; 21G4; 41A4
Thurgarton, Mid, 16C3
Thurgoland (Goods), GC, 42E3
Thurlby, GN, 17E1
Thurnby & Scraptoft, GN, 16F3
Thursford, MGN, 18D4
Thurso, HR, 38C3
Thurstaston, BJ, 20C5
Thurston, GE, 12C5
Thuxton, GE, 18F4
*Thwaite Flat Jc*, Fur, 24B5
Tibbermuir Crossing, Cal, 33E5
Tibshelf & Newton, Mid, 16B4; 41D3
Tibshelf Town, GC, 16B4; 41D3
Ticehurst Road, SEC, 5E5
Tickhill & Wadworth, SYJ, 21G5
Tidal Basin, GE, 40C2
Tiddington, GW, 10E3
Tidenham, GW, 8B2; 9F1
Tidworth, MSW, 4B5
Tilbury, LTS, 5B5
Tilbury Docks, LTS, 5B5
Tile Hill, LNW, 10A5
Tilehurst, GW, 4A2; 10G3
Tillicoultry, NB, 30A4
Tillietudlem, Cal, 30D5
Tillyfourie, GNS, 37F2
Tillynaught, GNS, 37C2
Tilton, GN&LNWJt, 16F2
Timperley, MSJA(CLC), 20C1; 24G1; 45B3
Tingley, GN, 21E3; 42B3
Tinsley, GC, 21G4; 42G2
Tintern for Brockweir, GW, 8B2; 9F1
Tipton, GW & LNW, 13B1; 15F4
Tipton St John's, LSW, 2B2
Tiptree, GE, 12F5
Tir Phil & New Tredegar, Rhy, 8A4; 43B2 *see also* New Tredegar
Tirydail, GW(LNW), 7A3; 43G1
Tisbury, LSW, 3D4
Tissington, LNW, 15C5
Tisted, LSW, 4C2
Titley, GW, 14E1
Tiverton, GW, 2A3; 7G5
Tiverton Junc, GW, 2A2
Tivetshall, GE, 12A3; 18G3
Tiviot Dale (Stockport), CLC, 45A3
Tochineal, GNS, 37C1
Toddington, GW, 9D4
Todmorden, LY, 20A1; 21E1
Toft & Kingston (Goods), LNW, 11C3
*Tolcarn Jc*, GW, 1D1
Tollcross, Cal, 44D3
Toller, GW, 3F2
Tollerton, NE, 21B4
Tollesbury, GE, 12F5
Tolleshunt D'Arcy, GE, 12F5
Tomatin, HR, 36E4
Tonbridge, SEC, 5D5
Tondu, GW, 7C5; 43D4
Tonfanau, Cam, 13B5
Tonge & Bredon, Mid, 16D4
Tongham, LSW, 4B1; 5D1
Tongwynlais, Car, 43C4
Tonteg Halt, TV, 43C3
*Ton-y-Groes Jc*, PT, 43F3
Tonypandy, TV, 43D3
Tonyrefail, GW, 43D3
Tooting Junc, LBSC&LSWJt, 39F5
Topcliffe, NE, 21A3
Topsham, LSW, 2B3
Torksey, GC, 16A2
Torpantau, BM, 8A5; 14G3, 43C1
Torphins, GNS, 34A3; 37G2
Torquay, GW, 2D3
Torrance, NB, 29B5; 44D5
Torre, GW, 2D3
Torrington, LSW, 7G3
*Torrisholme Jcs*, Mid, 24B3
Torryburn, NB, 30A4
Torver, Fur, 24A4; 26G2
Totnes, GW, 2D4
Toton Yard, Mid, 41G3
Tottenham Hale, GE, 40A4
Totteridge, GN(NL), 5A3; 11G3
Tottington, LY, 20A1; 24F1; 45B1
Totton, LSW, 4E4
*Touch South Jc*, NB, 30A3
Tovil, SEC, 6C5
Tow Law, NE, 27D5
Towcester, SMJ, 10C3
Tower Hill, LSW, IB5
Towiemore (Goods), GNS, 37D1
Town Green & Aughton, LY, 20B4; 24F3; 45F2
Towneley, LY, 24D1
Towyn, Cam & Tal, 13B5
Trabboch, G&SW, 29F4
Trafford Park, CLC, 20C1; 24G1; 45B3
Tram Inn, GW, 9D1; 14F1
Tranent, NB, 30B1
Travellers' Rest, TV, 43C3
Trawscoed, GW, 13D5
Trawsfynydd, GW, 19F3
Treamble, GW, 1D1
Treborth, LNW, 19D2
Trecynon Halt, GW, 43D2
Tredegar, LNW, 8A4; 43B1
Treeton, Mid, 16A4; 21G4; 41A3; 42G1
*Treeton Jc*, GC/Mid/SHD, 42G1
Trefeglwys, Van, 14C4
Trefeinon, Cam(Mid), 14F3
Treferig, TV, 8B5; 43C3
*Treferig Railway Jc*, TV, 43C3
Trefnant, LNW, 19D5
Treforest, TV & BRY, 8B5; 43C3
Treforest Halt, AD, 43C3
Tregaron, GW, 14D5

Tregarth, LNW, 19D2
Trehafod, TV(BRY), 8B5; 43C3
Treharris, GW(Rhy), 43C3
Treherbert, TV(RSB), 7B5; 43D2
Trelewis Halt, TBJ, 43C2
Trench Crossing, LNW, 15E2
Trench Halt, Cam, 20F4
Trenholme Bar, NE, 28F5
Trent, Mid, 16D4
*Trent Jc*, Mid, 16D4
*Trent Valley Jc*, LNW, 15E3
Trentham, NS, 15C3; 20F1
Trentham Park, NS, 15D3; 20F1
Treorchy, TV, 8B5; 43D2
Tresavean, GW, 1E5 (inset)
Tresmeer, LSW, 1B4
Trethomas, GW, 8B4; 43B3
Trevil, LNW, 8A4; 43B1
Trevor, GW, 20F5
Trewerry & Trerice Halt, GW, 1D1
Trewythan, Van, 14C4
Triangle, LY, 21E1
Trimdon, NE, 28D5
Trimingham, NSJ, 18D2
Trimley, GE, 12E3
Trimsaran (Goods), BPGV, 7A3
Trimsaran Road, BPGV, 7A2
Tring, LNW, 10E1
Trinity & Newhaven, NB, 30 (inset)
Trodigal Halt, CM, 29 (inset)
Troedyrhiew Garth, GW, 7B5; 43E3
Troedyrhiw, QYM & TV, 43C2
Troedyrhiw Platform, QYM, 43C2
Troon, G&SW, 29E3
Troutbeck, CKP, 26E1
Trowbridge, GW, 3B4
Trowell, Mid, 16C4; 41F3
Trowse (Norwich), GE, 18F3
*Trowse Upper Jc*, GE, 18F3
Troy (Monmouth), GW, 8A2; 9E1
Trumper's Crossing (for South Hanwell & Osterley Park) Halt, GW, 39D2
Truro, GW, 1E1
Trusham, GW, 2C3
Truthall Platform, GW, 1F5 (inset)
Tryfan Junc, NWNG, 19E2
Tucker Street (Wells, Som), GW, 3C2; 8E2
Tue Brook, LNW, 20C4; 24G4; 45F3
*Tuffley Jc*, Mid, 9E3
Tufnell Park (Goods), GE, 40B5
*Tufts Jcs*, SVW, 8A1; 9E2
Tullibardine, Cal, 33F4
Tullock, NB, 32B1
Tulse Hill, LBSC, 5B3; 40E5
Tumble, LM, 7A3
Tumby Woodside, GN, 17C2
Tunbridge Wells, SEC & LBSC(SEC), 5D5
Tunbridge Wells West, LBSC, 5D5
*Tunnel Jc* (Neepsend), GC, 22G4
*Tunnel Jc* (Salisbury), LSW, 4C5
*Tunnel Jc* (Worcester), GW, 9B3
Tunstall, NS, 15C3; 20E1
Turnberry, G&SW, 29G2
Turnchapel, LSW 1D5 and inset
Turnham Green, LSW(Dist), 39D3
Turnhouse, NB, 30B3
Turriff, GNS, 37D1
Turton & Edgworth, LY, 20A2; 24E1; 45B1
Turvey, Mid, 10B1
Tutbury, NS(GN), 15D5
Tuxford, GN & GC, 16B2
Tweedmouth, NE, 31C3
Twenty, MGN, 17E2
Twerton-on-Avon, GW, 3A3
Twickenham, LSW, 5B2; 39E2
Twizell, NE, 31D3
Twyford (Berks), GW, 4A1
Twywell, Mid, 10A1
Ty Croes, LNW, 19D1
*Tycoch Jc*, GW/BPGV, 7A2
Tydd, MGN, 17E3
Tyldesley, LNW, 20B2; 24F2; 45C2
Tylorstown, TV, 8B5; 43D2
Tylwch, Cam, 14C4
Tyndrum, NB & Cal, 32E1
Tyne Dock, NE, 28B5
Tynehead, NB, 30C1
Tynemouth, NE, 28B5
Tyseley, GW, 15G5
Tytherington, Mid, 8B1; 9F2

Uckfield, LBSC, 5E4
Uddingston, Cal & NB, 44C3
*Uddingston Jc*, Cal, 44C3
Uddingston West, NB, 44C3
Udny, GNS, 37E4
Uffculme, GW, 2A2; 8G5
Uffington (Berks), GW, 10F5
Uffington & Barnack, Mid, 17F1
Ufford Bridge, GN, 17F1
Ulbster, HR, 38E2
Ulceby, GC, 22E3
Ulleskelf, NE, 21D4
Ullesthorpe & Lutterworth, Mid, 16G4
Ullock, WCE, 26E3
*Ullock Jc*, WCE, 26E3
Ulverston, Fur, 24A4
Umberleigh, LSW, 7F3
Underwood Goods (Paisley), Cal, 44G3
Union Bank Farm Halt, LNW, 45D4
Union Mills, IMR, 23B2
Unstone, Mid, 16A5; 41B2
Up Exe, GW, 2A3
Uphill, NB, 30C3
*Uphill Jc*, GW, 3B1; 8D3
Upholland, LY, 20B3; 24F3; 45D2
Uplawmoor, Cal, 29D4; 44G2
*Uplawmoor East Jc*, Cal, 29D4
Upminster, LTS, 5A5
Upper Bank, Mid, 7B4; 43G3
Upper Batley, ON, 42B3
Upper Boat, AD & Car, 43C3
Upper Broughton, Mid, 16D3
Upper Holloway, THJ(LTS), 40B5
Upper Lydbrook, SVW, 8A1; 9E1
Upper Pontnewydd, GW, 8B3; 43A3
Upper Port Glasgow (Goods), G&SW, 29B3
Upper Sydenham, SEC, 40F4
Upper Warlingham, CO, 5C3
*Upperby New Jc*, LNW, 26 (inset)
Uppermill, LNW, 21F1
Upperthorpe & Killamarsh, GC, 16A4; 41B3 *see also* Killamarsh
Uppingham, LNW, 16F2
Upton (Ches), GC, 20C4; 24G4; 45F4
Upton & Blewbury, GW, 10F4
Upton & North Elmsall, HB, 21E4; 42D1
Upton Magna, SWN, 15E1
Upton-on-Severn, Mid, 9C3
Upton Park, LTS(Dist) & LNW, 40C2
Upwell, WUT, 17F4
Upwey, GW, 3F3
*Upwey Jc*, GW(LSW), 3G3
Upwey Wishing Well Halt, GW, 3F3
Uralite Halt, SEC, 6B5
Urmston, CLC, 20C1; 45B3
Urquhart, GNS, 36C1
Ushaw Moor, NE, 27D5
Usk, GW, 8B3
Usworth, NE, 28C5
Utterby Halt, GN, 22G2
Uttoxeter, NS(GN), 15D5
Uxbridge, GW & Met(Dist), 5A2; 10G1
Uxbridge High Street, GW, 5A2; 10G1
Uxbridge Road (Goods), GW & LNW, 39D4
*Uxbridge Road Jc*, GW & Met(Dist), 39C4
Uxbridge Road (Pass), WL(H&C), 39D4
Uxbridge Vine Street, GW, 5A2; 10G1

*Vale of Rheidol Light Railway*, VR(Cam), 14C5
*Vallance Road Jc*, Dist/WB, 40C4
Valley, LNW, 19B2
Van, Van, 14C4
Varteg, LNW(GW), 7A4; 8A4; 43A2
Vauxhall, GE, 18F1
Vauxhall (London), LSW, 40D5
Vauxhall (Yarmouth), GE, 18F1
Vauxhall & Duddeston, LNW, 13C4
Vauxhall Fishmarket (Yarmouth), GE, 18F1
Velvet Hall, NE, 31D3
Venn Cross, GW, 8F5
Ventnor, IW, 4G3
Ventnor Town, IWC, 4G3
Verney Junc, LNW & Met&GCJt, 10D3
Verwood, LSW, 3E5
Vicarage Crossing Halt, GW, 20E5
Victoria (London), LBSC(LNW), SEC&GWJt & Dist(Met), 5B3; 39D5
Victoria (Manchester), LY(LNW/Mid), 20B1; 24F1; 45A3
Victoria (Mon), GW, 8A4; 43B2
Victoria (Norwich), GE, 18F3
Victoria (Nottingham), GC&GNJt, 16C4; 41F4
Victoria (Sheffield), GC(LY), 16A5; 21G3; 41A2; 42G2
Victoria (Swansea), LNW, 7B4; 43G3
Victoria Basin Goods (Wolverhampton), GW, 15E3 (inset)
Victoria Park (London), NL & GE, 40B3
Victoria Park (Whiteinch), NB, 44F4
Vine Street (Uxbridge), GW, 5A2; 10G1
Virginia Water, LSW, 5B1
Vobster (Goods), GW, 3B3; 8E1
Vobster Colliery (Goods), SD, 8E1
Vowchurch, GW, 14F1

Wadborough, Mid, 9C3
Waddesdon, OAT, 10E3
Waddesdon Manor, Met&GCJt, 10E2
Waddington, GN, 16B1; 17B1
Wadebridge, LSW(GW), 1C2
Wadhurst, SEC, 5E5
Wadsley Bridge, GC, 21G3; 42G2
Waenavon, LNW(GW), 8A4; 43B1
Waenfawr, NWNG, 19E2
Wainfleet, GN, 17C4
Wakefield (Kirkgate), LY&GNJt, 21E3; 42C2

Wakefield (Westgate) (Goods), GC&MidJt, 21E3; 42C2
Wakefield (Westgate) (Pass), GN&GCJt, 21E3; 42C2
Wakerley & Barrowden, LNW, 16F1
Walberswick, SWD, 12B1
Walcot, SWN, 15E1
Waldron & Horeham Road, LBSC, 5F5
Waleswood, GC, 16A4; 41A3
Walham Green, Dist, 39D4
Walkden, LY & LNW, 20B2; 24F1; 45B2
Walker, NE, 28B5
Walkerburn, NB, 30D1
Walkergate, NE, 28B5
Walkeringham, GN&GEJt, 22G5
*Walkinshaw Branch Jc*, Cal, 44G3
Wall, NB, 27B3
Wall Grange, NS, 15C4
Wallasey, Wir, 20C4; 24G4; 45G3
Wallasey Village, Wir, 20C4; 24G4; 45G3
Wallingford, GW, 10F3
*Wallneuk Jc*, G&SW/G&P, 44F3
Wallsend, NE, 28B5
Walmer, SEC, 6C1
Walpole, MGN, 17E4
Walsall (Goods), LNW & Mid, 13A2; 15F4
Walsall (Pass), LNW(Mid), 13A2; 15F4
Walsall Street Goods (Wolverhampton), GW, 15E3 (inset)
Walsall Wood, Mid, 15F4
Walsden, LY, 21E1
Walsingham, GE, 18D5
Waltham, GN, 22F2
Waltham Cross & Abbey, GE, 11G3
Waltham-on-the-Wold, GN, 16D2
Walthamstow, GE & TFG, 40A3
Walthamstow St James Street, GE, 40A3
Walthamstow Wood Street, GE, 40A3
Walton (Northants), Mid, 17F2
Walton & Anfield, LNW, 45F3
Walton for Hersham, LSW, 5C2
Walton-in-Gordano, WCP, 3A1; 8C3
*Walton New Jc*, LNW/BJ, 45D4
Walton-on-the-Hill (Lancs), CLC, 20C4; 24G4; 45F3
Walton-on-the-Naze, GE, 12E3
Walton Park, WCP, 3A1; 8C3
Walworth Road, SEC, 40D5
Wamphray, Cal, 26A3; 30G3
Wanborough, LSW(SEC), 5C1
Wandsworth Common, LBSC(LNW), 39E5
Wandsworth Road, SEC(LBSC), 40E5
Wandsworth Town, LSW, 39E5
Wanlockhead, Cal, 30F4
Wansford, LNW(GN), 11F1; 17F1
Wansford Road, GN, 11A1; 17F1
Wanstead Park, TFG, 40B2
Wanstrow, GW, 3C3; 8E1
Wantage, WT, 10F5
Wantage Road, GW, 10F5
*Wantage Tramway*, WT, 10F5
Wappenham, SMJ, 10C3
Wapping & Salthouse (Liverpool) Goods, LY, 45 (inset)
Warblington Halt, LBSC, 4E2
Warboys, GN&GEJt, 11B2
Warcop, NE, 27E2
Wardhouse, GNS, 37E2
Wardleworth, LY, 20A1; 21E1; 45A1
Ware, GE, 11F3
Wareham, LSW, 3F4
Wargrave, GW, 4A1; 10G2
Wark, NB, 27B3
Warkworth, NE, 31F5
Warlingham, SEC, 5C3
Warminster, GW, 3C4
Warmley, Mid, 3A3; 8C1
Warmsworth, GC, 21F4
Warnham, LBSC, 5D2
*Warren Hill Jc*, GE, 11C4
Warrington, LNW(BJ), LNW & CLC, 15A1; 20C2; 24G2; 45D4
Warrior Square (St Leonards), SEC(LBSC), 6F5
*Warriston Jc*, NB, 30 (inset)
Warsop, GC, 16B4; 41C4
Warthill, NE, 21C5
Wartle, GNS, 37E3
Warwick, GW & LNW, 10B5
Warwick Road Goods, GW & LNW, 39D4
*Warwick Road Jc*, Dist, 39D5
Washford, GW, 8E5
Washingboro', GN, 16B1; 17B1
Washington, NE, 28C5
Waskerley Goods, NE, 27D4
Wassand, NE, 22D3
Watchet, GW, 8E5
Watchingwell, FYN, 4F4
Water Orton, Mid, 15F5
Waterbeach, GE, 11C4
Waterfall, IMR, 23B2
Waterfoot, LY, 20A1; 24E1
Watergate, SR, 7G3
*Waterhall Jc* (Cardiff), TV, 43B4
*Waterhall Jc* (Pyle), PT, 43E4
Waterhouses (Durham), NE, 27D5
Waterhouses (Staffs), NS, 15C5
Wateringbury, SEC, 6C5
Waterloo (Aberdeen), GNS, 37G4
Waterloo (Lancs), LY(LNW), 20B4; 24F4; 45F3
Waterloo (Liverpool) Goods, LNW, 45F3/G5
Waterloo (London), LSW, 5B3; 40D5
Waterloo Halt (Glam), BM(Rhy), 43B3
Waterloo Junc (London), SEC, 40D5
Waterloo Road (Blackpool), PWY, 24D4
Waterloo Road (Staffs), NS, 15C3; 20E1
Waterside, G&SW, 29F4
*Waterside Jc*, NB, 29B5; 44C5
Watford High Street, LNW(LE), 5A2; 11G1
Watford Junc, LNW(LE), 5A2; 11G1
Wath, Mid & HB, 21F4; 42E1
Wath-in-Nidderdale, NV, 21B2
Wath-on-Dearne, GC, 21F4; 42E1
*Wath Road Jc*, Mid/SK, 21F4; 42E1
Watlington, GW, 10F3
Watnall, Mid, 16C4; 41F4
Watsons Crossing Halt, LY, 21E2
Watten, HR, 38D2
Watton, GE, 12A5; 18F5
Wattsville, LNW, 43B3
Waverley (Edinburgh), NB(NE), 30B2 and inset
Waverton, LNW, 15B1; 20E3
Wavertree, LNW & CLC, 45F4
Wear Valley Junc, NE, 27E5
Wearhead, NE, 27D3
Weaste, LNW, 45B3
*Weaver Jc*, LNW, 15A1; 20D3; 45D5
Weaverthorpe, NE, 22A4
*Weddington Jc*, AN, 16F5
Wednesbury, GW & LNW, 13A2; 15F4
Wednesfield, Mid, 15F4
Wednesfield Heath, LNW, 15F4
Weedon, LNW, 10B3
*Weekday Cross Jc*, GC/GN, 16 C4; 41F4
Weeley, GE, 12E3
Weelsby Road & Hainton Street Halt, GN, 22F2
Weeton, NE, 21C3
Welbury, NE, 28F5
Weldon & Corby, Mid, 16G1
Welford & Kilworth, LNW, 10A3; 16G3
Welford Park, GW, 4A4
*Welham Jc*, LNW/GN&LNWJt, 16G2
Well Hall for North Eltham, SEC, 5B4; 40E2
*Welland Bank Jc*, MGN, 17E2
Wellfield, NE, 28D5
Welling, SEC, 5B4; 40E1
Wellingborough, LNW & Mid, 10B1
Wellington (Leeds) (Pass), Mid(LY), 42A2
Wellington (Salop), SWN, 15E2
Wellington (Som), GW, 8G4
Wellington College, SEC, 4B1
Wellington Street (Leeds) (Goods), GN, LNW&LYJt & NE, 21B2 (inset); 42A3
Wellow, SD, 3B3; 8D1
Wells (Norfolk), GE, 18C5
Wells Priory Road (Som), SD, 3C2; 8E2
Wells Tucker Street (Som), GW, 3C2; 8E2
Welnetham, GE, 12C5
Welshampton, Cam, 20F4
Welshpool, Cam(SWP) & W&L, 14B2
*Welshpool & Llanfair Light Railway*, W&L(Cam), 14B2
Welton (Northants), LNW, 10B3
Welwyn, GN, 11F2
Welwyn Garden City Halt, GN, 11F2
Wem, LNW, 15D1; 20G3
Wembley Hill, GC, 39B3
Wembley, LNW(LE), 5A2; 39B2
Wembley Park, Met, 5A2; 39B3
Wemyss Bay, Cal, 29C2
Wemyss Castle, NB, 30A2; 34G5
Wendlebury Halt, LNW, 10D4
Wendling, GE, 18E5
Wendover, Met&GCJt, 10E2
Wenford, LSW, 1C3
Wenhaston, SWD, 12B2
Wennington (Lancs), Mid, 24B2
Wensley, NE, 21A2; 27G4
*Wensum Jc*, GE, 18F3
Wentworth & Hoyland Common, Mid, 21F3; 42F2
Wenvoe, BRY, 8C4; 43C5
Wern (Goods), Cam, 19F2
Wern Las, S&M, 14A1; 20G4
Werneth (Oldham), LY, 20B1; 21D1; 45A2
*Werrington Jc*, GN, 17F2
West Auckland, NE, 27E5
West Bay (Bridport), GW, 3F1
West Bridge (Leicester), Mid, 16F4
West Brompton, Dist & WLE, 39D5
West Bromwich, GW, 13B2; 15G4
West Calder, Cal, 30C4
West Cornforth, NE, 28D5
West Cross, Mum, 43G3
West Croydon, LBSC, 5C3; 40G5
West Cults, GNS, 37G4
West Derby, CLC, 45F3
West Drayton & Yiewsley, GW, 5B2; 10G1
West Ealing, GW, 39C2

West End Lane, LNW(NL), 39B5
West Fen Drove (Goods), GE, 11A3; 17G3
West Ferry, D&A, 34E1 (inset)
West Gosforth, NE, 27B5
West Green, GE, 40A4
West Grinstead, LBSC, 5E2
West Hallam, GN, 16C4; 41G3
West Halton, GC, 22E4
West Ham, LTS(Dist), 40C2
West Hampstead, Met & Mid, 39B5
West Harrow, Met, 39A1
West Hartlepool, NE, 28D4
West Hoathly, LBSC, 5E4
*West Holmes Jc*, GC/GN/GN&GEJt, 16B1 (inset)
West India Docks, GE, 40C3
West Jesmond, NE, 27B5
*West Jc (Colwich)*, LNW/NS, 15E4
West Kensington (Goods), Mid, 39D4
West Kensington (Pass), Dist, 39D4
West Kilbride, G&SW, 29D2
West Kirby, BJ & Wir, 20C5; 24G5
West Leigh, LNW, 45C3
West Leigh & Bedford, GC, 45C3
*West London Extension Jc*, WL/WLE, 39D4
*West London Jcs*, GW & LNW, 39C4
West Marina (St Leonards), LBSC, 6F5
West Meon, LSW, 4D2
West Moors, LSW, 3E5
West Newport, NB, 34E4
West Norwood, LBSC(LNW), 40F5
*West Norwood Jc*, LBSC, 40F5
West Pennard, SD, 3C2; 8E2
West Rounton Gates, NE, 28F5
West Runton, MGN, 18D3
West St Leonards, SEC, 6F5
West Stanley (Goods), NE, 27C5
West Street (Gravesend), SEC, 5B5
West Street (Glasgow) Goods, Cal, 44F1 (inset)
*West Street Jc* (London), Met/SEC, 40C5
*West Thurrock Jc*, LTS, 5B5
West Timperley, CLC, 45B4
West Tinsley, GC & SHD, 42G2
West Vale, LY, 21E2; 42C5
West Wemyss, NB, 30A2; 34G5
West Wickham, SEC, 5B4; 40G3
West Worthing, LBSC, 5F2
West Wycombe, GW&GCJt, 10F2
Westbourne Park, GW & H&C, 39C5 and inset C1
Westbrook, GW, 14F2
*Westburn Jc*, Cal, 44C3
Westbury (Salop), SWP, 14A1
Westbury (Wilts), GW, 3B4
Westcliff-on-Sea, LTS, 6A4
Westcombe Park, SEC, 40D2
Westcott, OAT, 10E3
Westcraigs, NB, 30C4
Westenhanger, SEC, 6D3
Westerfield, GE, 12D3
Westerham, SEC, 5C4
*Westerleigh Jcs*, GW & Mid, 3A3; 8C1; 9G2
Western Jetty (Immingham), GC, 22E3
Westerton, NB, 44E5
Westfield, NB, 30B4
Westgate (Rotherham), Mid, 21G4; 42F1
Westgate (Wakefield) (Goods), GC&MidJt, 21E3; 42C2
Westgate (Wakefield) (Pass), GN&GCJt, 21E3; 42C2
Westgate-in-Weardale, NE, 27D3
Westgate-on-Sea, SEC, 6B2
Westham Halt, WP, 3G3
Westhead Halt, LY(LNW), 20B3; 24F3; 45E2
Westhoughton, LY, 45C2
Westhouses & Blackwell, Mid, 16B4; 41D3
Westmill, GE, 11E3
Westminster, Dist(Met), 40D5
Westmoor, Mid, 14F1
Westoe Lane, SSM, 28B5
Weston (Bath), Mid, 3A3; 8D1
Weston (Lincs), MGN, 17E2
Weston & Ingestre (Staffs), NS, 15D4 *see also* Ingestre
Weston-on-Trent, Mid, 16D5
Weston-sub-Edge, GW, 9C5
Weston-super-Mare, GW & WCP, 3B1; 8D3
Westward Ho!, BWHA, 7F2
Westwood, GC, 21F3; 42F2
Wetheral, NE, 27C1
Wetherby, NE, 21C4
*Wetherby E & W Jcs*, NE, 21C4
*Wetmore Jc*, Mid, 15C5 (inset)
Wetton Mill, NS, 15B5
Wetwang, NE, 22C4
Weybourne, MGN, 18D4
Weybridge, LSW, 5C2
Weyhill, MSW, 4B4
Weymouth, GW(LSW), 3G3
Weymouth Harbour, GW, 3G3
*Weymouth Jc*, GW, 3G3
Weymouth Town, GW, 3G3
Whaley Bridge, LNW, 15A4
Whalley, LY, 24D1
Whaplode, MGN, 17E3
Wharf Station (Towyn), Tal, 13B5
Wharram, NE, 22B5
Whatstandwell, Mid, 16C5; 41E2
Whauphill, P&W, 25C4
Wheathampstead, GN, 11F2
Wheatley (Oxon), GW, 10E3
Wheatley (Yorks), HHL, 21E2; 42B5
Wheelock, NS, 15B2; 20E2 *see also* Sandbach
Wheldrake, DVL, 21C5
Whelley (Goods), LNW, 45D2
*Whelley Jc*, LNW, 20B3; 24F2
Wherwell, LSW, 4C4
Whetstone (Leics), GC, 16F4
*Whickham Jc*, NE, 28 (inset)
Whifflet, Cal & NB, 30C5; 44B3
Whifflet Low Level, Cal, 44B3
Whimple, LSW, 2B2
Whimsey Halt, SVW, 8A1; 9E2
Whippingham, IWC, 4F3
*Whiskerhill Jc*, GC, 16A3
Whissendine, Mid, 16E2
Whistlefield, NB, 29A3
Whitacre, Mid, 15F5
Whitburn, NB, 30C4
Whitby Town, NE, 28F2
Whitby West Cliff, NE, 28F2
Whitchurch (Glam), Car, 43B4
Whitchurch (Hants), GW & LSW, 4B3
Whitchurch (Salop), LNW(Cam), 15C1; 20F3
Whitchurch Down Platform, GW, 1C5
White Bear, LU, 20A2; 24F2; 45D1
White Colne, CVH, 12E5
White Fen (Goods), GE, 11A3; 17G3
White Moss Crossing Halt, LY(LNW), 20B3; 24F3; 45E2
White Notley, GE, 11F5
Whiteboro', Mid, 16B4; 41D3
Whitechapel, EL & WB(H&C), 40C4
Whitecraigs, Cal, 29C5; 44E2
Whitecroft, SVW, 8A1; 9E2
Whitedale, NE, 22D3
Whitefield, LY, 20B1; 24F1; 45B2
Whitegate, CLC, 15B2; 20D2
Whitehall Road (Leeds) (Goods), LNW&LYJt, 21C2 (inset)
Whitehaven (Bransty), LNW&FurJt, 26E4
Whitehaven (Corkickle), Fur, 26E4
Whitehaven (Goods), Fur & LNW, 26E4
Whitehouse, GNS, 37F2
*Whitehouse Jc*, LY, 24E3
Whitehurst Halt, GW, 20F4
Whiteinch, Cal, 44F4 *see also* Victoria Park, NB
Whitemoor (Goods), GE, 11A3; 17F3
Whiterigg, NB, 30C5; 44A4
Whithorn, P&W, 25D4
Whitland, GW, 7A1; 13G2
Whitley Bay, NE, 28B5
Whitley Bridge, LY, 21E5
Whitlingham, GE, 18F3
Whitmore, LNW, 15C3; 20F1
Whitney-on-Wye, Mid, 14E2
Whitrigg, Cal, 26C2
Whitstable Harbour, SEC, 6B3
Whitstable Town & Tankerton, SEC, 6B3
Whitstone & Bridgerule, LSW, 1A4
Whittingham, NE, 31F4
Whittington (Derbys), Mid, 16A5; 41B2
Whittington (Salop), GW & Cam, 20G4
Whittlesea, GE, 11A2; 17F2
Whittlesford, GE, 11D3
Whitton (Lincs), GC, 22E4
*Whitton Jc*, LSW, 39E1
Whitwell (Derbys), Mid, 16A4; 41B4
Whitwell (IoW), IWC, 4G3
Whitwell & Reepham, MGN, 18E4
Whitwick, LNW, 16E4
*Whitwood Jc*, Mid/NE, 42B1
Whitworth, LY, 20A1; 24E1; 45A1
Whyteleafe, SEC, 5C3
Wichnor (Goods), Mid, 15E5
*Wichnor Jc*, Mid/LNW, 15E5
Wick, HR, 38D2
Wick St Lawrence, WCP, 3A1; 8D3
Wickenby, GC, 17A1
Wicker (Goods), Mid, 42G2
Wickford, GE, 6A5
Wickham (Hants), LSW, 4E3
Wickham Bishops, GE, 12F5
Wickham Market, GE, 12C2
Wickwar, Mid, 8B1; 9F2
Widdrington, NE, 27A5; 31G5
Widford, GE, 11F3
Widmerpool, Mid, 16D3
Widnes, LNW & GC&MidJt(CLC), 15A1; 20C3; 24G3; 45D4
*Widnes Jc*, GN, 15A1; 20C3; 45D4
Widney Manor, GW, 9A5
Wigan, LNW, LY & GC, 20B3; 24F2; 45D2
*Wigston Central Jc*, Mid, 16F3
Wigston Glen Parva, Mid, 16F3
Wigston Magna, Mid, 16F3
*Wigston North Jc*, LNW/Mid, 16F3
Wigston South, Mid, 16F3
*Wigston South Jc*, Mid, 16F3

Wigton, M&C, 26C2
Wigtown, P&W, 25C4
Wilburton, GE, 11B3
Wilby, MSL, 12B3
Willaston, LNW, 15C2; 20E2
Willenhall, LNW & Mid, 15F4
Willerby & Kirk Ella, HB, 22D4
Willersley Halt, GW, 9C5
Willesden Green, Met, 39B4
Willesden Junc, LNW(NL/LE), 5A3; 39C4
*Willingdon Jc*, LBSC, 5F5
Willington (Beds), LNW, 11D1
Willington (Durham), NE, 27D5
*Willington Jc*, Mid/NS, 16D5
Willington Quay, NE, 28B5
Williton, GW, 8E5
Willoughby (Lincs), GN, 17B4
Willow Walk Goods, LBSC, 40D4
Wilmcote, GW, 9B5
Wilmington, NE, 22 (inset)
Wilmslow, LNW, 15A3; 20C1; 45A5
Wilnecote, Mid, 15F5
Wilpshire, LY, 24D2
Wilsden, GN, 21D2; 42A5
Wilsontown, Cal, 30C4
*Wilsontown Jcs*, Cal, 30D4
Wilstrop (Siding), NE, 21C4
Wilton, GW & LSW, 3C5
Wimbledon, LSW(Dist) & LBSC&LSWJt, 5B3; 39F4
Wimbledon Park, LSW(Dist), 39E4
Wimblington, GN&GEJt, 11A3; 17G3
Wimborne, LSW, 3E5
Wincanton, SD, 3D3; 8F1
Winchburgh, NB, 30B3
Winchcombe, GW, 9D4
Winchelsea, SEC, 6E4
Winchelsea Harbour, SEC, 6E4
Winchester, LSW & GW, 4D3
Winchester Cheeshill, GW, 4D3
*Winchester Jc*, LSW, 4B3
Winchfield, LSW, 4B1
Wincobank & Meadow Hall, Mid, 21G3; 42G2 *see also* Meadow Hall
Winder, WCE, 26E3
Windermere, LNW, 26D1
Windermere Lake Side, Fur, 24A4; 26G1
*Windmill Bridge Jc*, LBSC, 40G4
Windmill End, GW, 13C1; 15G4
Windsor & Eton, GW & LSW, 5B1; 10G1
Windsor Street Wharf, LNW, 13B4
Winestead (Goods), NE, 22E2
Wingate, NE, 28D5
Wingfield, Mid, 16C5; 41E2
Wingham, EK, 6C2
Wingham Town, EK, 6C2
Winkhill Halt, NS, 15C4
Winnington & Anderton, CLC, 45C5
Winscombe, GW, 3B1; 8D3
Winsford, LNW, 15B2; 20D2
Winsford & Over, CLC, 15B2; 20D2 *see also* Over & Wharton
*Winsford Jc*, LNW, 15B2; 20D2
Winslow, LNW, 10D2
Winslow Road, Met&GCJt, 10D3
Winson Green, LNW, 13C3; 15G4 *see also* Soho
Winston, NE, 27E5
Winterbourne, GW, 8C1; 9G2
Winteringham, GC, 22E4
*Wintersett Jc*, GC, 42C2
Winterton & Thealby, GC, 22E4
Winton, NB, 30B1
Winton Pier, G&SW, 29D3
*Winwick Jc*, LNW, 20C2; 24G2; 45D3
Wirksworth, Mid, 16C5; 41E2
Wisbech, GE(WUT) & MGN, 17F3
Wisbech St Mary, MGN, 17F3
Wishaw, Cal, 30C5; 44A2
Wishford, GW, 3C5
Wistow, NE, 21D5
Witham (Essex), GE, 12F5
Witham (Som), GW, 3C3
Withcall, GN, 17A2
Withernsea, NE, 22E2
Withington (Glos), SW, 9E4
Withington (Hereford), GW, 9C1
Withington (Lancs), Mid, 20C1; 24G1; 45A3
Withnell, LU, 20A2; 24E2
Withyham, LBSC, 5D4
Withymoor Basin (Goods), GW, 13C1
Witley & Chiddingfold, GW, 5D1
Witney, GW, 10E5
*Witney Jc*, GW, 10E4
Wittersham Road, KES, 6E4
Witton, LNW, 13B4
Witton Gilbert, NE, 27D5
Witton-le-Wear, NE, 27D5
Wiveliscombe, GW, 8F5
Wivelsfield, LBSC, 5E3
Wivenhoe, GE, 12E4
Wixford, Mid, 9B4
Woburn Sands, LNW, 10C1
Wofferton, S&H, 9A1
Woking, LSW, 5C1
Wokingham, SEC(LSW), 4A1
Woldingham, CO, 5C3
Wolferton, GE, 17D5
*Wolfhall Jc*, GW/MSW, 4A5
Wolfs Castle Halt, GW, 13G1
Wolsingham, NE, 27D4
Wolvercot Platform, GW, 10E4
Wolvercote Halt, LNW, 10E4
*Wolvercote Jc*, GW/LNW, 10E4
Wolverhampton, GW & LNW(Mid), 15F3
Wolverton, LNW, 10C2
Wolverton Carriage Works, LNW, 10C2
Wombridge (Goods), LNW, 15E2
Wombwell, GC & Mid, 21F3/4; 42E1/2
Womersley, LY(GN), 21E4
Wooburn Green, GW, 5A1; 10F1
Wood End Platform, GW, 9A3
Wood Green (Middlesex), GN(NL), 5A3; 40A5
Wood Green (Staffs), LNW, 13A2
Wood Lane (White City), H&C, 39C4
Woodborough, GW, 3B5
Woodbridge, GE, 12D3
Woodburn, NB, 27A3
*Woodburn Jc* (Sheffield), GC, 41A2
Woodbury Road, LSW, 2B3
Woodchester, Mid, 9F3
Woodend, WCE, 26F3
Woodford (Essex), GE, 5A4
Woodford & Hinton (Northants), GC(SMJ), 10B4
*Woodford Jc*, GC/SMJ, 10B4
Woodgrange Park, LTS, 40B2
Woodhall Junc, GN, 17B2
Woodhall Spa, GN, 17B2
Woodham Ferrers, GE, 6A4; 11G5
Woodhay, GW, 4A3
Woodhead, GC, 21F2; 42F5
Woodhouse (Yorks), GC, 16A4; 21G4; 41A3; 42G2
Woodhouse Mill, Mid, 16A4; 21G4; 41A3; 42G1
Woodkirk, GN, 21E3; 42B3
Woodland, Fur, 24A4; 26G2
Woodlands Road Halt, LY, 45A2
Woodlesford, Mid(LY), 21D3; 42B2
Woodley, GC&MidJt(CLC), 21G1
*Woodley Jc*, NB, 44C5
Woodnesborough, EK, 6C2
Woodside (Aberdeen), GNS, 37F4
Woodside (Birkenhead), BJ, 15A1; 20C4; 24G4; 45F4
Woodside (Halebank) Goods, LNW, 15A1; 20C3; 45E4
Woodside & Burrelton, Cal, 33E5
Woodside & South Norwood, SEC, 5B3; 40G4
*Woodside Jc*, SEC/WSC, 40G4
Woodside Park, GN(NL), 5A3
Woodvale, CLC, 20B4; 24F4; 45F1
Woodville, Mid, 16E5
Woody Bay, LB, 7E4
Wookey, GW, 3C2; 8E2
Wool, LSW, 3F4
Woolaston, GW, 8B1; 9F1
Wooler, NE, 31E3
Woolfold, LY, 20B1; 24F1; 45B1
Woolston, LSW, 4E3
Woolwich Arsenal, SEC, 40D1
Woolwich Dockyard, SEC, 5B4; 40D2
Wooperton, NE, 31E4
Wootton, IWC, 4F3
Wootton Bassett, GW, 9G4
Wootton Broadmead Halt, LNW, 10C1; 11D1
Wootton Pillinge Halt, LNW, 10C1; 11D1
Wootton Wawen Platform, GW, 9B5
Worcester (Goods), GW & Mid, 9B3
Worcester (Pass), GW & GW&MidJt, 9B3
Worcester Park, LSW, 5B3; 39G4
*Worgret Jc*, LSW, 3F4
Workington, LNW, 26E3
Workington Bridge, LNW, 26E3
Workington Central, CWJ, 26E3
Worksop, GC(Mid), 16A3; 41B5
Worle, GW, 3B1; 8D3
*Worle Jc*, GW, 3A1; 8D3
Worle Town, WCP, 3A1; 8D3
Worleston, LNW, 15B2; 20E2
Worlington Golf Links Halt, GE, 11B5
Worlingworth, MSL, 12B3
Wormald Green, NE, 21B3
Wormit, NB, 34E4
Worplesdon, LSW, 5C1
Worsborough (Goods), GC, 42E2
Worship Street Goods, LNW, 40C4
Worsley, LNW, 45B3
*Worsley Jc*, LNW, 45B2
Worstead, GE, 18E2
*Worth Valley Branch Jc*, Mid, 21D1
Worthing, LBSC, 5F2
Worthington, Mid, 16E4
Worthy Down Platform, GW, 4C3
Wortley (Sheffield), GC, 21F3; 42F3
Wotton, GC & OAT, 10E3
Wrabness, GE, 12E3
Wrafton, LSW(GW), 7F3
Wragby, GN, 17A1
Wrangaton, GW, 2D5

*Wrangbrook Jc*, HB, 21E4
*Wrawby Jc*, GC, 22F3
Wraysbury, LSW, 5B1
Wrea Green, PWY, 24D4
Wreay, LNW, 26C1
Wrenbury, LNW, 15C1; 20E2
*Wrenthorpe Jc*, GN, 42C2
Wressle, NE, 21D5
Wretham & Hockham, GE, 12A5; 18G5
Wrexham, GW, 20E4
Wrexham (Central), GC(Cam), 20E4
Wrexham (Exchange), GC, 20E4
Wrington, GW, 3B1; 8D2
Wrotham for Borough Green, SEC, 5C5
Wroxall, IW, 4G3
Wroxham, GE, 18E2
Wryde, MGN, 17F3
*Wycombe Jc*, Mid/GN, 16D2
Wye, SEC, 6D3
*Wye Valley Jc*, GW, 8B2; 9F1
Wyke & Norwood Green, LY, 21E2; 42B4
*Wyke Jc*, LY, 21E2
Wyke Regis Halt, WP, 3G3
Wykeham, NE, 22A4
Wylam, NE(NB), 27B5
Wylde Green, LNW, 15F5
Wylye, GW, 3C5
Wymondham (Norfolk), GE, 18F4
*Wymondham Jc*, Mid, 16E2
Wynn Hall, GW, 20F4
Wynyard, NE, 28E5
Wyre Dock, LY, 24C4
*Wyre Dock Jc*, LY/PWY, 24C4
Wyre Forest, GW, 9A2
Wyrley & Cheslyn Hay, LNW, 15F4

Yalding, SEC, 5C5
*Yarde* (workmen), SR, 1A5
Yardley Wood Platform, GW, 9A5
Yarm, NE, 28F5
Yarmouth Beach (Norfolk), MGN, 18F1
Yarmouth South Town (Norfolk), GE, 18F1
Yarmouth (IoW), FYN, 4F4
Yarnton, GW, 10E4
*Yarwell Jc*, LNW, 11A1; 17F1
Yate, Mid, 8C1; 9G2
Yatton, GW, 3A1; 8D3
Yaxham, GE, 18E4
Yaxley & Farcet, GN, 11A2; 17G2
Yeadon, Mid, 21D2
Yealmpton, GW, 2E5
Yeathouse, WCE, 26E3
Yeldham, CVH, 11D5
Yelvertoft & Stanford Park, LNW, 10A3
Yelverton, GW, 2D5
Yeoford Junc, LSW, 2B4
Yeovil Junc, LSW, 3E2; 8G2
Yeovil Pen Mill, GW, 3D2; 8G2
Yeovil Town, GW&LSWJt, 3D2; 8G2
Yetminster, GW, 3E2
*Ynys-y-Geinon Jc*, Mid/N&B, 7A4; 43F2
Ynys, LNW, 19F1
Ynysddu, LNW, 8B4; 43B3
Ynyshir, TV, 8B5; 43D3
Ynyslas, Cam, 13B5
Ynysybwl, TV, 8B5; 43C3
Yockleton, SWP, 14A1
Yoker, Cal & NB, 29C4; 44F4
York, NE(GC/GE/GN/LY/Mid) & DVL, 21C5 and inset A4
*York North Jc*, NE, 21A4 (inset)
York Road (London), GN, 40C5
Yorkhill, NB, 44E4
Yorton, LNW, 15E1; 20G3
Ystalyfera, Mid, 7A4; 43F1
Ystrad (Rhondda), TV, 8B5; 43D2
Ystrad Mynach, Rhy, 8B4; 43B3
Ystradgynlais, N&B(Mid), 7A4; 43E1
Ystradowen, TV, 8C5; 43D4

*Zig Zag Lines Jc*, Rhy(BM), 43C2

## 7 Index to junction diagrams

**Note:** The numbers in this index refer to page numbers, not map numbers.

Abbey Holme 99
*Abbotswood Jc* 33
Aberavon 21
Aberdare 26
Abergavenny 25
Abersychan & Talywain 25
Aberystwyth 45
Acton 125
*Acton Grange Jc* 52
*Acton Wells Jc* 125
Addison Road 42
Adlington 75
Afon Wen 69
Alcester 34
Aldershot 15
Aldgate 128
Allerton 76
Alloa 108
Altofts 82
Altrincham 72
Andover 14
Andoversford 15, 34
Annan 99
Annesley 60
Apethorne 72
Applehurst 84
Ardrossan 102
Ash 15
Ashbourne 61
*Ashendon Jc* 35
Ashton 85
*Ashton Moss Jcs* 85
Askern 84
Avonmouth 24
Aylesbury 35
Bagthorpe 60
Bainsford 105
Balloch 105
Balquhidder 119
Banbury 38
Barnsley 80
Barnstaple 20
Barrhead 104
Barrmill 103
Basford 60
Basingstoke 15
Bassaleg 25
Bath 9
Batley 80
Bearley 34
Bedford 42
Beighton 58
Bere Alston 8
Berkeley Road 32
Berwick 110
Bidston 73
Biglis 29
Bilson 28
Birkenhead 73
Birmingham 44
Bishops Road 124
Bishopsgate 128
Blackburn 91
Blackburn Valley 82
Blackfriars 129
Blisworth 38
Blodwell 48
Boar's Head 77
Boat of Garten 118
Bodmin 8
Bonnywater 105
Bordesley 44
Bourne 68
Bow 130
Bowling 81
Bradford 81
Bradley Wood 81
*Brantcliffe Jcs* 134
Brayton 99
Brecon 48
Bredbury 72
Bricklayers Arms 131
Bridgend 29
Brierley 86
Brightside 82
*Brinnington Jc* 72
Bristol 24
Briton Ferry 21
Broadheath 72
Bromley 130
Bromshall 56
Broom 34
Broughty Ferry 118
Brymbo 30
Brynmawr 30
Builth Road 48
Bulwell 60
Burley 83
Burnham 25
Burton 58
Busby 104
Bushbury 51
Buttington 48
Buxton 53

Callander 110
Cambridge 42
Camden 129
Canonbury 131
Cardiff 27
Cardonnel 21
Carlisle 97
Carmuirs 105
Carnforth 90
Castle Douglas 99
Central Wales District 43
Chappel 39
Chard 9
Charing Cross (London) 131
Cheadle (Ches) 74
Chester 69
Chichester 15
Chorley 75
Chorlton 74
Cinderford 28
Clapham Junction 124
Cleator Moor 98
Cleobury Mortimer 34
Clifton (Lancs) 76
Clifton Colliery 61
Clown 59
Coalville 62
Coatbridge 119
Cockley Brake 38
Coed Talon 30
Cogan 27
Coity 29
Colbren 31
Coleford 28
Colne 81
Colwich 52
Connah's Quay 74
Corwen 69
Court Sart 21
Craigendoran 111
Craven Arms 45
Crewe 72
Crianlarich 111
Crofton 82
Cromer 67
*Crowthorn Jc* 85
Croydon 128
Cudworth 86
Cutsyke 82

Dalreoch 103
Devonport 8
Dewsbury 81
Dinnington 134
Distington 96
Dolgelley 49
Dolphinton 108
Doncaster 84
*Dove Jc* 58
Dowlais 26
Dowlais Top 26
*Drayton Jc* 57
Droylsden 85
Dudley 53
Dumbarton 103
Dumfries 99
Dundee 118

Eardisley 42, 49
Earls Court 42
Edenbridge 18
Edinburgh 105
Egginton 58
Elgin 118
Ellesmere 73
Epsom 18
Euxton 92
Evesham 34
Exeter 9

Farington 92

Fenny Compton 38
Fishguard 44
Fleetwood 93
Forest Gate 130
Forth Bridge 109
Frodingham 87
Frodsham 76

Gainsborough 62
Garstang & Catterall 93
Garston 76
Gartsherrie 119
Glasgow 135
Glazebrook 73
Gloucester 31
Godley 72
Goole 90
Grangemouth 105
Granton 105
Great Bridge 53
Greenhill 105
Gretna 99
Grimsby 87
Guide Bridge 85
Guildford 15

Hackney Wick (Goods) 130
Haigh 77
Halesowen 51
Halifax 81
Hammersmith 142
Hampstead Road 129
Hampton 50
Hartford 53
Hastings 18
Haughley 44
Havant 12
Haverhill 39
Hawes 91
Hay 49
Haydon Square 128
Haymarket 105
Headcorn 20
Heath 27
Heaton Lodge 81
Heaton Mersey 74
Hellifield 91
Helsby 76
Hereford 38, 42
*High Peak Jc* 53
High Wycombe 35
Highbridge 25
Highgate Road 130
*Hillhouse Jc* 75
*Hilton Jc* 115
Hincaster 91
Hindley 77
Holmfield 81
Hope 74
Huddersfield 81
Huntingdon 42
Hyde 85

Ibrox 102
Ilkley 83
Ingleton 91
Isle of Wight 13

Junction Road 130

Keighley 81
Keith 118
Kensington 142
Kentish Town 129
Kew 125
Kidwelly 31
Kilmarnock 102
Kilsyth 103
King's Cross 129
Kirk Sandall 84
Kirkbride 99
Kirkby 60
Knottingley 82

Laisterdyke 81
Lancaster 90
Langwith 59
Larbert 105
Lavender Hill 124
Leamington 39
Leatherhead 18
Leeds 80
Leicester 57
Leith 105
Leominster 38, 42
Lincoln 56
Liskeard 9
Little Bytham 68
Liverpool 139
Liverpool Street 128
Llancaiach 26
Llandilo 44
Llandovery 44
Llanelly 49
Llantrisant 30
Llanymynech 48
Lofthouse 82
Longhedge 124
*Longville Jc* 63
Loughborough 62
Low Moor 81
Lowestoft 66
Luffenham 57
Lugton 103
Lydbrook 28
Lydford 8
Lydney 28
Lynn 68

Macclesfield 72
Maiden Lane 129
Malvern 33
Manchester 93
Mansfield 61
Mansion House 128
March 68
*Marefield Jcs* 57
Margam 21
Market Drayton 51
Market Harborough 57
Marlborough 14
Marple 72
*Marsh Farm Jc* 45
Meole Brace 48
Merthyr 26
Methley 82
Midcalder 110
Middlewood 56
Midhurst 13
Millwall 129
Milner Wood 83
Mirfield 81
Moira 62
Monk Bretton 86
*Moorbridge Jc* 60
Morecambe 90
Morlais 26
Morningside 108
Morpeth 99
Mortimer 34
Mountain Ash 26
Muirkirk 104

Nantwich 51
Nantybwch 30
Nantyglo 30
Neath 21
Netherfield & Colwick 61
New Cross 131
New Mills 53
Newark 61
Newport (Mon) 25
Nine Mile Point 25
Normanton 82
*North Pole Jc* 124
North Wales District 68
North Walsham 67
Northampton 38
Northenden 74
*Northern Jc* (Braithwell) 134
Northfield 51
Northwich 53
Norton Bridge 52
Norwood 128
Nostell 86
Nottingham 61
Nuneaton 50

Oakenshaw 82
Oldham 85
Otley 83
Overseal & Moira 62
Oxford 39

Paisley 102
Partick 135
Partington 73
Parton 98
Pateley Bridge 83
Patricroft 76
Peasmarsh 15
Peebles 108
Pemberton 77
Pembrey 31
Penarth 27

Penistone 80
Perth 115
Peterborough 63
Peterston 29
Plank Lane 77
Plymouth 8
Pontardulais 31
Pontefract 82
Pontypridd 29
Pont-y-Rhyll 21
Poplar 129
Port Talbot 21
Portessie 118
Porthywaen 48
Portishead 24
Portsmouth 12
Preston 92
Princes Risborough 35
Purley 19
Putney 131
Pyle 20

Quainton Road 35
Quaker's Yard 26

Rainford 75
Ravenglass 98
*Ravenstone Wood Jc* 38
Reading 13
Red Hill 19
Retford 62
Rhymney 30
Rhymney Bridge 30
Roade 38
Robertsbridge 20
Rock Ferry 73
Romford 20
*Rosehill Jc* (Cumb) 96
Rothesay Dock (Yoker) 102
Roundwood 134
Rowrah 98
Ruabon 75
Rugby 39
Runton West 67

St Fagan's 29
St Ives 42
St Leonards 18
St Pancras 129
Salisbury 12
Saltney 69
Sandbach 72
Sandy 42
Savernake 14
Selby 83
Sellafield 98
*Shaftholme Jc* 84
Shafton 86
Shalford 15
Sheffield 82
Shepreth 42
Shipley 81
Shirebrook 59
Shireoaks 134
Shrewsbury 48
Siddick Junc 96
Six Pit 21
Sleaford 57
Smethwick 45
Snow Hill (London) 129
South Acton 125
South Kensington 124
South Lynn 68
South Tottenham 130
*Southern Jc* (Laughton) 134
Spalding 68
Spean Bridge 114
Spitalfields 128
Sprotborough 84
Sprouston 110
Stafford 52
Stainforth 84
Stairfoot 86
Stalybridge 85
Stamford (Lincs) 68
Standish 32
Stanley (Perth) 115
Stewarts Lane 124
Stirling 108
Stoats Nest 19
Stobcross 135
Stoke Prior 33
Stourton 87
*Strangeways East Jc* (Lancs) 77
Stranraer 98
Stratford-on-Avon 38
Stratford (London) 130
Strathaven 104
Strathord 115
Streatham & Tulse Hill 18
Stretford Bridge 45
Studland Road 42
Swansea 21
Swindon 14

Taffs Wells 27
Talyllyn 48
Tamworth 50
Tenbury 45
The Mound 119
Thorne 84
Thornhill 81
Three Cocks 48
Thrybergh 134
Timperley 72
Tottenham 130
Towcester 38
Treeton 82
Treforest 29
Trehafod 29
Tufnell Park 130
Turnham Green 125
Tuxford 62

Uttoxeter 56
Uxbridge Road 124

Verney Junc 35
Victoria Park 130

Wakefield 82
Walsall 45
Walton (Ches) 52
Wansford 68
Warrington 52
Waterloo (London) 131
Wednesbury 53
Welham 57
Wellingborough 42
Wellington (Salop) 45
Wells (Som) 9
Welshpool 48
West Kirby 76
*West Street Jc* (London) 129
Westbourne Park 124
Whifflet 119
Whitchurch (Salop) 51
Whitechapel 128
Whitehaven 98
Wichnor 50
Wick 119
Widnes 75
Wigan 77
Wigston 57
Willesden 125
Willington 58
Wimbledon 15
Wokingham 13
*Wolfhall Jc* (Savernake) 14
Wolverhampton 51
Woodford & Hinton 38
Woodgrange Park 130
Woodley 72
Woodside (South Norwood) 128
Worcester 33
Workington 96

Yarmouth (Norfolk) 66
Yarnton 39
Yate 32
Yeovil 12
*Ynys-y-Geinon Jc* 31
York 87